Drawing, Reconstruction of the Goworowo Synagogue. Approved 27 September 1922.

Courtesy of State Archives in Bialystok.

An opinion letter, accompanying the drawing, recommended approval by the City of Bialystok:

"City of Białystok, 27. XI. 1922
Reconstruction of the synagogue in Goworowo – Opinion.
The design of the new synagogue is artistically part of the type of modern buildings, a large number of which were erected in Ostroleka, allegedly based on Kurpie's architectural themes. The roof lines of this type of buildings are harmonious only in the drawings and visible from a greater distance, but in short, seen up close, leave much to be desired. Much more graceful to the eye, and to maintain the old Polish building traditions, are the roofs known from the reproductions of synagogues in Grodno, Wolpa, Zabludow, and in other Polish towns, ranking from Eastern Malopolska to Dzwina. However, the whole designed synagogue looks quite impressive. No objections are made regarding the erection of a new wooden synagogue."

The new Synagogue of Goworowo was destroyed in the September 1939 Nazi invasion.

Govorowo Memorial Book
(Goworowo, Poland)

Translation of
Goworowo; sefer zikaron

Original Book Edited by: Aviezer Burstin and Dov Kossovsky

Originally published by the Govorover Societies in Israel, the USA and Canada, Tel Aviv, 1966

JewishGen
מרכז עולמי לגנאלוגיה יהודית
The Global Home for Jewish Genealogy

A Publication of JewishGen
Edmond J. Safra Plaza, 36 Battery Place, New York, NY 10280
646.494.2972 | info@JewishGen.org | www.jewishgen.org

JewishGen is the Genealogical Research Division of the
Museum of Jewish Heritage – A Living Memorial to the Holocaust

MUSEUM OF
JEWISH HERITAGE
A LIVING MEMORIAL
TO THE HOLOCAUST

Govorowo Memorial Book (Goworowo, Poland)
Translation of ***Goworowo; sefer zikaron***

First Printing: July 2025, Tamuz, 5785
Original Yizkor Book Edited By: Aviezer Burstin and Dov Kossovsky
Project Coordinator: Lester Blum
Emeritus Coordinator: Martin Jacobs
Cover Design: Nina Schwartz
Layout, formatting and indexing: Jonathan Wind

Library of Congress Control Number (LCCN): 2025932199

ISBN: 978-1-962054-23-2 (hard cover: 524 pages, alk. paper)

About JewishGen.org

JewishGen, is a Genealogical Research Division of the Museum of Jewish Heritage - A Living Memorial to the Holocaust, serves as the global home for Jewish genealogy.

Featuring unparalleled access to 30+ million records, it offers unique search tools, along with opportunities for researchers to connect with others who share similar interests. Award winning resources such as the Family Finder, Discussion Groups, and ViewMate, are relied upon by thousands each day.

In addition, JewishGen's extensive informational, educational and historical offerings, such as the Jewish Communities Database, Yizkor Book translations, InfoFiles, Family Tree of the Jewish People, and KehilaLinks, provide critical insights, first-hand accounts, and context about Jewish communal and familial life throughout the world.

Offered as a free resource, JewishGen.org has facilitated thousands of family connections and success stories, and is currently engaged in an intensive expansion effort that will bring many more records, tools, and resources to its collections.

Please visit https://www.jewishgen.org/ to learn more.

Vice President for JewishGen: Avraham Groll

About the JewishGen Yizkor Book Project

Yizkor Books (Memorial Books) were traditionally written to memorialize the names of departed family and martyrs during holiday services in the synagogue (a practice that still exists in many synagogues today).

Over the centuries, as a result of countless persecutions and horrific atrocities committed against the Jews, Yizkor Books (Sefer Zikaron in Hebrew) were expanded to include more historical information, such as biographical sketches of famous personalities and descriptions of daily town life.

Following the Holocaust, the idea of remembrance and learning took on an urgent and crucial importance. Survivors of the Holocaust sought out other surviving residents of their former towns to memorialize and document the names and way of life of those who were ruthlessly murdered by the Nazis. These remembrances were documented in Yizkor Books, hundreds of which were published in the first decades after the Holocaust.

Most of these books were published privately, or through *Landsmanshaftn* (social organizations comprised of members originating from the same European town or region) that still existed, and were often distributed free of charge. The languages used to document these crucial histories and links to our past were mostly Yiddish and Hebrew. JewishGen has undertaken the sacred responsibility of translating these books into English so that the culture and way of life of these communities will be preserved and transmitted to future generations.

In 1986, a group of farsighted JewishGenners started a project to pool their efforts together in groups based upon their ancestors' towns and donate funds to translate the Yizkor books of their ancestral towns into English. As the translated material became available, it was made accessible for free at https://www.JewishGen.org/Yizkor . Hardcover copies can be purchased by visiting https://www.jewishgen.org/Yizkor/ybip.html (see section below).

It is our hope that the translation of these books into English (and other languages) will assist the countless Jewish family researchers who are so desperately seeking to forge a connection with their heritage.

Director of JewishGen Yizkor Book Project: Lance Ackerfeld

About JewishGen Press

JewishGen Press (formerly the Yizkor Books-in-Print Project) is the publishing division of JewishGen.org, and provides a venue for the publication of non-fiction books pertaining to Jewish genealogy, history, culture, and heritage.

In addition to the Yizkor Book category, publications in the Other Non-Fiction category include Shoah memoirs and research, genealogical research, collections of genealogical and historical materials, biographies, diaries and letters, studies of Jewish experience and cultural life in the past, academic theses, and other books of interest to the Jewish community.

Please visit https://www.jewishgen.org/Yizkor/ybip.html to learn more.

Director of JewishGen Press: Joel Alpert
Managing Editor – Peter Harris
Publications Manager - Susan Rosin

Notes to the Reader

The images in the original book were reproduced from photographs from the time of the first edition. These reproductions were already of poor quality, most being pre-war and others at least 60 or more years old. The images in the book are the best achievable.

A reader can view the original scans of the book on the websites listed below.

The original book can be seen online at the Yiddish Book Center website:

https://www.yiddishbookcenter.org/collections/yizkor-books/yzk-nybc313775/burstin-aviezer-kossovsky-govorovah-sefer-zikaron

OR

at the New York Public Library Digital Collections website:

https://digitalcollections.nypl.org/items/344b9520-0969-0133-3856-58d385a7bbd0#/?uuid=92ed6850-74fe-0133-cd7c-00505686d14e

To obtain a list of Shoah victims from **Goworowo (Poland),** the reader should access the Yad Vashem web site listed below; one can also search for specific family names using family name option. These lists are continually updated by Yad Vashem, so it is worthwhile to periodically search them.

There is more valuable information (including the Pages of Testimony, etc.) available on this website: https://yvng.yadvashem.org/

A list of all books available from JewishGen Press along with prices is available at:
https://www.jewishgen.org/Yizkor/ybip.html

Cover Photo Credits

Cover Design: Nina Schwartz, Impulse Graphics

Front Cover:

Shiffer family, 1932. Courtesy of Marion Stone. Patriarch Avram Yankel (Avraham Yaakov) sits at center, with daughter Hannah Shiffer Itzkovitch on his right and son-in-law Beryl Itzkovitch on his left. At far left are his daughter Ginny (Hinke) Shiffer and her nephew, Leslie Shiffer, both visiting from England. Behind Avram is an unknown woman, possibly his second wife, Toiva. The rest are unknown.
By 1932, three of Avram's children were living in England. Ginny came to Goworowo to persuade her father to emigrate, but he refused, saying he feared he would lose his Jewish way of life.

Background:

Diagonally opposite the supermarket, Goworowo, ©2010 by Ralph Schmeltz.

Back Cover:

Givner/Farba/Marcus wedding celebration, July, 1934. Courtesy of Alan Givner and Neil Farber. Zalman Farba emigrated to the United States with his older sister's family. He took her married surname and became Sol Givner. On June 23, 1934, Sol Givner married Rose Marcus in New York. This parallel celebration was held two weeks later, between the Farber, Givner, and Marcus families from Goworowo and Ostrów Mazowiecka.

Ruchel Leah Blum (right) with friend, ©1920, courtesy of Lester Blum.

Background:

Across Bridge Street from the Town Square, Goworowo, ©2010 by Ralph Schmeltz.

Geopolitical Information

Map of Poland showing the location of **Goworowo**

Goworowo

Goworowo, Poland is located at 52°54' N 21°34' E 51 miles NNE of Warszawa

	Town	District	Province	Country
Before WWI (c. 1900):	Goworowo	Ostrołęka	Łomża	Russian Empire
Between the wars (c. 1930):	Goworowo	Ostrołęka	Białystok	Poland
After WWII (c. 1950):	Goworowo			Poland
Today (c. 2000):	Goworowo			Poland

Alternate Names for the Town:

Goworowo [Pol], Govorova [Yid], Govorovo [Rus], Govorove

Nearby Jewish Communities:

Wąsewo 4 miles ESE
Różan 6 miles W
Czerwin 8 miles ENE
Długosiodło 9 miles S
Ostrołęka 13 miles N
Kosewo 14 miles E
Poręba-Kocęby 15 miles SSE
Ostrów Mazowiecka 16 miles ESE
Poręba Średnia 16 miles SSE
Brok 18 miles SE
Brańszczyk 18 miles S
Krasnosielc 19 miles WNW
Maków Mazowiecki 20 miles W
Śniadowo 20 miles ENE
Kamieńczyk 21 miles S
Wyszków 21 miles S
Szumowo 22 miles E
Baranowo 22 miles NNW
Pułtusk 23 miles SW
Kadzidło 23 miles N
Prostyń 24 miles SE
Małkinia Górna 24 miles SE
Łopianka 25 miles SSE
Andrzejewo 25 miles E
Zaręby Kościelne 26 miles ESE
Zbójna 26 miles NNE
Nowogród 26 miles NNE
Czarnia 27 miles N
Baczki 27 miles SSE
Stoczek 28 miles SSE
Zambrów 29 miles ENE
Łomża 29 miles NE
Piątnica 30 miles NE
Przasnysz 30 miles WNW
Jadów 30 miles S

Jewish Population: 1,844 (in 1897), 1,085 (in 1921)

Introduction

Growing up in a small town in South Texas, Corpus Christi, our father, Abraham I. Blum z"l often told us tales of his own childhood in Goworowo where he lived until age 15. When he immigrated in 1930 along with his mother and four sisters to join his father, who had previously immigrated to New York in 1923, he left his oldest sister, Ruchel Leah, her husband, their two daughters and his older brother, Moshe behind in Goworowo.

He gave us an expansive glimpse of the family's life in the shtetl which also included the loss of Ruchel Leah and the majority of the Goworowo relatives. This oral history was supported by letters received from Ruchel Leah from 1938-1941 which he had translated.

After his death, we further explored the fate of our family in Goworowo based on those letters as one starting point. Further research formed the basis for the book, *The Spirit of Ruchel Leah* which necessitated the translation of a few sections of the Goworowo Yizkor book. The information was invaluable in providing a foundation regarding the shtetl's individual residents, organizations – religious and secular, education, conflicts, and incidents in the shtetl's history including the Nazi invasion and the burning of the town.

We knew that the book contained more – a wealth of critical accounts that would be of interest to a wide range of readers including descendants of those who lived in Goworowo, researchers/historians and the general reader. This Yizkor book presents social, economic, political and religious information from those who experienced the life in the shtetl. To facilitate the availability of the articles in English, we worked as Project Coordinator with JewishGen to breathe life into the individuals (both living and deceased) and the bygone era.

By reading about their lives, culture and spirit, the translated book has given them back a voice they no longer had. The book will assist in understanding the magnitude of the tragedy of the Holocaust – the murder of six million Jews, the destruction of millions of additional lives, and the dismantling of a magnificent, vibrant European Jewish culture.

The essence of the Goworowo Yizkor book is encapsulated in the poem, *Goworowo* by Shabatai Chrynovizky z'l (1916-2022 Abraham I. Blum's first cousin)

> *My mother, may she rest in peace, was born in Goworowo town*
> *To Grandpa, Nathan-Kalman, bless his memory, and Grandma, Deborah, may she rest in peace,*
> *She was sent to Beit Yaakov School, where she studied Torah.*
>
> *She grew up under those circumstances, she grew up and met father – her husband.*
> *The town lay next to the river*
> *There Jews lived under difficult conditions, and it was horrible.*
>
> *Small businessmen and craftsmen barely could make ends meet.*
> *The Learning House was not far from there where Jews were quick to open in prayers.*
> *People affiliated with different parties, Zionists and Bund, were gathering and participating in endless discussions.*

The "market" was in the center of town
There people could buy and sell and also barter.

So lived the Jews until war broke in 1939, when Hitler raised to power, may his name be blotted out,
and the murderers arrived.
Jews escaped to the fields and forests, literally like terrorized animals.

They locked all the Jews in the Learning House and were going to set them on fire while still alive.
Babies, women and old people were crying, shouting "Hear O Israel" and hoping for a heaven-sent miracle.
Suddenly, without any reason, an SS officer ordered those in charge to open the doors and so they were saved.

So parted the Jews from their sacred and holy souls
They had neither a chance nor a choice
May their souls be bound up in the bond of everlasting life.

The survivors from the horrible terror will remember and remind all their lives, what happened to them.
They will tell and pass their whereabouts to the following generations
And will never forgive!!!

It is crucial for the current generation to study history (life in the Interwar years, during, and after the Holocaust) so that they can understand the present and make an impact on the future.

The Goworowo Yizkor book will ensure that the victims and survivors will not be forgotten.

Lester Blum

Elaine A. Blum

Acknowledgement

Recorded history primarily details the stories of large urban cities, monumental events, and world-renown individuals yet, it is the stories which emanate from the small villages, shtetls, which truly define the pulse of history. We wish to thank and acknowledge the original coordinators and authors of articles in the Goworowo Yizkor book for accomplishing the massive task of creating this memorial to a village and its people.

It is through the efforts of the JewishGen Yizkor Book Project, under the direction of Lance Ackerfeld, that these invaluable accounts of life and death in Goworowo have been translated into English to make this history available to a broader reading audience. The original book consists of articles written by various individuals of varying backgrounds, educational levels, writing styles and proficiency. We were privileged to have had the opportunity to work closely with Lance Ackerfeld during all phases of the translation process. His experience, guidance, expertise, and support contributed to this English version memorial to all who lived, worked, and dreamed.

The translation of the book was a daunting task accomplished by a trio of remarkable individuals – Tina Lunson and Sandra Chirirescu from Yiddish and Mira Eckhaus from Hebrew. Without your devoted work, we, the general reader, would never understand the world that existed in the Interwar years and what was tragically lost during the Holocaust. A mere "Thank You" is not sufficient.

The project would not be complete without publication. To that end, we wish to express our thanks to Nina Schwartz whose devotion and research resulted in captivating graphics for the book cover. Our deepest gratitude is extended to Susan Rosin and the entire team at JewishGen Press Publication for publishing this compelling and informative book about the shtetl of Goworowo.

Dedication

This translation is dedicated to the memory of Abraham I. Blum z"l who was committed to preserve and honor the memory of all the victims of the Holocaust.

Table of Contents

Memories and Episodes

Destruction and Mass Murder

Govorowo Memorial Book
(Goworowo, Poland)

52°54' / 21°34'

Translation of
Goworowo; sefer zikaron

Edited by Aviezer Burstin, Dov Kossovsky

Published by the Govorover Societies in Israel, the USA and Canada, Tel Aviv, 1966

Acknowledgments:

Project Coordinator

Lester Blum

Emeritus coordinator: Martin Jacobs

This translation of the Goworowo Yizkor book has been donated by Lester Blum and Elaine Ann Blum in honor of their father, Abraham Isaac Blum z"l in recognition of his dedication to preserving the memory of the victims of the Holocaust.

This is a translation from *Goworowo; sefer zikaron* [Yiddish: *Govorovo Yizkor-bukh*]
(Govorowo Memorial Book)
Editors: Aviezer Burstin, Dov Kossovsky, Publisher: The Govorover Societies in Israel, the USA and Canada, Tel Aviv, 1966
[*Irgunei yots'ei Govorovo beYisrael, Artsot habrit, veKanada*]
[Yiddish: *Govorovo landsmanshaftn in Yisroel, Amrike [sic] un Kanade*], Pages: 512 Languages: H,Y,E

Note: The original book can be seen online at the NY Public Library site: Goworowo

גוברובה ספר-זכרון
גאוואראווע יזכור-בוך

גוברובה
ספר-זכרון
נערך על-ידי
הרב אביעזר בורשטין
ודב קוסובסקי
הוצאת ארגוני יוצאי גוברובה בישראל, ארצות הברית, וקנדה
תשכ"ו * תל-אביב * 1966

[Page 6]

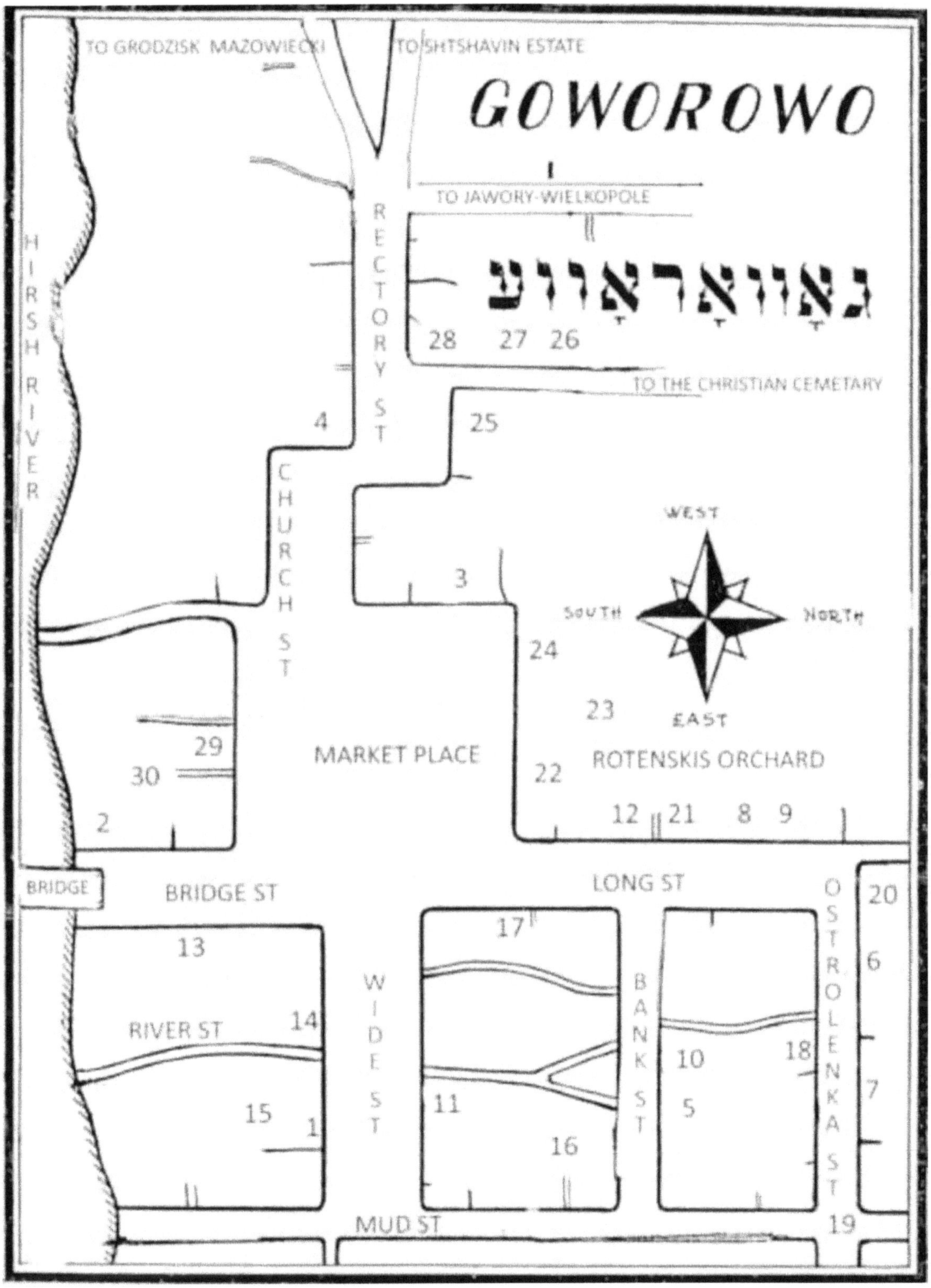
TO GRODZISK MAZOWIECKI
TO SHTSHAVIN ESTATE
GOWOROWO
TO JAWORY-WIELKOPOLE
גאָוואָראָווע
28 27 26
TO THE CHRISTIAN CEMETARY
HIRSH RIVER
RECTORY ST
4
25
CHURCH ST
WEST
SOUTH
NORTH
EAST
3
24
23
29
30
MARKET PLACE
22
ROTENSKIS ORCHARD
2
12 21 8 9
BRIDGE
BRIDGE ST
LONG ST
OSTROLENKA ST
20
13
17
6
WIDE ST
BANK ST
RIVER ST
14
10
18
11
5
7
15
1
16
MUD ST
19

Map legend

1 – Rabbi Alter Burstein Home

2 – Brick Synagogue built 1924/25

3 – Community Center

4 – Church of the Holy Cross

5 – Jewish Credit Bank

6 – Village Hall / Administrative Buildings / Prison

7 – Polish Public School

8 – Family Home occupied by Anschel & Ruchel Leah Taus

9 – Itche Yosel & Schwartza Dvora Taus Home Lazar & Feige Frydman Lived There

10 – The Merchant's Bank

11 – Mendel Chaim Rubin Home

12 – Mikhl (Max) Schmeltz Home

13 – Baruch Kuperman Home

14 – Chana Frydman Home

15 – Mikvah / Sauna Bath

16 – Avrom Meyer Schmeltz Home

17 – Bund & Peretz Library

18 – Village Slaughterhouse

19 – To the Goworowo Train Station

20 – Artisans and Retailers Bank

21 – Esther Shafran Colonial Store

22 – Kosher Restaurant

23 – Village Societal Hall

24 – Avromka Solka Home

25 – Christian Co-operative

26 – Post Office

27 – Police Headquarters

28 – Priest's Home

29 – Hotel & Restaurant

30 – Beit Yaakov School

Map and legend submitted by Lester Blum

[Page 7]

Oh that my head were waters, and mine eyes a fountain of tears, that I might weep day and night for the slain of the daughter of my people!

Jeremiah 8:23

[Pages 8-11]

[Table of Contents]

[Page 14 - Yiddish] [Page 12 - Hebrew]

Forward

by the Editors

Translated by Martin Jacobs

Edited by Gloria Berkenstat Freund

It is with holy trembling and a feeling of great responsibility that we have come to publish the *Goworowo Memorial Book*, which is to be a Book of Lamentation for our community, so tragically destroyed, and a worthy monument on the unknown graves of our dear martyrs, whose ashes and bones are scattered and spread across the woods and fields of Europe.

We are aware that a book is not sufficient to express the great pain and sorrow of a thriving Jewish community, so tragically annihilated by the German murderers, just as all the desolation of a surviving orphan cannot be engraved on a tombstone. And yet the tombstone must be put in place, and the horrible facts written down as a remembrance for us, for our children, and for future generations.

"Remember what Amalek did to you!"

It is our duty to remember and to carry the deep sorrow in our hearts, and it is also a sacred obligation to bear on one's lips an eternal curse for the Nazis and their assistants, who so brutally slaughtered a third of our people.

* * *

The collection and compilation of the material for this book was not so easily accomplished. All the historical sources and archives were destroyed along with the town. Those who died in the ghettos, concentration camps, and in exile can no longer speak. The select few who went through the seven sections of Hell, they too prefer to remain silent and not open the still bleeding, suppurating wounds, even though more than two decades have passed since the Holocaust. Few remain of the survivors who could have revitalized historical events from memory and set them down on paper. Only the feeling and strong belief that we have the sacred task and responsibility to perpetuate the memory of the destroyed town and of the martyrs, just as an orphan has the duty to say *kaddish* for his slain parents – only this has given us the courage and strength to begin the work, almost without resources and with our own powers.

With enormous effort, much patience, and great diligence we succeeded in procuring material – placing one brick upon another and erecting this monument. We have striven to give an objective reflection of the town – its institutions, parties, and organizations; rabbis, leaders, personages, and public figures; general descriptions, chapters on Holocaust and destruction, embroidering of town life,

[Page 15]

which strive to express what is specific and unique about Goworowo.

It must be mentioned that the financial means at our disposal to publish this "Yizkor book" were sufficient either to pay a professional editor (and then no money would have been left for paper, plates, printing, and binding, that is, we would not have a book), or to do everything ourselves, though with limited facilities. Of course we chose the latter course, and so it is quite possible that this book has not been edited in accordance with all accepted literary norms. But our goal was to build a monument and perpetuate the town, and this we believe we have accomplished. We therefore ask you not to look upon this book with a critical eye.

* * *

Although we have spared neither time nor effort in trying to make this work complete, we ourselves know that we are far from having achieved this. Much documentary material, and pictures of importance to the community, are lacking, as well as more detailed reports on institutions, on some political parties, and on important events. It is altogether possible that in "A Walk Through the Town" and in other descriptions and notes, as also in the list of those who perished, some names were left out, or were inaccurate. It may also be that some dates do not agree with reality. Unfortunately this could not be avoided. There were several reasons for this, several obstacles bringing this about. Chief among these were the weak response to our requests and solicitations and the incomprehensible indifference of our fellow townspeople, who unfortunately did not properly appreciate the importance of this book. You must also not forget that the entire gigantic task of publishing a yizkor book – the editing, to a great extent the writing itself, and even the technical work from beginning to end – was accomplished by just two volunteers, with their best efforts and purest motives. We therefore also cannot rule out the possibility that, as a result of the great burden they bore, errors may have crept in. These errors could perhaps have been avoided with greater teamwork. If anyone is disturbed by this and thinks that we have not been sufficiently objective, we ask pardon.

* * *

May this work be a monument to our dear martyrs and an eternal light for their souls, as well as a building block in the great structure of accusation against the world of evil and crime, and also against those who were in a position to provide for the world's welfare, but who looked on quietly and did nothing. May this yizkor book also be a contribution to Holocaust literature and a source for future researchers who will describe this terrible epoch.

The Great Synagogue
[Page 13]

[Page 16]

The *Shtetl*

A Chapter of History

Translated by Martin Jacobs

Edited by Gloria Berkenstat Freund

Goworowo, an entirely Jewish *shtetl* in Congress Poland[1], with a population of close to 500 families, lay on the Warsaw-Łomża Railroad Line, between the towns of Ostrow-Mazowiecki and Ostrołęka. Goworowo belonged to the district (*powiat*) of Ostrołęka, and for many years to the province of Białystok, and just a few years before the last World War the Polish Ministry of the Interior annexed the *shtetl* to Warsaw.

No official materials are available to us which would enable us to investigate how long the *shtetl* existed and since when Jews have lived there. The only historical source is a Polish geographic publication from 1881, *Slownik Geograficzny Krolewstwa Polskiego I Innych Krajow Slowianskich*[*], which states that Goworowo was already in existence in the 16th century. It says, among other things:

"Goworowo, a village on the Hirsh River (Polish name: Orz), Ostrołęka District, Municipality (*gmina*) and Parish of Goworowo, a distance of 20 verst[2] from Ostrołęka. Possesses a wooden church with a masonry chapel, which probably dates from the 16th century. It was renovated by the Bishop of Plock, Andrzej Stanislaw Zalewski, in 1729. The journal "Inżynierja i Budownictwo", April 15, 1881, provides information about a plan of development. Here were an elementary school, a municipal office, and a brewery. In 1827 there were 40 houses and 196 residents in Goworowo; there now are 101 houses and 1485 residents. The Parish of Goworowo, which previously belonged to Malawa and now to Ostrołęka, has 8100 residents. The Municipality of Goworowo has 4747 residents. The local court of the third district is in Czerwin, a distance of 12 ½ verst[3]. The following localities belonged to the Municipality of Goworowo: Goworowo settlement, and the villages of Brizhner-Vulke (Brzezińska Wólka),

[Page 17]

Guri (Góry), Grodzhisk (Grodzisk), Yemyeliste (Jemieliste), Yuzefova (Józefowo), Kotshko (Kaczka), Kobilin (Kobylin), Groys-Ponikve (Ponikiew-duża), Kleyn-Ponikve (Ponikiew-mała), Pakshevnitse (Pokrzywnica), Rembis (Rębisze or Rembisze), and also Govoruvek (Goworówek), Lipyanki (Lipianka), and Zabin (Żabin)[4]."

As can be seen, the Goworowo population figures in several periods are overall counts. No mention at all is made of Jews, although our parents and grandparents were already living in the *shtetl* in the last period, and there already was a lively Jewish life in the town.

According to oral tradition, Jews were among the co-founders of the *shtetl.* Older Jews could tell of a visit to the town of the Vilna Rabbi Abraham Danzig (1748-1820, author of "Haye Adam" and "Hokhmat Adam", as well as of "Tephila zaka"). It has also been determined that the famous rabbi of Posen (Poznan), Rabbi Akiva Eger (1761-1837), visited Goworowo on his way to Łomża at the end of the 18th century.

At the time of the Polish uprising of 1794 a Jewish rebel, Shmuel Tot, was well known in Goworowo. Old Jews reported that he became an informer, out of a great sense of Polish patriotism, and brought much trouble to the Jewish population. He had a sad end: the Russian government found him out and buried him alive.

We must assume that a large part of the Jewish population at that time lived in Wulki (Wólka), a little village on the other side of the River Hirsh from Goworowo. This fact is confirmed on its title page by an old manuscript of *Sepher Musar Haskel*; the book was published in Warsaw in 1857. Among other things, "Wulki-Govorovo" is explicitly written there. The fact that the cemetery was located not far from Wulki is evidence that there were many Jews.

At the time of the second Polish uprising, in 1863, the Jews of Goworowo contributed much to its success and fought side by side with the

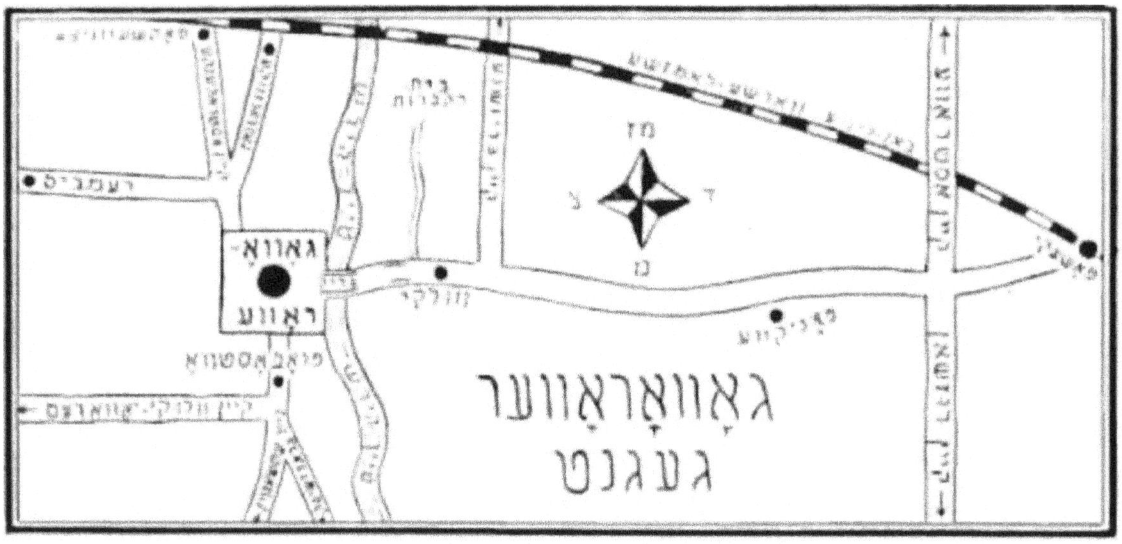

Goworowo area - drawn according to memory

[Page 18]

Polish patriots against the czarist satraps. It is said that after the suppression of the uprising the Jews hid the Polish rebels in their houses, dressed them in Hasidic garb, with *talis* and *tefilin*, and so rescued them from the Russian soldiers, who were searching for them throughout the area.

We found information about the size of the Jewish population in Goworowo at the end of the 19th century in the *Yevreyskaya Entsiklopedya,* vol. 12. It is stated there that the total number of inhabitants of the *shtetl* was 2139, of whom 1844 were Jews. These figures were confirmed by the German language encyclopedia published by Eshkol, vol. 7, which adds that in 1921 the total population reached 5299 residents but with only 1228 Jews.

* * *

In the first World War the *shtetl* suffered greatly from the retreating Russian army. Goworowo was the first town to be accused of espionage by the Russians, because of the so-called "eyruvim-telegraph"[5]. Because of this slander the last rabbi of Goworowo, Rabbi Burshtin, was arrested, along with several respected citizens of the *shtetl.* When others strongly intervened they were freed pending court appearance. The rabbi used this freedom to go to Rabbi Rubinstein in Vilna, whose efforts led to the annulment by special royal decree from St. Petersburg of the senseless slander. Nevertheless, before retreating from the *shtetl* on Shabos Nakhamu 1915, the Russians burnt the *shtetl*, and the entire Jewish population scattered to the neighboring towns and *shtetlekh* and some even fled deep into Russia.

After the occupation by the German army, some of the Jews who had fled Goworowo returned to the *shtet* and began to rebuild the ruins. The local German administration did not disturb them in this task. At the same time many sources of income opened up for the Jewish residents. With the end of the first World War, in 1918, those Jews of the town who had gone deep into Russia also returned, and a lively Jewish life again developed. It seemed that at last an era of peace and tranquility had arrived, but then new troubles started, from the new "masters", the Bolsheviks, and from the sadly famous "Hallerczyki" of the Polish Army of Awakening[6]. A flood of hostile decrees and persecutions were unleashed upon the *shtetl*, which were accompanied by levies, mishaps, beard shavings, incidents of Jews being thrown from trains, and attacks in general.

At that time the Bolsheviks arrested the Christian parish priest Goszczicki, nephew of Cardinal Kokowski of Warsaw. The leaders of the Poles turned to Rabbi Burshtin to intervene with the Jewish Bolshevik commissar on the priest's behalf. The intervention helped and the priest was freed. As an expression of thanks

[Page 19]

the priest sent the Rabbi a cordial letter with an solemn promise never to forget this deed. A short time later the priest was again arrested and the Poles turned once more to the rabbi for his intervention. This time however the rabbi had himself been arrested and sent with the prisoner convoy to Rozan fortress. The accusation carried with it the death penalty. As the rabbi sat in sadness in the detention center, reciting psalms in a loud voice, a Jewish officer came and said to him: Rabbi, we are quite a large group of Jewish soldiers and we will lie down under the horses if they try to take the rabbi from here to be shot. That same evening the door of the detention center opened and a quiet voice whispered from without: Rabbi, door and gate are open, flee! And in this way the rabbi was saved from certain death.

When the Polish forces took power there were pogroms against the Jews throughout the region. In Goworowo too the peasants gathered in the market place and armed themselves with axes and sticks. Then the parish priest appeared before the masses in his holy garments and said to the peasants, "Brothers! No Jew will be beaten in this town." The crowd dispersed and thus a pogrom against the Jews was averted in Goworowo.

* * *

During Polish rule and up to the outbreak of the last war life in the *shtetl* was relatively peaceful. There was no noticeable public antisemitism. Only with the latest "Owszem" policy[7] of the Polish government, when it officially called for suppression of Jewish commerce and businesses, was a quiet boycott and picketing of Jewish shops called. The friendly relations between the Jews and their Christian neighbors, long dear to the hearts of both, did much to weaken the boycott plans. Most of the antisemitic agitators came from outside the town. They looked resentfully at the peaceful relations between the Jewish and Christian populations.

Goworowo was considered a business town and had a greater economic base than neighboring *shtetlekh* of the same size. The middle class, consisting of merchants and craftsmen, provided the surrounding Christian villages with merchandise. These villages were thickly populated and relied greatly on the Goworowo merchants and craftsmen.

Among the Goworowo craftsmen, the cobblers, tailors, and hatters stood out. They exhibited their wares in fairs in the most distant towns and *shtetlekh.* These craftsmen of the fairs, the so called *tandeyters* (bunglers), produced rough goods, used only by the peasants. But there were also good craftsmen in the *shtetl*,

[Page 20]

who produced for the Jews of the *shtetl* and for a great many Christians of the surrounding area and who thought of themselves as more aristocratic than the *tandeyters*.

There was also in the *shtetl* a class of wealthier Jews who managed businesses and engaged in commerce with a broad scope. To this class belonged the brothers Neta and Iser Ritz, owners of the big steam mill and electric works of the *shtetl*; the brothers-in-law Isaac Kosowsky and Matisyohu Rosen (for many years also the latter's son-in-law David Segal), who used to deal in wood on a large scale and also held the lease on the saw mill from Glinka, the Christian owner of the estate. They cut the timber there and exported most of it. Later they were also in the business of the construction of wooden houses and they also dealt in building materials. Meir Wolf Tehillim was the owner of cement construction material businesses at the Pasheki (Pasieki) railroad station and of coal warehouses. To the wealthy class also belonged the merchants of manufactured and agricultural products, as well as the grain and meat dealers.

However, most of the residents were retailers, brokers, shipping agents, and craftsmen, who eked out their livelihood with difficulty. The support which relatives and fellow-townspeople sent from America contributed much to this class.

The banks contributed greatly to the economic development of the *shtetl.* The Merchants' Bank, "Bank Kredytowy", the "Artisans and Retailers Bank" and the Free Loan Society were active there.

The economic situation was relatively good and this was reflected in the spiritual and cultural development of the *shtetl.* In this field too Goworowo was an example for all other *shetlekh* in the area. In outward appearance alone the residents of Goworowo had already made an impression with their feeling for aesthetic purity and their pleasing sense of dress, their homes with uncrowded, beautiful furnishings, and their pretensions to elegance.

Many of the townspeople were well known for their philanthropy and hospitality. For many years the *shtetl* supported, at its own expense, a *yeshiva* with many students from the surrounding communities.

Goworowo selected as rabbis great scholars who could have had rabbinical chairs in the greatest cities in the country. Our generation well remembers the last three rabbis: the Gaon Rabbi Aaron Klepfish, author of *Bet Aharon*, a brother of the last Senior President of the Warsaw rabbinical court Rabbi Samuel Zeinwel Klepfish; the Gaon Rabbi Jacob Judah Cahana-Batshan, author of *VeShab HaKohen*, a distinguished scholar, day and night engaged in Torah study and prayer; and the last rabbi, the Gaon and Martyr Rabbi Alter Moshe Mordechai Burshtin, who was one of the leading Torah scholars of the last generation. His astuteness and sagacity were renowned. He commanded respect and was a successful leader of his congregation. The Rabbi was martyred in the Treblinka death camp in the month of Ab 5703[8].

[Page 21]

All communal and charitable institutions were active in Goworowo, as in all Jewish towns in Poland: a community administration with a president of many years, the Martyr Moshe Tennenbaum, and after him the Martyr Neta Ritz, and then the last one, the Martyr Moses Kosher; the burial society, having as its trustees Matisyohu Rosen, Isaia Eisenberg and Meir Romaner; a network of religious elementary schools, some under communal supervision; a *Yavne* school for the children of parents with Zionist inclinations, a religious *Beys Yakov* school, a *Tsish"o* for Bundists and Yiddishists, and a state elementary school where Jewish and Christian children studied together, which had two Jewish women teachers.

Preeminent among the charitable institutions were *Linas Hatsedeq*, which distributed medical aid to the ill; *Hakhneses Orhim*, for poor people traveling through the town; a Free Loan Society, *Hakhneses Kala*[9] and *Biqur-Holim*[10]. For several years starting immediately after the First World War the American "Joint" conducted its rescue work in the *shtetl.*

After the burning of the town in the First World War a temporary wooden prayer house (*beys-medresh*) was constructed; it could hardly hold the town's worshipers. After several years a splendid masonry synagogue, higher than all the houses in the *shtetl*, was built, on the initiative of the last rabbi, Rabbi Burshtin, with the active assistance of a Goworowo townsman (*landsman*) in America, Mr. Klass, and his wife Sore-Gitl.

In addition to the town's *beys medrash* there were other prayer houses and Hasidic *shtiblekh,* like the Alexander *shtibl,* the Gerer*shtibl,* Vurker-Atvatsker*shtibl,* the*Mizrahi-minyen*, the so-called "Smooth" *minyen* (where young men without beards prayed), etc. In almost every *beys-medrash* there were special study groups, such as the Talmud group, the Mishna group, the Psalms study group, the Torah study group, and others.

Organizations affiliated with all political parties in the country without exception were active in the *shtetl.* With their intensive activity, the organizations made an enormous impression on the party headquarters in Warsaw and therefore the latter had a very respectful relationship with them. Here were: the General Zionist Organization HaTehiya with its library; Po'ale-Tsion (right wing), Frayhayt, their dramatic circle and the Brenner library; Revisionists, Betar and their library; Mizrahi, HeHaluts-HaMizrahi, HaShomer-HaDati; Po'ale-Tsion (left wing); HaShomer HaTsa'ir; HeHaluts, and Ha'Oved. These parties together carried on the work of the communal benevolent fund (*Qeren-Qayemes*) and the Palestine foundation fund (*Qeren-HaYesod*) in the *shtetl.* In addition there were Agudas-Yisroel, Tse'irey Agudas-Yisroel, Bnos-Agudas-Yisroel and their Beys-Ya'akov school. The Bund organization had one of its biggest divisions in Goworowo, along with its youth organizations Tsukunft and Ski"f and the Perets library. There was also an illegal Communist party. All the above mentioned parties conducted lively cultural and social activities. At least once a week each organization arranged a lecture, a discussion evening[11], an athletic competition, entertainment, or a performance

[Page 22]

by its drama circle. From time to time the drama circles used to perform in the surrounding areas. The party headquarters used to send Goworowo the best speakers, well known personalities and instructors with many years of service in the party. The political and non-political press sold well, including *HaSfira*, *Haynt*, *Moment*, *Togblat*, *Folkstsaytung*, and all the other newspapers.

Despite the above mentioned parties, some of which openly claimed to be "free thinking", the *shtetl* was in general deeply religious, and the *beys-medrash* was always filled with people praying and studying. In the evening hours the toiling masses sat down around the long wooden tables and listened to Rabbi Betsalel Yusl teaching Psalms with Alshikh's commentary, with his sweetly haunting melody. Even ordinary people who understood no Torah shyly listened to the sounds of the Torah's holy words.

At the right side of the *beys-medrash*, at the windows which looked out on the river Hirsh, the "beautiful people" sat and studied the daily Gemara page together.

Around the two great tile ovens the *Holkhey-Nemishes* always gathered. Between a *kadish* and a *borkhu* they discussed the latest political news of the world. The coming of a preacher speaking of consolation and punishment drew much attention in the *shtetl*. People listened to him with baited breath.

Goworowo also had a reputation as a comfortable and peaceful town, where good relations among people reigned. This was especially evident at celebrations. If a Jew of the town made a wedding for his child, everyone felt like a relative; every woman considered it a necessity to come to the house of the celebrant. Some were occupied in baking and roasting, some helped dress the bride, and some simply gave their opinion. Marriages for the most part took place in the synagogue courtyard, and leading the bride and groom to and from the *khupe* used to turn into a real triumphal march through the town, with music, torches, fireworks, and dancing.

On Sabbaths and holidays, especially *Sukos* and *Simhas-Tora*, the town threw off all cares and joy was felt in every corner. The large yearly banquet of the *Khevre-Kadishe* was conducted with solemnity. It took place on the eve of the month of Shvat after a day of fasting and penitential prayers. At the banquet the community record book, in which were inscribed the important events of the year, was opened,. There too were noted the names of townspeople who had done good or ill, so that this day in the khevre-kadishe was a day of judgment for sinners, especially those who sinned against their fellow man.

The same reciprocity could be seen at sad events. If anyone in the town became ill countless people came to visit him and at night they divided into groups

[Page 23]

to watch over the patient. When there was (Heaven protect us) a funeral, everyone closed his business and considered it his duty to accompany the deceased at least across the bridge which led to the cemetery.

The cemetery was over a kilometer from the town. It was well tended, with trees and greenery, and surrounded by a masonry wall. Many of the grave stones were unreadable; due to their age the name and date of death of the deceased could not be determined.

* * *

Goworowo was a beautiful, peaceful, cordial town, full of life and Jewish charm. Strong invisible threads of love and respect tied the Jews of Goworowo to the town of their birth. Even those whom fate has driven abroad, across seas and wildernesses, have not cut the threads and have not been able to erase from their memories the place where their cradles stood, where they took the first steps in their lives.

The Goworowo associations and active *landsmanshaft* committees are spread across the world, from Canada and America to Israel. They see as their sacred goal maintaining a mutual fraternal contact and honoring with love and reverence the memory of their destroyed birthplace, Goworowo.

The location of the cemetery. Plowed under after the war.

* In publishing house of Filip Sulimerski and Władisław Waleski. Printed. *Wieku* [Century] Nowy Świat 59

A Chapter of History - Translator's notes:

1. In the late 18th century Poland was partitioned among Prussia, Austria, and Russia, and ceased to exist as an independent country. "In 1815 the Congress of Vienna . . . reassembled Europe after nearly a quarter century of warfare but did not see fit to restore Poland . . . . . The only change of importance was the curious creation of the Congress Kingdom of Poland. . . . this fragment of historic Poland was given a separate administration under Russian rule and allowed a considerable measure of autonomy. . . . The ruler of the Congress Kingdom was the Russian tsar who locally was deemed the king of Poland." From *The History of Poland* by M. B. Biskupski.
2. 13.3 miles or 21.2 km
3. 8.3 miles or 13.3 km
4. For Polish names see the *Słownik Geograficzny* and maps of the area on the web site www.pilot.pl.
5. During the First World War, the occupying Russians thought the *"erub"* was a secret telephone line for communicating with the enemy. See the English introduction to this book, pp. x-xi. (Although the matter is a bit more complicated than this, you can get some idea what an *erub* or *eruv* is from this definition in Weinreich's dictionary: "wire strung on the circumference of a town to classify it as enclosed private property in which objects may be carried on the Sabbath according to Jewish law".)
6. The Hallerczyki were the followers of Józef Haller, the first head of the Polish army after independence at the end of World War I.
7. "The infamous *owszem* or economic boycott politics began in June 1936, after being suggested in the inaugural speech of the new Prime Minister of Poland, General F. Slawoy-Skladkowski. This policy encouraged Polish customers to boycott Jewish businessmen, shops, handicraftsmen, and factories. Actively implemented by the nationalist extremists, the policy consisted of more than propaganda. It involved picketing Jewish stores and threatening Poles who dared enter, smashing store windows,

overturning stalls and pushcarts, destroying merchandise, and knifing and beating Jewish owners. " See http://davidhorodok.tripod.com/4a.html.
"As the Polish economy deteriorated during the Great Depression and the rise of Hitler and the collapse of the League of Nations in the 1930s underscored the fragility of Polish security, Polish society became increasingly concerned about unity and safety. Thus the Jewish situation deteriorated , especially after Piłsudski's death in 1935. Although Poland never passed anti-Semitic legislation, discrimination against Jews was widespread in administrative practice, including restriction to institutions of higher learning. Public outbursts of anti-Semitism, including economic boycotts and occasional street violence, were quite frequent in the late 1930s. It was a sad last chapter in the ancient tradition of Polish-Jewish cohabitation in the lands of the old Commonwealth."
From *The History of Poland* by M. B. Biskupski.

8. 1943
9. Philanthropic provision for the marriage of poor and orphaned girls.
10. Society for visiting the sick.
11. *kestl-ovnt.* I am indebted to Shane Baker for the meaning of this word. To paraphrase his remarks (Forverts Sho, 15 February 2003): several questions of current interest are written down and then selected for discussion by those present.

The transcribing of Hebrew words into English is full of pitfalls. Transcriptions that are readable are not accurate; those that are accurate are hardly readable. I apologize in advance for any inconsistencies in my own system.

Proper names pose a difficulty for the translator, since we cannot in general know from the Yiddish how the individual in question would have written his/her name in Latin letters. Again I beg the indulgence of the reader for any inconsistencies, as well as discrepancies from Latin letter spellings that are unknown to me but might be known to the reader.

[Page 24]

Goworowo Half A Century Ago

by Abraham Schwartzberg (Argentina)

Translated by Martin Jacobs

Edited by Gloria Berkenstat Freund

As far back as I can remember, the Jewish population of Goworowo was always religious. Every morning and evening the Jews filled the study hall (*beys-hamedresh*) for the morning prayer and the afternoon and evening prayers. Preachers would often come to the town to speak between afternoon and evening prayer and to give the people ethical instruction (*musar*). Weaving through their talks were sayings of the Sages (*Khazal*), suitable proverbs, Hasidic sayings, and topical stories. And so they reinvigorated the worshippers and did much to help sustain the religious spirit.

The residents were split between Hasidim and Misnagdim[1]. The great study hall belonged to the Misnagdim. The Hasidim were further divided into separate *shtibelekh*[2], each following its *rebe*[3], such as

Alexander Hasidim, Gerer Hasidim, and so forth. These *shtibelekh* were located in the same building as the great study hall of the Misnagdim and they all lived together in peace and harmony.

As a result of the differing opinions among the townspeople, problems with a new cantor, a ritual slaughterer, or a rabbi were difficult to solve. The Misnagdim wanted the religious officials to be from their group and the Hasidim from theirs. Meetings were held, assemblies were called, they discussed, they argued, they got angry, until finally, after long discussion and deliberation, an agreement was reached and again there was peace among Jews.

Children's education was in the *kheyder*[4]. When they were just four or five the children were sent to a *dardekey melamed* (teacher of the youngest children). Gradually they were led into the study of Talmud, together with *Tosfos* and other commentators. Most of the students, on finishing *kheyder*, went on to learn a trade. The brighter boys, I too among them, left in order to continue studying in the *yeshives* of Ostrowa, Lomza, and elsewhere.

Teaching the children writing was the task of the *rebe*[5]. In the larger *kheyders* one hour a day was set aside for this purpose. There was also a Russian school (up to 1917 Poland belonged to Russia[6]) for the Christian residents of the town and the surrounding area. The Jewish children were required to attend the school one hour a day, from 4 to 5 PM. There they were taught to read and write Russian. There was also a private Jewish teacher in the town who gave lessons in Yiddish, Polish, German, Hebrew, and arithmetic. The only existing organization was the *Khevre Kadishe*[7], which was concerned

[Page 25]

with cemetery problems. Once a year they held a religious dinner (*seudes mitsve*), which was only for members of the organization, where they dealt with matters concerning their activities.

There were no movements of a political nature in Goworowo, such as Zionism, Socialism, etc., and so there was no party activity to record. There were however individuals, workers, who were well versed in Marxist social theories, in other words, the eternal struggle between labor and capital. Their claim was that only social revolution could bring about the liberation of mankind. Being without followers, however, they kept apart from the community. The few *maskilim*[8] of that time also kept themselves apart. Evidently they were waiting for better times.

There was no library in the town. The entire reading material for young people consisted of books of stories about kings, princes, and other strange and fantastic tales, which were at that time in abundance. The youths used to get together in smaller groups on the long winter evenings at the home of a friend to read "literature", that of Shomer, Motke Khabad, Hershele Ostropoler, Simkhe Plakhte, and others.

Though since the end of the last century political Zionism as well as socialist movements had already begun to crystallize in the Jewish world, they had not yet penetrated to Goworowo. Only in about 1910 did the *Haskala* movement in the town begin to come out into the open and spread more and more among the youth. New winds began blowing, bearing a message for other times. A new era was beginning for the young. Among the older lads, those over 20, there was a small number of conscious autodidacts, keeping to themselves, not trying to spread their mode of thinking; they were waiting for the right time. "What reason cannot accomplish time will,"[9] they would assert, and that is just what happened. With the great fervor of youth they threw themselves into the *Haskala* movement, together with Zionist consciousness, which became their ideal for the future.

In many homes books by Mendele Moykher-Sforim, Isaac Leybush Perets, Abraham Reyzin, and others now appeared. Zionist literature was also already beginning to spread. Many were beginning to study Hebrew. A general revival was noticeable. A joy shone from the faces of the youth, an awakening to a new world, unknown to them.

I remember how, in spring time and in summer twilight, groups of boys and girls would go out for a walk on the road that led from behind the church (*probostwo*). They sang Yiddish songs by Perets, Reyzin, and also Moyshe Leyb Lilenblum, who was popular among the young at that time.

The older, more progressive youth had to put up with serious fights from

[Page 26]

their parents; these fights were often quite dramatic. The author of these lines used to witness, when he was a pupil of Yosl the *melamed*[10], how he would go after his son because of his *Haskala* ideas, and he gave his son some difficult moments. At the time, as a boy of 10, I already felt resentment towards my teacher for the emotional pain he so appallingly caused his only son.

At that time Benjamin Ginzburg, a son of Moses Joshua Ginzburg, appeared in Goworowo; he was a very knowledgeable and educated young man in his twenties. Benjamin came from Bialystok, where he was devoted heart and soul to the *Haskala* movement of that era. He was also active in the *hoveve-tsion* grouping, whose founder was Moyshe Leyb Lilenblum. Benjamin spread these ideas among the Goworowo youth, and he immediately won over the 13 to 14 year old Talmud students. He lavished attention on them and led them into a new world which was absolutely foreign to them. Ginzburg created concepts for them, concepts about the world and mankind, and at the same time they began to read Hebrew periodicals and newspapers of the time, becoming acquainted with Jewish problems as well as world politics.

All this, however was done privately and not within the framework of any organization. The reading, the discussions, the conversations were conducted during the walks in the twilight hours and on various other occasions. But their parents still found out about it and were angry with their children. The Rabbi too threatened the youth with various sanctions for straying from the true path. “Heretics, God forbid,” he said, “can bring misfortunes upon the town, such as illnesses and epidemics” and he went on and on. But no one took this seriously and in time it became just a habit; the anger gradually passed away.

The author of these lines, despite his participation in Benjamin Ginzburg's Enlightenment work, continued his Talmud studies in the *beys-hamedresh*. Because of my religious orientation, I was attracted by the Talmud melodies and the keen and subtle argumentation, as well as the interesting controversies among the authorities of the Mishna and the Gemara. The questions and answers of the various commentators especially sharpened my wits; among these were *Tosfos* and Maharsha. Every sentence contained wisdom and acumen. Young men, including those on *kest*[11], were found daily in the study halls applying themselves almost all day. There were also those who came only at certain hours of the day to “snatch” a page of Talmud for their spiritual satisfaction. The Talmud melodies could be heard coming from the study hall late into the night. They resounded all around. I was also fascinated by the discussions about Maimonides, Yehuda HaLevi, Baal Shem-Tov, and others, which were all new to me at the time, and so I was introduced to the great figures of past generations.

[Page 27]

The discussions about astronomy, cosmology, and other scientific concepts found in secular books, until then forbidden in Goworowo, were also very interesting.

During the First World War of 1914 the Russian military burnt Goworowo to the ground. After the German occupation the town was again beginning to be rebuilt; that was before it was under Polish administration. A new life began, especially among the youth. The Russian revolution of 1917, on which East European Jewry had placed much hope, especially had a great influence on the young. With all the fervor of youth they plunged into politics. Some even began to believe in the ideals of the Revolution. Most, however, remained loyal to the Zionist ideal and the directions in which it was going. Many, at first deceived by the beautiful revolutionary slogans, grew sober about the supposedly new ideas. The Balfour Declaration appeared and the activity of the Zionist parties was strengthened.

The wave of anti-semitism which penetrated the population with the approval of the new Polish government, and the boycott it carried on against Jewish crafts and trade, led to a great emigration by the young. Thousands of young people in Poland, among them from Goworowo, applied at the English consulate in Warsaw for entry visas for Palestine. Because of the great demand the English consul continually created new difficulties and restrictions, until emigration to Palestine completely stopped. Having no choice, the youth had to shift their emigration plans to the countries of South and Central America, and to wherever it was still possible to go to escape from Poland.

At the time agricultural training centers had already been set up in the villages, to which groups of Zionist youth were sent to work with farmers. For a set period of time they used to work in the fields and become familiar with farming, which they would need when they came to Palestine. The youth went to the agricultural centers with joy and with the idea and belief in a great goal, the ideal of the return to Zion. And this was the merit of David Ginzburg, to sow the seed among the youth of Goworowo which in time began to sprout, to grow, and to send down deep roots.

Translator's notes:

1. Hasidim are the followers of the religious leader known as the Baal Shem-Tov. Misnagdim are their opponents. Both groups, however, are strictly Orthodox.
2. A shtibl (plural: shibelekh) is a small Hasidic prayer house.
3. "Rebe" here means the leader of a Hasidic sect.
4. A Jewish traditional elementary school.
5. Here "rebe" means a teacher in a kheyder.
6. Actually only the eastern third of Poland, in which Goworowo was located. The remainder of Poland was split between Germany and Austria.
7. A volunteer burial society
8. Followers of the Enlightenment movement, or *Haskala*.
9. A popular saying.
10. A teacher in a *kheyder*.
11. The reference is to newly married men living with and supported by their in-laws so that they can continue their studies.

[Page 28]

Once There Was…

by Meyshe Granat, Israel

Translated by Tina Lunson

Once there was a little Jewish town Goworowo. The town was not distinguished with especially beautiful views of nature. It was on flat land with no hills, no forests nearby. But fields and gardens surrounded the town on every side. In summer it was bathed in green: fields of grain on tall stalks, and aromas from the fruit orchards and the lilac trees literally intoxicated the air. No smoke from factory chimneys choked us or made it difficult to breathe; factory sirens did not split the Eden-like quiet. The only whistle that was allowed to be heard two or three times over twenty-four hours was that of the Warsaw-Lomze train that stopped for a minute to take on and let off passengers. The whistle cut through the calm and cut into the pleasant stillness.

The town possessed two main streets: The Long Street, the Broad Street, and the market square. Besides those, there were a few small lanes that had various names or no name at all but were referred to by the name of a particular householder who lived there.

Goworowo had two suburbs: 1.) Vulke, on the other side of the river, over the two bridges. This was a poor village, which later separated from our Goworowo. The cemetery – which was beyond Vulke – originated long ago, when Goworowo was still a suburb of Vulke. 2.) Probosva, a tidy, lovely suburb after the Catholic church, where the Polish intellectuals lived. Also there: the priestly palace, the Polish cooperative with the inscription *"Svay do Svega"* on a plaque, the police station, the post office, the town doctor, for a long time the apothecary, and others. The whole environment possessed perfumy gardens and orchards. Some Jewish families also lived there, in houses they inherited from generation to generation since the beginning of time. We always wondered where Jews got the strength to settle themselves among so many gentiles.

The youth in both suburbs liked to stroll the streets in the evenings. Gentile youths concerned themselves with keeping Jews, heaven forbid, from crossing outside their defined area and wandering into the gentile territory. Very rarely did anyone oppose them.

[Page 29]

Therefore, Jews strolled up and down the long street; and since the civilization on wheels was a little delayed in coming to Goworowo they could take up the whole width of the street, from edge to edge. On Shabes day the strolling area was larger – during that day one could walk without fear all over the town.

The river in Goworowo ran through in three seasons of the year. In summer it shrank so that it was pitiful even to look at it. Every day someone remarked that it was "dying" a little. Even children could cross the river in summertime. They just took off their shoes, rolled up their trousers to the knee and without difficulty crossed the so-called "meadow". In autumn, when the rains began, and in spring when the snow was melting, the river grew wide and often over its banks. The river was at its full beauty then. In winter, when the river was frozen, people skated on it and pursued all sorts of winter sports. In order to haul water, it was necessary to cut a hole in the ice. More than one skater took a fall in such a *psheremblie*. Every winter they cut out blocks of ice and filled Meyshe Tenenboym's underground ice warehouse so that the town would have ice-cream and cool drinks in the summer. When someone had a high fever, another would run to the proprietor of the ice to request a piece of ice as a cure.

Beyond all that, the river had another assignment: When a food shop had an empty herring barrel, they would set it in the river, fill it with stones and after a time they took out a clean barrel, for making sauerkraut or to store water. And women sat the length of the river and washed their laundry. The population considered this a completely natural thing to do.

Every Thursday was a market day in town, and once a month there was a fair. The peasants came with wagons loaded with merchandise and filled up the market square, the broad street and other specified places around the town. On those days a "concert" of living voices was performed, from dawn until evening, enough to deafen. The Jewish grain-merchants – who earned their profit for the whole week at the market – ran busy and bustling from one wagon to another, touching and inspecting each sack of grain. They bargained with the peasants, and they slapped one another's palms once they had settled on a price and the transaction was closed. Where was there enough space in that small town to store so much grain? Potatoes, fruits, chickens and other items that the peasants brought in plenty. The shopkeepers also waited for market day: the peasants filled their shops and bought herring, salt, fuel oil, clothing, manufactured

[Page 30]

tools and all other necessary articles. The Jewish shopkeepers, like all the other merchants and dealers, lived the whole week from that day.

The Jews felt good in the town. There was no power that could change their way of life. Families had rooted themselves, bound themselves to one another and did not want to leave the town. If a family became cramped, they just built on another room, or raised another story, in order to stay in the same place.

The *Shabes* was one of the most beautiful treasures that the town possessed. A holy calm poured over everything and everyone. One moved from the weekdays into a zone of complete holiness. One threw off the heavy yoke of livelihood, forgot all worries. Hurriedness stopped, people began walking easily, with measured steps. They washed themselves well, dressed in their sabbath clothes and went to pray in a shul or in one of the [hasidic] *shtiblekh.* Some simply went for a sabbath walk. The table was set with Shabes dishes and tall candlesticks with burning lights that added a splendor and a mysterious mood. The whole family sitting around one table and the specific Shabes foods and songs created a particular impression.

Each holiday was celebrated according to all the laws and customs, especially the holiday of *Peysakh* [Passover]. Right after *Purim* people were already preparing ovens and bakeries where carefully-observed *matsos* would be baked. The week before Peysakh eve people took everything out of the house; everything was whitewashed, laundered, scoured, and the books were aired out. *Kashering* the utensils and burning the *khomets* [yeast-containing foods] was a special event in the town, particularly for the children. Jews in various locations in town tended kettles of boiling water and *koshered* the utensils that the wives brought them. One could smell the burning *khomets* all over the town, along with the "feather-dusters".

The interim days [of the eight-day holiday] were used for visiting. No one worked on those days. Teachers would go around in the streets and search out householders to give them a holiday greeting and then pester them into enrolling a *kheyder* pupil for the next term. Craftsmen negotiated with the worker-societies about prices. Each interim, they were supposed to get a few *zlotych.* The *Sukos* interim, as in *Peysakh* interim, was the "season" for the teachers, workers and servants in the household economy. The "contracts" were renewed and as a rule, with a raise. Jews had a good time during *Simkhes Torah.* They drank whisky, pilfered stews and honey-cakes, brought them into the *shtibelekh* and danced on the tables. And so they did on all the other holidays that were celebrated with such beauty and luster.

I recall *Tishe b'ov*: The congregation went to shul with burlap shoes on their feet, sat on over-turned benches and recited Lamentations with a weeping intonation. Everyone moaned with heartrending voices, both for the destruction

[Page 31]

of the Temple in Jerusalem and for their own problems. At the same time, it was more lively in the street. A group of boys had meanwhile prepared "forest-burrs" and thrown them into the hair of the girls' heads. They generally did hit their targets and the burrs remained stuck in the hair as if grown there. Only with much effort could the burrs be freed. The girls cursed, made believe that bandits would attack the boys, but they did not run away. Others just took care to cover their hair with head scarves.

The children all studied with private teachers, from the alphabet teachers up to the teachers of Talmud. When each boy turned four years old, he was taken with much ceremony to the alphabet teacher. The teacher showed the child, using a long, sharp-ended pointer, the first page of the prayer book and the letters of the blessing of the moon, and slowly elucidated the name of each letter separately. The father threw down from above, a large copper coin and called out with affected joy, "The good angel is throwing this down for you, may you be an observant Jew!" The father later gave the child some sweets in order to give him more desire to go to school.

At five years he was already learning to pray. At six years, it was *khumesh* [the Torah, five books of Moses] with commentary by RaSh"I, and explication of the Torah portion. At eight years he was studying Talmud. The sanitary conditions in the *khedarim* were far from any ideal. The teacher was always "a pauper with seven coattails" and the study room often also served as kitchen and even as bedroom as well. Besides the teacher who maintained the children in the stifling room from morning until evening, the children often had over them the teacher's wife, and on top of that, also his children who hungrily begged the *kheyder* pupils for the bread with butter, which their mothers had sent with them.

I recall an image of my *kheyder* that I will never forget: The room was very small. There were no windows, only a small window in the door. That light was barely enough to see the letters in the book. For a living, along with the teaching, the wife ran a dying business in the same room, and every time she stirred the dyes in the kettle with a long stick, the steam spread over the little room so that it was "as dark as it was in Egypt"; it also made such a stink as to take your breath away. The wife – understandably, as an advertisement for her business – wore all the colors and never washed them. She spoke with a mannish voice and all day cursed her husband and anyone else who, ostensibly, crossed her.

The teacher's tiny house stood a little higher than all the other little houses, and a few of the asymmetrical stones served as steps up to the entrance, which was narrow and low. The table around which we sat was narrow and long and made from unplanned boards. The children sat on long benches on both sides of the table with the teacher at the head. There was no recess

[Page 32]

for the children to play outdoors a little. Even in those minutes when the teacher was not expounding for the students, but only sat and adjusted his robe, the children had to sit quietly and look on with dread and fear at what he was doing. In the whole town there was not one playground. The little houses stood one next to the other on the narrow lanes, there was literally not any place to touch the ground. The teacher's whip even reached the far end of the table, but not always with the correct aim. It was no misfortune when instead of on the shoulder the pupil received the strike on his head. There was no better method of discipline at the time.

Anyone could be a teacher; one did not need any certificates to be one. Indeed, any ne'er do well could take it up. The majority were those who knew little more than they themselves learned as children. So, the alphabet is what one learned from them. The teachers did not love being asked questions too often. In providing answers they themselves, poor things, were not big experts. In the *khumesh* they skipped all the passages that dealt with problems of "she" and "he". The teacher was not able to find the correct explanation for the secret-filled passages. So he read through those passages quickly, like a Torah-reader recites the list of curses – in one breath – without any interpretation. The children understood that this was uneven, but avoided asking questions. Only a few years later, when they studied the Talmud – *Kadushim, Gitin, K'suvos* and *Nida* – did the pupils reach the secret that evaded them all that time.

The teaching of girls was full of complications. They did not go to any *kheydarim*. There were some women who taught the girls to pray from the prayerbook but that was done without any system. The more capable taught praying and how to read a book in Yiddish. The majority, though, did not know that either. Only in the last decades before the *khurbn* did the girls (even from religious families) start to seek out the government folk-schools, where they received a secular education. The progressive parents also sent their boys there.

Because of the striking antisemitism that dominated the Polish schools from the side of the teaching staff, the majority of school children did not finish to graduation. The religious youths did not sit out the entire time in the yeshives either (with few exceptions). After a year or two of study they threw off the yoke of Torah along with the long caftan and the black cloth cap, and traded the Talmud for Mendele, Sholem Aleykhem, Perets and others. They donned a modern hat and with the same enthusiasm that cooked in Abaye and Rava they threw themselves into Party discussions on Hertzl, Borokhov, Zshabotinski and Medem. They helped the ignorant, with one leap, to learn all the problems

[Page 33]

that beset the Jewish people. They took no time to search for a personal goal, but were always busy with Party issues and communicating their ideas.

The town experienced all the rises and shocks as did every large town although with barely any financial resources and intellectual power. The youth took up the chant of the new organic Jewish literature, and indiscriminately swallowed up the works of Perets, Balzac, Goethe and others. All that mixed together in their minds and built up a chaos of thoughts and concepts. The local political venues were always full of noise and tumult, beginning with Scouts, *Frayhayt, Poaley-tsien,* to *Tsukunft* and the *Bund.* It was the same in all the other organizations such as *Betar,* Left *Poaley-tsien, Ha'shomer ha'tsair,* General Zionists, *Mizrakhi, Aguda* and Communists. On Fridays they held checkers evenings, where the audience inquired and the speakers answered questions and "solved" problems such as the state ministers had been unable to solve. Party representatives, brought in from as far as Warsaw, spoke on *Shabes* during the day. The local venues were packed. Opposing parties heckled them and often disrupted gatherings. More than once that led to opposing fistfights.

Shabes evenings there was theater, or a "dance evening". The modern dances had not reached the small towns. The musicians were Christians, one with a swollen eye and the other with a lame leg. The youth loved dancing. They danced in the locals, even on the roadway that led to the train station and on the wooden bridge. Both the *Bund* and the Left *Poaley-tsien* had their own drama circles that presented pieces from

Goldfaden, Gordin and others. Both occupied the same artistic level. If one had a good comic, the other had a good tragic actor; if one had a good songstress the other had a lovely prima donna. There was always tumult in town on Shabes night. Children came to the presentation with the needed requisitions: a fur hat, a man's overcoat, a candlestick or tablecloths and other things, all to cover the price of entrance without a ticket. A member, a carpenter, had built a stage. For a lack of boards it came out narrower and shorter. An artist had to cover gaps in the stage, and it wobbled like a mattress in the middle. The evenings were successful for the most part and were the topic of conversation for a long time.

Besides entertainments and theater presentations which the party organizations conducted with their own resources (outsiders were rarely brought in) there were no other diversions in the town. In recent years a Polish initiative brought in a cinema apparatus that showed films in the Polish folk-school. That was an important event for the town. The majority of the guests were Jews. Although

[Page 34]

the offerings were of the cheapest genre – stale films from the old film societies – they still drew the attention of the population who found in them a distraction from the monotony of life.

The town had a name in the whole area for possessing good speakers. The neighboring towns often invited them for lectures, with the goal of building up or strengthening their own political organizations. One town, with a much larger population than Goworowo's, borrowed lecturers and announced them with huge posters with large-type letters "A Mass Gathering with the Participation of Friend Pluni-Almuni from Goworowo!" and the audience came *en mass* to see and to hear. Almost every party had its own library where most of its membership borrowed books to read. The party was something holy and each one did its work with enthusiasm. The walls of the party venues were full of slogans, painted and drawn by its members, in which was a bit of an inherent homey art.

Once a party had the whim to bring the first radio into the town. The audience came to hear and see "God's wonder" for, of course, a payment of a ten *groshen* entrance fee. But the radio had so many operators – almost as many as there were members there – and each wanted to show that only he understood the secret of the mechanism and the correct settings, that the radio lost its "tongue".

When the *Bund* divided into the *Bund* and *KomBund,* and *Poaley-tsien* split into Right and Left, the Zionists – of *El Ha'mshomer and Et levones* and the *Tsirey tsien* moved from the Right *Poaley-tsien*, it all boiled over in the small-town kettle; the arguments invaded every house and affected every family. On *Shabes*, when the father led the table and sang *zmiros*, he had to listen with stifled anger to the discussions of his sons and daughters who tried to convince one another that only his party had the monopoly over the whole truth and justice, and that the opposing party had wandered off into the darkness…

I remember how, in a stormy *Bund* meeting where we were supposed to decide between *Bund* or *KomBund*, and to which a speaker who had been dispatched from Warsaw preached in favor of *Bund*. A member from the ranks stood up and called out in a loud voice, "In truth it must remain *KomBund*, but, since we have a member all the way from Warsaw, who incurred expenses and says *Bund*, let it just be the *Bund*.

The young were hungry for knowledge and "swallowed" everything that was offered. Along with the drive for knowledge there was also, in no smaller measure, the impulse for community organizing. It is no wonder that the youth fell into communal work with their full fervor. Every call for *Erets Yisroel*

[Page 35]

was fulfilled with enthusiasm. Members went out in the rain and snow, tromping through mud and deep snow, going from house to house to collect the poor pennies for *Keren kayemet l'yisroel.*

The youth were crammed and stuffed with Zionism. They looked with dreamy eyes toward the unreachable land. Any news in *Haynt, Moment, Dos Vort*, about a cow arriving in *Ayn Herod, Beys Alfa or Nahalal* was an important event in the town. If a messenger came from Yisroel he was embraced with love and warmth, and his every word was imbibed with mystical ecstasy. When they heard that someone from a nearby town had made *aliya to Erets Yisroel* the jealousy was huge. The first members who violently tore themselves away from the town traveled illegally, claiming to be tourists. That was in 1932. A year later that was recalled in our town and several certificates were distributed.

The Pioneer movement also contributed to the rooting of Zionist thought in town. And one fine morning in 1925 there appeared in town two barefoot young men and a woman, with baskets in their hands. They had come to collect food products for a preparatory *kibuts*, which just a day earlier had enlisted a neighboring prince's estate. The town looked at them as an evil wonder. The youth encircled them and recognized that they were students from Warsaw who had decided to exchange their studies for work in Erets Yisroel. It had the effect of an electrical current on everyone and was the only topic of conversation for a long time.

The first *Shabes* after that, half of the young people in the town went to see them in the *kibuts*, in order the look with their own eyes and see how the process of preparation took place. A few days later the town also had a Pioneer organization and went out for preparatory training. They went through all the difficult preparatory work that was obligatory then in order to make *aliya.*

The party organizations make several attempts to organize various cultural institutions in town, such as Hebrew courses for evenings, kindergartens and so on but those did not last long. The householders who were more or less good financial founders, did not understand the project. Rather, they called it strange to “start at the beginning”. The party did not have a large sum of money at its disposal and the initiators were hounded from every side. The struggle of the parents was a quiet one, but a bitter one. The parents felt that in the uneven fight against their children, they were being forfeited. They scolded the children, often with slaps, but it did not help. While they wished the children welded into chains, they tore out of the chains and freed themselves. The youth smelled freedom and protested against the deep-rooted monotonic life that

[Page 36]

did not fit in the frame of the new, free and very promising life.

In the larger towns the youth had long been triumphant and carried the banner of light with arrogance. For us, though, the winds came a little slower. And so the struggle was hateful, bitter, and the youth put everything at stake in order to win quickly. To this day I do not understand how it came to the Goworowo youth to be so dynamic and vehement, awake and alive about the thing.

Later the parents became envious of the youth, and in a certain hindsight decided to take them as an example. Thus, the artisans founded an artisans' union and concentrated around their artisans' bank; the merchants' union grouped themselves around their merchants' bank. And for the poor population, a *gemiles-khesed* [interest-free bank] was later established. So, almost everyone in town who needed a money “injection” clung to their bank and someone else helped with a guarantee co-signature. The merchants' bank was operated with order, had a good official apparatus and in a short time even succeeded in moving into its own building.

Everyone possessed a warm heart, none allowed anyone else to fall. If someone was pinched, a sum of money was quickly collected and given as a "loan" even if never repaid. The good name of the town often drew needy people even from distant lands. Not only in material things, but also in the area of politics there were requests for our party strengths from other towns; that strength assured their success and we never denied them, but gave with a broad hand. Heart and soul were found in our town, and one helped another in whatever way they could.

* * *

My life in the town ran by me like a lovely film. One image chased the next. I retain a feeling of sweetness, accompanied by longing for those pleasant 24 years of mine there, which went by so quickly. The eye wants once again to take in that town, the feet – to walk on its homey lanes, the hands – with a tremble to touch everything that was so dear to me. But – there was a little Jewish town, and it is no more. An evil hand erased it along with the proud Jewish life. Erased forever.

[Page 37]

A Walk Through the *Shtetl*

Translated by Sandra Chiritescu

Edited by Gloria Berkenstat Freund

Donated by Lester Blum

Goworowo was connected to the big world via two train stations along the Warsaw-Lomza line: Pasek and Goworowo, and also via three main roads which led towards Ostrow Mazowiecka, Rozan, and Ostroleka. The distance from Goworowo to Warsaw was 90 kilometers, and to Lomza 60 kilometers. The Hirsh River, a run-off from the Narew River, cut through the shtetl coming from the southern side and separated it from the village of Wolka (*Wólka Brzezińsk*), which also had Jewish residents.

The Szczawin estate was located at a distance of about 2 kilometers. It belonged to the wealthy nobleman, Glinko. North of the shtetl was the village Goworówek: not far from there was the Rembish estate, which was for a certain period of time was owned by the Jewish noblemen Stein and Fein who were from Jedwabne. Aside from the estates mentioned above, the shtetl was surrounded by the following estates: Zambrzyce, Ponivke, Brzeźno, Suchcice, Gucin, Czernie, Kruszewo, Jawory, Danilowo, Pakshevnitse, and others.

When you entered the shtetl on the main street and crossed the bridge you were greeted on the left side by the impressive, red brick prayer house. On the right side there was the two-story brick home of the pharmacist, Goszczyński, and the post office director, Rasul. In the neighboring large wooden building Reb Velvl Blumstein, the watchmaker, an energetic community leader, lived. He was a Gerer Hasid and member of the synagogue council. His wife Feige Nekhome, a pious woman, was famous in the shtetl for her intelligence and acumen. His neighbor, the tailor from Vengrov, Reb Velvl Vaysbord, drew everyone's attention with his broad build and patriarchal looks. His son Khone, who lives in Columbia today, was a founder of the Ze'irei Zion (Youth of Zion) organization. His other son, Avrom, who was active in the leftwing Poale Zion youth movement was killed in the Warsaw ghetto. For many years, Reb Yoysef Velvl Gutman also lived there. He was a tinsmith, respected for his knowledge among the Gerer Hasidim. He lives in Israel today.

To the left side of the house was the home of Reb Baruch Kuperman, a synagogue council member and an activist/leader among the artisans. His wife Chana Ruchel distinguished herself through her pious deeds and anonymous charity. The bakery of Reb Yoyl Yelin was located in the next house. He was an Aleksander Hasid, a charitable man and hospitable person.

[Page 38]

His nephew, Yeshaye Rosenberg, who was considered his heir, lived and worked with him. In this small two-story home, Reb Menashe Holtsman had his colonial *(food and other consumer goods)* and paint store. He was among the most important bosses (*bale batim*) in the shtetl, a long term synagogue council member, a prayer leader, a peacemaker and an exemplary man.

The Kościuszki Street

The adjacent corner building which bordered Kościuszki Street, known as the "Wide Street" belonged to the stringent Aleksander Hasid, a learned man, Reb Yoynesn Zilbertson from a respected Warsaw family. He ran an iron business. His son-in-law, Reb Yoysef Dovid Ostshover, a Hasidic young man, owned a grocery store.

In the next house on Kościuszki Street was the flour and fur store of Reb Yeshaye Ayznberg, a learned man, full of spirited witticism, the founder and protector of the Aleksander sect's location for communal prayers (*shtibl*). His house was open, a place where learned men gathered. On the other side of the house his father-in-law, Reb Nussan Mozes lived. He was among the heads of the shtetl's committee to ensure that animals were slaughtered in accordance with the laws of Kashrut. Today he lives in the United States. His sons Moshe and Yankev were educated young men who had mastered the Lithuanian yeshivas.

Next to them lived Reb Efroyim Boynes, a blind man who went to the study house by himself every day and even prayed from memory on Rosh Hashanah and Yom Kippur at the synagogue lectern. His son-in-law Fayvl Mal lives in the United States today. In the other half of the house, Reb Mordechai Gurka had a bakery. He was a learned man and a Gerer Hasid. His wife Dvora ran the bakery. The other neighbors were: Nekhamye Kas, a shoemaker at the marketplace, and the widow Chana Frydman, the mother of Lazar Frydman, who was the founder and supporter of the Peretz library. In some Christian buildings there were apartments of: Avrom Roznberg, a tailor whose brother Yankev Roznberg from Rozan was among the first Jews shot in Goworowo by the Germans, and also Anschel Engel, a saddler.

The little street which led down to the river was nameless. It started with the house of Reb Zaynvl Berliner, a shoemaker, and his son-in-law Reb Yisroel Leyb Kruk, a learned man and wonderful prayer leader. Next to his house was Noyekh Karvat, a baker, who today lives in Israel (his wife Miriam, the daugther of Reb Mordechai Gurka died in Russia), and Hersh Berliner, the owner of a machine for cleaning wool. Their neighbors were: the butcher Pinkhes Dende; the so called "cold glazier", Mordechai Likhtman who owned a hand operated wringer for laundry and before Passover - a matzah bakery; Lazar Bielik, the shoemaker whose son, Tevye was a partisan during the war in the Polesia forests, and Dina Dende, the mother-in-law of Lazar Bielik.

On the other side of the street, the following people had apartments: Liberke Bresler and his son Yekl, a shoe maker, who now lives in Israel and Artshe Thservin, the baker, who also lives in Israel. Next to them lived: Berl Tsirman, a teacher of young children,

[Page 39]

and his daughter Brayne with her husband Avrom Skshinia, a market shoe maker from Makov.

In the neighboring small, caved-in house lived Avrom Yekl Shifer, the sign maker together with his daughter Chana whose husband was abroad every year: from there he sent her the first gramophone in the shtetl which impressed everyone. Across from them lived Bendet, the tailor from the Szczawin estate and his son Alter who was known as an "enlightened" Jew and poet, who has lived in Lodz the last few years.

The corner house on the Wide Street was owned by Reb Fayvl Brik, a shoemaker by trade, one of the most important men in the shtetl; even though he eschewed giving honors in the study house, he was always elected as *gabbai (one who assists with the reading of the Torah)* at the study house and vice-president of the burial society. During the last years he dedicated one of his rooms to hosting guests. His wife Esther Rivka also distinguished herself with good deeds.

The neighboring, nicely built house was the Rabbi's house. There, in a comfortable spacious apartment the Goworowo rabbi lived for the last 12 years. This was Rabbi Alter Burstein, may G-d avenge him. This house was the central focus of societal Jewish life in the shtetl. In the Rabbinic court, community meetings were held, conferences and all kinds of other community gatherings. From the Rabbi's house a narrow path led to the city's ritual bath and sauna.

The city's wealthy residents the brothers-in-law Reb Itzhok Kosovski and Reb Matisyahu Rozen lived in the neighboring two-story house. These brothers-in-law who were in the wood business were among the most well-respected businessmen in the shtetl. They were active in village society: Kosovski was a co-founder and activist of the credit bank for merchants, named Bank Zydowski Kredytowy, his son, Chaim was a student at the yeshiva in Lomza; and Rozen, an Aleksander Hasid was a manager, for many years, at the burial society. For many years their business partner was Dovid Segal who also lived there. His wife, Yehudis, co-founded in 1917 the Zionist organization in the shtetl. Their son, Khonen studied at the Polish gymnasium in Ostroleka. Today he lives in the United States. The last years Hershl Krulevitsh, a mechanic and scoffer and Leybl Kapesh, a wheat merchant lived in that building. Today they both live in the United States.

The other neighbor was Reb Yeshaye Hertsberg, wheat merchant, a Gerer Hasid who was a religious fanatic. His daughter, Miryem Ruchel, was the president of the Bnos Agudat Israel and among the principals of the Beit Yaakov School. For many years, Reb Moshe Mendl Farbarovitsh, an Otvotsker Hasid, also lived there. He greatly entertained people at celebrations, especially during the holidays. In the last years, he moved to Wolomin.

The following house belonged to Reb Leybke Schmeltz the bathhouse attendant who was a devout Jew and Aleksander Hasid. His son-in-law, Motl Ikultshik was a tailor. In the last front facing house on this side of the Wide Street lived Reb Shloyme Shtern, a learned Jew; his son Mendl studied in the yeshiva in Novaredok for many years, as well as being the head of a yeshiva for many years. He was known as one of the so-called *ba'alei musar (a religious movement based on introspection)*. In the back

[Page 40]

part of the house lived Chaim Oyslender, the broker, and Reuven Barnshteyn, a shoemaker.

Towards the river lived the carpenter from Wolomin, Yankev Kersh. His son Leyb was one of the founders and leaders of the Bund in the shtetl and later was among the prominent leaders of Poland's Bund where he was the leader of the youth movement. He distinguished himself with his strength as a speaker and his sharp pen. He was murdered as a hero in the Warsaw Ghetto. The brothers Peysekh and Yoyne Kersh lived in Wolomin a few years before the war; the latter lives in Israel today. Right at the river lived Esther Malke Bengelsdorf, a fruit seller and her daughter Chaya Razal with her husband Meyer.

The Other Side of Kościuszki Street

The other side of Kościuszki Street starts with the corner house of Reb Menashe Fish, a wheelwright. In the back part of the house lived Avrom Bresler and Moyshe Kalmen Shpitolevitsh, both shoemakers. After the house of the Christian meat merchant Felix Duro, who felt at home with his Jewish neighbors, lived the brothers Velvl and Leybl Taus, market merchants, and across from them lived Mendl Chaim Rubin, a shoemaker who raised a dairy cow for additional income. Meyer Shvarts, a shoe maker, lived in a front facing house and, in the back, his tenants Rivke (Ferls) Shpitolevitsh and Brayne Roznberg who together ran a fruit stall in the street market.

In the neighboring house lived Chaim Taytlboym, a saddler. The street next to his house led to a big passageway court where the following people lived - Reb Chaim Leyb Leybman, a stringent Gerer Hasid, a small seller of farm products, his wife Chana Yite had a street stall; Avroml Taytlboym, a coachman; Avrom Ruzhe, a shipping agent, and Khone Alek, a butcher. Next to them lived Reb Chaim Berliner, a shoemaker, a good-natured man who for many years he was the village magistrate. His son Leybl was the first victim of the German bombardment. In the second half of the house lived his father, Reb Yisroel Shabatai, also a shoemaker. There also lived Reb Shloyme Leyb Shakhter, of the Otvotsker Hasidim, a lover of Torah, a wheat merchant and wine producer; Noyekh Tshervin, a butcher who lives in the United States today.

A little further lived Reb Mordechai Trushkevitsh, the sexton in the prayer house. He was a learned man who knew entire tractates of the Talmud by heart. He would always sit and study a holy book. He was shot by the Germans soon after the first day of their invasion of the shtetl. His son-in-law was Mordechai Solka, a shoemaker, a good tradesman and knowledgeable in Jewish books who lives in Israel today. In the rest of the front part of the house lived Reb Yisroel Meyer Mishnayes, wheat merchant, a learned man who was a fervent follower of the Enlightenment, a dandy, member of the important Mizrahi movement *(religious movement within the World Zionist Organization)* His son Matisyahu was a well-known young man, co-founder of Beitar, who lives in Uruguay today. Next to them lived Yosel Engler, a saddler by trade and his grandson Nakhmen Taytlboym, a tailor.

In the next brick house lived Chaim Tsimerman, a good men's

[Page 41]

and women's tailor, from Pultusk; Moshe Kopetsh, a wheat merchant who lives in the United States today; Getsel Kersh, a carpenter, and others. There also lives Moshe Taytlboym, a saddler and horse merchant; his son Shimen, one of three triplets who lived in yeshivas for many years and died as a young man shortly before the war; his other son Hershel was sentenced for being a Communist and died in Russia.

Their neighbor was Chana Levin with her children. They later moved to be with her husband and father, Reb Avrom Levin in Cuba. Today they live in Israel. Next to them lived Chaim Frid who owned a colonial store who lives in Israel today. And Tsipore Zilbershteyn, whose husband Avrom Dovid left for America after their wedding. Later Sholem Fraske, a cattle merchant, moved in. The neighboring two-story house was owned by Itzhok Tsirman who returned from the United States. His daughter Feige also lived in an apartment. She was married to Leybl Makover. His tenants were Yantshe Fishman, a butcher, Yekl Zhelozni, a saddler, lives in Israel today; Feige Yente Daytsh and Avrom Meyer Schmeltz, a tailor. On the top floor was the local headquarters of the Za'irei Agudas Yisroel. For many years the rabbi's son-in-law Rabbi Arn Taytlboym also lived there. He later became the rebbe in Vurker-Narazhin.

In the neighboring brick building there was a restaurant and liquor store operated by Yekhazkl Khen from Sniadow. He was a learned Jew and a good leader of prayers. His neighbors were the owner of the building, Alte Tsveybak and her son Hershel, who also had a large tailor shop there. Next to them, in a separate house, lived Reb Avremele Grudko, a learned Jew with a sharp mind, a teacher of older boys; his son Dovid Arn, a merchant and co-owner of the first passenger bus from Goworowo to Warsaw. He was co-founder of the Zionist organization as well as, for a short time, a member of the community council. His other son Yehuda Grudko, a baker, and Yisroel Bielik, a shoe maker also lived there. The latter two live in Israel today. At the top was the local headquarters of the Mizrahi party. Nosen Mankete had his colonial store there. He was a Gerer Hasid who often sat at the rebbe's table. The neighboring house belonged to Malke Vishnia, she died a few years ago in Israel; the last years there, her second husband Chaim Batshan also lived there. He worked in accounts receivable and accounting at the Artisans and Retailers Bank.

The Long Street

In the two-story corner house where Kościuszki Street ended and Long Street began lived Rabbi Reb Naftuli Gemore, a Gerer Hasid and a teacher of Torah. Today he is a Rabbi in Haifa. His neighbors were Moshe Shpitalovitsh who worked in a mill and Zelig the shoe maker from Czerwin, the son-in-law of Fraske. Next to them was Leye Govoritshik's colonial store. She lived with her son-in-law Dovid Shulman, a Hasidic young man who was a bulk merchant. In a separate house in the courtyard Reb Bertshe Granat had a tailor shop. He was a modern tailor, a man with a stately appearance who died a few years ago

[Page 42]

in Israel. His apartment was later taken over by Reb Berish Barnshteyn, a shoe-leather worker. His son Simkhe was studying in yeshivas in Warsaw. Also living in the same courtyard were Klara Niks with her sons and Avrom Klas whose half-paralyzed son Shloyme was a volunteer assistant to the Polish post man. Even though he was illiterate, he would look at the letters and, with a special sense, recognize to whom they belonged.

Further on the front side of the street Moshe Potash had a small soda and sausage factory with a candy store. Next to him lived Reb Nosen Shran, a grand wheat merchant who lives in Israel today. On the top lived Itzhok Dovid Tehilim who also lives in Israel today and Yekl Dovid Nayman's daughter, Tsirl Kleyn with her husband. In the second half of the top floor was the Bund and Peretz libraries.

Then there were the houses of Reb Chaim Boruch Shakhter, a shipping agent, and an Otvotsker Hasid; Reb Velvl Yagodnik, a good-natured and lovely man, who taught Talmud and was a *meged (wandering preacher whose sermons contained both religious and moral instruction);* his grandson, the son-in-law of his daughter Nekhome, is Rabbi Bagard, the chief Rabbi in Beit She'an. Velvl Yagodnik and his wife were among the first victims shot by the Germans.

In the courtyard Lazar Korn from Kremenchuk also had his apartment. He also was among the first victims shot to death. His daughter Leye died in Israel. His neighbor Reb Chaim Itche Hetsran was a learned Jew who knew tractates of Talmud by heart. His sons, Yekhielke and Bertshe left for Russia and took high offices there. The neighbors were Chaim Niedzhvitski, an Otvotsker Hasid, wheat merchant; Yoysefke Barnshteyn with his spice store; his son Peysekh and Dovid Glogover, a tailor.

The Bankove Street

The corner house bordering Bankove Street was owned by Reb Yankev Shtshetshina, a Gerer Hasid, teacher, leader of prayers, wise man and popular arbitrator in the shtetl. Then there is the house of Reb Moshe Zindl, a furrier and his sons-in-law, Reb Naftule Tsimberg, a tailor who lives in Israel today and Nisn Frid, a shoemaker.

Next to them lived Reb Yeshave Nosn Kruk, a teacher who also owned a dye factory. His daughter, Zayftl, a widow who later married Hersh Berliner, his son, Menachem Kruk, a tailor also lived there. In the large courtyard stood the grain mill building of Reb Avrom Kruk next to the house in which he lived. His neighbor was Dan Dshiza, a peddler, the son-in-law of Brik and Mrs. Chava Sura Sarne, the widow of Reb Yeshaye Yom Tov Sarne of the Amshinaver Hasidim. Across from them was the building in which Reb Yekhezkl Tshekhanover used to have his brick and roof tile business. Later the building served as a garage for the first passenger bus in Goworowo. The last house belonged to Reb Hershl Brik, a shoemaker, the brother of Fayvl Brik.

The other residents of Bankove Street were Shloyme Dzhize, a business partner in Kruk's grain mill, the son of Shmuelke Dzhize; Yankev Gurko, a baker who lives in Israel today; Velvl Doytsh, the coachman who caused a stir in the

[Page 43]

shtetl with the first coach using rubber wheels; Moshe Alek, a butcher and Reb Hershl Rubin, a candy maker and cookie baker, a Gerer Hasid and cofounder of the Beit Yaakov school, who was burnt by the Germans with a Torah in his hands in Wyszkow. In the courtyard lived Esther Fraske, the widow of Reb Chaim Leyb, a butcher. He was a nice and happy type of person, a strong man, killed by a Christian in the forest near Dlugosiodlo. Their neighbors were his son Sholem, also a butcher who lives in the United States today; Sura Gitl Brik, the widow of Velvl Brik whose son lives in the United States now and a daughter who lives in Israel; Yisroel Levkovitsh from a village called Baraves; and Ansel Zimon in whose new house the Poale Zion (right wing) organization and library named after Y.H. Brenner was located. A little further lived Leyb Tshervin, a butcher; Yekl Gurman, a coachman the brother of Mikhl from Beyger; Hersh Itzhok Malavoni, a teacher with his mother-in-law; and Yekl Schmeltz, a butcher.

To the right of Bankove Street was a side street that bordered on Bobovskis field, the so-called Mud Street. There lived Ayzik Roytman, the coachman, his son-in-law Yosl Ogrodnik, also a coachman with his elegant coach; his son Leybl Roytman, Yekl Taus' son-in-law who together with the Christian, Sabotko brought the first truck to the shtetl and drove it – today he lives in Uruguay.

The Other Side of Bankove Street

On the other side of Bankove Street lived Mordechai and Baske Alek. He was a butcher. Both died in Israel. In the courtyard was the house of Reb Yovel Levkovitsh, a peddler. He was an interesting man with a stately appearance, a learned man, leader of prayers, and a tall broad shouldered, strong man. Whenever he had free time, in the middle of the week and during the Sabbath, he would always sit with a holy book in the study house. He died in Israel. The neighbors were Reb Shloyme Gordon, a Vurker Hasid, master builder of wooden buildings; Arn Yankev Zilber, a shoemaker for special elegant work; Sura Fraske, a widow who made a living whitewashing houses; Yehoshua Taus (Kavner) who returned from the United States; and Leybl Gure who had his own carpentry shop there – he died in Israel. Next to Yekl Alek, a butcher lived Reb Yankev Shprintses, a teacher of young children and synagogue sexton. Next to him was Reb Shloyme Chaim Tsimbal, Meyerl's son-in-law, synagogue sexton and gravedigger as well as Reb Abbale Podgurevitsh, a teacher of the Torah, shofar blower in the Gerer study house. He was a small, lively, and happy Jew who would always entertain the audience on Simchat Torah.

Next stood the separate building of the Merchants' Bank and in the next building lived Yekl Taus, a coachman. In the courtyard the following people had their apartments – Reb Yehoshue Molovani, the teacher and Mrs. Elke Shapiro, the widow of the rabbi from Tsherniv, Rabbi Reb Fishl Shapiro, in memory of the righteous.

In a nice brick building lived Reb Meyer Volf Tehilim, a big merchant

[Page 44]

and renowned wise man. Many Jews in the shtetl would come to him and ask advice regarding private and business matters. His courtyard was full of building materials and coal for burning. His neighbors were Berl Visotski, a wheat and fur merchant; Sikhe Taykhman, a shoemaker; his son-in-law, Leybl Sandale; Arn Shloyme Schmeltz, a butcher; Itzhok Azdaba, the son of Reb Dovid Azdaba, both smiths. Across from them lived his brother, Reb Kalman Azdaba, also a smith who married his daughter to a learned young man from Warsaw, Reb Fayvl Lubelski, a certified teacher who lived on the top floor. Next to them lived Shmuel Dzhize, a shoemaker and frequent visitor at the courthouse. He loved to get mixed up in quarrels between Jews and Christians. Also, Reg Hershl Glogover, among the respectable Jews in the shtetl, a Vurker Hasid, musician and good Talmudic teacher; his son, Itshe Glogover, a wheat merchant who lives in Israel today; and Hersh Berl, the shoe leather worker, the son of Mendl Melamed lived there.

In the front lived Hersh Brik's son, a tailor. Next to Alte "the Carpentress" lived Reb Yisroel Itzhok Shran, a Gerer Hasid who was among the zealots in the shtetl, a butcher whose customers were the most strict in observance of Kosher laws; his son Dan Shran who worked at Galant's soda water factory; Reb Ben Tsien Sandale, a merchant of whatever was on hand, Gerer Hasid and leader of prayers; his son Yossl survived the concentration camps of Auschwitz and Dachau who lives today in the United States; and Lazar Barnkevitsh, a shoemaker.

The Continuation of Long Street

The second house on the corner of Bankove and Long Streets belonged to Reb Yekl Alevorzh, a shoemaker; his brother Reb Hersh who spent many years in prayer, penance and fasts who later became the Zamoshtsher Rebbe in Lublin. Because he served many years in Czar Nicholas' army, he took particular pity on Jewish soldiers. He would read Torah for the common people and lead them on the path of *Yiddishkayt (Jewishness)*. He died before the war and his son, Reb Meyer took over the dynasty. In the second house lived Reb Itzhok Reytshik, known under the name Itsele Reytshik, a Gerer Hasid and learned man. He had a textile factory all these years and at the end was also a teacher. Next to him lived Yitke Gurman, a hatmaker; Mikhl Gurman, from Beyger and in the courtyard, Yisroel Arn Shults, a glazier; Moshe Brakhonski, a low boot shoe leather worker; and Lazar Vaknyazh, a peddler. In the neighboring apartments were Reb Yoysef Batshan, the grandson of the old Rabbi, a learned man and teacher, his wife and children. Today they live in Israel.

The new building in the front belonged to the important men – Reb Zalmen Verman, an Aleksander Hasid, textile merchant who had studious sons and Reb Pinkhes Shikara, an iron merchant whose son Aviezer was among the founders of the Beitar. At the top, above Shikara lived Moshe Dovid Malavoni, co-owner of the small mill. Today he lives in Israel. In the little house next to him lived Yehude Leybl Kas, the shoemaker. Further along

[Page 45]

Long Street lived Shashke Gitl Alakevitsh who traded in fish. Her children lived in the United States. Dovid Shvarts, a shoemaker also lived there. Next to them lived Reb Hershl Dovid Zilberberg, a setter of cobblestones, one among a few Jews who could pave roads and avenues. He was an Otvotsker Hasid and a leader of prayers.

The Ostrolenko Street

The next house which stood on the corner of Ostrolenko Street belonged to the Goworowo cantor /slaughterer, Reb Chaim Leyb Marianski. He came from Sniadowe, was the town cantor, a Gerer Hasid and prayed in the big study house. Together with him lived his son-in-law, Reb Yisroel Itzhok Bramberg, a young man, very learned who studied to become a slaughterer. The cantor had two other sons, Moshe and Shloymke, a Yeshiva student. The whole family died in Zembrów. In the next house on Ostrolenko Street lived Yudl Kakhan, the son-in-law of Reb Leybele Reyder, a smith. In the second half lived Leybl Brik, a tailor and Yekl Kakhan, a milk delivery man who would pick up at the noble men's courts and deliver them to Warsaw. He also had a grocery store.

In the same row of houses there was also the one of Reb Yekl Malavoni, a smith and his son-in-law, Arn Aronson, a teacher and preacher – author of a holy book. Reb Arn would drive around the country giving sermons and tell nice little stories and fables. When he would return to the shtetl, he would have much news to tell of his travels. His older son, Eliezer is in Argentina now. His younger son, Mordechai was a Yeshiva student and very learned. His son-in-law Hershl Sandale also lived there. He was a tailor.

After several Christian houses stood the last Jewish house belonging to Bendet Viroslav, a wheelwright. From the Ostolenko Street, there was a path down to the Glinkes, there was the mill of Reb Arnke Malavoni and the city's slaughterhouse. Before World War I, there was also the city bath and mikvah there. From Ostrolenko Street a wide street lead to the Goworowo train station and the villages of Goworowek, Rebisze, and others as well as to Ostrolenka through the village Borowce. These streets served the Goworowo youth as a meeting point and a walking path, especially on the Sabbath afternoons and in the evenings for lovers.

The Other Side of Ostrolenko Street

On the other side of Ostrolenko Street there were no Jewish homes. There was the city public school, the local city council buildings, the so-called administrative offices and the prison where the rebellious Goworowo population were imprisoned for administrative crimes. Next to those was the house owned by a Christian, Virembek where, for many years,

[Page 46]

the local Zionist organization, Ha'Techiya and its library were located. Then there are Jewish houses again. In a nice brick building that was exactly across from the Long Street lived Feige Rivke Gutman, owner of a grocery store whose husband Reb Volf Gutman was a well-known Gerer Hasid and respected Jew called the Rebbe. Also there were Reb Gedalive Grinberg, boss of a big bakery who was an enlightened Gerer Hasid; his wife Chana lives in Israel and his two sons, in the United States. At the top lived Matisyahu Frid, a wheelwright.

In the neighboring big courtyard there were several big houses which belonged to Reb Yosl Verman, from Zilar and his family. Reb Yosl, a rope maker and fish merchant, was among the powerful men in the shtetl. For a long time he was the manager of the synagogue. He was short, known as a busy body with a resounding squeaky voice. He scared all those who were praying. His son, Shapse Verman owned a wood warehouse and was very active among the merchants being an important member of the Mizrahi party. His son-in-law, Reb Sholem Pltake from Rozan was a Gerer Hasid and a founder of the Artisans' Bank that was located in the courtyard. Reb Yosl also had his daughter Tsirl Leye and her husband, who helped his father-in-law make rope, live with him.

In one of Reb Yosl's small houses there was also the first Yiddish school with its founder, the teacher Alter Hokhshteyn (together with Motl Ramaner). Hokhshteyn came from Luninets and made his way to Goworowo after World War I. He thought of himself as a real intellect, a tall, fat man, intensely balding and always with smiling eyes. He very much enjoyed working with children, pinching their cheeks and petting their heads. His clients were mostly girls, female students and boys. In particular he taught written Hebrew and Yiddish, math, and calligraphy. There was a religious teacher in the city's public school. He loved celebrations full of effects. On Lag Ba'Omer he would take a walk with all the children in the forest. They were all decorated in blue/white paper streamers and he sang with them ÒEli EliÓ. He also had a hobby of reading cards – telling fortunes.

To the left, deep into the courtyard was a house and grain mill of Reb Yankev Hersh Vengrov and his son-in-law Reb Moshe Kasher, the last president of the Goworowo Jewish community. This house with its wide footprint and size was impressive. Reb Yankev Hersh was far from a wealthy man. The two blind horses that pulled the massive and heavy mill wheel could not earn him a living. Reb Yankev Hersh was a typical Hasid from the Amshiniaver school – always in a good mood. Happy, loved to drink a bit of alcohol and entertain his fellow Jews.

Next to his house was the small, low, half sunken house of Reb Abale Likhtman, a glazier and coachman on the Goworowo – Rozan line. He was a real happy poor man. His half dead mare only walked at speed when he sang her Lecha Dodi or another prayer. His neighbors

[Page 47]

were Reb Avzik Rozen, an honest and kosher butcher. After the war he left for Canada to be with his son, Khone Meyer and died there. His brother-in-law, Bendet Shetsekh, the wheelwright who returned in the 1920s from the United States and brought with him the American manners. Reb Betsalel Yosef Kavrat, a learned and wise Jew, a good Talmudic teacher who was shot by the Germans immediately on their first invasion of the shtetl also lived there.

The Other Side of Long Street

The corner house on the other side of Long Street belonged to Reb Bertshe Viroslav, a wheat merchant who was among the cheerful Aleksander Hasidim. He never earned enough to make a living and loved Kiddush and the meal after the Sabbath *(considered the fourth meal of the day).* His daughter, Tsipe and her husband, Simkhe, the wood turner along with their children were killed by the Germans on the first day of the invasion of the shtetl. His son, Itzhok was among the fanatical activists in the Zionist Socialists who died in the Bialystok ghetto.

Next to them lived Reb Shmuel Krvietski, a shoemaker whose son, Yekhezkl died during the Bolshevik invasion in 1921. His other son, Baruch, a hair dresser, lives in the United States today.

In a large two-story building lived Reb Yehoshua Rozen, a synagogue council member for many years and considered an influential person. He was active among the artisans and their bank. He died not too long ago in Israel. His sons-in-law, Reb Meshulem Golovinski of Rozan, a learned man had an oil pressing factory in the courtyard and Matisyhau Oyslender, a wheat merchant and milk delivery man are both in Israel now. Another two sons-in-law, Shloyme Gerbard, grandson of the Vishkover rebbe was a yeshiva student in Kletsk and Barzilai from Ostrow were killed in the war years.

There was another house where Reb Itche Yosel Taus, the gravedigger lived with his wife, Devora. He was a leader of the burial society along with his son-in-law, Lazar Frydman, a baker. A little further, where the street bordered Ratenski's fruit garden, lived Reb Sholem Greyner, a locksmith who with his three sons are today in Israel. Next to them lived Yekl Markus, a peddler.

At the front, in a brick building, lived Reb Avrom Luzim, a smith who raised cows and sold their milk for additional income. Thanks to his efforts with his relative Sura Gitl Klass in the United States, she sent large sums of money which allowed the building of the new big synagogue. On the eastern wall of the synagogue, a special plaque was hung in her honor. His neighbors were Hershl Alek, a butcher who lives in the United States and Lipman Drevienko, a peddler.

Nest to them, at the front, lived the widow of the shoemaker, Blum, who died in America *(at the time Hilda Blum was living in Goworowo, she was not a widow. Shalom Joseph Blum had immigrated to the United States in 1923. She followed with the minor children in 1930. Shalom Joseph died in Fort Worth, Texas on May 7, 1959).* Her son-in-law, Anschel Taus, a first rate shoemaker, quiet and intelligent person died in a German concentration camp next to Lublin.

Further lived Moshe Horovits, a baker who was among the respected leaders of the Bund and later a council member of the synagogue in the community and Naftule Schmeltz, a butcher who today lives in Israel.

[Page 48]

A brick building, in the style of the big city, was built by Avrom Kruk, the former village magistrate. His wife Tslave was among the first victims shot by the Germans. The Beitar organization was located in his house for many years and for a while there was also a Talmud Torah founded by the Rabbi to take the children out of the Christian public school. There also lived Yekl Zhelozni, a saddler who lives in Israel today and Tsalke Azdaba who had a grocery story. Along with his wife Henie, he lives in Israel today. In the neighboring apartments lived Shimen Vaser, a wood turner; the wheelwright, Reb Leybl Karlinski, a Gerer Hasid whose three sons and one daughter were killed by the Germans with one daughter who lives in Israel; and Avzik Rubin, the butcher. They all lived in the house of Reb Yankev Shapse Trukhnavski and his son-in-law Reb Avrom Shafran. Reb Avrom was among the respected men in the shtetl, an Otwocker Hasid, learned, wise, and intelligent man. He had a colonial store which was among the biggest in Goworowo. His son Simkhe Bunem studied in the Lomza Yeshiva in his younger years and with the Rabbi. Later he was the leader of the Socialist Zionist movement in the shtetl. He married Neta Rits' only daughter and became a business partner in the big mill. Afterwards he left for Wolomin where he died. Reb Avrom's two other sons, Moshe and Dovid were killed by the Germans. His first born, Binyumen and Mendel, as well as Itche, a student at the Lomza Yeshiva, a pedagogue and leader of the Beit Yaakov School live in the United States today. His daughter, Rivke, her husband Shmuel Roznberg as well as his son Yisrolke, a tailor who was among the Bund activists in the shtetl live in Canada.

In a small house lived Mordechai Sierota a tailor from Makov, the son-in-law of Avrom, the synagogue sexton. He bought this house from Shmuel Volf Broyner, a soldier in the Polish army who made his way to Goworowo after World War I to save the local train bridge and later married the daughter of Yekl Grinshteyn, the locksmith. Broyner's house was a meeting point for the shtetl youth where they listened to gramophone records and folk songs. He died several years ago in the United States.

Next to him lived Reb Chaim Dovid Shran, an Otvotsker Hasid, a wheat merchant who along with his wife, Chaye Beyle were killed by the Germans in their house on the sad Friday evening. The old couple Yoske and Ruchel Shmuelke who were well respected on the noblemen's estates, lived in the same house. In the other house lived the shoe leather worker, Yekhazkl Mendl . Next to him lived his father Reb Yisroel Eliezer Zamelzon, a leather merchant, strictly observant Jew always well dressed with a well-groomed beard and a gold chain shining from his vest. Reb Yisroel Eliezer's second son, Yudl was off with the Bolsheviks in Russia at the time and was killed there during the cleansing of 1937. His son Yankev lives in Argentina today. In the same house lived his son-in-law, Itzhok Sniadover who returned

[Page 49]

to the shtetl from Argentina shortly before the war and died there. Their neighbors were Reb Yakev Leyb Aleyorzh, a shoemaker – relative of the Rebbe from Zamoshtsh and in the front lived Reb Yehoshue Yekhiel Nayman, an Aleksander Hasid, the so called *shaye khil, with the bill* Despite his small, wiry body, he had a healthy, nice voice and was a respected leader of prayers in the Aleksander prayer house. From trading with the noblemen's estates he made a lot of money which later he suddenly lost it all. His son, Leybl was an actor in the Warsaw Yiddish theater. His son-in-law, Yidl Gurfinkl, a watchmaker, was a homebody who did not earn much. Yidl's two children, a boy and a girl, managed to hide in a village somewhere behind Zembrow until 1944 and were later killed by Poles.

Deeper in the courtyard lived Reb Avrom Potash, the rope maker, his two daughters both educated in the Beit Yaakov School married in Israel Rabbis from South Africa and America. At the front, in a nice house, lived Reb Yisroel Shvarts, a wealthy tailor of old clothes and Mikhl *(Max)* Schmeltz who later died in the United States. His children live in America and Brazil today. Reb Mordechai Schmeltz, the butcher built a nice brick house where his apartment and shop were at the bottom and at the top lived Zelig Hertsberg, Reb Baruch Kuperman's son-in-law, a wheat merchant. Next to them, Reb Chaim Horovits an activist in the Mizrahi party had his grocery store and sold milk.

The Market

The corner house that bordered on the market was owned by Reb Yehuda Sheynyak, a textile merchant. He was among the stringent Gerer Hasidim and among the good prayer leaders. He was also occupied with community matters. His son, Chaim died during a German bombardment in the shtetl of Serock. In a neighboring two-story building Reb Shmuelke Tsudiker had his apartment and oil pressing shop. He was an enlightened Aleksander Hasid, among the Mizrahi activists and a synagogue council member. The neighboring house belonged to Reb Shoyel Potash, a Vurker Hasis who had a kosher restaurant. His daughter, Brayne had a big haberdashery and confectionary store there. Later Yisroel Hersh Yablanko lived there. He was a wealthy wheat merchant who with his wife and children live in Israel today.

In a large two-story family home lived the family of Reb Yankev Berl Blumshteyn with his son-in-law, Reb Zelig Papiertshik and his two sons, Reb Yekhiel Meyer and Reb Gershn. Reb Yankev Berl's home had a reputation of Torah and greatness in one place. He was among the elite Vurker/Skernievitser Hasidim and raised his sons that way. His respected sons-in-law, Yekhiel Meyer had a leather store and Gershn was a wheat merchant. Reb Zelig Papiertshik had a textile store and traded with noblemen. Today he lives with his family in Israel. He is active in society and leads the Yeshivat Atarat

[Page 50]

Zkenim in Yad Eliyahu and is related to the Chief Rabbi of Israel, Rabbi Yehud Iser Unterman, may he have a long life, Amen.

In the courtyard lived the Tinsmithess, Chaye Zelde Klempner who as charity all these years, supported the shtetl's water carrier, Shloymo Akiva Beserman. Shloymo Akiva was not of sound mind since childhood but he was popular with everyone. He was always in a good mood, happy, a melody on his lips and distinguished himself with a wonderful memory. He was musically talented and a grand eater. There was not a single event in town where Shloymo Akiva did not attend and helped prepare but, at the same time, you had to watch his hand or he would eat up a big portion of the prepared dishes.

At the front, in a brick building lived Reb Avrom Itzhok Galant, the so called Kvosknik *(came from Kvas)*. He was well respected in town and among the enlightened Aleksander Hasidim. He had a popular candy store and sausage and soda water factory with was a popular meeting place for the youth where they would get together over a glass of beer and a sweet bite. There was a lot going on Friday and Saturday evenings there when Reb Avrom Itzhok would trustfully extend credit to everyone. His son, Moshe, a yeshiva student, was tortured by the Germans in Ostrow and his daughter, Rivke is said to have been in Russia having reached a high officer rank in the Red Army. At the top lived Irl Apelboym, a good women's tailor who immigrated to Israel after the war and died there. His wife and two children live in Israel today. His youngest son, Mordechai was killed by the Germans. In another small house lived Reb Avrom Kiris, a shoemaker as well as his son, Itche Velvl, also a shoemaker. Today he lives in Israel. Next to them lived Yosl Zilbershteyn, a hairdresser.

After Ratenski, the Christian butcher, stood the house of Reb Dovid Dranitsa, a tailor and his son-in-law, Reb Noske Kan, who traded in fish. For several years he was the village magistrate. He lives today in the United States. In the courtyard stood the house of Reb Moshe Dranitsa, a merchant, president of the Zionist organization and synagogue council member. Today he is the head of the religious council in Bet She'an, Israel. In the same courtyard there was also a big wooden barrack that belonged to Moshe Dranitsa which had a grain mill. In later years the barrack served as the city's social hall for big meetings, theater shows and other events/ cultural happenings.

Next to the small house lived Reb Mikhl Liver, a shoemaker and Yehudis Kas, a shipping agent. Next to them lived Reb Yankev Dovid Nayman, a shipping agent, Vurker Hasid among the respected men in town, He also had the exclusive right to sell yeast in the entire area. In the other half of the house that bordered on the priest's garden was the prayer houses of the Amshiaver, Otwocker, and Vurker Hasidim.

Back to the front of the market, there was a row of houses that stood in

[Page 51]

the center of the marketplace. The first one was Reb Asher Kutner's with his haberdashery store. He was among the Otwocker Hasidic zealots and gave them space for a prayer house as a gift. Next there was the house of Reb Avrom Mordechai Fridman, among the old Gerer Hasidim, an honorable and learned man, former councilman and among the respected men in town. He owns the largest textile store. He and his wife, Reytse were well respected even among the surrounding Christian population who trusted them deeply. Their sons, Shloyme and Henech lived with them as well as their son-in-law, Reb Levi Varshaviak, a Gerer Hasid and leader of the Agudah, among the founders and activists of the Beit Yaakov School. Today he lives in Israel. His place was later taken by Reb Yisroel Burshtin, a young man from Warsaw. He was a Gerer Hasid, big religious leader and leader of the Beit Yaakov School. He was shot by the Germans in the village of Duvanek.

In the neighboring two-story house lived Itche Solka, the son of Avromka, the synagogue sexton, who had returned from Cuba and opened a shoe store; Devora Mashenzon, a widow who had a hair salon; next to them Reb Avrom Yisroel Trushkevitsh, son of Reb Mordechai, the synagogue sexton - a learned man – typical student of the Lomza yeshiva who had a colonial store. At the top Reb Avrom Solka had his apartment the last few years. He was the usher of the Rabbinic court. He was a small Jew from Zhvave with a long beard. He was a big shot, mixed up in the town's affairs and knew everyone's secrets. He was among the most capable matchmakers in the area. Later when his children from the United States generously supported him, he did not forego the post of the Rabbinic court's usher.

The Kasztelno Street

In the nice corner brick house that bordered the Kasztelno Street lived Reb Elkhonen Fridman, among the enlightened ones and a founder of the Mirzahi party in the shtetl. He had a candy store and was also the bookkeeper at the Jewish Credit Bank. He son, Shapsl was among the leaders of the Beitar. He, his wife, three sons and two daughters were all killed.

The right side of the street was inhabited exclusively by Christians. At the end of the street was the priest's palace and fruit garden.

Probostwo

On a big square across from the church stood a big brick building where the Polish People's House stood and the first Christian cooperative which was in intense competition with the Jewish merchants. A little deeper into the field was the Christian cemetery. After another row of Christian houses there was a side street where several Jewish families lived including Reb Mordechai Shniadover, owner of a wind mill that stood a little further. There was another wind mill next to it that belonged to the partners

[Page 52]

and owners of the small steam mill – Reb Chaim Krulevitch, a good-natured man and Reb Yehoshue Drozd, among the respected Aleksander Hasidim, a good prayer leader and learned man.

Behind there, in the rest of the Probostwo area lived the wealthy brothers, Note and Iser Rits, owners of the city's electric power company and the big steam mill that produced flour for the entire area. Reb Note Rits, a learned man, was for several years, the president of the Jewish community. Reb Iser Rits, a Gerer Hasidic, was very hospitable and gave generously to charity. They were highly respected men in the shtetl. With them lived their children and son-in-law of Reb Iser Rits, Reb Shloyme Ekiezer Botshan, a student in the Lomza yeshiva from Rozan.

From the Probostwo a path leads towards the fence of the Christian nobleman, Glinko's residence, a palace in the estate, Szczawin. He was one of the wealthiest men in Poland and many Jews from Goworowo and the surrounding area conducted large business transactions and generated their income from him.

The market and the Kasztelno Street as it looks today
In the center: The memorial to the murdered residents

[Page 53]

On the way back to the shtetl there was the house and big colonial store of Reb Chaim Potash, a Vurker Hasid and musician. Next to it there was a meeting place of the Poale Agudas Yisroel Party. Then there was the city's post office and next, the shtetl's police headquarters. After the house of the Christian town doctor, Glinko stood the big parish church and the priest's palace.

The Other Side of Kasztelno Street

After several Christian stores stood the house where Reb Yekhiel Gerlits had his colonial store. He was a learned man, well versed in Hebrew and Yiddish literature, a friend of Nokhem Sokolov, knowledgeable in Polish and Russian. He used to write request to the government offices on behalf of the shtetl's Jews. Together with him lived his son, Chaim Gerlits founder of the city's interest free loan charity. Today he lives in the United States. Next to him also lived his older son, Itzhok Velvl Gerlits, the son-in-law of Reb Velvl Blumshteyn, owner of the iron store and mechanic workbench.

The Other Side of the Market

After Ratenski's big Christian textile store stood a small wooden house where Reb Shmuel Avrom lived, a tailor, with his son-in-law Reb Shimen Azdaba, a wheat merchant, Gerer Hasid and reader of the Torah in the synagogue. Next to them lived Sura Zilbershteyn, Reb Fayvl's widow, a stringent Otwocker Hasid, a learned man. Across from them lived the tailor from Radzilow, Reb Velvl Zilbershteyn, an honest man and large charity donor who died in Israel. His neighbors were Reb Mendl Botshan, the son of the old Goworowo rabbi, an impressive personality with a patriarchal look, a Hasid and honest man. In the front Reb Gaviel Yaloviets had his bakery. He was a good natured man. Later Yankev Kasher from Vonseva [Wąsewo] took over the bakery. In the next house lived Velvl Barg, a shoe leather worker from Pasheki.

In a nice two story building, Reb Moshe Tenenboym had his hotel and restaurant. He was president of the community for many years and an activist in the Mizrahi party. Next to him was the iron store of Reb Baruch Mints, a Vurker Hasid. The Hasidic rebbes would usually stay with him when they visited the shtetl. In the same house also lived Mrs. Eytshe Mints, a textile merchant and Reb Peysekh Shachter, a slaughterer. Their neighbor was Reb Itche Meyer Yaloviets, an Aleksander Hasid who traded in wheat. In the courtyard lived Reb Chaim Ber Grudke, the shipping agent considered to be among the respected Jews in town. An Aleksander Hasid, he was the shofar blower in the big synagogue.

In the front of the house lived Reb Gedalye Pshisusker, an Aleksander Hasid who owned a textile store and Hersh Berl Fayntsayg, a hat maker. His daughter, Blimtshe was an accomplished actress and his wife, Teme died in Israel. Then there was also the house and colonial store of Reb Meyer Ramaner, a Gerer Hasid an

[Page 54]

learned man who was an activist for community needs, for many years a synagogue council member, a learned man and an arbitrator for lawsuits at the rabbinic court.

The following house belonged to Reb Nosn Farba, a well-known Amshinaver Hasid who worked in the stone business. Together with him lived his sons-in-law, Nakhmen Yarzhambek and Rabbi Nakhmen Belfer, among the best students of the Lomza yeshiva. Today they live in Canada. Next to them lived Reb Yisroel Itzhok Tsudiker, a wheat merchant and Aleksander Hasid. In the courtyard there was the new big synagogue that was built in the year 5685 *(1924/25)*, the old wooden synagogue, the Talmud Torah, the Aleksander and Gerer prayer houses, the Beit Yaakov School, the interest free loan bank, and the welcoming office *(where strangers to the shtetl were welcomed)*.

Further along the front of the market, Reb Yekl Klepfish had his colonial store. He was the son of an old Goworowo Rabbi, the Beit Aharon and his son-in-law Reb Dan Rosenberg, a big textile merchant who had the power of attorney for the Jewish National Fund. He was an activist for the interest free loan bank. Next to them lived Reb Moshe Skurnik who was among the enlightened ones and Lovers of Zion. He was a speaker and affable person who immigrated to the Land of Israel in 1935. He died a few years ago. In the second half of the house lived his brother-in-law, Reb Elizer Kshanzhko, an honest man, Aleksander Hasid who traded in wheat. His wife and daughter live in Israel. There also lived Reb Chaim Mitsnmakher, a hat maker, son-in-law of Rabbi Reb Fishel Shapiro from Tshervin. His wife and children live in Israel today. Also Reb Moshe Mozes, a young, learned man who was a wheat merchant lives in the United States today.

In Wolka

On the other side of the river, in the small village, Wolka lived the following Jewish families: Reb Bendet Viroslav, a wheelwright who recited psalms in the study house. His daughter lives in Israel today along with his son-in-law Nakhmen Yarzhombek also a wheelwright. Also in the village were Yekl Budne, the smith and Moshe Taus, owner of a workbench for repairing agricultural machines.

In Pasheki

At the train station of Pasheki, 5 kilometers from Goworowo lived the following Jewish families: Meyer Likhtenshteyn with his son, Yoysef today in Israel. They operated a grocery store together with his son-in-law, Yoysef Rekhtsheyd. Leybl Barg also owned a grocery store. His children live in Israel. Leybl Thilim was a shipping clerk.

In Suchcice

In the village of Suchcice lived a few Jewish families. In the remaining villages of the Goworowo area no Jews were living the last few years.

[Page 55]

Rabbis

R' Solomon Zalmen Klepfish
May His Holy Memory be for a Blessing

by Moses Zinowits, Israel

Translated by Mira Eckhaus

Edited by Tina Lunson

R'Aron Solomon Zalmen was born in the city of Nemirov in the district of Brisk d'Lita, to his father, R' Yakil Klepfish, a great scholar, Torah teacher and a respected person. Authors of his time described him as: "a great rabbi in the Torah, he learned and taught and did a lot, his deeds and exploits were known to everyone, and he was highly respected by all his loved ones and acquaintances". In order to benefit the public and increase and glorify the Torah, R'Yakil published important books, among them: *Zayit Ra'anan*, *Margaliot HaTorah*, *Mlo A'omer*, *Meshivat Nefesh* and new interpretations on the Maharal, the Gaon R' Aryeh Leyb Zunz, the Rabbi of Plotsk.

At the end of his life, R' Yakil moved to Warsaw and became one of the city's most beloved and respected persons. His house became the Torah salon in the capital city; and also for his famous sons, the great Torah scholars, well-known people, who publicized the Klepfish family all over the country.

His eldest son, the Gaon R' Shmuel Zaynvil, was a rabbi and a judge in the Warsaw community and was among the great teachers. His students served as rabbis and judges in large communities in Poland. He served in his high position for dozens of years. His second son, R' Avrom Mayer, studied with the Gaon R' Yosef Dov Halevi Soloveitchik and the Gaon Hanatziv at the Volozhin yeshiva, and later he was appointed Rabbi in the city of Yablonka, near Visuki Mazovia, in Lomzshe district. His son R' Shmeril was not engaged in teaching, but he was considered one of the greatest of the city of Warsaw and one of its sharp and brilliant scholars.

His son, R' Aron Shlomo Zalmen, was a Gaon, sharp and well versed in all aspects of the Torah. He was appointed as a rabbi in the city of Vizna in his youth, and later received the position of the *Av Beit Din* [Head of the Jewish court] in the city of Goworowo.

R' Aron Shlomo Zalmen received his elementary education from his great father in his native city of Nemirov and when they moved to Warsaw, his brother the Gaon R' Shmuel Zaynvil took care of his education, and under his supervision and guidance R' Aron Shlomo Zalmen grew up and rose to great heights in the virtues of the Torah. He amazed his family and acquaintances with his great perseverance and excelled as a sharp mind and great author of new interpretations, with only a small part of his work reflected in his composition *Beys Aron*, which contains wonderful interpretations on Talmud tractates.

When he reached the age of marriage, the famous rabbi R' Tsvi Halevi Levinsky of Stevisk, chose him as the son-in-law for his dearest daughter, and there he continued to study Torah with wonderful diligence and perseverance. (Rabbi Tsvi Halevi Levinsky immigrated to Jerusalem at the end of his life and is the father of the esteemed Goelman family of Idvovna, Stevisk and Bnei Brak).

In the year 5626 or thereabout, R' Aron Shlomo Zalmen was elected, through the intercession of his influential father-in-law, as rabbi in the city of Vizna. In this city he completed the writing of his book *Beys Aron* and was crowned with the approval of the Gaons R' Khayim Elazar Vaks, *Av Beit Din* of Kalish;

Rahal Rakovsky, *Av Beit Din* of Plotsk and R' Yosef Heber, *Av Beit Din* of Idvovna, the father-in-law of his brother R' Avraham Mayer. The aforementioned Gaons

[Page 56]

praised and glorified the young author, and this is what R' Chaim Elazar Vaks wrote about him: "A great rabbi in Torah and reverence, and I have seen the great men of the land who testify and say about him that he is like a spring that increases in everything related to the Torah and reverence". And the *Av Beit Din* of Plotsk further added: "I already know him for several years and I know that he studies Torah also at nights and he is full of knowledge of the Torah".

Although this book was ready and arranged for printing in Vizna, the author was unable to publish it, probably because of his poverty and oppression, because the salary he received from the city of Vizna was not enough for his livelihood. Therefore, he accepted the offer of the city of Goworowo, a bigger and richer city than Vizna, and moved there to serve as *Av Beit Din* in the mid-1930s.

At the beginning of his tenure in Goworowo, he fulfilled his life's mission and founded a yeshiva for talented students. His idea was to establish a large yeshiva in a national format, which would bridge the Judaism of Lita and its methods of studying the Torah, with hasidic Polish Judaism. Even though he was a staunch "opponent" and never allowed the Sephardic version to be included in prayer, even though many Ger Hasidim were concentrated in Goworowo, Vurke and Alexander. Nevertheless, he appreciated the glory of Hasidism and wanted to complete it with the in-depth study of the Lithuanian learning system. However, this wonderful idea of his did not come to fruition due to a serious illness that put him on the deathbed for many years. Indeed, this idea was adopted by the great rabbi R' Elieyzer Shulevitz, who founded the great yeshiva in Lomzshe.

Details on the rabbi's illness were written, with the consent of his brother the Gaon Rabbi Shmuel Zaynvil, in his book: "Even though he has been ill for more than ten years, nevertheless he gathered his strength and continued to write new interpretations and record them in his book". This consent was written in the year 5645 and was attached to the above-mentioned essay when it was published in the year 5646.

R' Aron Shlomo Zalmen passed away in 5645 and he did not reach old age. He was not privileged to see his book published, and it was published only after his death, by his son R' Moshe, and his son-in-law, R' Yaakov.

His son R' Yakil, a Torah scholar and God fearing Jew, lived all his days in Goworowo and perished during the destruction of the city during the Holocaust.

[Page 57]

R' Jacob Judah Kahana-Butsian

May His Holy Memory be for a Blessing

by Moses Zinowits, Israel

Translated by Mira Eckhaus

Edited by Tina Lunson

He was a descendant of a privileged family of Gaons and rabbis, generation after generation, back to Shimon the righteous. His father, R' Tsvi Aryeh Ha'koen, was a rabbi in Nemirov and author of the books *Tahalichot Hayabsha*, novel interpretations of Jewish law for walkers on both weekdays and on Shabbat and for those who travel in carts drawn by horses, as well as on the *Pareve Mashin*, which are scattered throughout the Talmud and commentaries, and in the first and last *Shulkhan Orekh*, as well as the book *Tahalukhot Hamayim*, laws for sailors. He was the son of the holy Rabbi R' Yitzchak Isaac, known as "*Kohen Gadol*", who authored the book *Sha'arey Yitskhak* on the wisdom of *Kabole*, and was a student of R' Mordechai Malkhovits, and the grandson of R' Yaakov Yehuda Kahana, *Av Beit Din* of Valpi, who was a diligent student of the Rebis R' Shlomo of Karlin and R' Yaakov Yosef of Ostra, the author of *Toldot*, and later he was a loyal student of the *HaKhozeh* of Lublin.

Although the family's origin was from Polish Lithuania, the whole family adhered to the Hasidic movement and remained loyal to it and its leaders all their lives, and thanks to their greatness in the Torah they added grandeur to the movement and were honored even by its great opponents such as R' Hirshel Orenstein, *Av Beit Din* of Brisk, R' Aryeh Leyb, the author of *Yefei Einaym*, and R' Shaul Epstein, *Av Beit Din* of Kosova, father of the mother of the Gaon and author of *Khazon Ish*.

Rabbi Yankev Yehude Kahana, *Av Beit Din* of Goworowo, authored in his youth the book *Veshav Hakohen*, in which he resolves all the doubts of the authors of the commentaries about the Talmud that remained unsolved. Because of his great humility, the author asked not to be relied upon with the Law and signed his name only with his initials. There are two approvals for this book: from the Gaon R' Eliyahu Shik, *Av Beit Din* of Lida, Yager and Kobrin, and Mr. Shmuel Zaynvil Klepfish, a judge in Warsaw, who was a close relative.

His first position in the rabbinate was in the city of Yandziev in the Ostrov Mazovietski district. From there he moved to serve as a rabbi in the city of Stradyn, however, in the rabbinic world he is known as "the author of *Veshav Ha'koen* of Goworowo", a place where he worked for decades, and where he was also known as a saint and an exemplary man. He was appointed a rabbi in Goworowo after the death of R' Aron Shlomo Zalman Klepfish.

R' Yankev Yehuda brings up the matter of a special regulation that was set up in Goworowo in the matter of ritual slaughter, which was prohibited and boycotted by all the important householders: "the ritual slaughterers are not allowed to butcher the cattle each by themselves, they are obliged to be together during the *shekhite* and the inspection and to show their knives to each other even the for the sheep and goats. And if a slaughterer and an inspector are not both in the house, the other slaughterer and inspector and is obligated to show his knife to the R', *Av Beyt Din*, before he performs the *shekhite*, besides what is required to show his knife to R' Damta as is customary. In addition, each and every one of them must bring the lungs before the rabbi for examination". The writing was done in front of the *Maharilag* (perhaps it was Rabbi Yehuda Leyb Gordon, *Av Beyt Din* of Lomzshe)

[Page 58]

and it is presented in the book *Be'er Moshe* by Rabbi Moshe Nachum Yerushalimski from the time he served as *Av Beit Din* of Ostrolenke.

Rabbi R' Yankev Yehuda was in contact by letter, regarding questions and answers in Jewish law with the greats of his generation, with the Gaon R' Malkhiel Tanenbaum, *Av Beit Din* of Lomzshe, the author of *Divrei Malkhiel*, with R' Moshe Nakhum Yerushalimski, the author of *Birkat Moshe*, and with R' Nissan Kupershtok, *Av Beit Din* of Makove, the author of the book *Ani Ben Pakhma*.

In the book *Stirat Zkeynim* by R' Khayim Mordkhe Bronrot, *Av Beit Din* of Tskhekhnov and the Chief *Av Beit Din* of Tel Aviv, R' Yankev Yehude Kahana is described as a Gaon, an innocent saint, and an exemplary man who was well known for his sharpness and depth of knowledge of the Torah.

ספר

וישב הכהן

ווארשא

ВЕШОВЪ ГАКОГЕНЪ

ВАРШАВА

1879.

The cover of the book *Veshav Ha'koen* by R' Kahana-Butsian

The rabbi's eldest son was R' Shmuel Ha'koen, known as Shmuel'ke Stradiner. He exalted in Torah and Hasidism, and his daughter Feyge Motl was the wife of the R' of Tskhechnov. His second son, R' Menachem Mendel Ha'koen, persevered day and night on the Torah, and his work and the Torah were his profession (*Torato Umanuto*). He served for a period of time as a ritual slaughterer and inspector in Goworowo and endeared himself to the public with his noble ways and in his handsome patriarchal figure. He achieved greatness and passed away in the city of Bialystok in 5700, where he had fled from Goworowo because of the oppressor.

[Page 59]

A Few Memories of the Old Rov

by R' N. Talmud, Israel

Translated by Tina Lunson

I had the privilege of spending nearly one year in the close company of R' Yankev Yehude Batshan, the old Goworowo rabbi. I was reckoned among the young men who studied with the Rov in his daily Talmud lesson. He was already a man of many years. Very tall, a lean, slender figure with a high forehead and a sparse little beard. He moved slowly, walking step by step, and spoke quietly and carefully, as if he were counting every word. I never saw him angry; he smiled often and although he was occupied with his study, he always loved a witty word and a jest.

The material situation of the town at that time was not bad. Trade with the Christian princes brought in a good revenue. And the relationships with the gentiles were good. The old Prince Markvitski, from Brizshnia, had a custom of sending wagons of free potatoes to the Jews on the eve of *Peysakh*. The Rov's material situation was therefore also good and secure.

The Rov's apartment was communal – two rooms built onto the wall of the *beys-medresh* [study-house]. The Rov's son Mendl and his family lived in one room and in the other room, which was divided off by a curtain, half served as the *beys-din* [Jewish court] and the other half as the Rov's sleeping chamber.

Above the Rov's apartment, the next story, were the prayer rooms [*shtiblekh*] for the Ger and the Aleksander Hasidim. The Hasidim of both Rebis' dynasties were mutually intolerable and disputes between them were constant. But the Aleksander Hasidim were richer and stronger than the Ger, among them well-heeled and eminent proprietors, and they supported the Rov in every way possible, because the Rov was an Aleksander Hasid and very respected in the Rebi's court. It was said that for each difficult question in the Aleksander court, the "Joy of Yisroel" told them to ask the Goworowo Rov. He was the jurist for the Aleksander Hasidim.

The Rov ran his house very frugally, although he was well situated, and had married all his children and grandchildren to wealth. One of his

[Page 60]

grandchildren was R' Branrot, the Tshekhanover Rov and later the head of the *beys-din* of Tel Aviv.

I once sat with the Rov during a lawsuit before the rabbinic tribunal. When the two litigants laid their 10 *groshen* judgement fees on the table, the Rov quickly took the money and put it deep in his pocket. The thing made me wonder. I asked him why he put the fee away. He smiled and answered, "Once I decided a case when the losing litigant grabbed his fee and ran off. Since then, I am more careful."

Another time I accompanied him on a Friday night to an event for a new born son at Bertshe Kolodzsher's on Long street. Passing my house, the Rov stopped and told me to go home. I moaned, "I want to go with Rov to the house, because a Talmud scholar should not walk alone at night for apprehension about demons."

The Rov laughed. "The Goworowo demons do not consider me a Talmud scholar."

The town in general held the Rov in high esteem because he was by nature, good and he rejected glory, hated disagreement and he did not shout. The town also recognized his scholarship and honesty, which was an example for all the neighboring towns.

[Page 61]

The Last Rov

by A. Avinoam, Israel

Translated by Tina Lunson

Even in the previous generation, the generation before the Holocaust, there was rarely to be found a person with so much influence as was incarnate in the personal charm and noble characteristics as was the last Goworowo Rov, Rebi Alter Meyshe Mordkhe Burshtin, may God avenge his blood. A wonderful patriarchal figure, a person with tact and feeling, sharp-minded and magnanimous. Full of impulse and creative energy. His scholarship and shrewdness were well known throughout Poland. Indeed, he was called upon from far corners of the land to settle complicated and difficult issues of Jewish law, and people from near and far came to him for advice on Jewishness, community and business matters and found solutions and consolation.

For almost 30 years the Goworowo Rov steered his congregation through still waters and calm and stormy eras. Sure and firm he held the rudder in his hand and laid his seal on the entire community and even on the personal lives in the town.

He was not only the greatest spiritual leader of the generation, he also loved the town and its householders. He rejected with disdain more than one proposal to take over a rabbinic seat in larger towns. When they proposed, early on in his 30-year stay, that he take the rabbinic position in Ostrow-Mazavietsk after Rebi Mayer Dan Plotski, although it was a large town and a heritage rabbinate – he expressed his wish in front of his intimate friends: As long as the proposal is not carried out, because it would be hard for him to part from the quiet, idyllic life in this lovely, venerable little town.

The Rov operated his "realm" high-handedly. He took himself to be, and felt it himself, that he was the leader not only of the religious Jews but of all the Goworowo residents. When he found out that the local Bund was burning the electric light on *Shabes*, he sent for the Bund leader Leybl Kersh, and convinced him that in Goworowo one may not violate the sabbath. When a soccer team wanted to arrange a match on a *Shabes* and he was not able to convince them in a good way, the Rov organized a group of Jews on the sports field who drove them away. Although a pursuer of peace, he was prepared to go through fire for a just cause, not considering sentiment or relationships.

[Page 62]

R' Alter Meyshe Mordkhe Burshtin may God avenge his blood, the last Goworowo Rov

The last Goworowo Rov had great strength in delivering sermons. Even a simple everyday conversation with him was a delight. His witticisms and aphorisms went the rounds from mouth to mouth. But he personally enjoyed nothing as much as sitting and studying. People said about him, he never stopped learning. He spent all his free time studying and writing innovations on Torah and was not pleased if someone disturbed him in his daily lessons. It was a special pleasure for him to study with the youth. On the long winter evenings, he studied with scholarly young men and boys, from midnight until the grey early morning.

Even gentiles were drawn to the Rov with great respect. At times, his interventions with the local or provincial authorities were helpful.

The Rov's home was a community house for the town Jews and for guests from outside it. There were always people in his court room, some with a question to ask, or a community issue, or simply to pour out their hearts. The Rov's house was run with generosity and hospitality and served as an example for the inhabitants of Goworowo.

[Page 63]

R' Alter Meyshe Mordkhe was born in Ruzshan near Narev, in *sav-reysh-lamed-tes* by his father Rebi Issakhar Dov Burshtin (Ostrozshinski), a Talmud scholar and observant Jew, and his mother Rivke.

From childhood he was seen as a genius for his clear head and sharp sense. His innovations in Torah surprised scholars. R' Petakhiye Harenblum, the Warsaw Rov once heard a repeat of one of his explications and sent for him to come to Warsaw to spend a long time and could not be separated from him. The "Ruzshan genius" did not want to travel away to study in a *yeshive*, as he could not be parted from his beloved parents. He sat for whole days and nights in the town study house and studied with diligence.

At 17 he married his wife Genendl, the daughter of the great *goan* Rebi Avieyzer Shikara, one of the great scholars in the area, the son-in-law of the Vale Rov, Goan R' Avrom Aron Hendl, the rebi and teacher of the Ger Hasidic court and of the Radzin Rebi may God avenge his blood.

He boarded with his wealthy father-in-law for two years. Afterwards he was invited by the Amshinov Rebi, R' Menakhem, and took up the task of rearing and teaching his children. Hasidim continually tell of the great affection that Rebi Menakhem demonstrated to the "Rozshaner genius". They considered him as their child and protected him like a treasure. After Rebi Menakhem's passing, he was further retained as fellow-scholar by Rov Yosele Amshinov of blessed memory and a house-friend of the entire Vorke community. He was the one who examined the education of all the candidates for sons-in-law in the Vorke court, and later also for other Hasidic courts.

In *sav-reysh-samekh-tes* R' Alter took up the first rabbinic post in Tshervin after the Tshervin Rov, R' Branrat. He remained there for three years, and earned so much love and friendship that up until the Second World War the Tshervin Jews clung to him as to a father.

His second rabbinic seat was in Goworowo, where he spent the First World War. The town was burned down. He contributed his portion to the rebuilding of the town and protected it from the evil demons of destruction from the Russians, Germans, Bolsheviks and Halertshikes.

His first daughter Blume was married to the Vorke-Narazshine Rebi's son R' Arele Tenenboym, a grandson of Yeshresh Yankev. Her second husband was R' Borekh Tshizsheves' grandson Butshe Eydlshteyn, from the richest family in Mlove. The other daughter married a young Hasidic scholar and prosperous merchant.

At the outbreak of the Second World War, he remained in the town until the last of the householders left the place. He spent a few months in Bialystok, then he went to Vilna where he developed a wide community activity. His home was the gathering place for all the rabbinic refugees, and was united in great friendship with the *goan* R' Khayim

[Page 64]

Ozer Grodzenski, Rebi Elkhonen Vaserman and with the official town rabbi, R' Sender Itsik Rubenshteyn. The president of the Lodz Jewish council Leybl Mintsberg often came to his home as well as senator Trakenhaym from Warsaw. When the Germans took Vilna the Goworowo Rov experienced the contemporary beatings and was in the ghetto there for several weeks. He was rescued by a miracle and fled in a German automobile to Grodne. There he was taken in as the rov for the ghetto. From Grodne he fled back to Bialystok and remained in the ghetto until its liquidation.

For 17 days in the month of Av, that month of sadness and devastation, the filthy hands of the Nazi murderers prepared the Goworowo Rov, while he sat and studied. And they took him to the death camp, Treblinke. May God avenge his blood.

The Rov's daughter Yeta with her husband
Meyshe Goldfeder, may God avenge their blood

The *Rebitsn* Rokhl
of blessed memory

The Rov's Blume,
may God avenge her blood

Rokhl (left) and Zelda, the Rov's younger daughter,
may God avenge their blood

[Page 65]

R' Alter Meyshe Mordkhe Burshtin

by *R'* Samuel Aaron Halevi Pardes

Editor of the monthly Rabbinical File – Chicago

Translated by Mira Eckhaus

Edited by Tina Lunson

The *Gaon* R' Alter Meyshe Mordkhe Burshtin, *Av Beys Din* of the Goworowo Jewish community in Poland, was one of the greatest rabbis, a genius and a magnificent sage, a hasid and a humble and wonderfully knowledgeable man in all the Torah professions.

He compiled a large essay of "queries and responses" from questions that had been sent to him from all over Poland, which was never published, and was burned in the torching of the town of Goworowo in the year 5700 (1939).

He served in the town of Goworowo for nearly thirty years. Many communities, among them large and important ones, appealed to him to accept the position of *Av Beys Din* there, but he refused to part with his town where he lived in peace and honor, devoting all his time to studying the Torah.

The Rov may God avenge his blood was highly respected among all strata of the people of his town and the surrounding area. His beautiful appearance and his stature left a great impression on everyone who saw him. The late Rov of Amshinov, R' Yosele said of him that, like previous righteous men, he also did not blemish anything in the image of God that the blessed God did endow him with.

When the damned Germans occupied Goworowo, they looked for the Rov may God avenge his blood and wanted to kill him. He managed to hide, and from his hiding place he led his community onward. But he did not want to leave it, until they deported the entire population of the town, and then he fled to Bialystok, and from Bialystok to Vilna.

In Vilna he was one of the leaders of the committee of refugee rabbis who fled from enemy lands; he excelled in his good qualities, in saving and leading that committee. The late *Gaon* R' Khayim Ozer Grodzhinski liked him very much. He often called him to his home to enjoy his teachings and to consult with him on all the questions that were brought before him.

Due to family reasons, the Rov may God avenge his blood did not flee to Japan and remained in the Vilna ghetto during the terrible hardships. He was the first to escape from the Vilna Ghetto to Grodno. In Grodno he was appointed as the *Av Beys Din* and served there for over a year. When the enemy arrived in the Grodno ghetto, he returned to the city of Bialystok. In Bialystok his house served as the place for the committee of sages. All the rabbis and members of the yeshives who sought refuge in Bialystok, always gathered at his house. Also, the famous civic activists Reb Leybl Mintsberg, who was a delegate in the Polish Sejm and the head of the Lodz Jewish community, as well as the senator Reb Yankev Trokenheim, always consulted him and were like members of his household.

The Rov of Goworowo strongly supported the Jewish resistance fighters in Bialystok. Together with R' Yitzhak Levin, the son-in-law of R' Mishkovski of Krynik, they were engaged in founding an armed society of young Torah students. The teacher from the Beys Yankev school for girls, Ms. Kaposta, bought guns outside the ghetto and placed them in the Rov's house, in order to distribute them among the Torah students. He strengthened the hearts of the Torah students with passionate sermons to stand against the wicked with sword and bow.

In the month of Av, 5737, the holy Rov was taken to Treblinka. May God avenge his blood.

(From "*HaPardes*", booklet 12, year 21, Elul 5707 - September 1947)

[Page 66]

The Religious Life

Jewishness in the Town

by Yosef Gurka, Israel

Translated by Tina Lunson

As in most cities and towns in Poland, so too in Goworowo, religious Jewishness stood in the center of Jewish life. Everything in the little town, without exception, turned around that act. The *shul* was the central gathering point for the entire population. There, and in all the Hasidic *shtiblekh* [prayer rooms] one could always hear the voice of Torah; people sat day and night and studied. The heads of the community, with the rabbis at the top, devoted most of their activities to religious interests. One could say that the private life of each individual was controlled, directly or indirectly, by the council members and the Rov, whenever he was not entranced by the secrets of the *Shulkhan Orekh* and other religious writings.

The greatest attention in the town was given to the religious education of the younger generation. That concern and dedication occupied the highest place of all the management issues because that dedication is, indeed, the foundation of Jewish existence, as the wise men say: "No kids, no goats". Goworowo had recorded great successes in the area of education. There was a network of *khedarim* [religious schools] for boys and a *Beys-Yankev* school for girls. The level of instruction was high.

Besides that, Goworowo possessed a large number of *yeshiva* boys [advanced pupils] and dedicated students of Torah who studied in the large *yeshives* of the land.

Goworowo residents excelled with their love of Torah, and generously supported the Torah scholars of the town and beyond it. The majority of the householders were concerned that their sons become Talmud scholars and strove to marry their daughters to scholars. For that goal they spared no trouble and no money. They took great efforts to maintain their sons-in-law in their homes for years so they could sit and study without other worries.

In the last years before the war broke out, R' Aron Vladamirski from Vishkove – known in *yeshive* circles as R' Aron Stelner – founded a Novoredok *yeshiva* in Goworowo. It was temporarily located in the study-house and children from the local areas studied there, such as Ruzsha, Ostrove,

[Page 67]

Ostrolenke, Makove and others. Those students "ate days" with local residents who provided their meals.

Many contributed to the religious institutions of the town, the rabbis, all the important Torah personalities who planted love for Torah and love for Yisroel among the householders and called them to do *mitsves,* good deeds; in particular the last Rov was famous for his astuteness and sharp-mindedness, standing head and shoulders above others. All the rabbis, the religious leaders, and teachers, gave the greatest part of their time and energy to spreading Jewishness, planting love of Torah and concerning themselves to help the young generation to study in the big *yeshivas.*

Even in the years after the First World War, when the winds of the Enlightenment and free-thinking began to blow through the Jewish street and of course Goworowo was not exempted from that, our town did not lose its specific Jewish religious outlook. There were, indeed, many young men who put the Talmud aside, but an opposing reaction was soon created on the other side. The religious youth organized, rented a space, and conducted a strong enlightenment campaign. That was a large group of *kheyder* boys who later went to *yeshivas* and continued to study.

One of the greatest merits that distinguished Goworowo was that the inhabitants, with few individual exceptions, were not inclined to extremism. There were no radicals. Thus, the observant Jews did not "crow" on the rooftops and the free Jews did not "needle" the young. That is how the whole town stayed homogeneous and for the good of religion and tradition, or as they say: Torah and tradition.

[Page 68]

Among Hasidim

by Avrom Levin, Israel

Translated by Tina Lunson

Every time when I meet Jews from the former Goworowo at the yearly remembrance of the tragedy or at a happy occasion, after the Holocaust, my eye scans the town's *beys-medresh* [study-house] and the Hasidic prayer rooms – the entire town with its little houses and lanes, along with the figures who illuminated the town and were so tragically cut down.

Although I have not lived in Goworowo for more than 20 years (from 1907 to 1927) everything is still etched in my memory and in my reckoning, these were the best years of my social, intellectual, and social life. Neither the 25 years of living in far off wealthy Cuba, nor the years of my being here in our land Yisroel, can compare with the beautiful Jewish life of that small, poor town Goworowo.

We always talked about the brotherliness and homeyness of that time, of each dear Jew like Fishl Shapira, later the Tshervine Rov of blessed memory, and others. Sitting with R' Fishl and talking and learning was a true spiritual pleasure. Another great pleasure were the gatherings every *Shabes* morning with R' Yoelke the baker, where we drank tea and commented on the traditional texts. Although the tea had the smell of *tsholent* [sabbath stew] it still was better than the coffee that I drank in Cuba or in America.

Dear beloved Jews were in that town, whose like I have never met in any other place. Although R' Fishl was always tiring himself out with the money exchanges and usually running around seeking an interest free loan, he was still happy and whenever one went to his home you found him deep in study at a table full of open books, such as the Talmud, *Yore deye*, *RaMBaM* and others. He always greeted people with love and friendship, and when someone came whom he could talk to and study with he would not let them leave.

I recall an interesting event. Once Fishl arrived back from a trip to Tomashov, where he was attending to some merchandise matters (he dealt in manufactured goods). As usual, I asked him what he was doing. He answered me, "Go tell Yonatan (Zilbertson) that I have an interesting piece of merchandise for him." I did not understand what he meant, because he had not yet received the merchandise that he had just bought. Nevertheless, I went to Yonatan and said that Fishl had told me to fetch

[Page 69]

him and had a good piece of merchandise to show us both. Yonatan reoriented himself quickly and said that it must certainly be something to do with learning that he had asked about in Tomashov. And so it was. He told us with enthusiasm about a question on the Commentators that someone had asked in Tomashov and happily told us how he had answered. That is how involved in learning R' Fishl of blessed memory was. As it is written, "He asks and responds, replies and derives."

At home, when a customer came to call and was waiting impatiently, he did not close the Talmud volume but laid his red handkerchief over it and spoke with the customer with the same intonation of Talmud study. Peasants who came to buy from him approached him with respect. I was with him at home once when a peasant, a familiar Sobieski, came to buy something and stopped him in the middle of study. Fishl asked him what he needed, and he told him, "You pray, I can wait." And he did sit for a little while until he closed the Talmud.

The finest pleasure was *Shabes* and holidays when we made *kidush* together. Each one had contributed some part to the feast, according to their abilities. One brought dessert from home and many times also a *Shabes* stew to R' Fishl and mixed all the *kugls* together. How pleasant it was, sitting together and spending time in happiness and with songs. Although they tired themselves all week with finding a livelihood, on *Shabes* and holidays they were carefree, all worries were forgotten. For the third meal of *shabes* we were pampered and did not want to go over to the weekday, so after "ushering out the *Shabes* queen" we also ate together. On holidays we did not want it to end either but gathered – sometimes at R' Fishl's and sometimes at R' Yonatan ¬ to drink a toast and be joyful together.

When *Khanike* came around we were very merry. Every evening we would meet in another place ¬ sometimes at our home, or Yonatan's or at Metayes's (Rozen) or Fishl's and spend fraternal time together. First we would set up card games and take a few *groshen* from each "circle", and when we had collected enough to buy a bottle of 90% and a few herrings, someone dealt the cards, made a "*l'khayim*" and we celebrated the feast. The householders honored us with potato pancakes and we sang "*Maoz tsur*" [O mighty stronghold of my salvation, to praise You is a delight].

Here is the story of what happened once. It was *Shabes* night of *Khanike* when we were gathered at R' Fishl's to bid the *Shabes* queen farewell. As it was in winter, R' Fishl asked his wife to cook up some groats in order to warm us up. Meanwhile we set up a card game and as usual took a coin from each "circle" to buy whisky and herring. When the groats were ready someone went to Potash and bought the whisky and herring. We washed, drank a *l'khayim* and enjoyed the groats. Then we sang about the *Shabes* night of *Khanike*, talked about our study, recited the blessings after meals and so it went on until after midnight. When we went

[Page 70]

outdoors to go home we were gripped by a fierce cold, deep snow and a wind that stung our eyes and it was hard to take a step. After a quick discussion we decided not to go to our homes and make our wives get up and go to open the doors for us, but to go into the Aleksander *shtibl* and stay there for the night. Say and do. We headed for the Aleksander *shtibl*, but, when we tried to open the door we could not. It was closed from the inside with a wooden bolt. We understood that someone was sleeping in there and did not want to open it for us. There was another door on the other side of the *shtibl*, but in winter it was covered with boards. Since there was a small window above this door we decided to lift one of us so that he would be able bend back the obstacles, crawl inside and then open the door. Since I as the smallest, it fell to me and without an alternative I had to carry out this piece of work. When I got inside, I encountered a poor man sleeping soundly behind the oven, and he had bolted the door so that no one could, heaven forbid, could steal his poperty. After removing the obstacle, in came Yisroel Mayer (Meshnius), Nosn Mayer (Rokhl Shmuelke's) and Yonatan. After the big meal we had no desire to sit and study so we resumed playing cards. At dawn we heard someone walking on the steps. It was Yisroel Itsik Tsudiker, who had been sleeping and was now coming to the *shtibl* to study. We did not wait for him to ask why we were there so early, but quickly left and went to our homes so that no one would see us on the street because we were all still wearing our *shabes* clothing – long satin coats and so on. Early on Sunday Shprintse, Rokhl Shmuelke's daughter, Nosn Mayer's wife, came to my wife Khane Leye and asked her, "Was your little angel at home last night? My man did not spend the night at home, he just recently came home, what do you say about that? We've seen a lot, who knows, did they play cards all night long?" My wife smiled, because I had taken care to tell her everything, and she called out to her, "So what? He hasn't disappeared yet!"

"And you're laughing about it?" Shprintse shouted, "Don't you know what that means, playing cards a whole night long?"

My Khane calmed her down. "It's still not so terrible, *khanike* comes only once a year, they can still make a living." Thus everyone was generally happy, and although most of them were great paupers, they all had modest needs. People always felt a spiritual satisfaction.

I want to mention some saints, Yisroel Yitsik Tsudiker's son. His business, which had to do with salt, herring and fuel oil, was run entirely by his wife and he could

[Page 71]

always be found in the study-house or in the *shtibl* philosophizing. Once on a market day, a Thursday, someone came to request vindication and said, "You stand here and talk nonsense and there are many customers in your shop, your wife is alone there and cannot offer advice, and the customers are going away."

"Should I buy another few pounds of salt, or another couple of quarts of oil, or another few herring? Eat a piece of herring? I do not want to eat a piece of herring and I don't want to go work with the peasants!"

Once his father R' Yisroel Yitsik invited all the Aleksander hasidim in his house on the night of *Shmini atseres* after the Torah circuits for *kidush*. It was prepared with all good things: whisky, herring and so on. We had a good time there, dancing and singing. Khaye his wife called out, "Anyway, Avrom, Yisroel Mayer, Yonatan, dancing and being merry with the Torah, they study all year, but Ruven, Yehoshue Ber's son, why isn't he dancing? Perhaps because he's been making '*kekles*' all year?" They then explained to her that, when a brother gets married all the other brothers rejoice with him, and...let's just party!

Another episode is etched in my mind. When Metayes Rozen moved into the *smetelikhe* in his apartment he invited the Aleksander hasidim to his home for *Shabes kidush.* Khayim Yosl the scribe was among those invited. He was a Jew whose whole life was full of troubles, an established pauper, always lived in squalor and could make *Shabes* only with a great effort. But he was happy nonetheless. And indeed, at that very *kidush* he made toast after toast, took a little more, and another drop, and in his tipsiness began dancing on the table and singing "One God in heaven and on earth" and we helped him out with "We learn about our beginnings, happy are we in our service, our lives are sugar sweet".

And Khayim Yosl's everyday conversations were wonderful. If someone gave him potatoes to eat, he would say, "Ay, what a shame! If you could press the potatoes out a little more and give me the whisky from them, I would like it even better."

R' Avrom Leyb the phylactery seller often traveled to Goworowo from Vengrov or Kalushin with his merchandise of *t'filin*, *mezuzes*, *tsitsis* and so on. As he was Khayim Yosl's competitor, they would frequently tell one another off. Once he came to Goworowo during a great freeze. He went right into the Aleksander *shtibl* with his merchandise, snowed on, frozen, with pieces of ice in his beard and moustache. He headed straight for the warm oven, laid a cheek on the oven, and began to moan. We, a few

[Page 72]

young men, were sitting in the *shtibl* studying. Khayim Yosl the scribe was also there. We asked Avrom Leyb, "What happened to you?"

"One of my teeth is frozen and is as soft as butter" he replied. We understood that he wanted us to put something on it because we knew he was a big jokester. Khayim Yosl did not move but said that he had heard that a tooth was supposed to be soft. Avrom Leyb said, "Don't you believe it? Then tap on the tooth and convince yourself." As Khayim Yosl reached out a finger, then, he was bitten. "You want to stick your finger in someone's mouth?!" Avrom Leyb said to him.

Khayim Yosl was a dear Jew. He used to complain, "When I was young, I thought that when one is young, with warm blood, it is hard to fight the impulse to evil; but, when I would be old and the blood a little cooler, it would the easier to overcome the impulse. I am, thank God, older now and what has happened? If it's not enough that the younger impulse did not go away, now an older impulse to evil has arrived too."

The joyfulness of the *Shabes* and holidays was unforgettable. I remember another event. We were all gathered at R' Fishl's for a Sukos water drawing observance. We had a barrel of beer with herring, we were rejoicing and joined in a circle and began dancing. In the middle of the dance Nosn Mayer fell from our hands when a board broke in the floor, and he fell through. We did not think much of it and kept on dancing. Only when Khayim Yosl started yelling that Nosn Mayer had fallen down into the cellar did we all run to see what had happened. But the plaintiff stood up as though nothing had happened. We all went back upstairs and went back to dancing and Khayim Yosl sang to us, "We are happy, with our service, for our life is sugar sweet…"

There were many Jews in town who dedicated their time and energy to community work and for poor people. One of them was R' Meyshe Yehoshue Ginzburg, who was himself a poor Jew and therefore also a sickly man and gave much concern and time to the creation of a "hospitality house". R' Meyshe Yehoshue put a lot of work into that house; every Friday he went around to every house and collected a few pennies from everyone and with those small sums he established a study house at the "hospitality house". There were several *minyonim* there every day and Jews went there to study.

R' Meyshe Yehoshue also collected money for the paupers who arrived in Goworowo. In those days when there was a scarcity of small change, he was a great help to them. Because in many of the poorer houses people would stall, using the excuse "I don't have any small change", Meyshe Yehoshue made receipts for *groshens* and half-*groshens* and put them into circulation. Each pauper

[Page 73]

who came to town exchanged several *gilden* from Meyshe Yehoshue for receipts and with those he could get change to use. Plus, proprietors would come to him to exchange money for receipts. That way those who collected for charity could receive more money than usual, because even a poor resident who could not afford to give a whole *groshen* had the possibility of giving a half *groshen*. Even after leaving the town some paupers returned to exchange Meyshe Yehoshue's receipts for the current tender.

And there were women devoted to caring for the sick and needy, among whom Rokhl Shmuelke and Khane Rivke Shmelts excelled. When there was a poor pregnant woman in town or just a sick person, the women were concerned for them. They already knew who would give a piece of chicken or a good bowl of soup in order to strengthen the patient. No one in town knew who the food was for.

The same women also occupied themselves with charity for poor brides. When a poor girl was getting married, they put together a dowry and also clothes and other items for the trousseau.

The *bikur kholim* for visiting the sick was also active in the town. They would send two people for night duty to sit by the patient. After the First World War, when there were so many cases of infectious diseases like typhus or even influenza that caring for a patient was dangerous, no one refused that *mitsve*. And the *mitsve* was always dutifully carried out. The entire town revolved around the same few hundred rubles. Today I borrowed from someone, and tomorrow someone may borrow from me. Anyone who had a few *rubles* or *zlotych* in the house knew that if a Jew came to borrow, he would have to give it. Wednesday, before a market day, the grain merchants borrowed from the shopkeepers; Sunday, on the other hand, when the shopkeepers had to travel to Warsaw for merchandise, they borrowed from the grain merchants. And that is how the wheels turned.

Although, as stated, making a living was not easy, a congregation still needed a cantor for *Shabes*. I recall what happened in town when they started saying that R' Shmuel Nosn the ritual slaughterer was already old and they would need a new slaughterer and cantor. The hasidim said that they only needed a ritual slaughterer and not a cantor; one can get by without a cantor. But the opposition maintained that they wanted a cantor in the study house on *Shabes* because it was very pleasurable. The old Rov of blessed memory wanted his son R' Mendl to be the slaughterer. The Rov had taught him the laws of ritual slaughter and Shmuel Nosn the slaughterer had shown him how to slaughter. The Aleksander hasidim, of course, held with the Rov and with R' Mendele because they we all Aleksander hasidim. Besides that,

[Page 74]

the hasidim said, why bring in an outside ritual slaughterer at a time when R' Mendl is a respectable, honest Jew and regularly sits and studies. But the opponents were against the will of the hasidim and R' Mendele did not want to take it on, and they demanded a cantor/ritual slaughterer in one person.

One time, on the morning of *Hoshane-raba*, when the Aleksander *shtibl* was in the middle of prayer, several Jews came in with an unslaughtered goose and let it loose on the floor. The goose walked around, and blood was running from her neck. Although such a case could happen with any ritual slaughterer, they used the opportunity to shout, "Just look at your slaughterer!" R' Mendl was in the *shtibl* then, standing there, pale and stricken, and wanted to pay them for the goose, which was now *treyf*. But they stuck with their "We do not want Mendele as our slaughterer in any way or form!"

Another time there was a case in the same Aleksander *shtibl* when on *Rosh-hashone*, during the afternoon service, those opposing Mendele tore up the steps to the *shtibl* and left those praying up there. They wanted to teach the hasidim something for their support of R' Mendele. The news traveled to our wives and after a few hours of sitting in "arrest" they were able to locate someone who could put the steps back. That event was then topic of the day. The town "went off its wheels".

Not wanting to create a serious feud they finally decided to bring in a cantor/slaughterer from outside. Several cantors came each for a *Shabes*, prayed at the cantor's stand, sang in the study house, and went away with nothing. They did not please the congregation. Until the cantor Itshe came with two choir boys, whose praying on *Shabes* did please and he remained as the cantor/slaughterer. His two choirboys were one a grown man and the other a small boy with a beautiful, resounding voice. On their first *kaboles shabes* the younger boy sang *m'kadeysh meylekh ir melukhe* and everyone was inspired. And the Aleksander hasidim agreed on R' Itshe because he was one of their hasidim, and in particular, as he came to Goworowo at the recommendation of the Aleksander Rebi. The two choirboys were given 'eating days' and there was peace and serenity in the town.

After R' Itshe's departure R' Melikhel from Moscow was taken on as cantor/slaughterer. He was a Ger Hasid and was loved by all, even by the Aleksander hasidim. He was a Torah scholar and a good cantor/slaughterer, with a pleasant voice.

After the passing of the old Rov of blessed memory, R' Burshtin may God avenge his blood was elevated as town rabbi in Goworowo. He immediately founded a Talmud study group and each day, between afternoon and evening prayers they arranged the tables and learned with R' Burshtin. Anyone who got a difficult passage parsed it with the Rov.

[Page 75]

A few months before *Peysakh* everyone read the same passages in order to be able to celebrate *erev Peysakh* properly and thus to free the young men from fasting that day. In finishing that study, the Rov connected the end of it with the beginning of the next chapter with a lovely explication. Then the young men brought whisky into the study house, drank a *l'khayim* toast and wished one another a kosher and happy holiday.

During the First World War the whole town, along with the study house, was destroyed in a fire and the few Jews fled. At the end of 1915 some Jews returned to Goworowo. We returned in 1916. The few dozen Jews including the Rov, lived on Probostva Street. The prayer room was in the Rov's house. I recall that when I arrived at the Rov's for the first time, he embraced me with such love and friendliness, and tears showed in his eyes from his being so moved. He repeated several times, "thanks God that we are seeing one another, I longed for my householders". He cited the Talmud, "in *Peysakhim p"z*, the meaning is that when one is a Rov, one is no longer a regular householder for himself and one is dependent on the opinion of others, the opinion of the community, on the opinion of the proprietors, but I still missed my householders."

When more Jews came back to Goworowo and there was still no study house, they prayed in a shed in the middle of the market square, and some prayed at Yoelke the baker's. Later, Yisroel Mayer Mishnayos, Matisyahu Rozen, Itshe Kosovski, Meyshe Tenenboym, Khayim Ber Grudke, Khone Fridman, Shmuel Volf Broyner and Yoni Besukhem created our house of prayer at Avremele Grudke, where we prayed every *Shabes* and holiday. That is where we also founded a *Mizrakhi* organization for the town and from the center in Warsaw received propaganda materials, writings, literature and so on. From time to time a speaker from *Mizrakhi* visited us, and we met there openly and our movement grew continually. At Avremele's we spent good time in a friendly atmosphere; of course, we also studied a page of Talmud and on *Shabes* or holiday we made a *kidush* together. Meyshe Mendl Farbarovitsh also prayed with us. He was a merry pauper and could sing very well. When a holiday came it was pleasant to spend time over a glass of whisky. He never got tired of singing and dancing. I remember a *Simkhes-Torah* how he danced on the table and sang songs; he could go on for that long.

That is how I remember the life of my little town Goworowo during my 20 years living there. Those years were the best and happiest in my life and will remain etched into my memory forever.

They were dear and beloved Jews, those mentioned above and all the others, with their merits and even with their flaws. "Woe for those who have been lost but are not forgotten."

[Page 76]

Der Beys-medresh
The Study House

by Yosef Gavati, Israel

Translated by Tina Lunson

The *beys-medresh* served as the central meeting point for the Jews in the town. Beginning in the earliest hours of the morning until late into the night, it was dominated by a lively movement of people. Before dawn, when the stars were still in the sky, one could already see the *hashkome* Jews, mostly artisans and peddlers, who came to offer their duty to the Creator of the world, before their going out to work. They recited the psalm of the day, studied a chapter of *Mishnayos* and prayed with intention. Later the shopkeepers began to come in, who opened their businesses later because any early morning revenue was poor anyway. The merchants and Hasidic Jews prayed with the last *minyonim* which drew on well into the day. No one came late to prayers because when one came into the study house there was always a *minyen* going on. Those praying came from every stratum of the population. You could encounter the sharpest hasidim (their *shtiblekh* were mostly closed in the early morning weekdays) to the "common folk", and even the so-called "worldly" Jews – members of the socialist parties in town.

The study house was open the entire day. Sitting and learning there were young men living with their fathers-in-law; young men just returned from the *yeshives*, or those who could not travel to a big *yeshive* for whatever reason; old Jews who no longer had worries about livelihood, having given their businesses to their children; those who lived on a pension from America; and ordinary Jews, not scholars, who came to the study house to read a chapter of psalms. From time to time, you could also see young merchants who used the weak sales of the early hours in their businesses, left their wives there and came to catch a page of Talmud. At the same time, they got into conversations with the young husbands and *yeshive* men about various world problems, general political questions and local community issues.

The greatest movement into the study house was in the early evening hours. Streams of Jews hurried in from every direction, so as not to be late

[Page 77]

for *minkhe*, the afternoon prayers. Between the afternoon and evening prayers Jews of every social level sat around tables. Around the table on the south side, where the windows looked out toward the river, sat the town scholars, who studied the Talmud page of the day. Opposite them, at a table on the north side, sat mostly artisans and dealers who listened to their *rebi* explain the Torah portion with *ALShiekh*, studied a chapter of *Mishnayos* and so on. Regular scholars sat at another table, studying Talmud with commentators, *Yore Deye, RaMBaM, Perkey musar*, or other holy books. At that table there were also zealous boys who repeated the Talmud that they had learned in *kheyder* during the day. Behind them, around the ovens and near the entrance door, stood plain Jews and young men who caught a chat about the latest world politics and international events. They also did not neglect a little town gossip.

When a traveling preacher came to town, one of the especially well-known *magidim*, who came to speak in the study house between afternoon and evening prayers, everyone pressed closer to the *bima* to hear better. The preacher would often relate various histories, parables and stories, interweaving them with sayings of the wise men of blessed memory and ethics. There was special interest in town when a guest speaker came from *Erets Yisroel*, or a religious speaker from the central who would lecture about issues in Zionism. Then the study house was packed with people of all stripes. Even upstairs, in the women's section, many women came to hear the speakers. For hours after the sermon there were still Jews standing in the market square discussing and explaining to one another what they had just heard. It was also a sensation in town when young cantorial talents came to town and attended the prayers in the study house. They prayed for tickets. The doors of the study house were locked, and entrance cards were sold at the door. When the *vunder-kind* cantors came it was sufficient to put up just two or three placards with their pictures, which were hung on the corner houses, and their success was certain. The study house was full from end to end and even the women's section was packed.

The *beys-medresh* was open until late at night. Then one could find diligent young men, or old Talmudic experts, who studied by candlelight (as is known, the electricity in town was on only until 11 at night).

On *Shabes* the study house got a very different look. Dozens of electric lights and very bright oil lamps illuminated the large room. The tables were covered in white, the Ark was covered with a red velvet curtain onto which were sewn in golden thread two lions holding the crown of Torah. Fathers and children dressed in their *Shabes* clothing filled the study house. The Rov arrived dressed in a

[Page 78]

long silk coat with a thickly woven silk sash, white stockings and low black boots, and a large round, fur *Shabes* hat on his head. With the Rov's arrival a hush fell over the whole study house and everyone stayed in his place.

On Friday evening, as well as on *Shabes* morning, a large contingent of young men attended. There were also Bundists and even Communists, just dissuaded from the Zionist groups. Possibly, they had dressed up out of respect for their parents. Sons of hasidim who no longer wanted to pray in the Hasidic *shtiblekh* also came.

If the whole study house prayed either in the Safardi mode or in the Ashkenazi mode, on *Shabes* the mode of prayer was Ashkenazi. That originated from the time of the learned R' Klepfish of blessed memory, who introduced the mode to the *shtetl* and so it remained over the years. Generally, the congregation drew from only the *misnagdim* and their mode was Ashkenazi. The hasidim had their *shtiblekh*. In later years the permanent cantor of the large study house was R' Khayim Leyb Marianski, the cantor and ritual slaughterer. He himself was a Ger Hasid and, of course, prayed in the Sephardi mode, although in the study house he prayed in the Ashkenazi mode.

On *Shabes* during the day there were often sermons by traveling speakers who stayed in the town overnight. The Rov held his traditional sermons twice a year in the study house: *Shabes shuve* , the *Shabes* between *Rosh-ha'shone* and *Yon-kiper* when he appealed to repentance and good deeds, for peace and love of one Jew for another, to pardon and to ask for forgiveness, and to strengthen Jewishness; and the second sermon the Rov gave was on *Shabes ha'gadol* right before *Peysakh* and dedicated to that holiday and its laws and he strongly called for the observance of *kashrus*. The entire population of the town came to the Rov's sermons, all the *shtiblekh* were closed, the streets and houses were empty, and the women's section of the shul was overflowing.

* * *

The *gabeyim* of the study house were R' Dovid Dronitsa, R' Yosef Verman, R' Fayvl Brik, R'Yehoshue Rozen, R' Mayer Shvarts and others. R' Menashe Holtsman used to lead the morning prayers, *Rosh-ha'shone* and *Yon-kiper*. The last years the shofar blower was R' Khayim Ber Grudka. Torah readers were R' Avromke Tsalke, R' Mordkhe Trushkevitsh and others. The *shamosim* were Berl Tsirman, Yekl Shprintses, Mordkhe Trushkevitsh, Shleyme Khayim Tsimbal and others. The *shames* for the *beys-din* was R' Avromke Tsalke.

* * *

That beautiful study house was built in *sav-reysh-pey-hey* thanks to Ms. Gitl Klas from America, who sent great sums of money to Goworowo for that purpose.

[Page 79]

The Aleksander *Shtibl*

by Yosef Zilbertson, Israel

Translated by Tina Lunson

The largest Hasidic *shtibl* in town was the Aleksander, which existed for many years before the First World War and was probably one of the first organized *shtiblekh* in Poland, whose hasidim traveled to the first Aleksander *rebi* the *AdMoR* Rov, Rebi Khanukh-Henokh Ha'koen of blessed memory. The old Aleksander Hasidim who are here with us in Israel tell that before the First World War there were as many as one hundred Aleksander Hasidim in Goworowo, which was a significant percent of the population as a whole.

The Goworowo hasidim were very eminent with the old Aleksander Rebi, the master *Yismakh Yisroel* who was very fair with them. Among the old Aleksander Hasidim who traveled to *Yismakh Yisroel* were R' Yisroel Yitsik Tsudiker, R' Shmuel Nosn Rozen the ritual slaughterer, Nakhum Kshanzshka, R' Fishl Shapira later the Tshervine Rov (we write about separately), R' Manes Domb the miller, R' Nakhum Meyshe Galant, R' Yekhiel Gerlits who besides being a Jewish scholar was also a *maskil*, an Enlightener; R' Yekhezkel Tshekhanover and R' Yoske whose wife Rokhl Shmuelke was known as a great saint who occupied herself with community work and did good deeds with love. The old Rov, R' Yankev Yehude Batshan and his son Mendl are reckoned among the Aleksander Hasidim.

The Aleksander *shtibl* served as a place of Torah throughout the years, where people sat and studied. Among those who learned there before the First World War were R' Berish Tunkelank, Yankev Berl's son-in-law; R’ Zalman Verman; R’ Avrom Levin (today in Israel); R’ Yisroel-Mayer Mishnayos; R’ Fayvl Zilbershteyn; my father R’ Yonatan Zilbertson, and many others.

During the First World War, the Aleksander *shtibl* went up in smoke along with all the other houses. When the Jews returned to Goworowo after the war, the Aleksander Hasidim organized and reestablished their *shtibl*. But they did not have a permanent place and

[Page 80]

could not even dream of a building of their own at that time. Because of the large number of hasidim they divided into groups: some prayed with R’ Yekhiel the baker and some with R’ Yonatan Zilbertson. R’ Hershl Niks also hosted a *minyen*. At times they also prayed at R’ Yeshaye Ayzenberg's. Later they rented an apartment from Yosl the harness-maker and that served as a *shtibl*. Because there were so many *Mizrakhi* members among the Aleksander Hasidim, they split off and created their own *minyen* with R' Avremele Grudke, where they prayed the whole time. Only in the last years were the Aleksander Hasidim successful in constructing their own *shtibl* above the old study house, where most of them prayed. Young men and older boys studied there during the day.

The Aleksander Hasidim occupied a large place in the community life of the town. The long serving president of the Jewish Council was R’ Note Rits, an Aleksander Hasid. The *gabay* of the Burial Society, R’ Matisyahu Rozen, was an Aleksander Hasid. There was not an institution in the town where Aleksander Hasidim were not represented.

I will mention some outstanding Aleksander Hasid here:

R’ Yonatan Zilbertson, my father, was among the well-respected hasidim in the land. Even as a young man he used to travel to the Aleksander Rebi R’ Yekhiel. He was a sharp scholar and an expert in Talmud and scriptures and one of the finer Jews in the town. The hasidim prayed with us in our house for many years.

R’ Yeshaye Ayzenberg, for many years the *gabay* of the *shtibl*, would study every *Shabes* in the study house with the *Olam khumesh* with *SL”H*. He enjoyed inviting a large number of hasidim to his home every *Shabes* night for a glass of tea and everyday conversation.

R’ Yekhiel Gerlits, a great Talmud expert and master with permission to act as a rabbi, was a standard prayer leader for the *yomim norim* in the *shtibl*. He was treasured and revered by everyone.

R’ Yehoshue Mordkhe Drozd, a partner in the small mill. A scholar and in awe of heaven, a brilliant prayer leader with a warm voice.

R’ Note Rits, a partner in the big mill and in the electrical work. A clever Jew, he sprouted with humor, was known for his generosity and welcoming of guests. As mentioned above, the president of the Jewish Council.

R’ Matisyahu Rozen, one of the rich and eminent proprietors in town, full of wisdom and sharp-minded, loved to do favors for people. He had a claim to being a *Khasen Torah* and as already mentioned, was *gabay* of the Burial Society for many years.

R’ Bertshe Viroslav, a sharp Aleksander Hasid, although he

[Page 81]

Matisyahu Rozen of blessed memory

made a parsimonious living, he still lived with confidence. He had a claim to praying *p'suki d'zimros.*

And others, and more dear hasidim, warm Jews in whom the quality of love for Yisroel was planted deep in their hearts and who were far from any blind fanaticism. They found their place in the Aleksander *shtibl* as sworn Lovers of Zion and hasidim, who were far from Zionist philosophy; sharp scholars, along with the simple "Jew from the whole year".

R' Avrom Levin

It should be noted here that along with us in Israel is one of the then eminent Aleksander Hasidim, good prayer leader and master singer, R' Avrom Levin. Rov Avrom still learns today with a group, every day between afternoon and evening prayers, a Talmud lesson in one of the synagogues in Tel Aviv.

[Page 82]

The Ger *Shtibl*

by Yosef Gur, Israel

Translated by Tina Lunson

It is not known exactly when the Ger *Shtibl* was founded in Goworowo, but it is well known that Ger Hasidim were already in the town even in the time when the first Ger Rebi, *AdMoR* Rov Yitsik Mayer Alter may his sainted memory be for a blessing, the *Hidushey Ha'rim.*

In the time of the second Ger Rebi, *AdMoR* R' Yehude Leyb may his memory be for a blessing, the master *Sfas Emes* was already known since in town there was a fine organized group of Ger Hasidim who were very prominent in the Ger court. It is also known that there were Goworowo hasidim at the *Sfas Emes* table who went there to stay for months at a time and the Rebi would take them under his wing. I have heard here in Israel from old Ger Hasidim who themselves remember and confirm the fact that there were young Ger Hasidim from Goworowo among those at the Rebi's table.

Of the known Ger Hasidim in town who were among the entourage of *Sfas Emes*, we know about these: Yosef Zishe and also Motl Likhtenshteyn, who later moved to Ostrove and was popular in the Ger hasidic circles as Motl "Ostrover". In his later years, the same R' Motl – already in the time of the third Ger Rebi, *AdMoR*

R' Avrom Mordkhe may his saintly memory be for a blessing – was sent to Erets Yisroel as a messenger from the Rebi in 1921. The rebi was building houses in Yafo then and R' Motl settled in Tel Aviv. Later, when the Ger Rebi established the *Sfas Emes* Yeshiva in Jerusalem, R' Motl moved there, where he lived out the rest of his years. R' Motl was famous as a great scholar, giver of charity and doer of good deeds. In his last years he was interested in the refugees from Goworowo. And his children and grandchildren stay in contact with those from Goworowo (R' Motl was a father-in-law with the Grudke family). He passed away a few years ago in Jerusalem at a ripe old age.

Also, part of the Goworowo Ger Hasidim were R' Sholem Azdobe, who left the town more than 50 years ago, for America. R' Sholem came to Israel a few years ago, settled in Bney Brak and continued his activity in the Ger Hasidic circles. Those old town Ger Hasidim also

[Page 83]

include R' Yekele Karlinski and R' Yitsik Ayzik Gutman.

After the First World War, when the town began to rebuild after the big fire, no hasidic *shtibl* was successful in finding a building for itself, and the Ger Hasidim had to pray in private homes. For the first years after the war their *shtibl* was at R' Velvl Blumshteyn's, where the hasidim gathered on *Shabes* and holidays, prayed and studied and occupied themselves with strengthening the Jewishness of the town. Later they went over to R' Yankev Shtshetshina's house to pray. Although they did not have their own prayer rooms the Ger Hasidim stayed united, well-organized and traveled often to their Rebi in Ger. Because there was no wealth among the hasidim it took a very long time until they acquired their own building. They only achieved that when all the other hasidim had already had their prayer rooms for years. The Ger Hasidic *shtibl* was located in the courtyard of the study house above the *Ha'keneses orkhim.*

The quarters of the Ger *shtibl* were not large – there were not many hasidim, but their influence in the town was very apparent. The Ger Hasidim took an active part in communal and in political life. Many of the Ger hasidim were prominent in the town in many institutions and establishments. Ger Hasidim were among the first members of the community after the First World War: R' Yehude Sheyniak and R' Mayer Ramaner, the latter who served as vice president of the Jewish Council. The Ger Hasidim were among the first founders of the *Agudas Yisroel* and the *Tsirey Yisroel* as well of the *Beys Yankev* school for girls and the *Talmud Torah.* They were very active in the group *Shomrey shabes* where R' Yeshaye Hertsberg was especially recognized. R' Yeshaye was known as a fanatic, he led the camp of honoring the *Shabes* and disbanded the soccer players on *Shabes* and so on. The Ger Hasidim, as in other towns, were the founders of the Talmud Group where they studied the *daf yomi,* the page of the day.

Of the prominent Ger Hasidim, it is worthwhile to mention the following:

R' Avrom Mordkhe Fridman, who was counted among the descendants of a family that was among the founders of Goworowo. He had great knowledge of the Talmud and was one of the rich Jews in the town;

R' Mayer Ramaner, one of the prominent proprietors, a Talmud scholar, and a clever man, who played a large role in community life. He was also one of the founders, and very active in, the Merchants Bank, and as mentioned earlier, vice president of the Jewish Council;

R' Velvl Blumshteyn, one of the sharp Ger Hasidim in the town. An influential Jew who took an active part in communal matters. He traveled often to the Ger Rebi and was one of the most prominent Jews in town;

[Page 84]

R' Yehude Sheyniak, one of the eminent Ger Hasidim and proprietors, had great knowledge of Talmud and often traveled to *Sfas Emes*. He was counted among the zealots and a fighter for strict *Shabes* observance;

R' Yitsik Reytshik, a modest Jew, who usually sat and studied. He was an expert in mystical texts and *kabole*, one could often find him in the *shtibl* poring over the *Zohar*;

R' Mordkhe Leyb Gurka, one of the old hasidim, a scholar who studied for years in the Lithuanian yeshivas. After his marriage he became a frequent visitor to *Sfas Emes* and stayed with him for months. A clever Jew who did not like mixing in politics, but was devoted to the ideas of *Agudas Yisroel*;

R' Iser Rits, one of the rich Jews in town. Part owner of the big mill and of the electric works. A devoted Ger Hasid, a great giver of charity and welcoming guests;

R' Yankev Shtshetshina, one of the old hasidim. A prominent, clever Jew, a prayer leader in the Ger *shtibl*;

R' Yeshaye Hertsberg, one of the sharpest Ger Hasidim, active in the *Agudas Yisroel* and cofounder of the *Beys Yankev* school for girls. As already mentioned, Rov Yeshaye was very active in the group *Shomrey Shabes*;

R' Yisroel Yitsik Shron, one of the old hasidim, a respected Jew and a prominent proprietor. He was faithful to and dedicated to the Ger tradition;

R' Yisroel Yitsik Shron, may
God avenge his blood

R' Khayim Leyb Leybman. A sharp Ger Hasid in the full sense of the word. He was devoted heart and soul to hasidism. His whole life was dedicated to Ger Hasidism. Although he was poor, he always lived with confidence.

[Page 85]

I should mention two other Ger Hasidim who distinguished themselves and are with us in Israel:

R' Naftali Gemora

R' Naftali Gemora, one of the prominent Ger Hasidim in town, a great Talmud scholar and a shrewd man. He was the prayer leader for the afternoon prayers for many years in the Ger *shtibl*. Today he is in Haifa and is active there as a rabbi;

R' Leyvi Varshaviak

R' Leyvi Varshaviak, the son-in-law of *A. D. R'* Mordkhe Fridman, a devoted Ger Hasid, one of the establishers of *Agudas Yisroel* in the town and of its meeting points in Pasheki. R' Leyvi was also one of the cofounders of the *Beys Yankev* school for girls. He now lives in Tel-Aviv.

[Page 86]

The Vurke *Shtibl*

by Avrom Holtsman, Israel

Translated by Tina Lunson

The late Vurke *shtibl* was actually an amalgamation of Skernievts, Amshinov and Vurke hasidim. Until the First World War, they were dispersed according to their rabbis, and they prayed separately. Thus, the Skernievts hasidim prayer at R' Yankev Yehoshe Kiri's, headed by the *gabeyim* R' Yankev Berl Blumshteyn and R' Menashe Holtsman (the father of the writer of these lines) who was also the prayer leader there, along with many other eminent householders.

The Amshinov *shtibl* was located in the study house building and the leading hasidim were R' Yesheyahu Yom-Tov Sarna, R' Nosn Farba, R' Mayer Volf Tehilim, R' Yankev Hersh Vengrov ("the *kasha* maker), R' Aron Aronson and others. It is worthwhile adding that the last Goworowo Rov, R' Alter Meyshe Mordkhe Burshtin may God avenge his blood, was also an Amshinov Hasid and from time to time he would pray in the *shtibl* on *Shabes*.

I do not know the exact reason why those two *shtiblekh* were liquidated; but it is a fact that the Skernievts and Amshinov hasidim have warm feelings for the Vulke hasidim, apparently because of the relationship of their rabbis: The Skernievts *Rebi*, R' Shimele of blessed memory (who passed away in *sav-reysh-pey-daled*), was a grandson of Rebi Itsikl of blessed memory, the founder of the Vulke dynasty and author of the book *Ohel Yitskhak*. In turn, Rebi Itsikl's two sons, Rebi Yankev Dovid of blessed memory was the *AdMoR* of Amshinov, and Rebi Mendele of blessed memory was the inheritor from Rebi Yitsik, the *AdMoR* of Vulke.

Before the First World War, the Vulke *shtibl* was in the building of the large study house, the same as all the other *shtiblekh*. After the war, all the returning hasidim began to organize and created temporary *shtiblekh* in private homes. The Vulke hasidim also prayed in a private residence, but not a permanent one. Once they prayed at R' Borekh Mints', another time at R' Shaul Potash's and they often made a second *minyen* in the study house. That went on for so long, until the Vulke Rebi himself – R' Avrom Meyshe of blessed memory (a son of Rebi Simkhe Bunim of blessed memory, who passed away in Tiberia), came down to Goworowo for a *Shabes* (he stayed with R' Borekh Mints) and

[Page 87]

it was decided to construct their own building for a *shtibl*.

The inheritors of R' Avrom Fayvl Neyman – the son of R' Yekl Dovid, and R' Asher Kutner, son-in-law of Rivke'le, R' Avrom Fayvl's daughter – donated a place for that goal, that bordered the priest's garden. A building committee was immediately created, made up of the following persons: R' Khayim Dovid Shron, R' Khayim Potash, R' Shleyme Leyb Shakhter and R' Menashe Holtsman. The building committee set to work energetically, they sold "bricks" and wrote a *seyfer Torah* under the name of the Vulke Rebi R' Simkhe Bunim of blessed memory. And sold [alphabet] "letters". After a certain period of time the building was ready, and for the *yomim-norim* they prayed in their own building for the first time.

The prayer leader for that first morning prayers was R' Avrom Boynes, and he also blew the *shofar*. R' Khayim Potash led on the second day and R' Avrom Shafran blew the *shofar*. R' Menashe Holtsman led the afternoon prayers, *kol nidrey* and *ne'ila*. One must also attribute the excellent leaders R' Yankev Hersh Vengrov, R' Hersh Glogover, R' Khayim Borekh Shakhter and others. The Torah reader was the great scholar and teacher R' Avrom Shafran who also taught a lesson from the Talmud to the congregation.

R' Avrom Shafran

R' Meyshe Mendl Farbarovitsh (father-in-law of Meyshe Dronitsa) was a talented musician, fine prayer leader and also a merry hasid. When he would come back from Warsaw for a *Shabes* in the town, the Vulke congregation enjoyed his special praying and the addition of new hasidic melodies.

Among the congregation were R' Pinkhas Shikara may God avenge his blood, and, may they have a happy life R' Nosn Shron and R' Meshulem Golavinski (today both are in Israel), and others.

[Page 88]

The "Progressive" *Minyen*

by G. Yosef, Israel

Translated by Tina Lunson

The "progressive" *minyen* was distinctive among all the houses of prayer in the town. That *minyen* was an original creation of the Goworowo youth who had decided that there was no place for them in the various Hasidic *shtiblekh*, where they were strange because of their clothing, their shaved faces and perhaps also because of their snatching a side conversation during the prayers.

Among those in the "progressive" *minyen* (in the shops they also called them the "casual" *minyen*) there were people from all the circles of the secular youth in town, beginning with Zionists of all splinters, those with no party affiliation and even Bundists. Among the creators of the *minyen* were Yankev Kasher (the baker), Dovid Aron Grudka, Meyshe Dranitsa, Yankev Gurka, and the Bundist activist Yosl Zilbershteyn. The prayer style, as well as the customs of that *minyen* were in a strong traditional spirit (in Goworowo a reform *minyen* was never even thought of), just as in all the other Hasidic *minyonim* in town. Among the local prayer leaders were Dovid Aron Grudka, Meyshe Dronitsa, Dovid Glogover, Yankev Grudka and Avrom Holtsman, of the many boys who prayed in that *minyen*.

Although that *minyen* did not represent any party affiliations it still was conducted in the Zionist spirit; almost all the money donations were designated for *Keren Kayemet l'Yisroel*. They collected money for Zionist funds at every opportunity. At a *kidush* or any other *Shabes* or holiday gatherings they sang Zionist songs.

Those praying in the "progressive" *minyen* were considered a united and locked group. They stuck together and from time to time arranged various cultural, religious presentations. For the first *slikhes* they usually presented a *malave malke*, for which Yankev Kasher had a tradition of creating a roasted goose in his bakery. Also, the "circuits" on *Simkhes Torah* took place with full fanfare, including the singing of nationalist songs.

The *minyen* took a large place in the community life of the town. In the last elections to the Jewish Council, before the outbreak of the last war,

[Page 89]

that *minyen* produced its own slate. The candidate for their list, Meyshe Dronitsa, was elected to the Jewish Council, where he took a chairman position in the ritual slaughter committee. He fought to bring a Zionist spirit to Council life. Indeed, in the last budget there was a special item for 200 *zlotych*, an expense for the Goworowo Council for *Erets Yisroel*.

Most of them shared the fate of all the Goworowo Jews. A few were saved by some miracle and are now in Israel and other countries.

From right: Leybl Kaptsh (with bicycle)
Sitting: [from right] Zelig Hertsberg, Mayer Goldberg, Yitskhak Dovid Tehilim, Dovid Glogover, Itshe Glogover, Sholem Fraske, Matisyahu Oyslender and Meyshe Dranitsa
Standing: [from right] Yosl Zilbershteyn, Irel Apelboym and Dovid Doharn Grudka

[According to the photograph, the occasion was Yitskhak Galagaver's [Itshe Glogover?] departure]

[Page 90]

Kheydarim un Melamdim
Religious Schools and Teachers

by Yosef Gurka, Israel

Translated by Tina Lunson

In their concern for the education of the children, a line of teachers took upon themselves the assignment of teaching Torah and Judaism to the young generation. Those teachers – beginning with the alphabet teachers and up to the Talmud instructors – who educated the young between the two world wars, were well known to all of us. All of the youth in town, without exception, went through their schools. For some, reading a page of Talmud was enough, and some further expanded their learning in the *yeshivas*. The knowledge acquired in childhood which he received in the *kheyder*, no one ever forgot.

In the following lines I will try to depict the intellectual situation of these educators, as I remember them.

Elementary Teachers

The *dardiki-melamdim* in the town were: R' Berl Tsirman who, as a *mitsve*, went around every Friday as the *Shabes* eve approached, and called out *"Yidn in shul arayn!"* {"Jews to the shul!"}; R' Yekl Shprintse, who in his later years became a beadle in the study house; and R' Yeshaye Nosn Kruk, a meticulous person before whom the boys trembled if he even blinked, and especially at his whip.

Of the elementary teachers, who planted Jewishness in the hearts of the very small children, the brothers R' Hersh Itsik and R' Yehoshua Malavani had a special approach to the children and taught them with heart and soul.

R' Aba'le Podgurevitsh

R' Aba'le – people called him that [diminutive] because of his small build – was a Torah teacher. Most of the Goworowo youth passed through his *kheyder*. He was an unusual educator, awaking respect in his pupils and was devoted to them heart and soul. R' Aba'le cared for his pupils like a father, and his wife, the *rebitsin,* was faithful to them. The boys treated them the same – they were bonded to their *rebi* and loved him very much. It was very rare for him to use a whip.

For years after leaving his *kheyder*, his pupils felt an obligation to visit their beloved teacher. He was a God fearing and acute Hasid and traveled often to the Ger Rebi.

[Page 91]

R' Hershl Glogover

The Talmud teacher R' Hershl Glogover, or, as he was popularly called, Hershl "the fop", was a good Jew, a teacher and commanded respect, if only for his extraordinary appearance. Always dressed in neat, clean clothing, with a finely combed beard, he made the impression of a wealthy lumber merchant rather than a teacher. His pupils were boys who had already studied Talmud with Commentators and were preparing to travel out to a yeshiva. R' Hershl had been teaching even before the First World War.

R' Yisroel Leyb Kruk

R' Yisroel Leyb Kruk occupied an esteemed place in the education of the Goworowo youth. He was a real Talmud scholar and was gifted with rare pedagogic abilities. He was also a talented teacher and guide, not comparable to any teacher of the old cut. R' Yisroel Leyb kept to the modern and progressive, and strove to educate his pupils in the spirit of the times – according to the example of the modern Talmud-Torah. Himself a student of the great Lithuanian yeshivas, he taught his pupils in the *Litvish* style, in a scholarly manner. It was a great merit for the student when R' Yisroel Leyb accepted him into his *kheyder*; and not everyone was taken. He sought pupils with good heads and with a strong will to study. It is no wonder, then, that the majority of his pupils continued their studies in the *yeshivas*, and the more local *yeshivas* also considered his pupils.

R' Yisroel Leyb Kruk, of blessed memory

[Page 92]

R' Yisroel Leyb was also an important member of *Hoveyvi-tsion*, and one of the founders and leaders of the *Mizrakhi* movement in town. Disregarding that the Hasidic circles looked askance at Zionism, and in some instances chased the *Mizrakh-ists* out, he stayed firm in his membership in *Mizrakhi.* He would propagandize for Zionism, sell *sheklim*, work for *Keren kayemet l'Yisroel* and lead flaming discussions with his friends in the *Agudas* circles. R' Yisroel Leyb Kruk died in the war years.

R' Avrom'le Grudke

Also reckoned among the important teachers in Goworowo was R' Avrom'le Grudke. Once he was a big grain merchant, but when he was older he took up teaching. R' Avrom'le was a great Talmud scholar and Enlightener although his outward appearance gave the appearance of an idler. He was full of Torah and wisdom, a master of Hebrew grammar, knowledgeable in *TaNaKh*, an expert in philosophical books, knew chapters of *Guide for the Perplexed* by heart as well as Yehuda Haleyvi. He was also very well versed in world literature, knew the Enlightenment books well, was interested in history, natural science and so on.

R' Avrom'le loved to take a break during teaching and tell the pupils of the great wonder of God's world: about the wisdom of physics, chemistry, and other secular knowledge. On the long winter evenings when the sky was full of stars, he sometimes walked around outdoors with his pupils, pointing out stars with his finger and calling them by name: Mars, the Chariot and others, explaining their paths and thereby demonstrating an expertise in astronomy. About the meaning of the science, as in, is there life on Mars, he explained, "Just as in our world everything is green, so it is on Mars that everything is red, because its [Hebrew] name is *Madim* is from the word *adom*– red." The pupils swallowed every word that came from the mouth of their beloved rebi.

R' Avrom'le Grudke had the habit of ending the studies an hour early on Friday, closing the Talmud and sitting back to relate various histories. Each week he chose a different theme. He would tell the pupils about great Jewish personalities and historical figures, and thus weave in whole chapters of Jewish history. If it was about Rebi Avika or Bar-Kokhba, how energetically he depicted the Bar-Kokhba rebellion and the role of Rebi Akiva; whether it was about the era of Babylonia with its princes, the figures of Yehude Ha'nasi, Hilel the Old and others; the sources of the *ganoim*, the wonderful stories about RaMBam when he was the chief doctor to the Egyptian king; the story about Ibn Ezra who presented as a poor man and traveled all around the Jewish world; the tragic history of the expulsion from Spain, the decrees of the 1400s and others.

[Page 93]

When he talked about *Erets Yisroel* he did so with much enthusiasm, and hardly knew when to end. He often sat for more than two hours later than usual. He offered about the Turkish Sultans, how they uncovered the Western Wall, which had been shadowed in mist for so many years; about the Cave of the Patriarchs which no one dared to go inside of because a mysterious wind blew out of there; about *Rokhl's* Tomb, the graves of R' Simion ben Yokhay and his pupils and all the mystic stories that were woven around the kabalists in Tsfat. When he touched on the story of the revival to life of *Erets Yisroel* and the *Khibat tsion* movement, he literally shone. He spoke spiritedly about Baron Rothschild, who bought land and established colonies with Hebrew names; about Moses Montefiori, the great Jewish intercessor who was received by powerful Tsar Nikolai and managed to lighten the burden for [Russian] Jews, and about his activity for *Erets Yisroel*. With his conversations and chats he brought a great coherence to Jewish history, a love for *Erets Yisroel*, for knowledge and a will to learn.

R' Avrom'le did not merit coming to *Erets Yisroel*. He was murdered along with all the Goworowo victims in the area of Slonim, may God avenge their blood. Only his son Yehude with his daughter Tsipora managed to come to *Erets* a few years after the outbreak of the war. His younger son Khone, the *Beys"Ri*, who a short time before the war prepared to go to *Erets Yisroel* by foot along with the Ripel Group, did not manage to realize his dream. He, along with all the other family members, were murdered with all the martyrs, may God avenge their blood.

R' Yitskhak Reytshik

R' Yitskhak Reytshik, or as people used to call him, R' Itsele, was also in his older years. He turned to teaching after he was forced to liquidate his manufacturing business.

R' Itsele, a fine scholar, a very pious and observant Jew, took pains to educate his pupils in his spirit. He died during the war years.

* * *

Besides the above-mentioned “permanent” teachers there were are also “temporary” or “part-time” teachers for whom teaching was nearly a livelihood or a seasonal occupation.

R' Beytsalel Yosef Karvat

R' Beytsalel, or as we called him Tsale-Yosl, belonged among the “temporary” teachers. In fact, he was a merchant. He dealt in fish, grain, leasing orchards and so on. But he did not make a good living from all that,

[Page 94]

and he had to turn to teaching. He was a scholar, with a sharp mind and agile comprehension, who did not like to think for long but to answer quickly and get to the point. In general, he was impatient and a quick decider. He had modest needs and did not worry about himself too much. When he did not have any great success at teaching, he threw himself into trade, and vice versa. He gave private lessons in Talmud with the Commentators to pupils in the town.

R' Beytsalel Yosef was one of the first victims of the Holocaust in Goworowo. He was shot right on the first Friday when the German murderers had just come into the town.

Heads and with a strong will to study, it is no wonder, then, that the majority of his pupils continued their studies in the *yeshivas*, and the more local *yeshivas* also considered his pupils.

R' Beytsalel Yosef Karvat

R' Yankev Shtshetshina

R' Yankev Shtshetshina, the son-in-law of R' Beytsalel Yosef, was a "temporary" teacher. He drew his main livelihood from his haberdashery business on Long Street. R' Yankev was a fine, noble Jew, with a long beard and a constantly smiling face, with friendly glances. He was not supported by his teaching but was a teacher out of need – the shop did not bring in the full livelihood for his household. And since he was a man burdened with children, he had to seek additional income. In poor health, he was not able to give over his knowledge to his pupils, and despite his scholarship and good humor his *kheyder* was not very large.

Right after the great fire in the town R' Yankev left for Ostrove. There the Germans caught him and forced him to clean the water closets with his bare hands. Later they shaved off half of his beard crosswise and he had to

[Page 95]

walk around that way. He would not shave off the other half of the beard under any excuse. He died in the war years.

R' Yankev Shtshetshina,
of blessed memory

R' Yosef Batshan

R' Yosef Batshan was also a "temporary" teacher. He was the grandson of the old Goworowo Rov, the *v'shev ha'koen* and son-in-law of R' Yehude Sheyniak. R' Yosef was really a grain merchant, but, since he did not make a full living from that trade, he often also occupied himself with teaching. He was known as a Talmud expert and Enlightener and considered himself one of the eminent proprietors in the town.

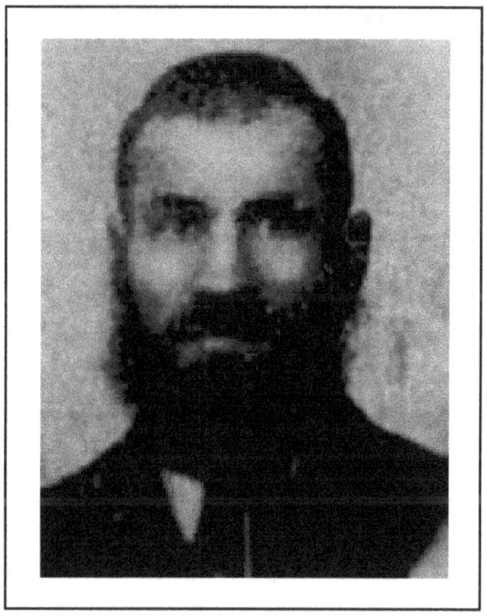

R' Yosef Batshan,
of blessed memory

[Page 96]

R' Aron Aronson

Especially famous and well-known all over the land was R' Aron Aronson, author of books of his sermons. For the most part he traveled around over the towns and villages of Poland and presented his sermons, which were distinguished by their sincerity and folksiness. Masses of people gathered in the study houses of every town when R' Aron spoke. His stories and parables had a good reputation in the world of traveling preachers and more than one of the famous preachers repeated his sermons and often used his stories and parables that were then continually used by the audiences.

I will mention a characteristic case: One of his sons, who was of the idealist Socialist bent and far from being religious, from time to time used to become "someone else". Then he let his beard grow. He traveled around the country for several months repeating his father's sermons. He delivered the sermons with such talent that it was hard to differentiate between father and son. When the writer of these lines was studying in one of the *yeshivas*, far from Goworowo, I accidentally happened upon one of R' Aron's son's sermons. It is worthwhile citing the witticism that he wove into a sermon and as he characterized the revolutionary common people: The "song of glory" which is sung on *Shabes* after praying, and which begins with the words "I weave songs and poems", he translated as what would be said when the Messiah comes. When *Moshiakh* comes there will be "songs of the meek" when the poor will sing "songs" and "murder the rich" – that is, the wealthy who have never reckoned with the poor, oppressed them and not helped them, will then find no place, and will be killed.

R' Aron used to leave the town after *Peysakh* and return from his wanderings over the Polish countryside a year later, for our *Peysakh.* When he wanted to spend a year's time with his family he packed in a few pupils and became a teacher. Being a permanent pauper, he had no great aspirations and sufficed with a small number of pupils. In his free time, he was busy writing additions to his sermons. R' Aron was probably killed in Lomzhe, where one of his sons was the cantor and ritual slaughterer.

R' Velvl Yagodnik

Goworowo had another "teacher-preacher" in R' Velvl Yagodnik or as people called him, Velvl Brizshnier. R' Velvl was a tall, hearty Jew with broad shoulders, a sharp glance and a high, scholarly forehead. He was a teacher of average boys who had just begun to study Talmud.

[Page 97]

Although he was a scholar with a broad knowledge of secular things, he still kept himself apart, did not like to "intrude", not mix in politics, and was not a fervent Hasid but a simple, common person. Thus, he was very devoted to his pupils. He necessarily chatted with them, preached *Mussar*, led them to love the Torah, to desire learning and to be honest Jews.

He spent a lot of time traveling around the land, delivering sermons, and calling the audience to be good and pious. He considered himself a bit of a socialist and in his sermons he preached for charity, justice and equality and not to, heaven forbid, exploit one another. R' Velvl was also one of the first victims from our town. He was shot by a German near his house on the first Friday of their invasion.

R' Aba'le Likhtman

One must also count R' Aba'le Likhtman among the town's teachers, who for many years tutored children. He was a learned Jew and talented in song and music. He was also the bathhouse attendant for several years. In his last years he gave up both his professions and became a wagon driver on the Goworowo to Rizshan line. From all his livelihoods he remained a complete pauper.

R' Leybke Shmalts

R' Leybke Shmalts also dealt in teaching for many years. He was a fervent Aleksander Hasid and often traveled to the *Rebi*. On *Rosh-ha'shone* and *Yon-kiper* he led shul services. For a certain time he was also a beadle. As a Jew he was a doer of good works and a giver of charity. In his last years R' Leybke was a bathhouse keeper in the town.

R' Leybke Shmalts,
may God avenge his blood

[Page 99]

The "Kosher" *Kheydarim*

by Yosef Gurka, Israel

Translated by Tina Lunson

Before the First World War, during the time of the Russian Tsar, may he rot in hell, there existed three "kosher" schools for children in Goworowo, and three "ritually impure" schools. Do not laugh, gentlemen, it is indeed curious, but such was the fact.

Why "kosher" and why *treyf*? I will explain:

Under Russian rule there was a decree that in each *kheyder* or school where children were taught, there must be hung a portrait of the tsar and of his wife, and that the children must be instructed in the Russian language and grammar for at least two hours every day. Among the parents were some who, without an alternative, agreed to teach the children a little Russian. But there were other fathers who said, under no circumstance would they allow their children to be taught *goyish*. Therefore, there were two kinds of *kheydarim*, the "kosher" ones with the teachers Yekl Shtshetshina, Hershl "the fop" and Yosele Melamed; and the "*treyf*" ones with the teachers Mendel the Lame, Niske and Aba'le.

Both sides having a claim, both the kosher and the *treyf*, had to give the Christian director of the schools, Stankius, a bribe in order for him not to tell the Russian inspector what was being done. The *treyf* schools Stankius covered over completely, as if they did not exist, and for the kosher ones he notified the teachers the day before the inspector was to arrive; they cleaned everything up, hung the pictures of the tsar and the tsarina, and at the hour the inspector came they seated the Yiddish-Russian teacher Kovkevitsh and his wife, and the children recited the prayer in honor of the tsar and studied a little Russian.

There was a time when the kosher *kheyder* children really did have to go to the general school for two hours each day and study secular subjects. This was designated for 11 to 1 o'clock. Those children had to pay their "debt" later by studying until 10 at night.

The teacher Yankev Kovkevitsh and his wife, very intelligent people, strove to spread education in the town. But they were forced to do the will of the most strictly religious householders. The teaching couple were also busy giving private lessons for boys and for girls in their parents' homes. Their son Lazar Kovkevitsh, who was born in Goworowo, also became a teacher of Yiddish and Russian. The Kovkevitsh family was in town until the Great Fire. After the First World War they never returned to Goworowo.

[Page 100]

Yeshiva People

by Yosef Gurka, Israel

Translated by Tina Lunson

After the First World War, when Jewish life in town was beginning to stabilize again, many parents sent their children to study in *yeshivas*. The first *yeshiva* swallows were: Meyshe Sarna, Aron Shron, Bunim Safran, Avrom Holtsman and Meyshe Aron Granat. Although they did not remain in the religious framework, their religious education still had a great influence on them. The rejuvenated emancipation, the national and revolutionary movements on the Jewish street, pulled many students away from *yeshivas* and Torah teachers, and threw them into community work. They, the *yeshiva* people, helped to build almost all the political parties and cultural movements in the town. They were also the leaders and the educators of the youth organizations. The level of knowledge constantly rose through them.

With the infiltration of the Novoredok Yeshiva into Poland, the so-called *Musarniks* established similar *yeshivas* in the towns around Goworowo, like Ostrove, Ostrolenke, Vishkove and others. The *RaShI* Yeshivas and directors who went around to the towns and villages to recruit students, also visited Goworowo. They conducted a large enlightenment operation among the youths and indeed did recruit many young men. Already in 1924-1925 some of the best students from R' Yisroel Leyb's *kheyder* traveled to the Ostrove Yeshiva, and they later developed a large *yeshiva* movement that took in a significant number of the growing youth.

Mendl Shtern

One of the first young men who went to the Novoredok Yeshiva was Mendl Shtern, the son of R' Shleyme Shtern. He was one of the best pupils and very much involved with *Mussar*. In later years he held an important position in the Novoredok Yeshiva world. He traveled around and founded *yeshivas* and himself served as *yeshiva* head in several of the *yeshivas* that he had established. R' Mendl Shtern was killed in the war years, may God avenge his blood.

Fishl Krulevitsh

Fishl, the son of R' Khayim Krulevitsh of the small mill, was considered

[Page 101]

one of the best men of the central Novoredok Yeshiva in Bialystok. He was a great scholar, was known as an innovator in Torah explication and refinements and was well versed in the new Hebrew literature. Fishl Krulevitsh died two years before the last World War and left behind many manuscripts and explications on Talmud, as well as poetry in Hebrew.

Yerakhmiel Verman

R' Zalman Verman's son Yerakhmiel was one of the best *yeshiva* men that Goworowo produced. He studied in many *yeshivas* and everywhere he excelled and advanced. He was a very assiduous student, sitting almost day and night to study and also became very pious; his outward appearance was as a typical Hasid, with a beard and *peyes*. (Goworowo was considered a half-Litvish [Lithuanian] town, and it was rare for the *yeshiva* men to go around in hasidic garb, and beard and *peyes*. Most of them wore modern dress, in the Litvak style.)

Yerakhmiel studied in many *yeshivas*, among them Bialystok and Lomzhe. In later years he was a pupil of the Lublin Rov, R' Mayer Shapira may his memory be for a blessing. When the Lublin Rov founded the famous *Yeshives khokhmey Lublin* in Poland, he selected students for his *yeshiva* from the best geniuses of all the *yeshivas* in Poland. Yerakhmiel belonged to that group and had the honor of studying in that *yeshiva*. He was killed in Shtshigove, where he lived the last years after his marriage, may God avenge his blood.

Meyshe Mazes

Meyshe Mazes, the son of R' Niske the ritual slaughterer, was also one of the best young *yeshiva* men in town and a great Talmud scholar. While still a young man, people were addressing him as "Rov" in the town of Vonseva [Wąsewo], but he did not take the yoke of rabbinics upon himself. After his marriage he became a big grain dealer. He was also a leader in the *Tsirey Agudas Yisroel*. He is now in America, along with his wife Sima, the daughter of R' Khayim Potash, and their children.

Yitskhak Shafran

The youngest of that group was Yitskhak Shafran, the son of R' Avrom Shafran. At the beginning he studied in the Novoredok, later in the Lomzhe Yeshiva and more recently in the hasidic *yeshiva* in Warsaw, where he became authorized to act as a rabbi. Yitskhak, or as we called him, Itshe, besides being learned in Torah, was also a politically orthodox leader and community activist. He was one of the founders of the *Tsirey Agudas Yisroel* in town,

[Page 102]

was the head of the *Beys Yankev* school for girls, and others. Itshe got out of Poland through Vilna and Japan and is now in America, where he holds a rabbinic office.

Yekhiel Nayman

Yekhiel, the son of R' Yekl Nayman the shipping agent, came back from the *yeshivas* in his free time. He had set aside studying in the Otvotsk *shtibl* and then helped his father in his business. Yekhiel was also a community activist in the *Aguda* circles. He was killed during the deportations to Soviet Russia.

Yerakhmiel Dronzd

Yerakhmiel Dronzd, the son of the great scholar and hasid R' Yehoshe Mordkhe, also studied at various Novoredok yeshivas, until he was mobilized in the Polish Army. When he was freed from military service, he did not return to the *yeshivas*, but helped his father in his business at the small mill. When the *He'haluts ha'mizrakhi* was organized in town, he became active in the *Mizrakhi* movement. Yerakhmiel Dronzd, along with his entire family, were murdered among the victims of the war years, may God avenge their blood.

* * *

The above recalled group of *yeshiva* men brought a revolution to the life of the younger religious youths. The bigger boys who had finished *kheyder* could see only one goal and ideal - to travel to a yeshiva. In a few houses arguments took place between the children and the parents, who opposed their sons becoming "bench squeezers". They would rather that they learn some trade, or even help the father earn a living. But the children, who believed in learning, were jealous of the first group and wanted, like them, to go to another city to study and come home for a holiday after a semester, soaked with Torah and the *yeshiva* spirit.

The movement brought about the departure of several dozen youths for surrounding *yeshivas* in 1926. Ten boys went to Vishkove alone, among them the writer of these lines. A comparable number traveled to Lomzhe. The following students belonged to that second group:

Simeon Taytelboym

Simeon, the son of Meyshe Taytelboym the harness-maker, against the will of his parents, tore out of the house and took off to the Vishkove Yeshiva where they were happy to take him because of his good mind for learning. Simeon excelled in his refinement and diligence in study. He was very friendly

[Page 103]

and helped weaker pupils understand the lessons. The *yeshiva* took very good care of him, knowing what kind of home he came from and how he had come to them. Later he went on to larger *yeshivas*, and in the last years was in Bialystok. Perhaps because of his poor health condition he should not have been out in the world, especially in living conditions that were hard for him. In 1938 he became very ill and died.

Khayim Kosovski

Khayim Kosovski was the closest friend of Simeon Taytelboym in R' Yisroel Leyb's *kheyder*. They were a "pair" who studied together and R' Yisroel Leyb was always proud of his two best pupils. He always used them as an example, emphasizing Khayim as son of R' Itshe Kosovski the rich lumber merchant, and Simeon as the son of Meyshe Taytelboym the harness-maker. Khayim did not go to the small Novoredok Yeshivas where everyone had "eating days" in someone's home and often had to sleep in a bench in the study house. His parents sent him to the big Lomzhe Yeshiva on their own account. Khayim pursued his studies for several years in Lomzhe Yeshiva, where he grew into a scholar and pious man. He dressed in modern clothes and also studied secular subjects. After returning to our town, he helped his father run his businesses and was also active

Standing, from right: Khayim Kosovski may God avenge his blood, Fishl Krulevitsh of blessed memory, and Yerakhmiel Drozd [sic] may God avenge his blood
Seated: Yekhiel Nayman of blessed memory and Yitskhak Shafran

[Page 104]

in the *Tsirey Agudas Yisroel.* Shortly before the war he was married in Lomzhe to the daughter of the well -known family Hendlish, of the manufacturing branch, and was killed along with all the Lomzhe Jews may God avenge their blood.

Yehoshe Leybman

An interesting type among the *yeshiva* people was Yehoshue Leybman, the son of R' Khayim Leybman, who was a great pauper. At eight years of age Yehoshue was already known as a genius. His father, who was a keen Ger Hasid, wanted to educate him in that spirit. He allowed him to wear *peyes* (rare in Goworowo), a long coat and a sash. At ten years of age Yehoshue was taken into a *yeshiva* and over one term he leapt several levels and studied with much older boys.

Later, Yehoshue began reading secular books, not wanting any more "learning", and made friends with boys who were far from the *yeshiva* circles. His religious parents suffered from him and literally chased him out of the house. He stopped being religious, made friends now with the "left" circles and positioned himself near the Communist Party. They provided him with red literature, which he used to read in his uncle Mayer Volf Tehilim's attic. Not having anything to do, he decided to become independent and to teach himself some kind of trade.

On a certain day he received a radical rupture in his life - he decided to return to the faith, in the full sense of the word. He went back to the famous *Musar yeshiva* in Mezritsh where he told the whole truth to R' Dovid Bliakher (known as a great master of Musar) and demanded that he make him whole. Yehoshue took upon himself a vow of silence for several years, did not sleep in a bed (and for a time with a stone for a pillow), studied day and night and in general, distanced himself from the pleasures of this world. He was patient and determined and did everything properly. Over that time, he grew into a great Talmud expert and became very observant.

Yehoshue then traveled around to cities and towns in Poland and founded *yeshivas*, and the last two years of the war he himself became head of a *yeshiva*. It is interesting to relate that during all those years he did not visit Goworowo; he did not want to recall what were for him unpleasant times. However, he supported his parents and family, and brought his two younger brothers to live with him. The whole family Leybman was murdered in the war years, may God avenge their blood.

[Page 105]

Mordkhe Aronson

Mordkhe, the son of the preacher/teacher Aron Aronson, was one of the outstanding *yeshiva* students. He spent all the years up to the outbreak of the war studying in *yeshivas*, especially in Bialystok and in Lomzhe. He was very diligent and expert, and had, like his father, distinguished himself with a talent in public speaking. Mordkhe gave modern lectures, and a bright future was predicted for him. During the war years he was seen in Samarkand, Uzbekistan, Russia. His further fate is unknown.

Nosn Levkovitsh

Nosn Levkovitsh was one of the good students in the *yeshiva*. It was hoped that he would grow into a big scholar. But even in his young years he distanced himself from the *yeshiva* and joined the General *He'haluts*. Nosn left for *Erets Yisroel* just before the war, where he lives to this day.

Dovid Fridman

Already at ten years of age Dovid stopped studying in the *kheyder* because his mother Khane Fridman, a widow, did not have money to pay his tuition. She sent him to learn to be a hairdresser and he gradually earned a little money. He went back to Avrom'ele in his *kheyder*, where he had been so good in his studies. At thirteen years he went to a *yeshiva*, where he was one of the best students. He studied in many *yeshivas*, and the last years, in the Novoredok Yeshiva in Warsaw, where he received a rabbinic diploma. He was married before the war, lived in Warsaw, and was murdered there, may God avenge his blood.

Shleyme Marianski

Shleyme, the son of the Goworowo cantor and ritual slaughterer R' Khayim Marianski, studied all his life up to the war in the Lomzhe Yeshiva, where he grew into a scholar. When he returned home, he learned ritual slaughtering from his father. He was also gifted with a beautiful voice and dreamed that he might inherit the cantor/slaughterer position in the town. In the war years he along with his family were in Zembrove, where they were all murdered may God avenge their blood.

The Brothers Yudl and Motke Rits

Yudl and Motke studied in various *yeshivas*. They were two of the richest children in Goworowo. Their father, R' Iser Rits, a keen Ger Hasid, was the co-owner of the big mill in town.

[Page 106]

After a time, they returned from the *yeshivas*, joined *Betar* and helped run the mill business. They, along with their large, multi- branched family, were all murdered by the Germans. Of the entire family Rits, no trace remains may God avenge their blood.

Mayer Verman

R' Zalman Verman's second son, Mayer, also spent many years studying in *yeshivas*. A few years before the war he returned to town and became a shipping agent. He traveled to Warsaw and back every day. Mayer was active in *He'haluts ha'mizrakhi*. He was killed in the war years along with his family may God avenge their blood.

Meyshe Galant

Meyshe, the son of R' Avrom Galant, was a fine young man. Because of his poor health condition, he did not study for long in the *yeshivas*. He helped his father in his business and was among the religious circles. He was also active in the *Tsirey Agudas Yisroel*. Murdered along with his family may God avenge their blood.

Standing, from right: Shleyme Goldberg (Yehoshe Rozen's son) of blessed memory; Aron Yehude Batshan (great-grandson of both Goworowo Rabbis, Klepfish-Batshan); and Mordkhe Aronson
Sitting, from right: Shleyme Marianski, may God avenge his blood; and Yankev Mozes and Yosef Gurka

[Page 107]

Yankev Mozes

Yankev, the second son of R' Niske Mozes the ritual slaughterer, was one of the scholarly young men in the town. He studied in the big Lithuanian *yeshivas*; in the last years, in the Kletsk Yeshiva. He, along with his family, are in America today.

Yosef Gurka

The writer of these lines, the son of R' Mordkhe Gurka, one of the keen Ger Hasidim, studied for many years, almost to the outbreak of the war, in various *yeshivas* in Poland, among them several years in Warsaw. He is located today in Ramat-Gan, Israel, where he is active in *Ha'poel ha'mizrakhi*. He is also correspondent for *Ha'tsifa* and holds a position at *Yedies Ramat-Gan*.

Akhieyzer Burshtin

The last Goworowo Rov's son, Akhieyzer was considered a genius from his childhood and excelled in his broad understanding of study. He studied in the large *yeshivas*, including the *Mesivta* in Warsaw.

Akhieyzer later studied at the famous *Yeshives Khokhmey Lublin* of Rov Mayer Shapira, from whom he received a rabbinical certificate. He was one of the only Goworowo people who made it through the Hitler hell in the concentration camps and survived. After liberation he was one of the leaders of the *Shiras ha'pleyte* refugee efforts in Germany and served as the head of the *Vad ha'hatsola* rescue group. Rov Akhieyzer Burshtin is in Israel now, where he is leader of the trade and *yeshiva* school *Torah v'melukhe* in Kfar Citrin near Haifa. He is the author of several books and is also active as a journalist.

Yosef Zilbertson

Yosef, the son of R' Yonatan Zilbertson, studied in one of the *yeshivas* for a few years. Later he was forced to return back to the town and help his father in his iron business. He was active first in the *Tsirey Agudas Yisroel* and then in *He'haluts ha'mizrakhi.* He is in Kholon today, where he is active in *Ha'poel ha'mizrakhi*. He is the only survivor from his entire family.

* * *

Besides those mentioned here, there were also the following *yeshiva* boys: Yosef Kshanzshka, the son of R' Leyzer, who studied until the war in various *yeshivas*, and today is in Germany; his brother Avrom also studied in several *yeshivas*, today in America. The brothers Ayzik and Elieyzer Verman, R' Zalman's children, the last of the best students in the Kletsk Yeshiva; they were murdered together with their families. Khayim Skurnik, the son of R' Meyshe, studied in several *yeshivas*; he came to Israel after the last war where today he lives in Haifa. R' Yisroel Leyb Kruk's son Yankev returned

[Page 108]

home, founded the *Ha'shomer ha'dati* in the town and was active in the community; in the war years he was in Russia and apparently killed there. His brother Khayim Avigdor Kruk, one of the town scholars, was murdered in Vilna; Yosef Sandale, a long-time student in several of the big *yeshivas*, was one the few Goworowors to make it through the German death camps; he is in America today. Dovid, the son of R' Yisroel Itsik Shron, a fine young man, studied in various *yeshivas*, was killed with his whole family. Nosn Hertsberg, son the R' Yeshaye, very industrious, studied well, was murdered with his whole family. Noske Mankete's son Shleyme studied in a lot of *yeshivas* until the outbreak of the war, he and his whole family were murdered. The brothers Shmuel and Yeshaye Shtshetshina, the children of R' Yankev, studied in several *yeshivas*, and are today in Canada. Both of R' Yekhiel Mayer Blumshteyn's sons, Leybl and Noyakh, studied at the Slabodke Yeshiva [Kovno] for a long time; both brothers were killed during the war years. Khayim Zilbertson, R' Yonaton's son, a *yeshiva* student, one of the great scholars, was murdered along with his large, multibranched family. Avrom and Shmuel Mazes, R' Niske the ritual slaughterer's sons, studied for a time in *yeshivas*, and are now in America. Simeon Leybman and his younger brother, the children of R' Khayim Leybele, were also Lomzhe Yeshiva men; they were murdered with their families. Also, *yeshiva* students, the brothers Shleyme and Mordkhe Apelboym, Yitskhak Granat, and others.

* * *

I have endeavored to give a picture of the *yeshiva* people of Goworowo. All the above mentioned are far, far, from all of them. It would be no exaggeration to say that nearly a hundred young men studied in *yeshivas* in the years between the two world wars. Because of the long period of time that has elapsed, I can certainly not mention them all. I have, heaven forbid, no bad intention here.

Still today, I meet Jews, great Torah scholars, who studied with Goworowo men in various *yeshivas*. Our youth were found in dozens of *yeshivas* in Poland. Judging by their number, one can discern what a great town Goworowo was. Only a few individuals remain alive. The much larger part was murdered by the German persecutors.

May my words indeed be a gravestone for the dear Goworowo children who were killed as martyrs. May God avenge their blood!

[Page 109]

Two Brothers

by the Daughter of Yankev Dov

Translated by Mira Eckhaus

Edited by Tina Lunson

Two brothers with a small difference in their ages; two brothers, one tall, broad shouldered and good looking, named Aryeh; and the other short, with a thin and delicate face, named Neyekh.

Two brothers, sons of one father and one mother, the crowns of their family, loved and honored by all; both studied at the Slabodke Yeshiva.

The father worked hard at his job, but he sent his sons everything, packages of food and money to fulfill all their needs, so that they lacked nothing and could study Torah diligently. When they visited home for the holidays, their father immediately sent them back to the Yeshiva, so that they would not stop studying Torah. And so their father, the late Reb Yekhiel Mayer, who is my brother, used to say: "It is enough that I am busy most of the day with idle things, in negotiations, but you should learn Torah: from your studies I draw strength and great encouragement."

Even in the terrible days of the outbreak of World War II, the parents did not take their sons from the *yeshiva*, so that they did not stop studying Torah.

When the Nazis captured Goworowo, and I moved with my family to the town of Zembrove, which was under the rule of the Russians – my brother, the late Yechiel Meir, moved to the city of Bialystok. One bright day, my cousin Neyekh came to me; he came to ask after my parents. I brought him home and shared the meal with him. After a few days he went to his parents, and as always, the parents sent him back to the *yeshiva*.

Days and months passed. Their father was caught by the Russian authorities in his attempt to cross the border to Vilna. He was banned and sent to Siberia. The rest of the family members were also sent somewhere in Russia. The two brothers were still at the Slabodke Yeshive [in Kovne/Kaunas].

Day followed day, and night followed night, the air smelled of gunpowder, and the sword of the angel of death was outstretched. The life of every Jew was in danger of death. Blood stains, the smell of burnt bones, cries and wails, pain and agony, light and darkness were all in confusion and the sounds of murder did not stop.

The two brothers, Aryeh and Neyekh, died as martyrs to God; the two brothers, Aryeh and Neyekh, sacrificed themselves with purity.

We stand before the Almighty to ask for forgiveness and atonement for the people of Israel, and we pray for gathering all the people of Israel and the return of the sons to their borders. May their souls be bound in the bundle of life.

[Page 110]

The *Beys-Yankev* Schools

by Rov Yitskhak Shafran, America

Translated by Tina Lunson

When Sora Shenirer, of blessed memory, had just begun establishing the network of *Beys-Yankev* schools in Poland, Goworowo was among the first towns who quickly saw the light contained in that genial idea, and the religious leaders promptly decided to create such a school. Sora Shenirer herself came specially to Goworowo, presented a lecture for women and for the male leaders, and the *Beys-Yankev* was opened with much fanfare. Although everyone knew that *Agudas Yisroel* supported and directed those schools, all levels of the town's population sent their children there. The school took on a general and non party character and was concerned only with the religious cultivation and education of the pupils.

Goworowo had a special merit in the *Beys-Yankev* Central because for our school they selected the best qualified women teachers from the Krakow *Beys-Yankev* seminary. The first teachers were Khane Berliner, Frume Shremer, Rokhl Dhan, F. Orlanska and others. Indeed, the studies were on a very high level. After a short time, the girls could pray and read and write Yiddish and Hebrew; and in the second year were already studying *TaNaKh*, Judaism, Jewish history and so on. The huge success of the school could be seen in the open exams at the end of the school year which took place before the observation of the parents and of the head rabbi. All were, literally, inspired, hearing the fine smooth responses from the children and their deep knowledge of the material. A special impression was made by the pupils from the higher classes, who recited whole chapters of Isaiah by heart, well interpreting every verse and the main idea of the chapter.

Even today, in better times and in wealthy countries, community institutions fight hard for their existence. All the more so in those times in poor Poland. Yet in no large city was a *Beys-Yankev* school closed for a deficit or lack of funds. Thus we can be proud of our poor town, or better said, with the recollection of our town, which supported the school, without disagreement, for the whole time until the outbreak of the war.

Various leaders were involved with the school and the management of

[Page 111]

it for the whole time of its existence. I will note here the names of the most vivid directors to thank for the beginning and development of *Beys-Yankev* in our town. First of all - our *Rov*, our learned rabbi and genius, Rov Alter Meyshe Mordkhe Burshtin may God avenge his blood, who was from the founding through the end, the head and director and chief manager of the school. Every important decision was made only with his approval. Thanks to the *Rov*, the *Beys-Yankev* had a free town venue, without rent. When the school did have a deficit, he helped with the Council and moved to even out the budget.

A group of pupils[a] with their teacher Frume Shremer in the middle
About 1928

R' Leyvi Varshavniak also had a large part in the founding of the *Beys-Yankev* school and in the first years of its existence went to much trouble regarding its support. After R' Varshavniak made *aliya* to *Erets Yisroel*, where he still is to this day, a young man from Warsaw, R' Yisroel Burshtin may God avenge his blood, took over his business and along with the shop, all of R' Varshavniak's leadership. Within a short period of time, he became one of the towns biggest community activists in every area. I personally never saw a leader with so many problems. The man did not rest one hour of the day. He neglected all his private business in order to help someone with a favor, a good bit of advice and everything else possible. Even his tragic death was tied to his willingness to help a hungry Jewish child. I will

[Page 112]

relate here the sad story of the death of that undauntedly good man, R' Yisroel Burshtin:

It was a Thursday, the 7th of September 1939. In and around the town, skirmishes were taking place between the Polish voluntary army and the Germans. The residents ran into the nearby fields and lay on the ground to avoid the flying bullets. People did not move from their place for hours at a time. A young girl was crying that she wanted food. R' Yisroel Burshtin could not bear the crying of a Jewish child, so he got up from his place and went to take a piece of bread to the little girl. A murderous bullet struck him right in the heart. After a few days he was buried in the town cemetery. R' Yeshaye Hertsberg, who had helped with the burial, had found a ring of keys in his pocket. When he showed them to me, I quickly realized that they were the keys to the *Beys-Yankev* school.

A group of pupils[b] with their teacher F. Orlanska in the middle
1932

I will return to the history of *Beys-Yankev*. On a particular day at the beginning of 1932, R' Hershl Rubin may God avenge his blood, and a messenger from the *Rov* came to me and asked me to come to him right away. At the *Rov*'s courthouse I encountered a meeting of activists who managed the situation of the *Beys-Yankev* school. Suddenly the *Rov* called out to me, "Itshe! I want you to be the secretary and treasurer of the *Beys-Yankev* Shule". I was not expecting such a surprise.

[Page 113]

I tried to defend myself: "I am just a young man, it is not appropriate, the town will talk…" and so on. By chance, the famous preacher Rov Mordkhe Barbateles was also sitting in the *Rov*'s house. This was a Jew on fire. He burned, in fact, with love for Yisroel and awe of God. He stood up and cried out "What?! Hasidic simpletons! You drink Jewishness and you have to save it!" Naturally, I accepted the post and held it until the end.

The last two *Beys-Yankev* teachers who worked under my term of office were thank God, saved. Leye Gulevska - today, Rebitsin Epshteyn - worked in the Goworowo *Beys-Yankev* and brought the school to a higher level. Working that last summer before the Holocaust was the teacher Yenta Vrubel - today Rebitsin Mones of Cleveland, America. I met her in Lomzhe after the outbreak of the war and crossed the border into Lithuania with her.

I recall the *Beys-Yankev* school, the pupils, the teachers and the directors. I could weep and lament for the lost ones, but we must also thank *Ha'shem* who is to be praised for those saved.

A group of pupils with the teacher Rokhl Dhan in the middle

1933

Notes from Lester Blum:

a. Norma Blum (Hoffman) - 2nd row from the bottom 1st one on the left
b. Surcha Taus - 1st standing row - to the right of the teacher

[Page 114]

The *Shomrey Shabes* Group

by A. Inbri, America

Translated by Tina Lunson

The concept and the name of this group could make the false impression that there were breaches in observing the sabbath; that there were those who, heaven forbid, did business, traveled, worked on Shabes or kept their shops open. No! In Goworowo the Shabes was absolutely the sea of rest and joy, the holy Shabes Queen held her white wings open over the town the whole 25 and one-quarter hours, with all the supplements before and after. There was not one man in the town, a boy or an elder, a Bundist or a Ger Hasid, who would not go to *shul* to pray, both Friday evening and Shabes morning. Even Freethinkers and Communists fought over *aliyes* to the Torah in the study house. I myself was witness when a Leftist party leader raised his fists to Avromke the beadle when he thought he had not given him the *maftir aliye* on a *yortsayt* date.

I recall another story about a hairdresser who, not far from the study house, tried to infringe a little on the Shabes. The *Rov* was walking to shul and by chance noticed that the door of the hairdresser's shop was only half closed and there was movement inside. The *Rov* did not hesitate but burst into the shop, shoving the door open. Indeed, there was a young man with a soaped face, and the hairdresser in his white apron was shaving his beard. The *Rov* gave a roar like a lion, "*Shabes*!" The soaped-up man dashed out the back door and the hairdresser received a slap from the *Rov* that made him see stars.

But that was a rare event, because the same hairdresser would later put on his new overcoat and go to *shul* to welcome the Shabes.

Indeed, it was not the fundamental purpose of the *Shomrey Shabes* society to protect the Shabes from desecration. The reasons were quite different, one could say - educational, which was in the framework of Jewish education. Basically, the group could have called itself "observing modesty" or "observing tradition", and their activity could apply to all the days of the week. But who has time on an ordinary Wednesday to give attention to public things? Then who would be concerned with livelihood? So, it was put aside until Shabes evenings. Rested, having prayed, having eaten,

[Page 115]

the members of the *Shomrey Shabes* went out over the streets to conduct their activity.

I recall an example of those Jews, who sought something lost at night in the study house courtyard. Passersby asked him, "What do you seek?" He would answer, "I have lost a purse with 50 *zlotych*. Really, I lost it by the river, in the mud, but go look in the mud at night? Here it is light, clean and dry - I search here for my lost things."

The assignment of the *Shomrey Shabes* was to go around on Friday evenings in all the streets and lanes of the town and keep an eye on the strolling youths, so they would not, heaven forfend, do anything to desecrate the *shabes*. A boy and a girl should not be alone together, and when midnight neared, they drove the boys into their houses.

In the early weeks of this activity, the boys were a little shocked. They stayed in line and like good children they went home and went to sleep early. But later they resented it. Their young blood revolted, and they began a quiet, bitter fight with the *Shomrey Shabes* folk. They hid in the dark corners, in the attics, clucked and crowed like chickens, and made a mockery of the modesty and Shabes protectors. The *Shomrey Shabes* chased them, ran after them, but go chase the wind! The business began to be tiring until the group was dissolved.

That same *Shomrey Shabes*, with the *Rov* at the helm, once reacted sharply when one Shabes evening during the ten days of repentance between *Rosh Ha'shone* and *Yon Kiper*, a theater troupe arrived in town to perform. The actors became stubborn and wanted a lot of money. The *Rov* shouted and turned the world, "What?! You want to do theater during 'remembrance of the covenant' week?! Not possible!" The show was to take place in the hall of the church. The *Shomrey Shabes* folk stood at the entrance of the hall and did not allow any Jewish guest to enter. The theater troupe had a big failure and left town in disgrace.

There was another time the *Shomrey Shabes* had an opportunity to do something on a certain Shabes afternoon, when a Goworowo sports group was set to play a soccer game with a Christian team. A special messenger woke the *Rov* from his Shabes afternoon nap and told him the story. The *Rov* alerted the members of *Shomrey Shabes* and they all went to the sports field on Ostrolenke Road. Some of the sportsmen fled in fear. Shayke Hertsberg delivered a hearty slap to the shameless players.

After that incident, there was no more open desecration of the Shabes in Goworowo.

[Page 116]

Khevre Kadishe
The Burial Society

by Bar Bey-Rav, Israel

Translated by Tina Lunson

The only community institution in town that was always prospering and had a large stable revenue was the *Khevre Kadishe*. No one could compete with that society, and as it was not yet time for God to swallow up death forever, everyone was a potential candidate, at some time, later or sooner, to fall into their hands.

The large revenues that streamed into the treasury of the Burial Society came from burial money that the society took from deceased rich people. If the wealthy person was a bit of a charity giver in life, the society related to him with care. But when he was a stingy, with a closed hand – after death he had to pay the coin along with a percentage. Often such a stingy rich man was left to lie a day and a night because of the haggling of the inheritors – stingy children of the stingy – who did not want to give the large sum that the society requested. It started a whole set of transactions, with shouting and threats, people ran to the *Rov*, until they came to a certain compromise and the corpse could be buried, late at night by the light of lanterns.

The large sums of money that lay at the disposal of the Burial Society were always turned over for the maintenance of the cemetery. A Christian watchman with a yearly stipend sat in a house that the society built for him on the land of the cemetery. He guarded the graves and tombstones, planted trees, kept order and cleanliness, and took care of the hedge that surrounded the cemetery in order to keep the nearby gentiles from turning the cemetery into a pasturing field for their cows. The larger part, though, of the society's revenues went to benevolent and philanthropic ends. In the area of the very respectable new study house, the guest house, in the interest free loans till, into the *kheydarim* – every place got money from the Burial Society. Of course, it was not easy to get a coin from the society. Because, whoever knew the secret of whatever was put in, no more could be taken out. And the *gabay* was also somewhat of

[Page 117]

a rich man, an influential man, a hard nut to crack, and did not give in easily. But, after a little negotiation, they gave the needed funds. Did they have a choice?

One day a year was completely sacred for the Burial Society; that was the eve of the New Moon of the month of *Shevet*. On that day the Society members dressed in their holiday satin coats and prayed in a special *minyen*. The had fasted, calling it a little *yon-kiper*, with special fasting prayers and songs. That night the famous *Khevre Kadishe* feast took place, one that made a huge impression in town and which people talked about for weeks afterwards.

The feast was under preparation for months, buying up good things and all things that are good and the choice of the land. Fishermen brought in the biggest carp and pike. Goose dealers fattened up heavy geese, and so also with calves. The fattest breast and rib meats were sought out, and *kishkes* and male fish roe. Non compassionate women cooked that, in the name of a *mitsve*, in big pails and filled the *kishkes* with cow brains and the finest flour. The sharp, sweetish smell of roasting meat wafted over the whole town including those, poor things, perked the appetites of these Jews who did not merit being Society folk. For the second *gabay* people cooked oat grits in large pots and carrot *tsimes* with bees' honey. Liquors were produced, fit for a king, and necessarily, the sharp drink – vodka, 96 proof, and also Haverbush beer.

On that historic night, no one in the town could sleep. Everyone was standing outside windows of the *gabi's* house and looking enviously in, as the Society folk wiped their grease- stained moustaches and sang in tipsy voices "There is no one like our God".

At the annual *Khevre Kadishe* feast, the *gabay* for the next term was selected. Many men were interested in the fine, honorable post. However, in order to be chosen one had to have the merits of a little inherited prestige plus some "prestige" in the pocket. After all, whom can be trusted with so much money, if not a wealthy person?

Of the Goworowo Jews who had the merits to be *gabays* of the *Khevre Kadishe* between the two world wars, one must mention R' Yankev Hersh Berliner, R' Yeshaye Ayzenberg, R' Fayvl Brik, R' Mayer Ramaner, R' Velvl Blumshteyn, and Matisyahu Rozen. The last mentioned was *gabay* for several years, he devoted a lot of time to the Society and also spent a lot of money.

The *Khevre Kadishe* book of records served as the community record book at one time, where all the statutes and important events of the town were written. The record book was as big as a Vilne Talmud volume, bound in black leather with a decorated and beautifully painted cover. It was always stored at the *Rov's* among his holy books, and was burned along with the town, which the Germans set afire, soon after the outbreak of the last World War.

[Page 118]

Community Bureaus and Institutions

The Local Council

by Bar-Even, Israel

Translated by Tina Lunson

The Goworowo *gemine* or local council was also free of Jews in the good old years. Although the town was populated almost completely by Jews, the district functionaries found an ingenious idea; they included in the town all the close-in and further-out villages and thus craftily created an out weighing Christian majority. The result was that both the president and the secretary and all the officers were recruited from only the Christian population.

Mostly the local council was nominated from the district office, and no one asked the Jewish population who should serve with them. The [Jewish] councilmen Avrom Mordkhe Fridman, Zelig Popiertshik and Khone Fridman served only a few limited terms on the local council.

The local council had a weak influence on town life and took little concern with its needs. Even the records for the Jewish residents such as birth certificates, death certificates and marriage certificates, were also administered by the *Rov*. When there was an important announcement to make, or an order from the government, that was done through the mediation of the so called Jewish "village magistrate". In the years between the two world wars, Hershl Niks, Avrom Kruk, Khayim Berliner and Niske Koen served as that Jewish *soltis*.

That said, no bad relations, and often good ones, ruled between the local council president and the Jewish population. It depended on the person who was president. Most of the time he was a native -born merchant, or well settled in the area who lived well with the Jews, and further maintained the same friendliness as when he took the office.

Often the town Jews had to bear chicaneries on the part of the local police. A policeman actually had great powers in his hands. He could – for no reason, to anyone, any time – punish a Jewish merchant or a household proprietor with a large cash fine, and later there would be big trouble to shout down the order, or to repay those injured. More than once

[Page 119]

in fact, the police commandant let loose his helpers on the town, and signed dozens of reports with large fines for various crimes. Later in the same day the *Rov* had to invite the commandant and all his "brass buttons" to his home and offer them snacks with alcohol until they became "soft" and tore up all the reports.

R' Khayim Berliner,
may God avenge his blood

At the disposition of the local council and the police was a jailhouse, which people called the *koze*. It was a kind of wooden building with a small window with bars, in which they placed someone suspected of some crime, or as a kind of punishment. Mostly those sitting in the *koze* were Christian drunkards; and rarely, a Jew. But, when a Jew was sitting in there, his wife would keep him company all day, chatting with him through the little window and passing food to him through the bars. It was a rare thing for a Jew to spend the night there.

The peace judge was located in the nearby settlement of Tshervin. From time to time, for special trials, the judge would come over to Goworowo, and conduct sessions and deal with them there.

All tax issues were in the hands of the local council in Ostrolenke. For the annual valuation of the volume of business of the Goworowo merchants, assessors representing all lines of business would sit with them and explain the terms of the assessments.

Some of the assessors were Menashe Holtsman, Avrom Rozenberg and others.

The local council was very busy with one thing, especially in the last years before the war, taxing Jews to buy weapons for the Polish

[Page 120]

Army. In this the president and the secretary of the *gemine* were fierce patriots. They came to the *Rov*, invited the wealthy householders and took trouble to get more money from them for that goal. The last collection action was designated for the L.A.P., the League for Air Defense.

R' Niske Kohn

The chairmen of the local council after the First World War, were Karolak – later, Tshekhovski, Frontshik, Voytshik and others. In the last years, already under the new order, Sobotka served as chairman.

Stamp of the *Voit* and a letterhead

[Page 121]

The Jewish Community

by A. Bar-Even, Israel

Translated by Tina Lunson

Life in our town was conducted through our own sovereign authority, our own statutes and ordinances, which had nothing in common with the surrounding, one could say, hateful, atmosphere.

The organized Jewish community was the representative agency, both outwardly and internally, for all matters in the town, and its influence, along with the influence of the town *Rov* – was decisive and not regulable. It goes without saying, the ritual slaughter of animals for human food, laws of *kashrut* and specifically religious matters, but even questions of personal and general character were also governed by the Jewish community administration, and everyone had to be obedient, despite not having disposal to any police and other enforcement organs.

Before the First World War, under the Russian regime, Yehoshua Bar Venger, the son-in-law of Yekl Klepfish and father-in-law of the old Goworowo *Rov*, held the office of president of the Community. The members of the Council were Yudl Sheyniak, Yesheyahu Hertsberg, Dovid Dranitsa, Borekh Mints and Yekl Shtshetshina. Yekhiel Gerlits was employed as secretary. The then Goworowo *Rov*, the brilliant Rov Yankev Botshan, rarely mixed into the politics of the Council's activity. The birth records of the population were also in the hands of the Council. The local municipal tax was in general collected by force – with the help of the *voit*, when the town mayor's men with the shiny chains across their chests, went around to the houses demanding the money.

The later, and last, Goworowo *Rov*, the brilliant Rov Alter Burshtin may God avenge his blood was very active in community life. All of the Council meetings took place in his home, and it was usually he who saw through all the accepted decisions and resolutions. It was rare for anyone to rebel against the decisions and the wishes of the *Rov*.

In the later terms of the Council, after the First World War, the heads of the Council were: Menashe Holtsman, Matisyahu Rozen, Velvl Blumshteyn, Mayer Ramaner, Yehoshe Rozen, Borekh Kuperman, Yankev Hersh Vengrov, Avrom Shafran, Naftali Gemora, Yankev Kasher, Meyshe Dranitsa, Dovid Aron Grudke, Shmuel Tsudiker, Matisyahu Oyslender and Meyshe Horovitsh. In most of the terms of the

[Page 122]

Council administrations there were representatives of the religious parties and the various strains of the Zionist parties. Only in the last term were there also some from the *Bund* (the last Council secretary was Khone Fridman).

The Council imposed a direct municipal tax on each family. Besides that, it had revenue from ritual slaughter, birth certificates, the cemeteries, and so on.

The chief assignment of the council was to have oversight over the general and religious institutions, such as the study houses, *kheyderim*, ritual bath, hospitality, distributing social help, and hiring religious professionals – rabbis, ritual slaughterers, cantors and beadles.

Just before the First World War, the Council hired the last Goworowo Rov, our learned rabbi and teacher Burshtin may God avenge his blood, who was formerly the *Rov* in Tshervin. That *Rov* was hired in a peculiar spontaneous method. He came, along with all the local rabbis, to the funeral of the previous *Rov*, the *vashev ha'koen*, and delivered a eulogy in the *shul*. His representation and his appearance and good name that accompanied him as a genius and wise man made a great impression on the councilmen, and soon after the burying of the *Rov* they encircled him and congratulated him. The later Council consisted of Itshe, the cantor and ritual slaughterer; Malkhial, cantor and ritual slaughterer, who later moved to Vishkove; Khayim Leyb, cantor and ritual slaughterer, and Niske, ritual slaughterer.

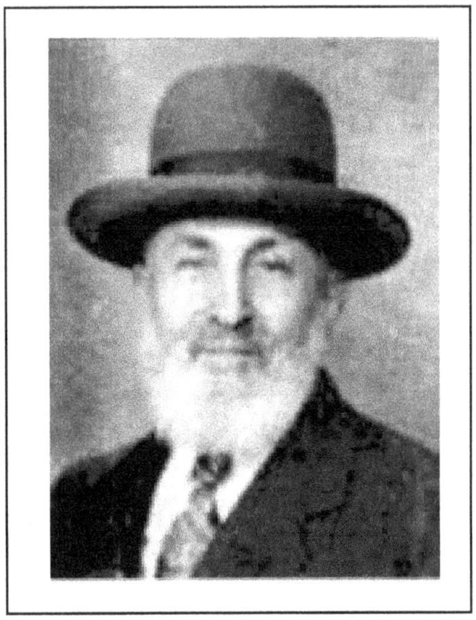

R' Borekh Kuperman, of blessed memory

R' Dovid Dranitsa, of blessed memory

In the last days of the German occupation and right after the First World War, the Council developed a large activity in aid for rebuilding the town, with help from the American Joint Distribution Committee. Then for a long time a representative from the Joint was posted in Goworowo, who, under the direction and oversight of the Council, distributed aid to the needy.

[Page 123]

R' Avrom Tsalka,
may God revenge his blood

Under the German rule in the First World War and during the Bolshevik invasion, the members of the Council suffered greatly and were arrested several times under the threat of the death penalty; but they bore with bravery and honor the high office which the town had laid upon them.

R' Nisn Mozes,
ritual slaughterer

[Page 124]

Schooling and Education

by A. Boki

Translated by Martin Jacobs

Edited by Gloria Berkenstat Freund

The only secular institute of learning in the town was the general state elementary school (*szkoła powszechna*), where Jewish and Christian children studied together. There was no secondary school (gymnasium), vocational or commercial school, or even evening courses for advanced studies in Goworowo. Anyone who wished to continue his studies after completing elementary school had to go to a larger town, or take private lessons from the same local teachers. Not everyone could afford this.

The *powszechna* was supposedly compulsory for every boy and girl from 7 to 14 years of age, but this was not actually the case. In the time of Russian rule, and even afterwards at the beginning of Polish independence, many parents got out of sending their children there. In the case of the Christians it was because of their own weak desire for learning and knowledge; they themselves were uneducated (many of them were illiterate), nor did they care if their children learned anything either. The motivation of the Jews, however, was piety; they did not want their children to become "Gentiles". Boys and girls should not sit together, and boys should not be without hats. (The Jewish pupils were excused from going to school on Saturday.)

The Jews looked for various ways to get around the compulsory education law. The very orthodox parents not only did not send their sons to the school, but not even their daughters. The more "enlightened" sent

[Page 125]

Jewish and Christian students from the elementary school (4th class) with their teacher

their daughters only. At one time under Russian rule, Jewish children were permitted to attend the state school for only an hour or two a day. For this purpose they were excused from *kheyder* and their only subject was Russian language. For other subjects they had to turn to private teachers. In the time of Polish independence, Jewish parents who wished could, with the "assistance" of the director of the state school, completely avoid sending their children there.

In the last dozen or so years before the outbreak of the war, it became more and more difficult to get around the law. Parents had no choice but to send their children to the school. The more religious parents only sent their daughters there (even those who were attending the *Beys-Yakov* school) and continued to use various ruses to keep their sons out. Many sent their children to *yeshivas* and in this way solved the problem. The "free thinking" parents also sent their sons, especially in the last years, when there was a push for secular education and knowledge.

A group of students from the elementary school with their teachers (1932)

[Page 126]

A class from the elementary school with their teachers (1934)

Instruction in these state schools was at a high level. Most of the students were Christian, from the town or the surrounding area. The teaching staff was also Christian (in the last years even a bit antisemitic), with the exception of two Jewish women, Taub, from Przemyśl, and Genia Shchavinovitch, from Kolno, both of whom taught for many years in the Goworowo *powszechna* school. After the First World War the state school was temporarily located in a large building on *Probostwo*. It was only at the beginning of the twenties that a splendid building on Ostrolenka Street, near the town council house, was built for it. It had a specially built athletic field, and at the top was the residence of the director, Stankius.

The teacher Genia Shchavinovitch

[Page 127]

The school comprised seven classes, some of them double classes, as well as a pre -school, with the necessary facilities.

* * *

In addition to the state school mentioned above there was a private school in the town, run by Alter Hochstein, a teacher. Hochstein came to Goworowo in 1916 or 1917, from Russia, with the

Henekh Friedman, may his memory be blessed

Alter Hochstein, may God avenge his blood

Motl Romaner, may his memory be blessed

Girka family. He himself was originally from Palesia. He settled in the town and opened a school. It was at first located in Shmuelka Dzhiza's (Khizak's) house; later he moved, with his school, to *Probostwo*. For about a year he ran the school in partnership with Motl Romaner. The latter taught Polish and German, and Hochstein taught Russian, Hebrew, Bible, Yiddish, arithmetic, and other subjects. Later Romaner left and gave lessons privately. Romaner died before Passover of 1918.

Hochstein was then the only teacher left. He had so much work he had to get in an assistant. Henekh Friedman became his assistant teacher and they worked together for a long time. Friedman especially took care of the younger children. After some time Hochstein moved his school to a separate cottage in Shabtse Werman's courtyard. He taught there for many years.

Hochstein ran his school in an ethnic spirit. Children who, for whatever reason, had avoided going to the general state school, as well as those who had attended it, studied with him; they acquired Jewish knowledge and learning from him. He taught the younger children in the morning and he organized afternoon classes for adults. In the evening he gave private lessons for students in their own homes. Hochstein also used

[Page 128]

The teacher Hochstein and his students (in about 1918)

First row (from the right): Butsha Granat (?), Eliezer Lewin, Patasz, Hershka Granat (?), Ruchl Gurka, Khone Alek, Miryam Papiercik, Golda Teitelbaum, Neiman (?), Khava Burshtyn and Breyna Bruchanski
Second row: Bunda, Khava Blumshtein, Feyga Sheiniak, Miryam Cudiker, Pesha Teitelbaum, Khava Alek, Breyna Rozen, Ester Lewin, Etl Niks, Bluma Rozen, Khava Gurka
Third row: Zelig Hercberg, Yekl (Avraham the hairdresser's son), Henekh Fridman, Mendl Teitelbaum, Mates Rubin, Hochshtein, Itshe Kiris, Khaya Kersh, Zelda Burshtein, Ester Goworczik, Ruchl Burshtein and Liba Proska
Fourth row: (a Dlugoshadler), Yekl Alek Avraham Romaner, Nakhman Teitelbaum, Moshe Lewin, Velvele Rubin, Hershl Alek, Miryam Bielik, Yehudis Proska, Miryam Rubin, Sura Romaner and Miryam Birk

[Page 129]

to write personal letters, in several languages, for uneducated Jews, for which he received a fee, but he could not manage on that alone. For several years he was also a religious instructor in the *powszechna.*

All this time Alter Hochstein led a lonely life. It was only in his later years that he married. He and his wife, who came from Wiązów[1], perished along with all the Jews of Goworowo.

With the strengthening of the ethnic spirit in the town, pressure to learn the Hebrew language also grew. Hochstein did not have the time to handle everything himself. Goworowo needed especially good teachers of Hebrew.

In the early twenties the Hebrew teacher Zerah Brick, who was from Lomza, came to us. He organized afternoon and evening Hebrew classes, divided into groups. He also gave private lessons, both for young people and for adults. He taught in the town for several years and was also active in the Zionist Organization.

After Brick came Greenspan, a teacher from Długosiodło. He too stayed in the town for a few years, teaching several Hebrew language classes and also giving private lessons.

At the beginning of the thirties Moshe Levkovitch, from Przasnysz Makowa[2], came to Goworowo to teach Hebrew. He was strong on initiative and organizational abilities. He started an afternoon Hebrew school as well as evening classes. He also led a young people's drama circle, which gave performances in Hebrew.

When Moshe Levkovitch left Goworowo after a few years, his father Rafoyl Levkovitch from Przasnysz came to the town. A relative of Matisyahu Rosen, Reb Rafoyl had by then a stately appearance and a full beard. He was learned in the Torah, a scholar, and a *maskil*[3], a good pedagogue and an expert on Hebrew and its literature. He also had musical training; he had played for a while in the Warsaw Symphony Orchestra.

Reb Rafoyl, like the teachers mentioned previously, gave both private and group lessons. He also taught the violin, and he created Hebrew courses, in which adults and young people from the Zionist organizations studied.

It is interesting to add that for some time during the years when Greenspan was the teacher there was also an Esperanto teacher in the town, a native of Plock, who came from Ostrow-Mazowieck. He taught only Esperanto and had great success.

Aside from the teachers mentioned above, who were, so to speak, apolitical, at certain times the political parties on their own responsibility brought in teachers, organized classes, opened kindergartens, etc.

In 1930 the right wing *Poale-Tsion* opened a Yiddish pre -school.

[Page 130]

A group of students from CYSZO[4] with their teacher, Peshka Goldman (above on the right)[a]

It was organized by the *shul-kult*[5] teacher, Bialostotska (she now lives in Israel), but only lasted a short time.

In 1931 and 1932 Asher Gilberg (Ben-Oni), a Hebrew teacher from Mizocz, Volhynia, was also active. He was sent by the Betar commission in Warsaw, exclusively to teach Hebrew to Betar and Revisionist Zionists in the town. The Bund, also, in the early thirties, created a kindergarten and also organized courses for young people and adults, where reading and writing Yiddish were taught. The Tsisho teacher, Sheyne Rudnitska (she now lives in South Africa), administered everything, but it, too, did not have a long existence.

After a lengthy interruption, a kindergarten and an afternoon Yiddish language school were organized by the Bund in 1938. The afternoon school kept going up to the outbreak of the war. The Tsisho teacher, Peshka Goldman of Kobryn, directed it. She perished during the war years.

In 1937 the Mizrahi organized a Yavne school, led by Magid, a teacher from Brest-Litovsk. It did not last more than a year.

In the years 1937 – 1939 there was also a Hebrew afternoon school in the town, located in Kruk's home in the Long Street, conducted by Portnoy, a teacher from Bialystok. The students wore special uniforms and blue-and-white caps. The school had been founded by Moshe Dranica, Jacob Kosher, and Yosl Silberstein.

At the beginning of the thirties an attempt was made to start a private Hebrew kindergarten, organized by Royter, the kindergarten teacher from Rutki, who was related to the Kosovsky family. The kindergarten lasted a short time.

(We have written in previous chapters about the *Haredim* and the *Beys-Yakov* school.)

Translator's notes:

1. Yiddish *Vonseve*.
2. Yiddish *Prushnits-Makave*.
3. Maskil: An adherent of *Haskala*, the Jewish Enlightenment movement.
4. The "CYSZO" was a Jewish-Socialist-Yiddish school network that operated in Poland between the two World Wars.
5. "Shul-kult" is a reference to the School and Cultural Union, which sponsored schools emphasizing Yiddish and using the so-called "Utrechian" curriculum.

Note from Lester Blum:

a. Elka Taus - bottom row 2nd from the left

[Page 131]

The Merchants Association

by D. Ben-Yitskhak, Israel

Translated by Tina Lunson

The Merchants Association in Goworowo was founded about 1925. This was during the time when the premier and the finance minister in Poland was the sadly well-known Vladislav Grabski. Grabski wanted to stabilize the economy of Poland and secure the Polish *zloty*, so he imposed a taxation system, especially on Jewish merchants and shopkeepers, that was then unbearable. His financial politics brought about a rupture in economic life of the Jews in Poland. His doctrine caused many Jewish merchants, unable to sustain the burden of the taxes, to liquidate their businesses. Grabski's tax screw gave impetus to the *aliye* to *Erets-Yisroel*, the so-called fourth *aliye* from Poland. After Pilsudski's coup d'etat (1926) when Grabski lost his financial portfolios and became a professor at the agricultural college in Warsaw, his tax system still remained, further and mercilessly oppressing the Jewish merchants.

The heavy tax burden by Abratovi, Dokhodovi, Mayiontkovi and others did not, of course, miss our town. And our merchants, the majority of whom were middle-income based, broke under the heavy load of the *podatkes* with the various names. Because of their unbearable situation, it was necessary to unite and use that common strength to resist the attack. Their main task was the taxation problem.

A group of merchants headed by Zelig Papiertshik took the initiative upon themselves and created the Merchants Association. Indeed, the Association had much to do. Because of the huge tax evaluations, as already mentioned, that had been laid on the Jewish merchants and shopkeepers in Goworowo, they had to send local merchants, from several branches of business to Ostrolenke, to the assessment commission in order to fight and argue with the officers and oppose their will. This was not easy work. The delegates often had to decline those assignments because their mediation was not generally successful,

[Page 132]

and the shopkeepers had received large tax assessments.

But the Merchants Association was always standing watch, and they did everything within their possibilities. An intervention was generally necessary, a written or oral one, an intermediary, a delegation, and so on.

With a strong sense of the antisemitism in Poland, fired up by their newspaper *Sprava kaolitska* which also did not avoid our town, new decrees and orders came out that had as a goal to make life harder for the Jewish merchant, shopkeeper and small retailer. So, in the beginning of the 1930s, an order came out to write on the shop signs the full first and family names of the owners of the relevant business. The intent was simple – one should know that the proprietor was a Jew. The Jews who had Polish family names made use of various ruses. They just wrote the first letter of their first name with a large letter, ending with very small type and the whole family name in large letters. Such family names were rare in our town, and it did not even help.

Later, in the era of the *ovshem* [allowed antisemitism] politics of the Polish government, there began a chapter of boycotting Jewish businesses. Signs appeared with slogans such as *swoj do swego* ["yours to yours"] and calling for Christians not to buy from Jews. If in other towns that brought about side taking fistfights, in Goworowo it showed a weaker character, but there was still a boycott with pickets in front of the doors of Jewish businesses. The Merchants Association also had much to do here – pleading, intervening and sending delegations to the relevant organs of authority became a daily event.

The Merchants Association existed until the Second World War.

The Credit Bank

In order to lighten the economic situation for the merchants, a financial institution was created under the name *Bank Kreditovi* G.M.B.A. The bank was founded at about the same time as the Merchants Association. Among the founders were the president of the Merchants Association Zelig Papiertshik, Matisyahu Rozen, Itshe Kosovski, Mayer Ramaner, Yankev Shtshetshina, Shmuel Volf Broyner, and others. The office of the treasurer was entrusted to Itshe Kosovski, who held it for all those years for no payment whatsoever until the destruction of the town. At first all the bank operations were carried out by him in his home. Later they rented a location from Velvl Blumshteyn in his little brick house, which was on the Market Square (near Irl Apelboym). From there they moved over to Avrom Grudke's and continued their activity.

[Page 133]

In 1929 the bank built its own masonry building, in an alley that ran from the Long Street to Bobavski's Field, which was actually called Bankove Street later on.

The bank was joined with the central cooperative movement in Warsaw on Rimarske Street 6, in whose control the bank lay. The capital for the bank consisted of a large loan from the central bank, private deposits held in trust and from *payen* – partly from the members with a certain sum which was deducted when taking the loan. The loans had to be approved by two persons and be paid back in weekly installments. The bank also had an account in the P.K.A. (number 65,477).

The bank prospered well, having income from changing money. Its revenues were small. But the bookkeeper and the beadle received salaries and all the others worked completely gratis.

Over the years the managing members changed. Meyshe Dranitsa, Shmuel Tsudiker and others were part of the last administration.

The bank's own building

* * *

[Page 134]

The bank's first bookkeeper was Meyshe Levin, who managed the work of the bookkeeping and the secretariat. When Dr. Khayim Shoshkes, the well-known activist, writer and world-traveler, came as an inspector from the central bank to check the books, he was impressed by Levin's bookkeeping. Shoshkes recommended him to a better paying post in a bank in Grudshondz. Levin really did, in 1928, leave town and go to work in the Grudzshondz [sic] bank. From there he moved to be bookkeeper in the famous firm of the rubber works, P.P.G. In 1930 he left Poland and traveled to his parents in Cuba. A few years ago, he was in Israel for a time and is now in America.

After him, Hershke Granat took over as bookkeeper and secretariat of the bank; he had worked earlier in the Artisans' Bank. He was also a very precise and self-reliant professional, to the satisfaction of the management and the interested parties. He died at the young age of 20, in 1932. Later the energetic and capable professional Khone Fridman took over the books and all the other bank operations. He held that post until the fall of the town.

* * *

Finally, I must mention the devoted beadle of the bank, Shleyme Klas. Although badly disabled, he would always run around with the receipts, receiving exchanges and installment payments, calling members to meetings and keeping order in the bank. He was an honest type and carried out his work perfectly. He along with his family were murdered with all the other Goworowo Jews may God avenge their blood.

[Page 135]

The Artisans Association

by Meyshe Granat, Israel

Translated by Tina Lunson

The chief assignment of the activities of the Artisans Association in town was to curb the antisemitic outbreaks that aimed to attack the branches of livelihood of the Jewish craftsmen.

From the Polish newspapers and from other propaganda mouthpieces one could daily hear an open hatred that demanded the establishment of trade guilds and, that members could only be the tradesmen who have completed trade and educational exams. Of course, those demands were very clear; the total extermination of the Jewish artisan and an end to the Jewish work competition both by means of the power of the fist and from the economic standpoint.

Big posters in very large type *swoj do swego* ["yours to yours"] were hung on the Christian businesses. Only thanks to the watchfulness of the representatives of Polish Jewry, Hartglas, Tshernikov and others, were they successful in temporarily repealing the decree.

Because of the frequent chicaneries, both from the central Polish government and from the provincial and local administrations it was absolutely necessary to stand watch to protect the interests of the Jewish artisans.

The artisans lived in constant fear, afraid of the *goyishe* officers. That latter tricked them, felt that they were self-ruling. The artisans often worked for them without pay. In our town one who helped a great deal with his wisdom and knowledge was my brother Hershke of blessed memory, who would push against every attack intended to oppress the Jewish artisan. As the first bookkeeper and secretary of the Artisans Association, he stood watch against the general decrees and against the too large tax evaluations.

There were times when my brother Hershke sat day and night and wrote well composed letters to the appropriate authorities with requests and explanations. More than once he involved me in that work too. Of course, all that was done with good relationships and with the agreement of

[Page 136]

our father, R' Bertshe of blessed memory, who was one of the most impressive activists (the chairman, even) of the Artisans Association. Those letters, when they were received by the relevant office, made a big impression and were for the most part acted upon.

R' Bertshe Granat of blessed memory

Concerning the local administration, when it required a personal intervention, in the council or with the police, my father dealt with it promptly and always won. When someone came to my father and told him about his problems, he right away put on his overcoat, straightened his well kempt little beard, took his walking stick and with a prayer on his lips was off to conduct his mediation. Only the thought that someone could be helped by his deeds gave him courage and energy.

In such cases he did not like to let it lie until morning, or even for an hour later; an inner instinct to do and to help inspired all his positive actions. He spoke to them in their folk language. He was to them the usual Jew. The *goyim* loved him because of his open heartedness and logical approach and so did not oppose him. The “nerve center” of the artisans was my father's house.

The assignments of the artisans were split in two directions:

On the outward front, the contact with the government offices.

On the internal front, the Artisans Bank, which helped the members in their financial difficulties. The two things were done with honesty and devotion, under the leadership of my father, may he rest in peace.

[Page 137]

R' Irl Apelboym of blessed memory

The town was lightly populated and had no signs of manufacturing for those who chose work and without a higher school for those who had chosen to study. Many sent their children to learn Torah in the nearby Lomzshe Yeshiva, or to other places. Those who returned from those places comprised the so- called intellectual part of the town. But those parents who had sought a purpose, turned their children over to an artisan and in time, there was an overabundance of trade workers. Every year there were new artisans until in time there was fierce competition among them. They worked from early until late at night by the light of an oil lamp and with difficulty drew a livelihood from it. Some traveled from town to town for the fairs. They were soon better situated. But most of them were dependent on heaven – if the winter was cold and the summer rainy, then the tailors could sell their short jackets and the shoemakers, their boots.

In their time of need the bank helped them and many times got them "back on their feet". Of course, the bank could not address all needs. The loans were limited and without the appropriate guarantees it could not give a loan. At the time when the Merchants Bank gave loans to everyone, the Artisans Bank remained faithful to its task and gave credit exclusively to its own members.

I never heard of any cultural activity that the Association conducted. But I knew that because of their connection to the Central Bank in

[Page 138]

Warsaw, they sent representatives from time to time to address trade topics. Discussions in the area of labor took place in the study house before and after prayers.

The Artisans Association and its bank were bound together. Some of the activists were in both places. After my father, Idl [sic] Apelboym was elected president and even later, Meyshe Tsimerman. Kalman Azdaba was also president and bank cashier for a long time. Mayer Shvarts was also a cashier. Later the bookkeeper was Yitskhak Velvl Gerlits; the last was Meyshe Khayim Botshan. The council members Yehoshua Rozen and Borekh Kuperman were activists for the artisans, as well as Sholem Plotke, Shmuel Grinberg, Avrom Rozenberg and others.

The bank changed its location one time. Early on, the bank operations were conducted in Kuperman's home; later, at Meyshe Dranitsa's, and after that at Avrom Kruk's and from there, at R' Naftali Gemara's. Close to the Second World War, when people already felt that a catastrophe was approaching, the last bank chairman Mordkhe Shmelts turned over all the bank materials to the bookkeeper Khayim Batshan and with the help of the Association's chairman Kalman Azdaba they distributed the funds to the members. Thus they, with their own hands, liquidated the Artisans Association and the bank, which had helped the craftsmen for so many years in the struggle for their existence. One day later, Nazi Germany began exterminating Polish Jewry.

[Page 139]

The Free Loan Society

by B. Alef, Israel

Translated by Tina Lunson

There were indeed two banks in Goworowo that gave larger loans to merchants, artisans and small retailers, with the goal of increasing their volume of trade and developing their workshops but, the money was procured only after long formalities, against a cash deposit, and for interest, and not everyone was able to procure the required guarantees and endorsements.

Their large concern about the poorer strata of the population awakened the idea in the minds of some of the town's social activists, to establish a *gemiles khesed* fund, that would specifically help the small merchants and poor craftsmen with an interest free loan, to be paid back in short or long term installments and without the complicated provisions of the regular banks.

The chief initiators of the *gemiles khesed* fund were Khayim Gerlits, Dan Roznberg, Pinye Shikara and others. For that purpose, money was gathered from individuals, a subsidy from the Jewish Community Council, and a large sum contributed by the central *gemiles khesed* treasury in Warsaw.

The fund was operated from a two room space in the old *shul*, which had been specially remodeled for that purpose. It developed wonderfully over a short period of time, the number of members grew, and it became an important factor in the economic life of the town. Those using the fund were those in the middle and the poor retailers and artisans, and all of them paid back their loans in the exact installments.

Already at the beginning the fund was grounded on the basis of free will and without any administrative expenditures. Therefore, in the first times Khayim Gerlits did all the fund's bookkeeping himself. But, when the operations broadened, and demanded longer hours of work, Gerlits alone was not able to manage it all. He thought up an original plan. He taught bookkeeping to several of the yeshiva men in the town and they happily carried out the whole job, with keeping the books, giving out the loans and accepting the installment payments. That plan was very successful and became an example for other towns.

The *gemiles khesed* fund existed until the destruction of the town.

[Page 140]

Hospitality

by B. Avi-Eyzer, Israel

Translated by Tina Lunson

Due to Goworowo's location at the center of Jewish settlements, with its own train station, with roads and highways that made it easy to get to the town and also because, since Goworowo Jews had a reputation in the whole region as charitable and generous with alms, the town attracted all sorts of beggars and poor people from all over the land.

The arriving paupers would go from house to house collecting alms. It was rare for such a person to knock on a Jewish door and not receive a two cent coin, a *kopek*, a snack, a warm lunch or a dinner.

The poor folk were mostly single persons, the head of a family who was trying to make his three *zlotych* (a daily wage for a laborer), would spend the night and move on. But often a whole poor family would descend on the town, with a horse and wagon, a man and a woman with children. They would settle in for a few days, and not leave until they had assembled money worthy of them and some used clothing in addition.

Some did not belong to that category of needy person - traveling preachers, emissaries from *yeshivas*, messengers from hasidic *rebis* for "community money" and "footloose" cantors. For preachers and cantors, they set up a table at the door of the study house after prayers and did not let anyone out until they paid the "exit fee". For *yeshivas* and "fine Jews" they found a couple of esteemed proprietors to go around the town collecting money for them. Of course they gave them a much larger donation; they collected 20 to 25 *zlotych*, and sometimes more.

For esteemed guests they generally found a town proprietor to invite them home for the night, opposite the regular poor folk who spent the night on a hard bench behind the oven in the study house.

Avrom Tsalke, the head *shames* of the study house, busied himself with the poor who stayed for *Shabes*. He would give out "tickets" to householders, each poor man according to his dignity. A poor man who was knowledgeable in Torah went to a householder of the same mind, they could speak of those Jewish things at the *Shabes* table; and an ordinary poor person was sent to a simple householder. His "tickets" were generally honored by everyone. In case a

[Page 141]

guest arrived in the late afternoon and did not receive a "ticket" from Avrom'ke, he was placed by the door after prayers and always found a host who took him home for the *Shabes* meal.

The *mitsve* of hospitality to guests, especially before the First World War, had a very devoted doer in R' Meyshe Yehoshe Ginzburg, a Jewish scholar and Enlightener, who later dealt in holy books. He would also take in guests to his home and concern himself with all their needs. There was a time when there was a shortage of small coins in the country and that served as a good reason to aid a pauper with very little to live on. Meyshe Yehoshe "invented" a "poor people's bank" and published a "money issue" with his signature on it. Householders could purchase such small "banknotes" from Meyshe Yehoshe in order to give to the paupers, and they, the poor, could exchange them for cash.

In the last years before the Second World War the Jewish Council constructed two large rooms by the *shul* for a guest house. There were a large number of beds with straw mattresses where the poor men could sleep the night and spend their free time. Gitl Leye Mikhalovitsh concerned herself with the poor women, who could spend the night in her own poor home, cook a little food and wash their clothes.

Great contributors to this hospitality were Fayvl Brik who in the last years designated one of his rooms for poor people; Velvel Zilbershteyn (the "Radzshilover tailor") who built out a special room in his apartment and ran a "private" guest house for the poor; and Yoel'ke the baker who had a *kalbe shavue* from before the sack of Jerusalem. There was not one hungry person who went to him and did not leave sated. His whole bakery and sales counter were at the disposal of the poor.

There were also two guest houses, so called hotels, where one could spend the night for a payment, with Meyshe Tenenboym or Shaul Potash. Although these hotels charged a fee, they did also manage the *mitsve* of hospitality, with their good heartedness and a good situation. Many times a Jew slept there without money, and also received a bite to eat.

Goworowo Jews knew well the words of the wisemen: "Welcoming guests is greater than receiving the face of the *shekhina*", and they valued them and fulfilled them with their whole hearts.

[Page 142]

Housing Poor Travelers and Visiting the Sick

by A. Avi-Uriel, Israel

Translated by Tina Lunson

Goworowo did not possess its own town hospital and no sanitation department or health institutions existed, not through the local council or the Jewish Council. The population itself upheld cleanliness standards and also concerned itself with medical help for a sick family member.

When someone in a family got sick, one immediately consulted with the neighbors, made up a few "grandma's remedies" and sent for Gitl-Leye so she could ward off the evil eye. When all those incantations and amulets did not help, one called for the *feldsher* [unlicensed medical practitioner]. As soon as he looked at the patient, he had his prepared remedies - for stomachache, a little castor oil; against a pain in the back, ten cupping glasses; and for headache, a couple of leeches or some bloodletting.

If this was a passing illness, the patient got up from bed anyway, though weakened a little from the cupping and the bleeding. In the case of a serious illness, and the patient was still sick after the *feldsher's* treatment, then it was a real illness and one soon sniffed danger. Then there was no other choice but to call the doctor.

For a dangerously ill patient the doctor alone did not suffice, one went to pray fervently at the holy ark, brought in *kheyder* boys from the *shul* to sing psalms and "measured" graves. One trembled in fear at a hospital; a hospital smelled of the cemetery. Better to call in the Gutshine doctor, who was also known as a bit of a miracle worker; or bring doctors from Warsaw, Lomzshe or Ostrolenke, just not to send any patient to a hospital.

There was a Jewish doctor in Goworowo before the First World War, but he did not have longevity. The Christians practically boycotted him, and he could not make a living from the Jews alone, so after a short time he had to leave the town. Generally, the people preferred to call the *feldshers* with their home remedies, than the doctors. In those times Goworowo had two *feldshers*, Moshtshikhovski, an ethnic-German who could speak Yiddish and was also a hairdresser; and the second one was good, a converted Jew.

[Page 143]

Their advertising signs consisted of three shiny brass trays that hung by the entrance of the house.

After the First World War, the doctors Zalevski and Kozlovski came from Ostrolenke each week and saw patients in the pharmacy. Later Dr. Tshepita worked there more permanently. In the later years Dr. Glinka treated Goworowo and the surrounding area and also served the members of the sick fund. He still lives in the town today. The midwives Miryam and Khaye Sore, daughter of Shmuel'ke Dovid, were active in the town for long years. Later there was also a Christian midwife.

Permanent teeth doctors or dentists were not usual in the town. For a few years the dentist Manye Hofman from Warsaw worked with Avrom Grudke. Later the woman dentist Dara, from Rembis, worked with Meyshe Tenenboym. In the last years a woman dentist came from Vishkove once or twice a week. Plus, a dentist from Ostrolenke came to work in Goworowo frequently.

As stated, the people of Goworowo turned to a doctor only when the "knife was at their throat". But even a doctor did not cure an illness with his hand. One had to buy a prescription, a rubber warming bottle, an icebag, a thermometer, and other medicinal herbs. Someone also had to sit with the patient, spend the night by him and so on. Therefore, there was not any difference between a poor person and a rich one, each one needed help in the time of illness. Thus, the Goworowo householders, headed by Gadliahu Tsudiker, Mendl Gutman and Kosover, took the initiative and created a *linus ha'tsedik* [lodging for the poor]. Several pairs of people set out over the town to collect money and with a subsidy from the Jewish Council they purchased the necessary utensils, which were lent out for the ill for a pledge.

For many years in Goworowo there was also a *biker kholim* [society for visiting the sick] which had more or less the same assignment as the *linus-ha'tsedik.* Both organizations had as their one goal to help the sick in all manners and with all means. They were active in the town for many years and their work was of great use to the Goworowo population.

[Page 144]

Parties and Organizations

The Zionist Organization

by K. Ber, Israel

Translated by Tina Lunson

When in the years before the First World War the idea of Zionism had already struck deep roots everywhere, and there were Zionist organizations in many large and small towns, Zionist idea had not yet reached Goworowo.

In truth, there were a few individuals who had been infected with Zionist thought. The youth had discussed the topic on their strolls outside the town, in meetings in private homes, but no organizational activity or open steps or official work had come out of it. For that they had to recreate "the story of Genesis" which already smelled of heresy, of revolution, of conversion may God help us! – and for that that one must have much courage and energy to enter the struggle with the more observant population of the town. Not all of the youth wanted to do that. Not everyone wanted to enter an unequal competition.

The old *Khoveyvi tsion* tried something out. R' Meyshe Yehoshe Ginzburg used to collect money from the nationally minded Jews and buy land in *Erets-yisroel* through *Keren kayemet l'tsion,* for the sake of the *mitsve* and in private, but after a certain big loss, they stopped their activity.

R' Meyshe Yehoshe's son Binyumin was almost the only one who did not stop for any pitfalls, bravely propagandized his Zionist stand, against others, and was persecuted by his religious parents and by the extremely fanatic environment. So did the conscious young man Avrom Horovits endure many chicaneries and insults from his father R' Yosl the teacher. For Nakhman Tshekhanover there was the case when he collected money for the *K.K.L* on *Purim* and his observant father R' Yekhezkel said that with that act he had turned the merry *Purim* into *Tishe b'ov*. Even the *Ha'tsefira, Haynt* and other Zionist newspapers were *treyf*, forbidden, and one had to read them in secret. So, it was no wonder that in such an atmosphere it was difficult to organize and establish a Zionist organization.

[Page 145]

It is possible that with time they would have come around. As the saying goes, "what the mind will not solve, time will solve". Then Zionist thought and consciousness did finally ripen in our town and could appear in the open without fear; but then the First World War broke out, the town was burned down, and the population fled in every direction. Only in 1917, when the refugees began to return and began to construct a new Jewish life again, then Zionist thought got a new attire. A large number of people were already coming to the conclusion that our own land was a necessity. Truly, the religious Jews still held to their own, but the youth revolted and engaged them in a struggle.

* * *

At that time, the town already had a non -partial library at Yehoshe Ber Leviton's on Broad Street. All the young people attended there, without differentiation of party views, including the religious. That library was the place where lectures and discussions were held on various themes, and to the point – Zionism. Binyumin Ginzburg was the main speaker. Also, Yekhiel Pshisusker, Khone Vaysbarg, Yehoshe Vengrov and many others stepped up for the Zionist idea. Meyshe Regazi came often from Ruzshan and spoke about the *Bund*. Each one there had his word and preached for whatever he liked. The Zionists were the majority however, and decided to take matters into their own hands.

Indeed, one can read in *Ha'tsefira* (No. 34 from 1917) that during the interim days of *Sukes* there had been a Zionist gathering in which about 100 people had taken part. The assembly had unanimously voted to establish a Zionist organization, to arrange Hebrew evening courses and lectures on Zionist and secular issues, as well as to organize an entertainment evening, and agreed to establish a library. The following were elected to the council: Binyumin Ginzburg, Nakhman Tshekhanover, Mendl Farbarovitsh, Peysakh Trukhnovski, Yehudis Rozen and Zalman Fridman. Khayim Matisyahu Evron and Bunim (probably Dine Boynes) were elected to the revision committee.

The administration took to their work energetically, carrying out the decisions of the general assembly. They also procured a large number of books, laying the foundation of a Zionist library. The teacher Hokhshteyn came to their aid too, offering his school venue for their use until they would later move over to a private apartment of Dvashe and Borekh BRH"B on Long Street.

[Page 146]

First row, right to left: Zlata Fridman and Yehudit Rozen
Standing, from right: Tsipe Boynes, Rokhl Fridman and a Jewish teacher of Polish

After the publication of the Balfour Proclamation (November 1917) the ranks of the Zionists grew and in time became a force. But gradually with the October Revolution in Russia, which took place at the same time, Socialist thought also stole into the minds of the youth. They soon began pull Zionism and Socialism together.

Although the legitimization was in the name of the Zionist organization, that did not stop the members from introducing their approaches. It often happened that *Tsirey-tsion, Poaley-tsion* and others came up in the Zionist organization's discussions about Zionism. With the return of the brothers Hershl and Simeon Farba from Russia, the propaganda for *Tsirey-tsion* increased. Other possibilities, of other shades. One tried to persuade the other and despite the differences in meaning it turned out to be a revival for the Zionist activity.

During the long period of time when the Zionist organization's library was located at Dvashe's, they further pursued the religious circles. The latter demanded that the Zionist evenings (for exchanging the books and so on) should take place separately for men and for women and various other demands that the youth opposed. The point was that the observant parents, whose children were already involved in the organization, became active and so wanted to prevent their sons

[Page 147]

from "disgrace and spoilation". The Zionists used to come together often in other private homes. From time to time, they would also meet at Meyshe Granat's (a nephew of Bertshe Granat), who belonged to the "triplets" – B. Ginzburg, Y. Pshisusker and M. Granat of the cultural activists.

* * *

During the two years of the Polish Independence, the Zionist organization led an animated activity – as against the time of the Bolshevist invasion (1920) when there was a void in the town. The Zionists were afraid to conduct any work openly and also the use of the library had to be stopped. The youth had to literally hide themselves. Anyone who wanted to exchange a book had to travel to Ruzshan. In that short era, a non- party library was created at Shoshke Gitl and Avrom Alakevitsh's on Long Street. Those active there were Yankev Gurka, Meyshe Dovid Malavani, Yitskhak Dovid Kuperman, Yankev Zamelzon, Leybl Kersh and others. Binyumin Ginzburg also helped them. Later a leftist *Poaley-tsion* evolved from it, under the leadership of the brothers Shlazer and Yankev Zamelzon, and a *Bund* headed by Leybl Kersh.

When the Red Army left Goworowo, some of the youth left with them to Russia, and the entire group work, especially the Zionist activity, had to be reorganized anew. But now the new Polish government organs began to look askance at them and suspected everyone of sympathy with Communism. It is worthwhile noting the following incident.

During that time in Goworowo, the leaders of the *Tsirey-tsion* Binyumin Ginzburg, Yankev Karvet and Hershl Farba also, some of the *Ts. K.* members of the Zionist organization like Shvalbe and others, were arrested in Warsaw. Those arrests took place in relation with a circular from *Ts. K.* in which a conference of Zionist delegates was called in Warsaw, which was, in short, indicated only with two letters.

Given that by chance, on the same day, the Communist International had called a conference in Vienna, the Polish authorities in Ostrolenke understood the two letters as indicating Vienna. They were certain that everyone was Communist and masquerading under the Zionist organization's legitimization, as the *Tsirey-tsion* was under one legitimization. The Polish patriots in Ostrolenke made a resounding blow about that, covering a large area all the way to Warsaw. They wanted it to appear that only they were successful in uncovering a Communist cell. Only after the personal intervention by Yitskhak Grinboym in Ostrolenke was the senseless libel cleared up and the arrested were freed.

[Page 148]

Meyshe Dranitsa

In about 1923, Binyumin Ginzburg left the town and other leading members also went away. The leadership of the Zionist organization was taken over by Meyshe Dranitsa, Yankev Karvet, Yehudis Rozen, Dovid Aron Grudka, Borekh Kravietski, Dovid Glogover and others, as memorialist and librarian, Khayim Gerlits. And the Hebrew teacher Zerekh Brik served in those same roles for a long time.

The religious Jews would still not leave them in peace. The town *Rov* also inspired them. Because the Zionist organization was officially legalized, that brought about the following collision.

The organization was based then at Yosl Engl's (the harness-maker) on Broad Street. The religious Jews intervened with the town police commandant, Grushka, and one evening he drove all the attending members out of the place and had the place locked, ostensibly because they were Communists. A delegation with Meyshe Dranitsa and Yankev Karvet went right away to the *Ts.K.* in Warsaw and pleaded for their intervention. The delegation brought back two letters from the *Ts.K.,* one to the police commandant and the second to the *Rov*. The commandant promptly turned over the keys and the venue was reopened. The commandant, for his unlawful act, was forced out of his office. And the religious got their verdict. But the *Ts. K.* was not interested in aggravating those relations and was silent about the matter. Except the *Shomer Shabes* group visited the venue frequently, checking to see that they had not lit a lamp on *Shabes* or were smoking on the holy day.

[Page 149]

Dovid Aron Grudka,
may God avenge his blood

But not only were the Zionist members pursued by the religious, the householders, too, who rented them space were harassed. The thing was now attracting attention from both sides. The Zionist organization had to turn to a Christian. They had to rent a venue from Virembek on Ostrolenke Street. They were there for many years.

Over time the pressure from the religious got much weaker. The Zionist organization (*Ha'tekhiya*) conducted its work in the calmer atmosphere. Zionist thought was already penetrating among all levels of the population. The work of the national funds and the sales of *sheklim* grew stronger. The Zionist members took part in theater performances, whose revenue was designated to purchase books for the library. The administration now consisted of Bunim Shafran, Meyshe Aron Granat and others. Avrom Holtsman was secretary and librarian for a long time. In 1925 [he] helped to found the agricultural training *kibuts* in Tshirnia.

Meanwhile the Zionist organization continued to hold discussions and member chats about the various currents in Zionism. In March 1927 a split occurred and the *Poaley-tsion* Zionist Socialists separated from the Zionist organization. (See further *The Rise of the 'Poaley-tsion' Zionist Socialists*). A new administration was chosen. Meyshe Dranitsa was again elected as president, Dovid Aron Grudka as vice president, and B. Kasovski as treasurer-secretary, and others. The first active librarian was Matisyahu Mishnayos, and later, Avieyzer Shikara and also memorialist.

[Page 150]

A group of members of the Zionist organization

Sitting, from the right: Hine Leye Romaner, Yete Burshtin, Nemi Tsudiker and Devore Romaner
Under them: Sore Givner and Blume Farba

At the end of the 1920s, with the rise of the Revisionist movement, the Zionist organization got pushed over to the Revisionists, who had for years conducted their activity on the legalization of the general Zionist organization *Ha'tekhiya*. (See further "the Revisionist Movement")

In the 1930s the Zionists entered into various institutions in town. Active as members of the Jewish Council were Dovid Aron Grudka, Yankev Kosher and for the last term, Meyshe Dranitsa. The latter also belonged to the management of the Merchants Bank, the credit bank, before the destruction of the town. The Zionists collaborated in other areas as well. The founders, main leaders and most of the congregation of the Progressive *Minyen* were also recruited from the General Zionists.

Unfortunately, the majority of the leaders and ordinary members who had for years led the struggle for Zionist thought did not live to see its realization. They were killed with the six million Jews in the Holocaust era, may God avenge their blood.

[Page 151]

My Activity in *Tsukunft* and the *Bund*

by Rokhl Brestel-Grudke, Israel

Translated by Tina Lunson

The younger generation of the *Bund*, to which I belonged, was led by the earnest comrade Simkhe Zilbershteyn. He was our teacher and educator, and we were drawn to him with love and respect. His assistant was Meyshe Alek. He was usually in a good mood, with smiling blue eyes; he cared for us like a father for his children, and we found in him a sure support in all our doubts.

The recognized and general leader of the *Bund* was the dear comrade Leybl Kersh. He had a special soft spot for young people. He hugged children and kissed them as if they were his own. He inspired us with his personality and under his influence we were ready to carry out the toughest assignments without getting tired.

One must single out some distinguished members of the *Bund*, Comrade Itshe Kiris and his wife Sheyndl, today in Israel, who were already standing by the *Bund* in its cradle in Goworowo; and the unique comrade Leyzer Fridman who served us all as an example of devotion and self sacrifice for an ideal. It is enough to mention the fact that Leyzer Fridman constructed the Perets Library in Goworowo with his own weak energies. He denied himself a new suit or buying shoes and used the money to procure books for the library. And Khone Olek, Mayer Shmelts and Meyshe Karvet were some of the most active members.

I, myself, eventually became active in *Tsukunft*, the youth organization of the *Bund*. I threw myself into the work with my whole youthful energy and evolved in every area.

In the early times the *Bund* did not have its own venue. We, the youth, would gather outside the town, under the open sky near the railroad. Later the comrades rented a place from the Christian woman, Vengelska. But that was curious. Many of the older Friends did not agree that the youth should be all together in one place. Simkhe Zilbershteyn was angry with us and protected us so that we would not "fly off" into other organizations which were

[Page 152]

beginning to conduct a large agitation among the youth. Finally, Simkhe Zilbershteyn found us a place in the Perets Library where we carried on our activities.

Leyzer Fridman

Moyshe Olek

Simkle Zilbershteyn

The young energy in the *Bund* developed and grew. By the next elections we had readied two members for the administration, Yisroel Shafran and the writer of these lines.

First row, from right: Simkhe Zilbershteyn, Avrom Romaner and Yosef Yagodnik
Second row, from right: Sholem Praske, (unknown), Leybl Kersh and Shmuel Shetsikh
Standing, from right: Sore Shmelts, Itshe Kiris, Sheyndl Karlinski, Meyshe Olek, Mendl Taytelboym, Brayntshe Rozen, Leybtshe Gemora and Malka Viraslav

[Page 153]

Later, the underground Communist organization stole members from us. Then the parents also understood the importance of the youth organization and they began to offer a lot of respect and attention.

The *Bund's* Perets Library possessed 6,000 books in Yiddish and Polish languages and was the largest library in town. It served every level of the population, from *Beys-Yankev* school girls and *yeshiva* boys to Communists and even Poles. There was a special department for children and youth books. I was a librarian for a long time, as was also Sore Romaner.

First row, from right: Meyshe Shmelts and Khone Olek
Second row from right: Ziske Toyz, Mendl Taytelboym, Simkhe Zilbershteyn and Yisroel Shafran
Standing, from right: Leyzer Fridman, Velvl Rubin, (unknown), and Noske Karlinski

The *Bund's* dramatic circle was very successful. It set a high, fine artistic level and played the best creations of the time, *Got fun Nekome, Der Toyber, Dorfs Yung* and other pieces that had great success. The director was Yosl Zilbershteyn and myself, as assistant. The town was lacking in entertainment venues, so our presentations were always well attended.

In the area of popular education, the *Bund* also recorded large achievements. The Perets Library opened evening courses for the young and for adults, beginning classes and advanced classes. The *Bund's* pre-school and afternoon school were also a big success. The teachers were

[Page 154]

Sheynke Durnitska and later, Peshke Goldman from Kobrin.

A large group from the *Bund* and the Perets Library

The latter teacher, Goldman, was lodging at Meyshe Horovitsh, the *Bund's* member on the Jewish Council. I recall an incident. I went to see her on a Friday evening and found her on the bed wailing in tears. I was quite shocked. She explained that she came from an observant Jewish home, and she knew that right now her father was reciting the *kidish* and the *Shabes* candles were lit on the table, and it broke her heart. I promptly took her to my house. When my strictly observant father came home from the Ger *shtibl* and encountered the *Bundist* teacher, he did not remark but just said "Good *Shabes*". I told him the story and she was allowed to stay with us. My father, of course, had to take some ribbing from the Ger Hasidim, "How does it happen that a *Bundist* teacher is staying at your house?" – but he brushed them aside: "A Jewish child is a Jewish child". Later she went to live in Shayke Hertzberg's house.

In general, Goworowo had a liberal approach to one another's ideals. The many views and party positions did not disturb the community's idyllic living together. On one "press day" Yisroel Burshtin, the fanatic *Agudas-nik,* even bought a copy of the *Folks-tsaytung* from me; and when the *Beys Yankev* girls' school presented a play, I bought a ticket.

People in the Bund's Warsaw Central were drawn to Goworowo with great respect. The circulation of the *Folks tsaytung* and the "press days" was so great it was like that in the well known big cities and we often received commendations for them. The Central sent such "big fish" of the Party as H. Erlikh, V. Alter, Y. [?] Pas, B. Shefner, Dine Halpern and others, to Goworowo. I. I. Kruk and B. Malkin

[Page 155]

visited us with their lectures. The artist Holtser also visited us.

I present these details here which come to mind, writing these lines. Of course I have left much out and forgotten much because of the tragic war experiences. It causes pain and it cuts the heart when one recalls the dear friends who were so horrifyingly murdered by the Hitleristic killing squads. I want to mention a few names of friends whose images appear before my eyes, Meyshe, Khone and Khave Olek, murdered in Zelve, near Slonim; Leybl Kersh, killed at the end of the ghetto rebellion in Warsaw; Simkhe Zilbershteyn, killed near Baranovitsh; Meyshe Karvat, killed in Slonim; Naske Karlinski, killed in Baranovitsh; Sholem Praska and Gishe Olek, murdered near Minsk; Yenkl Olek and Golde Daytsh, killed in Russia; Anshel Toyz, murdered in Treblinka; Yosl Zilbershteyn, killed in Kartuz-Bereze: Meyshe Horovitsh, killed near Minsk; Yosl Ogrodnik and his family, killed in Russia; Leyzer Fridman, killed near Nashelski; Anshel Engel and his wife and daughter, murdered in Russia. Dovid Vishnia and his wife Masha; Oleyarzsh Yisroel Nakhum; Leybl and Velvl Toyz as well as Ester Greyner and her brother Berl – all murdered in the bloody war years.

May my lines be a gravestone for their sacred memories!

[Page 156]

The Rise and Development of the *Poaley-tsion* Zionist Socialists

by Meyshe Granat, Israel

Translated by Tina Lunson

The movement for a laboring *Erets Yisroel,* which stood for the task of building the Land on a socialist foundation, captured a large part of the youth in the 1920s. They understood that in order to make the economic life of the Jews a healthy one, they must stratify the people onto other foundations, become stewards of the land, live in communes and not refuse any physical labor.

In 1925 the Right *Poaley-tsion* merged with the Zionist socialist *Tsirey-tsion.* That was an important event then. Better reports began arriving from *Erets yisroel*, which created a base for a broad branched effort among the laboring masses.

Zionist-Socialist ideas began to infiltrate our town after some delay. We were still all grouped together in the General Zionist Organization. Discussions often arose about the end goals of Zionism, about Socialism, and so on. Meanwhile the ranks of the General Zionists continued to grow. We ourselves had not expected such large success. Since the idea of being independent was ripe, of no longer being the kept son-in-law of the General Zionists, we were ready to pull away from their guardianship.

That happened in March 1927. Several members took the initiative, rented a space and laid the first foundation stone for the party *Poaley-tsion* Zionist Socialists in Goworowo. We grew quickly. It was necessary to create our own library, which would serve as the cultural life center for the members. The leadership circle grew. We could envision that we too had the potential for good, influential work.

The continual gathering of new books and all the other tasks that are tied to maintaining a party drove us to large expenditures. The financial difficulties robbed a lot of our time. For that reason, the party created a dramatic circle which would bring in some revenue. And there, it turned out that we possessed an arsenal of precious

[Page 157]

human resources. Our own members and delegates from the Central in Warsaw arranged evenings for checkers and dancing. But our budget problem was always a worry. It was never real, but ever "patchy".

The Executive Committee of the "*P.Z.- Z.S.*"

First row from right: Zelig Hertsberg, Yankev Drozd, Aron Shron, Meyshe Sorge and Bunem Shafran
Standing, from right: Yitsik Viroslav, Feyge Kuperman, Sore Skurnik, Yitsik Blumshteyn, Sore Plotke, Sore Sarna and Henekh Fridman

Each member carried out his work without payment. All the work of the chairman, secretary, librarian, theater director as well as the simple work of chopping wood and carrying water, everything was done voluntarily, with joy and without self-interest. They often contributed their hard work by giving the best hours of the day for the success of the whole venture and enterprise.

The space was always full in the evenings, where one could find a lively community. There was always a happy and friendly mood there. The leaders were interested in each member, always knowing "whose shoe was pinching". Everyone felt as if the place was their own home. Someone was singing, someone laughed at a good joke or at a merry story and someone was embroiled in a political discussion.

Sometimes, at a lecture or a presentation, the police on duty paid a visit. Although we always announced the "innocent" topics to the police and used "kosher" content, we never used such terms as "socialism", "communism", "proletariat" and others.

[Page 158]

It also happened, if a gentile, a self-styled protector of the law, happened to overhear a word that he could not quite digest, then he dissolved the gathering, dispersing everyone away.

For special celebratory events there were also Poles gathered in the streets. Those culture angels were drawn by comrade Avrom Holtsman. He turned out precise and polished work, creating new forms of the Yiddish alphabet. His posters drew extraordinary attention. They shone with the names of lecturers and topics in huge letters or the name of the play. The poster was also decorated and adorned with various ornaments in more vivid colors.

Good reports were coming from *Erets yisroel*. Every Jew's dream was to move there as soon as possible. Zionist Socialism was a significant factor in our national revival. With the establishment of *kibutsim* and collective living we saw our auto-emancipation, the shift to a healthier foundation. Great self-sacrifice and tremendous perseverance would be necessary in order to carry this out, and the Zionist Socialist movement provided that. Thus, people welcomed the party with deep respect and credibility. The party grew and broadened its strata. From that framework there blossomed the youth group *Frayhayt* and also a younger movement, *Skoytn* [scouts].

The relationships of one party with the others were not always ideal. There were often squabbles between them. Each party stood unwilling to concede. Mostly it came out as a sharp push-back with words. Rarely did it turn to opposing fistfights. Better we should live with the Zionist thinking parties. Something still united us in a common goal – we had a partnering feel for Zionistic responsibilities.

He'khaluts and *He'khaluts ha'tsair* were absolutely outspoken *Poaley-tsion* comrades. We were in good relations with the General Zionists, from whose school we had emerged. We held the *Ha'shomer ha'tsair* in the same regard. We often held cultural events together. One did not attack the other. Rather, the opposite – we helped as much as possible. Our paths were, really, different, but the goal was the same. We stood a great distance from *BeTaR*. They were essentially fine people who were fed an extremely conservative diet. They were hot-headedly governed in every step by their leadership, followed militaristic rules and stood always ready to take orders from above. When Jabotinsky threw out the slogan "Stop!" they fled the General Zionist world organization and kept to their own doggerel. They unloaded their repressed impulses in the poor, silent *K.K.L.* charity boxes. But we were patient and never engaged them in battle, believing that they were just going through a temporary phase.

[Page 159]

But it was worse with the *Bund* and the Communist party. Each of our meetings was accompanied by their shout-outs. The only goal of their presence was to disturb and disrupt our meetings. We never visited their meetings. If one of us wandered into one, it was not with the goal to disrupt them. It seems that they could not accept our strong growth and the large influence of the P.Ts. party. Because we had risen above them in every area except "fisticuff argumentation" and in gifts of handicrafts. There was also a *Mizrakhi* party in town, an *Aguda*, a left *Poaley Tsion*, but we were not in contact with them.

Officers of the First of May Gathering, 1930

From the right: Yitskhak Blumshteyn, Avrom Holtsman, Khave Segal, Bunem Shafran, Yankev Drozd and Yitskhak Viroslav

Despite our negative relationship with the *Bund*, we did have one area of work together - the respect and care for the Yiddish language. The *P.Ts.–Ts.S.* party was principally for "school culture", whose task was to help those in the Diaspora to live their lives in the mother tongue Yiddish; but at the same time to introduce the Hebrew language through the front door. The party rejected the case of the Yiddishists, as it neglected the continuing problems of the laboring masses in the Diaspora, through its positive stance for Hebrew. And from the General Zionist side, it rejected that with the recognition of the Yiddish language, it stepped out against the accepted decisions of the Zionist Congress. The party found itself between the hammer and the anvil. For a long time

[Page 160]

A group of *Frayhayt* members

Below: Meyshe Shafran
Second row, from right: Grinberg, Meyshe Granat and Yitskhak Viraslav
Standing: Elin, Viroslav, Kahan and Shmuel Blumshteyn

the question did not come up in the columns of the newspapers. There were heated discussions in the evening meetings about the problem. Until the *Ts. K.* decided to give the question over to the free hands of the members. Indeed, both languages were declared national languages by them. We supported both the "school culture" and the Yiddish School Organization. Of course, our work was intertwined with that organization's work. The *Bund* was the autocrat, not letting anyone reach a verdict. We therefore stopped relations with them for the sake of peace.

I was delegated as representative for the party in the Yiddish School Organization committee, was in good personal relations with them, especially with their party leader Leybl Kersh, a young man with good qualities and a faithful server of the labor issue. I had always had respect for the Yiddish word, although Hebrew was on my horizon. I then considered and at every opportunity expressed my personal opinion that, working closely with the *Bund* in other areas of community life was not excluded. In a calm, relaxed atmosphere one could take on many partnering strengths, creating a single energy for educational institutions, theater, libraries, professional unions and so on.

A special chapter must be dedicated to *Frayhayt*, the youth movement of the party. The older members carried the yoke of the financial tasks of the organization. They were the splinters of *K.K.L.*, the *Keren ha'yesod*, *P.O.F.*, and helped maintain the local venue, the library and other expenditures. However, the

[Page 161]

Frayhayt movement was not so burdened financially. The older members took care in particular to educate intellectually. There had to be the followers, the future party. That *avant garde* gave us great hope. A young group ranging in age from 14 to 16 years, impulsive, conscious, a majority of them very adept, with independent behavior and sure steps, ready for any call. Future leaders of the movement.

And we created another youth movement in the 1930s as well, the *Skoyt* [Scouts]. This was for the "infants of Ruben", the youngest children. In order to prepare new cadres for the movement it was necessary to begin with *alef.* These were children of 11 to 14 years old, who were barely out of *kheyder*. Some of them were apprentices and there was a danger that we would lose those children if we did not keep them busy; in particular, when we saw a similar tendency in the *Bund*. We did not stuff them with dogma. We put more emphasis on the physical development, helping to draw a living color to their pale, fallen-in faces. We kept them outdoors, had frequent spot events, exercises and sport competitions. The rest came from them. They were bound to the local venue, stopped being shy, took part in conversations and enjoyed happy events. In time they put down good roots. Each year we celebrated the transfer of the grown Scouts to the *Frayhayt* movement with a parade.

A large group of *Poaley-tsion* Zionist Socialists and *Frayhayt*

The *Frayhayt* and *He'khaluts* were like Siamese twins who could not be separated. At their gatherings one could

[Page 162]

usually see the same friends. No event took place in the area of *Erets Yisroel* where one did not find the appropriate, comprehensive handling. The leaders of the local party took pains, life and limb, sacrificed, for their permanent development, and they certainly carried out all the duties that the movement had laid on them. The ideological activity had achieved its goal and a large number of them made *aliya* to *Erets*. Overall, Goworowo was considered a fortress of Ts. S. thought. The Central in Warsaw regarded us highly.

Our library, named for A. N. Brener, had an interesting history. As I mentioned at the beginning, we were all sitting together in the General Zionist Organization and were partners in the library anyhow. But when the idea of Zionist Socialism was ripe and we pulled away from the Zionist Organization and created a party of our own, we also demanded that the library be split percentage-wise according to the number of members and that we should receive our part. The General Zionists did not agree to this. As security against our stealing the books, they hung huge locks on the door and on the bookcases. But that did not help. During *Rosh-ha'shone* night in 1927 four of our members, with the help of duplicate keys, got into the space and took the larger and better part of the books. The surprise was on us and the police took everyone forcibly and threatened them with jail. No one betrayed the other. We stood trial twice in Tshervine court but because of a lack of evidence we were all freed. A year later, when the story was almost forgotten, the members, in the middle of the night, dragged the books, which had been buried in sacks somewhere in Probostvo near the Jewish windmill the whole time, to the venue. Thus was our library enriched with a large number of books, thanks to that "literary" theft.

There was also a kindergarten among us for a time, which was run by the party. The woman teacher, Bialastotski (today in Israel), also a party member, who was sent from the Central *Shul-kult*, conducted her work with devotion. It was a pleasure to look in on how the little children played, sang and danced, surrounded with care and warmth from the teacher. Unfortunately, the school was not long-lived because of a lack of funds; the small number of children enrolled could not sustain the kindergarten.

Our daily organ *Dos vort* and the weekly publication *Bafrayung-arbeter-shtime* as well as the *Frayhayt* all had wide circulation. The fervent followers of our party could not wait for the mail carrier

[Page 163]

A farewell picture at the departure of Sore and Yitskhak Blumshteyn and Aron Shron to *Erets Yisroel.*
August 1932[a]

[Page 164]

to bring the newspaper to their homes but made a special trip to the post office to get it.

And the party was very innovative in the area of sports, particularly in soccer. Mostly the younger members played. The town did not have any special sports field, so the team gathered in the evenings outside the town near Mordkhe Shniadover's windmill and played there. Various sports appliances were installed at the local venue. But the sports were always in another place, after the political activities.

The young people strove body and soul for the idea of freedom, for the dream to realize the *Erets Yisroel* ideal. The ideal captured them completely, there was no time for anything else. They enjoyed little else in life because everything was just a springboard to the end goal – *Erets Yisroel*. Unfortunately, the majority of the members did not live to see it. Honor their memories!

Finally, I must recall the members who stood at the head of the movement:

Bunem Shafran, Yitskhak Viroslav, Yankev Drozd, Zelig and Feyge Hertsberg, Meyshe Shafran, Rokhl Klepfish, Alte Zilbershteyn, Shmuel Blumshteyn, Leybl and Perl Sandale (all murdered); Meyshe Sarna, Meyshe Granat, Aron Shron, Khave Segal, Avrom Holtsman, Yankev Gurka, Yehuda Grudka, Yisroel Kutner (all in Israel); Yitskhak and Sore Blumshteyn, Hershl and Khave Krulevitsh (in America).

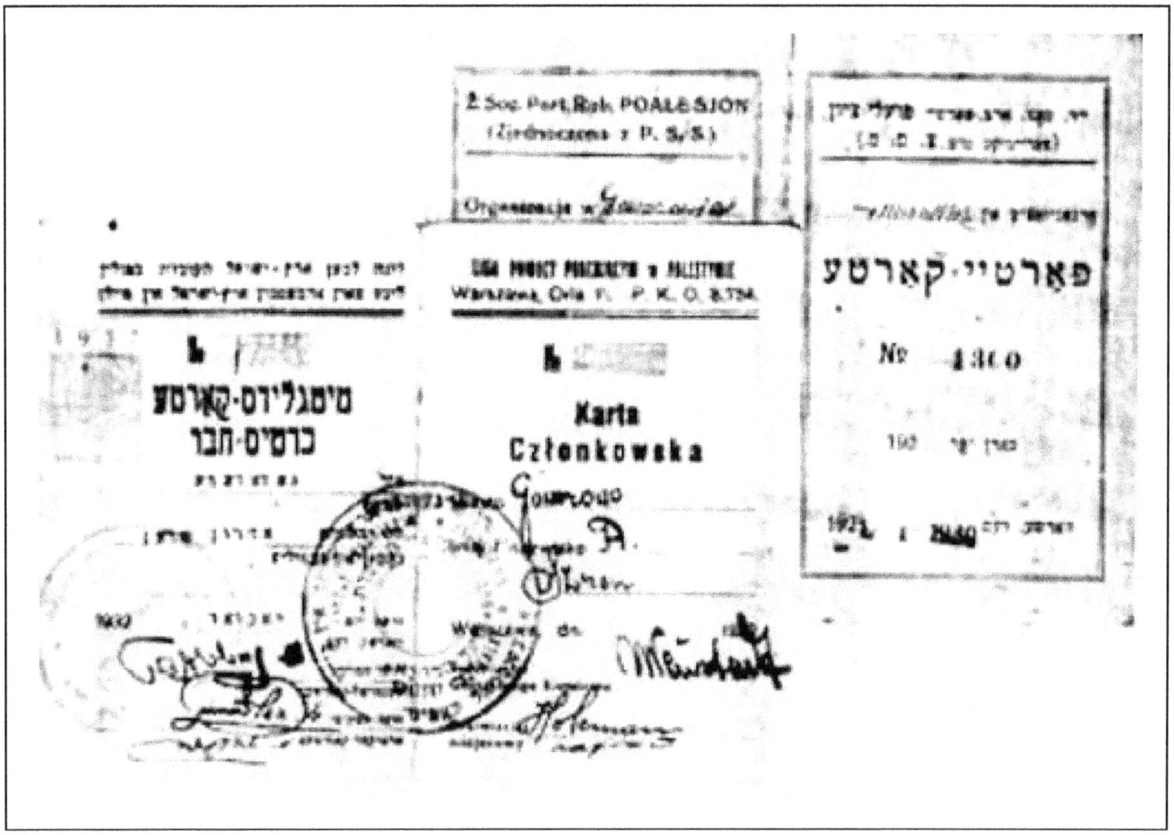

Membership cards for *Poaley tsion* and for the League for a Laboring *Erets Yisroel*

Note from Lester Blum:

a. 2nd row from the top, 4th person from the right - Reuben Schmeltz

[Page 165]

The Revisionist Movement

by B. Kosovski, Israel

Translated by Tina Lunson

The Revisionist idea infiltrated the town first at the end of the 1920s. After being in the framework of the General Zionist Organization *Ha'tekhiya*, we created a Revisionist group named *Ha'shakhar* through the initiative of members Matisyahu Mishnayos (Uruguay), Tzedek Farba (America), Avieyzer Shikara (may God avenge his blood), Khave Burshtin (Israel), the writer of these lines, and others. That was still during the time when the three Zionist factions, *Al ha'mishmer*, *Et livnos*, and *Revizionistn* still belonged to one General Zionist umbrella organization; so we conducted our activities within it. Matisyahu Mishnayos often presented lectures in the same venue, propagandizing the ideas of Jabotinsky. The issues of Revisionism were also treated in other presentations. Within a short time, our strength and influence grew and the writer of these lines was officially elected as secretary of the General Zionist Organization

Ha'tekhiya. Later we even became a majority and both the local space and the library were under our authority. For many years we had made do, for the powers that be, with the official legitimization of the Zionist Organization. We often arranged for lectures, discussions and checkers evenings and other presentations.

In about 1930 a representative from the commissioner of *Betar* in Warsaw came, and the *Betar* was founded in our town. Yehude Rits was designated as Commander and the command consisted of Khave Burshtin, Shabsay Fridman, Yosef Krulevitsh and later also Yosef Drozd and Mordkhe Rits. The head of the *HaTsaR* was Avieyzer Shikora.

By the end of 1931 the commissioner of *Betar* sent the instructor and Hebrew teacher Asher Gilberg to Goworowo, from Mizatsh in Volyn, who carried on the work of the commandant of *Betar*. During the year that Gilberg was with us the Revisionist movement grew in size and strength. He also presented frequent lectures and open multi-party discussions. He taught Hebrew, history and conducted conversations about actual issues among the members.

First row at top, from right: B. Kosovski, Khave Burshtin, Yosef Krulevitsh, Shleyme Apelboym and Dovid Blumshteyn
Second row, from right: Avieyzer Shikora, Yehude Rits, Shabsay Fridman, Yosef Drozd and Mordkhe Rits. (all murdered)

[Page 166]

After Gilberg, *Betar* sent Yitskhak Mak (Ben-Dovid) from Warsaw as our instructor. He would not have any open presentations but worked exclusively within the party. He taught the *Betar* members marching, sports and military training. It seems as though, because of money difficulties, he could not stay with us for long, and after about half a year he left Goworowo.

During that year I returned temporarily from Warsaw where I had studied and worked and was chosen as commander. I held that office until the very outbreak of the war. Although I was more in Warsaw than in the town, the most important decisions were made with my knowledge and agreement and all current issues of the movement in Goworowo were taken care of by me personally with the authorities and the circles of command in Warsaw. In my absence the work was conducted by the lieutenant and assistants, Shabsay Fridman, Yosef Krulevitsh and later, Shleyme Aplboym. In the last years Dovid Blumshteyn and later Elkhonen Kosovski, Hershl Gerlits and others were also added to the presidium.

The *Betar* recruited from level C, 18 year olds who automatically belonged to the *HaTsaR*, from level B, youth from 14 to 18 years old and level A, up to 14 years. Each *Shabes* afternoon in the local venue there was a parade where all members were present in their uniforms; later, an *oneg shabes*; and each Friday evening a “checkers evening”. In the summer months, after the parade, we would

[Page 167]

meet outside the town, give lessons and talk over actual Zionist issues, as well as do exercises. Each year on the 11th of Oder a Trumpeldor assembly took place, with readings, declarations and so on. The *Betar* also published a wall newspaper called *Tel-khay*. We had our own library. Besides the books that were given to us by the General Zionists, we had also bought new ones, and of course various party literature.

Until our entrance into the World Zionist Organization we had distributed *sheklim* and actively worked for the *Keren ha'yesod* and the *K.K.L.*, taken part in all the actions and undertakings and events at the head (first or second place) of the *K.K.L.* gatherings. It did not disturb us to conduct our activities for *Keren Tel-khay*. Besides the several actions we also emptied the three cornered, blue and white charity boxes every month, as well as organizing “flower days”.

* * *

At the end of 1932, Yosef Krulevitsh traveled for agricultural training to Ushtshilug-Lokatshe, Volyn, Ludmir Regiment. After working there for a year, he received a certificate from the “Palestine Office”. Jabotinsky was then against the individual certificates that were distributed to the Revisionists. He wanted them to be given as a Party, exactly as all the other parties did and so we ourselves would have disposal to them. Jabotinsky then issued an order (ms 60–?) that one should not accept any individual certificates. Krulevitsh had to resign from that and did not make *aliye* to *Erets*. (Today he is in America.)

A group of *Ha'tsair-Betar* with teacher Gilberg in the center

In front, *Beys-rim* from Regiment A (from right) L. Tenenboym may God avenge his blood. Gutman, M. Fridman may God avenge his blood, A. Govortshik and Kh. Segal

[Page 168]

Since the dealings with the certificates was a long-lasting one, we searched for various other ways to make *aliye*. The following from *Beys-rius* took the available opportunities.

Tsipora Grudka (today, Klibarski) left town in August 1932, with an excursion to the *Makabi* games which was organized by the engineer Zshelinski from Lodz;

Menukhe Grudka (today, Zeltser) came to the Land a few months later, also with an excursion organized by the Polish travel agency *Arbis;*

Rokhl Shapira (today, Zakharyahu) came to the Land after *Sukes* 1936 with the group of motorcyclists from *Betar* in Israel, who came to Poland with the aim of making fictitious marriages and returning with their "wives";

Idel Skurnik left for *Erets Yisroel* in 1936, along with her family;

Ester Gutman (today, Kantarovitsh) also traveled illegally.

Beys A khinus Betar in Ostrov-Mazieki, Lag b'oymer 1932. The P.V. exercises.

First row, from right: Shabsay Fridman and Yosef Drozd
Second row, from right: Avieyzer Sandala, Yosef Krulevitsh, Yehoshe Tenenboym, Dovid Blumshteyn, Gadol Botshan and B. Kasovski
Standing: Yehude Rits and the instructors Zshalandzsh and Ben-dror

* * *

In about 1933, we created a *Betar* -like agricultural training company subcommittee, like a branch of Ruzshan. The company commander was Elieyzer Treshtshanski

[Page 169]

from Bielsk-Podlask, an intelligent young man who also conducted the cultural work and often gave lectures. The *Betar* members did all the hard work in order to support it. They worked with Rozen and Kosovski in the sawmill and did not even reject chopping wood. Of course, our members helped in the work and the most interested one was Shleyme Apelboym.

The flourishing existence of the company and the sympathy that it got from the Goworowo population was not lost on the Leftist parties. They did everything they could to disrupt us and to drive us out of the town. They would incite the *goyim*, saying the *Betarim* would take their work and livelihood, and that led to oppositional fistfights. Once in such an incident Apelboym was wounded, receiving a blow on the back.

Then the police stepped in, who arrested several Jewish boys and prepared a trial, which had to take place in the Ostrolenke county court. The prosecutor wanted to make it a political trial. They judged it political terror, illegal activities, and so on. The Left circles threatened our members for giving witness. Shleyme Apelboym was warned in particular, and he had to leave town; he went to Bialystok and entered a *yeshiva.* When our members saw that the judgement could end with years of prison for the Jews, they withdrew their witness testimonies, and the beaters were freed just before the trial. About six months later the company was dissolved.

* * *

Despite our conflict with the certificates with the Jewish Agency, as seen above, the agricultural training proceeded. In 1934 a special proclamation about traveling to the training colony was made through our organization. Called up from our cell were Shleyme Apelboym and Avrom Mazes, who were taken for training to Zelve (near Slonim-Volkovski), where they stayed for a year. After their return to Goworowo Apelboym, as lieutenant commander, took over the work of the cell until he would make *aliye* in December 1937. He went with the Third *Aliye* of the *F.L.P.* In *Erets Yisroel* he rose to company commander in *Rosh Pina*, where he was very busy. After the verdict of Shleyme Ben-Yosef, Apelboym went over to *Ramat Gan* and became active in the ranks of the *TsAL*, directing very weighty assignments. Today a prominent member of *Heyrut*.

* * *

The Goworowo *Ha'tsair* and *Betar* participated in various national conferences which took place in Warsaw; and other such gatherings and meetings. Thus, the *Betar* cell participated in a regional gathering in Ostrov-Mazavietsk during *Lag b'oymer* 1932; in a gathering in the summer of that same year, in Bialystok

[Page 170]

with the participation of Yosef Klorman and others. In the summer of 1938, the cell took part in a *Betar* camp in Dlugashkov along with the cells from Ostrov-Mazavietsk, Ostrolenke, Vishkov and Ruzshan. We often met with the *Betar* members from Ruzshan in the Shtshavine forest on the summer *Shabosim.*

From time to time we brought in speakers from Warsaw, who presented open lectures. In most cases, we would rent large halls for these. Sometimes we sought out Dr. A. Lipman, Asher Zelig Lerman from the *Keren Tel-khay* (Asher Naur, the recently-deceased coeditor of *Yediot Akhronot*), Y.Sh. Peker, Yosef Krust, Yosef Krelman, and others. In 1934 we had a visit from Herr Yitskhak Gurion from *Erets Yisroel,* there since the Second *Aliye*, today a prominent leader, who came to Goworowo to visit the family of Yoel Levkovitsh.

During the 1935 plebiscite about creating a new Zionist organization (N.Ts.A.), everyone voted for Jabotinsky. There was no *Brit ha'Kanaim*, the so-called *grosmanistn* , in town. Despite the small "Fascists" and "Guns and Swords" we continued to grow. The Revisionist movement reckoned among the large parties in town. In our ranks were many youths from the *yeshivas*, and young women from the *Beys Yankev* schools, from the *folks shule* and youth from every stratum of the population. During our nearly ten year existence we struck deep roots. We were recognized for our active work by the *HaTsaR* and the *Betar* commissioner in Warsaw. I often used my

A large group of *Ha'TsaR* and *Betar* members

[Page 171]

personal contacts with them. To cite our carrying out our commands and for our active work for *Keren Tel-khay*, we received a golden token to add to our banner. Especially, in 1936 we, the writer of these lines, Shleyme Apelboym, Yosef Krulevitsh and Avrom Mazes Â, received the *Simon Ha'nedar*.

A group of *Betar* members from Level B

(From right): Gutman, Ester Gamora, Khone Kosovski, Sore Haravits, Hershl Gerlits, Ester Drozd, Eydl Skurnik, Brayne Grudke and Dovid Drozd

* * *

This is, in short, the history of the Revisionist movement from its founding; its rise and activity until the destruction of the town. We have mentioned only the persons who were the leaders the whole time. But we have not forgotten all the members not named and all the little brothers from Level A up to the older members who handed over the Revisionist movement idea and loyal Jabotinsky's ideals. The goal that they fought for, heart and soul, they were not able to realize. The Hitleristic murderers destroyed everything. Only a small part survived the gruesome war and by various ways and byways arrived in Israel. Few found their way to other lands. The largest number, though, did not avoid

[Page 172]

the bestial German-Nazi hands and shared the fate of the Six Million Jewish martyrs.

Let us stand silent for a while and remember with reverent honor all those who are no longer with us. May God take revenge for the spilling of their innocent young blood!

A document for *Betar* and for *Agudas Izrakh Tsioni* (*N.Ts.A.*)
Above center: the *Simon Ha'nedar*

[Page 173]

Mizrakhi, He'khaluts-Ha'mizrakhi, and *Ha'shomer-ha'dati*

by Y. Avi-Sore, Israel

Translated by Tina Lunson

The *Mizrakhi* organization in Goworowo was one of the first Zionist organizations in the town. The members recruited from the *hasidic* and *maskilish* [enlightened] circles and though they were few in number, they held a respected place in the communal and cultural life of the town.

Echoes of the intensive activity of the *Mizrakhi* soon after the First World War was evident in the reports and correspondence of the Central *Mizrakhi* organ *Ha'mizrakhi*, which was published in Warsaw. In number 19 of that organ, of January 1922, it was stated that the authorities had legalized the activities of *Mizrakhi* in Goworowo and that at a general meeting a committee had been elected, consisting of six members, Avrom Levin, chairman; Ali Grinberg, vice chairman; Y. L. Tandetshazsh (son-in-law of Mayer Romaner) secretary; Khonen Fridman, treasurer; Yisroel Leyb Kruk and Shmuel Tsudiker, administrative members. In a second correspondence there was a report about the cultural activity that the *Mizrakhi* was conducting in the town; in a new venue for the organization, they had founded a circle for studying Torah, *mishnayos* and Talmud; and they had created their own *minyen* for prayer. The visit by *Mizrakhi* representative Zalkind â€“ a son of the Kharkov Rov, was a great success. His brilliant lectures had drawn big crowds and thanks to him, 25 new members joined the *Mizrakhi*.

A great stir was caused in town by the visit of the *Mizrakhi* political leader Rov Hager, the Rov of Sosnovets. He presented several lectures in the great *shul*, which was packed full of men. And the women filled the women's *shul*. He was hosted by our *Rov* in his home, and although the *Rov* is not a *Mizrakhi* sympathizer, he still, in honor of the Sosnovets Rov and his grandson from Vizshnits, came to *shul* to hear his speeches. The great ideological leader of the *Mizrakhi* also paid a visit to Goworowo; the Tshekhonov Rov Mordkhe Bronrot, who himself stemmed from Goworowo and later became the Rov of Tel-Aviv.

The *Mizrakhi* members participated in the General Zionist activities; collected money for the *Keren kayemet* and *Keren ha'yesod*, dispersed

[Page 174]

sheklim and actively took part in the community, economic and cultural life of the town.

Y. L. Tandetshazsh,
may his memory be for a blessing

The proclaimed leaders of *Mizrakhi* were the scholar and *hasid* Reb Yisroel Leyb Kruk; the community activist and Enlightener Reb Elkhonen Fridman; Reb Shmuelke Tsudiker, who for many years occupied the office of delegate for *Keren kayemet* and member of the Jewish Council for its last term; a fine and honest community leader, the Aleksander Hasid Reb Yisroel Mayer Mishnayos; the timer merchant Reb Shabsay Verman; Reb Sholem Plotke from the artisan activists; Reb Dan Rozenberg, also a deputy for

Keren kayemet; and Reb Meyshe Skurnik. The latter was a brilliant speaker and colorful personality who played a large role in the town's life.

In 1935 many *yeshiva* folk who had gotten the Zionist idea after being in *yeshivas*, enrolled in *Mizrakhi*. They entered the youth departments *He-khaluts* and *Tseirey Mizrakhi*. The leaders were Yerakhmiel Drozd, Yosef Gurka, Yosef Zilbertson and Mayer Verman.

The *Ha'shomer ha'dati* was founded in Goworowo in 1936 (in Israel it is called *B'ney Akiva*). Among the founders of *Ha'shomer ha'dati* were Yankev Kruk, Gedalye Tsudiker, Mordkhe Apelboym, Yankev Rozen, Shmuel Shmelts and others. The *Ha'shomer ha'dati* developed itself, had a significant number of members, among them many *yeshiva* men. They conducted a multi-sided program in many areas and were recognized by the Warsaw Central.

For a long time the Goworowo *Ha'shomer ha'dati* published their own wall newspaper with artistic drawings by their leader Yankev Kruk.

The *Mizrakhi* venue and its youth organization were located on

[Page 175]

Bankova Street at Reb Mayer Volf Tehilim's for many years, and later on Koshtshushki Street at Reb Avrom Grudka's. The venue always bristled with activity and life and various exhibits. Sometimes mass meetings were held in the *Mizrakhi* venue with the participation of dozens of personalities from around the country. I recall the mass meeting against the British Agency after the publication of the *Aliye* Decree. Dozens of speakers were presented from the Central office and *Mizrakhi* members from Goworowo, one of them from *Ha'shomer ha'dati*. The hall was packed full and many people stood outside because of the lack of space.

There were almost no older *Mizrakhi* members left alive after the *Shoah*. And the majority of the young members were killed by the murderous Hitlerists in the war years.

A pity for those who are lost and are no longer with us.

The administration committee of *Ha'shomer ha'dati*

[Page 176]

Tseirey Agudas Yisroel

by Rabbi Yitskhak Shafran, America

Translated by Tina Lunson

As the religious Jews in Poland had organized themselves under the banner of *Agudas Yisroel*, some leaders in Goworowo, especially from the Ger Hasidim, took the initiative to create a section of *Agudas Yisroel* in the town. They brought in a speaker from Warsaw, called a meeting and several dozen men signed up to be members. But there it stayed. They did not do any specific work and no one felt their influence in town until the creation of *Tseirey Agudas Yisroel*, an organization of effervescent youth with fresh young energy. They rented a space, ordered a stamp, printed forms, hung up a sign and developed feverish activity that was soon felt in the town peoples' every step.

The *Tseirey Agudas Yisroel* in Goworowo was first founded in the 1930s and came as a reaction against the free youth organization of the left and right socialist parties and later, the Revisionist youth section *Betar*. Those youth societies had roiled the town, igniting a fire of conflict between the older and younger generations. Fathers attacked the local venues, destroyed their furniture and beat the children; the *Rov* created a scene. Of course, the children won. Their success was huge. A boy, a girl of 13 years, already belonged to an organization. The parties developed big propaganda programs and worked to win over more members. In the local venues they entertained themselves with songs and dance, with reading books and listening to speeches, which had a wildly attractive pull for the younger generation. The result was indeed that the study house was empty and many *yeshiva* boys left the *yeshivas*.

Some *yeshiva* boys decided to start a fight and to use the same weapons as the free organizations. If the others sing and dance, they could sing and dance. The only remaining question was a suitable place and what kind of name to give the new youth organization. Meyshe Ziltsertson suggested *Mizrakhi*, others wanted *Tseirey Agudas Yisroel*. In order to remain non-political, they decided on *Tiferes bokhurim*.

That compromise was not approved by Reb Leyvi Varshaviak.

[Page 177]

He said that for him it was neither milk nor meat. He warned the Ger hasidim and agitated the *Rov*, that they must use the name *Tseirey Agudas Yisroel* instead. A council was quickly made up with Leyvi Varshavniak, Meyshe Mazes, Khayim Kosovski, Itshe Shafran and others. They rented a space and sponsored a celebratory opening with great fanfare. The *Rov* taught the audience the first page of Talmud for the *daf yomi* program, they sang and enjoyed themselves for hours around tables with tablecloths.

Later, a revolutionary idea occurred to one of us to create a *minyen* of only youths, where the cantor, Torah reader and *gabays* were all boys. The success was immense. Many respected householders supported the youth *minyen*. Such fine Jews as Mayer Volf Tehilim, Avrom Yisroel Trushkevitsh, Itshe Kosovski, Yekhezkel Kheyn, Menashe Fish and others. There were other regular attendees. They supported us and helped with everything. Rebi Naftali Gemora was our prayer leader for the Days of Awe and studied *midrash* with us every *Shabes*.

On holidays when the *yeshiva* folk came home, the local *Tseirey* venue was a very lively place. Half the town came to the *Simkhes-Torah hakofes* to see the fervent dancing. The whole house shook.

The position of the *Tseirey Agudas Yisroel* in the town became very strong; so much so, that at the last Jewish Council elections they set up their own slate and presented two council members. Thanks to the *Tseirey* , the *Agudas Yisroel* reorganized and became a stronger factor in town.

Tseirim from the area at the conference in Dlugoshodle, summer 1936

[Page 178]

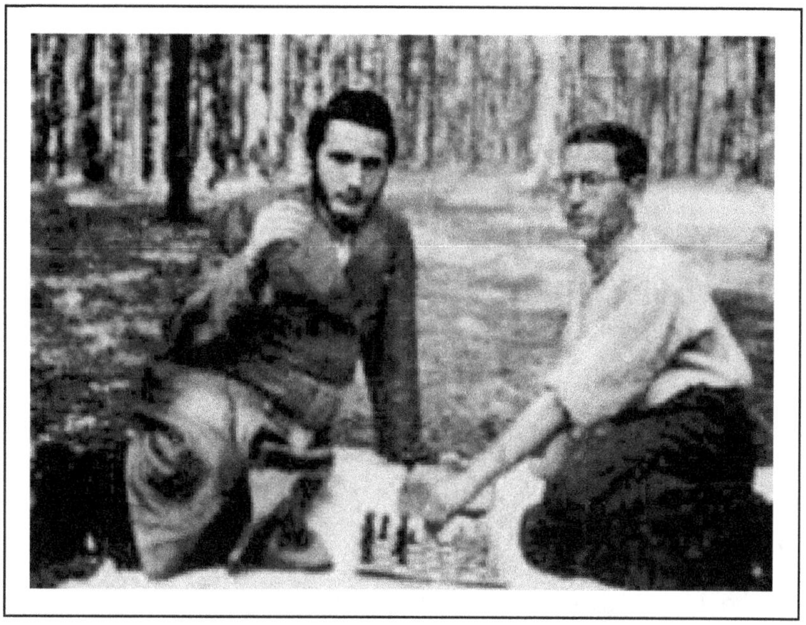

Yitskhak Shafran (right) and Menakhem'l Kalish may God avenge his blood, the youngest son of the Amshinover Rebi Rov Yosele of blessed memory, at a round of chess in the Dlugoshodle forest, summer 1939.

The memory of each murdered Jew in the town is sacred and dear to me but, here I will mention a few members of the *Tseirey Agudas Yisroel* in Goworowo for whom this article is the appropriate place. The member Leyb Hersh Holtsman of blessed memory, his simple honesty, his self-sacrificing work for the organization; when he sang *khevet m'shomayim v'roa* with this beautiful clear voice the entire town trembled. Who could forget such a good, fine friend as Khayim Kosovski, may God avenge his blood? We sat for hours immersed in sublimation, listening how he played heartfelt melodies on his violin. How could one not mention the sincere saint Reb Hershl Rubin, the candy-maker; his prayer leading, his teaching, his agility? He was a flaming fire for Jewishness.

I recall a story about him, which it is a *mitsve* to publish. It was the last year before the war, during the night before the eve of *Shavues*. I was by chance in his house and was unintentionally a witness to a spat between him and his wife. He wanted to travel to Ger for *Shavues*, to the Rebi, and she would in no way agree to that. In order to be certain that he would not leave without her knowing, she locked the door and put the key in her pocket.

What did he do?

In the middle of the night, he opened a window and ran off to Ger in just his housecoat. At the close of the holiday, in taking his leave, the Ger Rebi wished him “a good sealing”. Surprised, Reb Hershl wondered, such a blessing is appropriate for *Yon-kiper*, for *Hashone-raba*, but how does it fit into *Shavues*? The other hasidim who heard it also took it as a marvel.

A few months later, when the Second World War broke out, Reb Hershl Rubin fled to Vishkove. After the Nazis carried out the first slaughter of the Vishkove Jews, Reb Hershl was found in *shul*, shot to death, wrapped in a *talis* with a Torah scroll in his arms. May God avenge his blood.

[Page 179]

Basya and *Banos Agudas Yisroel*

by *Rabonit* Rivke Rozental-Shtshetshina, America

Translated by Tina Lunson

The Goworowo *Beys Yankev* school for girls was one of the first *Beys Yankev* schools founded in Poland at the end of the 1920s. Ms. Sore Shenirer, the founder of the Krakow *Beys Yankev* seminary and the school network across the land, came specially to Goworowo in order to attend the establishment and opening of the school.

The *Beys Yankev* school was a great success from its very first existence. Pupils from every level of the population enrolled, from very religious to secular homes, from wealthy positions and the poorer classes.

The program of the school was a rich one and had included all sides of Jewish life. It taught Torah, the Prophets and Writings, Jewish history and conducted discussions about Judaism and religious philosophy. All this was offered by qualified women teachers, permeated with belief and a sincerity which spoke to the hearts of the young women students. There was also a drama club connected to the school, which gave public presentations especially for *Khanike* and *Purim*.

Several male leaders concerned themselves with the intellectual form of the school and with its financial issues. Leyvi Varshaviak, today in Israel, made many contributions to the development of the school and later, the extraordinary young man, Yisroel Burshtin, may God avenge his blood, who was so tragically and cruelly murdered by the Nazi persecutors. In the last years Yitskhak Shafran, one of the leaders of the *Tseirey Agudas Yisroel* (today in America), managed the school. The above mentioned leaders and even more, devoted their work, heart and soul. They concerned themselves with the existence and broadening of the *Beys Yankev* school. Later they also

[Page 180]

Banos and *Basye* clubs of Goworowo and Ostrolenke during a gathering.
In the center, the teacher Leye Gulevski.
Summer 1926

founded a *Banos Agudas Yisroel* for grown girls which developed a broad activity in the area of Jewishness, culture, social questions and especially *Erets-Yisroel*. The council consisted of the following members: Rivke Shtshetshina, Eydl Kshonzshka and Miriam Rokhl Hertsberg may God avenge her blood. The *Basye* and *Banos* clubs

A large group of *Banos* and *Basye* clubs with the
Bas Yankev teacher Ester Obershteyn from Grodne in the center Winter 1938-39

[Page 181]

collected money for the *Keren ha'yeyshev*, made "flower days" and organized presentations for *Erets Yisroel.*

Today, after the Holocaust, when one makes an assessment, of what remains of the entire *Beys Yankev* movement, what became of the *Basye* and *Banos* organizations after the great tragedy, the summation is a sad one. Only a few survivors can be found in Israel, America and other countries today, but the majority of the girls were tragically cut down during the Nazi persecutions. I do not know if it is a consolation, but according to what I have heard, all the members of *Banos* and of the *Beys Yankev* school, sanctified God in their lives and deaths, and even in the worst situations did not forget that they were brave daughters of the glorious Jewish people.

May the memory of them remain always fresh in our memories!

From right: Brokhe Grudka, Yente Vrubel (Kalish), Feyge Mondra (Mlave), Miriam Hetsberg and Fraska

1939

[Page 182]

Ha'shomer ha'tsair

by Elieyzer Levin, Israel

Translated by Tina Lunson

The Goworowo cell of *Ha'shomer ha'tsair* was founded at the end of 1927. To tell the truth, we did not have great success. We had no money to rent a space and almost all the youth already belonged to some other organization, like *Frayhayt*, *Tsukunft* and others. But, encouraged by the help of the head of the cell in Ruzshan, Leybl Bukhner, we decided to create a cell in Goworowo and we were not disappointed.

A short time after the founding we already numbered about 100 young people of both sexes. The leadership consisted of Hershke Granat, head of the cell; Meyshe Levin, lieutenant and recorder; Feyge Sheyniak, Nekhe Shakhter and Rokhl Vaysbord. As we did not have a venue, our meetings took place in the open field outside the town. Once on the "New Road", often along the road to Pasheki, or even on the *Probostva* near the Jewish windmills. The meetings of the separate groups took place in the private homes of the cell leader, Yitke Rozen, Khave Molovani and others. We also often arranged for conventions in the Shtshavine

A group of *Ha'shomer ha'tsair* after its founding in 1927[a]
The leadership sits across the front.

(From right) Nekhe Shakhter, Hershke Granat, Feyge Sheyniak and Meyshe Levin.(a)

[Page 183]

First row, from right: Hershke Granat, Nekhe Shakhter, Ruven Shmelts, Leybl Shvarts and Yosef Krulevitsh
Standing: Leye Zilber, Yetke Rozen, Leye Grudka, Blume Govortshik and Yitskhak Blum

1928[b]

Forest with the Ruzshan cell of *Ha'shomer ha'tsair*. We would hear speeches, do various exercises and get advice from them, the older cell about our future activities.

Over time, we became a factor in the town. We contributed to the total of the General Zionists, who sometimes allowed us to use their venue. In general, most of our meetings took place there. Later we had a long-term place with the Right *Poaley tsion*. We were representatives in the council of the *K. K. L.* and were in first place as collectors. Besides the work of emptying the blue and white charity boxes each month, carrying out "flower days" and wedding gatherings, we also made money at other opportunities. We once gave a presentation under the name *The Cantonists*, in which the main roles were played by the writer of these lines, Nekhe Shakhter and Shleyme Apelboym. From that, we gave half of the revenue to the *K. K. L.* In 1929 the *Shomrey Shabes*, headed up by the town *Rov*, decided to make the *eruvim* for the town anew. They installed large poles around the town and planned to lay the wires across them. But there were no experts in climbing the poles available. When I learned about that little piece of work, I went to the *Rov* and proposed that for a certain sum contributed to the *K. K. L.* (that was – one *zlotych* per post), I was prepared to climb up and lay the wires. The *Rov*, who was an opponent of Zionism, did not agree with that, but, having no alternative, he had to give in to the "business".

[Page 184]

I do not remember how many *zlotych* I earned for the *K. K. L.*, but according to the currency of the times it was a large sum.

In 1929 the Mlove branch of *Ha'shomer ha'tsair* to which we belonged, arranged a summer camp in the village Alatave Pagaze (?), under the directorship of member Haykl. About one thousand *Shomrim* participated there, from Ruzshan, Ostrov-Mazieki, Ostrolenke, Mlove and many other towns. We were about 20 members from Goworowo. The course, which was run under a strict military discipline, lasted for two weeks.

First row, from right: Sore Dine Engel, Nekhe Shakhter and Rivke Grinberg
Standing: Leye Olek, Khane Likhtman and Leye Zilber

1931

We were involved with sports, learning to march, listening to various speeches and lectures and getting accustomed to hard pioneer training conditions. When we returned to town we were inspired to carry on our further work. We marched through the town in full uniform several times, with our banner, to the tune of a trumpet, like soldiers.

Our cell was in full bloom for several years. With the death of our cell leader

[Page 185]

Hershl Granat, who died at a young age in 1932, our work was weakened. It still existed officially for a while, but in about 1933 the cell dissolved, and the youth melted into the other existing Zionist youth organizations.

From right: Leye Rotshteyn, Leye Gurka, Feyge Ozdoba. Elieyzer Levin, Khave Molovani, Nekhe Shakhter and Hershke Granat

Notes from Lester Blum:

a. Abraham I. Blum - standing 19th from the right.
b. Abraham I. Blum - on horse far left of the picture.

[Page 186]

The Left *Poaley-tsion*

Neyekh Karvat, Israel

Translated by Tina Lunson

The Left *Poaley-tsion* in Goworowo was founded in about 1923. The first constitutional meeting and member gathering took place at Leyzer Aleyarzsh's home, with the attendance of the later famous historian Dr. Emanuel Ringelblum, delegated from the Warsaw Party Central. The following people were voted onto the committee: Avrom Vaysbord, Neyekh Karvat, Tuvye Kas, Khaye Vaysbord, the teacher Alter Hokhshteyn and others.

Although few in numbers, the members with their conscious ideas conducted broad cultural and party related activities. We took part in almost all the Zionist actions in the town. From time to time, we also brought in speakers, party activists from the Central who presented in rented venues in town. As well, we were visited and given readings by Yankev Zerubavl, Peterzeyl and others.

The party developed poorly, because we did not have any young people. No new members came to take the places of members who had immigrated or left the town. We did not even have the means to rent our own space, and all our activities were held in the private homes of the members.

In the last years we conducted our activities together with the *Poaley-tsion* organization in Ruzshan. We held joint gatherings in the Shtshavine forest. At one such gathering, the well-known *Poaley-tsion* leader Yankev Zerubavl took part.

Over the two decade existence of the *Poaley-tsion* newspaper, *Arbeter tsaytung*, we distributed the paper around Goworowo. We also made large sums of money for the *Palestiner arbeter fund.*

The organization in town numbered about 35 members. Only a few individuals survived. The majority were murdered along with all Polish Jewry.

[Page 187]

The Brener Library

by Avrom Holtsman, Israel

Translated by Tina Lunson

The library named after Yosef Khayim Brener was created after the *Poaley-tsion* Zionist Socialists separated from the General Zionist Organization. Previously, there had existed only the General Zionists library *Ha'tekhiya* which had just been created before the end of the First World War by Binyumin

Ginzburg with the managing partner Meyshe Dronitsa (Israel), Khayim Gerlits (America) and Dovid Aron Grudke may God avenge his blood.

I still recall the times when not only a book, but a simple newspaper was looked at askance by the religious fanatics. This happened to my father Menashe of blessed memory. In 1913 during the Beylis Trial he once took a copy of the *Moment* newspaper with him into the Vurke *shtibl* and the watchmaker Yankev Yosef Plantshok glanced at it to see details about the famous judgement. By chance Avrom Fayvl Nayman noticed it and started a big to-do. "How is it possible! desecration, sin and evil doing against the rabbis..." When my sister Yetke wanted to read a booklet, she had to subscribe to the Ostrove Jewish Library.

The first kernels of the *Ha'tekhiya* library also had to sustain sanctions from the Goworowo religious fanatics who influenced the town *Rov* not to allow the library to be located at Ms. Devashe's. In those times the confused, over-heated religious "Cossacks" wanted to serve by example for the neighborhood and they tore into the local library and burned all the books. In court they maintained that they were prepared for "martyrdom", to take any punishment upon themselves. In Goworowo it did not come to that. The *Ha'tekhiya* library found a space and began to conduct their activities anew.

I was then studying at the Lomzshe Yeshiva. There too, I read books in secret and made friends with Simkhe Sapershteyn, the correspondence for *Haynt* newspaper for the Lomzshe region. When I returned from the *yeshiva*, I took over the library office from Khayim Gerlits and at the same time was elected secretary of the Zionist Organization.

I began conducting an intensive task of putting in order and cataloging,

[Page 188]

binding books and organizing a reading room for the Jewish press, *Haynt, Moment, Ilustrirte vokh, Literarishe bleter*, *Velt shpigl* and others. We arranged literary and entertainment evenings with the participation of the members, Meyshe Sarna, Meyshe Granat, A. Holtsman, Bunem Shafran may God avenge his blood and Yitskhak Viroslov may God avenge his blood. We ourselves created a humoristic newspaper with parodies on small town types and general events, then fitting them to suitable melodies from theater and presented shows in the town and in the area. That brought in a lot of revenue for the library.

At that time the younger Zionist members began grouping to *He'khaluts* from the Right *Poaley-tsion*. People communicated in secret with the Central at Dszhike Number 11 in Warsaw and they sent the representative Kh. Tiger. A committee of members was elected, Meyshe Granat, A. Holtsman, Meyshe Sarna, Zelig Reytshik, Aron Shron, Yisroel Kutner, Simkhe Bunem Shafran may God avenge his blood and Yitskhak Viroslav may God avenge his blood. Our group began drawing many young people from the wealthier circles to itself. That called up opposition, both among the older members of the General Zionists who saw in us as rebels and renegades, as well as among the leadership of the *Bund* who held themselves as the only representative for the Jewish laborer. Once when we were preparing for a lecture from Dr. Gliksman, a group of *Bundists* headed by Leybl Kersh showed up at our venue and obstructed the speaker. By chance the policeman, Lada was just passing by, and he deflected and punished the disruptors.

The General Zionists' space was too tight for us, so we, at *Purim* 1927, rented our own venue, from the midwife on Ostrolenke Road. At the same time, we proclaimed the founding of the *Yosef Khayim Brener Library* with a celebratory reception where one could also greet and wish well to the members Meyshe Granat and Shmuel Rozenberg (the husband of Rivke Shafran) who were traveling away for Pioneer training.

We began a recruiting action for new books for the Brener Library. At the same time we turned to the General Zionists, for them of give us a portion of the *Ha'tekhiya* Library and take over the debts that we still owed for books.

But a surprise awaited us there. The General Zionists simply laughed at us and cynically answered, "We don't take anyone back from the cemetery".

That response boiled our blood. It angered me especially, because I personally had bought the books, bound them, and I was registered at the money exchanges which involved a fee to be paid at the beginning of each month. We decided not to let the matter rest.

Meanwhile we had moved into a two-room space at Katervos's. All the members had striven to clean and organize the venue. We had

[Page 189]

acquired wood by "taking" it at night from the wood warehouses of Kosovski-Rozen and Shabsay Verman and we ourselves built the tables, benches, cabinets and a stage with decorations. I got oil paints myself from my father's shop (we maintained that for a cultural goal one may "acquire" things by stealth).

As on the 20th of *Tamuz* there would be a commemoration evening for Hertsl, I arranged for the event to take place at the General Zionists' venue. My comrades were angry with me, but I had an intention for it. While the speeches were going on I made an impression of the key in chewing gum. Member Hershl Krulevitsh, a locksmith by trade, fashioned a key, and I and members Yisroel Kutner, Hershl Krulevitsh and Yankev Drozd may God avenge his blood, worked out a plan on how to take the books from the *Ha'tekhiya* that had been so unrightfully taken from us.

On the eve of *Rosh ha'shone* in the year *tes-reysh-pey-khes*, at night, I went with my father to recite *slikhes* in the Vurke *shtibl*. My father was the cantor and I helped him with the singing. In the middle of the service, I disappeared, and along with the above mentioned members "checked out" from the *Ha'tekhiya* Library several sacks of books and buried them near Yankev Drozd's windmill.

Having done that bit of work, I went back to the *shtibl* and, along with the congregation, beat my heart at the recitation of the *al kheyt*. My alibi was ready.

In the morning the town went off its wheels. A sensation – books stolen from *Ha'tekhiya*. Soon witnesses were found who had seen me carrying the books at night.

A lawsuit was processed in the Tshervine court. The main witness to the accusation was Leybl Kersh, whom I think just wanted revenge for the seven days' arrest he got for disrupting Dr. Gliksman's lecture.

But the witness got lost. He did not know who else took part in the event. I could not have carried all the sacks alone. He only saw me from a distance and how could he say he recognized me by my looks. The essence, I was set free and had the right to complain against him for claiming false witness. I, of course, did not use that privilege. We did not need to draw out the matter.

Around Passover 1930, in partnership with *Ha'shomer ha'tsair*, we rented a large hall and made a celebratory opening. Then we dug up the "booty" and took the books to the Brener Library.

Of course, today we look back with different eyes on those events. A little older and more sedate. But I do understand those times of youth, burning hot, that did not know of holding back and restraint when dealing with an idealistic goal and a community issue.

[Page 190]

The Agricultural Training Camp *Pulkha* in Tshirnye

by Aron Shron, Israel

Translated by Tina Lunson

Although the Agricultural Training Camp *Pulkha* in Tshirnye only existed for little more than six months, it notes a fine chapter of Zionist work. I will therefore describe here the history of its development and activity up to its dissolution.

It was 1925. We, a group of the Right *Poaley-tsion,* had just joined the General Zionist Organization. In many members, the idea of making *aliye* to *Erets Yisroel* was already ripe. We turned to the *He'khaluts* Center in Warsaw to send a few members for agricultural training. Their answer was negative, as they did not have any free training positions available, but they suggested that we ourselves should create an agricultural training point in our area and they would help us make it so.

We asked the *He'khaluts* Center to send us more candidates. In Goworowo we already had the following, Bunem Shafran, Zelig Hertsberg, Yitskhak Shpitolevitsh (all murdered), Zelig Reytshik (today in Belgium), Meyshe Sarna, Yisroel Kutner, Berl Tsudiker and the writer of these lines (all in Israel).

From the beginning, we pushed against financial difficulties. We needed money to purchase various work tools and cooking equipment; and then we had an ingenious idea. At that time, the new building for the study house was just being finished. Yitskhak Blumshteyn and I went to the town *Rov* and asked him if he would give us the job of painting it. The *Rov* agreed. We received 120 *zlotych* for our work. For that money we could buy the necessary things, and in a few days we were ready to travel.

[Page 191]

First row, from right: Aron Shron and Zelig Reytshik
Second row: Yente Viernik, Malke Shtern and Garnek
Third row: Berl Tsudiker, Zelig Hertsberg, Tsvi Poyzner, Kalman Kurapotve, Ash and Yitskhak Shpitolevitsh
Fourth row: Yisroel Kutner, Meyshe Sarna, Ester Mandra (from Vishkove), Khaye Blume Vonsiak and Bunem Shafran

We hired a horse and wagon and we, the above mentioned eight boys, took the household goods and set out for Tshirnye. I recall that we had a large procession. The whole town came out to the bridge to accompany the first pioneers for Pioneering work. Arriving at the place, a disappointment awaited us. The apartment that the Prince had promised was not yet ready. We were left without an alternative and turned to the local blacksmith, Reb Borekh Frid (his son Khayim and his family are now in Israel). He put us up, temporarily, above his smithy shop and his wife cooked a lunch for us. More than once we woke up smeared with soot, with faces like *Purim* players. Some of the time we slept in the grain barn on straw, beside the Prince's horses. We greeted all this with love and got up very early to the work in the fields. After ten days our two room barrack (half sunk in the ground) was ready.

We were in contact with the Central again, reported about our work and asked that they send more people to us. A few days later the following members arrived from Warsaw, Tsvi Poyzner and Yosef Novina; from Otvotsk, Tsvi Plint; from Vishkove, Ester Mondra (all in Israel); from Mokove,

[Page 192]

Khaye Blume Vansiak; from Ostrolenke, member Ash; from Dlugoshadle, the women members Malke Shtern (today in Israel), Yente and Bernalts Viernik; and the male members Kalman Kuropatve and Holtsman; from Yadove, member Garnek and others. We became a group of 25 Pioneers and could run a good operation. We chose an administration in which our members Zelig Reytshik and Meyshe Sarna were involved. Tsvi was elected as secretary. He was an intelligent young man, knew Hebrew well and had already done practical agricultural work (he came from Russia). We were also already doing cultural work, learning Hebrew, conducting member discussions, making a small library and so on. And the Center sent out more people from time to time who presented lectures.

Each day another daily pair (a boy and a girl) was designated, whose assignment it was to keep the residence in order, cook and bring breakfast to the members in the field. Three times a week the daily pair was given a horse and wagon by the Prince, and they traveled to Goworowo to buy products such as meat, bread and other necessities.

During this time we became accustomed to the hard physical work. We cut the grain, hay and handled the separators. Three men from our group, Hertsberg, Shpitolevitsh and I, went into the woods and cut down large trees, loaded them onto wagons and brought them to the estate with horses. We were taught how to handle the Prince's horses. The estate manager was pleased with us. Indeed, we did no worse than the Christians at the work.

The non Jewish workers tried to scare us, saying that when it came to the cutting we would not be able to handle it and would run away, because standing in the field the whole day and cutting wheat is hard labor. But we had the strength for that too. Some of us went through a short course in cutting with the scythe and quickly grasped the rules of it. The Christian workers kept us specially in their midst during the cutting to keep us in place. Other members then were occupied with gathering the cut wheat, binding it in sheaves and standing them in rows for drying. That was also not light work. We did it all with industry and will, knowing the goal, and to see that everyone can work.

The order of the day was full to overflowing. Up to go to work at dawn. After working for two or three hours, the pair on duty brought us breakfast. For lunch we came back to the house to eat and rest a little. At sunset we ended work and came back home. After washing and a little rest and after the evening meal, we had a lesson in Hebrew. Then a general discussion, singing and dancing. From time to time some

[Page 193]

friends came for an evening, as for a *Shabes*. We were free to go to the town to visit the family and friends. Besides that, almost every *Shabes*, some friends from Goworowo visited us.

The group *Shomer Shabes* from Goworowo decided to hold oversight of us over *kashrus*. Right on the second Friday, as we were just back in our own apartment, Reb Yesheyahu Hertsberg may God avenge his blood paid us an official visit. He was staying with the Frid family and we were observing *Shabes* faithfully and properly. We all welcomed the sabbath, made *kidish*, sang *zmiros* and ate a *Shabes* feast, with fish and all the other dishes. Of course, he also visited our kitchen, inspected the meat and dairy utensils and expressed his satisfaction.

A month later Reb Avrom Shafran may God avenge his blood came to visit for a *Shabes*. He was with us, eating the cold dishes with us (we did not have any *tsholent* to serve), and in the evening he went back home. Also, my father Reb Yisroel Yitskhak may God avenge his blood visited us often. But, in order to spare him any unnecessary trouble, I asked him to come during the week. After returning from such a visit, he paid personal visits to the parents of the Goworowo Pioneers, to tell them that he had checked and that everything was in order. We did indeed observe *kashrus* and avoided as far as possible desecrating the *Shabes*, so that our observant parents would not have any unnecessary anxieties. It was a fact that even in the midst of "cutting season" we took *Shabes* rest.

On *L"g b'oymer* we got a vacation from the Prince. We used it and went through the forest on foot to Dlugoshadle. We attended a concert there that evening

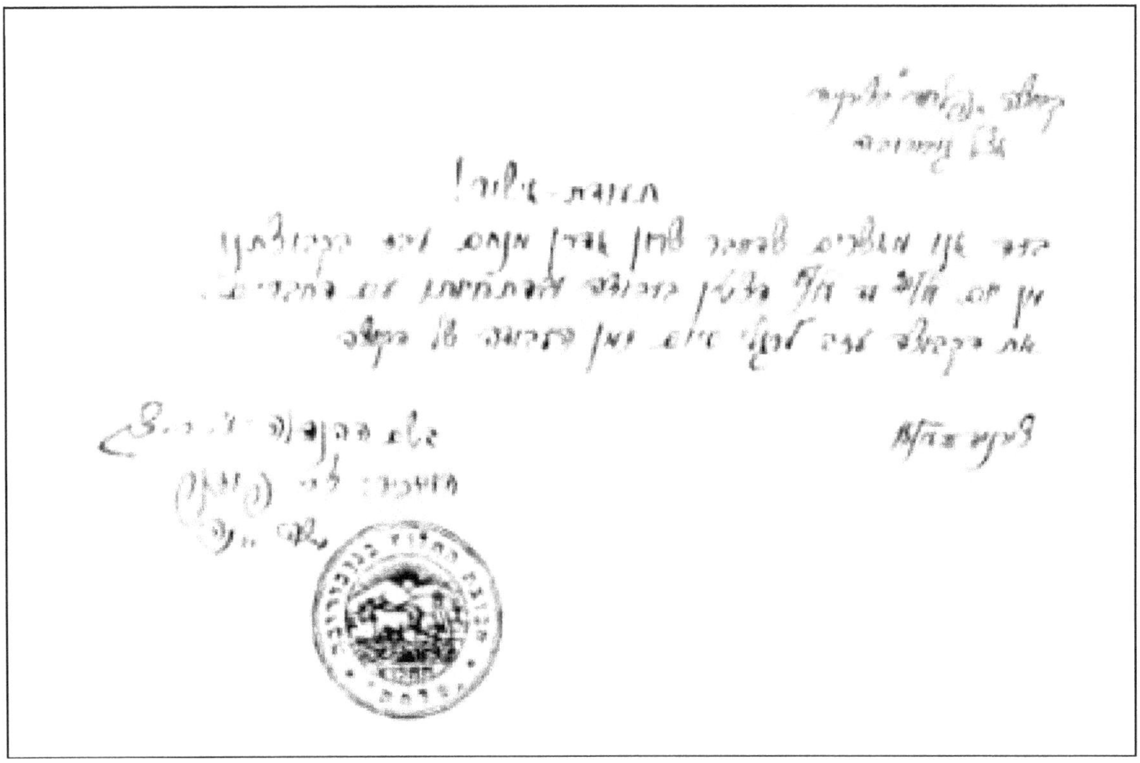

A certificate for our settlement after finishing the agricultural training

[Page 194]

(we had members with artistic abilities) and the town took us in with great enthusiasm.

After working for half a year, our agricultural course ended, and we received the appropriate certifications from the Prince. A member came down from the *He'khaluts* Center, conducted examinations among us and gave testimonials to a number of members, so they could then make *aliye*. It is worth noting, that not all could sustain the heavy physical work and had gone back home after a while.

The agricultural *kibuts* in Tshirnye was then liquidated and we shipped the whole inventory (tools, utensils, dishes, books) to the Center in Warsaw, along with about 100 *zlotych* that we had managed to save up.

Because of the opposition from his parents, Meyshe Sarna did not travel to *Erets Yisroel.* And I could not make *aliye* because I was called into the Polish military service, where I stayed for two and a half years. When I came back and inquired at the *He'khaluts* Center for my certificate, they refused it and told me to go to agricultural training again. I refused and went to my sister in Ostrov-Mazowiecki, where I became active in the party *Poaley-Tion* Zionist Socialists and in the dramatic circles. In 1930 I went back to Goworowo and continued my activities in the movement and in the dramatic circles. In August 1932 I finally made *aliye,* along with my wife Devore and others who also used the [tourist] excursions to the *Makabi* games in *Erets-Yisroel.*

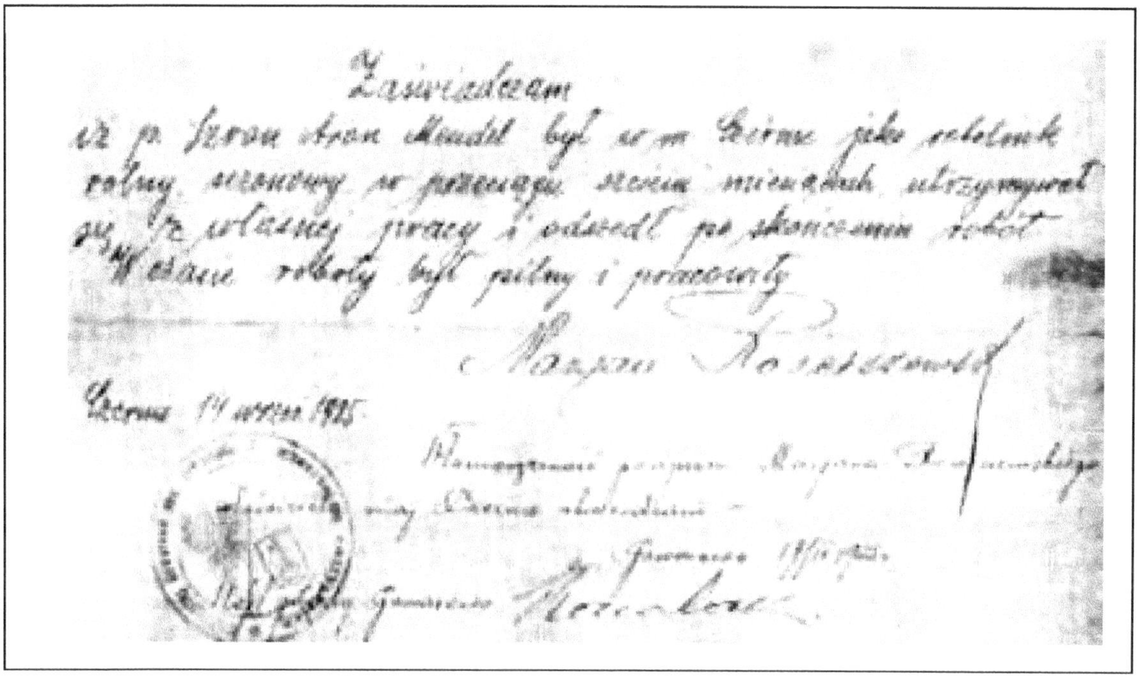

Zaświadczam

Certificate from the Tshirnye Prince Rashtshishevski after completing the agricultural training. His signature was confirmed by the village mayor Karolak with the stamp from the community council.

[Page 195]

The Preparatory Training Point in Pasheki

by Leyvi Varshaviak, Israel

Translated by Tina Lunson

The preparatory training group named after the famous *Aguda* leader and *Sejm* deputy Rov Eli Kirshboym, in Pasheki, was created at my initiative in 1934. Twelve members of the *Agudas Yisroel* in Poland took part in that Pioneer colony, including the following four members from Goworowo, the writer of these lines as founder and chairman, Meyshe Mozes, Yosef Tehilim may God avenge his blood, and Meyshe Galant of blessed memory.

The work place for the training was in a concrete factory at the train station in Pasheki, that fashioned blocks, sidewalk tiles, water pipes for wells and so on, and belonged to the Goworowo proprietor Reb Mayer Volf Tehilim. The goal was that the training members would learn the concrete trade, which at that time was extremely useful in *Erets Yisroel.*

The members worked eight hours a day in the factory, after which they spent time as a community, prayed as a group, studied Torah lessons and listened to readings about various topics.

I personally participated in the training for only four months. I was ousted by the Palestine Office in Warsaw because of a certain injustice by the son-in-law of Mayer Posheker, who willfully reported to the Palestine Office that I left the training each Thursday in order to trade in the marketplace.

The best lie is a half-truth. It was, truly, a correct assertion because I used to travel each Thursday to Goworowo to the market to purchase food products and other needed things for the training point. But the inspectors from the Palestine Office who came to Pasheki on a certain Thursday and did not find me there, did not comprehend the motive and ousted me from the training. I went on to another training point near Warsaw.

Of those at the Pasheki training there remain only two members, myself and Elkhonen Lubart, who lives in Kriat-Motseki.

I will take this opportunity to provide a few moments from my community activities in Goworowo. I would like to list to my credit the founding of the *Beys-Yankev* school, for which I was almost the only one standing by the cradle at the founding. I will only mention the huge assistance of the town rabbi,

[Page 196]

Rov Alter Meyshe Mordkhe Burshtin may God avenge his blood and of the Rebitsn Ginendl of blessed memory who devoted much time and energy to the school and produced financial help; and thanks to them the school could develop and bring about an intellectual revolution in the town. The enthusiastic assistance of many of the town's Jews came later. It was from the *Beys-Yankev* school that the youth organization *Basye* was created as well as *Banos Agudas Yisroel.*

The training group with Leyvi Varshaviak in the center

On the left: Meyshe Moses and Meyshe Galant of blessed memory
Standing above on the right: Yosef Tehilim may God avenge his blood

I had many helpers in the broadening of the Ger *shtibl*. When I arrived in Goworowo the Ger *minyen* was in a private residence at Velvl Blumshteyn's. After a completed action a space was rented at Yankev Shtshetshina's, and after that, with the help of Rov Burshteyn may God avenge his blood, they built their own building.

The *Tseirey Agudas Yisroel* organization, which numbered about 30 to 40 members soon after its beginning, was founded at my initiative. The founding council consisted of the following five members, Leyvi Varshaviak, Yitskhak Shafran, Avrom Yisroel Trushkevitsh may God avenge his blood, Tsvi Rubin of blessed memory, the candy-maker and Khayim Kosovski may God avenge his blood. I was also elected as representative from *Agudas Yisroel* to the administration of the town *Gemiles khesed* fund.

After my *aliye* to *Erets Yisroel* in January 1936, I also stayed in close contact with Goworowo Jews and was always curious to know what was happening there.

[Page 197]

The training group at work

The Goworowo members in the picture are: Leyvi Varshaviak (third from left), Meyshe Mozes (fifth from left),
Yosef Tehilim may God avenge his blood (second from right) and Meyshe Galant of blesses memory (fifth from right)

[Page 198]

The Drama Circles

by Avrom Holtsman, Israel

Translated by Tina Lunson

The first performances in Goworowo began with the cantor Yosef Khayim, who lived in the town just before the First World War. The older generation remembers him well, the merry cantor with his group of performers. They performed on the days of *Purim*, with gay little songs and various artistic skits and went around from house to house for little gifts of food or money. The money was given exclusively to benevolent ends, like the Passover fund, the fund for poor brides, the poor house and others. Later when the number of needy people multiplied and they could no longer wait from *Purim* to *Purim*, they performed at every wedding. They sang, imitated various types of people and otherwise entertained the guests. They showed how a Cossack would chat with a Jewish elementary school teacher, with a little Russian, a little Polish and, of course, a little Yiddish. This brought out a lot of laughter from the audience who were happy to toss contributions into the charity box.

After the First World War there were already modern performances coming to the town. They played pieces in an appropriate venue with scenery, with make-up and sets. In those days, Meyshe Bengelsdorf (Ester Malke's son) came from Russia, where he had completed an acting school. He performed in Goworowo with a group of amateurs, to great success. For a few years there was also a youth choir under the direction of Meyshe Brukhanski (a younger brother of cantor Malkiel). He was a good cantor and singer. The choir had many public performances.

In 1922 the play, *Di shekhite* by Yankev Gordin was performed with the participation of Binyumin Ginzburg, Yekhiel Pshisusker, Peysakh Trukhnovski, Eydel Levitan, Dovid Glagover, Feyge Feyntsayg and others. Other performances were also presented. The revenue was designated for the library at the Zionist organization. Various evenings of entertainment with artistic programs were also arranged for the same goal. For the 11th of Oder, they also produced the one-act play, *Der shoymer* by Z. Vidervisht; *A doktor – a soykher* by Sholem Aleykhem, with the participation of Sore Gemora, Avrom Romaner and others.

[Page 199]

The number of amateurs increased during that time; and their artistic abilities developed. We had our own director, a make-up technician, a parody writer, a promoter and so on.

In 1926, the acting troupe Shitarski–Brofman–Noyman arrived in Goworowo from Warsaw. The Zionist Organization made an agreement with them, that they would help with technical and human resources and so receive a certain amount of the revenue. Under their direction we then put on *Di rumenishe khasene*, *Vu zenen mayne kinder*, *Der dybbuk*, *Der greyser moment*, *Di shvartse khofe* and *Khashe di yoseyme* which went off with great success. Our local resources who took part were Bunem Shafran, Leybl Kersh, Aron Shron, Avrom Holtsman, Simkhe Zilbershteyn (promoter), Sheyndl Karlinski, Sime Shakhter, Sime Potash and others.

The drama circle of the Right *Poaley tsion*

First row from right: Aron Shron, Blume Fayntsayg, Sore Sklornik, Avrom Holtsman and Reyzl Shniadover.
Standing: Sime Potash, Shmuel Blumshteyn, Sime Shakhter, Meyshe Granat, Nekhe Reytshik and Yehude Grudke.

After a short while, the hairdresser Yosl Zilbershteyn from Pultusk arrived in Goworowo. He was a young man with artistic and organizational abilities and could also direct and do makeup. He created a non-party drama circle of the earlier mentioned people and of Meyshe Dovid Malovani, Feyge Shetsekh, Leybtshe Gemora, Kalman Klepfish and Khaye Zilbershteyn. That troupe, under Zilbershteyn's direction, put on *Devorele meyukheses*, *Di farblondzshete neshome*, *Hertsele Meyukhes* and others.

But this idyll did not last. A split took place in 1929, which I caused. The story was during *Purim* 1929,

[Page 200]

while we were performing the play *Der batlan*. I was playing the role of the teacher Bronin, a *Bundist*, also a sympathizer with a wealthy man's daughter. When it came to the words that Bronin says "If Zionism possessed no more than that one merit, which a person like you does not have, then that alone would be worth being a Zionist...", I added a few words, in keeping with *Purim*, "and traveling to *Erets Yisroel* and not looking at a ninny like you...". Well, that started a huge uproar. Yosl Zilbershteyn reacted from behind the scenes. He demanded I, because there were also many *Bundists* among the audience, publicly apologize for conducting agitation for traveling to *Erets Yisroel* and right now, in the middle of the play, or else he would stop the production. Although I did not consider my deed to be criminal, I agreed to apologize, but after the end of the play. Because of the fact that the entire revenue was designated for the fund for the poor at Passover, I did not want to become a subject of mockery. After the play, I did indeed come back to the stage, but instead of apologizing I came out with the announcement that a new drama circle was being formed at the Brener Library, and that I had made that declaration on my own responsibility and without consulting the other members. Some of them scolded me for "burning the pudding", others supported me. But all the same, how could I come up with a play and then have it prepared in such a short time?

But then an ingenious idea came to me. At the *Skala* Theater in Warsaw they were playing *Gebrokhene hertser*. Thanks to my acquaintance with a collaborator at the *Haynt* newspaper, I was able to get a copy of that script, already censored by the Polish ministry of education, and brought it back to town with me. We immediately distributed the roles and began to act it out. Participants were Bunem Shafran, Aron Shron (also Dezshi), the writer of these lines (in the main role of Avigdor and Grim), Shmuel Blumshteyn, Dovid Khetsron, Blume Fayntsayg, Nikhe Reytshik, Reyzl Shniadover, Alte Zilbershteyn, Sime Shakhter, Sime Potash, Sore Skurnik, and others. The piece was produced with much moral and material success. With that revenue we rented a large venue for the party (*Poaley tsion* Zionist Socialists) with the Brener Library, at Fayvl Shron's.

Later, Aron Shron was successful in bringing the piece *Umshuldik shuldik* from Ostrov Mazieki, which he taken a part in there. That piece was presented in our own venue, during *Peysakh* week 1930. We produced that play several times and people even came from the surrounding area to see it. After that we played *Der fremder*

[Page 201]

Invitations, announcements and programs from the theater presentations produced by the drama circle of the Right *Poaley tsion*

[Page 202]

by Yankev Gordin on 31 January 1931, *Tsulib a kind* by Rikl Shlumke, 28 February 1931.

At that time, some artists from America were playing guest roles in Warsaw and had great success in staging *Zayn vayb's man* (*Seme Lets*). I was able to bring the play down to Goworowo and a few times it played with me in the main role of Seme Lets. Leye Rozen and Malke Tsalke also took part in the play.

We went from success to success. We later produced *Di brider Luria*, *Di shtif-muter*, *Di Royber* by Fridrich Shiller, *Der feter* by Staynberg, and others. We also presented one-act plays, sketches, monologues, recitations and so on. All the revenues went to purchase books for the Brener Library.

That lasted until the end of 1932, when our main amateur artists got married and moved away, the majority making *aliye*. We could not produce any more shows. So we arranged for *khanike* that year, a grand ball with an artistic program - "Humorous Newspaper", sketches, parodies and so on, which were in the main directed by myself.

After the above mentioned split, Yosl Zilbershteyn had organized his drama circle anew, but now under the shingle of the Perets Library of the *Bund*. Over the years they staged *Got fun nekome* by Sholem Ash, *Der Toyber* by Dovid Bergelson, *Tsvishn tog un nakht* by Sh. Anski, *Hersh Lekert* by H. Leyvik, *Afn altn mark* by I. L. Perets, *Der dorfsyung*, *Afn veg to Buenos Ayres*, *Di konspirative dire* and others. All of those productions were carried off with great success. Participants were Tsipora Khetsron, Sheyndl Karlinkski, Mashe Molovani, Leybtshe Gemora, Yisroel Shafran, Leyb Niks, Khane Olek, Libe Gemora and others. For a time Rokhl Gemora helped with the rehearsals and promotion.

Besides those described, drama circles also existed in smaller forms in other places. The *Beys Yankev* school had an active drama circle of only girls, who also played the male roles. At the end of the school year they also gave performances on historic themes. They presented *Makires Yosef*, *Meylekh Akhashveresh*, *Shimshon un Dlayle* and others. The performances were given in the women's shul or in a barn at the Rozen-Kosovski lumber yard or other places. Their presentations were well attended.

The *Ha'shomer ha'tsair* produced *Ha'khutfim* (Cantonists) in Meyshe Tenenboyms's hall, with Nekhe Shakhter, Elieyzer Levin and Shleyme Apelboym in the lead roles. They also performed several one-act plays.

[Page 203]

Almost every year on the 11th of *Oder*, *Betar* also mounted pictures, enactments and other artistic performances that were connected to the memory of Yosef Trumpeldor.

It is worth mentioning that the largest number of presentations in town were presented in Meyshe Dronitsa's barn.

Membership card for the drama circle of the *Poaley tsion* Zionist Socialists.

[Page 204]

The Work of the National Funds

by A. Sh. Menakhem, Israel

Translated by Tina Lunson

Keren kayemet l'Yisroel

The work of the *K.K.L.* was carried out by all the Zionist parties. In that work all the party bickering and political discussions disappeared. The sole common goal was to create more money for the Fund.

The main revenues for *K.K.L.* came from the blue and white *pushkes* (charity boxes). The town was divided into three regions and each month a different party was assigned another region to empty the *pushkes*. That system was instituted in order not to do anyone injustice, since not all the regions brought in the same amount. That job was done mostly by the youth.

Besides the donations made for *aliyes* to read the Torah by the Zionist disposed congregants, we also carried out "flower" collections at weddings and other celebrations. From time to time we had various inter party presentations, whose revenue went exclusively to the *K.K.L.*

The work of the *K.K.L.* was very intensive, Each party had to try to produce more money. At the first places of collection, the *Betar* and *Ha'shomer ha'tsair* stood in the almost the same proportion as the population and the Goworowo Jews reckoned as the biggest collectors and donators. At the *K.K.L.* Central in Warsaw, our town took a prominent place.

[Page 205]

For especially large events, the main office of the *K.K.L.* sent out speakers to us, which mostly took place in the large study house, with speakers on the topic of the day. We were visited by Pinkhas Fogelman, Avrom Bialistotski, Yekhiel Frenkl, Tenenboym and others. The council of the *K.K.L.*consisted of party delegated members. For a long time the following members worked there: Meyshe Dranitsa (General Zionist), Yitskhak Viroslav (*P.Ts-Z.S.*), Meyshe Granat (*He'khaluts*), B. Kosovski (*Betar*), Hershke Granat (*Ha'shomer*) and others. Later others were active: Avrom Holtsman, Avieyzer Shikora and others. For many years the head of the *K.K.L.* was Dan Rozenberg, the last leader was Shmuel Tsudiker. Both belonged to *Mizrakhi* and were voted in unanimously.

Keren ha'yesod

The work of *Keren ha'yesod* became unstable, and it was not an official committee anyway. The administration of *Keren ha'yesod* was connected to larger sums of money and the larger part of them could not be allowed. From time to time though, they produced very important events. Then, the Central *Keren ha'yesod* in Warsaw would send special messengers who gave lectures in the large study house and explained to the audience the importance of the undertaking. From those declared sums we could underwrite promissory notes for longer terms. During those special events we were visited by Asher Kolodny, Rov Hogar and others. About the importance of the national funds, we often heard lectures in the study house from the hospitable speaker and *Mizrakhi* leader Meyshe Skurnik.

The Zionist youth organizations rarely took part in the action for *Keren ha'yesod.* Only the adult members of the parties were active; they were well-known activists who were among both the collectors and the donors.

[Page 206]

Scholars, Leaders, Types and Personalities

Naske Goworower[1]

by I. I. Trunk, America

Translated by Tina Lunson

When the Hasidic *shtibl* was constructed, Pinkhas Likhtenberg began to gather a congregation for his *shtibl.* He did not want it to be the sort of rag tag hasidic spot as the big *shtibl.* In the end he was surrounded by merchants in the courtyard. Even the rich, Germanic wool spinners from Lodzsh came to him. He also did not want too much wrangling with his Germanic wife. He certainly wanted peace in the home. So, he set out a list of who should pray in his *shtibl.* He wrote out the list at home, in his office. The list was written in pearly, scholarly handwriting, and he placed it carefully between the covers of a *Guide to the Perplexed.* One must admit, Pinkhas Likhtenberg had expressed masterfulness even in that area.

Nevertheless, he had seen to it that Reb Leyvi Kahan would pray with him. With that, he wanted to snatch the rose from the big *shtibl.* With that he also *kashered* the *shtibl* in the eyes of his German wife, who was always angry at that wild notion of making a hasidic *shtibl* right under her nose. Publicly, before everyone's eyes, she had therefore worn her own hair as a protest. Let everyone see what she, Dobzshinski's daughter, thought of Pinkhas Likhtenberg's dark deeds. R' Leyvi Kahan wanted to make her shut

[Page 207]

her mouth. However, if the old Baron Hayntsl was not ashamed to be friends with Reb Leyvi, to speak with him in Yiddish and to ride with him over Pietrikov Street in the rich aristocrat's coach, why must she, Dobzshinski's daughter, not benefit from the honor if R' Leyvi Kahan was seen with her in the courtyard. Pinkhas' wife was indeed a little quieted when she heard who would be one of the first of the congregants in the *shtibl.* Secondly, he would let everyone hear, along with R' Leyvi himself, which *shtibl* Pinkhas Likhtenberg intended to make in his house. Torah and greatness in one place.

Each person whom Pinkhas chose as one of his prayers was a true attraction. And I will intentionally dwell on some of them.

For *shtibl shames* he chose Naske from Goworowo. To explain who Naske was, is not one of the lighter things. And among the rare Lodzsh Jews, Naske was a rare Jew. What livelihood Naske had before he became *shames* in Pinkhas' *shtibl* is also hard to say, because Naske was the typical anarchist of any who ever lived in this world. He did not honor any order of any kind or organization, no kind of legal community and no kind of community obligation of people to people. He was an individualist of the most extreme sort and livelihood would certainly fit in with a community order. He chose his livelihoods according to the need of the moment. Here he was a teacher, there he threw over teaching and began carrying a can of oil around to rich people's houses, or pushing wagons across Pietrikov Street along with all the simple porters although everyone who knew Naske, also knew what a sharp *hasid* and sharp scholar he was. Naske did not take anyone into account, he did not recognize any duties and any conventions around the community.

Naske himself was a tall Jew with fiery flaming red hair, with a fiery red beard and flaming red *peyes*, which he always had tied together under a velvet hat. No one knew why or when, Naske would suddenly stand up in the middle of the house or in a noisy street, and with rash impatience untie the *peyes* and let them out from under the hat. It looked like two streams of fire falling down on both sides of his face. And Naske went around for a while with his *peyes* unbound. People looked, but Naske did not look at people. Until he would stop still and tie the *peyes* back under his hat.

I believe that no person had ever seen Naske's eyes. He held them, with fierce stubbornness, heavily lowered, both when he spoke with someone and when he was walking in the street. I always wondered how Naske knew where he was going if he did not look and walked with his eyes lowered. Looking at someone, like looking around oneself, is a kind of partnership with someone. And that was something he did not do. Even

[Page 208]

his language was different. He spoke his own dialect, and pronounced the Yiddish words in his bizarre way. Because language is a specific commonality among people, Naske did not accept that. Naske spoke in his own *Naskish* language and one had to know him well in order to understand him. For example, he did not say "*shoyfer*" but "*sheyfer*"; not "*yoytse zayn*" but "*yeytse zayn*". Every Yiddish word sounded different from Naske's mouth. A true anarchist.

Thus, Naske had never succeeded in traveling out of Lodzsh, although he had several times chosen to travel to his hometown of Goworowo. Why he suddenly needed, out of the clear blue sky, to travel there no one knew. He only said, "I'm going to Goworowo". But he never did manage to go. Because Naske was never able to believe that the train really left from Lodzsh on a regular schedule, and it did indeed keep to its schedule. That kind of regulation that was under this nose and in relation to his trip to Goworowo, would be absolutely contradictory to Naske's spirit. When people told him that the train left, for example, from Lodzsh at ten minutes after four o'clock. Naske, in his great surprise, untied his flaming red *peyes* from under his hat and they fell around his cheeks. He looked sharply at the floor through his lowered eyes and finally arrived at the train two hours later. And he was still surprised that the train had actually left according to the schedule. What a crazy world! Nevertheless, Naske believed that what happened today was just a wild chance, that the train left according to the schedule. Tomorrow it would surely leave anytime it felt like it. Naske arrived again three hours after the scheduled time. That way, he was expressing his trust that the train was not crazy and went in his *Naskish* manner. When, in his disappointment with the train he repeated this for several more days and Naske saw that the train was not making a joke with the schedule, Naske reconsidered. He would not go to Goworowo after all.

That was the kind of Jew that Pinkhas Likhtenberg had chosen for a *shames* in his *shtibl*. When everyone asked him, how is it possible that such a strange wild man was to operate the *shtibl's* accounts, sell *aliyes* and in general run the economy of the *shtibl*, Pinkhas smiled quietly and said that it would soon be fine. How would it be fine? Already in the first weeks of his job Naske demonstrated his anarchism and did so with none other than the powerful tsarist government, in this way. Pinkhas had installed gas lighting in his *shtibl*. When the first bill arrived to pay for the gas, Naske did not believe that the state gas facility meant it for real. He did not believe in paying bills. Naske threw the official gas bill into the trash. Eventually the last deadline came. The gas facility sent an

[Page 209]

official, who turned off the gas meter and hung a lead seal bearing a Russian eagle from it. A fine threat to Naske Goworowo! When twilight came and they needed to light the gas lamps in the *shtibl*, Naske did not make any long evasions. Before everyone's eyes, he went to the gas meter, ripped off the government lead seal and opened the meter again. The Jews shouted that not only would Naske go away in chains for that, but that Pinkhas Likhtenberg would be dragged off to prison with him. Naske did not respond.

In passing, I want to add: In Goworowo, in 1918 when the Germans suffered a defeat in the First World War and the population in all the Polish towns disarmed the German military, Naske suddenly ran out of the *shtibl* and into Pietrikov Street. He let loose his red *peyes* and with his eyes lowered ran up to a German soldier. The German was shocked and handed his rifle over to Naske. Naske went back into the *shtibl* and placed the German rifle near the holy Ark.

[from the book *Poylin*, Volume 3]

Orignal footnote:

1. Naske Kats, the old Brilant's son-in-law.

Reb Meyshe Yehoshe Ginzburg
of Blessed Memory

by Meyshe Granat, Israel

Translated by Tina Lunson

The sources for books in town were exclusively at the party associated libraries, the General Zionist Organization's *Tekhiye*, the *Poaley tsion* Zionist Socialists' named for Brener, the *Bund* named for Perets, and others. There were also some who subscribed to books directly from the Warsaw publishers. But there was also a bookstore in town, which was owned by Meyshe Yehoshe Ginzburg. In truth, it was not a bookstore in the full sense of the word, but one could find quite a good assortment with him. It was not a front business with shelves of sorted books, just a private residence where the books were strewn in dozens of places. It was a symbol of disorder there. It was also no wonder. Reb Meyshe Yehoshe was already an old man and not having a wife, he had to all the household work as well; so, he could not always manage it all.

Reb Meyshe Yehoshe was a great scholar and a lover of books. Usually, he sat and consulted a holy book and it was hard for him to tear himself away from it. He did not begin to do anything in the house until he had finished with the book.

[Page 210]

So he sat, either by himself in a room or in the hours of prayer in the *shul,* always bent over a book, squinting his left eye and not seeing what went on around him. He swam with his whole being in the secret worlds. He was an expert in the entire Talmud and Commentators and also loved to read the Hebrew secular press. When Reb Meyshe Yehoshe came into the *shul*, even the *Rov* stood up for him. If someone needed to ask a legal question or lay out a negotiation, they turned to him. He did not need to think, quickly gave an answer, not once taking his eyes off the book.

He was a very old man, but he did not yet wear glasses. His shoulders were already hunched from always sitting bent over books. He lived on the Broad Street, across from the town *Rov*, in one room. In one corner stood a wooden bed which was hardly ever made up and in the other corner was the kitchen, with utensils around it. Books, holy books mixed up with the novels, lay about everywhere - on the bed, on the table, on the chairs and even on the floor. When someone came in to buy a book, it was also hard for him to tear himself away for the book and talk with the customer. He gave the impression that he would rather get rid of the customer and get back to his book. So, people did not like to buy books from him. It was difficult to discuss matters with him and to consult with him about what book to select. Mostly the customer himself had to take the trouble to look over all the books as they were, scattered about, until he found something.

I bought my first books from him, picking them out myself. I had the opportunity to look around and to familiarize myself with more books. My being in his room for hours did not disturb him at all. I did not need to pull him from his occupation. Overall, he did not see me at all.

His son Binyumin, already an adult man, was the first intellectual in town; it was the custom of the youth, even before the rise of the political movements among us. He was a person of high education who brought the Zionist thought into Goworowo. He frequently gave lectures, and he educated a generation of party leaders.

[Page 211]

Reb Avrom Mordkhe Fridman
of Blessed Memory

by A. Bashan, Israel

Translated by Tina Lunson

Every Jewish community in Poland wanted to be able to boast such a respected proprietor as was Reb Avrom Mordkhe Fridman of blessed memory. A distinguished scholar in the full sense of the word, a clever man in many areas; people asked his advice in the most complicated business matters and in personal problems; a leader in supporting the Jewish community as well as a wealthy man who came to it through his extraordinary honesty. He was the synonym of the honest merchant. His word was holy, both for Jews and for the *goyim*. Jews treasured him and *goyim* thought more highly of him than their own priests. One could say of him that his house was "a place of Torah and greatness in one place" and even if he had lived in Warsaw, he would also have been reckoned among the finest and most prominent proprietors in that great capitol city.

As the Talmud says in verse *Eyzer kenagdu* (Genesis 2:18) "It is not good that man is alone; I shall make him a helpmate opposite him." Reb Avrom Mordkhe did indeed merit and his wife Reytse was also distinguished with virtues and good qualities and was much beloved in the town for her good heartedness and love of people. He was a member of the local council for a time and she sought to help orphans and widows; he gave to charity and to community work, and she gave many anonymous gifts and other social aid. Indeed, their house was a meeting place, and the town was proud of them.

Reb Avrom Mordkhe was born in Goworowo in 1860 to his parents Shabsay Dovid and Khaye Ester, who operated a manufacturing business in the town. He studied in the town study house, and clung to the Sokhstshove *rebi*, the *avni nazir*, from whom he received his "model" of learning. He married his wife Reytse, the daughter of Yitskhak Dovid and Rive Openheym, owners of a restaurant in Tshekhonov.

After the wedding Reb Avrom Mordkhe took over his father's manufacturing business, which brought him large profits. His wife Reytse devoted herself to the business while he studied Torah or did deeds of charity. He was a passionate *hasid* and often traveled to the *rebis* of Novominsk, Parisov, Sokhotshev, and finally, to the Ger Rebi, Rov Avrom Mordkhe'le Alter may his memory be for a blessing. He was an avid follower of the *Agudas Yisroel* Party and supported all their activities.

Reb Avrom Mordkhe passed on in 1930 in Goworowo, and his wife Reytse further maintained the business along with her son Henekh.

The wife Reytse was murdered along with her sons Elkhonen and Henekh and their wives and children, in Slonim, by the murderous hands of the Nazis.

[Page 212]

My Father the Cantor & Ritual Slaughterer

by Eliahu Yankev Brukhansky, Israel

Translated by Tina Lunson

My father R' Khayim Malkiel stemmed from an aristocratic family in Lomzshe. The first rabbi in Lomzshe, the well-known saint Rov Zalmele Hasid, was his great grandfather. My father's father, Rov Eliahu, was reared in Stalptse. He studied in the big *yeshivas* and was known as a scholar and he was also very talented musically. In his youth he sang in the choir of the famous composer Nisn Belzer. After his marriage to my grandmother Gite Sheynkop, he became cantor and ritual slaughterer in Sokhotshin, near Plonsk. My grandfather, however, did not remain in a community post his whole life, but returned to Lomzshe, opened a food store and drew his living from that.

All his children possessed native talents for music and my grandfather educated them further and taught them singing and composition. His son Menakhem was cantor/ritual slaughterer in Sarotsk and in Kreve. He sang in a fine baritone and was also capable of learning. The second son Yankev Kopl was a genius in his youth. He was ordained at 18 years of age from *Hofets Khayim*. In his youth he inspired wonder with his singing. He sang in the largest *shuls*, standing on a bench because he could not reach the cantor's stand. He also did not want to stay in the small town as a cantor. He became a Hebrew teacher in a Lomzshe middle-school. Later he went off to America and became a lecturer in a rabbinical seminary. The younger son Meyshe was a phenomenal singer. He spent a lot of time at home with my father. For the holidays he would come to us in Goworowo to help my father with the services. He married a Goworowo girl, Rokhl, a daughter of Yisroel Leyzer Zamlson. For several years after the wedding he lived in Goworowo and tutored a youth choir. He prayed the high holidays in a Lomzshe shul. He and his whole family were murdered in the Holocaust in Lomzshe.

Their younger son Shleyme was also a beautiful singer. He would sing with my father in Goworowo and later, in Vishkove. Today he is in America.

But the most talented singer of all the brothers was the firstborn, my father Khayim Malkiel of blessed memory. My grandmother used to say that even as a child in the cradle his little voice sounded so sweet, that they soon recognised that he would grow up to be a great cantor. His voice was wonderful, his coloratura and feeling literally enchanted people. When he sang for the cantors Nisn Blumental and Pinkhas Minkovski in Odessa, they were inspired by his

[Page 213]

talent. Even gentiles came to *shul* to hear him sing. When he was cantor in Makove there was a separate gallery for the gentiles of the high-ranking *natshalstva* circles, who came to *shul* and waited through all the prayers until he would sing.

Khayim Malkiel Brukhansky
of blessed memory

My father, however, did not much like the glory that people granted him. By nature he was a modest person and loved the ordinary folk. He had great friends in the musical circles. Among his good friends were Menakhem Kipnis from Warsaw, Birnboym from Tshenstokhov, conductor Ayzenshtat from the Warsaw synagogue, conductor Dovidovitsh from Nashik's *shul*, the cantor Hirshov and other great cantors.

He himself authored many compositions and many hasidic *nigunim* which he sang at the tables of the Ger Rebi.

In his youth he studied in the Mir Yeshiva. After his marriage to my mother Rokhl Leye, he took on his first post as cantor/ritual slaughterer in Seratsk near Warsaw. He did not make much of a living there and after a year went

[Page 214]

to Novidvor and from there to Makove. He was cantor/ritual slaughterer there for six years and always took care that the essence and the flavor of the prayers be at the appropriate level. He was meticulous in that area. Recognizing that the Makove Rov, Yisroel Nisn Kupershtokh, was also an extraordinary master of prayer, my father particularly helped him in *Neile*, when the *Rov* prayed in the famous Makove *shul*. But he did not make a living there either and remained a pauper.

Then the Goworowo householders Mayer Romaner and Shayke Hertsberg, whose families stemmed from Makove, proposed that he be cantor/slaughterer in Goworowo. They promised him the best conditions and a large sum of money to pay his debts.

For *parshas sheklim* 1911, my farther traveled to Goworowo with a choir of 12 persons, in which his two brothers Menakhem and Meyshe also took part. He prayed the *Shabes* prayers so beautifully that the Goworowo Jews were ecstatic. They decided to hire him at any price. Soon after that *Shabes*, a delegation of Goworowo householders headed by Dovid Liver to represent the working people and artisans came to Makove with a purse of money. Father accepted the post.

In Goworowo we first lived in a three room apartment in Dovid Liver's building, until we were well oriented. The love of the Goworowo Jews for us was indescribable. Every night in our house was like a joyful holiday. On *Shabes* and actual holidays it was even more joyous. All the householders, hasidim and "enlighteners", came to us to rejoice and drink a little whisky. Our house was full of song. The cantor flowed together with the town as one body. Everyone sang along with father's "little pieces", *Ha'ben Yakir li Efroym, Ha'teoreru, Kaboros* and a bit of *V'hu yasmieynu* were the most valuable merchandise in town. Several youths and boys from Makove who were studying singing and ritual slaughtering with my father also came with him and were literally snatched up by the householders, such as Gavriel Yalovitsh, Avrom Mordkhe Fridman, Itshe Mayer Fridman and others. Especially noted were the boys Binyumin Mundzak with his lovely solos; Hersh Leybl Shtern from Ostrolenke, a brother of the poet Yisroel Shtern; Meyshe Binyumin Rzshepka, a *yeshiva* man who had a beautiful bass-baritone voice and was a good soloist. From Goworowo itself were Henekh, a relative of Yehoshe Rozen, a good soprano who later moved to America; Yisroel Niks, a soprano; Leyb Hersh Fleysher, the cap-maker and Khayim Leyb Proske's son-in-law, a tenor; two brothers from the Lis family, tenor and baritone; Khonen Vaysbord, a baritone, and later, Avrom Holtzman, Motl Lerman and others.

[Page 215]

For the Days of Awe my uncle Meyshe also came and it was a full ensemble, which enchanted the congregation. Even hasidim in the *shtiblekh* hurried to finish their prayers in order to catch a few tones from my father.

It was a tradition in Goworowo that the cantor make a feast for the proprietors of the study house after *Shabes*, after *slikhes*. But for my father the hasidim did not want to miss the pleasure and they also came. A big dispute grew out of that. Reb Dovid was alarmed, "You have the little reflectors! Soon they will take our cantor from us, too!" My father smoothed it over and then there was peace.

At that time the old Rov Kahana-Botshan of blessed memory, was still alive. He only studied Torah and did not mix into any community matters. My father had to fill a double function – to represent the *Rov* in all matters. Livelihood was abundant and usually happy and cheerful.

The gentile population in Goworowo also valued my father very much. When, during the First World War, the *Rov* and the proprietors were arrested for the accusation of the "*eruv*-telephone" case, they treated my father with respect. The police commandant was passing the house and said, "This is where our beloved *shpievik* and *zsheshek* lives." Because of that many people staying at our house were saved.

It was during that time that the local council introduced the oversight of *shkhite* [ritual slaughter of animals for food] because of the money involved and the hygiene. So the police always kept the *sheykhet's* slaughtering knife and gave it back only for a slaughtering in their presence. Of course, the *sheykhet* had another knife for slaughtering whenever he wanted or if someone needed it, without the knowledge of the police. But the commandant had a good excuse to look in on us, drink a little glass of whisky with snacks, and visit a little with my father.

Although my father was a staunch Ger hasid, he still loved *Erets Yisroel* very much. He collected money for the emissaries from the *yeshivas* in *Erets Yisroel* and he took the Zionist youth under his wing. The town Zionist leaders Binyumin Ginsburg, Yekhiel Pshisusker, Shmuel Fridman, Dovid Fridman and Khonen Vaysbord often came to him to hear his songs of Israel.

My father found it very stimulating to hear the Torah read by a good and exacting Torah reader. Thus, he went to hear R' Yekl Klepfish read. That was a real *Shabes* pleasure for him. For *shofar* blower my father always chose Khayim Ber Grudke (later my father-in-law) who was a good blower. He was also very pleased with Menashe Holtsman's morning prayers during the Days of Awe. He used to say that Menashe Holtsman prayed well at the stand and could adjust the prayers. For the third meal of *Shabes* all the musicians gathered at the *Rov's* house and sang *zmiros* together.

Those were good years in Goworowo. The idyll did not last long, before the town was burned and ruined in the First World War.

Even after that, when the town began to be rebuilt, there was no livelihood for my father. With a heavy heart, he had to leave there and take over a post in Zakrotshim. In 1921 he came to Vishkove as cantor/ritual slaughterer. Here my father had the opportunity to conduct his cantoring on a larger scale. My brother Hersh Yosef and I assisted him in his work. My brother was also a ritual slaughterer. And my sister Brayne Dvore and her husband Mikhael Brame were musical.

All this ended with the great destruction of Polish Jewry by Hitler. My father had the merit to die in his own bed, in the Lomzshe hospital, on the 18th of *Shevet* in 1940. He was buried in the Lomzshe cemetery near the grave of the *Rov*. My whole family – mother, brother and sister with her husband and two children, were murdered as *kidush-ha'shem* martyrs in Slonim.

May God avenge their blood.

[Page 216]

My Father Reb Yonatan Zilbertson

by Yosef Zilbertson, Israel

Translated by Tina Lunson

My Father Reb Yonatan descended from a very illustrious family in Warsaw, where his parents, wealthy hasidim, had lived for many generations. He came to Goworowo as a son-in-law of Khayim Elieyzer Koen, may he rest in peace, whom he had taken for his daughter Khaye Leye.

Reb Yonatan ran a big iron business and was the chief purveyor for the local princely estates. My father figured among the wealthy people of the town. Despite the fact that he lived in this small place for decades, in his essence and in his day-to-day dealings he remained a big-city type, who had a hard time fitting into the narrow frame of the small town householders. He strove to get the Goworowo householders to take him as an example, not the other way around.

His house had been renovated with large, airy rooms and a permanent *suke*, with a roof that opened and other large town comforts. He went out on the street in a finely tailored long coat, with never any stains on his clothes and wearing shiny leather boots. His beard was always properly combed. All this was far from the concepts of the *shtetl* householders, who were accustomed to having their *kapotes* shine and not their boots.

[Page 217]

He was loved and accepted by everyone, especially the better part of the *shtetl* population. Going past his house, especially on the long winter nights, one could generally hear the voice of Torah. That was Reb Yonatan studying the lesson with his grown sons, Mayer and Meyshe. The passer-by would listen for a while and think to himself, "that is called Torah and greatness in one place".

My father was one of the most eminent Aleksander Hasidim in the land. As a young man he traveled to the old *rebi*, Rov Yekhiel may his memory be for a blessing. The *rabeyim* of the Aleksander line who used to visit Goworowo generally stayed and conducted their "tables" in his house. He was a relative of the Amshinov Rebi, and when it was time for the *rebi's yortsayt* he went to Rov Burshtin, may God avenge his blood, who considered himself an Amshinov *Rov*, for a blessing.

The *yortsaytn* of the Aleksander *Rabeyim*, which were generally connected with a feasting *mitsve* or an end of Shabes meal, took place in his home. On the seventh day of Passover the congregation usually came to his home for *kidush* and when it came time for the ceremony of drawing water – which took place in his spacious *suke* – the people stayed until late in the night with a little keg of beer and singing, dancing hasidim. By the way, his neighbors always ate in his *suke*, Reb Yeshaye Ayznberg, his son-in-law Yosef Dovid Ostashever and long may he live Reb Niske Mozes, the ritual slaughterer. For me, sitting in the *suke* with such a large and merry group is etched into my memory and belongs to the most pleasant memories of that time.

Along with the fact that Reb Yonatan was one of the old-time pious hasidim, he was also a sharp scholar, an expert in Talmud and excelled, noted for a special logic in learning. The *Rov* often consulted with him on difficult questions of observance.

Reb Yonatan took pains to educate his children in his way. Indeed, his sons were all Talmud scholars and at the same time devoted lovers of Zion, loyal to the idea of religious Zionism.

My father died in his bed in Warsaw, in *Tevet sav-shin*, just before the ghetto was opened. But his sons Mayer and Meyshe with their families, and his younger son Khayim Elieyzer, a remarkably dear boy, died in the Warsaw ghetto. Yosef Dovid Ostashever, his son-in-law and his wife, his daughter Yetke and their four children were killed in the slaughter of Slonim. May God avenge their blood!

[Page 218]

Reb Matisyahu Rozen
of blessed memory

by B. Itshes, Israel

Translated by Tina Lunson

Reb Matisyahu Rozen of blessed memory was born to his parents Reb Yisroel Yitskhak and Rivke Royze Rozen of blessed memory. His father was one of the town's prominent proprietors and rich Jews. He had a grocery store on the market square and also dealt with the local noble landowners.

At the beginning of this century, Reb Matisyahu married Sheyne Kosovski (one of Yitskhak Kosovski's sisters) and then began to deal in the lumber trade, along with his father-in-law who was already in that business. After his father-in-law Yitskhak's marriage, they bought a place on Broad Street where they built a spacious building and left space under it for a lumber warehouse. Both partners dealt in large lots, buying up whole *dzsholkes* of forests from the local estate holders, had them cut in Glinke's sawmill and sent the largest part to export. A small portion they left for the local market. They got rich from the large business and were considered the rich men of the town.

Reb Matisyahu ran a generous home on a big-town scale. It was always full of guests, the majority were merchants from outside, customers from the area, as well as noble landowners with whom he had business ties.

Reb Matisyahu was an Aleksander Hasid although, I do not recall if he ever traveled to the *rebi*. It is possible he took up his hasidism as an "inheritance" from his father Reb Yisroel Yitskhak who was a fiery hasid, traveling to the old Aleksander Rebi together with Reb Yoske Piontnitsa (or Pshenitsa – he was known as Rokhl Shmuelke's husband). Reb Matisyahu did first pray in an Aleksander *shtibl*, but later went over to a *Mizrakhi minyen*.

As a wealthy Jew, he usually spent generously on benevolent goals. If someone set out to build a community building, he would always donate "wholesale"; and if the foundation was ready and they were really constructing it but did not have the means to finish it, he took care of the roof. He very often donated a *kidush* to the *shtibl* and for special occasions he invited the congregation to his home. Of course, the refreshments were the best – fit for a king.

Reb Matisyahu had a claim to be the "Torah groom" which he would buy for any price. Although the hasidim specially pressed him to spend money knowing that he would not relinquish the *mitsve*, he did not

[Page 219]

resent it and paid the largest sum and after *musaf* held a *kidush* at his home.

His wife Sheyne
may God avenge her blood

His daughter Yehudis

Reb Matisyahu Rozen
of blessed memory

He was a member of the Merchants' Union, of the Merchants' Bank and was also for a time, a councilman for the Jewish Community Council. Though one must say that he did not like it and rejected the office after a short while. The community work often brought him into conflict with other people, which he did not know or want. He was good-natured and generally avoided controversy. He was also *gabay* of the Burial Society for several years but, that was an honor for him, an honorary position and no more. He also spent money there.

Reb Matisyahu was meticulous about his appearance. When he had to travel to see a prince about trade matters, he put on his holiday clothes in order to make the proper impression. He did not stand against the wealthy landowners on price. He also bought with an open hand. "It should be for everyone", he would say after every acquisition from the forest. And that was just how it was. He and his father-in-law earned a name as honest merchants among the princes and the name went before them all those years.

Reb Matisyahu was a clever Jew. He also had a sense of humor, loved to joke and liked to hear and retell a cheerful story. When he traveled to Warsaw to the merchants to settle accounts, he always brought home gifts for his family members. Although he was never concerned about purchasing them, he always brought them home as "bargains", saying that he paid less for the things. "Both parties are happy", he would quip, "the merchant from whom I bought the things and those who will use them."

[Page 220]

After a long illness, Reb Matisyahu died a few years before the war.

May his soul be bound up in the band of the living.

* * *

His wife Sheyne was quiet and unassuming, good-natured and a very efficient housekeeper. She was known for her good works but did not want people to talk about them. Her home was always "open". If anyone needed help with anything, they went straight to Sheyne. She gave with an open hand, as was appropriate for a wealthy woman.

She ran her home in a rich way and everything there was in order. Her husband Matisyahu sponsored a *kidush* after his being called to the Torah as a standard practice, which was precisely prepared. Sheyne always had integrity; she simply knew no other way. She avoided gossip and lived in peace with all. No one ever heard a sharp word from her.

They had a single daughter, Yehudis. The daughter, a picture-perfect girl, received the appropriate rearing and education, and was counted among the intellectual young people of the town. She inherited the good qualities of her parents and was beloved by everyone. In 1917 she was among the founders of the Zionist Organization in Goworowo. She was active in community affairs for many years. In the beginning of the 1920s she married Dovid Segal from Kharzshl, a scholar and an Enlightener. His father Yekhezkel was a prominent Aleksander Hasid there and a good prayer leader. After their wedding the young couple moved to Warsaw and opened an amber business. They were not successful however and returned to Goworowo. Both fathers-in-law took Dovid in as a partner in their lumber business, where he worked mostly in the sawmill. At the same time Segal took his proper place in the community.

They left Goworowo in the middle of the 1930s and moved with their three children to Ostrolenke. During the outbreak of the war they – along with their mother Sheyne Roze – found a place of refuge in Slonim. Sheyne, Yehudis, Dovid and their two children Hele and Meyshe later shared the fate of all the Slonim martyrs may God avenge their blood. Their older son Khone succeeded in surviving the war and today is in America, with a wife and two children.

[Page 221]

My Parents

by B. Kosovski, Israel

Translated by Tina Lunson

My Father Reb Yitskhak of blessed memory

My Father Reb Yitskhak or, as people called him, Itshe Kosovski, was a son of Khone Alter and Frume Kosovski from Ostrov-Mazovietsk. My grandmother's father, that is, my father grandfather Reb Neyekh Yashinovski of blessed memory, a great scholar, was an in-law of the Makover *Rebi* Rov Fishele may his sainted memory be a blessing. His son Yitskhak (a brother of my grandmother) married the Makover *Rebi's* daughter Reyzele. Yitskhak and Reyzele died in *Erets Yisroel;* were buried in Tiberias (or Tsfat) more than a half century ago.

Our family should, in all probabilities, stem from the village Kosove back from the time when our great-grandparents took on the family name and from then on, the name Kosovski.

The family Kosovski was multi-branched and spread out over numerous large towns in Poland. They were found in Warsaw, Bialystok, Grodne, Volkovisk, Ostrov- Mazovietsk and other places. In the last century, also in other countries.

My grandfather Reb Khone Alter, a Talmud expert, stemmed from Ostrov-Mazovietsk. He dealt in lumber and also had a *maydan*, a special oven to extract turpentine, in Yarzshombek near Ostrov. He became wealthy from those businesses. My father himself, of all the children, took over the lumber trade.

As shown in the official documents, my father was born in 1880 but in fact, he was younger. That was done specially in order to avoid serving in the tsar's military. At the time there was a decree that of a set of twins, only one had to serve; well, he was a twin and that served him well. But he was still called up for the Russian-Japanese War, because the "green ticket" only freed him in times of peace.

My father came to Goworowo apparently after the marriage of his older sister Sheyne to Matisyahu Rozen, in the beginning of this century. Then Matisyahu joined the lumber trade and dealt in partnership with my father, whom he already knew. After that they worked together for many years.

Soon after the wedding, which took place a few years later,

[Page 222]

my parents lived at Borekh Mints' house. A little after my father, in partners with Matisyahu, bought the place on Broad Street from a certain Mendl Khana'tshe's and there built a fine double house as well as a lumber warehouse.

Reb Yitskhak and Dina Kosovski of blessed memory

We went through the First World War with my grandfather in *Maydan*, where my grandfather died in the meantime. Only in about the 1920s did we return to Goworowo. By then my father along with my uncle Matisyahu managed to rebuild the burned house and also prepare lumber for the market.

They dealt in huge volumes and were reckoned among the few wealthy men in the town. They purchased entire *dzshalkes* of forest from the local landowners, especially from the richest estate owner, Glinka, who cut the lumber in his sawmill for which they held a lease for many years. And the majority of the prepared material was exported. They kept a small portion for the local market. They employed dozens of gentile day workers, beginning with skilled workers in the sawmill up to various laborers like choppers, sawyers (*tratshes*), wagon drivers and so on. Further, in the seasons of cutting the trees, they hired many more workers, in particular wagon drivers who drove the trees out of the forest on small sleds and brought them to the sawmill.

In buying the forests and in extracting the maximum from each tree, and in cutting in the mill, my father was a specialist (perhaps he was more of a tradesman than merchant). Once he had laid the "gauge" on the trunk of a tree he already knew by eyeing it, what and how much the tree would offer. He rarely made a mistake.

[Page 223]

Although we had people busy working for us, my father worked hard, literally from sunup to sundown. Especially in the winter months the work was "hot" – they had to try to cut and take out the timber while the frost and snow remained. In those months my father sold on the spot all the branches and some firewood, and came back with a good daily ransom. We often exclaimed when he came home so late.

My father was a good man through and through. Not only with his own did he have good relationships, but also with the gentiles, his workers. He pretended "not to see" when a gentile took a little wood or someone "forgot" to repay a debt. He also did not stay in disagreement with them, avoided disputes, and simply did not allow them to pick a quarrel. He made an effort, in general, not to make any enemies, because, in the end, being in the woods for years with the gentiles, that could make for danger.

Prepared wood (boards) was often bought by the big Warsaw merchant Rubinlikht. He sent us his "man", Shedletski from Dlugoshadle (today he is in Israel) and he would take over the material. After such a customer I would, or my younger brothers would, sit for hours with the cubic meter booklet and try to figure out from the tables how many meter lengths of wood was in the transport.

* * *

As already said, my father was an industrious person and loved order. When he had a free hour or so he would go into the lumber warehouse and call us children to come and help him put back and sort the various kinds of wood that over time had been tossed around and gotten mixed together. On *Sukes* he had regular folks who came to borrow boards for their *sukes* and would return them after the holiday. If someone brought them back with nails (*tshvekes*) in them he did not say anything. It was also our tradition every winter for our partnership business to distribute tens of meters of firewood as gifts to the needy.

* * *

Our house was a religious national one and participated in a broad range of charitable gifts, as was appropriate for wealthy people. My father himself,

[Page 224]

except for his "Jewish" cap, wore a short coat with a cravat and a cropped beard. He first prayed at the Aleksander *shtibl* but with the founding of the *Mizrakhi minyen* he went straight over there. He considered himself one of the *Mizrakhi* men and one of its leaders.

Except for my brother Khayim may God avenge his blood, we, the other three children, were active in the Zionist Revisionist movement. When Khayim decided that he would go to the Lomzshe Yeshiva to study, father happily accepted it but in no way would he allow him to "eat days" [in other people's homes] but supported him privately. After we finished the *folks shule* our father sent us to continue our education with private Polish teachers, even though this was very expensive. I still remember that for a long time, before my move to Warsaw, Beytsalel Yosl came to our home and studied a chapter of Talmud and commentaries with me.

* * *

My father was one of the members and activists of the Merchants' Bank – the *Bank Kreditovi* in town. Though the management changed over the years, my father continued the work without interruption – at its founding in the mid 1920s up until the decimation of the town. All those years my father was active as treasurer, winning the trust of everyone. The bank operations involved many thousands of *zlotych*, and, well, who else could you trust but a rich man?

My father was a modest and honest person and always trod a straight path. What he decided to do, or to tell someone, that was his intention. He loathed betrayal, telling lies, dragging a matter out. He avoided gossip and disputes and distanced himself from them. For helping someone and doing good deeds , he was always ready.

More than once he left his private businesses and literally ran to the bank to take care of matters of some pressing loans, or to avoid someone's promissory note being contested. He very often paid from his own pocket for someone's note, or just as an act of charity; to say nothing of the small or larger charities he liked – because in our house one never forgot.

* * *

My Mother of Blessed Memory

My mother Dina was several years younger than my father and came from Piontnitse, near Lomzshe. Her father was called Berl Leyb Koviar and her mother, Leye. My mother's family were Lomzshe Enlighteners, eminent in the whole region. That grandfather of mine was also in the lumber trade. He worked with forests of immense proportions and had many brokers and workers. It is possible that the trade relationships of both my grandfathers brought about the marriage match of their children.

[Page 225]

My mother was quiet, refined and very modest. She was devoted not only to us, her own, but to everyone she came into contact with. Very often she stood in the shadows. She cared first of all for others, taking care of something for another was first in place, and then she did for herself.

She had "her" poor folks. They came regularly, every week, for prepared, cooked meals and for produce. And she gave very generously.

My mother was a model of justice and fairness. She could not tolerate any injustice. She was a person with a warm Jewish heart and with many good qualities and served as an example for others.

Ours was, as they say, "an open house". A guest in the middle of the week, or on *Shabes*, was a frequent event. During that time when children from outside came to study in Goworowo, my mother gave two or three boys "eating days" during the week. She also did not neglect their clothing when the pupils were clearly in need.

* * *

After the outbreak of the Second World War, my parents wandered to Bialystok. In 1940 they were sent north by the Russians, along with all the *biezshentses*. My father's mother too – that is, my Grandmother Frume – was with them and died in exile at an old age. Afterwards, when they freed all the Polish citizens in 1941, my parents traveled to Uzbekistan. They did not survive until the actual liberation and end of the War. My father died on the 22nd of *Elul* 1942 (*tes-shin"beys*), and my mother a half year later on the 8th of *Oder* 1944 (*tes-shin"daled*). They were buried there in *Kalkoz Kalin*, Kadzshavade Region, Andizshan Oblast. Their bones remain in a strange land.

May their souls be bound up in the band of the living.

Grandmother Frume
of blessed memory

Khayim and Khaye'tshe
may God avenge their blood

Nakhman
of blessed memory

[Page 226]

I want to mention at the end my youngest brother Nakhman, who died in Warsaw after a short illness in 1935 at only 13 years of age; my brother Khayim and his wife Khaye'tshke (nee Hendlish), who were murdered with her parents along with all the Lomzshe Jews; my uncle Zalman Kosovski, of Ostrolenke, and his wife, daughter, son-in-law and grandchildren, as well as his brother Velvl; my mother's large family Kovior in Warsaw, several family members from the family Lavski from Zambrove and all the other relatives who were part of the fate of the 6 million martyrs.

May God avenge their blood!

Reb Meyshe Tenenboym
May God Avenge His Blood

by A. Bashan, Israel

Translated by Tina Lunson

Rokhl
of blessed memory

Reb Meyshe
may God avenge his blood

In community life one may encounter a leader with such inborn characteristics that it would not occur to anyone to doubt his political determination; it was self evident to everyone that this man should hold the rudder of the town in his hand and stand at the top of the community and its council.

Such a sort was the penultimate head of the Jewish Council, Reb Meyshe Tenenboym.

In the era between the two World Wars, he interrupted his positions at the center of Goworowo community life as president or *parnas* of the Jewish Council and was the cofounder of all the Jewish establishments and institutions in the town.

[Page 227]

Reb Meyshe Tenenboym possessed a great deal of personal charm, which helped him to have an impressionable effect on people and thanks to that, he had the necessary influence on the Goworowo residents, both Jews and gentiles. By his nature alone, a goodhearted and affable man, he created a lot of friends and followers in town who stood by his side to help in each community activity. He never used his high position to impose his will on anyone but, used well chosen words to try to persuade one and it always came out his way.

Reb Meyshe Tenenboym made his living from a wine bar and inn that he kept in his large two story house on the Market Square, an inheritance from his parents, Yehoshe and Hinde. With that business he worked up to a wealthy, comfortable position. But he neglected that business because of his community work and later became a bit impoverished. But no one noticed that about him. He was always smiling and with a good word on his lips.

Reb Meyshe Tenenboym was born in Goworowo in the late 1880s. He married in 1910, to Rokhl the daughter of Khone Alter and Frume Kosovski. He had two children with Rokhl; Khane, today in America, and Yehoshe who died tragically young in 1935. After the death of his wife Rokhl in 1920, Reb Meyshe married again to Sheyne Hene Kremer from Mishenits who bore him the children, Borekh Leyb, Shleyme and Yisrolik.

Yehoshe
of blessed memory

Reb Meyshe with his three sons

[Page 228]

A picture of Reb Meyshe Tenenboym and Rokhl's wedding, with their families and guests. 1910

[Page 229]

Reb Menashe Holtsman of Blessed Memory

by Avrom Holtsman, Israel

Translated by Mira Eckhaus

Edited by Tina Lunson

With awe and reverence, I light a memorial candle for the soul and memory of my father, teacher and rabbi, the late Reb Menashe, the son of Reb Mayer Holtsman.

He was a worthy Jew, honest and kind in heart, a *hasid*, humble and pleasant in his ways and kind to all, a seeker of peace and involved with those around him. My late father acquired most of these virtues from his father, Reb Mayer, a rich and generous timber merchant, who was also well known for his learning, honesty, modesty, and his great virtues.

My late father was born in the year 5634. He received his education in the *kheyder* and in *yeshivas*, and at the same time did not neglect a general education; he learned the languages of the country, Polish and Russian, as well as bookkeeping.

Even in his youth, my father was gifted with a pleasant voice, knew the prayers and led services, was well versed in *hasidic* melodies and poetry. He followed the *rebis* of Vurke, and often chanted at the "study tables" of the *Rebi* of Skernievts, whom he respected and liked very much.

When my father once sang the song, *Shir Ha'malos* at the *Rebi's* table when he was an eighteen year old boy, he was heard by an old *hasidic* man, Reb Dov Pizman, the uncle of Rov Yankev Shleyme Pizman, Jewish judge and arbiter in Ostrolenke. He was fascinated by my father's personality, by his singing and by the *Rebi's* affection for him and he chose him as a son-in-law for his daughter Sarah, who is my late mother of blessed memory.

The grandfather, Reb Dov Pizman, was only privileged to participate in the joy of my parents' engagement, as immediately after the engagement he became ill with an illness from which he never recovered. Before his death, he said to his family, "I leave you in trusted hands, in the hands of my son-in-law Menashe, although he is not married yet".

In 5652, my father moved to Goworowo and opened a trading house for groceries, notions, oils, paints and chemical products. My father managed his trade with honesty and justice and immediately won the hearts of the owners of the estates in the area. They became his constant customers and heeded his advice. Among the customers were the nobleman Glinka from Shetsvin, Roshtsishevsky from Tsirna, Mrakbitsky from Bryzhna, Zemzhitski from Ponikba, all the local police and government officials. In a short time, my father managed to be very successful in his business and became rich.

However, my father did not only invest his efforts in trade. He also gave his share in civic affairs. He was chosen as the community leader immediately after the establishment of the independent state of Poland. He excelled as a peacemaker between rivals. Through his efforts, neighbors were reconciled and people in dispute compromised; he made peace between a man and his wife, between ritual slaughterers and butchers, and especially became famous as a lobbyist with the government authorities. With his pleasant manners and his gentleness of speech, he knew how to persuade the people in power and whenever there was trouble for the individual or the public, he worked to cancel decrees and lighten the sentence. From the reign of Tsar Nikolay until the outbreak of the war, he did not stop speaking well of his people before the police chiefs, the Russian Kolan Movits; the Germans Knut, Molsklaski and Knoblich, during the first [German] occupation in 1918; and the Poles Laskovski, Grushka and Nikel. Many of them already had the custom of visiting my father on Saturday evenings and tasting the *gefilte* fish. When they were about to recruit young Torah scholars for the army, my father made the acquaintance of the district doctors

[Page 230]

The late Reb Menashe Holtsman

Kozlovsky and Zaleski and they released from the draft anyone he requested.

At my sister Yetta's wedding, the chief priest of the town sent a special messenger with a congratulatory letter, to honor the honest and decent *Strozkunni Pan Manash*.

Once a Christian woman accused my father of selling cigarettes without duty and excise tax. This evil woman hired false witnesses and her whole intention was to deny my father the government license in order to win it for herself. The priest invited the secretary of the district court, from whom he learned the names of the witnesses. He called on them and influenced them not to testify falsely. The case of the prosecution was worthless and my father won the case.

My father always prayed in the house of the *hasidim* of Vurke. There he led the prayers on *Shabes*, on *Rosh Khodesh*, and for the holiday *musaf.* Once it happened that in the Great Synagogue the leader of the morning service of the Days of Awe became ill; the rabbi and the community begged my father to fill his place in the *shakhris* prayers. Since then, he always prayed the *shakhris* service on the Days of Awe in the Great Synagogue in the Ashkenazi style, in addition to a *musaf* and the *Kol Nidrey*, which he prayed in the house of the *hasidim*.

When I immigrated to Israel in the year 5693, my father gave me a letter to the *Rov* of Bnei Brak, the son of the *Rebi* Rov Shimole Kalish of Skierniewice, in which he expressed his heart's desire to be privileged to immigrate to Israel and live in the *Rebi's* vicinity, so that he could enjoy his brilliance and be one of the guests at his table.

My father was not privileged to fulfill his heart's desire. He passed away abroad, in the steppes of Russia, on the eve of *Rosh Khodesh Sivan*, 5702.

May these words of mine serve as a candle to the holy memory of my late father.

[Page 231]

Avrom Shafran
May God Avenge His Blood

by Sh. Yitskhak, Israel

Translated by Tina Lunson

Reb Avrom and Ester Shafran may God avenge their blood

Reb Avrom Shafran was born in Dlugashodle in 1882. He father, Elieyzer Gedalye was of the settlers of the village in Vurke; a keen *hasid* in the Kotsk style, but he only went to the Mitel Vurke *Rebi*, Rov Mendele and later to *Rebi* Simkhe Bunem who died in Tiberias. Reb Elieyzer Gedalye was a great scholar and was the first teacher of every Vurke child. The *Rebi* Avrom Meyshe may his sainted memory be for a blessing, even when he was already the *Rebi*, used to stand up in his presence. The current Vurke *Rebi*, Rov Yankev Dovid Kalish may he have a long life, who lives in Brooklyn, New York, says that he had his *Rebi* Reb Elieyzer Gedalye of blessed memory to thank for everything that he learned. His son Avrom was an observant *hasidic* young man who well knew how to study and always went with his father to the Vurke *Rebi*.

When Avrom was about 18 years old, Reb Yankev Shabsay from Goworowo took him as a son-in-law, for his 17year old daughter Ester. When he was taken to an examination in his knowledge, the examiner said that Avrom knew more than he did.

Reb Yankl Shabsay was a wealthy Jew and he tried to buy up fine sons-in-law. He himself was a big "Enlightener". People said that when Reb Yankl Shabsay considered a future son-in-law who was a slim and refined young man, he would ask him, "How will those skinny

[Page 232]

fingers of yours be able to make a living?" His wife Khaye Sore, who was a real saint, would answer, "Him for sure, with those refined fingers, he is the one I want for a son-in-law for my daughter Ester Yakhne...plus a large dowry, three or four years living with us for free on *kest*, a Vilner Talmud, and the big Lemberg *Shulkhan Orekh*. And before he comes for the wedding, he must buy an expensive *shtreyml* for *Shabes* and holidays."

For those years living with the in-laws, he sat in the Goworowo study house and learned. In those years the study house was literally a big *yeshiva*. Young men from all the bigger towns in the area came to Goworowo to learn. Although Avrom was a scholar he was not considering any rabbinical post. "Too great a responsibility", he would say. When the Goworowo Rov was not in his home, the women generally came to Avrom with their questions.

After the years of *kest* he turned to trade and was successful. His businesses kept getting better, until he became a big merchant and a rich man. His honesty was well known. Despite the fact that he was always busy with trade, he still sat every day and studied. He was the prayer leader in the Vurke *shtibl*, Torah reader and in later years also studied the "page of the day" with the congregation.

He did not want to mix in the matters of the Jewish community. In the last election for the Jewish Council (in 1937) a delegation came to him for *Agudas Yisroel*, beseeching him to allow them to add his name to their slate of candidates. After much effort, they managed to make him agree. He was elected and for the first time became a council member, taking the office of treasurer. Everyone was happy with him because of his objectivity and honesty.

Reb Avrom, along with his wife and their sons Meyshe and Dovid were murdered in the slaughter of Slonim, probably on the 24th of *Kheshvan, sav-shin"beys*, which is the day the children observe the *yortsayt*. Their son Simkhe Bunem with his wife Devore'le and child were shot in Kosov-Latski. May God avenge their blood.

[From right] Bunem, his wife Devore'le, Meyshe and Dovid Shafran may God avenge their blood

[Page 233]

Five Generations

by Khave bas Yankev Dov, Israel

Translated by Mira Eckhaus

Edited by Tina Lunson

Reb Yankev Dov Blumstein
of blessed memory

Our extensive family struck deep roots in the town of Goworowo and the glorious chain continued for five generations. My mother's elderly parents also lived in the town, followed by my grandfather Reb Mayer'ke of Tiktin and grandmother Khave Tove, my father of blessed memory Reb Yankev Dov, the son of Aryeh Blumshteyn, and my mother, my sisters and brothers and their descendants. These generations were born, educated and raised in the town; engaged in trade, built houses and branched out, until the evil Hitler may his name be blotted out came upon them and destroyed the toil of generations. I lost a sister and a brother with their families and the rest were scattered all over the world.

The rest of the four generations, whose bones were buried in the cemetery of the town, was interrupted as well. Our Polish neighbors craved the fertile land on which the cemetery was located, so they climbed onto it with a tractor, turned and plowed the land and sowed grain seeds to feed and satisfy their bodies from the bones of our loved ones.

Tears are flowing from my eyes for the tragedy that happened to my people and my family.

The figures of my parents are always in my mind. I see my late father, tall, upright in stature, shining face, radiating energy and courage, and a restrained smile on his lips. I see my late mother, modest, quiet, managing her spacious home with humility and nobility and seeing everything with her vigilant and clever eyes.

My mother's father was a great scholar with lofty idealism. He belonged to the "Tiktiner of noble birth" movement, who studied Torah day and night, in order to bring about the Messianic era. He passed away at a young age, when his daughter, that is my mother, was only six months old. When she grew up and reached

[Page 234]

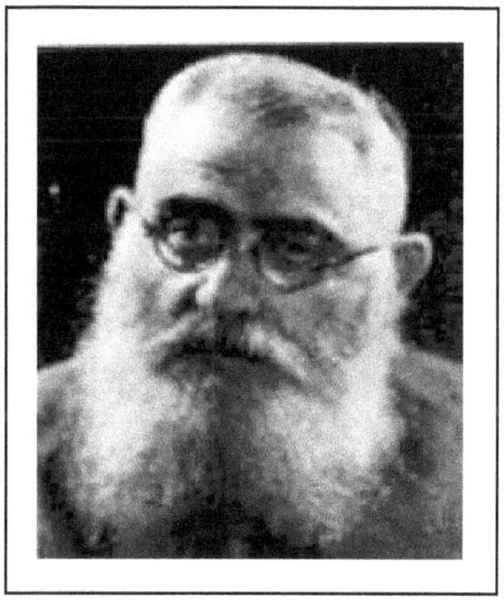

Reb Zelig Papirtsik

the age of marriage, she was engaged to a *yeshiva* boy from the city of Vengrov. On her first visit to the home of the groom's parents, she heard the groom's family sing a song that she did not like. She returned home heartbroken and expressed her refusal to marry the groom in question. The groom did not agree to sever the relationship and sued her. However, due to her being an orphan, the verdict was given in her favor. A short time after, the groom passed away.

My father was the chosen groom and although he was not promised a dowry, he agreed to the match because of the nobility and beauty of the bride. When they got married, the children did not live a long life. Rabbi Nakhum'ke of Bialystok advised asking for forgiveness from the deceased. And so, one night after midnight, my father went out with a *minyen* of Jews to the cemetery, prostrated himself on the grave of the deceased and asked for forgiveness. Since then, the bad luck passed and my father was privileged to have a generation of blessed righteous sons, who follow his ways, the way of Torah and *mitsve*. After a few years my father was able to establish commercial ties on a wide scale with Polish nobles who owned estates in the area, through which he came to great wealth. Thanks to his loyalty and honesty, the owners of the estates trusted him with all their hearts and he became both their personal and economic advisor. His livelihood was not easy at all. Etched in my memory is that dark winter night. It was already midnight and father had not returned from his trip to the Polish estate owner. The roads during this period were disturbed by bandits and wild animals and he was alone in his tiny sled in a dense forest. Mother was anxious and she looked out the window every moment. And here the sound of the ringing bells was heard. Father came back completely frosted and he reassured us, “Here is the gun I received from Kolomiec, the police chief, there is no reason to fear”. However, with this he whispered a secret to mother, “I must risk myself. I have to manage a large house, educate sons, give charity to the poor – the blessed God will help me” .

My father was a very charitable person and my mother also fulfilled that *mitsve*. “She opened her arms to the poor and extended her hands to the needy”. In honor of every *Shabes*, she would send me with *Shabes* dishes to bring to the homes of the poor. I remember the desolate poverty I saw in many homes and how they were happy to see my mother's gift that was presented to them in a modest and humble way.

[Page 235]

Reb Yekhiel Mayer and Leye Blumshteyn of blessed memory

My late father was an enthusiastic *hasid* and the *tsadik* Reb Nakhum'ke of Bialystok used to stay in his house when he passed through Goworowo. Even though my father was a *hasid* of Rebi Shimol'e of Skernievts and was treated as member of his household, he still showed great respect to Reb Nakhum'ke because of the above act.

The older daughter, my sister Esther, married a Torah scholar from a famous family in Israel. He is Reb Berish, the son of Reb Fayvl Tunkenlang of Warsaw, the grandson of Rabbi Motele, a teacher in the capital city of Poland, and the brother-in-law of the Rebi of Alexander and the Rebbe of Yablonka. The wedding took place in Goworowo and it was magnificent. All the nobles of the area gave their carriages to bring the many guests who came to the feast. The beautiful bride wore a sapphire and diamond necklace and an expensive silk dress. Everything was fit for a king.

My brother-in-law Reb Berish was a scholar and a *hasid* and he was supported by my father for ten consecutive years. After that he moved to the city of Warsaw. In his book, the late Rov Mordkhe Bronrot, the head of Tel Aviv judicial system, gives a faithful overview of this distinguished family.

My sister Esther's eldest son was named after his grandfather Reb Motele. He was a tall and handsome man. He had three sons. The eldest son was raised and educated for a long time by my father. The second son, Yerakhmiel was one of the Warsaw Ghetto fighters and died a heroic death fighting the war of his people with the German soldiers. My sister Esther herself died of starvation in the ghetto.

My second sister, Hanna also married a groom from Warsaw, Reb Zelig Papirtsik, a *hasid* and a Torah scholar from a privileged family. He also received a large dowry and food. He invested many years in the Torah and the work. We, the little children at home, fell asleep and always woke up to the sound of his Torah and his pleasant voice while he was studying the *Gemora*. My father housed him and his family in a luxurious apartment in his apartment building in the city center.

My brother, Reb Yekhiel Mayer Blumshteyn, suffered a lot during his short life. He was born during the great fire of the town. All the houses in the town went up in flames, and my father moved my mother and the newborn baby to a farmer's house in a nearby village. On the first *Shabes* night there was no *minyan* to make *shalom v'yisker*, and my father regretted it very much. During the First World War,

[Page 236]

Reb Gershon and Dvore Blumshteyn may God avenge their blood

as a child, my brother contracted smallpox. Due to the lack of doctors and medical treatment, his life was in danger and his face was disfigured. This caused him great suffering.

At the end of the First World War there were fluctuations in the Jewish youth. The Socialist and Zionist movements and the revolution in Russia greatly influenced the youth to divert them from the paved and occupied path, while my brother Yekhiel Mayer remained firm in his position - loyal to the Torah, the religion and the sanctities of the people.

He married his wife Leye, a modest and kind-hearted woman from Ostrolenke and opened a trading house for leather and supplies for shoemakers. He had five sons and a daughter. He invested efforts in educating his children in the way of Torah and *mitsves*. When the boys grew up, he sent them to *yeshivas* and generously provided them all their needs.

My brother Yekhiel Meir reciprocated kindness to people, greeted everyone and gave charity beyond his means. When the town was occupied by the Germans, he fled to Russia, and after the war, he emigrated to America and died there. May his soul be bound up in the bond of everlasting life.

My brother Gershon Blumshteyn may God avenge his blood, fought the war of truth all his life. For every injustice which was done to someone that he knew about, he reacted in acute form, without hesitation and without bias. All his days, he stood by the weak and fought his war and even endangered his life. When, in his youth, Polish boys attacked Jewish boys, he launched a counterattack.

He married Dvore, the daughter of the Rov of Tshervin, a wonderful and innocent man; his daughter was also modest in her manners, and meticulous in *mitsves*.

I remember that last night of the destruction of Goworowo. My brother Gershon clearly showed his bravery and his kindness when he risked his life to save the sick and the children of Israel. It was after a day of enemy aerial bombing. Many people gathered to find shelter in the house of his neighbor Reb A. Y. Galant. Suddenly wounded soldiers appeared from the front and announced that the enemy was about and to flee the town. There was a great commotion and panic. A horse and cart were worth a lot of gold. Everyone wanted to run as fast as possible. My brother Gershon harnessed his cart and loaded it with sick people and children, without taking anything from his possessions. And so, he set out to save souls, abandoning all his possessions.

[Page 237]

Mayer Zev Tehilim

May God Avenge His Blood

by Yitskhak Shafran, Israel

Translated by Tina Lunson

Reb Mayer Vulf (Zev) Tehilim was descended from the Vurke *Rebi* Rov Itsikl and traveled to the Amshinov *Rebi* of the Vurke line. He did truly love the Jews of Vurke but in his temperament and acuity he surpassed even Ger and Kotsk.

Reb Mayer Vulf was a wholesale dealer on a large scale, a big risk taker in trade. He would buy a lot of wagons full of coal, kerosene, cement, mortar and so on. Mostly his dealing was successful. He made a good living and became rich; but more than once it happened that he lost money on a transaction and had to take out another interest free loan. But he was never defeated by that, always cheerful, went on making big deals and got back on his feet. People never knew when he earned and when he lost.

As for community matters, especially for the charities like the fund for poor brides, help

[Page 238]

for a pauper, he was always ready to work with all his strength. It was at his initiative and assistance that the *Tseirey Agudas Yisroel* renewed the activity of the *Lines ha'tsedik*, of acquiring a lot of medical equipment which they lent out to poor, sick Jews.

He gave charity with an open hand. He usually donated more than another person in the same position. During the rush of the Fourth *aliye*, he was the first to buy land in *Erets Yisroel*, through *Agudas Yisroel* and sent his elder son, Yitskhak Dovid there. He had a big failure there, lost a lot of money, and his son had to return but, his love for *Erets Yisroel* was not diminished. With the blossoming of the agricultural pioneer movement, he was the first to invite *Agudas Yisroel* to open a training station in his cement factory in Pasheki.

Reb Mayer Vulf was an observant *hasid*, preserving Jewishness in every detail. Most recently he was praying with the *Tseirey gudas Yisroel minyen*. On *Simkhes Torah* he tended to make the priestly blessing in the morning prayers because of the tumult that dominated the afternoon service. The circuits of dancing with the Torah scrolls went on so long in that service and the praying went so late, to about four o'clock. They could not prevail on him, though, to make a *kidush* sooner. Only when people had finished *musaf* did he make *kidush*. Very characteristic of his conduct was his remark about the quote "*Tov met b'kavone, m'haraba sh'lo b'kavone*", which simply means that one must do something, but with intent, or do a lot, without intent but, he used to say just the opposite, "One must do a lot, even without *kavone*, because, a lot without *kavone* still produces a little *kavone*".

Reb Mayer Vulf was a short Jew, with no special indications of strength but, he had a voice, literally the voice of a lion, which could be heard from afar. I was once witness in the study house when Reb Mayer Vulf shouted loudly, complaining about justice in some particular matter. The alarm was his last weapon when someone refused to agree with him.

People say that during the last World War, Reb Mayer Vulf wandered over to White Russia, it seems, not far from the train station in Minsk. When the Russians deported the *bezshenikes* to Siberia and other places, the transport trains went through White Russia and sometimes stopped at the train station where Reb Mayer Vulf lived. He would often come out to the trains and search for familiar faces and relatives. When he found a Goworower, he tried to approach and offer some help. The N.K.V.D. guards did not allow this however. So he would stand at a distance and feel pity for those from his town whom the Russians were persecuting. But the fates were otherwise. Many of the deportees survived the war while he and part of his family were murdered. May God avenge their blood!

[Page 239]

A Memorial Candle for my Family

by Menukhe Zeltser-Grudka, Israel

Translated by Mira Eckhaus

Edited by Tina Lunson

Reb Khayim Ber, his wife Brayne, and his daughters:
Rokhl and Brokhe may God avenge their blood, and Menukhe may she live long life (on the left)

My father Reb Khayim Ber, of the house of Grudka, was from a loyal *hasidic* family and he himself was God fearing and observed every *mitsve* and custom of Jewish tradition.

I remember the holidays at home. Feelings of joy and elation were on my parents' faces and a festive atmosphere filled the house. In the Days of Awe, Father served as a *shofar* blower in the great synagogue that was next to our house. He prepared himself with great respect for the exalted role of a public messenger before the Creator. On *Purim*, the neighbors used to gather at our house and my father read aloud in front of them from the scroll with his pleasant voice and captivating emphasis.

It still echoes in my ears, the sound of the Talmud that my father read aloud while he was sitting and studying in any free time, whether it was day or night.

My father was a working man and struggled hard to support his family with dignity. However, he was always calm and cheerful and a warm smile never left his lips. He was full of hope and faith in a better future. He was a good and benevolent man to the people and his family and loved by all, children, adults and elderly, regardless their religious opinion.

My mother was a woman of valor, she inspired her daughters and her family with her spirit. She also worked hard as a housewife, educating the girls, and even assisted my father in his efforts to provide livelihood.

When the two girls immigrated to Israel, mother did not rest and was not quiet until she used all her efforts and connections so that the girls would not be missing a thing in their first steps in Israel.

I see in my mind my kind and dear sisters, young women full of life and joy, who had only just begun to taste the tree of life and here they were murdered in their youth by bloodthirsty murderers.

It is hard for me to come to terms with the bitter and passing idea that I will no longer see my loved ones, my family members, who perished in such a tragic way. May these lines serve as a memorial light for their souls.

[Page 240]

Reb Borekh Mints
of Blessed Memory

by A. Boshon, Israel

Translated by Tina Lunson

One of the prominent, refined types in Goworowo was Reb Borekh Mints. He occupied an honored place in the town. He behaved in a very bold, forward way and had a wealthy man's generosity, of a big city scope. He gave the impression of a refined Jew from an earlier time. Always clean and tidily dressed, a nice rosy face with a wide spreading snow-white beard, a silver walking stick in his hand, he walked down the street slowly, with an expression of dignity.

It was a pleasure to go into Borekh Mints' house. Everything there spoke of wealthy comfort - fine, massive furniture, plushy divans, a silver and crystal cabinet. Everything made an effective impression- he himself in his house, in a flowery silk house jacket, soft slippers with a squeak, and carrying refreshments for the guests.

He was no great Talmud scholar, but he loved to hear "a Jewish word" and to honor a Torah scholar with his whole heart. He liked the idea that the Talmud says, "adorn yourself with *mitsves*". He did not receive any money to shine and polish the holy utensils, but for a good deed. On *Sukes* he used an artistically worked little box for the citron. He had a *khanike* lamp, also of silver, more than one meter high and he had a fine Turkish *talis* with a silver collar. For every Jewish thing, he bought the most beautiful and best, sparing no cost.

Reb Borekh had an iron business on the Market Square and for a long time was quite rich. He later lost his wealthy status but still ran a lovely home, gave generously to charities, and maintained his custom of handing out candies to children.

Reb Borekh Mints was an ardent *hasid* to the *rebis* of the Vurke line. When any of the Vurke grandchildren happened to come to Goworowo, he acted as an inn and set out a table suitable for a *rebi*. We all remember the visit to Goworowo by Rov Avrom Meyshe'le Otvotsker, who stayed at Reb Borekh's house. The whole town attended the *Shabes* tables, giving notes to the *Rebi* and asking for blessings. Although the house and furniture had gotten shabby, Reb Borekh was pleased and glowed with pride.

Reb Borekh did not mix in town matters and did not want to be a councilman or a community activist. Only for the building of the Otvotsker *shtibl*

[Page 241]

did he get involved. He so liked to live his own life, calm and quiet, not letting the outside disturb him.

He was born in Goworowo and died there in the early 1930s.

Reb Mayer Romaner
of Blessed Memory

by A. Boshon, Israel

Translated by Tina Lunson

A scholar among scholars, a wise man among experts as well as a folk figure, respected by everyone – for such circumstances one must have specific characteristics and many good qualities.

Reb Mayer Romaner or as we called him in town, Reb Mayer'l, for his small size, was without doubt worthy of such an estimation. In the town, he was both loved and respected. Indeed, for his distinguished personality, Reb Mayer'l was always at the top of the council leadership. He himself did not seek out honors. Rather, he was a proper "originally modest" person, who spoke in a quiet voice, distanced himself from conflict, was measured and sensible, as is the character of a true Talmud scholar. But those very qualities impelled people to elect him as a councilman in every term of office and as a representative in many community institutions. He felt a deep responsibility to community matters. He gave much thought to his social obligations. Indeed his advice was generally weighty, "weighed and measured". He stated his case with very few well-honed words, with a smile on his lips, and accompanied by a clever aphorism.

Reb Mayer'l was born in the 1860s, to his parents Reb Avrom Yitskhak and Freyde Romaner, proprietor of a haberdashery and food shop in Makov-Mazavietsk.

Reb Mayer'l learned in the Makove town study house, with great diligence, it appears, because he achieved a higher level in learning that particularly showed his clear, logical comprehension and analytic power of understanding. People say that Nakhum Sokolov, the famous editor of *Ha'tsefira* and president of the World Zionists, was also studying at the Makove study house at that same time. Reb Mayer'l married his wife Reyzl, the daughter of Avrom Mendl Koen, who operated a tavern in Makove.

After the wedding Reb Mayer'l moved to Goworowo along with his in-laws. They went on operating the tavern and Reb Mayer'l sat in the study house and learned.

Reb Mayer'l was an important leader of *Agude* in town, and of

[Page 242]

the founding of the *Beys Yankev* school for girls. He held one of the most honored places in the Ger *shtibl*. He guarded the "page of the day" like a treasure and never missed a day of studying that page of Talmud.

In later years he opened a haberdashery business from which he drew an abundant living. And of course he had a fine, respectful home, and was devoted to community service.

With the outbreak of the war Reb Mayer'l fled back to the town of his birth, Makove, and died there on the 9th of Kheshvan, sav" shin. His wife Reyzl, his daughter Hinde Leye and her husband Shleyme Khayim Tsimbal and their little boy Itsikl were murdered in Slonim, may God avenge their blood. Their daughter Freydke Tandaytshazsh died in 1925; her husband Yitskhak Leyb, in 1957 in Argentina.

[from right] Reyzl Romaner may God avenge her blood, Yitskhak Leyb and Freydke Tandaytshazsh of blessed memory

[from right] Sh. H. Tsimbal may God avenge his blood; their children and his wife Hinde Leye may God avenge their blood

[Page 243]

Reb Yankev Hersh Vengrov

by A. Boshon, Israel

Translated by Tina Lunson

Since he looked at a person with an acute eye which was rather practiced in godliness, one could easily recognize that Reb Yankev Hersh had a relationship to the Vurke *kheyder*. It was simply on his face, which poured out so much love for the Jewish people, such goodness and good-heartedness, that one could easily see the old *Rebi*'s doctrine of "judging all mankind on the side of merit", of using the right side of the coin, that one cannot go through the world with anger and not with hardness; even a transgressor among Yisroel is still a Jew and one must act towards him only with goodness.

I do not believe that any Goworowo Jews had ever, at any time, seen Reb Yankev Hersh in a bad mood. Even though his personal circumstances were not happy ones. The two blind horses that he used in his little grain mill could not make him a complete living and, a confession, could not make a dowry for his daughters. But what had livelihood to do with state of mind? A Jew needs to be happy, always brave and cheerful, if only because one was created a Jew, as the Talmud says, you must make blessings as much as for bad as for good.

Reb Yankev Hersh was a fervent *hasid*, like those one -time pioneers of *hasidism*. Anyone who saw his zeal at the *erev Peysakh* guarded matsos, or at the hasidic welcome of the *Shabes* Queen, he shone with holiness. He did not like to rely on another. He laid the fire himself, he put on an apron to peel the potatoes, and he cooked up *hasidic* groats that had a thousand flavors. And while doing so, he sang the old Vurke melody with such ecstasy that it touched the heart.

Reb Yankev Hersh had such a folksy house, an entire house with a garden, fenced and with hedges, like a prince's estate. He also had his own harness team, a horse and wagon which he often used to take *hasidim* to a *rebi* who had come to a nearby *shtetl.*

He married his elder daughter to a young *hasidic* mercantile man, Meyshe Kosher, who later became president of the Goworowo Jewish Council in its last term.

Reb Yankev Hersh was probably sent by the Russians to their camps. The fate of his family is not known to us.

[Page 244]

Reb Fayvl Brik

May God Avenge His Blood

by A. Boshon, Israel

Translated by Tina Lunson

Reb Fayvl Brik was one of the big community activists in the town. There was not one Council action or undertaking, in which Fayvl did not have a large part. He was a member of many institutions in town and had real concern for their existence.

He was a quiet and separate person, not pushing himself to high places and not seeking any glory. Quietly, without to-do, he did his fruitful work in the name of heaven and for the sake of the *mitsves*. In his Council position he liked to sit in a corner, wrapped in his heavy calico robe and listen to what others said. He only offered his own opinion when they asked him for it.

Reb Fayvl Brik had life wisdom bored into him. It was a pleasure to converse with him. One had to take his ideas into consideration. The Rov often consulted with him on community affairs.

Fayvl put a lot of his energies into the building of the town's new study house. But when they wanted to make him a *gabay* he did not agree. He hated disputes to the bottom of his heart but, if someone had to fight, he was ready. He was also involved with the Burial Society and for a while was the *gabay* of that group. He was particularly dedicated to the *mitsve* of welcoming guests. He was the builder of the town's hospitality house. Besides that, he devoted a room in his less-than-spacious house to an inn for poor people who spent the night there and ate.

Reb Fayvl was a shoemaker by trade. He especially worked on peasant shoes and boots and was quite well off. But he did not pursue riches. He loved to search out favors to do for people and help another in a time of trouble.

Reb Fayvl was the pride of the town's artisans. They extolled him because he was one of the most honored and respected craftsmen in town.

Fayvl or as people called him, Fayvl Yermiahu's, was murdered during the war years, may God avenge his blood.

[Page 245]

Yoel'ke the Baker

by A. Bar-Even, Israel

Translated by Tina Lunson

There were legends going around in many towns of Jews, spiritual heroes, who breathed with love and devotion for the people and were prepared to sacrifice their own lives for the salvation of the community. That strength burgeoned especially in difficult moments for the folk, when the destroying angel held his gleaming sword over Jewish heads, threatening to drink up a Jewish settlement in blood.

Those Jews were necessarily simple, everyday people, different from the crowd, who did not mix into Council matters, who did not request anything from anyone or demand anything of anyone. Yet, when the moment for miracles arrived, their risen personas of strength and heroism came into full view.

Reb Yoel'ke Yelin, or as he was popularly known "Yoel'ke the baker", belonged, without any doubt, to that brave constellation. The Goworowo residents mention his name to this day with a sacred shudder and with honor and carry his image deep in their hearts, as a synonym of devotion, strength and self sacrifice.

Yoel'ke had lived in the town for many years. His wooden, several storied house stood in the middle of the Market Square, between the houses of Borekh Kuperman and Menashe Holtsman. In that house Yoel'ke had his bread bakery, the selling counters, and a large room that served as a tea house. His apartment was up on the next floor; where he lived with his wife Rivke'le.

During the years of the outbreak of the last war, Yoel'ke must have been sixty-odd years old. His strength must have been waning. He alone baked the goods, sold the products and could still lift a sack of flour on his shoulders with the ease of a young man.

Beginning with just his appearance, one could easily make a mistake and suppose that Yoel'ke was a stickler, an impatient Jew. The yellow/grey little beard that ringed his thin face was hard and usually dusted with flour; the pale grey eyes were obscured by thick yellow brows. His stooped height, the hoarse, rough voice, and his severe, piercing glances gave his face an angry hardness.

In fact, inside Yoel'ke there beat a good, sensitive Jewish heart – full of love and friendship for all people.

Yoel'ke's personal life was permeated with pain and worry. He had almost no pleasure from this world. His wife Rivke had birthed him thirteen

[Page 246]

children and not one of them remained alive. Yoel'ke and his wife went around like shadows, ashamed, locked into themselves and depressed.

Yoel'ke found his entire comfort in helping Jews; supporting the needy and rescuing a person in trouble. He performed that help through modest work, without noise or fuss, and with a heartfelt naturalness.

His tea room was usually full of guests, poor people, traveling preachers, couriers, who received their "snacks" and "dinners" completely free, with a smile on their lips.

At night, the tea room was turned into a "hotel". Yoel'ke pushed the tables and benches aside; Rivke brought in bed linens, and however many guests there were, there was a place for everyone to sleep. No one was asked for legitimization and no one was asked hard questions.

The tea room was not meant for only indigent guests. Even the "high class" of Jews who wanted a hot, well-sugared glass of tea, sat at one of the wide oak tables and drank as much as their hearts desired.

The biggest commotion at Yoel'ke's was a Shabes morning. It swarmed with people, like a beehive of coming and going. Every hasid who was returning from the Shabes cold *mikve* beat a path to Yoel'ke's to drink a boiling glass of tea. Even Enlighteners who did not go to the *mikve* from one *erev yon-kiper* to the next did not lose out on drinking a glass of the warmth at Yoel'ke's on Shabes to warm the chilled, sleepy bones from the cold night.

This Shabes tea drinking was set out for self- service because at the same time, both Yoel'ke and Rivke were busy portioning out bubbling hot water for the children and maids to take home to their houses.

The town Jews very much appreciated Yoel'ke's broad hand and his good-heartedness. But no one imagined that he was capable of showing such valor as he demonstrated that Shabes in the month of *Elul* in 1939.

It was in the week that the Germans took Goworowo and they elected that Shabes day to make the bloody accounting of the Jews.

Just before dawn, when the town was still sunken in a deep sleep, the murderers started a wild, hellish tumult. They opened with heavy gunfire, shooting, breaking down doors and ordering all the Jewish residents to leave their houses. Anyone who did not hurry was shot on the spot. All those Jews were herded, with brutal force, into the big *shul*, and soldiers were posted on all sides. The entire Jewish population of men, women, children were shoved in, cramped, pressed together.

Around lunchtime the S.S. men set fire to the town, each house

[Page 247]

individually. With devilish smiles they assured the Jews jammed into the *shul* that the soldiers would soon be there to set fire to the *shul*, along with all the people.

The screaming, a lamenting that filled the study house space split the heavens. Especially heart rending was the cries of the hungry children, who had had nothing in their mouths since the previous night, for in the great chaos the mothers were unable to bring any food with them. And the children were pulling at their parents: Mama!

Mama! Food!

Everyone saw the children's suffering, heard their cries, but no one dared to even think of going out on the street to find food. The S.S. order was exact and clear, “Anyone who appears on the street will be shot without further warning”. No one doubted the sincerity of that order.

Yoel'ke sat in a corner of the *shul*, immobile, looking on at the wailing children and quietly murmuring psalms. After a while he stood up, pushed himself through the packed together mass of people and approached the door. His hard -bitten lips showed a firm determination. He threw the door open wide, went through it and disappeared outside.

A deadly quiet settled over the study house. A convulsive shudder of horror gripped everyone. Then soon was heard the murderous shot, aimed by the Germans into the body of Yoel'ke.

In the joint dead silence, one could hear the crackling of the burning houses and the wild shouting of the agitated murderers.

Through the large paned windows of the study house, Yoel'ke could be seen running fast, crossing the street, going into his bakery. After a long time, he came back out bent under a heavy sack that he was carrying on his shoulders.

The despicable eyes of the guarding soldiers were blinded. They did not even see the old Jew with the heavy sack slowing walking, his flaming face that of a martyr who strode with proud steps, with such certainty and inner calm as if he were walking to a joyous occasion as a *mitsve*.

Yoel'ke entered the *shul*. “Here are *khale* loaves for you, Jews!” he said with such matter-of-fact modesty, “Take them, Jews, give it to the children, today is Shabes!”

Reb Yoel'ke felt nothing of how much super human strength, courage and self-sacrifice lay in the lofty deed that he had done so naturally and so simply.

And, after his deed was done, a high ranking German officer driving by had ordered the release of the Jews from the burning study house, everyone ascribed to the merit of Yoel'ke the baker for his huge self-sacrifice in order to help the suffering Jewish children.

[Page 248]

In memory of my father R. Moses Skurnik
May His Memory be for a Blessing

by Khayim Skurnik, Israel

Translated by Mira Eckhaus

Edited by Tina Lunson

Reb Moshe Skurnik
of blessed memory

When I come to reminisce about our city of Goworowo and about my family there, I recall the prayer leader's plea on *Yom-kiper* before *musaf*, "I am poor in merits, I am agitated and afraid". I am also agitated and afraid of the great role of the commemoration enterprise in memory of our town. I bow my head to the initiators of the commemoration and I pray - May all those who added a pillar to the memory of the glorious Judaism in Poland, for our sakes and for our children's sake, be strong.

What do I start with? With the wonderful youth in our town; the vibrant youth, who aspired and fought with all their might to break the enslaving shackles of man as an individual and of the Jewish people in general. Although the youth of our town was divided into all kinds of parties such as *Poaley tsion* left and *BeTaR*, its aspiration was only one - return to Zion. The ways were different and unalike, but the goal was one – a Jewish state.

I remember one Saturday afternoon. My father, Reb Moshe of blessed memory, sat in the synagogue and as usual studied a page of *Gemora* and we, the youth, gathered around him. He stopped studying for a short while and spoke to us about the return to Zion and the duty of being ready to leave the Exile quickly. It was as if my late father, in the back of his mind, felt the need to hurry, lest it be too late.

My late father was a passionate Zionist from the very beginning of the Zionist Organization. According to him, he once received a letter of thanks from Herzl himself for his help in conducting propaganda for the spread of the Zionist idea among the broad strata of the people. He was a talented orator, with great persuasive power, and his speeches always attracted a large audience. He was among the founders of *Mizrakhi* and its youth movement in Goworowo.

When Ze'ev Jabotinsky founded the new Zionist Organization, my late father joined the movement. He preached in the synagogue and explained that they would not hand over the state to us on a silver plate, and that there would be

[Page 249]

a need to fight for it and make sacrifices on the altar of its establishment. And indeed, when he was privileged to immigrate to Israel, he extended his help to the underground, fighting with the British mandate. In his home, in Haifa, he hid underground fighters with weapons and risked his life for the idea he believed in.

My late father was born in the city of Lodz in 1882 and after his wedding moved to Goworowo. He immigrated to Israel in 1936 and died in Haifa in 1952.

Our town Goworowo excelled in the generosity of its residents and readiness to lend a helping hand one to another anytime and anywhere. Perets' story comes to my mind, *If Not Higher* still. There were quite a few in our community about whom we could say, if not higher still.

Unfortunately, our town was burnt and no longer exists. We are commanded not to forget Amalek and what he did to us. We will tell our children about the glorious Judaism that was destroyed in such a cruel way. Let our children tell their children until the end of all generations.

The day will come and God will take our revenge on the damned Germans.

Rov Khayim Mordkhe Bronrot
May His Sainted Memory be a Blessing

by Sh. D. Yerushalmi, Israel

Translated by Mira Eckhaus

Edited by Tina Lunson

The *Rov* Reb Khayim Mordechai Bronrot, may his sainted memory be a blessing, was born in Ostrolenke in 5641. His father, Reb Nosn Tsvi, a bookseller, lived for many years in Goworowo, sent him at a young age to study with the Gaon *Rov* Avraham of Sukhtsov and then with *Rov* Eliyahu Singer, *Rov* of Kalish. He was authorized to teach while he was still young by *Rov* Malkhiel Tanenbaum, the author of *Divrey Malkhiel*, the *Rov* of Lomzshe, *Rov* Moshe Nakhum of Yerushalimski, the *Rov* of Kalitz and *Rebi* Shimon Dov of Shedlets. He married Figa Matel, the daughter of Reb Shmuelke of Stradin, the daughter of *Rov* Yankev Yehude Butsian of Goworowo.

The first rabbinate he was appointed to was in Tshervin, Ostrolenke district (5668-5674). Afterwards, he was appointed as a *Rov* in the city of Khorzel but, after a short time, when the First World War broke out and all the Jews of the city, which was close to the German border, were expelled from it, he arrived as a refugee in Warsaw and stayed there for two years. For the time being, he devoted himself to public affairs and was one of the heads of the refugee aid committee. In 5676 he was appointed as a *Rov* in Tshekhonov and served in this rabbinate for twenty-five years, with a break of two years (5682-5683), during which he was in America on a public mission together with *Rov* Troyev of Kutne. While he stayed in America, he also served as *Rov* of the synagogue of the Lubavitsh Hasidim in Chicago. In 5699, about two months before the outbreak of the Second World War, he traveled again on a public mission to England and due to the war, he was forced to stay there for several years until he was able to immigrate to Israel.

In Poland he was considered one of the great rabbis, he was great in Torah and well-versed in public affairs. For many years he was a member of the executive committee of the Association of Rabbis in Poland. He was popular and cherished in the rabbinic circles and closely associated with the courts of the *rebis*. Although he was an Aleksander *hasid* and even commented on the family of the Aleksander *Rebi*, he was a loyal Zionist and among the first rabbis in Poland who united

[Page 250]

Rov Reb Khayim Mordkhe Bronrot

around the *Mizrakhi* organization. He was very active in the movement in writing and speaking and held positions in the administration of the movement. For a certain time, he was a member of the working committee of the *Mizrakhi* organization in Poland. At his initiative, the Knesset of the *Mizrakhi* Rabbis in Poland was founded, and he headed it. During his stay in England, he served as the vice president of the *Mizrakhi* there, participated in the world *Mizrachi* conferences as well as in the 12th, 13th, and 14th Zionist Congresses.

He visited Israel in 5686 and 5696. He settled there in 5703 and was appointed the head of the Tel Aviv judicial system. He served in this position until his last day. He was also appointed as the chairman of religious education in Tel Aviv. After the death of the chief *rov*, *Rov* Moshe Avigdor Amiel, may his sainted memory be a blessing, he was active in the *Mizrachi* movement in Israel and spread Torah widely. He published many articles in the movement's periodicals in Israel and abroad, *HaMizrakhi*, *Di Yidishe Shtime*, *HaTsofue*, and many more. He authored many books on *halakha* and *droshe* [interpretation of the Bible], a large part of which remain in handwritten form.

The ones that were printed: *Oytser Ha'khayim*, *Pietrikov* (5690), *Kidushim in Halacha and Agada*, *Omer Ve'dvarim* (5695) sermons on the parshes of the week in the books of Genesis, Exodus and Leviticus (the rest were left in handwritten form), *Stirat Zkenim* (5708) on the articles of our learned teachers in *halacha* and *agada* (the rest was left in handwritten form).

He also published *halachic* articles clarifying the question of milking on Shabes (5706); *A trip by Airplane on Shabbat* (*Sinai*, vol. 14, pages 129-135), with special attention to the problems of the time zones and the need to build the renewed Jewish community.

Rov Khayim Mordkhe Bronrot died in Tel Aviv, 7th Adar 5710 (1950). May his soul be bundled in the bundle of the living.

[Page 251]

Rov Avrom Mendl Galant

May His Blessed Memory be for a Blessing

by Meyshe Khayim Galant, Canada

Translated by Tina Lunson

My father *Rov* Avrom Mendl was born in Goworowo, to his parents Yitskhak Yankev and Malka Perl Galant, may they rest in peace. The father, a Vurke Hasid, was a scholar and a very pious man and they reared their son in the spirit of *Yiddishkayt*; he was a very diligent student who studied 18 hours out of every 24. Whenever one might go to the study house, they would find him sitting and learning. He did indeed become an expert in Talmud and its commentators. He later married in Ostrove, to the daughter of Yeshaye, Talis maker, who gave him a generous dowry plus free room and board in order for him to sit and study, with the prospect of becoming a *rov*. But he did not want to be a *rov;* not willing to make the Torah into a source of income, so turned to trade and also prospered. In the early days, he also continued to study in his free time.

During the First World War he became impoverished and under guidance from the Vurke *Rebi*, to whom he had traveled, agreed to become a *rov* and found a post in a small town near Ostrove.

In the Second World War he, along with his family, wandered into Russia where he suffered terribly because of his religious observance. He got through the days with a piece of bread and water and when it was available, some potatoes. And so he spent several years. After the War he was evacuated back to

Poland. From there to a camp in Germany where he acted as *Rov* until he merited making *aliye* to *Erets Yisroel* and passed away herein a good place, the 25th of *Tevet sav-shin-tes "vov* at the age of eighty.

[Page 252]

Hasidic Personalities

by Yosef Zilbertson, Israel

Translated by Tina Lunson

Reb Yeshaye Ayzenberg
of Blessed memory

Reb Yeshaye Ayzenberg, long term *gabay* of the Aleksander *shtibl*, was a type of keen *hasid* who was characterized by a great love for the simple Jews. Every *Shabes,* after lunch, people saw Fayvl the Lame walking to Reb Yeshaye's to call him to come and study Torah and *kabole* with the congregation in the large *shul.* Reb Yeshaye put on his heavy satin *kapote* and his high velvet hat, wrapped his throat with his red kerchief and went off to *shul.* The congregation "swallowed" his every word.

Reb Yeshaye ran the *gabay* office in the *shtibl* with authority. If he decided that they must recite various liturgical poems during their prayers, such as *Shira* on Passover or the Ten Commandments during *Shavues*, the protests from the older hasidim from one side did not help nor did the younger hasidim on the other side, who complained that Reb Yeshaye was introducing new customs into the *shtibl.* The hasidim did indeed recite these "creations". As revenge the group caught any "errors" in Hebrew during his leading the afternoon prayers on *yom-kiper*, which Reb Yeshay had claim to pray from the cantor's stand. But despite those incidents, he was much beloved by all.

Reb Yeshaye had a flaw of fabricating Torah proverbs on the spot; if the congregation demanded more whisky and cookies at *kidush*, he would say, "If you eat, you must pay, but there is no money". In his trade with pelts, he would interpret the verse in *Megiles Ester* "there was light and joy for the Jews" as, "the Jews laid on furs" (from the word for light). *Simkhe v'sason*, as "when there is joy and happiness"; *v'ikar* as "the pelt will be expensive".

Etched into my mind from boyhood are the *Shabes* nights when hasidim gathered at Reb Yeshaye's house to drink a glass of tea with sugar. Among the regular guests were Yisroel Leyb Kruk the elementary teacher, Avremele Grudke the teacher, Meyshe Skurnik the expediter, Yudl the clockmaker, and others. We, the children, waited all week to hear the wonderful stories that were told around the table, beginning with the beer dregs at Nikolay, the demons and ghosts that used to terrify at the guard post, up to the actual political issues of the day. They talked about everything and everyone around the table and Brayne his wife, may she rest in peace, stood by alert and ready to pour everyone's tea.

[Page 253]

Reb Yeshaye merited dying in his own bed. His wife Brayne (they did not have any children) died being transported to the Siberian boreal region, during the last World War.

Reb Yekhiel Gerlits
May God Avenge His Blood

Reb Yekhiel Gerlits was one of the more interesting types of the Aleksander *shtibl,* an Enlightened Jew, Talmud scholar, authorized to act as a *rov*, and a colonial merchant. He was a man of letters and affairs, knew Russian and Polish and wrote petitions to various government offices in those languages.

In his youth he was friends with Nakhum Sokolov, who even proposed that he become his secretary. After he moved from Makove to Goworowo he still maintained contact with him through letters. They carried on that correspondence for many years.

Reb Yekhiel was an optimist by nature, always tidying up and taking everything with a joke and a smile. He was one of the regular prayer leaders for the Days of Awe in the *shtibl*. He perished in the war years.

Reb Note Rits
May God Avenge His Blood

Reb Note Rits, the co-owner of the big mill and electric works in town, was a tall, big-boned Jew who bristled with good health and an energetic appearance. He was reckoned among the eminent hasidim of the Aleksander *shtibl* because he was also a wealthy man and was very generous in the area of *mitsves*.

On certain occasions Reb Note invited the congregation to his home for *probostva* and the hasidim never regretted the long trip that was imposed on them. He compensated them with a lot of whisky and plenty of cooked dishes too for, as mentioned, Reb Note was half owner of the mill.

Reb Note excelled with his hearty, folkish humor, which bubbled up in him. When he told a good joke, even the most gloomy person had to burst out laughing. He was president of the Jewish Council for a few years and much loved by all the Jewish residents, as well as by the Christians. He and his whole family were murdered by the German Hitlerists.

Reb Avrom Yitskhak Galant
May God Avenge His Blood

Reb Avrom Yitskhak Galant or as he was popularly known, *der kvashnik*, was considered one of the most intelligent of the Aleksander hasidim. He read a Zionist newspaper, was a little bit of a philosopher, loved to ponder every issue and did not take things too lightly.

[Page 254]

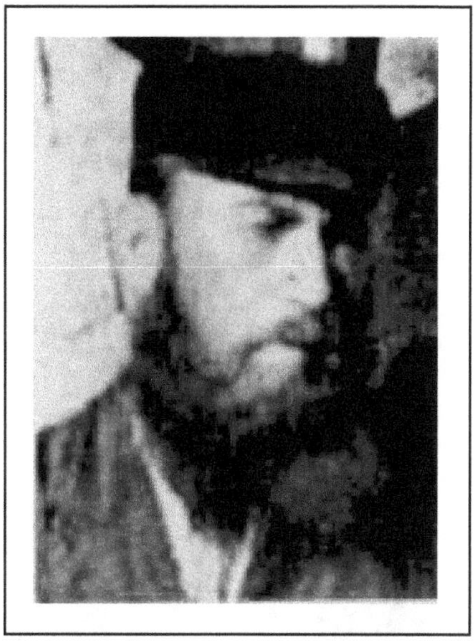

Reb Avrom Yitskhak Galant
May God Avenge His Blood

His delicatessen shop and even his private residence were meeting points, especially for the religious nationalist youth. On the weekdays of the summer months they ate delicious ice cream with him and a good glass of soda water and on Friday and Saturday nights a cold glass of beer.

Reb Avrom Yitskhak was an outstanding master of song and one of the good prayer leaders in the Aleksander *shtibl*. His son Meyshe was one of the first victims - the Germans caught him in Ostrove at work and then

[Page 255]

Reb A. Y. Galant's children

threw him into cold water, from which he was badly chilled and he died. Reb Avrom Yitskhak and his family were murdered in the last war.

Reb Bertshe Viroslav
May God Avenge His Blood

Reb Bertshe Viroslav was a true example of an old time, old *hasid.* Although his livelihood was hardly large, he was always in a good state of mind. He loved to hear and to tell hasidic stories, tales about *rabeyim* and religious Jews. He was also a champion for a good drink of whisky, 95 proof, at the hasidic celebrations that were frequent in the Aleksander *shtibl.*

Reb Bertshe had right of possession to the "verses of song" for the Days of Awe. He sang in many voices and before he had even finished the blessings he was already hoarse.

He and his entire family were murdered in the last World War.

Reb Aba Likhtman
May God Avenge His Blood

Reb Aba Likhtman or, as people used to call him, Aba the wagon driver, was always a neat and happy Jew, a kind of "merry pauper". He maintained communications between Goworowo and Ruzshan with his half dead horse and broken down wagon. A trip with Rev Aba was not known for its comforts. No trip went by without a wheel breaking in the middle of the road or the horse going on strike. Then one received a full recompense of his "artistic" entertainment for the passenger.

Reb Aba, with his developed taste for humor, liked to put the passenger in harness. If he was going uphill, he asked the passenger to do the favor and agree to the *mitsve* of helping push the wagon up the hill. Sometimes he set the passengers up as soldiers in the "Aleksander Troop" in which he himself had served for many years and singing an up-beat military march, would march a nice few kilometers with them. When he could already see the Ruzshan bridge in the distance, then it was really not worthwhile to get back into the rickety wagon.

Reb Aba was a learned man, and for the Days of Awe he usually served as prayer leader in a village not far from Ruzshan. On *Simkhes Torah,* Reb Aba good heartedly sang the "bits" from the Days of Awe prayers and repeated the sermon that he had given before the *shofar* blowing in that village. He told us the following story about something that happened to him. Once, as he stood praying aloud at the cantor's stand, he saw through the window that his horse was wandering

[Page 256]

around eating grass. Then he suddenly saw that the horse was wandering off. His poor spirit sank – a cantor cannot walk away in the middle of prayers and here, the horse was going further and further. What to do? A solution occurred to him. With each word that he sang, he sang out *prrru, prrru, prrru* with a screaming, whining tune, until the horse heard it and came back. The village householders absolutely loved the new style of *davening.*

He was murdered with his whole family in the last war.

R. Avrumke Tsalke,
May God Avenge His Blood

by A. Bashan, Israel

Donated by Lester Blum

Edited by Tina Lunson

As a general rule a *shames* in a small town is typically an unassuming, quiet man, who is thankful that no one bothers him. He likes to flatter the important men of the town a little and he dies of hunger three times a day, except for Sabbaths and holidays.

Avromke Tsalke was, indeed, a *shames* in Goworowo, but the above mentioned characteristics were lacking in him; he was not unassuming, he was not quiet, he flattered no one; in fact important men flattered him. He was also rich and had lots of money.

So what did he need to be *shames* for? Really just for his own pleasure. It was his nature to have to know everything that everyone in the town was doing. As official town *shames* he had entry everywhere. He was at the Rabbi's house and at all gatherings. He took part in all meetings of the congregation and was a buddy to all the town elite. You could say that he was the pulse of the town and everything that went on had to go through him. All the stories and happenings in the town, general and personal, came to his attention, and he knew where to react and where not.

He liked things to be stirred up a bit in town. A bit of a dispute between *Hasidim* and *Misnagdim,* or between two citizens eager for honor, that really was just what he was looking for. Just for fun, he took care that the dispute did not die down too quickly.

In the town *beys-medresh* he was like a "king among his troops"; he gave an *aliye* to whomever among the important men he chose to give, and to whomever he did not chose, he did not give one. He was the leader of prayers,

[Page 257]

the reader for the Torah, and the provider for poor travelers in town. Although there were two other *shamasim* he did not forego the privilege of accompanying the Rabbi to and from prayers and everywhere else the Rabbi had to officially visit.

R' Avrom and Leye Tsalke, may God avenge their blood

He was by nature a good-hearted and cheerful man, welcome in every house.

Reb Avrom was born in Goworowo. His father's name was Nosn Kalmen. After his marriage he graduated and worked hard to make a living. Only when his children were grown and had left for America did his situation improve. His children sent him a lot of money and in time he came to be considered one of the town's wealthiest men.

From time to time one of his children would come from America to visit him. Then he would be quite an exciting figure in town – an American "Lord" with a bright checkered suit, a Panama hat, and a fat cigar in his mouth. He was the center of attention, which gave Avromke bucketsful of pleasure.

Avromke took no money for being a *shames.* He did it as a good deed, and indeed, also for his own pleasure.

After the outbreak of the war, Reb Avromke and his wife, Leye moved to Slonim where they were killed. He was then approaching 80 years of age.

[Page 258]

History of One Family in Goworowo

by Yitskhak Vardi-Rozenblum, Israel

Translated by Mira Eckhaus

Edited by Tina Lunson

Goworowo, the typical Jewish town in the center of hasidic Poland, was no different in its character and style of life from the rest of the Jewish towns in its vicinity. It was blessed with all the characteristics of a *shtetl* with all its virtues and demerits; respectable homeowners, Torah scholars on the one hand and precious Jews with their simplicity and kindness on the other. Life developed and was managed in the small, low wooden houses that were scattered around the market square and in several streets that branched off from it. The reins of the public administration were held in the hands of towns' *Rov* and the community leaders; all social activity was carried on in the synagogue and in the hasidic *shtiblekh,* which were dominated by respected *gabays*, those who know how to debate matters of Jewish law and tradition and those who were influential due to the power of their money.

A normal day of the week for a Jew went as follows: he would get up to worship the Creator, walk hastily to his study house or to his *shtibl* to pray with the crowd, and finish with a review of a page of the Talmud or a chapter of *Mishnayos* , *Ein Yakov* or a chapter of psalms, each man with his custom; afterwards he would return home for his morning bread and then turn to his daily matters in order to bring livelihood to his home.

The daily businesses from which the Jews of the town made their livings, were not particularly distinguished by their diversity. They extended over very limited areas, mainly in the retail trade and in a number of craft branches that Jews maintained for generations. The trade was mainly concentrated in the market square with its shops and stalls, with goods, a little of this and a little of that - sugar and salt, oil and tar, notions and other minor, incidental items. Their livelihood depended mainly on the kindness of the tourists, at that time - the Gentiles of the surrounding countryside, who would go to the town to sell their produce and do their shopping, during all days of the week and especially on the market days. The small grocer and the craftsman did not see much benefit in their work; the nature of the villagers was to bargain, to buy small quantities and often even buy on credit and skip their payments. In order to earn his livelihood, the small grocer or the craftsman in the town had to work and toil, together with his family members, from morning until evening.

However in this landscape, there were a few exceptional Jews in each town, whose economic situation was better and their status was respected in the eyes of mankind, and they were the forest merchants, the grain merchants, who were involved in big business. The forest merchants would buy whole forests from the Polish landowners and the owners of the estates and cut them down. The trees would be poled in rafts across the Polish rivers to export them abroad; or they would buy grain from the granaries, collect it and send it in wagons to different countries. These merchants for the most part lived in a spacious walled house, behaved generously and charitably and their opinions were accepted by the townspeople. A similar status was also granted to the traveling merchants, the "agents", who spent most of their days in the big city in the wholesale trading houses and with the main agents of the factories, from whom they would order and buy all kinds of goods for the owners of the shops and stalls in the town. Even this trade was conducted on a considerable financial scale and profit.

Reb Shmuel Rozenblum's family was also among the class of grain merchants in the town. Reb Shmuel himself was born in Goworowo and his expertise in the grain business was inherited from his father's home

[Page 259]

along with a "right of possession" and a good name among the farmers and the owners of the estates, who sold him their grain and the fruit of their orchards and gardens. He was especially successful in trading in grain, which he sent in large quantities to Danzig and with God's will, there was great produce in the fields and barns and even the prices in the world's markets were good, so that his economic situation was usually good. But that was not the only reason Reb Shmuel was respected in the town. His greatness in the Torah, knowledge of the Talmud and rabbinic literature, made him well-recognized outside the boundaries of the town, and he was often asked by important rabbis from the surrounding towns to come and serve as an arbitrator and in complicated matters, especially among the people of large- scale commerce. Reb Shmuel spent time in the court of the Aleksander *Rov* and was always among those closest to him. Reb Shmuel was known as a charitable person and his house was always open to anyone, to help them in a difficult time with money, advice and encouragement. He performed all his actions with humility, brotherhood and kindness. So it is not surprising that for many years he served as the community leader and was accepted and loved by all strata of the public.

The family's place of residence was on Long Street (*Lange Gas*). The house had spacious and handsome rooms that always bustled with vibrant life from the large family, the commerce and the general involvement. One of the rooms was set aside as a Torah study area where he spent his free hours and in the late hours of the night. In this room there were cupboards and shelves full of holy books, books of *responsa* and rabbinics, books of hasidism and exegesis, and among them all, in its leather binding, the *Shas Vilna* edition of the Talmud, which in those days was literally considered a valuable asset, shone out. His late wife Sore, the daughter of Reb Meyshe Mints, managed the household affairs and helped her husband in his activities, both in matters of trade and in giving charity openly and secretly. In particular, she made sure to make the stay of the poor who were invited into her house pleasant and fed them with the best food in the pantry. She devoted most of her energy and attention to educating her children in the Torah and good deeds while she served as an example and role model for them and for that their love and admiration for her were without limit.

However, this family has also known troubled and bad days. The big fire that broke out in Goworowo on *Shabes khazon* of the year 1888 did not pass over Reb Shmuel's house either but consumed the house with everything in it and the grain warehouses that were in the courtyard of the house, which were full to overflowing. Like many others in the town, they managed only to save their lives and they remained without any property. In a difficult and depressing situation, they were forced to move to another house on Market Street, the inheritance of his wife Sore from her father, Reb Moshe Mints.

The fire disaster that hit this family brought in its wake an even more bitter disaster. In the fire, Reb Shmuel caught a cold and fell ill with a fatal illness, from which he never recovered, and on the 24th of *Kheshvan* of that year, he passed away, while he was still in his best years, leaving behind a widow and ten children. The four older children were indeed married and were independent while the father was still alive; however, the education and finances of the remaining six children, small and tender, fell on the shoulders of a destitute widow after the fire.

With no choice, the mother Sore had to start all over again and continued trading in grains. The Polish landowners and the owners of the estates treated her with great respect and helped her by bringing her the grains themselves, so that she would not have to go to their villages. They especially appreciated her honesty and diligence. However, this trade in grain, which was also associated with hard and tiring physical work, weighed heavily on her and she had to convert it into a trade in butter and eggs, which the owners of the estates

[Page 260]

brought to her house and she would send them to Warsaw to different merchants every day. Little by little, she was able to restore the family's financial security and raise the children in Torah, in awe of heaven and good manners.

And so, days and years passed and the family of Reb Shmuel Rozenblum, who was born and raised in Goworowo, spread out and branched out in all directions.

The eldest son, Reb Khayim Leyb, of blessed memory, moved to Mishnits. He was a great scholar and as his father, he was one of the distinguished Aleksander hasidim. In Mishnits, he was considered among the respectable houseowners. His late daughter Rivke married Reb Mordkhe Yosef Rosenblat and stayed on to live in Goworowo. Both of them perished in an epidemic that raged at the beginning of the 20th century in Goworowo and its surroundings. They left behind three little orphans who were gathered into our home and educated in our family as brothers and sisters for all intents and purposes. The third son, Reb Mordkhe Menakhem of blessed memory, served as a judge and teacher in Kosov-Telaki and he was also known to be great in Torah and hasidism.

The fourth daughter, Zeyftl of blessed memory, married Reb Eliyahu Orzhekh, one of the well-known forest merchants in Poland. Their home in Warsaw, at 22 Muranowski Street, was notable for its wealth and aristocratic customs. They left behind two daughters, who perished in Hitler's Holocaust may his name be blotted out.

The daughter Brayne may God avenge her blood, married Reb Khayim Ber Grudka, may God avenge his blood, from Goworowo, who was well known and remembered by all the townspeople, as a wise Torah scholar, smart and intelligent, with a distinguished face, with a constant smile of kindness and joy of life upon his lips. Reb Khayim Ber was one of the "traveling merchants" (agents), he would send foodstuffs to Warsaw and bring all kinds of goods from there for the grocers and the stall owners in Goworowo. Reb Khayim Ber had daughters, some of whom started families in Goworowo and lived there. Only two daughters remained from his entire family that was destroyed in the Holocaust and they are in Israel - Mrs. Elka, who married Reb Eliyahu Brukhansky, the son of the cantor Reb Malkiel and Mrs. Menucha, who married the native Reb Moshe Zeltser. Both established respectable families in Israel.

The son Reb Dovid of blessed memory, was the pride of the whole family. Even in his youth, he was famous among the rabbis and scholars in the area as someone who was great in the Torah and has noble virtues. While he was still a young man, he was ordained to teach by the rabbis of Ostrolenke and Tshervin. With his great humility he resolutely refused all offers to appoint him as *rov* in one of the towns. The late *Rov* Avraham Yosef Tsinovitsh, who served as a rabbi and judge in Ostrov-Mazovietski (the author of the book *Salsalot Yosef*), noticed the exceptionally great scholar, highly educated and handsome young man, and took him to his home as a groom for his daughter Naomi. This match of a hasidic man to a

Lithuanian rabbi was a rarity in those days. Reb Dovid was supported by his father-in-law and was close to the great rabbis and personalities, who visited often the house of Reb Yosele Tsinovitsh in Ostrov and then he was appointed as rabbi and a judge in Lomzhe. Reb Dovid was engaged in commerce and at a certain time, when he lived with his family in Roshan, he served as a certified supplier for the Russian army. He had an abundant and dignified livelihood and despite his many troubles, he never missed a single day of his regular lesson in the Talmud. With exceptional devotion he took care of his children and educated them in the Torah and good manners and was privileged to see the results of his investment in his lifetime. His eldest daughter Rokhl, who was a kindergarten teacher in Lomzhe and active in the Zionist *Histadrut* there, immigrated to Israel, married Reb Shlomo Slutsky (the owner of carpentry factory *Erez* in Tel Aviv). The son, Reb Shmuel Khayim, also born in Goworowo, continued the family's golden chain and was considered one of the young and well- known prodigies among the members of the *yeshivas* and rabbis. At the age of 18, he had already published a book of questions and answers called *Bikhurey Shakhar*,

[Page 261]

which deals with *halakhic* negotiations with the *Gaon Rov* Khayim Ozer Grodzhinski of Vilna, the *Gaon Rov* Yosef Rozen of Rugtsuv, the *Gaon Rov* Mayer Simkhe of Dvinsk and many more. In their answers they crown him with such titles that even veteran rabbis would flaunt and boast about them. During the ghetto period, he served in the rabbinate in Lomzh, acting as the substitute of the elder Rabbi, *Rov* Yosele Tsinovitsh may his memory be for a blessing. He perished in the Holocaust along with the rest of the family, his parents Reb Dovid and Naomi, his brother Pinkhas and his sisters Mishka and Zipora, may God avenge them. The son Yisroel Yitskhak Verdi (Rozenblum), studied in the Lithuanian *yeshivas* of Slonim and Lomzhe, he was one of the leaders of the *He'khaluts Ha'mizrakhi* and *Ha'shomer Ha'dati* in Lomzhe and until the year of his immigration to Israel, in 1936, he worked at the center of the *Mizrakhi* movement in Warsaw. In Israel he first worked in the executive committee of the *Ha'poel HaMizrakhi* and was active in this movement and a member of its central institutions. He now works as a senior official in the Tel Aviv Municipality, as chief examiner in the audit department.

The daughter Devushe, may she live long life, was the first who, being still a little girl, left the family house and moved to the big city of Warsaw, where she was educated by her cousin Khane Kroytman. One neighbor, who owned a grocery store, noticed her because of her quickness and knowledge in commercial matters and invited her to help her in the store's business. In exchange for her work, she provided for all her needs and even deposited for her every month one ruble to a reserved fund. On all kinds of occasions, she would give her additional sums of money, which were also deposited in this fund. In a short period of time, about forty rubles accumulated in the reserved fund, a substantial sum in those days. One day, mother came to visit and found her working in a store, she did not like this and returned her to Goworowo. Being already “wealthy”, Devushe began to trade in confections herself and at about the age of 17, she became an independent merchant in the town. In 1912, she married Reb Baruch Baharav, the son of the *shochet* Reb Mordkhe Moyshkov and they opened a confection store there. During the First World War, when the Russians entered Vishkov, the Cossacks attacked the store and looted it, leaving nothing of all the property they had accumulated with great effort. Destitute and with no property, they returned to Goworowo and there they started trading in foodstuffs. In 1921, her husband, the late Reb Baruch, passed away and Mrs. Devushe remained a widow with three small children.

At that time, the Zionist spirit penetrated Goworowo as well and the towns' young people and some respectable homeowners established a Zionist organization there. Mrs. Devushe was one of the first to join this organization and was even a committee member. She was very active in collecting funds for the Land of Israel, selling *shekels* and also signing on a subscription for the *Tsefira* newsletter. In 1920, they established a library which was located in Mrs. Devushe's house. The Goworowo *Rov*, who opposed Zionism, did not view with favor the establishment of the library and the fact that the youth would gather there for debates and cultural actions. The situation reached such a point that the *Rov* threatened to boycott Mrs. Devushe, the library and its visitors. The secretary of the Zionist organization at the time was Reb Binyamin Ginzburg. At literary evenings organized by him, he would read from the works of Mendele, Sholem Aleykhem and others. Reb Binyamin also excelled in singing and with his pleasant voice, he sang at the social gatherings. The best young people in the town were active in this Zionist organization, such as Yehudis Rosen, Dovid Aharon Grudke, Dovid Hirsch and his brother Naftali Mints, Yehiel Peshisuskar, Khayim Alter, the son of the tailor Bendt, Rachel Mints, Sor Tannenbaum, Beyle Rosen, Esther Tshekhanover, Khane Fridman and more. There was a drama club near the *Histadrut*, which presented the play *The Sale of Yosef* the proceeds of which were dedicated to the Land of Israel. Years later, Mrs. Devushe came back to

[Page 262]

Vishkov and renewed the confection shop there. And so, she raised her children in an atmosphere of public activity and Zionist affairs. In 1935, she immigrated to the Land of Israel. In the same year, an exhibition opened in Tel Aviv and she set up a beverage kiosk there. With the establishment of the Tel Aviv port, she set up a cafe and restaurant for the port workers on its premises. After many wanderings and hardships, she succeeded several years ago, together with her husband, Reb Israel Khayim Osenholts, may he live a long life, in establishing a flower shop for them in Bat Yam, which provides them with a decent living. In all her places of residence, her acquaintances and neighbors knew and know to tell about, her good deeds and her good heart. The people of the towns of Goworowo and Vishkov, in their distress, turned to her for help and received it from her with a warm welcome and generosity, even at times when she herself was in need. Of her three children, only the eldest son immigrated to Israel and settled in Givatayim, where he works as a gardener and owns a flower shop. Her daughter Feyge and youngest son Aron remained in Poland and perished in the Holocaust.

The fifth son, the late Berish, was the only one in Reb Shmuel's family to pass the Russian army test and was accepted, however, as was the custom among young people in those days, he also fled to America, worked there and toiled hard, until he reached the status of an affluent merchant. For many years, he would send sums of money every month to support his mother and the rest of the family in Poland. He himself was an honest man, pursuing justice and with a generous heart. In 1958, he passed away in the United States.

The youngest son was Rabbi Reb Aharon. Although he was born in a hasidic family and was educated as such, he chose to study in Lithuanian *yeshivas* rather than in a *shtibl.* He left home at a young age for the most famous Torah places, such as Radin Yeshiva (the place of *Hofets Khayim* may his memory be for a blessing) and later, at the great Lomzhe Yeshiva, where he was also ordained to serve in the rabbinate by *Rov* Y. L. Gordon and *Rov* Yosele Tsinovitsh. At the Lomzhe Yeshiva, Reb Aharon was known as "the Goworower".

First row (from the right): Sore Tanenbaum, Khane Fridman
Standing: Devushe Rozenblum, Esther Tshekhanover, Beyle Rosen

[Page 263]

My Uncle Reb Efrayim Leyb Boynem

by Yankev Gurka, Israel

Translated by Tina Lunson

Before the First World War my uncle, Reb Efrayim Leyb Boynem, maintained a fine, wealthy home, and was considered among the "seven best in the city". His business was a wholesale trade in food products. He imported whole wagon loads of rice, sugar, oil and matches from Russia and sold them to the retail merchants of the town. Later he bought up a large area of forest near Ruzshan from a Russian General, hacked down the trees, cut them into railroad track sleepers and exported them to Germany. In my uncle's forest

[Page 264]

there were many gentile workers, under the direction of Shabsay Kuper and his son Shmuel, from Dlugoshodle. I recall an incident when, in that very forest, gentiles robbed and murdered two Goworowo Jews, the brothers Avrom Yitsik and Leybl Altarzsh who were grain merchants and buried them alive. The murder was discovered later.

My uncle was a big Talmud scholar. He had a set of the Vilne Talmud and a large case of holy books. He was always studying or consulting some book. He would often travel to the Vurke *Rebi* and was an eminent *hasid* in his court. The Braker *Rebi,* who was known as a master of miracles, came twice a year to Goworowo and stayed in my uncle's house. His apartment had six rooms and they were all full of people who came to beg the *Rebi* for salvation. Besides the *Rebi* himself, he was always accompanied by a sexton and his two sons. The *Rebi's* elder son was matched in marriage with my uncle's daughter Dina, who was already a child "requested" by the *Rebi.* In the first years after their wedding, my uncle did not bother the children. The Braker *Rebi* told him to dress Dina in white clothing. Dina wore white clothes until she was fifteen. The *Rebi's* remedy helped, because Dina and the other daughter, Tsipe, grew up lovely and healthy, which people accepted as a miracle from the *Rebi.*

My Aunt Tsirl, a small and sensitive Jewish woman, ran the household and also helped my uncle in his businesses. She was known as a very charitable woman, helping poor people and making weddings for poor brides in their home.

My uncle retained a teacher for the two daughters, one who taught them Hebrew and Torah, as well as teachers for German, Russian and Polish. The elder daughter Dina was very well educated and spoke several languages.

With the outbreak of the First World War my uncle's family migrated deep into Russia and when they returned to Poland they found everything burned down and ruined. Even the forest that my uncle had bought from the Russian general had been confiscated by the Polish government. They did him one favor, though; they left him wood to build a house for his and other families. From those troubles my uncle was left blind, and Aunt Tsirl died from grief.

Even as a blind man, my uncle further pursued learning with perseverance from the outside; he did not mediate the public praying and did continue as *shofar* blower for the Vurke *shtibl.* He died in 1932 or 1933.

The elder daughter Dina with her husband and three accomplished children were tragically murdered by the Germans in the Holocaust years. The younger daughter is in America today, with her husband and two children.

[Page 265]

Reb Velvl and Feyge Blumshteyn

May God Avenge Their Blood

by A. Boshon, Israel

Translated by Tina Lunson

Reb Velvl and Feyge Nekhame Blumshteyn may God avenge their blood

As a *kheyder* boy, when the *rebi* studied the verse with us, "See, I have called by name Beytsalel the son of Uri, the son of Hur, of the tribe of Judah", we imagined in our fantasy Beytsalel the master of the *mishkan* as Reb Velvl the clockmaker, tall, erect, with a long white beard and spectacles sliding down his nose. Just as Beytsalel made all the artistically complicated utensils for the Temple in the desert – the breastplate, the tunic, and all the priestly garments – so was Reb Velvl a craftsman with silver and gold, fashioning stone and wood, as stated in the verse.

That was not just a childish fantasy. That was also true in reality. Such artistic sense and God blessed hands as Reb Velvl had, were rare to encounter. A unique goldsmith, a first-class clockmaker, and even an architect on a high level. Anyone who saw during the construction of the town study house how he managed the gentile builders and Jewish carpenters would agree. He was not an insignificant person, yet they all obeyed him as an expert and authority.

But Velvl was not only a person of artistry, he was also a person of the community, an honest public figure. He was elected to the Jewish Council in almost every term and no town regulation was made without Velvl's agreement. Reb Velvl was a true observant Jew, a fiery Ger *hasid*, but not with fanaticism and extremism. He

[Page 266]

valued everyone's feelings, not insulting anyone, but for himself he was meticulous and rigorous.

His wife Feyge was an unusual type of Jewish woman. Intelligent, always happy, with a lot of energy that she put to use for charity and social work for women. She was one of the main spokespersons at all the meetings for women's issues called by the *Rebitsin* Genendl of blessed memory. She was an extremely clever woman and men also had to recognize her sensibilities.

They, along with their daughter Rokhl and her husband Yitskhak Velvl Gerlits and their children, as well as their son Shmuel, were murdered during the war years, may God avenge their blood.

A family portrait. In the middle – a tourist from America.
1936.

Reb Mordkhe Leyb Gurka

of Blessed Memory

by Y. Ben-Khasid, Israel

Translated by Tina Lunson

Reb Mordkhe Leyb Gurka of blessed memory was considered one of the most honest, modest personalities in the town. Although he was a great Talmud scholar and a man of deep conscience, he still held himself apart, liked to live separately, far from glory and not mixing in any community matters.

Reb Mordkhe Leyb was born in Ostrolenke. He came to Goworowo when he married his wife Dvore, of the well known family Potash, who were among the founders of the town. His parents were simple Jewish artisans. His four brothers and two sisters

[Page 267]

were professionals. His parents had also sought out a "purpose" for him, but he was drawn to learning. At the age of eleven he went off to the Lomzshe Yeshiva, which had just been founded and from there to a Lithuanian yeshiva in Agustov, where he studied until his marriage. In the *yeshiva* he was considered among the most industrious students, studying day and night and seldom traveling home. He was called the "Ostrolenke genius". Even his *bar-mitsve* took place with great fanfare in the *yeshiva*.

Reb Mordkhe Leyb and Dvore Gurka of blessed memory

At age seventeen Reb Mordkhe Leyb married his wife Dvore. Her parents had promised him a large dowry and several years of room and board. In Goworowo Reb Mordkhe Leyb, the Lomzshe Litvak, made friends with *hasidic* young men who were traveling to the Ger *Rebi*, master, teacher, *rov*, *Rov* Yehude Ari Leyb, known for his book *Sfas Emes*, may his sainted memory be for a blessing. One time Reb Mordkhe Leyb traveled with them to the *Rebi* and the *khasidus* school of thought appealed to him and he became a fervent Ger *hasid*. He sat months long and learned from the *Rebi* and learned the system of *khasidus*.

That period did not last for long. About two years after their marriage, his wife's parents died and he had to tear himself away from study and become a merchant. He dealt in huge volumes of flour and salt, which he imported from deep in Russia. He brought in whole wagonloads of flour and salt from Kharkov, Yekaterinaslav and other sources and sold them in the whole region around. In his free time, he continued to study and also did not forget to visit the *Rebi*, especially during the Days of Awe.

With the outbreak of the First World War Reb Mordkhe Leyb of course left all the merchandise and wandered with his family to Pinsk. After their return to the town, he

[Page 268]

could not go back to his trading and his wife Dvore took up the yoke of their livelihood. They now had eight children in the home (six girls and two sons) and the debts were continually growing. His wife would not stand for such a situation and began dealing in whatever was left, if only to bring some money into the house. Reb Mordkhe Leyb helped her in all this. When all the merchandising ended, Dvore became a sweets-baker. They were successful at that and ran that business until the destruction of the town.

I will offer a detail here that the general public probably does not know about. Reb Mordkhe Leyb spent all his years fasting on Monday and Thursday. And on the other days of the week, he first ate at 12 o'clock. Because of the work, he necessarily went late to the study house and was literally the last one to return. He customarily recited all the psalms and also studied and so that took up half the day. He gave charity and private loans generously, especially helping out his hasidic friends when they needed help.

In any free minutes, besides his newspaper *Dos yidishe togblat*, he liked to read *Haynt*, *Moment* and even the *Bundist Folks-tsaytung*. He also read any secular books that their children brought into the house.

Every *Shabes* morning the scholarly hasidim came to him to drink tea with sugar. Some of the regular visitors were Yankev Yehoshe Ginzburg, Khayim Leyb Marianski the cantor-ritual slaughterer, Mayer Romaner, Yankev Shtshetshina, Shayke Hertsberg, Aron Aronson, Yisroel Mayer Mishnayos long may he live, Nisn Mazes the ritual slaughterer, and others, where they chatted about current matters.

With the outbreak of the Second World War, Reb Mordkhe Leyb and his family moved to Bialystok. There he was among those who did not have a Russian passport and others advised him to procure one. For that "sin" he and many other Goworowers and their families along with thousands of other *biezshentses* were deported to the deep forests of northern Russia. His house there was a gathering place of the Jewish intellectuals. They came to hear what the "old Mr. Gurka" had to say. Himself, a man of faith, he comforted and encouraged everyone, assuring each that the Redemption would come and they would be released from that place. Knowing Russian well, the N.K.V.D. commandant often came to discuss things with him. He also took pains to observe his Jewishness. He was even arrested for organizing a *minyen* for *Rosh-ha'shone* and *Yon-kiper*. But he was proud of that.

After the liberation, which was thanks to the famous agreement between Sikorski and the Russian government, Reb Mordkhe Leyb did not feel well and saw that his days were numbered. He moved to a Jewish settlement where there was a Jewish cemetery, in order to be buried in a Jewish grave. He wanted

[Page 269]

to go to Buchara, Uzbekistan. While traveling there, with a Polish military troop, they went through the little town of Kermine, Uzbekistan, a Jewish settlement since the time of the Second Temple in Jerusalem, with a cemetery from that era. Reb Mordkhe Leyb wanted to get off there, but the train went on. Despite the very difficult circumstances, he was able to travel back there. A short time later, the 11th of *Kheshvan, sav-shin"beys* (the 3rd of November 1941), he passed away and was laid to rest in a Jewish grave in the Kermine Jewish cemetery.

His wife Dvore, of blessed memory, who was known for her charity and help of the needy, accompanied him all of those years. In the hardest moments of their life, she helped him carry the yoke of the family. She passed away like a saint, in the town of Samarkand, Uzbekistan, the 23rd of *Tevet, sav-shin-khof"giml* (1st of January 1943) and was buried there in the Jewish cemetery. Their eldest daughter Rivke Beylis may God avenge her blood, along with her family, were murdered by the Germans. Their daughter

Miryam Karvat of blessed memory died in the war years in Russia, the 16th of *Elul, sav-shin"beys*, near Katakurgan.

Their children who survived are Yankev and Yosef Gurka and Rokhl Brestel in Israel; Khane Krulevitsh, Leye Last and Nekhame Epshteyn in America.

Reb Hershl Glogover
of Blessed Memory

by M. Rimon, Israel

Translated by Tina Lunson

Reb Hershl Glogover was the greatest Talmud teacher in the town. People called him "the fool" because he always wore his *Shabes* clothes and no stain was allowed on his clothing. He was polished and adorned like a prince. He really looked like a monarch with his long white beard down to his belt. He looked with concern after every hair of his beard and he always behaved with dignity.

No one ever saw him smiling. He spoke little and was very fussy. Almost the opposite of what the verse says ,"a stickler is no teacher". But he was a good *melamed.* For him, every boy must know the Talmud page. If it did not go well, he took it out in anger. He was not overly selective. If he had to give a little slap along with a pinch, he did not spare anything, as long as the boy would understand what the Talmud says. And indeed, his pupils went to the Lomzshe Yeshiva and had nothing to be ashamed of in their learning.

Reb Hershl was also a fine prayer leader and singer. He sang Vurke melodies with much heart and gusto. It was a pleasure to hear.

[Page 270]

Reb Elkhonen Fridman
May God Avenge His Blood

by M. Rimon, Israel

Translated by Tina Lunson

Khone Fridman was an effervescent, dissatisfied type, a person with a lot of knowledge and education and very clever, almost a diplomat. People called him Khone Reytse's, after his mother's name. His father was also called after Reytse's name. The town followed the precept not to recognize names and family names from the actual birth certificates. For the town, the person himself and his popularity ruled. Reytse was the *Mirele Efros* of the family. Khone Fridman was a shrewd merchant in the grocery line. He did not bring any abundant livelihood, either because the town did not have the power to support it or because of the unrest that nested in him and did not allow him to attend the business. He loved to be out in the street and know all the happenings of the town and to catch a side job. He roamed around outdoors until he managed to capture a real pony.

Around that time the Rits brothers from the steam mill received a concession for an electric station that would provide electric light for the town. Khone Fridman became the electrical master director, who was to install the electrical connections in the houses and in the streets. How did he manage that? Possibly, because of his acquaintances in the government circles. He took to the work energetically and with the help of his son Shepsl, that whole job was done to the satisfaction of all the residents, who were tired of the sooty oil lamps.

Khone Fridman was one of the founders and activists of the *Mizrakhi*, a good bookkeeper and petition writer. He was active for a long time as secretary of the Jewish Council.

He, along with his wife and five children, were murdered in Slonim may God avenge their blood.

[from right]: Wife Feyge and the children: Shepsl, Yehoshe, Rivke, Sore and Meyshe Fridman may God avenge their blood

[Page 271]

Reb Yisroel Yitskhak Shron

May God Avenge His Blood

by A. Inbar, Israel

Translated by Tina Lunson

A war cannot be fought with generals alone. One must find ordinary soldiers who present their hearts for the enemy's bullets and are ready to go under fire for a just cause.

Reb Yisroel Yitskhak Shron did not occupy any official position in the Jewish community. He did not strive for leadership. But wherever there was a conflict or a struggle for a Jewish issue, he stood himself on the front lines of the battle for his truth. Whether it was a complicated violation of *Shabes* by a soccer team, or a question of educating the younger generation, Reb Yisroel Yitskhak was one of the first to "take a position", without personal interests or calculations. Reb Yisroel Yitskhak was a conservative, honest Jew from the fine Ger Hasidim and his whole life earned his living by manual labor.

His father Reb Yosef, also born in Goworowo, was a butcher by trade and was very wealthy because all the local princes bought

Reb Yisroel Yitskhak may God avenge his blood and Khaye Beyle Shron of blessed memory

Standing, from right: Reyzl, Dan and Dovid Shron
Below, Dan's child Sholem Hershl may God avenge his blood

meat from his butcher shop, which was the largest one in town. In his younger years Reb Yisroel Yitskhak did not work in trade but sat in the study house and learned. Even after his marriage to his wife Khaye Beyle from the merchant family in Ostrov-Mazavietsk, he still continued to sit there and study. But then when his father became old and weak, he had to learn the butcher trade and he took over the butcher shop.

When the war broke out, the Shron family fled the town and crossed into the Russian border area. His wife Khaye Beyle died in that strange place, in the town of Dambrovitse, near Rovno. Where Reb Yisroel Yitskhak died is not known. Their children also died - Dan with his wife and their child, and Dovid, may God avenge their blood.

[Page 272]

Reb Khayim Dovid Shron
May God Avenge His Blood

by A. Inbar, Israel

Translated by Tina Lunson

Reb Khayim Dovid Shron was an ordinary, honest Jew with great faith in wise men, shrewd merchandising and authentic good heartedness which could provide an example for others. He operated his grain and flour business fairly and straightforwardly. A word was a word. And thus, he had a good livelihood and an honorable, lovely Jewish home.

Reb Khayim Dovid stemmed from an old well established Goworowo family. And his father, Reb Yosef, was born in the town and married his wife Tsirl, the sister-in-law of *Rebi* Avieyzer Ruzshaner, who was the father of the Goworowo *Rebitsn.*

In his youth, Reb Khayim Dovid sat in the study house and learned and also traded a little. Due to his honesty, he acquired some possessions. He married Beyle from Ostrov-Mazavietski, the daughter of Nosn and Rivke Gitl, who had a tanning business.

Reb Khayim Dovid was a fervent Vurker Hasid, and from time to time would travel to the *Rebi* in Otvotsk. He also prayed in the Vurke *shtibl* and was considered one of the fine hasidim.

Reb Khayim Dovid and his wife Khaye Beyle were among the first victims of the Nazi persecutors soon after their taking of Goworowo. They were tragically murdered on that sad Friday evening; may God avenge their blood.

[Page 273]

Reb Khayim Leyb Marianski the Cantor-Ritual Slaughterer

by Y. Avi-Sore, Israel

Translated by Tina Lunson

Reb Khayim Leyb served as cantor and ritual slaughterer for about twenty years in Goworowo. He was hired for that position by Reb Malkiel at the end of the First World War. Earlier, he had been cantor-slaughterer in Shniadove. He joined the competition, which was announced by the *gabeyim* of the *shul.* He was taken over all the other candidates because of his strong voice and his beautiful style of reciting the psalms.

Although Reb Khayim Leyb came from a Lithuanian town, he was a devoted Ger Hasid. He often traveled to the Ger *Rebi* and reared his children in the same spirit. He was a Talmud scholar and an expert in ritual slaughter.

Reb Khayim Leyb was a tall, big boned man with a pointed grey beard. Always dressed impeccably, with polished boots, a red kerchief tied around his throat out of concern he would become chilled and ruin his voice. For the most part he prayed in the study house, but from time to time he came to the Ger *shtibl* and learned *Sfas Emes* along with the Talmud page of the day. He was good natured and friendly. He stopped to talk with everyone and said a kind word. He was loved in all the circles of the town. His house was open for everyone. He was especially occupied with his children's friends. When the writer of these lines became *bar-mitsve*, being a friend of his youngest son Shleyme, Reb Khayim Leyb organized a reception in his home for all our friends. Reb Khayim Leyb and his wife fussed over the reception just as if it were for their own child. Of course, my father made a *kidush* for the hasidim in the *shtibl*. It was a pleasure to come to Reb Khayim Leyb's home and hear him tell his good stories. When anyone needed help, either morale or financial, Reb Khayim Leyb was prepared to help him.

Reb Khayim Leyb had four children, one daughter and three sons. The eldest was married in Zambrove. Meyshe, Leye and Shleyme were in the home. All the children were educated in the religious spirit. Once Meyshe was no longer studying, he got him into training to learn a trade, to be sure that he did not leave the Jewish way. The youngest son Shleyme was a diligent student. He sent him to learn in the Lomzshe Yeshiva.

[Page 274]

Shleyme excelled with many good qualities. He was a Talmud scholar, strong in religion and in modern life. He was also gifted with a beautiful voice. The last years before the war, he learned ritual slaughter and also prepared to become a cantor. For his daughter Leye, Reb Khayim Leyb took in a son-in-law, a young *hasidic* man, a good Talmud pupil and a music student, Yisroel Yitskhak Bromberg from Volomin.

When Goworowo was taken by the Germans, the Marianski family fled to Zambrove, to their son, who at the time ran a grain mill. I encountered them there, depressed and broken. They all were murdered there as martyrs. There is no trace left of them. May God avenge their blood.

[Page 274]

Reb Tsvi Aleyarzsh
the Zamoshtsh *Rebi* of Blessed Memory

by A. Ben-Even, Israel

Translated by Tina Lunson

In Lublin they called him the "Zamoshtsher *Rebi*," but in fact he was born in Goworowo, to the family Aleyarzsh. His brother Mayer Yankev's two sons, Hershl and Khayim Leyb and their children lived in the town for many years. His wife, the *Rebitsn* Nekhe, was one of Menashe Holtsman's sisters.

Rebi Tsvi did not descend from any rabbinic dynasty. In his younger years he adhered to the *Rebi's* courts in Vulke, Radzimin and the Ruzshan grandsons. With them he soaked in the aroma of *khasidus* and thirstily swallowed their Torah. It was with his own strengths that he worked up to the high level of being a *rebi* among Jews.

In Lublin he held court in a several storied house in one of the ghetto lanes. His hasidim consisted of simple people, laborers, craftsmen, small dealers, porters, wagon drivers – Jews hardened by hard life, who found with their *rebi* an hour of spiritual pleasure, a little hope and comfort in their worry.

The old *Rebi* passed away at the beginning of the 1930s. His only son and heir apparent Reb Mayer'ke became his substitute. Reb Mayer'ke was a genuine, refined young man, a man of austerity, in great awe of heaven. He was marked for his great love of the Jewish people. He loved his hasidim as his own family. The hasidim would often come to the *Rebi* to cry out their bitter fates, or to share their joy with their *Rebi.*

[Page 275]

Our master, teacher and *rov*,
Rov Tsvi Aleyarzsh may his sainted
memory be for a blessing

It was very agreeable to see the honest, raw sincerity of his hasidim, natural people who meant what they said and who believed in the *Rebi* with their whole hearts. The effect of the *Rebi* on them was large indeed.

His wife, the young *Rebitsn* Khane (by the way, he had married one of their cousins, the daughter of Bunem Yitskhak Holtsman from Kharshal) was an example of a Jewish wife and mother. The had one child, a girl, who went through a serious illness and was left a vestige of herself. The *Rebitsn* also helped the *Rebi* conduct his court with wisdom and tact.

The young *Rebi* also had many followers in other places. He maintained a broad correspondence with them. They sent him little petitions from America and gifts and requests for advice and blessings. Before the Days of Awe or public holidays, when dozens of letters would arrive, the *Rebi* asked us to help him answer the letters. I enjoyed doing that, because he was a truly loveable person with a big heart and sensitivities. It was a pleasure to visit in their home.

The *Rebi* and his wife and child were murdered by the Nazis in one of the Lublin concentration camps, may God avenge their blood.

[Page 276]

Reb Yankev Shtshetshina
of Blessed Memory

by A. Boshon, Israel

Translated by Tina Lunson

A person with feeling and tact, a wise man among the wise, bubbling with humor and sharp mindedness, a Talmud scholar with a representative appearance – these were the characteristics of Reb Yankl Shtshetshina of blessed memory, a long-established Goworowo settler, one of the most respected in the town.

It is clear that, if not for his poor material situation and his heavy worries about livelihood, Reb Yankev would have achieved a high position in the Council leadership, for his wisdom, clear analytical understanding and power of persuasion. But what did the wise men say? "The wise remain poor." Although Reb Yankl possessed his own house with several apartments for renters, a grocery and haberdashery business in a good location, it was difficult for him to draw a livelihood for his household. He had to teach *kheyder* boys in addition. In passing, the teaching of children did not suit his essence, character or nature. He could not come down to the level of *kheyder* children. That was not his place. He felt good when he was sitting beside the *Rov* as an arbitrator in a very complicated case of Jewish law. Here he could juggle with ingenuity, discovering errors of logic to vindicate his side. He was certainly one of the most esteemed arbitrators in town.

Reb Yankl was a Ger Hasid of the liberal kind, not the extreme kind. He could find a common language even with heretics. His witticisms and smile made an impression on everyone.

Reb Yankl was born in Ruzshan to his parents Yitskhak Arye and Sore Dina. He spent his youth learning in the study house. He married into Goworowo. With his first wife he had their daughter Rokhl, who married a young hasidic man from Vishkove. He married his second partner Khane Elke, the daughter of Reb Beytsalel Yosl Karvat may God avenge his blood.

With the outbreak of the Second World War Reb Yankl and his family went through the whole thorny path of the Exile. He was transported to northern Russia. There he was extremely exhausted and suffered hunger. He passed away on the fourth interim day of *Peysakh, tes-shin"alef* and was buried in a forest near the grave of his one-time neighbor Reb Yitskhak Reytshik of blessed memory.

(See picture on *[Page 95]*)

[Page 277]

Reb Yeshaye Hertsberg
May God Avenge His Blood

by Yosef Gurka, Israel

Translated by Tina Lunson

Reb Yeshaye Hertsberg was not Goworowo born yet, he was bound with the town like one born of many generations. His family was from Makove and he married Tsipe, Miryam Rokhl's, who was an orphan and was reared by her uncle, the well known wealthy Reb Itsl Mints. He considered her his own daughter and married her to Reb Shayke from Makove. Reb Itsl promised him room and board and treated him like a son-in-law. Reb Itsl Mints was, as stated, very rich. He owned a large part of the area of the town, which, after his death, was sold to Ratenski (the orchard and manor) and a larger stretch to Yankev Berl Blumshteyn.

Soon after his arrival in the town, Yeshaye became prominent among the *hasidic* youth. He was a Ger Hasid and often traveled to Ger, to the *Rebi*, and stayed there for some time. He did not have any worries about livelihood as he was living with Reb Itsl Mints. He lived in a beautiful apartment and his home was a central gathering place for the Ger Hasidim in town. *Kidushim* and dinners at the end of *Shabes* were held there and also meetings about community problems in the town. Reb Shayke was one of the instigators for bringing in the cantor-ritual slaughterer Malkiel from Makove. He traveled to Makove to influence him and when the townspeople refused to release Reb Malkiel, he came in the middle of the night with horse and wagon and stole him away from Makove while the residents of the town were still sleeping.

When the Ger *Rebi* ordered his hasidim to found the *Agudas Yisroel* organization, Reb Shayke became the most active member in town. He was also active in *Beys-Yankev*, *Talmud-Torah*, and in all the *Aguda* undertakings in town.

When they began organizing the soccer teams in town and would play on *Shabes*, Reb Shayke became one of the active *Shomrey-Shabes* members and went out to fight against desecrating the sabbath and did not allow them to play. He was not surprised when it even came to physical blows.

Before the First World War, Reb Shayke did not have any worries about income. After the war, when the town had been burned down, Reb Itsl Mints died and his son Mendl established an iron factory in Pultusk and the inheritors sold the possessions and the land, Reb Shayke built a house near Reb Matisyahu Rozen and began

[Page 278]

dealing in grain. It went well for the first few years. After that, as the Christian cooperatives took to boycotting Jews, he became impoverished and went through difficult times. His children helped him with his livelihood. The eldest son, Zelig, helped in the grain business; his daughter Miryam Rokhl learned wig making and hair dressing; the younger daughter worked for Reb Leyvi Varshaviak and later for Reb Yisroel Burshteyn and for Beyle Potash in their businesses.

He reared all his children in the Jewish spirit. The daughters were active in the *Beys-Yankev* school and particularly Miryam Rokhl. She was president of *Banos Agudas Yisroel* and a good public speaker. She also presented lectures in Warsaw. She was observant and refined and loved to do charity. She had two sons, Mordkhe and Nosn. Nosn was a religious *yeshiva* boy.

The entire family Hertsberg was murdered as martyrs in the war years, may God avenge their blood.

Reb Yudl Sheyniak
of Blessed Memory

by B. Avi, Israel

Translated by Tina Lunson

An authentic type of Talmud scholar who had no more in his world than the four walls of Jewish law – that was the eminent householder Reb Yudl Sheyniak of blessed memory. His chief occupation was to sit and study. His manufacturing business on the market square was run by his wife and children. Still, Reb Yudl found a little time to busy himself with community matters; for a while he was a member of the Jewish Council; after the First World War he did some rescue work and was almost always an assessor for the meetings of the tax evaluation commission.

Reb Yudl was born in Tiktin in 1870. He studied with the Tiktin *Rov* and was a very good pupil. He married into Goworowo at age 18 to Gishe, the daughter of Gedalye and Yetke who had an *aleyarnia*. Although Tiktin was a purely Litvak town, in Goworowo Yudl became one of the strongest Ger Hasidim and was a frequent traveler to the *Rebi*.

Gishe, Reb Yudl's wife, was also well known in the town for her good heartedness. She took interest in the poor and sick people and was a good, devoted mother to her children.

Reb Yudl died in 1929. They laid the table where he always sat, learning day and night, in his grave. His wife Gishe died during transport to White Russia, Communist S.S.R, in 1945.

[Page 279]

Monument to a Living Soul

by Khave Bernshteyn-Burshtin, Israel

Translated by Tina Lunson

My mother, the *Rebitsn* Genendl, was the younger daughter of the Ruzshan scholar and genius *Rebi* Avieyzer Shikora. My grandfather had four sons and two daughters and his biggest goal was that the sons be Talmud experts and his daughters marry great scholars. He carried out his efforts. The older daughter, my Aunt Shifre, he married to the famous genius *Rebi* Avrom Aron Hendl, *Rov* in Varshe-Vole and the *Rebi* of the Ger and Radzin *Rebis*; and the younger daughter he got for a husband our wonderful father, *Rebi* Alter Meyshe Mordkhe Burshtin, *Rov* in Tshervin and in Goworowo.

Even as a little girl, my grandfather was proud of his younger daughter. She was beautiful and smart and comprehended Torah like a *yeshiva-bokher*. Grandfather was wealthy and was not stingy about the dowry. So they looked to match her with the best lineage. But my grandfather chose his best student and their marriage took place when they were 18 years old.

Grandfather predicted that his daughter Genendl would be a *Rebitsn* and so he prepared her for that. He taught her himself and sent her abroad twice.

After a few years of room and board at grandfather's and in various *rebi's* courts, my father became *Rov* in Tshervin. The *Rebitsn* soon exhibited her elevated personality. The town Tshervin was once a town in dispute. Eventually an angel of peace came down. Everything "adhered" to the *Rov* and one became good friends with the other. My mother's position was thereby a very important one. With her good character, humanism, wisdom and great tact, she helped her husband ascend in learning and in livelihood from near and far.

In Goworowo my mother established a rabbinic household that was an example to all. Welcoming guests in a generous style. Poor and rich, she received everyone with a blessing and cordiality. She had an encouraging word for everyone and she offered needed, wise and fitting advice. Everyone who came into the house left it with thanks and happiness.

My mother took an active part in the religious and community life of the town. She was one of the founders of the local *Beys-Yankev* school for girls and the chairwoman of the committee and she did much in the area of dedicating the space for the school. [Founder] Sore Shenirer visited Goworowo twice. She was my mother's guest and they shared a great love.

There were cases when father came into conflict with a Jewish Council member

[Page 280]

or some other local leader. The *Rebitsn* quickly knew how to smooth things over and resolve the quarrel and in the end, the people became the *Rebi's* good friends. More than once father was helped by her advice in some complicated legal matter or in a community issue. Her advice was always pertinent and solid.

Mother always lead herself and recited all the prayers like a male person; and she learned from Sore Shenirer to get up the nerve for the standing *shmone-esrey*. She also never missed a day of reading the press, the *Togblat*, *Haynt* and even secular books.

I can still see that terrible day when the servant came to me at work and told me that mother had suddenly become very weak. I found her unconscious but, her lips were whispering a chapter of psalms. She suffered for one week. All her children and grandchildren were gathered around her bed.

Her holy soul ascended on the 2nd of *Iyar, sav-reysh-tsadi"vov.*

[Page 280]

Khane Papiertshik
of Blessed Memory

by B. P. Miryam

Translated by Tina Lunson

Khane, the daughter of Reb Yankl Berl Blumshteyn of blessed memory was well known in town. She was married at quite a young age to the great scholar Reb Zelig Papiertshik, a leader and a sage, of an aristocratic Warsaw family.

She bore him six children, all girls and despite her heavy task of educating them, she still found free time to do *mitsves* and good deeds. She would go around collecting money and food for the needy and also help a sick person in any way they needed.

Khane was very refined and possessed a warm Jewish heart. Her manner of speaking and her approach to people brought her honor and esteem. She befriended everyone, had a good word for everyone, respected others and so became respected herself.

She died in the month of *Shevet* 1928. The sum of her years was only 32 when after a short illness she was torn away from life. She left her children, some at such an age that they could not comprehend the measure of the tragedy.

Khane Papiertshik remains baked into the hearts of her children and family, who will never forget her. May her soul be bound up with the bond of life.

[Page 281]

Two figures – Rokhl Shmilke's and Khane Rivke

by Khaye bas Yankev Dov, Israel

Translated by Mira Eckhaus

Edited by Tina Lunson

Rokhl Shmilke's lived with her husband in the attic of our house. They were extremely old. He was eighty years old and she was seventy. He was called Yoske and she was called Rokhl Shmilke's.

For many years they lived together in the narrow apartment with love and friendship like a pair of doves. "My Yoske" - she was proud of her husband and he called her "My wife Rokhl".

The town treated her with great admiration and respect. And indeed, she deserved this appreciation. There was no limit to her kindness and noble mindedness. She always smiled, she spoke calmly and peacefully and she was always ready to help others with all her might and heart.

She was busy with public needs, in every sense of the word. She took care of poor brides, not only to find them a dowry and sources for the wedding expenses, but also to find grooms for them. For the sick and weak, she hid in her bag some chicken soup, a piece of veal, and medicines for healing. The old woman walked long distances every day. She went to distant villages to ask favors from the Polish landowners for Jews. With the fluent Polish she spoke she asked for things and also managed to get what she wanted. Almost every day she went from door to door asking for money for charity. Everyone responded favorably with great generosity. She never told who she was collecting the charity for and who needed help.

Even though she neglected her husband a little because of her involvement with the community's needs, Yoske never complained. He suffered but did not rebuke her about it. On the contrary, he even encouraged her to continue her good deeds for the benefit of the poor, sick and oppressed.

Khane Rivke

When someone at home got sick, had a sore throat or head and teeth aches, they first called Khane Rivke to come and check him. She looked at the patient with her deep eyes, looked at the tongue, checked the pulse, and determined the diagnosis. She also decided whether there is a need to call the doctor or not.

She lived in a dilapidated house in a side alley with a difficult access. Her husband and sons belonged to a family of butchers and were always busy slaughtering, purging and cutting meat, and removing what needed to be out of the sight of the veterinarian. Khane Rivke also helped her husband in trading. But when she was called for help, she responded immediately and with hasty steps went to provide first aid.

Due to the extensive trust that the town's residents had in her, she was able in most cases to bring medicine and cure to every patient and every disease. I was present when the Polish doctor consulted her as if she was in his position, what is her opinion on the disease and what medicine does she suggest?

However, not only the disease was treated by Khane Rivke. She also brought sweets and delicacies to the patient. Her words of encouragement had the power to raise a sick person from his bed and make him well.

Indeed, Khane Rivke was a wonderful woman. When she fell ill with a serious illness, she accepted the judgment upon her as a punishment from heaven and quietly bore her suffering without complaining and telling others about her sufferings.

When she passed away, the residents of the town paid her great respect, and told after her death about her praises and good deeds.

[Page 282]

Reb Borekh Kuperman
of Blessed Memory

by A. Beys, Israel

Translated by Tina Lunson

Reb Borekh Kuperman of blessed memory
and his wife Khane Rokhl, may she have a long life

Reb Borekh of blessed memory was a person with exuberant energy, a born community leader and devoted social activist. He was a Jewish Councilman for many terms of the administration. He was also one of the most proclaimed artisans' activists in the town.

He was born in Goworowo in 1883 to his parents Tsvi and Yenta Rivke. He studied in the Goworowo Yeshiva as a boy. Later his father took him into the shoemaking trade, from which he made a good living. He built a house on the market square with a large apartment and a workshop.

He married Khane Rokhl (of the parents Granat) who had a grocery business in town. She, his wife Khane Rokhl, excelled in her charitable deeds and discreet gifts. She was among the less pious women, she gave her charity modestly and quietly in the name of heaven.

Shortly before the last world war, Reb Borekh Kuperman and his family moved to America. There too, Reb Borekh participated in community activities and was a leading member of the Goworowo *landsmanshaft* committee. His wife and children are still in America to this day.

Reb Borekh Kuperman died on the 11th of *Kislev, sav-shin-yud"khes* and was buried in the Goworowo cemetery in New York. May his soul be bound up in the bond of the living.

[Page 283]

Reb Asher Kutner

May God Avenge His Blood

by *Rov* Avrom Alter Kutner, Chief Rabbi, Lod, Israel

Translated by Mira Eckhaus

Edited by Tina Lunson

Rov Asher Kutner, may God avenge his blood, was born in Warsaw in the year 5630 to his father, the famous *hasid* of Radzimin Hasidism.

In his youth *Rov* Asher studied in *yeshivas* and he was great in Torah and qualified to teach, although he did not serve in the rabbinate. He married his first wife in the city of Ostrolenke. After the death of his wife, he married a second time in the city of Goworowo.

He was engaged in commerce and had set times for Torah studies. He was a philanthropist, a *hasid* and had noble qualities. He was involved with those around him and his entire mindset and way of life were imbued with the spirit of the Torah and firm faith. While studying the Torah and worshiping God, his qualities improved until he ascended to a higher level of noble spirit in his kindness, goodness, love for humanity, and his willingness to help all those who fail in the war of life, with his good deeds. He did not chase publicity and recognition. He obeyed the orders of those who were great in Torah and reverence, and was connected with every fiber of his soul to the late *Rebi* of Radzimin.

During the deportations from the city of Goworowo he fled to the city of Slonim together with his wife and daughter and there the Germans executed him in 5702. May his soul be bound in the bundle of life and may his memory be blessed forever.

* * *

Translated by Tina Lunson

Reb Asher Kutner was one of the most esteemed householders in the town and one of the distinguished *hasidim* in the Vurke-Otvotsk *shtibl*. He himself was not a Vurke *hasid*. His father Reb Shmuel Zaynvl was reckoned as the finest Radzimin Hasid in Vurke. He led the morning service during the Days of Awe for the last Radzimin *Rebi*; and after his demise he was lain near the tomb of the *Rebi*. But as in Goworowo there were no Radzimin Hasidim, Reb Asher joined the Otvotsk Hasidim, to which his relatives belonged.

In his young years Reb Asher learned in the Radzimin Yeshiva. Later he helped his father to run the leather business in Warsaw. He would spend the evenings in the *hasidic shtibl*, learning a page of Talmud and talking about hasidim.

Reb Asher married in Ostrolenke, with his wife Yokheved. Her father Avrom Yisroel had a wine bar there. After several years living with his in-laws, Reb Asher began trading and taking merchandise to Warsaw.

With his second marriage to his wife Rivke, at the end of the First World War, he moved to Goworowo and opened a grocery business in the market square.

Reb Asher was a typical *hasid* with all the *hasidic* ways of life and was good humored in his relations with people. He spoke the Warsaw *Yakh* language in a singing tone and loved to dismiss the whole world with a wave of his hand.

He was one of the founders of the Otvotsk *shtibl* and along with Yankev Dovid Nayman donated the site for the *shtibl.*

He was murdered along with his family in Slonim, may God avenge their blood.

A. Ben

[Page 284]

Reb Shleyme Leyb and Reb Khayim Borekh Shakhter of Blessed Memory

by Tsipora Zaltsberg-Shakhter, Israel

Translated by Tina Lunson

Grandfather Reb Shleyme Leyb was known in Goworowo as a wise Jew and a man of learning, one of the fine Vurke Hasidim. He would often act as arbitrator for important Jewish court cases and was the best close friend of the Goworowo *Rov*. When he died the *Rov* eulogized him with the words, "My right hand has been taken away." He had five children - Leye, Peysakh, Khayim Borekh, Sima and Nekhame. Peysakh was a Talmud scholar and very observant. He prayed and studied and did not want to take any enjoyment from the world. After his marriage he became a ritual slaughterer. He died of hunger during the transports to Russia because he would not eat unkosher food. The elder daughter Leye was killed with the family in Sokolov and Sima and his family in Slonim. Only Nekhame survived because she was in Pioneer training and made *aliye* to *Erets Yisroel* in 1938.

My father Reb Khayim Borekh was born in 1900. He studied in the Makove Yeshiva. In 1924 he married my mother Yetke Holtsman and established a fine Jewish household. He could sing, my father. People stood under our windows for the *Shabes* songs just to hear his singing.

On that sad *Shabes* the Germans shot several of our neighbors in our building. Everything was burned and we were left naked and impoverished. For several days we wandered among the gentiles and then to Bialystok. My father was an energetic person; he established himself well in Bialystok but, for the crime of not getting a Russian passport we were transported to Siberia. We made it through four hard years there and it was thanks to my father's energy and initiative that we somehow held our own. My father did the hardest work, sawing wood in the 50 °C cold. Once a falling tree hit him in the head. He was badly wounded but did not lose his courage. I remember, before the holiday of *Sukes*, he went away into the deep forest with the head of the Pultusk Yeshiva to dig a pit and cover it with branches in order to fulfill the *mitsve* of *Sukes*, so that no one would know.

In 1944 we, as Polish citizens, were sent back to Ukraine and the heavens began to brighten. We could now see some rays of hope. So, standing on the threshold of liberation, our worst misfortune occurred.

[Page 285]

Reb Khayim Borekh
Shakhter
of blessed memory

My father worked with Reb Shleyme Gelbart in a sugar factory. One certain *Shabes* night, when my father was working the night shift, there was a gas explosion and both were tragically killed. My father was then at the blossoming age of 44.

May his name be sanctified along with all the Jewish martyrs.

* * *

by Mordkhe Shakhter

Translated by Mira Eckhaus

I woke up in the middle of the night to the sound of an explosion in the distance. My heart foretells evil. I heard noise and commotion outside. They said that there was a disaster at the sugar factory, two workers were killed. A shiver went through my body; after all, my father worked there on the night shift. However, I immediately rejected the terrible idea. It is not possible, I said. On the table was still the Pentateuch in which my father taught me the week's parsha before he left for work, and here the war was about to end and a new, happier and shining era was standing at the gate.

But the cruel news came to our house. "The old Jewish man was among the dead". My father was young when he died, only forty-four years old. The Gentiles called him "an old man" because of the black beard that adorned his face.

My world was destroyed. I could not accept the idea that my father would never come back and I will not see him anymore.

Since then, every day, in the morning and in the evening, in the heavy Russian cold and the strong winds of the Ukrainian steppes, I would run around in a hostile environment of Gentiles to gather a Minyan of Jews to pray and say Kaddish in his memory.

May his memory be blessed.

[Page 286]

Reb Gedalye Grinberg
of Blessed Memory

by G. Even, Israel

Translated by Tina Lunson

Reb Gedalye Grinberg of blessed memory and his wife Khane, may she have a long life

In Reb Gedalye Grinberg's bakery one could not only get a fresh loaf of well-baked goods but, one could also hear a fine funny witticism and a Torah commentary. The knowledge that Reb Gedalye had earned in the Lomzshe Yeshiva was not lost even though he worked hard in his bakery and did not have time to refresh his memory of his earlier scholarship. He was one of the esteemed Ger hasidim and prayed in the Ger *shtibl* all his years.

Reb Gedalye had a lot of pleasure from life and was always happy. In essence, he was a quiet, separate person, did not like to mix in community matters. In town, people honored and respectfully valued him.

Reb Gedalye was born in Goworowo in 1888 to his father Yitskhak Ayzik the baker and mother Sheyne Gitl. He studied in *kheyder* and in the Lomzshe Yeshiva. At the age of twenty he married his wife Khane Marmelshteyn from Ruzshan and opened a bakery in Goworowo which he maintained until the destruction of the town.

Reb Gedalye died in another place, fleeing to Lomzshe, on the 21st of *Kheshvan, sav"shin*. His wife, long years to her, is now in Israel.

[Page 287]

My Grandfather Reb Yankev Shabsay

of Blessed Memory

by Rivke Rozenberg-Shafran, Canada

Translated by Tina Lunson

I will try here to depict a typical Goworowo Jew, who was born there in 1850 and lived almost all his years in that town. This was my grandfather, Reb Yankev Shabsay Trukhnovski, may he rest in peace, who was known by the name Yankev Shepsl "the Litvak". I will record a few episodes about him and about his wife, my grandmother, Khaye, about whom I heard when I was just a child. I will also relate facts that I myself later observed and naturally did not understand and evaluate at the time.

Grandfather and his two younger sisters were free-floating orphans when they were little. He was nine years old at the time with no one to redeem him and no nearby family, because their parents were also each the only child of their parents and died very young.

Strangers, good people, who tended to the children in the name of a *mitsve*, took in my grandfather at ten years of age, to be an apprentice with a tailor. He was provided with food and a bed for three years. And he was instructed that he should do everything that the proprietor told him to do and even obey the wife too. Because here he was getting food and a bed and being taught to be a tailor. The ten-year-old tailor apprentice could really not understand that in order to be a tailor, one had to carry water for the wife, bring in wood, rock the baby, and when she was pregnant, he had to clean and sweep the house as well. He did not, heaven forbid, complain and of course not revolt because he knew that in the end, he would be a tailor and that meant earning money for profit and in time also becoming independent.

When the three years ended, he did, besides the food and bed, receive money. People did not get paid in those days in a small town (probably everywhere) every week; sometimes every month, but sometimes for the whole season. When the half year was over, he received enough money to be able to clothe himself from head to foot – that is to say, a *kapote* and a pair of shoes.

At eighteen years my grandfather was a complete tailor and made a good match with his wife, my grandmother Khaye, who descended from an excellent lineage. She was also a little orphan and had been reared by an uncle. The good uncle promised a dowry and the two orphans were married. Grandfather was then prepared to become an independent tailor.

So his disappointment was huge when grandmother's uncle, after the wedding,

[Page 288]

said to him, "How should a Jew, as poor as I am, get money to give you as a dowry? I have given you a precious, quiet and fine girl from prestigious parents, I cannot give you any more; livelihood is from God, however the One Above wishes, whether you become a "patcher" without the brides' dowry." And God did really will it, that what the bride's uncle said did actually materialize. It's true, it was not so easy, but after getting through all the difficulties he did, finally, work up to a good livelihood and my grandmother lived out her years in quiet and refinement. She was regarded with honor and was esteemed by everyone. When she arrived at the women's shul, the women stood for her. "Khaye the charitable" they called her. She bore grandfather eight children – four sons and four daughters. The eldest of them was my dear mother, Ester, may God avenge her blood.

Now I would like to return to my grandfather. Before their first child was born to them grandfather traveled off to Warsaw with the sole thought and ambition to save enough money and become a householder for himself. In Warsaw he worked in a tailoring factory with many other workers. At lunch time, when all the workers went to a restaurant to eat, grandfather hid so no one would see him and ate a little piece of bread. When his coworkers asked him, "Shepsl, where did you eat?" He answered, "Over there, in that other restaurant."

So he lived for several years with great thriftiness in Warsaw. When he would come from time to time back to grandmother in Goworowo, he went by foot in order to save money. After years of living in stinginess, he in Warsaw and grandmother in the little town where she earned money by baking bread and braiding *khale* for others, grandfather had gathered enough money to realize his dream. The last time that he came by foot from Warsaw he literally, right at the door, lost his strength and fell in a faint. He did not try to walk it again.

Once grandfather even proposed that grandmother and the two children that she had by then travel with him to live in Warsaw but, she rejected that suggestion categorically. "In Warsaw," she said, "even the stones are *treyf*." She did not want her children to grow up there as *goyim* . Grandfather concurred and promptly built a house on Long Street, bought two sewing machines, brought in merchants from Warsaw, acquired journeymen and worked 18 to 20 hours over two days. In Goworowo people whispered that Yankev Shepsl had found a treasure of cash in Warsaw and had struck it rich for, how could it be, that in those few numbered years he could make so much money? So the legend remained as long as he lived. No one knew in what kind of poverty he had lived.

Grandfather's tailor shop went very well. He sewed coats, jackets and suits for gentiles and went from fair to fair selling that merchandise.

[Page 289]

He won the trust of his customers. "The Litvak does not trick you," they said. For him that was the best advertisement, one that could not be bought for money and it brought him success. Even the wagon driver who drove him to the fairs believed strongly in him. I recall that all those years he had only one driver and he was called Piotr. When Piotr died, his brother Volek took over the reins. And with all his prosperity he still lived very frugally.

But my grandfather already had another goal in life. Not to give his children to tailoring but to study, providing them with big dowries and matching them to marriages of good lineage. To a certain extent he was successful. The first son, Khayim Zalman, made a marriage with Yeshaye Diment's daughter Rivke, from Ostrove. Reb Yeshaye was a learned man of a good family but he was very poor. Thus, my grandfather gave the dowry and not as it was done then, by the bride's father. The second son, Velvl, married to the Vonseva [Wąsewo] *Rov's* daughter Pesh'ke. The *Rov* barely made a living from his position. After the wedding Uncle Velvl had to report for military conscription. Then a big argument broke out between son and parents. Velvl said that he did not want to serve the damned Russian government and that he would rather go to America. Those words struck the parents like a clap of thunder in the middle of a clear day. This was at the beginning of this century, when

A family picture during a holiday

Sitting second from right, Yankev Shepsl's daughter Sore with her husband Shmuel Shtern.
Except the ones designated with an "X", all were killed.
Of the survivors: Yisroel Truknovski, next to him his wife Sore and their daughter Khave (Canada).
Standing near the soldier is Khaye Zeml (Israel).

[Page 280]

only thieves were going to America, criminals, revolutionaries, who had to flee from the tsarist government. How did that suit for a prominent proprietor's son who had just married a *rov's* daughter? In the end grandfather had to pay a 400 *ruble* penalty to the tsar for his son's avoiding conscription. But Velvl stubbornly stood his ground and said that if they did not give him any money to go to America that he would hang himself. The depressed parents saw that their son meant what he said, gave him money and he did indeed leave for America. "Better to have a living son in *treyf* America than a son who hanged himself," they decided.

Until more respectable people began to move to America, the parents were ashamed to say that they had a son there. They did not imagine what the times, with the later wars and the Hitler years, would bring. And indeed, thanks to the first pioneers of the family who went along the "slippery, un-Jewish" path to America, it was through him that many in the extended family were saved, and are still there. When the Vonseva *Rebi's* son-in-law first arrived in America he spent a few years in the "sweat shops". He said that it would be better sweeping the streets than working in any "shop". He did in fact wash windows and do various heavy jobs. He also pushed a cart, sometimes with frozen apples, sometimes with shoe-laces and women's stockings. He slept in a shoemaker's basement, paying fifty cents a month rent. Gradually he got into business and as is the American way, became very rich. Uncle Velvl is now an old man of over 85 years, may he live to 120, and has lived in America the whole time.

Grandfather's third child was my dear mother, Ester. He also married her according to his wish. Reb Elieyzer Gedalye, the great scholar of Dlugashodle became the father-in-law and the 18-year-old Avremele the genius became the groom. Grandfather added to it because he gave a large dowry. Three years room and board, he bought the groom a fur *shtreyml* for the wedding, made him a silk *kapote*, gave him a complete set of the Vilne Talmud, plus – a beautiful, accomplished 17 year old daughter, whom my father had not seen until the wedding. Grandfather and grandmother were sure that their son-in-law with his great learning ability would become a *rov*. But father, after three years of *kest*, did not become a *rov*. "I am afraid," he said, "that taking a position with Jews onto my shoulders is too great a responsibility before God."

My mother opened a shop and drew her livelihood from it for 38 years. They reared nine children and lived in peace and tranquility. Until Hitler and his hoards came and slaughtered six million Jews, and along with everyone else, my dear parents and my three brothers Bunem, Meyshe and Dovid, may God avenge their blood.

[Page 290]

My grandmother died in 1917, my grandfather in deep old age in 1928.

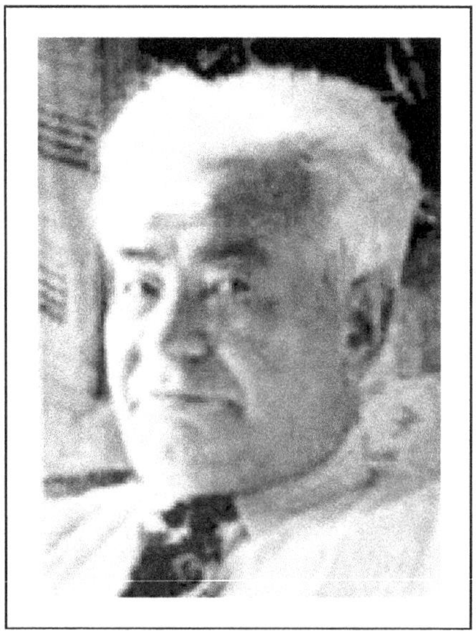

Velvl Trukhnovski

Reb Yankev Shabsay Trukhnovski was a fine type of religious Jew, an observant tailor who had a large workshop with workers, traveled to all the fairs with his prepared merchandise, worked hard all his life and still swore that he had to recite all the psalms every day for all the appointed occasions plus all the various Torah portions that were available in his big, thick prayerbooks.

The question was still, how can a Jew put so much time into it? But he found a simple bit of advice from *Genesis*: "then Jacob went on his journey" and right after midnight went straight to the study house and begin to recite. He prayed at dawn his whole life, with the first *minyen.* Coming home, he made a *l'khayim* with a little pure spirits and a bite to eat. After that he ate breakfast, which consisted of bread with some hot groats. That is how Reb Yankev Shabsay lived, whom people held as a wealthy Jew.

The Goworowo youth were well acquainted with that Jew. When they were coming home from strolling around half the night before going to sleep, Reb Yankev Shabsay had just gotten up from sleep and the friends saw how he turned on lights in the study house and began to recite the psalms.

His eldest son Velvl, who lives in New York may no evil eye harm him, already in his eighties, says that he can still not forget how his father would, in winter, in the freezing cold, in the middle of the night drag him out of his warm bed and force him to go to the study house to learn.

One of his other sons, Reb Yisroel Trukhnovski from Pultusk, who survived the war with his wife and children, lives today in Montreal, Canada.

A. Shin

[Page 292]

Reb Yehoshe Rozen
of Blessed Memory

by A. Boshon, Israel

Translated by Tina Lunson

Reb Yehoshe Rozen and his wife Alte of blessed memory

Reb Yehoshe Rozen, of blessed memory, was a type of energetic leader and social activist for general, religious, and professional matters in the town. He was a religiously observant and sincere person and very earnest in his tasks.

He was born in Goworowo about 1878, to his parents Yosef and Khave Rozen. He learned the shoemaking trade and married his wife Alte, the daughter of Yisroel Shabsay Berliner.

Soon after the First World War Reb Yehoshe got involved in community matters. He was a councilman in most of the Jewish Council terms and among the founders and member of the Artisans' Union and their bank. He was an active member of the Burial Society, the Psalm Society, one of the *gabays* in the Great *Shul* and one of the spokesmen for all Council matters.

With the outbreak of the Second World War, Reb Yehoshe and his family went to Russia. His youngest son Yankev, one of the members of the town *Ha'shomer ha'dati*, died there in 1942. He also lost his daughter Khave Galovinski there, along with his son-in-law Avrom Barzili. His other son-in-law Shleyme Gelbord

[Page 293]

was killed at the end of the War in Ukraine, along with Khayim Borekh Shakhter, in a sugar factory due to a gas explosion there. In 1956, in Israel, his daughter Sore Blume Oyslender died.

In 1949 Reb Yehoshe and his family arrived in Israel and settled in Bnai Brak. Being a natural leader, he soon began to be active in the *Poaley Agudas Yisroel* in his area. He became *gabay* of *Tikun Sufrim* and despite his old age contributed a lot to the *shul*.

Reb Yehoshe died in *Shevet, sav-shin-khof"daled*, and six months later, in *Elul, sav-shin-khof"daled*, his wife Alte died at almost the same age. They were both buried in the cemetery of *Zikhron Yakov* in Bnai Brak.

May their souls be bound up in the bond of the living.

Yankev Rozen
of blessed memory

[Page 294]

Reb Yankev Rozenberg
May God Avenge His Blood

by Y. Ben-Mordkhe, Israel

Translated by Tina Lunson

Reb Yankev Rozenberg may
God avenge his blood

Reb Yankev, the son of Reb Borekh Rozenberg may he rest in peace, was born in Goworowo in 1882. Although later, before the outbreak of the war, he lived in Ruzshan he still considered himself a Goworower. He would often come to town, where his mother Sore Gitl and brother Avrom Rozenberg lived.

Reb Yankev was a Jew in awe of heaven who loved the law of Torah, was a giver of charity and was known as a wonderful host of guests. When he did not have any guests for *Shabes* it was hard for him to sit at the table alone for the *Shabes* meal. He also belonged to various groups that studied Torah. He loved that very much.

Reb Yankev was very observant regarding *kashrus*. People said that during the First World War when he had fallen captive to the Germans, he lived for three years (1914–1917) on just bread and tea.

In Ruzshan, Reb Yankev became very active in the community. He was a member of the local Jewish Council, as well as a member of the Burial Society. He was treasurer of the Free Loan Society. He was a leader in public affairs with complete trust.

[Page 295]

With the outbreak of the Second World War, when the Germans neared Ruzshan, the Jews left their homes and began wandering from place to place. Reb Yankev and his family went back to Goworowo to his relatives. But here, what happened was horrible. On that gruesome *Shabes* at dawn, when the Germans drove all the Jews into the *shul* and began to burn down the town, Reb Yankev was murdered. A Nazi bullet put an end to his life. He was buried in the Goworowo cemetery. Many proprietors from both Goworowo and Ruzshan took part in his funeral.

Reb Yankev left behind a wife, Khaye Sore, who lives in Israel today. Also, their two daughters Ester Hadasa Klayn and Rokhl Rozenberg are in Israel with their families. Their son Borekh and his two daughters Brokhe and Khane, live in Russia. Their son Shmuel with his wife Rivke, the daughter of Reb Avrom Shafran may God avenge his blood, live in Canada. Shmuel Rozenberg, a scholar, already belonged to the conscious youth in Poland and became a community activist there. He and his wife are very busy in Canada among the Goworowo *landslayt* and have many supporters for the publication of this book.

* * *

Finally another mention, that Reb Yankev's son Mayer fell in the battle of the Russian Army against the Germans. His daughter Freyde died in Russia. Freyde's children Dov and his wife Tsipora and their two children, as well as her daughter Rokhl and her husband Ilan and a child, live in Israel.

Reb Yankev's mother Sore Gitl Rozenberg of blessed memory

[Page 296]

My Home

by Rivke Vinderboym-Proska, Israel

Translated by Tina Lunson

My large, many branched family was rooted in the soil of Goworowo for long generations. We ourselves lived outside the town, in a house on an open field, surrounded by green meadows and a lake. All our family members gathered often at our house, to enjoy the fresh air, spend *Shabes* and holidays together and celebrate happy family events.

Our house was blessed with a lot of children. My father used to say at the birth of each new child, "Now I am made richer with another treasure". My mother also never complained about her lot. There was nothing hard for her, for us children. She gifted us all of her best years and best energies. Our house was always full of children's clamor and children's laughter.

I remember the year when I started going to the Polish public school. It was not so easy for a Jewish child to attend that school. My father took pains and appealed to the school director for protection, so that I might be accepted there. A total of three other Jewish girls studied with me in that school. The jokes and laughter with which the Polish children received us still lie buried in my memory. They pestered us at every opportunity, and the Polish teachers did nothing to control it. That era was full of animosity and irritation. If not for my stubbornness and strong will to learn, I would not have been able to bear the animosity and indignity from the Polish pupils and teachers.

My father, Reb Khayim Leyb was a folksy, ordinary Jew. A tall, solidly built man with a beautifully combed beard, always with a smile, full of humor and witticisms, loved and respected by everyone. He earned his bread honestly. At first, he had a piece of land and a cow farm. Later he began to deal in cattle, then earned and led a simple way of life.

Until the terrible misfortune that ruined our home, even before the decimation of all of Polish Jewry, the murderous axe of *goy* was loosed on my father's head and tore him away from us before his time. It happened when familiar gentiles came to him and invited him to purchase some cattle for an agreeable price. My father suspected nothing. He harnessed his horse to the wagon, took some money with him, and drove to the village to buy the goods. He was supposed to come home by evening and did not come. It got to be late at night,

[Page 297]

we were getting uneasy, and alarmed people to go search for him. By morning the whole town was already on its feet. Artisans put their work aside, shopkeepers closed the businesses – everyone went out to search. Three days and nights they looked for my father, until they found him in a forest, lying in his wagon with his head split, the horse tied to a tree, robbed of the money that he had with him.

Our misfortune was as huge as the ocean. The whole area sank into a deep sadness. We had deep suspicions about a particular *goy*, that he was the murderer. Strong evidence led to him. We brought a lawsuit against him but the Polish court acquitted the case.

The misfortune completely broke our family. I remained in the house with another three sisters, except the married brothers and sisters.

We are three sisters in Israel since before the war. My mother, the youngest sister and the married brothers and sisters and their families were tragically murdered by the German persecutors in the gruesome years of the war.

Pesh'ke Goldman

by Kh. Sh. Kazshdan, New York

Translated by Tina Lunson

Pesh'ke Goldman worked as a teacher in Goworowo in the 1938-1939 school year. She worked in an afternoon school with children from the Polish folks school and the *kheyder*. She taught the children to speak Yiddish, to write and read it. In the evening hours she taught a group of *skipistn* (youth of the Bund), children from 12 to 16 years, all of whom already worked. She used Yankev Pat's *Mayn bikhl*. Her workday began at 10 in the morning and ended at 11 at night. From 10 to 1:00 she worked in an orphanage; from 1 to 7 in the evening in the afternoon school and from 9 to 11 with the *skipistn*. From a letter dated 20 November 1938 that she wrote to friends, she remarked, "As you see, I am toiling hard the whole day, without time to catch my breath."

Pesh'ke Goldman was born in Kobrin in 1908 (? – ed.). Her father was a glazier. In 1931 she finished the Jewish Teachers' Seminary in Vilne. During the years 1932 to 1939 she was active in the area of Jewish education.

She was first a teacher in an orphanage in Novidvar (near Warsaw) where she was also teaching in a Yiddish school, Botshan. Pesh'ke Goldman was also a teacher in Warsaw, Kobrin (her birth-town), Zshetl (near Slonim) and then in Goworowo. Where she died is not known.

(From The Teachers' Memorial Book)

[Page 298]

Reb Mordkhe Shmelts
of Blessed Memory

by Khaye Shmelts, Israel

Translated by Tina Lunson

Reb Mordkhe and Ester Shmelts of blessed memory

The family Shmelts was an old, well-established family in Goworowo. Reb Mordkhe was born in the town and he married his wife Ester, the daughter of a neighboring family. Soon after the wedding Mordkhe was mobilized into Tsar Nicholas' army and served a full four years there. While serving in the Russian military he received a heavy sentence for defending Jewish honor. This is the story. A Jewish soldier was standing praying in the barracks and a Russian soldier started annoying him and making fun of him. He was not satisfied with that and then poked him and badgered him. This boiled Mordkhe's blood, he warned the Russian soldier once, then twice, and when he did not quit he grabbed a stool and hit the hooligan over the head with it. The soldier was badly wounded and was taken to the hospital. There was a great uproar – a Jew had beaten a *goy*! A suit was brought against Mordkhe and he drew a heavy penalty. Mordkhe defended himself at the trial. He stated, "Imagine that there is a general in the regiment, everyone salutes him, but one soldier comes along and pokes him and teases and hits him. How would that look… Here stands a Jewish soldier, appealing to God for his king, for his people and for peace, and another soldier comes and tries to tear pieces off him…"

[Page 299]

Mordkhe was acquitted.

Soon after he ended his military service Mordkhe was mobilized again in the First World War. He fought with the tsar's army on various fronts and his entire regiment was taken prisoner by the Germans.

At the end of the war Mordkhe came back to the town and took up working in his meat trade. He had great success there and became rich. He was active in the artisans' union and was later elected as president of the Artisans' Bank. He made many contributions to the development of the bank.

By nature, Mordkhe was excitable and nervous. If there was a grievance, he would react with shouting and anger. But in essence he had a good, warm heart and loved to do a person a good turn; he lent money without interest, and regularly helped anyone he could. Once there was a situation in which he helped a Christian in a difficult situation and the priest in the church stood him as an example for the whole Christian population.

Mordkhe was on good terms with the high officials in the town. Therefore, the commandant wanted to take revenge on him. Once, one Passover eve, he punished him with a large fine for a little garbage in front of his house. Mordkhe shouted at him and shouted the truth in his face. The commandant complained about him in the district court for insulting a police officer doing his duty. Mordkhe could not get an attorney to defend him because they were afraid of the commandant. Mordkhe had to defend himself. He related the whole story of the revenge and since the commandant had bribed the Christian jurors with drinks at a wine bar, Mordkhe was freed, and the commandant had to leave Goworowo in great dishonor.

Mordkhe and his family went through great hardships during World War II. His wife protected the Jewish traditions with great soul-sacrifice. She starved and did not allow any non-kosher food in the house. They merited coming to Israel, where they lived another seven years.

In 1956 Reb Mordkhe died, and eight days later his wife Ester also died. The were both 74 years old. May their souls be bound up in the bundle of life.

[Page 300]

Binyumin Ginzburg

by Rifke Rozenberg-Shafran, Canada

Translated by Tina Lunson

Binyumin Ginzburg

Our town Goworowo had its own *Eykhad ha'om* [*Akhad ha'am*] in the intellectual personality of Binyumin Ginzburg.

His father, Reb Meyshe Yehoshe, stemmed from the famous Russian-Polish aristocratic family Ginzburg and was himself a great scholar. Still, the "evil tongues" said about him that he read "trashy, illicit" books and as proof, he could talk about many secular things and knew all the news that was unfolding across the world. So, from where would he know all of that if he did not read *Ha'melits* or other heretical newspapers?

Binyumin Ginzburg also learned Torah in his young years. It was said that he had a very good head for learning and would grow into a great scholar. But it was not to be as they foresaw. He later left off learning Torah and went into the study of languages, reading books, Jewish and secular literature, acquired higher education, and "new" thoughts sprouted in his head.

At that time, at the beginning of the current century, the Goworowo study house was full of young men and boys who sat and studied for the sake of Torah. Binyumin Ginzburg became friends with the "good heads" among the young men in the study house and introduced them to the new Torah. He told them about writers and books, about art and science, and they borrowed books to read, of course in secret and with much conspiracy.

Binyumin Ginzburg possessed great intellectual powers and spoke in a rich, multi-sourced language. His influence was soon remarked upon in the study house. Many young men were "soured" and "left the path", among them

[Page 301]

one of my uncles. I remember one time when my grandfather found a book in the house that my uncle had borrowed from Binyumin. The whole house grew dark. Grandfather was enraged and threw the book on the floor, then grabbed a huge tailor's scissor and sliced the book into pieces.

Of course, my uncle never brought any books into the house again but, that did not mean he stopped reading them. He just sought out places where his father's eyes would not find him.

I remember Binyumin as a little child, before the First World War. After the great fire he and his father left the town and returned again after the War.

Arriving in town, they rented an apartment in my grandfather's building. I had the opportunity to get closer and know him and marvel at his personality. I was then 11 or 12 years old. He loved to argue with me and often tried to convince me of the importance of reading literature and of establishing a library in Goworowo. I was overcome with a fear of the heretical thought. I was still young and religious then, reared by my parents and grandfather. Every night before sleep grandfather would sit down by the table read out a verse of *Shevet musar*, which depicted hell with all its details and the punishment that came for each sin individually. From those stories I had desolate dreams of burning pitch, tongues of fire and dancing devils. I was so terrified about the life of my "sinning" uncle. But when I saw how my uncle lived and that nothing bad happened to him, I began to understand that the danger was not so great. One could read a book and remain living too.

Binyumin's idea about founding a library in town became a reality. At first no one would rent him a space for that purpose, until the tailor Hersh Ber came back from America. Binyumin rented a space from him and founded the library, in the beginning with only his own books; later he created a committee and they bought new books until it grew into the big Goworowo library.

The first library in the town was the foundation on which the Zionist Organization was later built. The youth began streaming into the Organization which then divided into various splinters of almost every political party.

Binyumin Ginzburg stayed in Goworowo until the early 1920s. After that he went to Warsaw or Lodz and there became a bookkeeper in a large commercial firm. He was active as a journalist there as well.

He was killed along with all the Jewish martyrs by the German persecutors in the Second World War. Honor his memory!

[Page 302]

Leyb Kersh
May God Avenge His Blood

by Y. Sh. Herts, America

Translated by Tina Lunson

Leybl Kersh
may God avenge his blood

Born on the 5th of October 1902 in Shedlets – murdered in the Warsaw Ghetto Uprising May 1943.

His parents, Yankl and Treyne, moved from Shedlets to Volomin, a neighbor of Warsaw. The father, a worldly man, was a carpenter by trade. In 1917 the family settled in Goworowo, where Yankl was known by the name "the Volomin carpenter".

He had his first education in *khedarim* as well as a private school. In his young years he was sent to work; he became a tailor.

The short, thin little Leybl had an ocean of energy. His longish, good humored face gave evidence about a person who was ready to do good. He always looked for something to do. A type of born social worker. That same trait stood him well in the Bund.

He was a Bundist from his earliest years. Barely 15 years old in 1922, he founded an organization for young Bundists in Goworowo, *Tsukunft*. Later he was also active in the local Bundist party. It was to a large extent thanks to him that the Bundist movement in that small town in the Lomzshe region was effective. Leybl was not satisfied with just his hometown. He was not lazy and traveled to the neighboring villages and there helped with anything he could.

In 1932 the Party sent him to Biale-Podliask to direct

[Page 303]

the organization there. In that town he was also active in the professional unions. Among others he organized the wagon drivers and porters. With his patience and ability to get along with all kinds of people he succeeded in creating unity among the difficult and raw elements.

In 1934 Leybl settled in Warsaw, where he became secretary of the Artisans' Union. From time to time he traveled to the provinces as a Party emissary, to take care of organizational matters or deliver a lecture. He was dedicated to the Bund, heart and soul. Every job that he did, he did with heart. His name, which was very popular in the Bundist movement, can be found in the columns of the Bundist press, where he published numerous reports and correspondence.

Leybl Kersh was also killed in the horrendous years of the Second World War and the Nazis' orgies of murder. He was very active in the underground movement. He belonged to the directorship of the secret council of the professional unions and to the broader leadership (collective) of the Bundist organization in the Warsaw Ghetto. He worked in the Tobbens factory and along with his wife Sore (she stemmed from Radom, her birth name was Fridman) he lived on Zamenhofo Street in the Ghetto. During the selections several important Bundist activists hid in his apartment. He did a lot to save colleagues who did not have any work cards and hid them in the factory buildings.

When the time came to prepare for the Uprising, Kersh worked with the Jewish Fighters Organization. He was among the leaders of the active battle group.

Leybl Kersh ended his life as a fighter in the Warsaw Ghetto Uprising. He fell from a Nazi bullet around the 10th of May 1943 in Genshe 6.

(From the book, *Doyres Bundistn* [Generations of Bundists]

Reb Yankl and Treyne Kersh may God avenge their blood

[Page 304]

The Bundist Leader

by Feyge Sheyniak, America

Translated by Tina Lunson

The Bundist leader Leybl Kersh was always surrounded by his *hasidim*. His admirers went in groups around him with their ears pricked to be able to catch a "Torah" word from their leader. He himself was of small stature, thin, with a huge thick crop of hair, a long nose, hollow cheeks and a pair of expressive black eyes. His father, an ordinary, honest Jew, a cabinetmaker by trade, worked hard for his bit of bread. His mother, a pious Jewess, her wig pushed down almost to her eyes, constantly "talked" with God and praised his holy name.

Leybl Kersh had a huge drive for learning and had achieved everything with his own strengths. His assignment was to bring more teaching and erudition among his friends, men and women, who admired and venerated him. With extraordinary efforts, with the help of all the members, he established the "Peretz Library", the largest in the town. Leyzer Fridman, a simple bakery worker who worked hard for his living, played the largest role of his dedicated service for the Party library by constantly buying new books. Everyone knew that they could get such books there as were available in no other library. Leyzer Fridman used to say, "My head is not good for reading, but I believe my obligation is to work and provide an opportunity for others to enjoy the source of knowledge."

Leybl Kersh presented lectures on various political, literary and scientific topics. His voice thundered, his eloquence was powerful, full of pathos, in contrast to his weak body. When he spoke, the walls literally shook. His voice resounded widely.

In 1950, in Munich, Germany, I encountered his brother Peysakh in a hospital. He told me the following about him. Leybl was one of the leading forces in the Warsaw Ghetto and fought bravely against the Hitleristic murderers. He also inspired and encouraged others to fight against the enemy. With full passion, with all his strength, literally like a lion [*leyb*] he fought against the blood-thirsty animals. Later, seeing that the battle was a losing one and not wanting to fall into the hands of the murderers, he threw himself from the sixth floor. His small, worn, shrunken corpse lay without consciousness. (According to another source, the Germans shot him.)

[Page 305]

Memorial Light for our Distinguished Brother

by Moses Granat and Isaac Granat, Israel

Translated by Mira Eckhaus

Edited by Tina Lunson

Zvi (Hershke) Granat

More than 30 years have passed since Zvi (Hershke) passed away and the pain still pinches the heart and the space remains empty. The news of his death, which did not come as a surprise, shocked his family members, the Zionist movement in the town and all the residents of the entire town. He was a beloved figure, pleasant in manners and with a bright face, accepted by all. He was always alert to everything that was happening. His appearances in front of his fellow movement members and in all public appearances were appreciated and listened to, due to his intelligence, judgment and ability to analyze and his simple and radiating endearing approach. His brilliance and witty sayings became household word. His speech was measured and premeditated; each word was carved in stone without any excess whatsoever. He always knew how to fascinate those present, forcing them to listen to him to the end and accept his opinion. He knew how to penetrate the depths of the other person's soul. With his lifestyle he set himself as an example and a model. He was actively involved in the entire process of our social life and in the Zionist enterprise, the purpose of our lives. He merged in it not only the daily matters, but also the sacred and the beautiful things outside the framework of routine. He was looking for the harmony between the gray life and a life with meaning and value. He strove to bring together and blend emotionally with all the veins of his soul and to create perfection in everything that he attempted. His noble personality radiated around him devotion and zeal for the Zionist ideal. He knew how to sow the seeds of love for our homeland in the hearts of his students. He showed boundless loyalty, instructional wisdom and a wonderful organizational ability. He knew how to use up his extended knowledge and direct it to the right path. He did everything with modesty, outrightly, and without any prominence that disgusted him. He was always surrounded by friends, students and admirers who honored him with precious respect. The respect and admiration he received served as leverage for him for overcommitment to the values for which he worked and fought without hesitation and with an uncompromising conscience. He ignited the fanatic pioneering spark which turned into an ember.

A prominent expression of his active and lively life was his full and overflowing schedule, diligence in the continuity of his studies, reading, playing the violin, holding gatherings, meetings, lectures as the head of the nest of *Hashomer HaTzair*, his work at the Merchants Bank as a bookkeeper, while in fact, he also served as the actual manager, as the exclusive decision maker, who decided alone about every matter and without any consultation.

[Page 306]

He drew a yearning of holiness from the home atmosphere that was steeped in Zionism and from the tradition that was in the *cheder*, the Lomza Yeshiva and finally from his self taught studies. He inherited intelligence, wittiness, and innate intelligence from our late mother, Chaya z"l, who was known for her modest manners, noble mindedness and giving advice to those in need.

He absorbed his noble virtue of helping others from our father Reb Dov z"l, may his light shine, who was known for his open heart, who mobilized at any time to help the needy and sick. Some of them he rehabilitated with the funds he collected until they could stand on their own and some he hospitalized in hospitals until they recovered. I remember one rainy day. It rained non-stop and the flood literally threatened to repeat the time of Noah, the door suddenly opened without knocking and without saying hello, a Jew came in, wet to the bone, and with a short breath told my father about a critical patient who had just had a hemorrhage and there was an urgent need to hospitalize him in the district hospital in Ostroleka. My father changed his coat in a moment, took his stick and uttered, "Lord of the world, for the benefit of this sick stop the rain so that I can fulfill a great *mitzvah.*" When he left the house, the rain stopped completely. I saw in this the same miracle that happened with Yehoshua ben Nun, who prayed, "The sun will not set down in Gibeon" and the sun did not set down.

Zvi never resented if someone needed kindness and disturbed his rest outside the usual hours. These always came to their satisfaction. He also inherited his diligence and decency from our late father. People would deposit with our father, without any sign of receipt or any document, dowries, deposits, and simply money of the "parties" before the arbitration. And he kept these funds as if they were his possession without any differentiation.

And when I talk about him, I also remember this - he rebelled against his staff of teachers, the Poles, who did not excel with their love of Israel, by presenting them questions that they did not know how to answer. More than once, he exposed their ignorance. The teachers stood in front of him embarrassed, like a retarded student before his teacher. These phenomena lowered their prestige in the eyes of the other students, who were also faced with the riddle of the superiority of the diligent and wise Jewish boy. The teachers consulted on how to get rid of him. However, before they found a solution to their problems, Zvi stopped his studies at the school, as he did not consider it as an institution from which he could learn and progress and began an external study. Here, too, they immediately realized the strength of his personality, as every course he attended he finished with the highest excellency. In a relatively short period of time, he mastered completely the English language.

Once, he was banned with a group of his students near the railroad tracks far from the town. The Chief of the Police was notoriously known as a distinct anti Semite. He considered every Jew as a communist. They feared that this imprisonment would be prolonged. However, Zvi managed to enter into a lively conversation with the Chief of the Police and the latter, charmed by his brilliance, the strength of his spirit and the noble mindedness, was "convinced" that this was not a communist assembly, but a youth who loved nature and wandered in order to get to know nature and the beautiful scenery around it. Everyone was released immediately and the Chief of the Police invited him for more meetings in order to continue the interesting conversations.

I remember very well the correspondence between him and the cooperative center which plead him persistently to transfer to them and serve in a high position. He was promised a great future as the rising and promising star did not disappear from their eyes. But he was connected deeply to his family, to the bank, the child of his cares, and to the movement which he developed and nurtured.

[Page 307]

He was in constant tension, which eventually destroyed him while he was still young. He got sick. On his deathbed he fought hard with the master of death until he was defeated and passed away.

His work is continued by his students, who were saved from the Nazi inferno. In the project of building the country which continues, rises and develops, his memory and his wonderful and sublime image are bundled together. We will mourn his memory, that he did not get to see with his own eyes the fulfillment of his dream. May his soul be bound up in the bond of everlasting life.

* * *

He was head and shoulders above the crowd - although he was not of high stature. Even in his childhood he stood out for his unusual perception which was a "gift from God". From the following story that our mother, Mrs. Chaya z"l, used to tell, we can learn about his love for his people and his homeland. While he was in the public school, the teacher ordered the students to write an essay on some topic. Zvi took advantage of the opportunity and in his essay attacked the anti Semitism that prevailed in Poland and even wrote a hymn of praise to the people of Israel "who will return to their homeland". Of course, this was not to the teacher's liking and as a result, the headmaster of the Polish school, Mr. Stankius, came to my late father, Reb Dov (Bertshe) z"l, and tried to convince him that it was a waste of Zvi's time to study at the school, which was unable to contribute to his knowledge, as he "already passed the level that a boy can acquire in a public school", etc., etc.

Then began the affair of studies through correspondence. Besides his mother tongue, Yiddish Zvi was fluent in Polish, English and Hebrew. I remember how he gave a speech in Polish on the same evening when the famous hypnotist Professor Lessing appeared. The entire non-Jewish audience present in the hall was full of admiration for the polished language he spoke. Zvi proved his mastery of the Hebrew language to me in the speech I heard at the *Hashomer HaTzair* conference. By the way, he served as the head of the *Hashomer Hatzair* nest in Goworowo.

In our house there were dictionaries for English, French and more languages. He was able to sit down and read a book in a foreign language for hours with the help of a dictionary. He once commented that he takes it upon himself to learn any foreign language within a few months. The bookkeeping course, which he also studied through correspondence, was completed successfully by him and until his death he served as a bookkeeper at the Merchants Bank there. He was also the author of the newspaper *Ruch Spuldzilczy*, which was published by the cooperative movement in Warsaw. It is worth noting his handwriting - really a work of art.

Zvi was a man who pursued doing charity. He maintained a perfect order. He did not suffer any injustice. He had a warm heart and was ready to come to the aid of others at any time. Only after his death did we learn about things he had done, which he had never revealed in his life. People came to return money they had borrowed from him in their distress, of course without any interest. In times of need, they turned to him for help and they were always responded positively. This charity they received from Zvi, that's what the people claimed, really saved them. In addition to this, he would find time to educate others by giving lessons in various subjects. He never spared his strength and our mother z"l used to complain bitterly, that he did not eat on time and thus he neglected his health.

Zvi's holy purpose was to elevate the Hebrew youth, to train them to immigrate to the Land of Israel, in order to build it and make it an example for the nations of the world.

To the heartbreak of all of those who knew him, Zvi z"l himself was not privileged to immigrate to Israel. After a serious illness, Zvi passed away while he was only twenty years old (1912-1932).

[Page 308]

Elkhonen Kosovski of Blessed Memory

by D. Avi-Dani, Israel

Translated by Mira Eckhaus

Edited by Tina Lunson

Elkhonen, or as we called him, Khona Kosovski, was born in Goworowo in 1919 to a respectable and traditional family. His father Rov Yitskhak of blessed memory was one of the city's richest men, a public activist in the *Mizrahki* movement and one of the founders and directors of the Credit Bank. The children received traditional, Jewish and general education.

Early in their childhoods they instilled in their hearts the idea of Zionism and the love of Israel. It is no wonder, then, that Elkhonen at a young age found his place in the local *Beitar* movement. There he excelled in his devoted work to the movement and served as a symbol and example to the local youth with his elegant behavior, his manners and his Zionist work.

During the war, he was subjected to all the horrors of the Holocaust and after it ended, Elkhonen decided to immigrate to Israel and settle there. He married his hometown girl, his lifelong friend and member of *Beitar*, Rokhl, from the respectable Papiertshik family and at the end of 1947 he and his wife immigrated from Bergen-Belsen to Israel.

In Israel, he immediately enlisted in the IDF and fought the War of Independence until the foundation of the state. When he returned slightly wounded to his wife and little child, he said, "I helped with God's help to establish a Jewish state for my children, I have given my part…"

After quite a few difficulties, he got a job in the Ramat Gan municipality where he worked until his last day. In this work as well, he excelled in his dedication to the satisfaction of those in charge. As in Goworowo, he had many friends and was loved by his co-workers and all his acquaintances.

He died after a severe and prolonged illness on 16th of Adar 2, 5722 (22 March 1962), in his youth, at the age of 43.

With his death, the family lost a faithful husband and devoted father to his two children, Yitskhak and Mordkhe, a dear brother and brother-in-law, and a loyal friend to the people of his city and to all his acquaintances.

His life will serve as a symbol and example of devotion and loyalty, diligence in work, friendship and kindness to every person.

May his memory be blessed and may his soul be bound in the bundle of life.

[Page 309]

Memories and Episodes

I Remember You!

by Y. Zerubavel, Israel

Translated by Tina Lunson

Y. Zerubavel

The commotion does not let me rest.

The way they want to talk together and make agreements – they come together, the *shtetlekh*, the little towns of Poland, circling around me and pouring out their complaints and claims for me.

Why have you forgotten us and abandoned us? Do you not remember, what kind of importune guest you were, every time that you visited us, in whatever region of Poland that was? We welcomed you every time, accommodating you every hour of the forty-eight, early in the morning, or late into the night, in the middle of a week day, or even a *Shabes*, Friday evening, after lighting the candles, or at night after *Shabes*, after *havdole*; we hurried to welcome you on hot days, when the sun burned us and on the cold, frosty nights, in pouring rain, or in blizzards. There was no, heaven forbid, obstacle for us, parents and youths and even youngsters. Waiting hours long for your train, on the *kaleyke*, or on the ship, or when we had to ride in a farm wagon into town, or go by foot some round-about way so as not to upset the religious Jews, just because the lecturer arrived on *Shabes*.

Why ever have you forgotten us, why don't you mention us?

When the dark hour came, when Hitler's beasts occupied us, to annihilate all Polish Jewry, we struggled, each in his own manner. The little Jewish *shtetl* did not surrender to that whose name should be blotted out.

[Page 310]

We crawled into cellars, climbed into attics, dug ourselves into sheaves of wheat, hid out in pits and quartered ourselves in graves in the cemetery. You knew us then like a family member, homey, long-term, you knew, as we never disappointed you. Rather, in the bitter minutes we coddled the hope in you so our people would not drown and because a *Poaley-tsion* member must wrestle until the last breath is drawn. We had the certainty, that we would survive this Nazi *Haman* too. Many of us were killed, some, in the death camps, some among partisans in the forests, with weapons in our hands.

So then why have you forgotten us?

They write chronicles and histories about the big towns, full packed settlements, about select individuals, famous people, publishable things. And where are we? The *shtetlekh*, where is our *yisker*?

And so I hear the continuum, those voices, without stopping, that awaken the unease in me and do not let me rest.

I beseech them. Believe me in good faith, that you are mistaken. I remember you. Surely I remember you very well. You are baked into my heart and etched into my mind. Could I then forget the little town where and what would we be if not for the little towns that cultivated a generation of faithful, brave Jews, who with their deep Jewish love, with their thirst for life, formed a new, modern Jewishness. Not a generation of ignoramuses, that does not know why and how they are Jews. I remember your youth. Really, we were all young then and the youth nourished our dreams, visions, ideals. There were no Party professionals in the little town, no establishment by which the ideas could be turned into a source of livelihood. The revolutionizing in the little town was for its own sake. They meant their activity in her name, in truth. We were feverish with the ideal, we breathed in the imagination of redemption for Jews and for all mankind, "For our and for your freedom". I remember your plains, your forests, where we used to stroll, in order to carry our dreams about the future, in order to relate very secretly what the *Ts.K.* had conceived and what the *Ts.K.* had decided, and what it carried out. I remember that you welcomed with love every resolution and every instruction as soon as it came from the *Ts.K.* as if it were a Torah in its own right from Sinai. I remember how your eyes flamed, how your faces shone, how you rejoiced without end, when "someone came down from Warsaw", one of whom for years and years you only heard his name from a distance, read and reveled in a lengthy article, internally repeated a word, a witticism, an idea, or read a sharp polemic between political opponents.

I remember your houses, the poor homes with lovely warmth and

[Page 311]

friendliness, that never stopped beaming the whole time, that the guest from Warsaw was pleased with their Abraham-like hospitality.

I remember your families, who from childhood were boys and girls brought up in an authentic Jewish atmosphere and it was so truthful when later those youths declared that they had already become "fully Zionist" even in their mothers' bellies.

Unfortunately, I do not remember, off the top of my head, your every corner. In Poland there were so many far flung corners, where we arrived with our stirring message. But it is enough to remember just one name and soon a row of neighboring *shtetlekh* floats up, which snuggled up to the larger, better-known point and without an alternative we were forced to walk tens of kilometers in order to catch a lecture by a speaker who probably would not so quickly consider a visit to them in the even smaller place.

I remember you, poor, neglected *shtetlekh*, how you, with sincere love and a *hasidic*-like rapture, lit the lights of culture, initiated libraries and reading rooms where people devoured the creations of our writers, invented all kinds of societies and organizations for evening courses, for YIVO collections, for CYShO schools and theater lovers. I remember and remember...

But, as the years went by, since a cloudburst of blood spread over Polish Jewry, some *shtetlekh* have been lost into the community at large, it became hard to recognize and detach the singular *shtetl* with its group leaders and crowds of members, their official private names and their underground nicknames, while the memory is burning with one particular name, *Poaley tsion* in Poland.

He follows me like a shadow, a friend from the *shtetl*, and begs me: "*Fraynt* Zerubavel, write about Goworowo, write!"

I promise him to do it and put it off from day to day. Let us remember it well - Goworowo, a neighbor of Ruzshan, not far from Ostrolenke, on the road to Lomzshe.

Well, I certainly do remember. There was a joint gathering in the forest between Ruzshan and Goworowo. Right before me is Emanuel Ringelblum. Other speakers from Warsaw. I am there too and getting enthusiastic about the cultural activity of the groups, of their tenacity in distinguishing themselves and comparing themselves with larger places, not even considering the smaller Jewish population and remoteness from the main railroad line.

I painfully regret, that my mind is foggy, and I cannot recall individual names. Talking back is better. It is still, in sum, an accomplishment not of individuals, but of a party-collective, where every individual contributed his own and the collective created the whole.

[Page 312]

The collective in Goworowo, I remember. That and its accomplishments I will never forget.

No, I will not forget you, little *shtetlekh* of Poland. Your *yisker* is woven with bloody threads of scar into the whole, oy, how huge, *yisker* for the Polish Jew.

The only motorcycle in town

From the right: Velvl Barg, Yitskhak Kuperman, Khone Taytlboym (sitting on the motorcycle), Meyshe Malovani, Leybl Kersh and Yankev Gurka

1925

[Page 313]

A Jewish Town for the Folk

by Engineer A. Rays, Israel

Translated by Tina Lunson

Engineer A. Rays

Once there was a Polish Jewish realm, that numbered more than three and a half million souls; a Jewish settlement with a pulsing national and communal life, from which the rays beamed far beyond its borders and reached the farthest Jewish settlements spread all over the world. The beams were a fresh spirit for those settlements, which struggled with the invasive currents of assimilation and its comfortable familiarization of the Jewish people and strengthened them in the historic struggle.

A large part of Polish Jewry lived in the hundreds of small Jewish towns, *shtetlekh,* in Poland, in which, over the course of years, important energies generated which nourished the Jewish national life of Polish Jews. On one side, there was the religious part of the Jewish settlement, which had established itself in the *yeshiva*, in the study house, in the *shul*, in the *kheyder*, as with a steel Panzer against every foreign influence, and lived its own life for long generations. On the other side arose a Jewish youth which freed itself from the religious confinement, took up the new currents of the progressive world and bound them to their fervent will to fight for a position of equal rights in the larger family of world peoples, for the Jewish people.

The *Bundist*, the *Poaley-tsion* thought, the progressive Zionist thought in general, found fertile ground here for development and creation. Fresh energies came from the *shtetlekh* for the various social

[Page 314]

movements in the big cities; their leading institutions drew from the small towns the freshness, initiative, often also the pathos, for the heavy work. The *shtetl*, in point, gave the Pioneer movement in Poland its many thousands of members, who then wrote an important chapter in the history of the accomplishments of Zionism.

In the *shtetl* the emissary from the directing institutions met with a deep and sincere intelligence for the tasks and goals of the movement. There he encountered members with a folksy, honest sincerity, and who surrounded him with comprehension and love. In the little town one was often "warmed" by the spontaneous and honest enthusiasm that was displayed for every accomplishment of the Central office. Everyone, including those who thought otherwise, approached the representative from the Central authority with respect and did not guard against demonstrating it.

In the main, the lectures in the *shtetl* and the political gatherings were mass meetings and drew the notice of almost the entire town. Generally speaking, there was an established, lively Jewish national cultural activity that influenced every part of the settlement. Also in a small Jewish *shtetl*, there would be a Jewish library, a Jewish amateur theater club, a choir and cultural events of various character being presented regularly.

Thus, it was completely natural that the many great Yiddish writers and poets came from the *shtetlekh,* in just those little Jewish settlements were the courts of the important scholars and rabbinic teacher/leaders. Here great intellectual personalities were formed and crystalized, fulfilled and reinforced, intellectuals who in time became illuminators of Polish Jewry and often of the entire Jewish people.

In many of those Polish *shtetlekh* Jews had the fortune to be a high percentage and sometimes even the majority of the surrounding population. Many of the *shtetlekh* were almost purely Jewish. There were even some that had a Jewish mayor and in many of them, the majority of the council members were Jews. And so, it can be demonstrated that Jews and Poles had the ability to conduct a town administration together, no worse than the *goyim*, if not better than they. The Jewish town administration troubled to develop and build up the towns, not considering the obstacles that lay in their path, that is the local and state Polish authorities.

The Second World War shattered all that. With the murderous hands of the Germans and their helpers from the other nations, the Jewish *shtetl* in Poland was erased with fire and with blood.

Goworowo was without doubt one of the typical small Jewish settlements,

[Page 315]

that had its portion in the great achievements of Polish Jewry. Here, as in the other *shtetlekh* of Poland that showed the Jewish settlement the responsible comprehension to stand at the pinnacle of their tasks, as a national and cultural Jewish center. In Goworowo pulsed a warm Jewish community life. Despite that, the Jewish settlement there was bound with struggle for rights of the Jews in Poland, as a national minority.

All the Jewish parties that prevailed in the general life of Jews in Poland also prevailed in Goworowo. The Central Committee of the *Poaley-tsion* Socialist Zionists. The Zionist societal energies were especially active and in particular those of the Laboring *Erets-Yisroel.*

The *Poaley-tsion* Zionist Socialist Party in Goworowo has its rich page in the history of the Party in Poland. The Central Committee of the *P-ts.Ts.S.* always remarked on the devoted work of the local members. Without doubt the other parties had no less a foundation to draw the interest to the activities of their members in Goworowo.

Thus it is also worth noting the accomplishments of the remaining remnant of the Jewish settlement in Goworowo, who had the noble goal of eternizing the memory of those who are no longer with us and of their deeds. My memories of that devoted work done by the members in Goworowo justifies my telling this.

The administration of the *Poaley-tsion* Zionist -Socialists

First row [from right): Zelig Reytshik and Yehude Grudka
Second row: Bunem Shafran, Golde Shniadover, Yitskhak Blumshteyn, Sore Skurnik and Meyshe Granat

[Page 316]

Goworowo

by Israel Ritov, Israel

Translated by Mira Eckhaus

Edited by Tina Lunson

Through a thick fog which separates me from those years, I am brought back to the evening I spent in Goworowo. I was on a mission on behalf of my movement, *Poaley Tsion,* the Socialist Zionist movement in Ostrów Mazowiecki and from there I was invited to visit Goworowo for a few hours.

Unfortunately, only general, blurred outlines of this nice Jewish town remain in my memory. I remember the time I came to it; the great, extreme warmth with which I was received; the full, crowded hall where I lectured, and the same atmosphere around my visit. I brought the news of the Land of Israel and in particular, the working Land of Israel; the pioneer gospel and making *aliye* to live there; the gospel of the socialist Zionist movement in Poland and around the world; and on the other hand, lamentation for the situation of the Jews in exile, for the bereavement and failure and the lack of hope for the Jews, in general, and the Polish Jews in particular. Our heart prophesied things and did not know what it prophesied.

Only faint memories remain in my mind. But what is the practical implication? What, actually, is the difference between Goworowo and Garbulin, for example, or Grayevo or Garbovits or Grodno or any of the more than eight hundred Jewish towns and cities throughout Poland? There were differences in their size, in their shape, in the structure of their economy, in the number and nature of their institutions, but there were no, or almost no, differences between the Jews of Poland, about all of which Y. L. Peretz wrote, "This is how we walk, how we sing and dance, we – the great big Jews, Sabath and holiday, spirit-rich. This is how we go, our souls blazing."

There were certainly no differences during the Holocaust between the martyrs of Goworowo and all the millions of martyrs, whose souls and bodies both burned with the same flame, whose light was destroyed in our world.

* * *

I was in Poland, in the summer of 1939, on a mission of the movement. I went throughout the length and breadth of Poland and everywhere, in every Jewish community, I imagined the inscription of the horror, a sentence that has already been determined and cannot be reversed. You could almost hear the sound of impending doom. No one was able to imagine the full depth and dimensions of the disaster but, even a tiny portion of it, as seen from a distance, instilled fear of death. Indeed, there were those who, in the face of the anger of the tormentor, the despair, and the lack of sight of the horror, prayed for the near end, "we prefer that the war would break out and whatever should happen – happens!", but these were only a few, those who in their blindness thought that they had nothing to lose again. Aha,

[Page 317]

they had much to lose! And the Jewish people in Poland were surrounded by a sense of the eve of terrible days.

On the tenth of August I left Warsaw on my way to Geneva, to the Zionist Congress. At the train station I said goodbye to my accompanying crowd with a question in our hearts and in our eyes - will we see each other again?

Three weeks later the Nazi planes arrived and bombed Warsaw. The destruction of Polish Jewry began, the end of the thousand year history of Polish Jewry began.

* * *

Eight years have passed. The same eight years.

In the summer of 1947, I was again in Poland. Again, on a mission for the movement. In 1939 I came to three and a half million Jews; in 1947, to a few tens of thousands, those who survived the horrors.

I came to Warsaw and did not find – Warsaw. I found piles and piles of ruins. I passed through the "streets" and I didn't see – any streets. I tried hard but I could not find the streets Novolipki, Novolipia, Kremlitska, Dezilana.

About five thousand Jews were then in Warsaw; more precisely outside Warsaw in Praga. Most of them were not Warsaw people in their origin. About five thousand.

I would weave my way among the ruins, my eyes frozen, my heart petrified and all of me a cloud of *kaddish* - not a *kaddish* according to the bible, not a *kaddish* of the rabbis, *kaddish* over a dead nation.

I left Warsaw and traveled across Poland. I was looking for the survivors of the Jewish people. I found only a few.

I moved west. I could not go to the east. Gangs from the remnants of the *Armia Kraiova* and plain robbers and murderers wandered the roads and left their mark on anything and everything. And when they met a Jew, he would not get out of their hands alive again. On the roads as well as on the train. And I could not get to Bialystok, my beloved city, nor to many other places. I only managed to reach Łomża, and my friends scolded me for that too, "don't risk yourself!" I wasn't in Ostrov or in Goworowo and not – not in those hundreds of cities and towns, in which I was a frequent visitor.

I moved west. I moved like a shadow and I also reached Auschwitz. Here I found masses of my exterminated people. I did not find them. I found their souls and their luggage in the warehouses, the hair of the mothers and the sisters and the girls, hundreds and hundreds of thousands of shoes and clothes and children's shoes and *taleysim* and *tfiln.* I found many, many of them and the like in Auschwitz. In my loss of consciousness, in my loss of senses, the words of Shaul Tshernikhovsky's curse echoed in my heart:

Damn you, cruel Gentile!
Cursed be your name
Forever and ever, and the curse of God
Will be forever on your people!
Cursed are you of all men,
And a curse will be on you
As long as you live,
And it will follow you to the netherworld!
Your strength will be exhausted,
Cursed be every human emotion in you,
You have destroyed every emotion in me!
And you will drown in the blood of your sacrifices,
You will be immersed in the waters of tears,
And you will waken up night after night
By the cries of the dead, of the horrors.
God will send his plagues at you,
He will fasten the time of your fall,

the essence of life, your will dried up,
your soul will bear its sin forever.

And you will be terrified by yourself,
You will run away from yourself!

[Page 318]

These words echoed in my heart and they did not exhaust the full extent of the horror. After all, Shaul Tshernikhovsky did not see Auschwitz. These words of his (*Baruch from Magentsa*) about what had happened in the Middle Ages, do not express the crisis of our nation in these days. Is there an expression? Will it ever be found?

* * *

Another 12 years passed. Summer 1959. Again, I was sent on a mission to Poland. This time on behalf of the *Histadrut*, on behalf of the cooperative. This time, as a guest of the Polish government.

When I arrived in Poland, I noticed that a lot was already forgotten. Many wounds and scars healed while our calamity still remained in the full extent of its terror and it still cries out harder and harder.

This time the roads were safe both in the west and in the east but, as a guest of the government, I was subject to the traffic lines it had set and it turned out that I was once again moving west.

I traveled, in a convoy of cars, from Warsaw to Zakopane and back. I passed many settlement places, where in the past Jewish communities had flourished and prospered and now only cemeteries and more cemeteries – deathly silence. And why name these holy communities? Why?

I was also this time in Auschwitz and Birkenau. Here are the incinerators, the gas chambers, the torture chamber, the wall of death, the experiment house, the warehouses for luggage and clothes and glasses and prayer books; here, the train station, the selection areas, the pool where remains of bones are still floating; here are the houses and the barracks and the towers and the electrified wire fences, here is the "museum" with the findings of the camp, the photographs, the numbers – this is Auschwitz!

And you, as if you were not here yet, walk around stunned, bereft of senses.

* * *

Polish Jewry!

Original, rooted, vibrant, stormy and storm -tossed Jewry. Jewry of millions - multitudes of laborers, workers, toilers – "simple people" – "scissor and iron"; Jewry of merchants, shopkeepers; Jewry of men of action, with initiative and vision and energy, intelligence and resourcefulness; Jewry of great Torah scholars, greats of science, Torah and wisdom; a Jewry of the educated, writers, artists; passionate and enthusiastic *hasidic* Judaism, tortured and apostate, singing and dancing and rising to the highest heavens of poetry and joy and faith, which has no limit and has no end; a Judaism between the East and the West, drawing and sipping and basking in this and that and digesting in its essence and shaping a figure to itself – a Sambatyon figure - stormy and boisterous Sambatyon that emits from itself and throws out onto all its surroundings, blocks of initiative, Torah and wisdom, throws up to the cathedrals of major universities in the world, to the stands of famous *yeshivas*, to the stages of a multitude of theaters and orchestras, to the leadership of social movements and parties around the world, to the headquarters of revolutions, up to leadership in huge enterprises... Here was the popular Zionism, here were the movements of the workers, here was the socialist and pioneer Zionism.

Yisgadol v'yiskadeysh

* * *

I wrote the heading for these lines "Goworowo". I could have written any other name among the hundreds of names of the holy communities which were destroyed and no longer exist. What is the practical implication? One God created us, one devil struck us – What is the practical implication?

[Page 319]

The Betar in Goworowo

by Yosef Khrust, Israel

Translated by Mira Eckhaus

Edited by Tina Lunson

Yosef Khrust

I see the members of the Betar cell in Goworowo unclearly. The images have been blurred by time, decades and rivers of blood separate the moment when I write these lines and the few hours I spent among the young members of this cell. I am not sure that if I had a picture of Betar members, I would recognize those few members with whom I was in contact from time to time or those I had the pleasure of meeting in recent years and reminiscing about our youth and dreams.

But time did not blur the general picture - a typical Jewish town, small unstable wooden houses that looked as if they came out of a Chagall picture, a small room simply furnished, an unpolished wooden table, a few rough wooden benches, and two rows of girls and boys wearing brown shirts and their eyes burning with a strange shine which I had never seen before.

* * *

The cell in Goworowo did not produce generals. The members of the cell were literally woodcutters and water carriers. Their souls longed to immigrate to Israel and in order to be privileged not to the *aliyah* permit itself, but at the very least the mere hope of being a candidate for such an *aliyah*, it was necessary to obey one of the strangest regulations ever legislated by the Zionist institutions and to go to "training". They did not learn a profession there. There they suffered deprivation and hunger, similar to the deprivation they suffered from in their parents' homes. There they chopped wood and drew water, similar to the work that the unemployed among them worked on. They did everything they were ordered to do and they were shy and restrained and stayed in these trainings for months and even years. Only a few of these were fortunate enough to reach their homeland, and even those, did not arrive in the Land of Israel with immigration permits. The rest were murdered in the Holocaust, with the last words on their lips - Zion and Jerusalem.

Once upon a time, it must have been hundreds of years ago, their ancestors settled in the little town

[Page 320]

Goworowo. I do not know the history of this city, just as I did not know the history of my native city, Ostrów Mazowiecka, which was close to Goworowo. The same small houses, the same synagogues, which doubtlessly were used as temples to God or fortresses for protection against rioters. And their Jews were the same bent and thin figures, God-fearing Jews, who suffered for generations of gentile hatred and dog teeth, depraved Jews who were satisfied with a little from *Shabes* evening to *Shabes* eve.

How the concept of the national Zionist idea reached these remote towns is also a wonder we will never understand. The leaders of Zionism did not come to these towns and only few people from the town would go to the big city to hear a great orator when he came to talk about the building of the country. And the youth of Betar had to struggle from within and without. They heard the news of the renewed Jewish army, which is continuing the tradition of the Maccabees, they also heard rumors about a brave man named Ze'ev Jabotinsky, the founder of the Legion, the defender of Jerusalem and the prisoner of Acre. Somehow names like Patterson, Margolin and Trumpeldor reached them. The young hearts throbbed with enthusiasm under their long *kapotes*. The beautiful eyes of a Jewish girl who helped her mother behind the counter of the poor shop or near the stall in the market to earn her livelihood, squinted with excitement at the sound of disturbances in Hebron and Jaffa; a young *yeshiva* guy clenched his small fists with restrained anger and a determined decision to put an end to this humiliating situation.

But their parents expected to sit idly awaiting the coming of the Messiah, while outside, those who dreamed the dream of national Zionism were surrounded with contempt and hatred by all.

And I, a student at a Polish gymnasium, my heart also throbbed strongly, beneath my student's uniform, when I read the news about the rise of another generation and my most beautiful hours were the hours I spent with those girls and boys, poor seamstresses and *yeshiva* boys, at the Betar club. I often saw

From right to left: Khave Burshteyn, Ester Gutman, Menukha Grudka, Tzipora Grudka, Asher Ben-Oni, Leah Marianski, Malka Tsalka and Rokhl Shapira

[Page 321]

how, at the very last moment, a young man comes to the club dressed in a *kapote*, goes away for a moment to a side room and reappears from there wearing a Betar shirt, with his sidelocks tucked a little behind his ears, and I knew his story. This young man faces struggles even at his home, and God forbid if his father would know that his son is at this moment in the Betar nest. And then my heart would be filled with endless love for these young people. I was almost ashamed that my belonging to Betar was not connected with an everyday act of heroism like them.

The Betar cell in Goworowo did not produce generals from among its members; its members did not belong to the highest institutions of this movement and the history of mankind is first of all a history of kings and generals. As the Polish poet Maria Konopnitska says, “the king who goes to war and trumpets cheer him and Yash who goes to war and the trees whisper to him”.

However, the Betar cell in Goworowo produced heroes from it, few of whom in a later period were privileged to commit real acts of heroism, but most of them were privileged to live their heroism day by day, when they struggled even at their homes with their parents who were waiting for the arrival of the Messiah, and outside, with dazed youths who expected the Red savior and who surrounded the youth of Betar with a wall of hatred and contempt.

* * *

With three of my friends, I have had a closer meeting and I do not want to skip these meetings.

Khave Burshtin. To me, it was a wonder that this young woman belonged to Betar. At first, I did not know much about her. I only heard that she was the daughter of the local rabbi and I had some unpleasant experience regarding the attitude of rabbis to Zionist youth movements. I aspired with all my might to get to know this rabbi, the father of this girl, who belonged to Betar and even served in the headquarters of this cell. It is possible that there were many such rabbis in the Betar movement in Poland, I only knew one rabbi. It was Rabbi Yosef Wertheim of Rubishuv, whose children belonged to Betar and this with his full consent. I did not get to know Rabbi Burshtin. I heard that he was a smart man and a scholar and even one of the opponents of Zionism. But I knew his daughter Khave and her work. I knew and I better understand today, that she would draw from her father's house the same devotion, rootedness and loyalty to all the values of Judaism and I can not express what I feel towards that rabbi in the small town, who gave the Betar movement (perhaps not with his full consent) the most precious thing to him, his daughter.

* * *

One bright day, Dov Kosovski, the commander of the Betar camp in Goworowo, arrived in Warsaw. From the first moment I loved the simplicity and immediacy of this young man. As Jabotinsky said, “like a lion approaching a lion”, he intervened among us, the members of Betar's national leadership, without any feelings of inferiority and we were already well known “leaders” at the time and on the spot he gained our sympathy. In those happy days he often came to my little apartment and I even remember how he amused us with his beautiful paintings.

Then an entire world was destroyed. We heard a happy news. At the time I was on assignment in France, immediately after the World War, I learned that Dov was in a refugee camp in Bergen-Belsen. There, too, he immediately returned to activity. I will never forget the impression his first action made on me. He collected everything that was written at the time about the Holocaust, in the British part of Germany. The bibliographic booklet

[Page 322]

On the bridge of the "Hirsh" River

From right to left: Shabtai Fridman, Yosef Krulevitsh, Dovid Blumshteyn, Dov Kosovski, Avieyzer Shikora, Gad Butsian and Meyshe Rits

he published in Germany is a priceless historical document.

* * *

Zadok Parva arrived in my hometown but, he did not stay there for a long time. We quickly became friends but, we also parted ways quickly. He was among the founders of our movement in Goworowo and a short time later he immigrated to the United States.

Later, after I immigrated to Israel, the relationship between us was renewed. From the correspondence of letters between us I learned that even in the diaspora he kept his Judaism and principles, he made sure to educate his sons with a traditional and national Jewish education and that the home of Sol Givner (who is Zadok) and Reyka (from the Marcus family – also a Betar member) is a house for wise Torah scholars.

Later I arrived by a chance in New York, to the home of my old friends and found myself surrounded with an atmosphere of the Land of Israel, to the extent that such an atmosphere is possible in the diaspora. I have found myself among piles of Hebrew books, sitting between his two sons, Avraham and Nathan, who thirstily listened to every word about Israel and the owner of the house devoted his time to public affairs, to Hebrew education and the study of the Torah.

* * *

I said above that the Betar cell in Goworowo did not produce generals, but ordinary soldiers. The practice of history is that it is written not about soldiers but about generals. The names of all those ordinary soldiers have been erased by the wheels of history and this history would not have been written at all if it were not for those ordinary military men. And me, I dedicate these words to those simple soldiers whose names have been erased but, they wrote the Jewish history of our generation with their blood.

[Page 323]

The Amshinover *Rebi* in Goworowo

by Yisroel Rituv, Israel

Translated by Tina Lunson

The first Amshinover *Rebi*, *Rebi* Yankev Dovid'l Kalish, visited Goworowo twice. The purpose of his visits both times was to make peace in the town. The first time he came to calm a dispute about ritual slaughterers. There were two ritual slaughterers in Goworowo at the time, Shmuel Nosn Shub and Yankev Marianski, the father of our well known Khayim Leyb the *sheykhet*. The latter was also the town cantor and the town's proprietors were not happy with him as cantor. During the dispute, a large number of Jews would not eat from his slaughtering and even when the *Rebi* led the table and offered the traditional "remnants", several insolent proprietors did not want to take any food as a protest to the *Rebi's* peace efforts.

That same week a special obligatory feast had to be held, with the participation of the *Rebi*. The *Rebi* ordered that fish be prepared for the feast. The *hasidim* went to the gentile fishermen and asked them to catch fish. The *goyim* laid their nets in the river and could not catch even one little fish. Without any alternative, the feast was prepared with just calf meat.

While the *Rebi* was heading the table for the feast, he asked a question, "Why is there no fish on the table?" A *hasid* replied that the *goyim* could not catch any fish, on any account. The *Rebi* began to marvel, "Really!? How could someone not catch any fish? Are not there any fish in the whole river? Perhaps", the *Rebi* wondered to himself, "the fish did not want to be together on the table with the meat."

Hasidim promptly asked Reb Yankev, the ritual slaughterer, whether he had slaughtered the calf. Reb Yankev shrugged his shoulders. He had not slaughtered the calf. Reb Shmuel Nosn, the slaughterer, had not either. People started to investigate where the meat came from. It turned out that, because of the dispute, they had bought the meat from a Jewish butcher in a neighboring village. They quickly sent for an answer from the village butcher. He started stammering, "Here. There." In short, he confessed, that he himself had not slaughtered the calf.

They stopped eating the feast, no fish and no meat. The leaders of the dispute hung their heads in shame. They now saw what disputes can lead to and the peace was restored in the town.

By the way, the village butcher later converted and became a bell ringer and a beadle in a village church.

[Page 324]

The Excommunication

by Yitskhak Dovid Tehilim, America

Translated by Tina Lunson

When one depicts the history of a town there is generally a tendency to make the fine and honorable side of the town bold and bright and cover up the not-so-nice history. I believe that harm is done to the history if one hides the truth because he does not want to look at it; but, it is an obligation to also tell the fact that awakens an unsavory experience. I want to tell a story about an esteemed Goworowo proprietor who perpetrated an ugly deed, for which he paid dearly.

It was about ten years before the First World War, while the Goworowo *Rov* was *Rov* Yehude Botshan. One wintry Thursday evening the *Rov* was holding court, with Itshe Mayer as a complainant. The *Rov* heard his complaints and made his decision, that Itshe Mayer was not correct and had to pay a large sum as a fine. Itshe Mayer was furious and threw out the accusation that the *Rov* had not heard his complaints properly. So speaking, his lost control over himself and slapped the old *Rov* in the face.

The *Rov* did not react. He sat down on his bench and concealed his flaming face in shame.

The reverberation of the shocking report soon reached the *shul*, where young men and boys sat and studied. There was great commotion. The study house boys soon went all over town and called together the entire population, men, women and children, into the *shul*. They lit black candles, laid out the cleansing plank for the dead, the *shames* blew the shofar, and they declared Itshe Mayer excommunicated.

In the morning, Friday, the same young men went into the bakery, took Itshe Mayer's *khale* loaves out of the oven, tied them with string and dragged them all over town.

The town trembled before Itshe Mayer, would not speak to him or trade with him. Even the gentiles did not want to stand within four yards of him.

Several months later, Itshe Mayer's wife suddenly became ill and died. Itshe Mayer could not see any alternative for himself. He took off his shoes and went to the *Rov* with a wail, he should favor him and abolish the ban.

The *Rov* had pity on him, abolished the ban and requested the townspeople never to speak of that bizarre incident anymore.

[Page 325]

The *Eyruv* Affair

by Sh. L. Tsitron, Poland

Translated by Tina Lunson

Of all the libels that the Russian regime made against the Jews during the First World War, the one that takes on special significance is the libel about the *Eyruv* – the lines marking the areas Jews could walk and carry things on the Sabbath. The agitators latched onto the *Eyruv* wires strung across the poles, as the Jews talking in secret with the enemy and turning over all their military secrets. They could not hear that the wire of the *Eyruv* was not hidden anywhere outside and did not go anywhere inside; that it was just what you could see looking up and it ended and did not come down. To Vilne came the news from various small towns that that they searching for the wire *Eyruv*in and that it terrified the Jewish population. In some towns the Jews took the *Eyruv* down themselves. The Polish Jews suffered in particular with that. The Russians were not satisfied with just finding; there they arrested entire communities with the rabbis at the head and accused them of treason against the Russian state.

Once an officer came to *Rov* Rubinshteyn, the Vilne Chief Rabbi, and asked him, in the name of the regional commander, to come to headquarters at eight in the evening to meet with a general. Arriving there at the appointed time, he was greeted by a corps general who explained that, according to an order from the regional commander, he had been invited as an expert. The general was uncertain how to pose his question. He hesitated, not wanting to say outright what the expertise was, so that *Rov* Rubinshteyn would know immediately what his goal was in questioning him. Finally the general announced, "What significance does a wire line have for Jews?" *Rov* Rubinshteyn asked him to formulate his question differently. The general said again, "I am asking, what religious significance does wire have for Jews?" *Rov* Rubinshteyn immediately understood what he was dealing with here and said, "On that question I can answer, that Jews use wire to make an *Eyruv*." Then *Rov* Rubinshteyn enlightened the general with details and substantiated the purpose one makes an *Eyruv* according to Jewish law. The explanation was comprehensible in every detail. "If so," the general interrupted, "why did Jews in some areas use a wire net instead of an *Eyruv* wire?" *Rov* Rubinshteyn further explained that in many places in Poland they use a wire net for the same purpose as an *Eyruv*

[Page 326]

and further explained the Jewish law exactly and in detail. *Rov* Rubinshteyn's answer satisfied the general and he told him, "Now everything is clear to me. I'm satisfied with your response. I will pass it on to the reginal commander."

What was the effect of their calling on *Rov* Rubinshteyn's expertise? And what kind of impression did his explanations make? That would be known in a matter of days.

Two days after this incident, a delegation came to *Rov* Rubinshteyn from Goworowo, Lomzshe province, consisting of the town *Rov*, *Rov* Alter Meyshe Burshtin, and some of the local Jewish Council representatives. They had come to Vilne to find out what was happening with their case and to ask if someone could intervene for them.

The Goworowo *Rov* related the following:

Once in the middle of a Thursday night, while the whole town was already asleep, a commandant arrived from his station about seven versts away, with a company of soldiers, and made a raid on the wire net which, no doubt, the town Christians had pointed out to him. Locating the covered net work he immediately ordered that all the town leaders be awakened and driven together for a thorough examination. Uneasy and rattled they all answered that the *Rov* had made the net. The *Rov* confessed that he had made it according to the ordinances of the religion. But officer attacked him with terrible shouts, "You have made an underground telephone with the enemy and claim it is a religion! You will not fool me! You have not found any fool here!"

Seventy of the Goworowo Jews were arrested and driven away in the dark night to the commandant, seven versts from the town. Since there was not a place for everyone to stay there, they were not held for long. But they were informed that there would be a trial and that they were not allowed to leave the town.

The trial was turned over to Prince Tumanov, the high commander of the front and he turned it over to a general who would call in *Rov* Rubinshteyn as an expert.

From then on, the trial process stopped.

As the Goworowo *Rov* told it, in the morning after the expert came, the same general went to Goworowo to investigate the matter at the scene. He sent for the *Rov* who, with horror, repeated his same response, "This is a matter of religion." The general certainly corroborated it, "Yes! I know already that it is a matter of the religion."

The general ordered to give the *Rov* eleven of the twelve arrested

[Page 327]

"dangerous nets" and one "wire work" he ordered sent to Vilne.

Uneasy about the "net work" that was sent off, the deputation came to Vilne and as they discovered, the trial was voided. In the little town there was joy and rejoicing, a real holiday.

(*Vilner zaml-bukh*)

An Evening After *Shabes*

by A. Bar-Even, Israel

Translated by Tina Lunson

The reddish western horizon reflected in the high windows of the houses in the market square, slipped onto the white tin roof of the study house and waged war with the dark blue shadows that strove from all the dark corners. The scarlet rays of the setting sun stubbornly joined the blue rim of the heavens and did not let the sun disappear under the terrestrial globe. It was hard to distinguish them from the comfortable *Shabes* twilight mood, that had quietly restrained the town.

But, Jews were already going to make *havdole*, soon the kettles in hell would be heating up for sinners after the *Shabes* rest. Reddened with the shame that lay on them for the unpleasant work of burning sinful Jews, the rays ducked under the covering cloak of the earth, leaving the dark shadows to dominate the world.

The young folk strolled along the sidewalks of the market square, quietly discussing how they would be ashamed to disturb the dying wheezes of the holy day. One could literally hear the cry of pain from the *Shabes* queendom, who must now separate from her beloved husband, the "Congregation of Yisroel".

From the Ger and Aleksander *shtiblekh* up above the hospitality house and the free-loan society bank, strains of a sad, longing tenor voice sang *Bney hikolo* and in the Enlighteners study house, shadows trembled in the dark, rumbling *l'Dovid barukh ha'tsurey*.

The *shames* pounded his hand on the cantor's stand in the study house, "*Mayriv*!" "*havdole*!" Light flickered on in the houses, fathers made *havdole* over tea. And mothers piously whispered *Got fun Avrom.*

[Page 328]

The ritual slaughterer's son played *Ha'mavdil* on his fiddle and Yonatan's son-in-law, a red-bearded young man with large, round eyeglasses, was the first to open his shop, lending a Jew a cigarette, or a half ounce of tobacco for a whole week.

Brayne, Reb Yeshaye Shmuel Nosn's wife, lit the bright lamp and set up the samovar. Reb Yeshaye himself put on his flowery housecoat, smoothed his pointed grey beard, comfortably pulled on his slippers and seated himself at the table. Soon the crowd would come to drink tea, a custom in the town since ancient times. They drank tea at Yeshaye Shmuel Nosn's on *Shabes* night and only on *Shabes* night because the whole week Reb Yeshaye Nosn, a Talmud scholar and a wealthy man, went around angry and gloomy, spoke sharply to people, and even fought with his Brayne but, as soon as the holy *Shabes* arrived, he was completely another person. His language became calmer and softer, his flat weekday eyes took on a gleam, his furrowed forehead evened out, seemed higher; his dark grey beard was whiter and longer. A broad smile lay across his face and he loved his Brayne like two love birds – Brayne'shi and Yeshay'ele.

The contrast between the profane and the *Shabes* for Reb Yeshaye was so huge, like the difference between his two businesses, from which he drew his living, flour and furs. The flour was stored in long white boxes in the kitchen and dining room and the salted pelts lay in the vestibule of the back door of the house. The stink from the raw pelts assaulted the nose from a good distance.

But as the beloved *Shabes* arrived, the stink of the pelts disappeared and in their place the nostrils were tempted by the aroma of noodle pudding and the steamy smell of potato *tsholent* from Brayne's big, tiled oven.

The sanctity of the *Shabes* did not go away from Yeshaye with the *havdole*. The *Shabes* sparkle lingered for the whole *motsi-shabes* evening, until midnight, for the pleasure of the big crowd that came to drink tea for a "whole week".

The first one to open the door with a broad "Good week!" was Reb Yisroel Leyb, the Talmud teacher, a tall, bent-over, near-sighted Jew with a curly, blonde little beard, as if it might have been, heaven forbid, shaved. He loved to sing a tune and he always enjoyed himself. After him came a whole gallery of types from the town householders, Yudl the watchmaker, a short, thin little person, with a black wiry little beard.

He was unfortunately very poor and a glass of tea with sugar was something of a novelty for him. Really, from one *Shabes* ending to the next he

[Page 329]

ate hardly anything; then Khone Fridman, a red-bearded crafty and clever man. He wrote astonishing Polish and spoke with a Pole as a Jew talks to a Jew.

A view of the town from the bridge. On the left, the study-house.

Leybke, the baker, an Aleksander Hasid, who led the beginning prayers on the Days of Awe in the study house. He administered cupping glasses and could pronounce away an “evil-eye” but, from all his livelihoods together he could just barely make *Shabes*; Shayke, the grain merchant, who always held a bit of straw in this mouth, quick, irate and a PIKHAZ K'MAYIM. He prayed fast, ate in a rush and even slept in a hurry. Reb Avremele, the teacher, a small agile little Jew with sharp, darting eyes; a Jew with a keen mind, who loved to tell witticisms with a hoarse, whiney little voice; Reb Khayim Leyb, the cantor/ritual slaughterer, a tall and massive Jew, a majestic figure, with a short, wide, dark blonde beard that began growing under his chin. He was fastidious with appropriate manners; he always coughed a little, as if checking whether his voice had, heaven forbid, left him in the meanwhile. Reb Yekl, the old *Rov's* son, a sullen type, always spoke with the melody of a Talmudic question; and Reb Meyshe Skurnik, an Enlightened Jew with a beautifully combed, four pointed beard, and clever, sharp eyes behind a bone glasses frame, who could deliver a lecture with foreign words. He had a fine, resonating metallic voice, and could tell lovely, enchanting stories. Indeed, Reb Meyshe could fill up almost the whole program for the evening and after each story Brayne, Yeshaye Shmuel Nosn's wife, poured a fresh round of tea for everyone.

(“*Keneder Odler*”, 16 January 1959)

[Page 330]

A Wintry *Shabes* Dawn

by Yosef Zilbertson, Israel

Translated by Tina Lunson

A delightful *Shabes* calm had pooled over the *shtetl*. After a week of hard work, of trade and commerce, the town's residents are sunken in deep sleep and off in the realm of sweet dreams.

Here and there the night stillness was disturbed by figures slinking out of the lanes and yards. Enveloped in heavy winter coats, with shawls over their heads, they look like creatures not of this world. They are the "early morning prayer" Jews, who wake the day, they go alone to the study house when the world is still sunk in deep dreaming.

The silhouette of Mordkhe the *shames* slips out, with the high velvet hat on his head, and with the red scarf wrapped around his throat. Here goes Fayvl Brik with his brisk gait and from the Long Street comes Yosl Verman and his son Zalman, who is carrying a large volume of the Vilne Talmud under his arm.

The moon is still in her full beauty and looks down in wonder at the figures who slink now across the middle of the market. Their boots scrape and moan with each step on the frozen snow. One hears an echoing *kra, kra!* from the startled crows who have been diving in the snow.

A pleasant warmth embraces one when entering the study house. The two large caulked ovens stoked by the *Shabes goy* spread a loving warmth. The bright lamp illumines with a clear light. Over a short period of time the study house fills in. The group seats itself around the tables. In reciting *halel* the sad, sweet Talmud melody pours out from these learned Jews. At the tables near the ovens are seated the everyday workers perusing a chapter of psalms. The pain and suffering that they bear throughout the week of wandering over the villages and fairs, in the forges and workshops, they now pour into heartfelt psalms that King David, may he rest in peace, created for the pursued and plagued of his time.

We, young men used to get up at dawn on *Shabes*, not because the Torah burned in us but simply because of youthful curiosity and later to be able to brag to our friends about how early we got up.

We were especially drawn to the tables where the "Psalm Jews" sat. There we could hear the latest events of the week and various

[Page 331]

stories in a particular artistic manner that became woven into the songs in the psalms.

Here is an example:

Blessed is the man who does not walk in the counsel of the ungodly….

"There was a big fair in Dlugoshadle…"

nor stand in the way of sinners, nor sit in the seat of the scornful…

"...but the prices were deep in the earth..."

for only in the Torah of *ha'shem* is his desire...

"...the calf was a terrific bargain..."

and on His Torah he meditates day and night...

"...but the ritual slaughterer made it *treyf*..."

It was an easy and pleasant time spent, until the grey light of the day. Then the Enlightened Jews finished the early prayers and hurried home to a rich *tsholent* stew and *kugl* and then managed to grab a *Shabes* afternoon nap on the short winter day. The *hasidic* Jews did not pray in the study house but went off to Yoel'ke the baker where, already waiting for them, was hot tea that was just taken from the big oven. Although they could sense the aroma of the many *tsholent*s that were in the oven, they still drank the tea with much pleasure. After warming themselves with several glasses of tea with sugar they went to pray, each in their own *shtibl*.

So the *shtetl* lived from year to year, both winter and summer, until the Black *Shabes* of the 9th of September 1939 when the Hitleristic murderers poured their wild, persecuting wrath first of all on the "Dawn Jews". The first victim was actually Reb Mordkhe the *shames,* may God avenge his blood. The burned walls of the study house remained standing like a sad gravestone for the Jewish town. And they want to tell, that once there was...once...and the "once" now extends up to 25 years ago. There was a Jewish settlement that lived over several centuries, with its joys and sorrows and now, is no more.

Shabes at Home

by Feyge Sheyniak, America

In memory of my parents Gishe and Yitskhak Yudl Sheyniak

Translated by Tina Lunson

The table is covered, Mama lights the candles,
Whispering a prayer, hiding her face,
Her head is veiled, she recites a prayer –
Oh living God, health and prosperity!
The angel of *Shabes* is coming now,
Spreading her wings over the house;
The wine is red, the *khale* on the table,
And wonderful aromas of soup and fish.

Father makes *kidush*, hums a melody,
Beaming eyes, divine pleasure,
Holy songs, praise and blessing,
For kingly ease, for *Shabes* comfort.
The house is sparkling, clean and light,
In every corner *Shabes* tidiness.

The Jewish Queen, the lovely Princess,
She makes us forget the gloomy week.

[Page 332]

Memories of Youth

by Sore Tsimerman-Romaner, Israel

Translated by Tina Lunson

Our family came back to Goworowo from Makove in 1918. I was then of school age. I was told that there was a teacher in town, a certain esteemed person who taught Yiddish, Russian and Torah to children. He visited us in our house. To tell the truth, I did not like him at first glance. He spoke with a strange Russian accent and did not have a homey appearance. But when I began to study with him and I heard how he taught Torah with such a lovely melody, I changed my thinking about him. My brother Motl was also a teacher. He studied Polish with us, a group of girls. The school was in a half -destroyed building in the same courtyard as Yosl the herbalist. Really a miserable room, with no comforts, but we did not have any other opportunities for learning.

Around that time my brother suddenly became ill and died. His death was a terrible blow to our family and a great loss for all the school children of the town who had been studying with him. A year later the Polish folk school opened in town. The younger girls were enrolled in that school. For us, already a little grown-up, it was too late. We began to be interested in the organizations being created, the Zionist organization, the *Bund*, *Poeley-tsion*. A library was founded by the glazier Shoshke Gitl in her home. We could take books from there to read. The organizations arranged "checkers evenings" every Friday night. That gave our lives a little more content. My friends from that time were Ester Gavortshik, Reyzele Gerlits, Toybe Kuperman, Golde Shniadover and Khaye Potash; of all those, surviving are Toybe, Ester and Reyzele in America, and myself in Israel. When I write these lines I can see them before me. How dear and beloved they were to me, how lovely and fine the childhood years we spent together. It was really such an interesting era. Although we did not have the opportunity for a regular education, we managed to teach ourselves to study and to read literature, so that we would not remain behind the youth in other large towns.

[Page 333]

Unfortunately, to my great sorrow, all this was suddenly severed and there is no trace left of all that was precious and dear to me. I bow my head before their unknown graves. I feel somehow that I am a little guilty in this great misfortune but, how could I have helped them?

Our entire town was also destroyed. The Jewish houses with all the contents and the Jewish businesses are today in gentile hands. Sadly, we will now never see our beloved homes where we were born and reared.

I cannot forget the *Shabes* days when my father, may he rest in peace, would rise at dawn to study. I will never forget his touching melody while learning. Although an observant Ger Hasid, he understood his children with their new era longings. He did not disparage them in their communal life. Rather, he encouraged us to go socialize a little and entertain ourselves, in keeping with the possibilities of the little town.

I will write no more as my heart pains me too much when I recall the gruesome murders of my family-my parents, my sister Hinde Leye and her husband Shleyme Khayim Tsimbol and their children, Sore'le and Itsik'l.

May these written words of mine serve as the gravestone for their unknown graves.

First row, from right: Ester Gavortshik and Miryam Tsudiker
Second row, from right: Sore Romaner and Reyzl Gerlits
Standing: Rokhl Burshtin, Golde Shniadover and Zelda Burshtin

[Page 334]

Four Years in Goworowo

by *Rov* Menakhem Belfer, America

Translated by Tina Lunson

I arrived in Goworowo as a young man from the town of my birth, Lusk. While attending the Lomzshe Yeshiva, I happened to sit near a young man dressed in *hasidic* garb, whose name was Bunem Shafran, from Goworowo. It could never have occurred to me then that one year later, great changes in my life would be tied to that town. But what is that folk-saying? What the mind cannot solve, time will resolve. In 1935 I came to Goworowo as the son-in-law of Reb Nosn Farba of blessed memory.

To tell the truth I was a little shocked at the thought of settling myself and living in a *hasidic shtetl*. I was after all a pupil from the Lithuanian *yeshivas*, I dressed in modern clothes, and I imagined that all the Goworowo Jews, from large to small, wore long *hasidic* coats and round Polish caps, and were flaming *hasidim* for whom it would be a great *mitsve* to chase off a Litvish Enlightener. But after getting acquainted with the people I saw that my fear was a little overwrought. A large percent of the youth was modern minded and even the proper *hasidic* youth were also different than I had imagined. The proclaimed *hasidic* young men like the son-in-law of Reb Khayim Leyb (the ritual slaughterer), Yisroel Burshtin, who was involved with the *Beys Yankev* girl's schools and others were my dearest friends.

At this opportunity, I will also mention one of the things that distinguished the town of Goworowo. The town possessed one of the great *rabeyim* in Poland, *Rov* Meyshe Burshtin, may God avenge his death. With his learning, with his wisdom and shrewdness and with his stately appearance, he was an exception among the rabbis. Each time that we came to spend time with him in Torah study or everyday tasks, was a spiritual experience.

A little while after my arrival, another "Litvak" showed up in town. This was Reb Yekhezkel Khan, may God avenge his blood, who opened a wine and liquor shop. He was an expert Talmudist and an Enlightener. I had studied with his brother the Shniadover *Rov*, *Rov* Dovid Khan, in the Lomzshe Yeshiva. It was in his home that I

[Page 335]

became acquainted with the Makover *Rebi*, who came to Goworowo to establish a Makover *hasidic shtibl*. I, along with Reb Yekhezkel, prayed together in the *shtibl* until the outbreak of the war and I also studied a page of Talmud with a group there every day.

Thus life went in ease and calm until the horrible war came and put an end to that population.

I saw the first German with a murderous dog's face on Friday the 8th of September 1939. My wife Freyde Shifre, may God avenge her blood (she was killed in the summer of 1942 in the town of Dobrovits near Sarna, Volyn), and I along with another twenty Jews were visiting a landowner at his estate a few kilometers from town. We were sitting in a room. Suddenly the doors burst open and a German with a rifle pointed at us screamed out like a wild animal, "Hands in the air! You Jews wanted this war because Jews want Germans to fall on the battlefield." He turned around and left the room. That same day, Friday, we slinked back into town by round about routes. Hardly a moment passed when the Germans began catching Jews for work. We somehow avoided that capture and we sat in the dark until morning.

Shabes morning. The whole town was burning like the fires of hell. Dead Jews lay in the street. Germans caught me and started pressing me and another few hundred Jews toward Germany. We arrived in the town Ruzshan. They drove us into a bombed -out church and pressed us all into a small space. Pondering the bitter situation, I recalled a remedy from a great sage, that when one finds oneself in danger for one's life to recite the prayer *Nishmat kol khay* a certain number of times. Not thinking a lot, I began to recite *Nishmat*. After a few repetitions, a German came in and called out my brother-in-law Nakhman Yozshambek, may God avenge his blood, who was sitting near me. I kept saying *Nishmat* with strong intention. When I finished the whole number, my brother-in-law came back with two tomatoes. My heart felt a little lighter. I took that as a sign that the remedy had helped and that I would, with God's help, survive this trouble.

From Ruzshan we were forced headlong over many obstacles until on September 12 we were brought to a German camp in eastern Prussia. Several days after arriving in the camp, I dreamed this dream: I was already freed; an unknown person asked me how long I had been in the camp and I answered him, 17 or 18 days. The dream turned out to be correct. Exactly on the 18th day, *Shabes khol-ameyd Sukes*, the 30th of September, a German officer came to us in the camp and said, "Since Hitler does not like any Jews and does not want them found on German

[Page 336]

soil, we will drive all Jews to the new German/Russian border and all Jews must cross over into Russia. Anyone who does not follow this order will be shot."

That same day they took us to a train station, loaded us into beautiful train cars and took us to Ostrolenke. There, they told us to cross over to the Russians.

Two Neighboring Towns

by Yankev Kats, Israel

Translated by Mira Eckhaus

Edited by Tina Lunson

Goworowo and Dlugosiodlo were two towns that were close together and similar to one another. They had about the same population size, the same one story wooden houses covered with wall moss, and the same market square with streets surrounding it like babies wrapped in their mother's aprons. However, there was something specific in Goworowo that was not comparable in the neighboring towns. It was as if an atmosphere of nobility and generosity were poured over it. The residents appreciated their self-worth, were careful about their dress and language, and the youth in the town, of all shades, lived a lively life on the organizational and social level, aspiring to acquire an education and take care of repairing the world.

I was born in Dlugosiodlo and I had many relatives and friends in Goworowo. Not a year passed that I did not visit it several times. The distance between the two towns was a drive of about three quarters of an hour and I was always filled with excitement when I went to this sweet and charming town.

I remember my impressions of the figures I knew in Goworowo and who deserve to be commemorated in a book of remembrance, both those who sanctified the name of heaven and the name of the nation and perished in the terrible Holocaust and those who survived and live with us today.

I cannot forget the great Torah scholar, the magnanimous, pure and modest, Reb Fayvl Lubalski, one of the distinguished students of the *Gaon* of Warsaw, *Rov* Avremele Shtsutsiner, who was one of the greatest students of the *Rebi* of Sukhtsov, the author of *Avney Nezer*. Reb Fayvl was born in Warsaw and studied in his youth with the *Gaon* Reb Nosen Spigelglas in his yeshiva on Shliska Street in Warsaw and later studied with the aforementioned rabbi and was commissioned for teaching and rabbinical ordination. He married the beautiful daughter of Reb Kalman Ozdoba, a simple Jew, a blacksmith by profession, but modest and honest, God-fearing and of good character. He was awarded this magnificent son-in-law because of his love for the Torah and respect for the rabbis. For several years, Reb Fayvl was supported financially by his father-in-law, studied the Torah and rose in the fear of God. However, he did not aspire to become a rabbi and began to engage in the furniture trade. His trade was established and his financial situation was good, until the war broke out and he was killed along with his family as martyrs to God. May God avenge their blood.

[Page 337]

Over a page of Gemora
Sitting second from the right is *Rov* Avieyzer Burstein
Standing behind him is the author Yankev Kats

I remember the excellent young man, a clever scholar with lofty virtues, Reb Fishel Krulevitsh of blessed memory, the son of Reb Khayim, the owner of a flour mill. He studied with me at the *Beys Yosef* Yeshiva in Novoredok in Ostrów Mazowiecka. He had great and noble talents. He was very persistent, studied day and night, he was the first to come and last to leave the study house. Every Thursday night he was up all night, studying diligently. He had a wonderful memory and great morals. He suddenly fell ill with a serious lung disease and died before the outbreak of war.

During one of my visits to Goworowo, I influenced one young man, David Shron, may God avenge his blood, to go study at the magnificent Lomza Yeshiva. He listened to my advice and started studying vigorously and diligently. He soon became popular with the *yeshiva* boys and the overseer drew him very close. One day I noticed in the yeshiva's dining room that David was drinking an unusual amount of water. Being a *gabay* of *Ezras Kholim*, I told this to the overseer and he ordered me to take him to the yeshiva physician, Dr. Likhter, for an examination. The doctor determined that David had diabetes and his condition was dangerous. All medications were of no use and he perished at the beginning of the Holocaust.

May he live long life, the wonderful and excellent Torah scholar, Reb Yitskhak Shafran, one of the distinguished scholars of the Lomza Yeshiva. He had great organizational power, was settled and balanced in his opinion. He was one of the initiators and founders of *Tseirey Agudas Yisroel* in Goworowo and one of the activists of the *Aguda* ideal. He managed the ultra-Orthodox girls' school *Beys Yankev* with great success and was very popular among his friends. Today he lives in the United States.

For a short time, *Rov* Avieyzer Burshtin, the son of the town *Rov*, studied with me. He had a quick grasp of the Talmud. Even in his youth he tended to write and reminisce and his talent developed. Great respect to Goworowo who produced a writer, a scholar and a public figure who did a lot after the war in Germany in saving the surviving remnant. Even here, in Israel, he occupies a prominent place in the management of a large institution and writes articles in newspapers in Israel and abroad.

[Page 338]

Last but not least: My dear brother-in-law and sister, Reb Nosn and Dvora Shron. They had a grain and flour trading house in Goworowo and an apartment in the center of the town. My brother-in-law bought in advance the crops of the fields of the local Polish nobleman. He ground the grain in the Rits brothers' mill and sold flour to the town's bakeries, to Dlugosiodlo, and all the surrounding towns. During the market days, the house was like a beehive. Merchants from all branches of commerce came and went. One came in to offer goods, another came in to ask for charity, until well after the market. No one left empty-handed. Indeed, this merit was partially in their favor during the Holocaust.

When the war broke out and Hitler's soldiers entered the town, a terrible tragedy befell them. On the first day of their entry, the Nazis shot and killed my brother-in-law's father and mother and he buried them according to Jewish tradition. After this horrific event, they left Goworowo and moved to Dlugosiodlo, Tiktyn, then Bialystok, and finally arrived in Russia.

They also went through a big mental crisis in Russia. They lost two of their children while they were traveling on a crowded train. They searched for them all over Russia for a whole year until they happened to find them in the house of a man from Goworowo, Mr. Nuska Kohen. Only when they arrived in Israel did their troubles come to an end and they breathed a sigh of relief. They opened a trading house in Tel Aviv together with their children and, with God's help, they see the reward of their hard work.

There are many more stories about the town of Goworowo and its characters. It was a model and exemplary town. My eyes are tearful and my heart aches for the life of the town that was cut short in its prime.

A large group of *Shomer ha'dati*. See page 173.

[Page 339]

Martyrdom

by *Rov* Tsvi A. Slushts, Israel

Translated by Mira Eckhaus

Edited by Tina Lunson

I am close in my soul to the town of Goworowo, although I have never seen it in reality. Sometimes hearing about something is much greater than actually seeing it. I have heard so much about the town – about its rabbis, its *Hasidim,* and the people of action in it – that the image of the town is depicted in my mind in an illustration, as if it were my hometown and the place of my birth.

I am a great-grandson and grandson on my wife's side, of a great, noble man of the Jewish priesthood, *Rov* Mendl of blessed memory, a ritual slaughterer and meat inspector, who was the eldest son of the high priest, who was even greater than his brother, the *Gaon Rov* Yehuda Kahana Butsian may his saintly memory be for a blessing, who served for many years as the rabbi of Goworowo and its neighboring towns.

In the family tradition there is a history of the deeds and customs of the great elders that were passed, like a golden chain, from generation to generation, things that testify to their righteousness and greatness; and also, to the honesty of the townspeople with whom they lived for many years. It is impossible to talk about all the stories I have heard and the Sage's words are true, "if you haven't seen the lion, go out and see his descendants". I see the descendants who grew up in Goworowo and the surrounding towns, whose actions prove the glorious tradition they received in their childhood, and about them I say, Blessed is their homeland!

I heard about Goworowo's study houses, that were full of young adults and old men who were Torah scholars and God-fearing. I heard about people who did acts of charity and kindness, whose actions set an example for the near and far surrounding towns, and I heard about magnificent public institutions, which developed extensive operations in various areas, which also set an example for the nearby towns, and testified to the vigilance and ability of the people of Goworowo. Blessed are those who saw Goworowo in its glory!

The Jewish town of Goworowo no longer exists. Along with all the cities of Israel in Poland, it was ruined and the life in it stopped and still no mourners mourned its destruction and no tombstone was erected to its memory. And so, we are commanded as long as we have seen the great terror that occurred, to remember and remind ourselves and the generations after us, of the glory of its greatness while it existed, and the terrible tragedy of its destruction. Although the Sages stated, "The destiny of the dead is to be forgotten from the heart" – this destiny does not apply to a great city of Israel. The memory of a destroyed city cannot be forgotten forever. The Sages ruled on a dead person and not on holy and pure ones who gave their lives for the holiness of God and His Torah. The awakening of Goworowo's descendants to perpetuate the memory of their community that was and no longer exists, is the right thing to do. The current generation has the duty to carry out "so you will be able to tell your son and your son's son what the damned Nazis did to us", to provide reference material for future generations, who will link themselves in a lasting connection with the glorious past, and will recognize and know the colorful life of the town where a lot of the typical Jewish folklore is found, and they will learn a chapter in the life of heroism of the people of Israel.

[Page 340]

The widespread opinion among many historians is that one should be satisfied with the memoirs of capital cities and large cities, which have the power to express for generations the magnitude and the dimensions of the destruction. In their opinion, there is duplicity in bringing up memories of small towns, which do not add any material of historical value. The prophet Isaiah does not say so. The prophet emphasizes, "For thus says the High and Lofty One that inhabits eternity, whose name is Holy, 'I dwell in the high and holy place and also with him that is of a contrite and humble spirit, to revive the spirit of the humble, and to revive the heart of the contrite ones'...." (57, 15), and the Sages added, "From on high I am with those of humble spirit and the contrite ones upon whom I bow my *Shekhinah*". It was precisely in the dust of the small towns that precious pearls were hidden and they must be revived and immortalized for future generations because the *Shekhinah* is found precisely in the humble spirit and the contrite ones.

The commemoration of the town of Goworowo by discovering its hidden treasures of spirit and action will bring life to the next generation who continue to connect links in the golden chain of existence of the eternal nation of Israel.

[Page 340]

My Family

by Yitskhak Romaner, Israel

Translated by Tina Lunson

I remember my beloved grandfather,
May he rest in peace, in Eden,
The dignified face, the gentle glance,
He looked on people kindly.
Reb Mayer'l, head of the community,
Weighed his words on a scale,
Did not talk a lot,
What he said – said quietly.
Weighty, with logic and tact,
He stayed involved with people,
Livelihood, earned with work,
but above all, Jewishly and honest.

My grandma Reyzl, like those of her
time,
Full of just belief and trust,
Bearing the yoke, showing wonder,
Helping earn, rearing children.
Auntie Hinde Leye, a kosher soul,
Quiet, unassuming, very wise,
Happy with her man Shleyme Khayim,
Lived an idyl like good Jews.

On holidays, happy days, together.
Faithful children, father and mother,
The joy deep and wide,
The presence of God in the house.
The war put an end to that,
The good times all are gone.
Where are their holy bones,
Scattered over fields like stones.
My eye sheds a tear,
I will write no more,
Where can one find justice?
Where are you, yesterday?

[Page 341]

My Road to *Erets-Yisroel*

by Sore Blumshteyn-Skurnik, America

Translated by Tina Lunson

Even in my early childhood I was tortured by the thought that they do not like us and that Jews are superfluous in Poland. I was too young at the time to understand it was not only Poland that hated us, but the whole world did too.

Our family was the only Jewish family in a Polish village. My sister Rivke and I were the only Jewish children in the Polish school. The Christian children persecuted us at every step and chance. They hit us, threw stones at us and "honored" us with other troubles. My mother wanted to take us out of the school. "I will not have you there," she said, "and in any case girls do not need any school." But I was quite stubborn and decided, despite all the enemies, to continue in the school. Although my childish heart was full of pain, not so much from the blows I had to bear but, from the disgrace of being insulted as a Jewish child. In my childish way I decided to take revenge. When the Polish religion teacher came into class, I made a demonstration of not standing but remained seated in my place, as a response to their ugly insults.

Later we moved to Goworowo. As soon as the *He'khaluts* movement was formed in the town, I was one of the first to sign on as a member and when they began to collect money for *Keren kayemet l'yisroel* I went from house to house asking for money even though in those days it was very dangerous to go into an extremely religious house to ask for money for *Erets-yisroel*. It was very hard then to convince Jews that they needed a land of their own. Like the happy worm in the horseradish, Jews did not feel bitter about the Exile. When emissaries began coming from Warsaw to strengthen the *He'khaluts* Pioneer movement, I pelted them with questions about *Erets-yisroel*. I asked them so many questions that one responded to me, "This is too many questions for such a young girl, you must travel to *Erets* yourself to find out the answers to all your questions." It was evident that I wanted to know more than they could tell me.

I remember an incident. In 1929, when the bloody events broke out in *Erets-yisroel*, my father brought home the newspaper *Haynt*. Printed there was a call to Jews worldwide from Dovid Ben-Gurion to

[Page 342]

On the ship
Above on the left stand Sore and Yitskhak Blumshteyn and Aron Shron

save their brethren in *Erets-yisroel*. Everyone in the house wept in grief. I went to my mother and said, "Why are you crying? Let me go the *Erets-yisroel*!" My mother looked at me with pity and asked, "From what will we live in *Erets-yisroel*?" I was still too young to answer that question. But in my heart was etched a hot longing that when I got old enough, I would make *aliya* by myself and then bring my whole family. I was ashamed to say it out loud because I knew that they would laugh at me. As I got older and often said that I strove to go to *Erets-yisroel*, people gave me a nickname, Mistress of Dreams. But a strong will can break iron. All the difficulties were melted away by my strong desire. Ben Gurion's call was like a clock striking in my ears until I finally had the merit to make *aliya* to *Erets-yisroel* and to bring my father may he rest in peace, two brothers and two sisters over as well.

I feel the pressure of some guilt regarding my dear sister Gitl, her husband Ezra Bergman and their little daughter Sore, may God avenge their blood. He, my brother-in-law, was opposed to my plan to travel to *Erets-yisroel*. Not, heaven forbid, because he did not love *Erets-yisroel* but he maintained that the time for redemption had not yet come, in particular for a girl alone without her parents in a strange, distant land. My brother-in-law was a highly intelligent and educated person and could motivate what he said. That made me more vexed. We had many arguments. I could not convince him and he could not change my mind.

[Page 343]

Then my sister got mixed up in it. “Sore!” she said, “you can just ask us, we will send money for your expenses to come back home.” I became enraged and responded, “You will yet ask me to bring you over to *Erets-yisroel*!”

When the war broke out in 1939, I received a heart rending letter from my sister and brother-in-law. They begged me to save them. I promptly traveled to Jerusalem to the immigration department of the *Sokhnut*. The official looked at me as if I were out of my mind. He gave me to understand that I was the only one who had brought such a large family and from my side it was almost *khutspe* to ask for more certifications. I could not imagine then what kind of misfortune was being prepared for the Jews of the world.

My sister Gitl, my brother-in-law Ezra and their daughter Sore shared the tragic fate of all the Polish Jews. Unfortunately, I was correct in my response. But, *okh un vey* to being correct! How much would I give to not be correct.

The years have done nothing to heal my wounds. The graves of my sister, brother-in-law and daughter are still open. It is a terrible feeling to keep thinking about it.

May this Book of Remembrance be a gravestone for the dear suffering souls of our martyrs.

The third-grade class of the Polish *powshechna* school (1934)
At the left, teacher Genia Taub
(See page 124)

[Page 344]

With the *Rebi's* Approval

by Yitskhak Blumshteyn, America

Translated by Tina Lunson

During the last years of the Second World War[a] the situation of the Jews in Poland became unbearable, especially for the Jews in the small towns. There was, literally, nothing to do and nothing to take up for oneself. But the young people thought of a purpose; they were getting older, they should get married, build a Jewish home, and there were no prospects for how to accommodate this or to achieve any livelihood. The antisemitism increased from day to day. The Pollacks had robbed the Jews of all sources of livelihood, had simply torn the bread out of their mouths. The younger generation was orphaned and hopeless. There was no alternative left than to emigrate to another country.

We, a group of friends, men and women, members of *Poaley-tsion* and *He'khaluts*, decided that in order to emigrate sooner, the best place was *Erets-Yisroel*, the promised Jewish land.

But it is easy to say travel. In order to travel one must have money and a lot of it and money my father did have but would not give. A mediation on travel began in our house. Father stubbornly held to his side. A child should stay at home, for the pride of the parents. Who would be there to look after Jewishness? And in general, how could he send a child off on such a long journey? My mother looked at it with more distance, "What kind of purpose is it to sit at home with just room and board? How can the young people make a living in such a small town, with such antisemitism and with such competition?" In the middle of one such a heated discussion, my mother called out to my father,

"Velvl! Maybe by rights you should go to Ger to the *Rebi*, and see what 'May he Long Live' has to say?"

My father agreed.

Mother packed his satin *kapote*, some clean clothes, his *talis un tfiln* and father went off to Ger for *Shabes*.

Sunday afternoon father returned from Ger, but he did not mention what the *Rebi* had said, not yes and not no. I was very curious to hear what the *Rebi* had said. My mother also wanted to hear the holy word from the *Rebi*.

[Page 345]

Saying Goodbye

In the middle of the meal mother could not control herself anymore and blurted, "*Nu, Velvl!* What did the *Rebi* say?"

"You know what, Feyge Nekhame, the *Rebi* actually said? 'And if you would say NO, would that help you?' "

In that response from the *Rebi* father saw that the *Rebi* agreed to my journey and then I began to prepare to go to *Erets-Yisroel.*

Dvore Romaner and Tsipore Grudke set off. 1932.

Note from Lester Blum:

a. Should read "the First World War"

[Page 346]

A Jew Travels to *Erets-Yisroel*

by Aharon Shron, Israel

Translated by Tina Lunson

Since the *aliye* movement to *Erets-Yisroel* began in Goworowo in 1932, there had been a few unsuccessful efforts to travel to and settle in the land. At the beginning of the 1920s, Avrom Dovid Rubin and his wife Rivke Tsirl traveled to *E"Y* but in time they came back to the *shtetl*. People joked at their expense, that one of the reasons for their failure was that they had been tricked in *E"Y*, that instead of potatoes they had put oranges in their sack.

The second try was made in 1924 when the *Mizrakhi* members Yisroel Leyb Tandetshazsh (Avrom Romaner's son-in-law) who got to *E"Y* through Argentina; Khayim Sheyniak, who had learned carpentry for that purpose through a Christian tradesman in the *Probostvo*; and Yitskhak Dovid Tehilim. In 1925 a son of our town, Eliyahu Brokhonski traveled to the Land by way of the Vishkove *He'khaluts*. And that group also could not acclimate and came back to their homes after a time.

Tandetshazsh went back to Argentina and worked there as a teacher in the Bialek Schools until his death in 1957 (his son Yitskhak lives in Israel today).

The larger *aliye* to *E"Y* from our town began, as mentioned above, in August 1932. Technically that was an illegal *aliye* because no one had received certificates. They used the excursions which were organized in Poland for the *Makabiada* games in *Erets-Yisroel*. They came in as tourists and just stayed there.

In that first group there were my wife Devore (Romaner), Khave Segal with her husband, and Tsipore Grudke. Following them a week later were Sore and Yitskhak Blumshteyn as well as the writer of these lines.

What happened then in the *shtetl* was indescribable. The farewell evenings that were organized for us were impressive. Those leaving town went from house to house to say goodbye; it was literally unforgettable. The members of *Poaley-tsion* and *BeTaR* and other organizations, relatives and dear friends accompanied us to Pasheki. The *Frayhayt* came with their flags. Others

[Page 347]

traveled to Warsaw with us. The train platform was packed with people. The train did not move from the spot until we finished singing *Ha'tikva*. In Pshetitsh, Rivke Rozenberg-Shafran and Royzke Shniadover awaited us, who also sang heartily with us.

We stayed overnight in Warsaw and from there traveled by train to Konstants, Romania. On the way we also encountered other *olim* like us and together kept in close contact. On the ship we led a collective life with a common treasury. The head of our *kibuts* was a certain Gasner from *Rov*ne, already an older person, very much an intellectual and clever; we only ever called him "Aba".

At the farewell for Menukhe Grudka. 1933.

At arrival in the port of Haifa, none of us hesitated. Each of us had to find a way to accommodate ourselves on our own, even if just temporarily.

After a few days I went to the *Histadrut* to request work as a new émigré from Poland. But there was no work. They advised me to go to Rehovot, where I had a recommendation from my wife's parents, to a certain Avromitski. There they took me on temporarily and I went right to the office for an assignment. They sent me to an orchard. The manager looked me over, the new Pioneer with the short pants, and promptly detailed me to the appropriate work. He took me to a large yard with a lot of manure, told me to fill a sack with it, put that on my shoulder and fertilize each tree with a little of it. The manure was wet and heavy, and I got sweaty all over. As you can see, this was not the most

[Page 348]

aromatic job, but I welcomed it with love. I did that work as a contractor and earned 12 *piaster* a day.

During the time I was working in Rehovot, my wife was in Tel Aviv and gradually got work in her trade of tailoring. She worked for a woman with whom she spent the nights for a sum she would pay off, sleeping on the floor. I went to Tel Aviv every *Shabes*. As we together were able to save up a little money, we began to clarify our goals. We, along with Sore and Yitskhak Blumshteyn, who were after all staying for a while with their relatives, decided to create a joint place where we could live. We rented an apartment in neighboring Nordoy with a small kitchen and we all moved in. We bought a little furniture and some kitchen utensils and set up our joint household.

Around then I left my job in Rehovot and stayed in Tel Aviv.

My wife now earned 15 *piaster* a day and I could find no work in Tel Aviv. Then I remembered that in 1920 I had apprenticed to be a hatmaker with Leyb Hersh and tried my luck in that trade. I succeeded in landing a job in a hat business. For 10 hours – 15 *piasters*. Also good. My boss was happy with me and sometimes gave me a gift in the form of a pack of "Karmel" cigarettes for one half a *piaster*. After two months there I got a raise and now earned 18 *p.* a day. My wife and I together now earned

At the farewell for Rokhl Shapira [Shpira?]. 1936.

[Page 349]

33 *p.* a day, a good sum in that time. We decided to make a surprise for our parents in Goworowo. We sent them 2 pounds sterling (28 *zlotych* to a pound) as a gift. The town was then "going off its wheels" – in a short time would it be possible to save up money and send it home?

Sara and Yitskhak were working too, she in textiles and he as an "assistant" and painter, both making good money, so, we were each able to make separate residences. I rented a small apartment, "four by four", in neighboring Trumpeldor and paid 75 *p.* a month. We also bought furniture, a wardrobe for 4.5 pounds, a table for 1.5 *p.*, two chairs for 25 *piaster* and a kitchen table for 12 *p.* We both kept working and earning, lived for today and did not worry about tomorrow. We forgot about dinner and went out dancing until late at night.

When I demanded 25 *piaster* a day for my labor, my boss did not accept it. So, I left that place and through the office found work in construction. Indeed, I made 32 *p.* a day but the work was heavy. And later I even went up to 60 *p.* a day. My wife was also earning up to half a pound sterling a day and that allowed us to rent a larger apartment, for two pounds a month rent.

In 1933 Avrom Holtsman and his wife came to *Erets* and rented a two room apartment not far from us. They also rented a grocery store. Every *Shabes* evening all we Goworowers would meet at our house and enjoy the time together. Holtsman played the fiddle, we sang, and it was a fine time.

Some time later Holtsman bought a plot of land in Ramat-Yitskhak. He built a residence there and a grocery store and left Tel-Aviv. In 1936 when Sore's family (Skurnik) came to *Erets* and settled in Haifa, she and Yitskhak also left Tel Aviv and moved to Haifa.

We, the above mentioned, were the first Pioneers from our *shtetl* to stay in *Erets* despite all the difficulties. Later many others followed our example. Then the following families and individuals came. In 1933 – the family of Meyshe Granat and Menukhe Grudka; in 1934, Alek Proska (Viderboym) and Rivke Skurnik (Bar-Kokhba); in 1935 – the family Varshavniak, Alek Grudka (Brakhanski), Yankev Botshan, Dovid Mishnayos and Elieyzer Levin (from Cuba); in 1936 – the family Yehude Grudka, family Meyshe Skurnik, family Dov Tsudiker, family Bertshe Granat, Nomi Proska (Strasberg) and Rokhl Shpira [Shapiro?] (Zakhriahu). In 1937 – Shleyme Apelboym. In 1938 – Sore Romaner (Tsimerman), Nekhame Shekhter (Gelbfish), and Khave Molovani (Vayner). In those same years Aron Tehilim and Ester Gutman (Kantarovitsh) also arrived.

Since I had brought my sister-in-law Sore Romaner,

[Page 350]

there is an interesting chapter around that, and is worth noting.

As already mentioned, I did not come with my wife and in the official documents I was still figured as a bachelor. I used that and went to the immigration office of the *Sokhnut* to request a certificate for my "wife" Sore Romaner. I then wrote to Sore to send me a photograph of herself with the "appropriate" signature on the second side – "for my husband". I also asked her to send "love letters" with specific texts. I became a regular visitor at the *Sokhnut* so that they would put aside these "love letters" with the photographs and urged them to take care of my request.

When things dragged out for a long time with LEKH-V'SHUB I once caused a scandal, so that Usishkin, of blessed memory, ran into the room to see what was going on. When an officer (his name was Mikhaeli) became aware of what they were dealing with, he told him to do everything possible to get my "wife" quickly through the requirements.

A. Shron (left) with a friend at construction work

A short time later Sore was indeed called to the Palestine Office in Warsaw and given a certificate. When she arrived in *Erets* in 1938, also on her ship were Mikhaeli Dobkin and others. Dobkin viewed Sore as my “wife”.

And to this day when Mikhaeli (director of the public airport Dov) sees me, we smile at one another, recalling my scene that time in the *Sokhnut* office.

All of the above mentioned managed to came to *Erets* just before the outbreak of the war and all of them settled here (except for Sore and Yitskhak Blumshteyn who because of family preferences traveled to America in 1945). The majority of the Survivors after the war came to *Erets*, by any means possible. Today we number about 150 families, may they multiply.

[Page 351]

Goworowo in My Eyes

by Cantor Nosn Stolnits, Canada

Translated by Tina Lunson

Cantor Nosn Stolnits

Although I am not a native son of Goworowo, I am still tightly bound to the *shtetl* through family ties. I had a sister there, Khaye Beyle and her husband Yisroel Yitskhak Shron, may God avenge their blood, and also an aunt Beyle and her husband Khayim Dovid Shron, may God avenge their blood.

In my youth I visited Goworowo from time to time. I was inspired and affected by the prevailing atmosphere that was permeated with a deep religious spirit, filled with *hasidic* enthusiasm and love for the people, and everyone was connected and united like one large family.

The publication of this memorial book for the Jewish community Goworowo is a sacred mission. This will be a spiritual *mitsve* for that severed Jewish settlement that sprouted up and fermented with many sorts of activity, like many other spirited communities in Poland that were so savagely murdered and exterminated by the wild blooded Nazi regime, may their malignant names and memories be blotted out.

From the depths of my heart, I join in the grief for the children of Goworowo who lost their near and dear and who now go to build a monument to their holy memory and the memory of the *shtetl*. You may really be proud of the privilege with which the Omniscient God has gifted you, to be able to be actual co-builders on the sacred soil of our newly realized national Jewish home.

[Page 352]

A Story of *Khomets* and *Peysakh*

by A. B. Shoshoni, Israel

Translated by Tina Lunson

On one of the interim days of Passover in the year 1931 the famous publicist and beloved popular writer Yushzon-Itshele wrote an article in the Warsaw Yiddish newspaper *Haynt* titled *Yom-tov Sheyni*, in which he dealt with the character of *Yom-tov Sheyni* in the Exile, as it did not exist in *Erets-Yisroel* and was doubtlessly created for the lands of the Exile.

In that article the author did not have any intention to minimize, heaven forbid, the sanctity of the holiday on the last day of Passover. Yushzon-Itshele himself was a proper, observant Jew, a guardian of Torah and *mitsves*, and was far from any Reform ideas or insult to tradition.

The little Goworowo demons soon sniffed out that, from that article, one could make dainties for the editors of the *Agudist* paper *Dos yidishe togblat*, of which Yushzon-Itshele was a dangerous opponent who brought them a lot of trouble with his sharp pen. According to the general rule "hatred perverts justice", the Goworowo demons estimated that the editors of the *Togblat* would, in their great hurry and avid revenge, not check very closely, not be scrupulous about the details, and not use any logic and they composed an ostensible invitation to a certain person, that he should come to the Zionist Organization on the last day of *Peysakh* in the afternoon where a reception would take place and they would discuss Yushzon-Itshele's article. That invitation was written on an official letterhead with the stamp of the Zionist Organization. Then a letter was added to it from a supposed Goworowo proprietor who wept with bitter tears at the decimation that was taking place at the reception in the Zionist Organization, that people there ate leavened foods and drank beer and made ash and mud of the last day of *Peysakh* and, all of that, because of Yushzon-Itshele.

A few days after Passover, one fine morning, the bomb exploded with the train from Warsaw and the arrival of the *Togblat*. People opened it up and were furious. Across all six columns of the second page was a huge headline in out-sized letters, "Desecration of the holiday in Goworowo"; *Khomets on Peysakh* – look, you heavens!" The editor himself had blessed a large editorial article.

[Page 353]

Finally unmasking the very person who had led the Jewish masses away from the straight path. Rogovi poured pitch and sulphur on those who would lead Jews astray, who would make void the *yom-tov Sheyni*. Ayzik-Ber Ekerman wrote an article full of epithets and witticisms at the expense of Yushzon, "Uncle! We caught you at it!" The story itself was quickly served up on every plate, with the full text of the letter and the invitation, with witnesses who saw and witnesses who heard. The world was coming to an end!

The town was going off its wheels. One could probably believe the story themselves – there it was in black on white. But the address of the invitation – the town crazy, Shleyme Akive Beserman – already gave witness that this was a cooked-up event, an impish game with a far reach.

Soon telegrams were flying and retractions – no bears and no forest. First of all, everything was *kosher l'Peysakh*, the most stringent of the stringent, as was done in all the Jewish towns and second, no reception took place on that day.

The *Rov*, poor man, had to travel to Warsaw to take the stain of scandal off his community. He published a clarification in the *Togblat* that the whole story was a prank. Reb Meyshe Tenenboym sent retractions to the *Haynt* and the *Moment* in the name of the Jewish community. Yushzon-Itshele had good material for a new essay and the *Togblat* threw the guilt for the entire thing onto the Zionist Organization in Goworowo, for neglecting its letterhead and stamps and any little demon can subscribe to a good year. (In fact, they used a long ago stolen stamp from the Zionist Org.)

That story was the talk of the town in the whole country. Some gritted their teeth and lowered their eyes in shame and others, laughed into their fists at the impish joke that the Goworowo scamps had played.

Dos yidishe togblat –The Yiddish Daily

[Page 354]

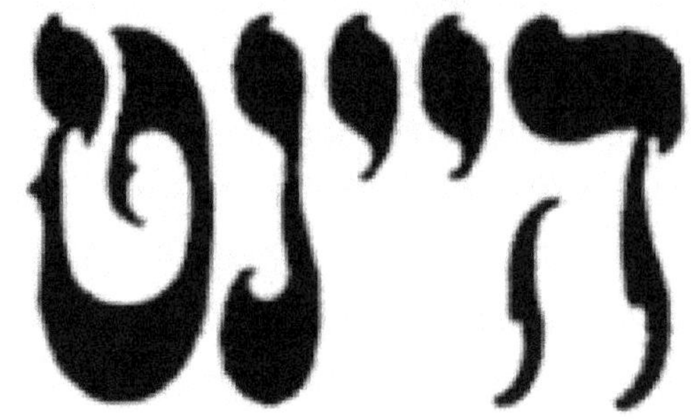

דער „יום־טוב שני"

ב. יאושזאהן

Der haynt –Today

The article *The last day of Peysakh* appeared in *Haynt* on the 4th interim day of Passover, 20th *Nisn, sav-reysh-tsadi"alef* (7 April 1931).

[Page 355]

Footnotes to an Essay

by H. Yustus, Israel

Translated by Mira Eckhaus

Edited by Tina Lunson

The uproar that arose and to be more precise, that was created by *Dos Yidishe Togblat*, the newspaper of the *Agudas Yisroel* movement following my late father's article *Der Yom-Tov Sheyni* [the second observed day of a holy day], should of course be examined taking into consideration the background of those days; taking into consideration the background of the fierce struggle that existed between the Zionist movement and the *Aguda*, and my father's part in it.

The attack which the *Togblat* came out with was unrestrained. The serious accusation that my father's intention was "to incite and lead astray", for the cancellation of *Yom-Tov Sheyni* was hurled without even leaving room for an oversight. And the intention was quite transparent. The campaign that my father led against *Agudas Yisroel* due to its stance towards Zionism and also towards internal problems which touched the lives of the community was fierce and at times its arrows were even aimed at the many *rebis'* courts; and the damage of my father's articles was severe, their influence was very great and one of the difficulties encountered by the counter-campaign was that it was impossible to raise against my father a claim of heresy or the like, that is, a claim of a negative attitude toward Orthodox Judaism or religion. Indeed, in the storm of polemics this tone was also sometimes sounded, but only half-heartedly, since my father was known as a religious Jew, observant of the *mitsves* and strict about the simple *mitsves* as if they were severe *mitsves*. And here, when the aforementioned article was published, the opportunity arose "to remove the mask" (as they wrote) and "reveal to all", that the truth of the matter is that there is nothing but a pretense, that here he even "proposes" the cancellation of a holiday!

And how far has the storm of the battle reached and how far has the fanning of the flames reached! On the *Shabes* day after the article was published, a group of *yeshiva* students burst into the synagogue of the "Talmud society" where we were praying and tried to attack my father; something that was prevented by the worshipers, who stopped them and expelled them. And if that were not enough, out of nowhere a proclamation appeared that imposed a boycott on my father.

The *Togblat* did not let up on the subject for many days and day after day articles appeared in it and a protest movement was organized in various cities and towns, which demanded to boycott the *Haynt* newspaper and forbid its reading by all ultra-Orthodox Jews. It was clear that this was indeed the main intention and trend; to impose the stamp of heresy on my father and on the *Haynt* as well.

By the way, I remember that one evening, on that same week, I went with my father to the *Haynt* editorial office. One of the owners of the newspaper, the S. Y. Yatskan of blessed memory, did not hide his concerns about the possible effect of this battle on the ultra-orthodox readers of the newspaper and out of absentmindedness, he commented to my father, "And why was it necessary…?" This comment made my father jump to an extent that I have rarely seen him like that, and he replied to

[Page 356]

Yatskan angrily, “If this is not to your taste, make the newspaper without me.” Yatskan justified himself and did not let go of my father until he made up his mind.

* * *

What motivated my father to write the article?

The answer to this must first of all be found in the fundamental feature that characterized his way of writing, his approach to writing, the trait that is the foundation of his personality; that he was never afraid to express what he felt. Writing was never a craft and a profession for him.

Father was good-tempered, friendly and had a soft and poetic soul. But nevertheless he had a solid character. Once he had reached his decision, it was impossible to change his mind. In public affairs he was not ready to make any compromises. He was unable to do things partially or in a shallow way, just as he was unable to write for lyrical beauty; he always strived for the essence of things and he always came to the reader with a consolidated and clear opinion. And it never occurred to him to consider if the idea he came up with would be popular or not, whether the reader will like it or not. In his writing he did not consider anything, except for one calculation, the soul-searching. And indeed, in this aspect he would consider a lot, consider and examine with the extent of his understanding and conscience. And that is it. Only this. Therefore, his writing was also a direct continuation of his personality and what he preached to others he carried out himself and knew no compromises even towards himself. He was a true man. It was his inner mindset that guided him and he knew no reluctance and this also led to the sharpness with which he wrote.

This article about the *Yom Tov Sheyni* is a drastic expression of this; for, as I mentioned, my father was observant and even strict and clear, because any idea of corrections was as far from him as the distance between east and west. The article itself repeats and emphasizes this point. The entire introduction of the article discusses the negation of the reform movement, “which began with minor corrections such as the removal of the second *Yekum Porkan* from the prayerbook and even led to the conversion of the Jewish *Shabes* to Sunday, which is the holy Christian day”. And indeed, even though it goes without saying that the article did not mean to be a “correction”, it was an injustice and a sin to attribute such intentions to it.

The article, which was written after a visit to the Land of Israel, mentions the strange feeling that arises “immediately on the second day of Passover, when everything around is secular, when Jews are traveling all around, there are merchants, workers, the shops are open, and in this secular hassle, there sits a group of Jews celebrating their holiday, exiled Jews who perform the *Seyder* as it should be… and the picture is even weirder on the last day of Passover you are in a religious house, all the members of the house are already under the secular hassle, the holiday for everyone is already over and only you must celebrate the holiday; the owner of the house prays a prayer from the afternoon service for the interim days with *Ata khonantan* (You have mercy on us) and from the service of the holiday with *Ata bekhartanu* (You chose us); the members of the household are already eating leavened foods and you are obliged to eat only matzah for an additional twenty-four hours… and all of this automatically arouses indignation and protest in you. Is it possible that that day itself will be holy for one Jew and secular for another?…”

In a sharp response (“crafty device”) to the *Togblat* attacks, my father wrote, among other things, “It is true that, as long as we are in exile, we must maintain it, but that does not mean that we must not regret it. Deep down in our hearts, we would certainly like for this *Yom Tov Sheyni* to exist. There are many forbidden things that after all are allowed to be desired. And so, the Sages say, 'Do not say I don't want to eat a pig meat,

[Page 357]

Reb Moshe Yustman - Yaoshson of blessed memory, the father of the author of the article

but say I want to, but what can I do as my Father in heaven has decreed on me'… Yes, we must not, for example, cancel *Tisha B'ov*, which even a Jew and the most religious Jew, would not ask to, and it will exist forever. As long as we are in the Exile, we must carefully observe and maintain the *Yom Tov Sheyni*, but this does not prevent us from seeing it as a heavy burden, a kind of punishment for the exile – and this is how our sages treated it, as shown in the wonderful article in the *Shir HaShirim Raba,* Chapter One in the verse 'Do not remember my sins and the deeds of evildoers'. 'The people of Israel said before the Almighty that I did not keep one *yom-tov* properly in the Land of Israel, but I kept two *Yomim Tovim* in the Exile. I thought I would get paid for both and I only get paid for one. Rov Yokhanan says about it (Ezekiel 4), 'and I also gave them bad laws'. This article of the Sages specifically emphasizes that the *Yom Tov Sheyni* is a punishment to such an extent that for observing the two-day holiday one receives a reward for only one day. And Reb Yokhanan even expresses and says that this *Yom Tov Sheyni* is under the definition of general "bad laws", a law which must be observed, although it is not one of the good and convenient things to the Jews. If the newspaper of *Aguda* existed at that period, can you imagine in your mind what kind of uproar they would have raised against Rov Yokhanan for this expression, "bad laws"!?…"

* * *

At the end of the article Der *Yom Tov Sheyni*, it is said, "God forbid, I am not advocating for a reform and the cancellation of this holiday… but I wanted to mention here the thoughts and reflections that arise in a Jew when he is privileged to celebrate a holiday in the Land of Israel and even more, when he returns from there to the exile".

And in this sentence lies perhaps the main motive for writing it.

My father saw in Zionism the literal national revival and he believed in its fulfillment with all his heart, even in the most difficult days that passed through the settlement and in the building of the country, he envisioned the future towards which every effort should be directed. His Zionism was self-inflicted in that he suffered the pain of the

[Page 358]

exile, the pain of the Polish Jews, their suffering, their poverty, the constant war for a loaf of bread, the persecutions they endured and the tomorrow that always stood before them in the heavy fog of an oppressive exile. All his writing was nothing but a call for rebellion, for not accepting this exile. And in his eyes, there was nothing more important than increasing the bond between the people and the country, than directing all the enormous forces embodied in Polish Jewry which he knew was its greatness and was connected to it with all the veins of his soul that were being consumed in the war of existence that reality forced upon it – to this goal, to this ray of light, which he considered as the rescue, the future.

And if, during his visit to Israel, the "strange feeling" during the days of *Yom Tov Sheyni* arose in him, it seems to me that indeed it also stemmed from this feeling that there is a difference between the Jew in Israel and the Jew in the exile and this feeling did not reconcile with his feeling and with his recognition of the necessity to bring about "change in the values" which will instill in the people the consciousness of the unreserved connection with the Land of Israel and the recognition of the centrality of the Land of Israel in their consciousness in practice.

שְׁמַד-שטיק

The article *Shmad Shtik* was published in the *Haynt* newspaper on April 12, 1931

[Page 359]

A Story with *Nadlitshbove*

by B. Dines, Israel

Translated by Tina Lunson

It was at the beginning of the 1930s, when young men of my age had to report to the military medical commission in Ostrolenke. Those were no longer the days of putting a "blowpipe" in your ears, claiming a "hunched" back, or cutting off a finger or a toe or imposing some other bodily flaw. One was most often just abandoned to fate and…money. I, as a son of wealthy parents, did not have to abandon much to fate, and happily chose the second path – evading military service with the help of *mezumen.*

My father, who had a brother in Ostrolenke, decided to travel to him and see the thing done on the spot. My uncle introduced my father to a "fixer" and for 100 dollars he undertook to "fix it" with the military doctor so that I would be completely exempt from the military. In order for the doctor to recognize me, he told me to stick a round, black bit of bandage on the right side of my face. Of course, since my father had given the payment to a third party and come home happy – it's a small thing? I would not have to be miserable for one and a half or two years.

The night before appearing before the doctor we, those obligated to the military duty, some dejected about the morning's fate and some encouraged (such as myself), began playing the traditional "dirty tricks". We took down Ratensky's sign with the painting of pig's meat processing and swapped it with the sign of a *hasidic* merchant; we took the wooden front steps from many houses, so that when the resident got up early in the morning his first step out would be onto the ground; we woke up people for *slikhes*; shouted "fire!", "thief!", and other silliness.

We arrived in Ostrolenke on the first train the next morning. We went directly to the military commission. I with my "symbol" went confidently to the military doctor, who examines me carefully from all sides and looks at me when he notices the requested mark on my face.

His going over me so long and so thoroughly really did call up

[Page 360]

a certain suspicion in me. I was almost certain that he could not find the smallest thing in me that he could misinterpret and he let me go (in the end I was completely healthy, without the smallest flaw). But I tried to drive away those doubts because 100 dollars is no small matter.

When I later received my confirmation, I stopped ruminating and philosophizing and saw that the deed was done. My acceptance into the military was not nothing – Category "A".

Of course, my father traveled straight to the "fixer" with a "willow branch" and many complaints about being led astray and so on. But go talk to the wall, it was all over. In short, it remained that the money was still on deposit and that he would "fix" me as a *nadlitshbovi*, that is, that I would not have to serve but remain a contingent. Also good!

But I did not go around as a happy fellow for long. A few months later I received a call-up notice from the military to present myself at the 81st Regiment in Grodne. I turned the notice on all sides, perhaps there was a mistake I thought, but no. It was all written in detail. Even the exact date and hour when I had to be in the barracks. My father went again to the "fixer" in Ostrolenke and this time with a bigger "willow branch"! But you can protest but it won't do any good, because a third scheme with new illusions could not be considered now. There was no alternative than to take the money back and keep quiet about it.

My father could not let this go by quietly and he began to investigate what had happened. It appeared that that "fixer" had collected a number of 100 dollar deposits for each military commission. Someone was often freed from service because of some weak physical condition and he kept the whole sum in his pocket. If there was a "patient" who was not freed, he still tried his luck to "fix" him as a *nadlitshbovi*, because keeping some as a contingent was also not an unusual occurrence. So, he also kept the deposit in such a case. And if the person was not released, neither here nor here, he gave back the deposited money. It was said that after each commission there always remained a good number of "clients" who were released or were over the number needed.

Possibly with a smaller number of "patients" he could share with the doctors and release only those who really did have some questionable condition but, with someone like me, without the smallest flaw, and especially in these times, he had to "work with his own hands", without partners and drew a fine livelihood from it, because what did he have to risk?

[Page 361]

As opposed to not taking any deposits! And if he had to give some "unsuccessful" clients their money back, he was certainly an honest person!

And I? I served the whole one and a half years in the Grodne 81st Regiment, like a fool.

Shtetl Pranksters

by A. Goworower, America

Translated by Tina Lunson

The pranks that we played in the *shtetl* in our childhood caused people many concerns but were of many flavors. Our "gang" ferreted out with our sharp little noses the weaknesses of this or that householder, found the "blister" where the shoe pinched and tried with all our might to make the sparks fly.

So, for example, we found out that Yisroel-Shepsl got a special pleasure from reciting *kadish* after praying in the study house. Therefore he remained sitting in the *shul* at night after the *mayriv* service until the last prayers and "knocked back" another *kadish*.

Yisroel-Shepsl was a Jew of 70 years, thin and tall, a long, drawn face with a small, thin nose, adorned with a sparse grey beard. In his young years he had worked as a shoemaker, making boots and selling them at the fairs. As he got old, his hands began to tremble and his eyes to tear and he gave up his trade and sat in the study house the whole day, in the summer in the large entrance hall and winter by the big, caulked ovens, at which he warmed his old, aching bones. He sat languishing all day, without a sign of life, not moving a limb, only when the cantor for *minke-mayriv* started the *oleynu* did he become lively at all, stand up to his whole height, stretch out his quavering throat and pronounce *yisgadol v'yiskadeysh* with much enjoyment.

We, the little gang, used to while away the long winter nights in the study house, supposedly to study a little Talmud; in reality, though, as soon as the last householder left the study house we began celebrating our "indolent fun", smoking cigarettes, jumping over the tables, or

[Page 362]

lifting a bench with our teeth. Yisroel-Shepsl stayed late at the *shul*. He did not hurry home to his cold, deteriorated little house. Better to sit by the warm oven in the study house and nap.

As soon as we saw the Yisroel Shepsl was sleeping, one of us would stand behind his shoulders and shout, "*v'ne'emar, v'haye es ha'shem, l'melekh al kol ha'orets...ha'shem eykhod*". And then someone else would call out "*Rebi* Yisroel-Shepsl! A *kadish*!" Yisroel-Shepsl stood up, stretched out his long neck and swayed deeply: "*yisgadel v'yiskadeysh*" and we crumpled into laughter. Until he went to sleep again and we would repeat the whole scene.

We kept up that "business" until one time, in the middle of such a *kadish*, Khayim-Leyb the ritual slaughterer came into *shul*. When he saw how Yisroel-Shepsl was cranking out a *kadish* and we were rolling with laughter, he made a very big fuss, "You insolent rascals!" he shouted, "God in heaven, worthless!" He threatened to tell the *Rov* about this. Then we left old Yisroel-Shepsl in peace.

The joke on old Yekl the butcher was more serious. He was also a Jew of 70 years, small, thin, skin and bones. He was the founder of a dynasty of butchers who provided the town with kosher meat. The old Reb Yekl in his younger years possessed a lot of energy and led the town by its nose. In his old age, his children and grandchildren had taken over that business and he was a regular figure at the study house. He sat by the oven and recited psalms, smoking his big pipe.

Although he was old and weak, people were still afraid to start up with him. First of all, no one had forgotten his former power, even though no trace of that strength was left. But secondly, his "mouth-piece" still functioned with the same steam as before. He could still deliver a stream of curses and one never knew where a door would open. He was a special master in that trade. So our gang did not like that so much.

But one evening when we were puffing away on cigarettes, he gave us a tongue lashing and threatened to tell our parents about us. We decided to buy him off with a portion of tobacco. Each day we had to bring some LO-YAKHRUTS tobacco for his pipe, so he would keep our secret. But we could not sate him. He was a passionate smoker and consumed a lot of tobacco. And his appetite seemed to grow with eating, becoming more and more. Our small change could not suffice to satisfy him and leave anything left for us. We decided, therefore, to wean him off of smoking. But how? We

[Page 363]

thought up a plan. We mixed a little gunpower from the caps for children's toy rifles into his portion of tobacco and gave it to him to smoke. We just sat back at a distance to see what would happen.

Yekl filled his pipe generously, lit it, and sat himself grandly by the oven, putting out large clouds of smoke from his mouth. He was so much enjoying the aromatic tobacco that he closed his eyes and lost himself in old memories, twirling the end of his moustache with great pleasure.

Suddenly – BANG! A shot was heard that, in the acoustics of the *shul*, resounded like the boom of a canon. The pipe went flying way far to the Torah ark and the old Yekl, poor thing, sprang up from the table in terror.

Anyhow, he shot off a few curses to the address of the Polish government and its tobacco monopoly, in case some help may be forthcoming.

When we finally recovered from laughing, we asked him with innocent faces, "Reb Yekl, what happened?"

"A black year on the Polish state for selling such tobacco. Tfoo on them! I was almost killed, heaven forbid! As they should be killed on some fine moonlit night." That was Yekl's response.

In short, our plan was totally effective. After several "explosions" Yekl stopped smoking.

* * *

The case of the false alarm could really have led to serious consequences. We did, indeed, protect ourselves for a long time, not telling anyone the secret of who had been the initiators of that "prank".

It was in the last years before the Second World War. Poland was earnestly preparing for a war and broadened its war industry. The population was taught how to protect themselves during an air attack. Our town planned for such an air attack by the enemy and the mayor had big placards nailed up, on which it was announced with giant letters that the attack would be carried out on the coming Monday. To that end a piece of iron would be hung on a pole in the market square. "When you hear the gong" the placard continued, "the population must quickly hide in their houses and remain there until the signal comes that all is calm."

The promised "alarm" in the town called up great observation. A whole week prior, little gatherings of people stood in the market and debated about the big "air attack" to come on Monday. Some acted as strategists for Poland and for Austria, pronounced their ideas about the 42-millimeter canon that the "Kraut thief" had and how the aeroplane mechanics would work in the air. In the trade unions, in *shul* and in the ritual bath, everywhere, that was the topic of the day.

[Page 364]

And it was evening and it was morning and Monday the "day of judgement" arrived. Since the placards did not state the time of the alarm, everyone got up very early. The men went to *shul* to pray with the first *minyen,* whatever happened, one should at least have finished their prayers; and the women ran quickly to buy baked goods and milk, so they would have something to grab for the tummies of the little children.

As we savored the tumult over the alarm, a wild thought occurred to us. We could hurry up the alarm and carry it out ourselves – said and done! One member of our gang brought a bell from his father's iron mongery; another went with him upstairs to the women's *shul*, and we all stood in different corners in the study house downstairs. The plan was that as soon as the bell rang, we would run to the door from all sides and make a lot of noise.

Soon the cantor began the loud *shmone-esre* and right after the *kedushe*, the bell suddenly rang and echoed. We took off running through *shul* like poisoned mice and made a terrible commotion. In the great confusion no one noticed that the bell ringing was coming from the women's *shul*. Everyone was certain that the alarm was from outdoors. The congregation began quickly putting away their *tfiln*, pulling off their *taleysim*, and shoving their way to the door. Some leapt through the windows with their *taleysim* still on their shoulders and raced in panic through the market to their houses.

When the people in the market saw the panic and the wild running, they quickly closed their shutters, closed their doors and ran away. Women shouted hysterically, "*Gevald!*" "Where are the children?" "*Vey iz mir!*" "Where is Shprintse?" "Where is Dvore – someone save her!"

The gentiles who lived around the periphery also followed the example of the Jews – closed their doors and shutters and went down to the cellar. Eyewitnesses reported that they themselves saw the police commandant run like an unyoked ox to seek protection from the air attack.

The opera was discovered after a whole hour of lying in the cellars. No airplane came and no one heard the announcing alarm. People became impatient, sticking just their noses outdoors, then pushing out their bodies to look into the sky – nothing there!

Only later did people realize that it had been the work of pranksters. The police commandant almost had apoplexy because of the annoyance. He offered a large cash reward for revealing the "criminal".

To our great joy, no one besides us ever knew who had made the false alarm.

("*Der amerikaner*", 8 November 1957.)

[Page 365]

Teaching an In-law a Lesson

by A. Goworower, America

Translated by Tina Lunson

Avreml was from boyhood considered a genius. His father, a fine, respected proprietor in the town, took pride in his accomplished son and always related the pinnacles of wisdom and novel interpretations by his little man, to his friends. He hoped, the father, that his son would become a great *rov* among Jews and did not stint with money for tuition fees. Avreml's teachers were also at a loss for enough words to praise their genius of a pupil. But they were silent about the prankish jokester part that the little genius had.

Small of stature with red little cheeks and small sharp eyes that restlessly moved around, Avreml roamed the streets of the *shtetl*, walking with his head swaying, thinking up ways to play a trick on someone. One *Peysakh* at the *seyder*, when the *rov* opened the door for Eliahu the Prophet, he stretched his hand with a long walking stick through the open door. One late Friday night, he stood at old Avrom-Yosl's window and imitated the voice of his cow. The old Avrom-Yosl, *nebekh*, got up from bed in his underclothes and went outside the house to look for his *lakishke* who meanwhile was sleeping quietly in her stall.

After he was *bar-mitsve* his father sent him to study in the Lomzshe *Yeshiva*. There, he thought, his old dream would be realized, that Avreml would become a great scholar, he would make a rabbinic marriage match, and he would have a son who was a great *rov* in Yisroel.

What happened was quite different. Avreml's restless essence did not allow him to sit in a *yeshiva*, it drew him out to the streets. There he met some friends. He read newspapers and books and became a Zionist.

The *yeshiva* was too small for him. The director looked at him askance. After a short while Avreml came back home to Goworowo. Supposedly he had already learned a lot from the *rov*, but his head was just not intended for study. So meanwhile he just thought about whom and how to play such a prank that the whole town would talk about it.

Avreml did not "work" alone. He had a whole gang

[Page 366]

of rascals who revered him and obediently carried out his plans. The "general headquarters" were located in the Vurke *shtibl* where he ostensibly went to study.

There all the pranks were invented, the plans worked out and the assignments distributed. When everything was "right and ready" they learned a little more.

Avreml always had his alibis ready. He was never caught red-handed, although everyone knew that the "little dew and rain" (what people called him because of his small stature) was the cause of all the trouble. Even the suffering "victims" themselves forgave him in the end for his dirty tricks, because everyone valued his fine learning, knowing that a genius had a clever mind, and one cannot have a lot of resentment for him.

His father tried to have an effect on him with goodness and with anger, but nothing helped. Avreml was truly enchanted with the matters at hand. He became very active in the Zionist Organization and worked for the *Keren-kayemet l'yisroel.*

During that time his pranks were mostly political. He had taken on the grievance that certain *Kana'im* had disrupted the Zionist work in the town and so would take out his revenge on them.

One of the big *Kana'im* who fought passionately with the Zionists was Iser the miller. There was a case when Iser was hosting a wedding in his house and as the usual case, members came to collect for the *K.K.L.*; he tore up the "flowers", snatched the blue-and-white charity box and literally drove the collectors away.

Iser was a sharp Ger *hasid* with a thick, wide, red beard, with thick grown-together eyebrows that half covered his eyes and gave an angry appearance to his countenance. He was a taciturn Jew, not looking audaciously in anyone's eyes, but was very stubborn and a "boiler" when he was enraged. Woe to those who made him mad. Iser lived outside the town, up on the *Probostvo*, where, together with his brother Note, he had a big steam operated mill and large warehouses full of grain. They were very rich. Iser had already grown children, among them a daughter who was now being presented to marriage brokers.

Avreml could not pass quietly over the chicaneries that he and his gang were ripening for the Zionists' opponents. He decided to pour out all his wrath on Iser, especially for destroying the flower collecting by the *K.K.L.* It should be remembered by his grandchildren.

Avreml took revenge on him in the following way. He had a large rabbinic wedding cards printed, in which it was stated that he, Iser, thanks to the beloved Creator, had lived to see the marriage of his daughter the maiden (the name here), with her chosen one, the

[Page 367]

preeminent (the name of the *haftore* here). The wedding, the printed card went on to state, "would take place, God willing, in a good and auspicious hour on Friday, Torah portion [not revealed in text] some certain day in Nisn. All friends and acquaintances are invited to come and rejoice on the *simkhe* and with God's help at their children's wedding may he, Iser, reciprocate them with the same."

That Friday was to fall on the eve of *shabes ha'gadol* in Passover, the first of April of the early 1930s. Avreml sent the wedding cards to all the many branches of the family all over the country.

Besides that, Avreml sent letters to the famous wedding musicians in Vishkove and Ostrolenke and to two well -known wedding entertainers that they not forget to come to celebrate the afternoon of the wedding, for which they would be lavishly rewarded. The entire action was held in strict secrecy from the townspeople.

That Friday (the First of April) turned out to be a beautiful spring day. A clear blue sky spread over the *shtetl*. The sun kindly warmed the houses around the market square and drew the people in them out onto the street. Along the wooden walks in front of the shops, the shopkeepers sat and warmed their chilled bones after a hard winter. The dogs laid stretched out lazily on their backs near the butcher shops. A cheerless quiet flowed over the *shtetl*.

Suddenly, from Bridge Street came pounding in with a clatter, two wagons with the famous Vishkove orchestra and went straight through the square to *Tifle* Street. Before there was even time to start to chew on that wild event, the sound of music came from Ostrolenke Street. That was the Ostrolenke orchestra, already playing on their instruments, sailing smoothly into town. Nothing much! Iser the miller was marrying off a daughter.

Soon after all that came the carts and *gumkes* from the train station, crammed with guests dressed to the nines, wives in silk, fur-lined coats holding children by the hand; men in long heavy coats, fur hats and round hats, and merry young men who had already drunk a *l'khayim* on the train.

"*Mazl tov!*" they shouted to the town Jews who stood in little groups around the square.

The crowd opened their mouths, shrugged their shoulders, having no inkling what was going on.

Seeing that everything was traveling toward *Tifle* Street, the crowd set out in that direction. Now they could see that the whole parade was going into Iser the miller's yard. Iser stood with his arms spread out, his red beard disheveled, not knowing what to do; here he was surrounded with joy, with his relatives and friends, kissing them, and then shouting and angry with the musicians, "What the hell do you want from me?"

[Page 368]

"What kind of visitation is this on me?" And they shouted loudly, "Mazl tov, in-law! God-willing to all your children!"

Anyhow, all the guests had to remain with Iser for *Shabes*, because there was now no way to travel back. And he had to settle with the musicians and the town of Goworowo had a merry *simkhe*.

Reb Iser promised his grandchildren, as of now, not to pester the Zionists anymore.

("*Der amerikaner*", Number 24, 24 June 1957.)

[Page 368]

Two Episodes

by Yankev Gurka, Israel

Translated by Tina Lunson

A Compromise with the *Rov*

It was in 1920, when the Bolsheviks were withdrawing from Poland. During the time that they had been in Goworowo, all the Zionist and social activities had been halted. And the library had stopped functioning. Whoever wanted to read a book had to travel all the way to Ruzshan. We, who were then among the young folk, took the initiative to reconstitute a library. We procured a legitimization from the regional office in Ostrolenke with no difficulty. We were also successful in assembling a few hundred books. But the hard part was finding a site. We were afraid to rent some kind of apartment because of the chicaneries of the very religious Jews. In the end we did rent an apartment from Avrom'ke the glazier on the Long Street. We quickly put together an administration with Leybl Kersh as chairman, Etke Fridman as librarian, Yankev Zamlson as treasurer, and so on. Almost every evening we exchanged books. Two or three times a week Binyamin Ginzburg gave lectures on science topics there. We also presented theater exhibitions.

We carried on our activities for a long time in that manner, until a group of fanatic Jews went to the town *Rov* and told him that we were meeting together with men and women and they must see that something be done, if it is not too late already.

[Page 369]

At first they took Avrom'ke the glazier to task about why he rented us the space. They even threatened to put him in official ostracization. But Avrom'ke had bound us with a contract and we could not be released from it; but then they came up with an ingenious idea. On one wintry Friday afternoon, they took the doors off and the windows out of our library's apartment and put us out of business.

Sitting, from right to left: Yitskhak Kuperman, Yankev Gurka and Kalman Klepfish
Standing: Zelig Hertsberg, Meyshe Dovid Malavani and Matisyahu Oyslender

We resented that deed very much. Promptly the next morning, early on *Shabes*, we went to the study house and did not allow the praying to continue until they would give us back the doors and windows. Right after the morning service Binyumin went up to the cantor's stand and began to speak and the others stood by the doors and did not let anyone out. Binyumin drew his "sermon" out especially long and that caused a lot of turmoil in the *shul*. Those praying saw that they would not be able to continue their prayers or to get out the doors to go home. But, since we blocked the exit they had no alternative but to jump through the windows and leave us alone. Then we decided to continue to stand up for ourselves; disrupt their praying as long as it took to give us back the doors and the windows.

The *Rov* was a shrewd Jew and he quickly saw that he would get nowhere with us with anger. He ordered us through Avremele the beadle to come to him with a delegation from the management. We chose the following persons: Leyb Kersh, Meyshe Dovid Malavani, Kalman Klepfish, Yitskhak Kuperman and the writer of these lines. The *Rov*

[Page 370]

gave us to understand that we absolutely must not have boys and girls meeting together and so on. We laid out our complaints, in short, and after a long transaction session arrived at a compromise. The females may come only to exchange books and not to stay there, and on Friday we must turn on the lamp before candle lighting time. With that our conflict ended. We received our windows and doors back along with peace in *Yisroel*.

It is worth mentioning that both of the *Rov's* daughters themselves, Rokhl and Zelde, borrowed books from us.

Reprimanding a Hooligan

This event unfolded in 1936. The time of the [Pro-Polish anti-Jewish *owszem*] "Yes" movement, and the picketing of Jewish businesses was already a daily manifestation. Even in our *shtetl* the antisemitism was already out in the open.

I was working for Yoel'ke the baker. One Sunday night I am standing in his shop and I look out the window onto the market square. Suddenly I see a drunken hooligan, dressed in his Sunday best and haranguing some Jews. He even pulled out a knife and was measuring Jewish beards. The hooligan even warned that some friends were coming to help him and they would stab all the Jews. It was easy to see that there would soon be an uproar in town, the streets were empty, and people were locked in their houses, sleeping.

The situation enraged me. I go out in the street and approach the scoundrel. It looks like this is Adam Shperling from Vurke, an incidental acquaintance of mine. When I made a remark about his behavior and told him, "If you are drunk, go sleep it off", he only replied, "Mangy Jew" and swiped at me with the knife.

I had been right in the middle of my work, my hands smeared with rye dough and holding an empty flour sack. I did not ponder for long and hearing the hooligan's response I "honored" him with the sack in the eyes, gave him a few blows with my hands thereby smearing his new suit and then ran away. In great shame the scoundrel also disappeared immediately.

But that did not last. Within half an hour he came back with a reinforcement of another five gentile ruffians. They came straight into Yosel'ke's shop looking for me, but, of course, I was not there. I had been off the street for a long time, being afraid of revenge. But it was worth it – reprimanding a hooligan!

[Page 371]

Wouldn't You Know It

(A True Story)

by Meyshe Sarne, Israel

Translated by Tina Lunson

Hoshane-rabe at night in the *shtetl*. Up River Lane blows an unfriendly wind. Light shines out from the gaps in *suke* walls. Jews, some dressed in white, are having a bite to eat after evening prayers. They will soon hurry back to *shul* to recite *tikun*. It is a holiday mood mixed with sadness. Not a small thing! *Hoshane-rabe* can be compared to *yon-kiper*. Heaven splits open and people lie there, awaiting the last stamp on their petition.

A pale moon is reflected in the little Hirsh River. Yankev Shleyme the blacksmith is outdoors to see if the moon makes a shadow of his tall, thin body. Something in the shadow he does not like. A bad sign. Who knows if he will get through the year in one piece.

Something makes a little splash in the stream. Yankev Shleyme shudders. He recalls what Beytsalel Yosl in the *khumesh* group taught, that on *Hoshane-rabe* night the dead swim around by the light of the moon, in order to get salvation from their sins.

A white figure suddenly appears before his eyes. Yankev Shleyme's mind becomes very confused.

"*A gut yon-tov* Reb Yankev Shleyme! I am Mashe Leye the wife of the glazier, your neighbor. My husband wanted me to ask you if you could wake him at dawn to go pray. He is not feeling well."

Yankev Shleyme had a hard time catching his breath.

"Good, yes, I will wake him soon."

Before dawn, before the rooster had even crowed, Yankev Shleyme knocked on the neighbor's window. He was glowing with fever and could hardly stand up. Mashe Leye quickly dressed and left for the *shul* with Yankev Shleyme.

Darkness enveloped the *shtetl*. It was still very early. A farmer's wagon loaded with hay appeared on the Market Street. Yankev Shleyme wanted to buy it and so did Mashe Leye. They began haggling. Yankev Shleyme became angry. A whole night without sleep, with empty dreams, he gave Mashe Leye a shove. Mashe Leye then grabbed a piece of wood from the wagon

[Page 372]

and hit Yankev Shleyme on the head with it. Yankev Shleyme's head spun around and he fell over in a faint. Violence! People woke up. People ran over. Mashe Leye disappeared without a trace.

The children of both sides came running up. Then they started, unfortunately, slugging one another like the *goyim*. It was a miracle that the *Rov* arrived just then. He was on his way to *shul* and he drove them apart.

But what! They fought for the whole of *Hashone-rabe*. First one side started it, then the other side. Faces bruised and beaten. Neighbors had no power to pull the opponents apart. Yankev Shleyme's heirs shouted, "Where is Mashe Leye?"

Evening approaches. *Shmini-atseres* is coming. River Lane forgets the story a little. It is a holiday after all. *Hasidim* still dance with the Torah, even into *Shmini-atseres*. Light shone through the windows. People heard *kidish* being made but did not see any light from Yankev Shleyme's and Mashe Leye's rooms were dark. It seems as though something is in the offing.

In the morning, early on *Shmini-atseres*, they found Mashe Leye dead. Did she suffer apoplexy from aggravation or, as some others said, they found signs of a beating on her body and her tongue was badly bitten. A sign. Yankev Shleyme's sons promptly disappeared. People had seen them leaving for America. Sadness in the town. There was no feeling for *Simkhes-teyre*. Children told stories about the dead, about demons and ghosts.

A few days later, Yeshaye Yom-tov left his little son in his spice shop on River Lane and she, Yeshaye Yom-tov's wife, was washing clothes in the pantry. Suddenly the boy screamed *Shema Yisroel*! and fainted. When he came to, he told a fearful story. No more and no less – Mashe Leye came into the shop and looked at him with huge, inexpressive eyes.

Then they found other witnesses, adult people, who had seen a white figure with a strange wide hat, like a head of cabbage, strolling the streets at night. Fear descended onto the *shtetl.* People inspected their *mezuzes*. They started sending messengers to the cemetery to beg forgiveness from Mashe Leye.

Yeshaye Yom-tov went to the *Rov*, "*Rebi!* Save us!" he yammered. "When night comes life is not a life…"

The *Rov* thought a little, and told him, "The next time that someone sees that figure, he must not fail, but grab it by the collar and look to see who it is."

That same evening, a group of youths were walking on the Broad Street.

[Page 373]

Suddenly, the white figure ran by. They remembered the *Rov's* words. They grasped one another's hands and ran after the figure.

Finally at Mud Street, out of breath, they grabbed the figure. Do you know who it was? Henrik the laborer, from Felix the gentile slaughterer's shop. He was enjoying playing a prank and scaring the little Jews.

Town Curiosities

by Khone Vaysbord, Colombia

Translated by Tina Lunson

A Corpse – A "Newbie"

Shmilke *Khizik* was not one of the big hotshots in town. Regarding livelihood, it was usually "narrow" with him. He was always a day short each week in being able to make *Shabes*. Indeed, his wife helped him to cover the "hole" in whatever way she could. In each season she sought some supplementary income. In winter she was busy plucking feathers and in summer, with picking fruit. She got better revenue in the summer *shav* season. She would get up at dawn and walk a kilometer or two outside the town, gather *shav* leaves in a sack and then sell it door to door. Here I will tell of an episode from such a *shav* gathering.

It was a summery day in about 1908. As usual, she, Shmilke's wife got up before dawn when it was still dark and went out on the road with an empty sack to gather *shav*. This time she chose the area near the Jewish cemetery, that was her idea. She walked bent over and gathered and gathered the sorrel leaves and she did not notice how close she was creeping to the cemetery.

As you might recall, at the very entrance to the cemetery there were the two tall gravestones of Itsl Mints and his wife, may they rest in peace. Shmilke's wife, seeing that she was now almost in the "good place", wanted to quickly retreat, because one must not gather from that place. But in her great hurry and conscience-lessness, her head got a bit confused and then she evidently saw that the two white stones were moving and that they were actually – corpses may God have mercy.

[Page 374]

She screamed out "*Shema Yisroel*" and started to run away. But her dress was caught on a small tree. She wanted to run forward but she could not, just as if the corpses were holding her back. She cried for help but go yell for help when there is no living soul around.

In short, she lost that whole sack of *shav* and she dragged herself home neither dead or alive. It took her some time to recover herself. Once she had rested a little, she told her husband the whole story. She also added that it was now clear to her why so many little children were dying in the town, because the corpses are walking freely around in the cemetery.

Shmilke, hearing this story from his dearest, ran to the current town *Rov*, the old *Rov* Botshan, and told him of the events with his wife. He begged him to make a great stir about it and to do something to halt the plague of children's deaths.

The *Rov* tried to calm him and made little of the whole story. He told him in the kindest way, that when someone dies and is buried, they cannot move any more and that the whole incident did not make any sense.

But Shmilke held his own. "*Rebi*", he said "I myself saw my wife's torn dress, which resulted from struggling with the corpses. Maybe" he shouted, "that very corpse was a new-comer and does not know the old laws."

God is Yearning for a Bit of Psalms

This was, if I am not mistaken, after the First World War. The town was being gradually rebuilt, and also the small wooden study house was already finished.

Once on a *Simkhes-teyre* afternoon, I am walking past the same study house and hear the sound of a sobbing melody, "Happy is the man who does not walk in the counsel of the wicked…". The thing intrigues me, thinking, who can that be? I am not lazy, I go inside and see that Yisroel Hersh is sitting with a psalter and reading the chapter in that sad tune.

"Reb Yisroel Hersh," I call out to him, "now on *Simkhes-teyre* when the world is rejoicing, merry, dancing in the streets, you are sitting here and reciting psalms, and even with such a mournful melody?"

"Yes," he answers me, "do you not know then, that, especially now, the Master of the Universe is longing for some psalms?"

* * *

[Page 375]

A Personal "Demon"

This happened on one dark winter night in the early 1920s. It was certainly after midnight and Binyumin Ginzburg was walking alone by the market and heard from a distance how someone was beating wash at the river.

If a simple Jew had heard that he would not have pondered over it but run off to the *Rov*, wakened him up, called a minyen of Jews and recited psalms. Because who could be beating laundry in the middle of the night, if not some demon, spirit or nogoodnik? But Binyumin was a worldly man of today, a conscious and enlightened young man to whom the thought of devils rarely occurred. He was generally, simply intrigued with what householder that could be, who had chosen the middle of the night to wash the laundry.

With no fear he walked in the direction that the sound of the pounding he was hearing. When he arrived at the place and looked hard into the darkness. He did not believe his eyes. Instead of a Jewess, as he had imagined, he saw a Jew with a big beard who was beating his wash on a stone with a *keyanke*.

"What is with you, Reb Meyshe?" Binyumin called out. "So late at night, you are sitting here doing your wash?"

"What do you want?" Reb Meyshe answered him. "Should I sit here in the middle of the day and wash along with all the women?"

Sh. Ts.

An outing on the Hirsh River

[Page 376]

Shleyme Akive, the Town Fool

by A. B. Shoshoni, Israel

Translated by Tina Lunson

There was no Jewish *shtetl* in Poland without its town fool. Just as a town had its own untrained doctor, bathhouse attendant, night watchman and midwife, so they had to find a town nutter, who belonged to the whole community and the public had to care for his subsistence.

Usually, the town fool was a half idiot, a melancholic, or some wild creature who did harm to the residents. Goworowo was lucky. Her town fool was of course good spirited, smiling, sang as he spoke, and was very useful by carrying water to people's houses, being responsible for himself and would do a favor for anyone.

Shleyme Akive Beserman was born in Goworowo of a fine respectable family. His father Reb Leybl, an honest Jew with a long white beard and a knowledge of the holy books was a teacher in town and a shofar blower at the big *shul*. His brother Avieyzer was a *rov* in Kamarove. His other brother Tsadok considered himself a philosopher, read literature and loved to discuss things.

As Shleyme Akive himself explained it; he fell from an attic as a child and since then his brain has been addled. His father dragged him around to all the doctors in the region. But nothing helped. It is possible that his supposition was correct. It could also be that he was born "touched in the head". One thing is clear, his father used every means to help him. So Shleyme Akive was very devoted to his father. After the passing of his father (*hSevet sav-reysh-ayin"giml*), Shleyme Akiva once went to the cemetery and tried to dig him up out of the grave. He wanted to will him back into the home.

Shleyme Akive stood for conscription back in the Russia era, before the First World War. The military authorities suspected that he had a special kind of disability, so that he should have been freed from military service. Yet they did not release him but sent him to one of their hospitals for observation. After six months they finally did release him and he came back

[Page 377]

to town well-fed, rested, happy and beaming with great joy.

Shleyme Akive poses for photographs during his work

Shleyme Akive had a phenomenal memory. He remembered old stories from childhood on and recognized people whom he had seen only once in his life and that years ago. He had a separate specialization for remembering *taleysim*. Among dozens of *taleysim* he could tell to whom each *talis* belonged and never made a mistake. There were incidents on *Simkhes-teyre* when various *taleysim* got mixed up and their owners themselves could not tell them apart. They sent for Shleyme Akive and he gave each person his *talis* without hesitation.

Shleyme Akive was also a great master in eating. His stomach could accommodate loads of food, literally without limit. He did not know any satiety. In general, he was honest and never touched anyone's property. But food was different. Here everything belonged to him. Woe to the Jewish wife who set the *Shabes* fish dish in the window to cool. Shleyme Akive would sneak it away and eat the entire kilo of fish and even two. Afterwards he just folded his hands behind him, self-assuredly strolled around the market square and sang to himself, "Aye was not Yente's fish delicious, a treat for the soul!"

[Page 378]

More than once the housewife discovered her misfortune only after hearing Shleyme Akive singing. Still, no one was angry with him. Everyone knew that if they left the fish on the windowsill without a guard, it automatically belonged to Shleyme Akive.

In his free hours, after delivering water to his clients, Shleyme Akive sat comfortably in the study house by the oven or in the Aleksander *shtibl*, napped a little or hummed a tune to himself. His good memory also served him in remembering the Jewish wordless melodies. He had a good talent for singing and remembered every song that he heard, like a real talent. It was enough to ask him, "What melody did Yisroel Leyb sing the *yetsue* to?" and he would answer right away and sing it. He often talked to himself or carried out a whole, endless dispute with himself.

On *Shabes* he ate a good feast with Yeshaye Shmuel Nosn. Afterwards he went around the houses and caught a bite of stuffed pastry, a little noodle pudding. Always a piece of *khale* was a good thing.

To do a favor for a person or help someone carry a heavy parcel, Shleyme Akive was always ready, even in the middle of the night, and not, heaven forbid, for any reward. The townspeople loved him. If he got sick, everyone cared for him, he lacked nothing in the *shtetl.* Once a peasant, a vicious person from a nearby village, threw him down several steps and left him there unconscious. The whole *shtetl* then went "off its wheels", wanting to punish the peasant. Porters and butchers "honored" him with a dead slug.

Shleyme Akive had his usual hostess in Khaye Zelde Klempner, the tinsmith's wife. That good woman kept him for the sake of the *mitsve*, gave him food, looked after him when he was sick, washed his clothes, and treated him as her own child. Thus he was very attached to her.

Shleyme Akive was murdered during the war years.

[Page 379]

Town Folklore

by M. Rimon, Israel

Translated by Tina Lunson

Names and Nicknames

It was rare to find a person in a *shtetl* who did not have a nickname in addition to his name and family name. The nicknames were given out in several categories. Most of them were according to the trade of the person in question. The family name was generally useless. It only served for the tax office and the letter carrier. So people were called, Yoel'ke the baker, Velvl the clock-maker, Ayzik the butcher, Zaynvl the shoemaker, Yosl the harness maker, Berish the peddler, Yankl carpenter, Leybke bath house attendant, Yisroel Leyb teacher, Simion wheelwright, Avrom Yosl the blacksmith, Note the miller, Yisriske the ritual slaughterer, Aba wagon driver, Mikhal the bender, Yankev Hirsh porridge maker, Avrom Yitsik *kvas* maker, Hershl candymaker, Bertshe tailor, Yosl Velvl the tinsmith, Khayim the tenant farmer, Dan the porter, Yosl hairdresser, Khaye the fisher, and so on. It also happened that the trade alone was still too little and an "addition" was applied. Because it could happen that there would be two blacksmiths with the same name in town, people had to distinguish them, the cold blacksmith, or the cold tailor, the cold shoemaker, the cold glazier and so on. That meant a bad artisan, without talent, without taste – a simple botcher. A few were referred to by their titles, like Shaye the Councilman, Khayim the Magistrate.

There was a category of nicknaming according to one's ancestry. That did not have to be a man or man's name. Thus, some were called Khane Reytse's, Yankl the Zavelikhe's, Mendl Tsipe's and so on. The women, after whose names the men were called, lived in a patriarchal style. So it was with the above mentioned Reytse, a clever woman, to whom many people came for advice. Also popular were Yekhiel Monise's, Shaye Shmuel Nosn's, Avrom'ke Nosn Kalman's, Rokhl Shmuelke's, Bertshe Kalodzsher, Meyshe Hinde's and others.

The physical side of people could decide it, such as the big Mordkhe, the tall Shames, the little Avremele, the small Mayer'l, Avrem'l dew and rain, the locksmith, and others. Some, because of their small stature, were just called Aba'le, Itsele and the like.

[Page 380]

There were also those who had traveled in from other towns. They were named according to the town of their origin; Dovid Ostrover, Velvl the Radzshilover, Meyshe Pashker, Velvl the Brizshnier, Yudl Makover, Velvl the Vengrover, or the Tsherviner shoemaker, the Makover tailor, and so on.

The color of someone's face often played a role, for example, the yellow Ayzik, the black Avremele, the black Dvore and so on. We also had some regular kosher family names like Gemora, Mishnayos and Tehilim.

A few women were called by the trade of their dead husbands. For example, Alte the carpenter'ke, Khaye Zelde the tinsmith'ke, Malke the capmaker'ke. Sore Gitl the blacksmith'ke, the chairman'ke and the like.

All these nicknames were to distinguish, not to elevate or put down. But there were nicknames that did indeed include a tone of insult. From a pure ethnographic, scientific standpoint they should be noted. Since I do not want to dishonor anyone here, what I have presented above will be sufficient, although the gallery is very large.

[Page 380]

Almost a Blood Libel

Translated by Mira Eckhaus

Edited by Tina Lunson

Ha'tsefira number 115, 1887

Goworowo, the 28th of *Iyar*. Yesterday morning a Christian woman came to their house of prayer with her six year old child and he immediately got lost and until the evening they searched for him and could not find him. And a thousand thanks to God, the Christians in our place live at peace with us. With all this, many of them have already said that they heard from their fathers that there was a case in the past that a Christian child was lost and they later found him hanged in the study house and of course even today the Jews may have carried him away and buried him in one of the places to take his blood. All day long the bell rang for the loss of the boy and his mother shouted outside for the lost boy. Until in the evening a Christian from the village of Zabin, which is near our town, came and said that the boy was there because he took the wrong path and when he was asked where he was from, he did not know how to pronounce the name of his town he was from and they assumed that maybe he was from this town. And so, the anger of the Christians subsided.

Well, we are obliged to thank God for the Christian children who are not lost.

Moshe Yehoshua Ginzburg

[Page 381]

Destruction and Mass Murder

On Polish Fields

By Binem Heler, Israel

Translated by Tina Lunson

Binem Heler

On Polish fields – scattered bones;
In old Jewish cemeteries – desolate stones:
Who do they have now?

The dead – this is how they left them.
They lie and are overgrown with grass:
Who will bury them?

Just as they were shot together,
The child wails yet for her mother –
Who will bid her stop?

Just as they were obliterated in the ghetto,
They lie tangled in sand and bricks:
Who will liberate them?

In village and town peace now reigns,
They sing songs and they cook their food,
And laugh as they eat,

And think that no one can waken the dead,
That anything one can cover with earth
Must be forgotten.

[Page 382]

"Although We Are Condemned to Death, We Have Not Lost the Divine Image"

by Dr. Arye Leon Kububi
Chairman of the Board of Yad Vashem – Israel

Translated by Mira Eckhaus

Edited by Tina Lunson

As we commemorate this year the six million who were murdered and the communities of Israel that were destroyed by the Nazis and their helpers, it is appropriate that we learn the lesson of the Holocaust this time in light of the notes and work of the historian of the Warsaw Ghetto, Dr. Emanuel Ringelblum.

What was the force that motivated Ringelblum and his group of assistants from operation *Oneg Shabes* to put down on paper every day, with a diligence that did not let them rest, what they saw and heard, as if this concern to record the tribulations and disasters and pass them on to future generations was the supreme commandment of their lives? It must have been the fact that they considered their action as a higher mission. And indeed we are allowed to see them as the heirs and successors of that "man who foresaw the great evil that was coming upon his people" because, according to Dubnov's definition, we are a people that is "historical at all times" and our historical consciousness stems from the recognition that, beaten, tortured, humiliated, and murdered we are never historical dust and that everything that happens to us has a deep meaning, a meaning for generations.

There was also an immediate goal for the Ringelblum group, which was to try to reveal the Jewish genocide to the world. Recently, the impression that was created is as if the nations did not know, during all the years of the war, about the disaster that befell us. It is true that until June 1942, a wall of silence surrounded the annihilation of our people and that Hitler succeeded in instilling fear in the Allies, lest something bad would happen to their struggle, if they showed interest in the fate of the Jews. But in June that wall was breached and on the 26th of that month, Ringelblum who was listening to a British broadcast, wrote, "In recent weeks, the English radio has continuously brought news about the cruelty towards the Jews of Poland - Chelmno, Vilna, Belzec, etc... we fulfilled our duty... even our death will not be in vain... we discovered the diabolical plan of the hater to destroy Polish Jewry, which he planned to carry out secretly... and if England stands by its word when it threatened retaliatory measures, then maybe we will be saved".

How did Ringelblum and his friends evaluate their lifestyle? We find the answer in an epistle intended for New York that he and Adolf Berman wrote on March 1, 1944, a week before his death, which begins with the shocking lines, "We are writing to you at a time when 95% of Polish Jews have already died in terrible agony" and in which they say, "The slogan of the Jewish social activist group was 'live with dignity and die with dignity'". And how do they detail these words? They single out a section for "the wonderful epic of armed combat, the heroic defense of the Warsaw Ghetto, the great struggle at Bialystok, the battles at Tarnow, Bendin, Czestochowa and other places".

[Page 383]

But they dedicated the main part of the epistle to acts of mutual aid and spiritual work. And so, they say, "[the slogan] was expressed in the widespread cultural action, which developed, despite unprecedented tyranny, hunger and hardship, and it grew in scope and depth, until the martyrdom of Polish Jewry". And so, Ringelblum wrote back in June 1942, without eliminating the shadows, about the acts of corruption and the treason, "And if the world asks, 'What did the people of *Musa Dagh* of the Ghetto Warsaw think, when they understood that death will not pass over them, as it did not pass over the Jewish settlements in the small towns', it will be said – even if we were condemned to death, we have not lost the image of God".

And how did they evaluate their death? Compared to the poor debate, the echoes of which are still heard today, if the deaths of the six million are to be seen as martyrdoms, it is worth bringing Ringelblum's testimony about his death and the death of his family. When it was revealed to him, on Saturday, while he was arrested in the Pawiak prison, about a chance of his salvation without the salvation of his wife and son, he responded, "I would rather die for the sanctification of *Ha'shem* together with them". And just as his family died for the sanctification of God, so all the families of the extinct people died for the sanctification of God. Ringelblum knew that the overwhelming majority of the six million, by refusing to give up human dignity, by identifying with the fate of their people, by devoting their remaining days to spiritual values and good deeds, would remain bundled in the bundle of our nation's eternal life.

A monument to the heroes of Warsaw Ghetto
(In the front – Mordkhe Govortshik)

[Page 384]

"I Seek My Brother"

by Yedidiye Frenkel, Israel

Yiddish translated by Tina Lunson

Hebrew translated and annotated by Jerrold Landau

With a heavy heart and with a burden on my soul, I traveled to Poland with the delegation from the State of Israel to the twentieth *yortsayt* of the Warsaw Ghetto Uprising, to search the remains of the great tragic fire, remnants of the great Polish *Judentum*, of the millions of martyrs and reified. Old and young, women and children, brilliant scholars and saints, rabbis and teachers, the devout and people of deeds, wise men of the Talmud and simple Jews, the honest and pure, working and laboring Jews, poets and guides, people of intelligence, heroes and dreamers, creators and warriors – all of that which the Nazi hoards murdered, burned, suffocated, gassed and wiped out from the world.

After thirty years of my leaving Poland I came to seek, if not my brothers, so to say, then the graves of my brothers! But even that, those the savages did not leave us. Their ashes are sifted and spread over the former death camps; the earth soaked with their blood has been plowed under; the schools and study houses mostly in ruins; the gravestones that told the thousand year history, a thousand years of great creative and intellectually rich Jewish life, they also are no more, they serve as pavers for the Polish highways.

Yes! As the prophet Yermiahu lamented, "The break is as big as the sea, who could heal it?" Yes! As big as the sea and deep as the sea and also as cruel as the sea! A catastrophe to the land, a destroying fire, an explosion, an earthquake; everything leaves some trace that something existed here, some lived and breathed here, but when there is a catastrophe over the sea, it is many times more tragic, because

[Page 385]

this was a ship of people that breathed and lived, with ambitions, with goals, with suffering, each one a whole world, and in a few minutes it is sunk to the bottom, and the sea, as if nothing had happened, flows on, plays with its flounces in the sun's colors, splashing its luminous waves, changing its blue colors, exactly as if, just a minute ago, a horrible tragedy was not played out, as just a few minutes ago, a mother and her young children did not choke on their last breath with a suffocating cry of distress.

That cruelty of the sea is the most terrible part of the tragedy of the *khurbn*. And the depth of the tragedy encountered! That Jewish ship, that Polish Jewry, was swallowed into the abyss, into the vast caverns, but the current of humanity streams on, as if we had not existed.

And it tears up out of the depths of our soul, the cry of pain from Rov Nosn Note Hanover, who lived during the time of the Khmelnitsky massacres and slaughters:

> *Aleph.* Where is the lions' den of the *Yeshiva* scholars
> Where is the alms house
> Where is the scribe, where is the weigher, who fences in *Meshovev Nesivos*[1]
> Where is justice between blood and blood, and words of dispute[2]

How were the hallowed stones poured out at the head of every street[3]
And the miniature sanctuaries[4] scattered like stones of the wall.

Beit. Poland, precious to Torah and the Law
From the day that Ephraim moved away from Judah[5]
Now is exiled, wandering, bereaved, and lonely.[6]

Gimel. What shall I take to bear witness to you, and to what shall I compare you[7] O Land of Poland
You have toiled in "These are liable to [the death penalty of] burning" and the chapter of "How does one hang"[8]
You have studied "These are liable to [the death penalty of] strangulation" and the chapter of *Chullin*[9]
And the chapter of "These are liable to flogging" and the chapter of "These are liable to exile."

Thus they lamented in those times and so we lament now, in our song of woe for Poland, the cradle of Torah and Hasidism:

Spirit, preciousness and source of good qualities,
Warmth, sincerity and full of ardor,
Still today sunken in the spheres,
Like a ship in a sea of destruction and persecution,
Murderers have abandoned you in a cemetery
That has swallowed the bodies and souls
You remain forever the greatest destruction of all destructions,
You have not lost any memory, like a cemetery without headstones.

The tragedy mourner has not been born, that could bring

[Page 386]

expression to the enormity of the destruction. The human language is too poor in words that could tell the beauty of the culture of the twentieth century Jewish world.

The world was not shaken, the sun did not stop its shine, the earth did not tremble when they hid thousands of living, struggling people in it, and cruelly suffocated their last death cries.

All nations compass me about;

They compass me about like bees; they are quenched as the fire of thorns; [Psalms 118:10 and 118:12].[10] All the nations, even those that mobilized their powers to extinguish the world on fire, approached our conflagration as if it were a fire of thorns and sticking shrubs, that no one is interested in putting out. That is the "love for humanity" of *goyishe* justice!

It was just that feeling that accompanied me for the whole trip and I had the feeling that for the entire time I was accompanied by millions of souls, with whom the air was full and who were demanding from me and from you an accounting of the soul! From me and from you! But not from the *goyishe* world. "You don't ask a Cossack for Justice". It would be ridiculous to request it. From a world which can indifferently tolerate such bestial, murderous eradication of tens of millions of human lives, one cannot make any moral and humane caricature and ask, "Why? And why?"

But this demand is from the self! You Survivors, remnant of Polish Jewry and these are also not young people, what have you done, that the heroic chapter of Polish Jewry does not become erased? If Goworowo has gone under, there should still be a *Seyfer Goworowo*!

When Moses, our Teacher, saw that the group who suffered at the hand of Amalek quickly forgot about it, so that he had to demand and shout, "Remember what Amalek did to you", urgently "Not to be forgotten!" God said to him, "Write the memory in a book", for the coming generations. Know who Amalek is! And do not let yourself be fooled by their "cultural" phraseology. A Book of Goworowo should record the luminance, the clarity, of the kosher Jews who, with fevered lips and mouths parched from thirst, went to their death with *Ani ma'amin* - I believe! In bunkers, in cattle cars, in primal forests, in dark frosty Siberian nights –*Ani ma'amin* ! In ghettos, in partisan units, in battle and in revenge –*Ani ma'amin* ! No power in the world can tear out that *Ani ma'amin*!

A *Seyfer Goworowo* should be written with the cry of those who cannot cry out until the great voice from heaven can be heard.

"Refrain thy voice from weeping, and thine eyes from tears; And there is hope for thy future; and thy children shall return to their own border."
[Jeremiah 31:15 and 31:16].[10]

Hebrew Translator's Footnotes:

1. *Meshovev Nesivos* is a halachic work by Rabbi Aryeh Leib Heller. The title itself would mean "the restorer of paths." The obscure phrase here seems to refer to a later commentary on that book, possibly from the town.
2. Based on Deuteronomy 17:8.
3. Lamentations 4:1.
4. A poetic term for synagogues.
5. A reference to the splitting of the Kingdoms of Israel and Judea – here referring generally to "times of old."
6. From Isaiah 49:21
7. From Lamentations 2:13
8. These are titles of sections of the Talmud, used here as references to the torment that the Jews of Poland endured. The next few stitches refer to other Talmudic chapters, with emphasis (and a double entendre) on those chapters that refer to various punishments that are to be meted out by a Jewish court (mainly from tractate Sanhedrin).
9. The Talmudic tractate referring to the laws of ritual slaughter of non-consecrated animals.
10. Translation of quotes from the Mechon Mamre Internet site.

[Page 387]

This Is How It Began

by Yitskhak Romaner, Israel

Translated by Tina Lunson

Fragments from a Lost Diary

27 August 1939. The town is cooking like a cauldron. Small groups of people on the streets and in front of the shops discussing – will a war break out with Germany or not? Dan, a tall, thin young man with a small, close- cut beard wants to convince his group that a war is an unbelievable thing. He bases this on various quotes from newspapers, that one should make nothing of it. Itshe Mayer, a Jew exactly the opposite of him, short with a sizeable belly, interrupts him, "What is he saying, the fool? I know that German like my own ten fingers. He still sucks the inspiration for war from his mother's milk. In the end, Poland will have the same fate as the other countries that Hitler has taken. How could it be different? Do our Poles have in mind an external danger? They fight only against 'Jewish community', that a Polish customer should, heaven forbid, not go into a Jewish shop. Such a people with such a government must fall at the first encounter of a hateful army, like a house of cards."

The little group grew and new people joined; small merchants who were bored from sitting and looking out for a customer and regular idlers and hangers-on who do nothing all day and now want to hear a little politics, some news.

1 September 1939. Just now the radio is again reporting the news that fascist Germany is attacking the Polish Republic. The speaker calls the population to be calm, order and courage. "We will show them the traditional hostility of Poland. Which means a Polish soldier." "We will not give them even one button."

The radio report traveled over the streets and lanes of the town as fast as lightning and already with a little extravagance. Each person added something. The German is already 23 kilometers into the country, near the border of Molave. He is going in several directions, one army in the direction of Goworowo. Women, carrying their pails of water from the new plumbing that is to say, the "artisanal well" stop a while and with a sigh listen to the latest news.

[Page 388]

They wring their hands and try to comfort themselves, that God will be merciful, and all will end for the best. With hope in their hearts each woman walks to her home and continues on with her day-to-day work, not giving herself any accounting of what awaits us.

5 September 1939. Today the first refugees arrived, from the surrounding *shtetlekh* that lie closer to the border. The residents took them in, as is appropriate for Jews. They gave them rooms and where it is a little tighter, even the beds and they slept on the floor, "Who knows how long we will occupy our places."

There is confusion on the streets. Young consider where to run to. Where is better, no one knows.

6 September 1939. Today we were rattled by the appearance of the first German airplanes. Their noise threw a fright into everyone. They flew very low and dropped a bomb near the *powshechna* school. One child was wounded lightly and one adult, severely. He died a few days later. This was the first victim of the Germans.

7 September 1939. The German Army is getting closer and closer to the *shtetl*. Consultations among the elite of the town take place in the *Rov's* home about what to do next - to remain and wait out the battles or flee to Vonseva [Wąsewo]. After long discussions they decided to leave the town.

When night fell, almost the entire town left in the direction of Vonseva. Each one prepared a pack of necessities and left. On the Ostrolenke side, the sky was red from the fires. Along the road we encountered solitary soldiers from the defeated Polish military. Despairing, we went on. Arriving in Vonseva it appeared that the Germans had already taken the little town and seemed to have murdered several Jews already. No one spoke of sleeping. We spent the night in whatever way we could. As soon as dawn came, the Germans issued an order that all arriving Jews must return to their places.

8 September 1939. The march back was a sad one. The people with backpacks dragged themselves tiredly. When Germans liked someone's backpack, they told him to stand still and they "liberated" it from him. May they take what they will, if only leave us the gift of life. Arriving back in town we found everything as we had left it. It was the eve of *Shabes* and everyone had prepared, as usual, for the *Shabes* meal. We eat in the half darkness and ponder what the night will bring or the morning. With melancholy thoughts we fall into a weary sleep.

[Page 389]

9 September 1939. At dawn we are awakened by a lot of gunfire. The Germans are shooting into the houses and anyone who does not run is shot. We run as if we are already dead. They drive us into the market square. The Germans have started a rumor that the Jews have shot two of their soldiers and as revenge they will burn down the town. Germans go around with fuel oil and bales. They douse the houses and set them afire. The fire flares up.

Meanwhile, we are gathered in the market. Around us, on the balconies, stand soldiers with machine guns aimed at us. An order to kneel. We think they will shoot us now, but they only photograph us. Then we are driven into the study house. The fires in the town flicker ever stronger and we, in the study house, crowded together and pressed, wait for the end. Also the courtyard of the study house is overfull and jammed. Soldiers watch us from every side and we must not run away. Where could we possibly run to? Into the water? The holy ark is open. The crowd pleads to God, weeps and shouts. The women are in spasms and the little children, not understanding what is happening here, complain very loudly. I sink into dark thoughts. Is this really the end already? Is the fate of the entire community of Jews to be burned in their own study house?

My thoughts are interrupted by the suddenly opened door. People push toward the exit and also jump through the windows. What's going on here? Are we actually saved? And what next? But there is no time to think. The congestion is ever stronger and I am pulled along by the current.

Barely out with all my bones and they drive us all over the bridge to the other side of the river. From the distance we see violent flames gushing from Tsudiker's little oil factory. The wooden house is burning with the fats from inside as if in hell. We realize our miracle. Several high ranking officers drove through by chance and did not allow us to be burned. That is how we won out over a certain death. We rest in the field where the cows used to pasture and again fear for the morrow. Oy, how we envied the cows!

[Page 390]

Diary of a Mobilized Soldier

by Yankev Gurka, Israel

Translated by Tina Lunson

Thursday, 31 August 1939

Thursday I was mobilized in the Polish Army. I had to report to Warsaw-Praga at Jagelanska 46. I take the train to Warsaw, which is already full of mobilized soldiers. From the Warsaw train station we are, under heavy military guard, driven to the appropriate gathering points. I arrive at the assigned place.

The disorder is huge. One can see that the entire military leadership is very unnerved. By ten o'clock at night they have barely managed to take care of a small number of mobilized. Each one receives a uniform, a rifle and a gasmask. There are still about 200 men, I among them. Quite hungry from a whole day of not eating, we were taken from there to a military kitchen two kilometer away. And then, to a large room to spend the night on the bare floor.

Friday, 1 September 1939

Early Friday a high officer delivered a lecture to us and two others informed us that the Germans had attacked Poland and battles were already taking place at the border and that each of us should see how quickly we could travel to our points. I was summoned to Lomzshe.

The train to Lomzshe only left at six in the evening. I take that opportunity to hop over to our Goworowo native Avrom Vaysbord, at Pavye 25. I barely manage to eat something with him and rest a little, when we hear Warsaw being bombarded by German airplanes. There are already many victims. The sirens blow constantly and the radio offers only “Upcoming”. There are disturbances in the tram communications and I barely arrive at the train station.

Women there are distributing food to all the mobilized. Only the militarily engaged are allowed on the train. We travel in darkened cars. When we pass through Goworowo I decide to get off, and there, at home, I will decide whether to stay or to continue the trip to Lomzshe. I arrive at our house at about two in the morning. There

[Page 391]

I encounter my wife's parents from Mishenits as well as refugees from Ruzshan.

***Shabes*, 2 September**

Since I have seen that the disorder in the military is so great, I decide to stay in Goworowo. But my father advises me to travel on because according to the reports one can receive the death penalty for not reporting to the military. Without an alternative, I went off to the train station. There I found Meyshe Tsimerman, also mobilized. There was no train running to Lomzshe, but we managed to ride in a locomotive to Shniadove. We arrived there at about two PM. From there we had to go by foot to Lomzshe. Meyshe Tsimerman promptly returned to Goworowo and I set out with my group to walk to Lomzshe.

Because of the fighting around Lomzshe the PKO was located in the train station. I promptly presented myself there. They immediately gave me a military coat and a function - to work in the kitchen and as soon as it began to get light, German airplanes began bombing our train. The train remained and was told to climb aboard the waiting train.

Around 2 in the morning we departed in the direction of Shedlets.

Sunday 3 September

On Sunday, as soon as it began to get light, German airplanes began bombing our train. The train stood still and we all ran into the nearby forest. Only a few hours later were we able to continue our journey.

Many people were gathered at each station. They threw food, sweets and flowers into the train cars. We arrived in Bialy-Podlask in the middle of the night. There was an airplane factory there and the Germans had already managed to make a pile of ashes out of it.

Monday 4 September

For several days in Bialy-Podlask we were in peasants' barns and then we were taken to be organized. We were divided into "companies" and "squads" and so on. We were assigned to grenade throwing, but the Germans detected us and began to bomb us from their airplanes. Some were killed outright and some wounded. We were told to run deeper into the nearby forest. There we were set up for the organization and we began to march forward.

The marching became chaotic. We received the news that the Germans were chasing us. We got an order to run in the direction of Brisk-Litovsk. The chaos became even worse. The night fell and in the dark we made various stumbles. Along the way I lost a shoe and could hardly keep up with them.

***Shabes*, 9 September**

Arriving in Brisk we, four Jews, separated from the

[Page 392]

Company, went into the town to buy something to eat. Meanwhile the Germans began to bomb the town. One bomb fell very close to our hide-out and by miracle we survived.

On our return, everyone (about 3,000 men) was ready to march further, to Kobrin. We got into rows and began to walk, but after going about two kilometers there came an order to requisition the Brisk fort (the famous Brisk fortification) and spend the night there. We stayed there for several days.

Thursday 14 September, the first day of *Rosh-ha'shone*

In the morning everything was organized again. Those who had full equipment and uniforms were to be sent to the front. I, who only had one shoe and others who lacked various things, remained behind. We were a couple hundred men. There I met Zelik the shoemaker (from Tshervin), Sholem Fraske's brother-in-law.

And now we stayed together. While establishing the new count, the Germans opened heavy artillery fire on us and many victims fell. Zelik and I still managed to slip out through a hole in the fort and then on all fours we crawled to the water. There we met other Polish soldiers and then we were a larger group. From that distance we could see that the fort was burning now. We went through fields until we came upon a train station. A railroad worker told us that Brisk was already occupied by the Germans and showed us the road to Vlodave, where we should direct ourselves.

***Shabes* 16 September**

We came to Vlodave on the Bug River on *Shabes* morning and the group prayed. The Jews gave us a room to rest and eat. That afternoon we refugee soldiers were reorganized there. They stood us in rows and we began to march in the direction of Khelm. Zelik and I decided to clear out. We left the rows unnoticed and went to a Jew's house. There we got civilian clothes and also spent the night with him.

Sunday 17 September

The Germans were already in Vlodave by early Sunday morning. Within two hours a fresh battle had begun between the Poles and the Germans. With many casualties and burned houses Vlodave was taken back again by the Poles. But a day later the Germans were back in town.

Tuesday 19 September

German soldiers are going around and collected all the young men, Jews and Christians. The Jews are driven into the *shul* and the Christians,

[Page 393]

into the church. Terribly crowded, without food or drink, heavily guarded, we were held there a full twenty four hours.

Wednesday 20 September

On Wednesday the Germans took 15 guarantors from the elite proprietors of Vlodave and freed us all. Zelik and I decided to leave, on our way home, back to Goworowo. We were not allowed to leave until six in the evening. We went straight out of the town, covered a few kilometers and spent the night in a haystack.

Thursday 21 September

To reach Goworowo we had to make a journey of 300 kilometers. To eat we had to go into the villages. By day we marched and in the evenings, which by the way were cold, we generally went to sleep outdoors on the haystacks. We went through Partshev until we came to Radzin-Podlask.

Friday 22 September, *Erev Yon-kiper*

On Friday morning we arrived in Radzin and went right to the *Rov's* home. The *Rebi* fed us lunch and told us to go home to our wives and children. We marched a good two days through Lukov and Shedlets, until we came to Sokolov. There we spent the night with a Goworowo family, a daughter of Shleyme Leyb Shekhter and her husband and children. From there we went to Kosovo, then Malkin, until we got to

Ostrove-Mazowiecki. In Ostrove we met my parents, sister and brother. My wife and children were in Ostrolenke.

I came to Ostrolenke and got right to work. A friend and I opened a small bakery and began baking goods. But the Germans learned about it and always took all the bread, until we had to stop baking.

One day the Germans issued an order that all the Jews had to leave Ostrolenke within 24 hours and move over to the Russian side. I stole over the border into Lomzshe. There I learned that my parents and the children were now in Bialystok. My wife, children and I came back and tried to reorganize, but it was not successful. Like all the other tens of thousands of *bezshnikes*, I could not get an apartment or a job. In a short time we went over the Volkovisk, where I could work in my trade.

That did not last for long. Those who had not received Russian passes were sent to the steppes of Siberia and the northern white bears. In 1941 the German-Russian War broke out and new troubles began. And the refugees who had taken Russian passes

[Page 394]

did not manage to escape. Many Goworowo Jews went through the hell in Slonim. We, like many others, succeeded in surviving the war, going through several transmogrifications. After the war I was in a displaced persons camp in Germany, along with my wife and children. In 1948 we arrived legally in Israel and are here to this day.

The Destruction

by Meyshe Molovani, Israel

Translated by Tina Lunson

Rumors were carried on the air, like black crows. The Germans were already on the march to Poland; they had already bombed here and there, sowing death. From everyone's eyes fear and chaos looked out. What to do? Where could one flee? Would one get out of the devil's paws alive? Waiting for Fate was no better than the fate itself.

A call went out for the mobilization of the military obligated. But, before then, Ostrolenke was taken by the Germans. Everyone sought a place to hide himself. Meanwhile, people went to the Christian suburbs, Goworowke, *probostva* and the surrounding neighborhoods. By Thursday September 7 the town was almost empty. The possessions that had been collected from generations of hard labor, people hid anywhere they could. They still harbored a spark of hope that perhaps they would be able to save it.

In the morning, early Friday, the Germans appeared in the town. They promptly posted announcements that all the Jews of military age must present themselves or else they would be shot. I first tried to hide myself, but in the end decided not to risk my life and presented myself at the gathering point. And those coming back from the surrounding villages were sent to concentration points in the market square. The peasants, children and parents, were invited to remain in the houses. They did not even disturb the women with concerning themselves with food for us. I saw that no good would come from sitting around there. I and a few others used the chaos and fled back into our homes. In the evening they

[Page 395]

collected them all into rows of four and under heavy guard led them to Panikve.

Shabes, around four or five in the morning, Germans opened wild shooting on the houses. Then I hear a clattering on the windows, accompanied by wild voices and shouts from the Germans, "Everyone out! Louse!" Anxieties befall me. I thought that it was over for me. They will surely shoot me. I hid from them. I got out onto the street and there I encountered a greater number of people killed. I recognized some of them, among them Mordkhe the *shames* and one of Yekl Kosher's sons. Christians were also among those shot, supposedly because they shot at Germans from their houses. We were ordered to gather all the dead bodies in the house of Yeshaye Ayzenberg. They were laid out in rows, one after another. At the same time the town was burning from three sides, from Fridman's side, by the church; from the Long Street and the Broad Street.

An order came to assemble at the market. The sick whom the Germans found in the houses, we had to carry to the gathering place. It came to me to carry our Yosl the ropemaker. My three children, who were among the living and fast asleep, had not heard about the whole action. Only when the Germans woke them with the butts of their rifles did they come running to the market. About eleven o'clock (before noon), the crowd was divided up. The Jews were taken to the *shul* and the Christians to the church. They held us in the *shul* for almost an hour. When the flames of the fires neared the *shul*, the Germans took out some men and placed us outdoors near the bridge. The terrible cries and screaming of the women in the *shul* tore at the heavens, terrified of being burned. Then an automobile full of high German officers drove through. When they heard the laments from the *shul*, they stopped. A general stepped out and asked the soldiers what was going on. When he heard that all the people there were to be burned, he did not allow it. The tension eased and they even allowed water to be taken in for our closed-in and fainting women and children to drink.

Meanwhile they led our men to Vulke. There, the German delivered a speech that only the Jews are guilty for the war and that the Jews are robbers, criminals, murderers and so on. He then told us to hand over our money and all valuable objects or else we would be shot on the spot. Of course, we carried out the order. They again placed us four to a row and marched us to Pasheki (five kilometers). The road was besieged by Germans. They made fun of us,

[Page 396]

running a finger across their throats, which had to mean that we were being taken to the slaughter. Soon another party arrived in Pasheki, from Vonseva, Jews and Christians, among whom were Meyshe Tsimerman, Yankev Kosher and others. They drove us all together to Ruzshan, to the door of the mayor there. From there we marched to the church. We sat there until evening in the worst misery, without food or water. A little later, another party of men arrived from Goworowo. From them we were first made aware of the fate of our women and children. They told us that only when the fire was already licking at the walls of the *shul*, the German sadists let them out and told them to go over to the other side of the river, through the water. Our minds were a little relieved, but still very worried about them. Would they be able to cope with this on their own? Finally in the evening they brought us bread and water.

Sunday at nine in the morning they put us into big trucks and took us to Makove. We found the town was intact, except for a few demolished houses. The Jews there moved about almost freely. Some of them brought food to the trucks for us. At first, we thought that the German wrath had subsided a little. But they soon showed their true ugly faces. When a young Jewish woman approached us with a little food, a German stabbed her in the leg with the bayonet affixed to his rifle.

We were held in a barn for fire fighters until five in the afternoon. They gave us bread to eat and coffee and another portion per three persons for the road. Outside the town tractors with small wagons attached to them waited for us, to take us further along the road. We were stuffed into the wagons like herring and we traveled to Prushnits. After a half-hour break, we continued the journey and around eleven at night we arrived in Mlove. The town is alight with fire. Thick clouds of smoke rise to the heights, the town has been burning for ten days without ceasing. After traveling for the entire night we arrived in Allenstein, Germany. When we stopped we were warned that for trying to flee, ten others will be shot. We were led under guard, by foot, to a highway and the Germans standing around made fun of us, "This is the march of the Jews on Berlin", one called out, and everyone exploded with laughter. They led us into a camp near Tannenberg, which consisted of wooden barracks and tents, fenced in with barbed wire and heavily guarded by soldiers. We met the other Goworowo Jews there, who had been taken from the market square. I recall a few of the names, Shmuel Tsudiker, Dan Rozenberg, Velvl Gerlits, Mordkhe the *shames's* son, to whom we had to relate the sad news about the gruesome death of his father, in order

[Page 397]

for him to say *kadish* and so on.

We spent *Rosh-ha'shone and Yon Kiper* in that camp and we performed the prayer services for the Days of Awe. A Jew from Shtshetshina recited *Kol nidrey*. His recital suited our sad situation and expressed what was in our hearts. We poured out bitter tears. The "Hear our voices, *HaShem* our God, spare us and have mercy on us" and the "Our God our King, tear prejudice aside" pulled violently at the Holy Throne. We did not get any food on *Yon-kiper*. "These shits do not get any food on such a day", said the Germans. Yekl Kosher, who was in the camp with me, asked me about his son, who had gotten lost in the great upheaval. But I was not able to make myself tell him the tragic report, that I had seen him lying in the Goworowo market square, shot to death.

There was a large number of Poles in that camp too. They had permission to rob us. They emptied our pockets, pulled off our clothing, shoes and so on. Socks. We gradually got used to the problem. One time the commandant of the camp called us together and gave us a lecture that Poland would be divided and the border between the Russians and the Germans would be the Vistula River. Goworowo would belong to the Russians. He told us to register ourselves and to state where we came from, so that each could be sent back to his place of residence. Of course, we all listed Goworowo. In three days he called us up again and shared with us that there had been a change in the border divisions and the border in fact was the River Bug and Goworowo would remain with the Germans. We were faced with a great proposal. If we had not earlier given Goworowo, we would no doubt be able to provide another town on the Russian side. But here we did not have any alternative. The third interim day of *Sukes* they took all of us registered Jews to the Allenstein train station and packed us into freight cars. We "German" Jews were given liberation certificates and sent off on the train to Ostrolenke. The camp director notified us that our certificates were only valid for three days and after that we must go over to the "dirty Russians". Arriving in Ostrolenke I found the town whole. I met more Goworowers there, among them Tsipore Mishnayos and others. From there we went by foot to Goworowo, a distance of 25 kilometers. My uncle's house, which was located on the *glinkes* and also our windmill, were standing untouched. The town was already burned, only the chimneys were left, and some unburned wood, heaps of bricks and ash. We returnees organized ourselves with Christians in the area. Gentiles brought me

[Page 398]

grain to grind and I had another week of work.

Eight days later, on a Sunday at ten o'clock, announcements were posted in the streets that all Jews must gather straightaway in the yard of the church. There were not many Jews in the town. The majority had already gone over the Russian border, which was near Tshervin, about 15 kilometers away. The *Rov* was already there and the ritual slaughterer Marianski and others. We all gathered in the church yard. Among us were the brothers Note and Iser Rits, the Krulevitshes, Shiadovers, Avrom Engel, Yisroel Aron the glazier and others. The mayor, the folk-German Busse, gave us a lecture, again in the same style, that the Jews were guilty for the war and so on. He advised us to go as soon as possible over the border to the "dirty Russians" because he could not give us any protection against the partying soldiers. In the end he insulted us further, selecting the following "pastime". He told the brothers Note and Iser Rits to fetch a wagon and brooms, to sweep the large plaza by the church and up to Yekhiel Gerlits' house, then load the manure onto the wagon, telling Note to harness himself and Iser to push the wagon from behind and haul the manure off home. For the older Christians this was interpreted as disgusting but the young were delighted to look upon it, as those two fine proprietors would be lowered down to the ground. A little later we were set free.

Naturally, we all went running to the Russian border. My brother-in-law and I bought a horse and wagon, packed in some personal belongings and by way of Brizshnia and Fisk, we crossed over the border at Tshervin, over to the Russians. I had just managed to "turn over" my windmill to Valdman, a folk-German, who also had such a mill in partnership with me. He also conducted himself respectably as regards the Polacks, who literally wanted to inherit it while I was still alive. There, we breathed a little easier, rested and slept calmly through the night. In the morning we went to Vishange Koshtshelne (Bialystok province) by way of Papatsh. There we met Shleyme Akiva. The Russians liked him very much and he was an entertainment for them. As usual, people could not fill him up here either. Once the Russians tried to fill him up by giving him eight loaves of bread (they did not have any more) to eat at one time. But he made them disappear into his stomach in nothing flat.

In my further wanderings, as fate would have it, I avoided Slonim. Many Goworowers had settled there and were later murdered by the German beasts.

I experienced a lot in the last world war. More than once, I saw death with my own eyes. By miracles I always lived through it.

[Page 399]

As I was destined to live, I overcame all the suffering and horrible experiences.

After the war, being in Poland, I decided to hop over to Goworowo. Some interior feeling drew me here, and although I had seen with my own eyes how the town was destroyed, I still wanted to give it a glance. At the same time, I wanted to finish certain personal matters.

It was in 1948. I did not meet even one Jew there. I spent the night with Dr. Glinka. His wife cried bitterly for me, that there were no Jews in the town anymore. I was not certain whether this was in sympathy for the murder of Polish Jewry or for the livelihood that they had lost. Jews ran to the doctor for the smallest concern. A gentile usually used some "grandma" cures. When he felt bad, they called the priest. But she continued to wail.

The Christians had managed to build houses on more and more places. So Voitatski had built a house and a haberdashery business on Gerlits's place. Manka, who had carried water to the Jewish houses, had built up a shop on Shaul Potash's place. Vavzshentshak, on Yoel'ke the baker's place. Kamienitski, on Klas's place. On Gemara's place, a *goy* from Yavares. And *goyim* from Vulke had built houses on more places. The new big *shul*, which was a magnificent building for the entire Jewish region, was being taken apart brick by brick, as the *goyim* used them to build their houses. Nothing remained of the synagogue – a pig market had been built in its place.

It happened that I was in the town another time, in the 1950s. It had acquired even more *goyishe* houses. I was seized by a fear of being one Jew among so many Christians. Although they looked at me with smiles on their lips, their eyes showed that they were thirsty for Jewish blood. I fled from there and ordered myself not to go there again. Nu, today I am in Israel in my own home.

Received by: **Meyshe Granat**

[Page 400]

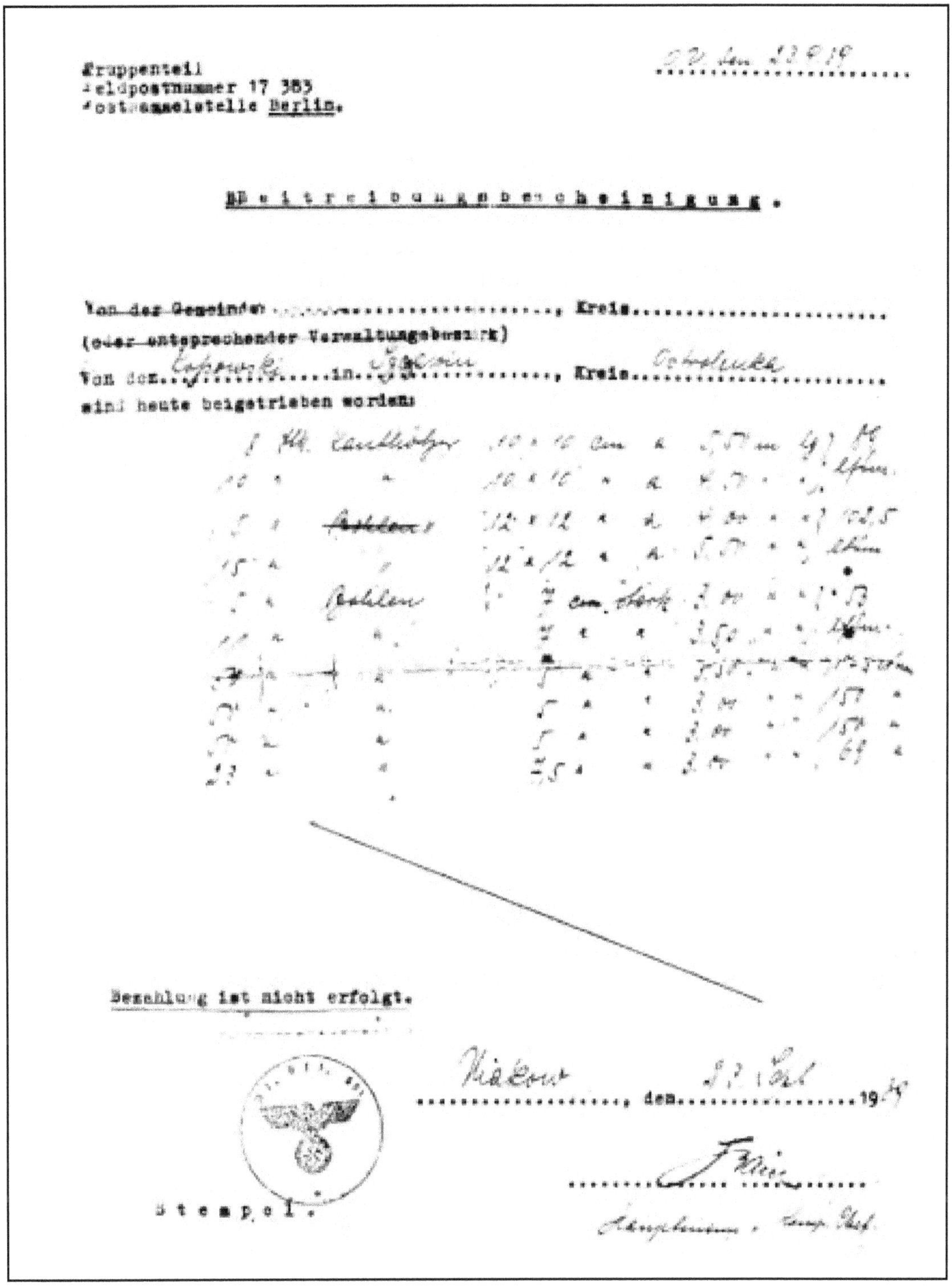

Truppenteil
Feldpostnummer 17 383
Postsammelstelle Berlin.

Beitreibungsbescheinigung.

Von der Gemeinde ...., Kreis ....
(oder entsprechender Verwaltungsbezirk)
Von dem .... in ...., Kreis ....
sind heute beigetrieben worden:

Bezahlung ist nicht erfolgt.

.................., den .... 19..

Stempel.

A German order for wood materials which they took from Kosovski and Shtshavin on 23 September 1939, with the added note that it has not been paid for.

[Page 401]

A Month with the German Beasts

by Shmuel Dranitsa, Israel

Translated by Tina Lunson

Friday, the 1st of September 1939, the day when Hitler/Germany declared war on Poland, I will never in my life forget. A great uproar overcame the town. Jews went around upset and did not know what they were about. In the morning, early on *Shabes*, when we were going into the big *shul* to pray, we saw through the windows the first refugees arriving in Goworowo from across the bridge. These were Jewish families from Ruzshan and other small towns that were closer to the German border. We helped them make temporary arrangements. But the anxiety among everyone grew from hour to hour. Sunday the arriving Jews fled further, some to Ostrove and some to the surrounding villages, where there were Jews. The chaos became greater and we could not determine what we should do – stay or run. One person looked to another. Only on Wednesday, the 6th of September, when the news arrived that the Germans were already in Vishkove and had shot a large number of Jews there, did we decide, finally, to move from the place. But it was now too late. The Germans were already chasing us. That same day, at about seven in the morning, the Hitlerist airplane flew through Goworowo and dropped the first bomb. It accidently fell outside of town, but the splinters hit Leybl Berliner (a son of Khayim the "mayor"), who later died from the severe wounds.

There were no thoughts of running away, because the German airplanes were flying very low and shooting the civilian population. For the moment, we decided to hide. My brother Meyshe and I, several neighbors and our families, went into Zambzshitski's cellar and hid there until the afternoon. Around five o'clock I went out of the cellar into the street to learn what was happening. Suddenly, I see Polish soldiers running from the *Probostva* side, who tell me that the Germans had broken through the partition line by the Narev and were already in Ruzshan. I run back to the cellar and tell everyone the news. We immediately fled to Vonseva with our wives and children.

[Page 402]

We arrived there at about eight at night. But the Vonseva Jews were packed up too. To our question "where to?" they answered, "Wherever our eyes lead us." There was no plan to remain there either and as soon as I heard that my sister Sore and her husband Noske Kahan and children were in the village Bogateles, we also went there. We arrived there late at night, where we heard that the Germans had already arrived in Goworowo and there was no place to run.

Friday the 8th of September the Germans entered Vonseva and from there they marched us to Ostrove. Because Bogateles lay near the main highway that led to Ostrove, the Germans shot up the village and several children were killed in that. We quickly left the burning village. But, where to go next? Without an alternative, we decided to turn back to Goworowo. Friday the whole day we walked in the great heat on back roads, in order to avoid the German soldiers who were on the roads. At night when we approached Vulke, we saw that the bridge was being guarded by Germans and were forced to go through the river. When we arrived at our homes, we learned from the shipping agent that just today the Germans had come into Goworowo and promptly posted signs saying that all men up to forty years of age must present themselves, Nosn Shron, Meyshe Tsimerman, Velvl Rubin and others had informed us. I could not close my eyes all night. I thought and I wept. At dawn on *Shabes* the 9th of September I go out in the street to find out what is new and hear shooting and the shout, "Jews, save yourselves!" But I notice that the Germans are also aiming at me. I succeed in running away and hide myself among the stalls that are still left from the Thursday market day. Running, I notice a lot of Jews shot, among whom I recognized Mordkhe the *shames*, Avrom Yekl, the "card-maker" and Yekl Rozenberg from Ruzshan who are lying dead on the ground. Meanwhile I am in among a crowd of Jews who are gathered together in the middle of the street and Germans with machine guns standing around guarding them. Women with children stand and weep, and heart- rending scenes are played out. I remark from a distance that Beytsalel Yosl Karvat is running to his daughter Khane Elke Shtetshine. Nearing her house on the corner of Bank Street, he was shot by a German. Across the way I see that the German bandits are standing near Velvl Brizshner's house and shooting into it. Velvl and his wife are murdered on the spot. Then Leye Korn runs out screaming that the Germans have shot her father Leyzer ("Krementshuk"). The blood gelled in my veins. These were the first victims

[Page 403]

who I saw with my own eyes. More Jews were killed in that slaughter of the Black *Shabes*.

We stood in the street like that until eight in the morning. Then came an order that all Jews without exception must go into the big *shul*. They stuffed as many as they could into there. Many remained outside in the yard. The lamenting from the women and children reached up to the heart of heaven. The Germans announced further, that men up to age 40 should voluntarily present themselves and those who did not, would be shot. There was no alternative and many obeyed. They arranged us outside the *shul*, near the bridge, under guard. Then I saw how Germans were driving around over the town and dousing the houses with fuel. Now there was smoke from the kasha maker's house and the whole town around it began to burn. The flames were already near the big *shul*. The cries for help and the heart -rending screams keep getting stronger and the Germans stand around with weapons and do not let anyone out.

The Germans tell our men to arrange ourselves by four to a row and we set off marching toward Ruzshan. They led us into a local church and there we sat until Sunday morning, the 10th of September. From there they took us by automobiles to Makove, where late at night they quartered us in a firemen's barn to spend the night. In the morning they put us in the autos again. Through a window I notice that two Germans with reinforced revolvers in their hands are leading Shmuel Blumshteyn. I do not know what happened to him later. From there they took us through Makove, Prushnits and Mlove to Germany. In Germany we were taken to Camp Allenstein, near Tannenberg (Eastern Prussia), which was meant for prisoners of war and civilian men intended for the military. The relationship of the Germans to us was still tolerable. They directed us every day to various work and that was our entire occupation. We slept on straw in wooden barracks.

They held us there until the 29th of September. On that day an order came that all Jews should be released from the camp. They gave out special "liberation passes" and took us to the train and set us in trucks prepared specially for us. They packed us in like herring. We could literally not move. Two days and nights we traveled, standing up, without food or water, until we arrived in Ostrolenke. There the Germans checked our "passes" and told us to go to Goworowo. When we arrived in Goworowo we could not recognize the town – everything was burnt, only heaps of ash. The majority of the Jews had fled and some were located with the Rits brothers

[Page 401]

in the mill. The meetings with our families were mixed with joy and weeping. They were worried about our fate, thinking that the Germans had murdered us right away and we were sure that they all had been killed in the flames of the burning study house. After telling them the history of our liberation, they told us about their miracles. This is how it went. When Nosn Farba's house was already on fire and the flames were already reaching the *shul* and the prayers and weeping of the Jews were up to the seventh heaven, suddenly from *Probostva* came running an automobile with high German officers and stopped by the bridge near the *shul*. The officers in the auto got out and asked the soldiers who was guarding the *shul*, what was going on there. When they heard that they were burning the *shul* along with the Jews, the officers said that they could not do such a thing and told them to free all the Jews. The soldiers carried out the order. They opened the doors and the windows of the *shul* and the Jews hurried out in great joy and through the river over to the other side. They were in a field for three days under heavy guard and then off to *Probostva* and other places.

The Jews saw a double miracle in that because they had wondered, how could an auto drive among the burning buildings?

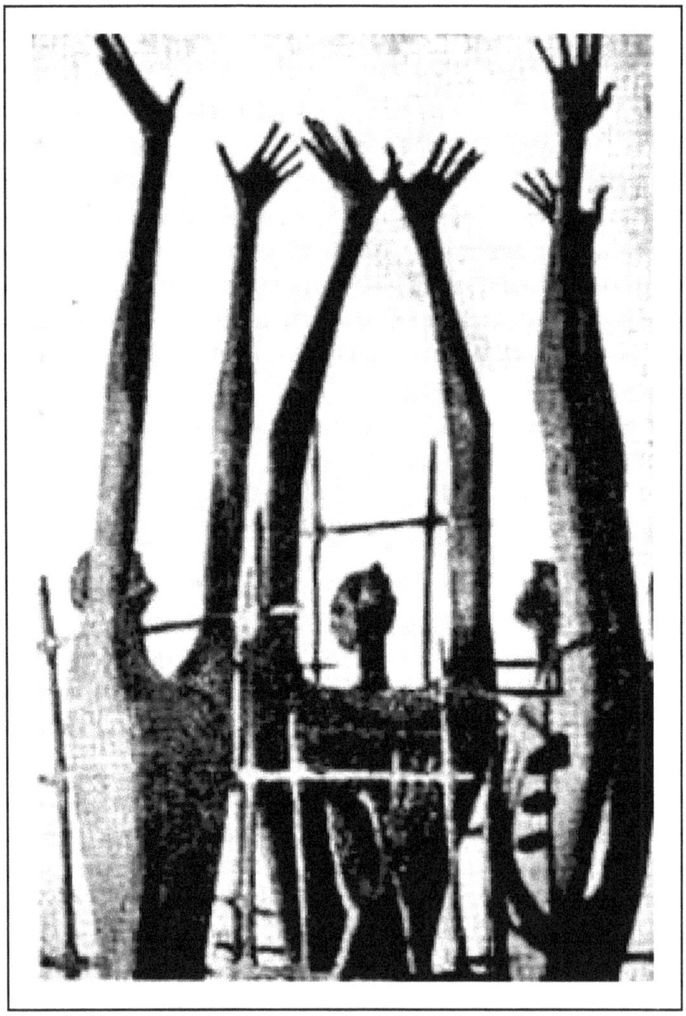

The memorial for the victims in Camp Auschwitz

[Page 405]

A Look Back

by Peysakh Tshervin, Israel

Translated by Tina Lunson

On Thursday the 31st of August 1939, the sun had just tossed her first rays onto the wet dew on the stone paved market square. Doors opened quickly and half sleeping figures appeared. People hurry – today is, as usual, the market day. Children are already going to school tomorrow; today is the last day before the new school year. They run, tanned and rosy from their summer vacation days. From the surrounding villages columns of wagons are drawn, packed with all kinds of produce, grain and animals that the peasants bring to sell in the town. Commerce begins. Here and there stands a Jewish craftsman slapping the palm of a gentile, wanting him to buy a pair of boots, a shirt or a hat. Women come and touch the chickens, measure the weight "by eye" and seek out bargains.

But this Thursday was different from all the other market days. Something was missing. Jews stood in little groups and whispered together; the air was uneasy. It smelled like a storm. A group of people suddenly started running to Felek the Polish butcher's, where there was a radio, to learn the latest news. Indeed, they did hear there a stern male voice, "We will not surrender even one button from a Polish uniform". Women began wiping their eyes with their aprons and the men sighed heavily. The peasants quickly harnessed their wagons and raced back home with a wild speed. The noisy and lively market square became empty and sad.

Although I was very young then and did not completely understand the seriousness of the situation, seeing the empty market square made my heart clench and I ran home crying. There I encountered a circle of women, all gesturing with their hands. Some were actually crying. Seeing me, my mother clasped her hands and burst into tears, saying, "What will become of us now, where will we go to? Losing a home, your father will be called up to the military."

Father came from the bakery covered in flour, but calm, and said to us, "Not to worry, we will get advice somehow. Meanwhile, we still do not know anything." I considered father's sturdily

[Page 406]

built body, with the two steel blue eyes, and came to the decision, yes, one could trust in him, with him we would not be lost.

Morning, Friday, women running, buying whatever they can, cooking, preparing for the sabbath, their sighing never stops. "May God guard and protect" is heard with every step. Suddenly the buzzing of an airplane can be heard and just after that, an explosion. Everything around us shook. A German bomb had fallen near the folks school and then we had the first victims. Now no one could doubt that the war had begun.

The day of *Shabes* was calm, but one felt that this was not for long. The whole week after that, many Jewish families came into Goworowo from the surrounding towns and *shtetl*ekh. Against that, many people fled Goworowo for some other place. The population of the town almost doubled. Every house took a refugee family. And the *shul* and other community places were over full. My parents were among those who left Goworowo and traveled to Ostrove. We took only the most necessary things with us and the rest we buried in our town. All of Poland was in chaos. People ran from town to town, always thinking that here is better. But every place was the same. The fear of the war and the fear of the Germans continued to follow us. The roads were full of retreating Polish military. Dusty and sweaty soldiers and officers were running in great disorder, stopping at every stream and well, hurriedly drinking even dirty water. After them came the Germans at a wild speed, chasing them in comfortable transports. Well-fed, well-rested, nicely clothed, they were in every area, singing, sowing destruction and death all around them. Poland fell and along with her, our town, our home. The instinct to live stayed with us though. Where to?

When we returned to Goworowo our little town already lay in ruins. Only the remaining, charred chimneys stuck up in the air alone, like orphans, and gave off a stink. It was quiet as a cemetery. The remaining Jews, from those who had returned after the fires, had settled temporarily in the *pasterunek* of the police. Dr. Glinka also lived there. Some had also organized themselves in the smaller and the larger mills. I went for a little stroll around the place, what remained of Goworowo. Everything, everything was burned. Not one whole house remained. Here and there a few unburned things still smoked. Almost everywhere there were posts bowed by the heat of the fire, bowls, iron bed frames, stands of sewing machines and other metal junk. Everything was erased, wiped, even with the earth. The effervescent little town,

[Page 407]

full of life, lay in ashes. The sole thing that remained as a vestige was the water pump in the middle of the market square. That was the gathering point for all who were searching among the ruins with the hope of finding some kind of valuable thing. Sad and silent, people greeted one another with glances and went away.

I spent a whole day circling around the streets, reminding myself that just a few days ago, children played hopscotch or with a ball, jumped over a rope and made the place merry. Here was Potash's candy shop, above it the Perets Library, a little further the bank lane, where the Yiddish school was too, and as a student I had to participate in a children's presentation. There is the teacher, a tall, dark charming woman, who started every day, before the lessons, checking to see that we had clean hands. Suddenly the figure of the wheelwright's little daughter from Vurke stole into my eleven year old mind. I walk and think and it seems to me that all this had been years ago, when I was just a child. The two weeks of war have made me more serious and mature.

I stroll further and in my mind, images of the not-distant past pass by; a *Shabes* summer day, the sun creeps lazily up on the horizon, just like the people from their beds. The week with its noise and the chase after livelihood is over, on *Shabes* people are too tired to think. Jews walk sedately to *shul*, leading their children by the hands. Dressed in clean, spruced-up clothes, I also walk with my father as is appropriate for a Talmud boy. But the seriousness vanishes in the middle. I am drawn to the river, where the water is so clean and pure, that I can clearly see the earth with its light pebbles. I steal out of the *shul* and then there I am at the river. In a minute I have swum to the other shore where the grass is so high and green and smells of many aromas. The meadow is like an embroidered tapestry, sprouting flowers of all colors.

I dream again - afternoon times. Shleyme Akive runs around from house to house to “work” the kugels and the potato casseroles. A little later, everyone is sunken in a sweet afternoon nap, but the youth are never tired. Some go to the iron train bridge to bath in the sun and swim in the river; some will just hide in the shadows of Stankius's orchard to enjoy some ripe fruit. Then it is soon *Shabes* evening. Electric lights already illuminate the houses and the streets. One can hear the voices of *havdole* from the houses. The young men with young women stroll around freely, openly, over the streets arm in arm, and provide topics for slander for the women who sit on the stoops and gossip about them as they pass.

In my fantasies I see the Spring days of Passover eves, the town

[Page 408]

cooking like a kettle. People lime their houses or cover them with paper. They clean, they *kasher*, and prepare for *Peysakh.* At Khaye's, the cold glazier house, there is a whole factory going on. They are baking *matses*. A clatter of wooden rolling pins and the little push of the piercing wheels. The "cold glazier" herself, mistress of all she surveys, stands at the flaming oven and shouts, " A *matse* in the oven!" Leybl her son, a youth like a giant, a master of it all, warns, "A *matse* to the pusher!" and sends a glance to the rollers. I wander around in all this and try to help each one, but they do not want my help. They put a hot, soft *matse* into my hand and sent me away from there.

The night of the first *seyder* everything and everyone smells pure and fresh. The silver candlesticks sparkle. Everything is merry. Father sits like a king and I ask the questions respectfully. As we invoke God's anger on our enemies, I fearfully open the door for Eliahu the Prophet. As usual I do not see him and I get a little mad and father laughs. In the morning, we go to appear before our friends, in our new suits and squeaky shoes. Where are they now, my friends?

I remember them, as we used to come together at Meyshe Dranitsa's barn and invent various games. Childish, naive games, but how nice they were. How many wars we conducted, how "heroic" we were as the boys from one street fought the boys from another street. Where are those boys now? Where did the streets disappear to?

Silence, no one answers, sad winds just moan and play on the wires on the poles. Broken, I turn back home. Life demands its own. My father has started baking bread and the women are cooking food [in a pot set] on two bricks stood on edge. People make plans, they think about tomorrow. What will happen next?

Then suddenly and with a lot of noise, five German soldiers on motorcycles rush by, steel helmets on their heads and with automatic rifles, heading for *pasterunek.* The crowd ran after them, in order to hear some news. The Germans began barking in their dog-like language and took to rummaging through the many rooms of the former police station. They found a police cap there, bullets, documents and various other things. They told the men to carry the papers outdoors and burn them, driving them out with the butts of their automatic rifles. Yekhiel Gerlits, a Jew already in his elder years, did not please the Germans for some reason and they pursued him mercilessly. "Faster, you cursed Jude", they screamed at him, while gesturing with the hand across the throat. Yekhiel fell down and a heavy Nazi boot came down on his face.

My father, as the youngest of the group, was accused of organizing a partisan group. One, a younger S.S. man with an iron

[Page 409]

cross on his breast, cruelly took my father and with curses and blows stood him against a tree and slowly placed his rifle on him. My blood froze and I did not know how to act. The other children were hiding around my mother and they all were weeping bitterly. I wanted to throw myself at the German, but my mother stopped me in order to avoid another victim. But then a miracle happened. In the yard there was a small little house for the gardener, in which a Polish family was now living. Suddenly the door opened there and a young woman came running to the place of the bloody spectacle. This was Vladka, the same

Vladka who used to wash our laundry and heat the ovens on the sabbath. Knowing Yiddish, she chatted with the German and pushed his rifle to the side. The German, smiling, directed a blow to my father's head and taking Vladka around, went off with her to the little house. How thankful we were then for the simple woman who, despite the full-blooming antisemitism, saved my father's life.

That same day we decided to leave Goworowo. Yosl Agradnik and his family went with us. We harnessed his droshky and set out in the direction of Shniadove, where the Russians were already. The horse went slowly across the bridge. I do not know why the wooden bridge was still there. My father drawled an old Russian farewell song. It became even more sad. I feel as if something in my heart is tearing. I feel as if I will never see Goworowo again. I close my eyes and disparate images like bits of cloud fly across my memory. I see myself among children in *kheyder* at *Rebi* Avrom Yisroel's. The *Rebi* catches a nap and we meanwhile play buttons. The *Rebi* wakes up and strikes out right and left with his belt. Winter, sledding, skating on the river, throwing snow at one another. We make snowmen, with two charcoals instead of eyes, a red carrot nose, and a broom at his side. Soon it will be winter days in the *shtetl*. The roofs decked in snowy hats, the market sparkling with thousands of diamond mirages.

I am wakened from my dream by the merry shout of a Red Army soldier's, "*Zdrostvoytye tovarishtshi!*" We are already in Shniadove, on the Soviet side. Now I understand that Goworowo, the town of my birth, is far behind me – as far as a dream.

I survived the war and today I am in Israel. But Goworowo, where I was born and reared and spent my finest childhood years, I will never forget! I will remember you eternally, my beloved *shtetele*!

[Page 410]

The Last *Kol-Nidrey*

by Khave Burshtin-Bernshteyn, Israel

Translated by Tina Lunson

The days between *Rosh-ha'shone* and *Yon-kiper*, the ten days of penitence, were sad and melancholy. The sun was obstructed behind a thick cloak of clouds. She was ashamed of the trouble and shame that we, the Goworowo Jews, had gotten for no kind of sin and evil. The town had been burned, ash and debris. The refugees were concentrated at the Rits brothers' mill, located just outside the town and it was thanks to that location it was not burned. The Rits brother had given all the rooms and residences on the estate of the mill for the burnt out and suffering townspeople. The others remaining rented rooms in the surrounding Christian houses. They clung together like sheep encircled by a pack of provoked wolves.

My family, which consisted of my father, my stepmother the *Rebitsn*, and myself, settled at Note Rits's in a comfortable, airy room. It is not possible to relate the sincerity and open-heartedness with which the family Rits approached my father of blessed memory. As a rule, everyone behaved as if we were one family. We literally shared what little we had and one helped another in whatever way he could. The troubles and experiences united everyone.

The holy day of *Yon-kiper* neared. There was nothing to feast on before the *Yon-kiper* fast. All of the flour reserves from the mill had been taken by the Germans. Everyone was worried and my father was very upset that Jews would not be able to do the *mitsve* of eating on the eve of *Yon-kiper* and could, heaven forbid, fall to temptation or become weakened on *Yon-kiper* itself. An idea occurred to me. I would go to

Sukhtshits where the former “mayor” Karolak lived, a great lover of Yisroel, and beg him for food. I told my father my idea. He hesitated. It was a long way to Sukhtshits. I would have to go by foot and the roads were considered very dangerous. He pondered it for a long time and glanced at me with fatherly concern. After a while he arrived at a decision. “Go, my child, and bring food for all the Goworowo Jews.” I no longer felt any fear and I set out on the road to Sukhtshits.

[Page 411]

I took Ester Leye Gemora with me and we sneaked along side roads but feeling the blessings that accompanied our important mission. To our great happiness we did not encounter any Germans along the way and we were successful in arriving at “mayor” Karola's house. We met him sitting in his simple house with his family. He fixed his pair of wondering eyes on us, as if he had seen living corpses. He ordered his wife to bake some bread and meanwhile he asked us with great interest how all his Jewish friends were doing. First of all, he gave us food to eat to our satiety and the whole time he comforted us with the thought that we would overcome this trouble. The bread was ready around lunchtime. We had to hurry in order to bring the bread before evening, for the last meal before the fast. Karolak gave us six large loaves of bread and he gave me a special bread and things for my father, the *Rov*. He asked us that if we were caught, we should not say that he had given it to us. With tears in his eyes, he accompanied us to the back road and told us to guard ourselves against the Poles just as from the Germans.

We got back to the mill in peace. All the Jews were standing on the road and looked at us as though we were the Messiah. In my father's eyes I could recognize signs of pain and a sting of conscience about how he had allowed us to make such a dangerous trip. But the joy of the return, to say nothing of the bread, covered the torture of his soul. The joy of all the people was huge. My father distributed the bread, to each his portion. The smell of the fresh bread quickened everyone's appetites and each rejoiced with the portion that he had received from the *Rov*, for himself and for his family after the fast.

We sat down to the erev *Yon-kiper* “feast”. Everyone was sunken in thoughts. Not long ago, one was a proprietor, of himself, a home, a family; and now, concerned for the future, and meanwhile such darkness; German murderers who seek Jewish blood, the Polish neighbors who became enemies overnight, and here we are homeless, dark before our eyes. Who knows if the Germans will want to use the holy *Yon-kiper* to torment the few Jews remaining in town, a little more. Our family was especially terrified because the news had reached us that the Germans were searching around for my father and it had already been said that one of the priests had denounced him, telling the Germans that the *Rov* was staying at the Rits brothers' mill.

Then we heard an automobile driving into the yard of the mill and heard wild screaming from the Germans. They ordered Note Rits to turn over the *Rov*. My father hid in the attic for a short while. But hearing that the Germans were not going away, he came out of his hiding place and bravely faced the Germans murderers. Several S.S. soldiers began to beat him and yank at his beard. An officer gave

[Page 412]

the *Rov* an order. In three days' time he must present the German office with several kilograms of gold and all valuables that remain among the Jews. He shot off his pistol and with wild laughter left with his band. There was panic, for where would they get gold, as there was not even one iron nail left from all their belongings. So they made a limit for the *Rov*, that if he did not present the gold on time, he would be shot and here it was already *Yon-kiper*.

The sun slid down and went on her way. Dusk came. People asked that each should pray by himself. My father did not agree, “If one still has the merit to recite *kol-nidrey* with the community, one must use it." In the large salon in Note's house they hung the window with a black cloth. The rescued Torah scrolls lay on the table. An eternal light flickered with a weak flame. People with swollen eyes slinked around like shadows. Children clung to their fathers, as they could perceive the great danger. There were not any holiday prayerbooks, so everyone prayed from their hearts and said their own improvised "prayer of acquittal". People did not plead for livelihood and pride from their children. People only pled for a bit of bald life and a quick redemption for the people of Israel.

There was not anyone to be a cantor for *kol-nidrey*. No one wanted to be the messenger from the community for such a broken congregation. My father began to recite *kol nidrey* with a broken voice. His face beamed with holiness. The women gathered in a nearby room, where the floor was wet with tears. We, the girls, myself, Libe Kosovski, Miryam Rokhl Hertsberg, the Gemora sisters and others, placed ourselves around the house outdoors, in order to sound the alarm if the Germans came near. That did not last long until we heard the sound of an automobile engine.

Germans with machine guns poured out into the yard. They chased everyone out into the yard, stood them in a row and aimed their machine guns at them. Everyone was certain that their last hour had struck. An officer called my father out from the row and said, "You 'godly man' come out!" They ordered him to take a prayer book in hand and a light. After that they called out from the lines Note Rits, Yoelke Beker, Itsele Reytshik and pointed their loaded rifles at them. People began reciting the last confession. A younger S.S. man sprang out with a motion-picture camera and made a photoshoot of the terrified Jews. They then shot into the air and went off to wherever they had come from.

People went back into the house to finish the prayers. Now no one wept, no one complained. This measure of trouble had already overflowed.

[Page 414]

So That You May Remember

by *Rov* Yitskhak Shafran, America

Translated by Tina Lunson

The commandment "that you may remember" is said about the departure from Egypt. It is a *mitsve* to remember and to relate the troubles and the miracles that the Jewish people experienced in *mitsrayim*; and that *mitsve* expands over the whole life of the Jewish person – in reciting *Shema Yisroel*, at the sabbath *kidush*, in blessings, at weekly, *Shabes* and holiday praying, in the *tfiln*, in weights and balance – everywhere. So that we may remember the day of our departure from the land of Egypt.

I have already asked many Talmud scholars, is the enslavement in Egypt a comparison to the distress that the Jewish people went through under the Nazis, may their names be blotted out? "No comparison" each one answered. Such enslavement, such torture, such terrible and bizarre deaths and such an enormous number of those tormented, 6 million martyrs, had not happened since the creation of the world. And the miracles of the rescued surviving remnant are also extraordinary, not to be comprehended. Every redeemed Jew can write an entire book about what kind of miracles allowed him to come alive out of the Nazi hell.

I was only under the Nazis for a few weeks and I was twice stood against a wall to be shot. The first *Yon-kiper*, at two o'clock in the morning, I was with my father Reb Shleyme Shafran in Ostrov Maziecki . Two Nazis broke down the door and came into the house. One shoved my father and me into a corner. In one hand he held a loaded revolver and in the other hand an electric lamp. He howled in a canine voice "Money, or I shoot you now!" Of course, I gave him everything. In another room the other Nazi, may their names be blotted out, encountered my cousin Malke Shafran from Ostrolenke. She was then twenty years old and a lovely woman. The Nazi wanted to rape her. But she put up a strong resistance and did not let him touch her. She told him that she was a religious woman, she would rather let herself be shot and not allow such a crime. When the Nazi came into our room, he told the second Nazi that she was very stubborn "Not to be had". When they finally left, my cousin said, "Yitskhak! I swear that he did nothing to me." My cousin and uncle, aunt and all the children were later murdered in the Slonim slaughter. May God avenge their blood.

[Page 415]

Today we have no Teacher Moses who can give us a Torah with *mitsves*, remember your departure from Europe. We have no Mordkhe and Ester who will write us a *megile* to read even just one time a year. Let us suffice in the meantime with what we have. We have fellow landsmen who publish a memorial book. Every landsman from every town and townlet should do that. Because each town has its own *megile*. How holy is a parent's *yortsayt* for us Jews? What kind of shake-up happened in our town when the first-born, sainted Yerukhim Fishl Krulevitsh died before the war? How sacred for hasidim is a *yortsayt* for their rebi? So then what should we do to immortalize the *yortsayt* for our *rebis*, *rabeyim*, brothers and sisters, colleagues, good friends and the community of Yisroel together, who were so cruelly murdered as martyrs to God?

The history of the departure from Egypt began with 70 souls, from whom the Jewish people developed. The decimation of our town when the Nazis came in on *Shabes* the 9th of September, began with the shooting of 70 people and the burning of the whole town. What kind of "so you may remember" have the wise men of this generation invented that one must do daily and one time a year in order not to forget all this?

We, the first generation of the Holocaust will probably not forget. I believe that each of us, wherever we live and whatever we do, even at night in bed, see the entire destruction before our eyes. But we must also think about our children and later generations, that they not forget either!

We are prohibited, however, from despair. Too much worry is a thing for Satan, because Satan's messiah Hitler, may his name be blotted out, wanted to drive us to despair and resignation. But as the Holocaust was so enormous and horrible, those few survivors are united by the great and extraordinary miracles. The survivors must thank God, may his name be blessed, for the huge miracles and marvels that happened to them. When the miracle is greater, so the joy is the greater.

I will never in my life forget the joyous events when, after the war, I came out from the Shanghai Ghetto in China, and finally arrived in America. Of course, every man for himself. We first mourned for our parents, relatives and the *shtetl* Goworowo where I had spent so many years of youthful education. But I had worked for six years in the *Beys Yankev* School for Girls as manager, secretary, treasurer, and myself gave lectures for the *Basye* and *Banos,* all without pay, as a gift. And when Hitler wiped all that away, I thought to myself Master of the Universe! Has my entire work for the sake of Torah, then, gone for nothing?! No trace remains, all gone to the devil?! A little while later I found in New York the ritual slaughterer's daughter Feyge Mazes, today Rozen, and Rivke Shtshetshina, today *Rebitsn* Rozental, the best of my students, members of *Banos*. My joy was beyond measure. I later found out that in Israel

[Page 416]

there were surviving members of *Banos*, the dear sisters Rokhl and Sore Zilbershteyn and others. Some members of the *Tseyrim* had also survived, the brothers Mazes in America and others in Israel. The *Rov's* only son, *Rov* Avieyzer Burshtin, was saved. All of them had already married, had children, conducted fine orthodox Jewish homes. And other men and women from our town had been saved. We see that the devil did not exterminate everything. Jewish continuity would be secure. All in all, may it be, that we have a beginning of the redemption. After thousands of years, we are credited to return to a Jewish state. All that comforts us and cheers our lamenting hearts.

We must make an effort toward a little joy, to demonstrate to ourselves and for the whole world, that the people of Israel lives, everlasting and forever!

Elegy

by A. Ben-Ir, Argentina

Translated by Mira Eckhaus

Edited by Tina Lunson

Tears flow from my eyes
for the city of Goworowo that has shattered life.
This is my native city,
where I grew up and was educated.
Now it is desolate,
wiped off the face of the earth.
Men and women, young and old,
Were burned like paper, slaughtered like sheep.
The hands of unclean people,
Thirsty for blood,
Like beasts of prey,
Stabbed them with the sword.
They went to death like messengers of the community,
To atone with their blood for the sins of the community.
They died for us,
And for our children,
And for all our people,
For generations to come.
Cursed be the murderers, their memory erased,
For all our enemies among us,
death awaits them, no blood will be shed,
peace will prevail between people and people.

[Page 417]

A Page of Talmud Saved Me

by B. Avieyzer, Israel

Translated by Mira Eckhaus

Edited by Tina Lunson

The camp in Belizin, Kielce district, contained four large manufacturing plants, where about two thousand Jews worked as forced laborers.

In this camp there were no gas chambers and incinerators like there were in extermination camps such as Auschwitz. Here, the Nazis used a different method: atrophy and annihilation through hard work and starvation. The prisoners worked hard at grueling jobs for twelve hours a day and received food rations so meager, that the amount that should have lasted a month was barely enough for one meal.

The terrible hunger that prevailed in Belizin left its mark on the miserable detainees after only a few weeks, swollen legs, a swollen stomach, an enlarged and swollen head, etc.

The commander of the last camp was a high ranking SS officer named Hertz, the son-in-law of an influential German general, thanks to whom he was able to escape from the front and with the excuse of commanding the labor camp, he remained in the home front without risking his own life. He himself did not raise a hand to beat a Jew and even prevented the *Scharführer* Buska, a sadist since his birth, from abusing the detainees in his presence, which was rare in these times, but did not lift a finger to change the killing regime in the camp; therefore, even the bravest of the detainees would not have lasted more than one year.

My place of work was in the knitting factory, where we produced and repaired woolen socks for the exterminators and the German civilian population. About four hundred Jews were employed here, divided into two shifts.

One day we noticed that the number of workers had decreased significantly and that many machines had been shut down due to lack of working hands. We were told that many were sick with the flu but, among the workers there was a rumor that this disease was a typhoid epidemic and that the Jewish doctors, as well as the *Stormbanführer* Hertz, were trying to hide the fact, out of fear lest the camp be eliminated because of this and then Hertz will also be sent to the front.

The ranks of the workers thinned out day by day but, the amount of food did not change. The healthy ones took advantage of this opportunity; each of them filled his bowl, which was hanged by a rope around his waist, several times.

One day, while I was swallowing a large portion of food, I suddenly felt that my body was becoming heavy. I tried to get up from where I was sitting and my head was spinning. Immediately I suspected that I was also trapped in a trap and suffered from typhus. With the rest of my strength, I dragged myself to the hospital.

The wooden shack where the patients lie down was once intended to be a stable for horses. It was about thirty meters long and nine meters wide. It had no windows but narrow portholes up the roof, through which pale and faint rays of light penetrated. On both sides of the walls stood two-story shelves

[Page 418]

and the sick were sprawled on them, crowded. Officially, the patients were under the supervision of a Jewish doctor and a nurse from among the detainees but in reality, the nurse did not do anything except wear a white apron and sit in the entrance hall. Neither did the doctor do much to improve the condition of the patients. And it is true that they had no possibility of helping the patients without medicinal drugs, when they alone were responsible for four hundred patients or more. Therefore, the patient himself had to take care first of all to find himself a place to lie down. If he had an acquaintance among the healthy people, who provided him with food to restore his soul, he could hold on somehow, and if not – then he laid down without food until he was well and could get up and take care of his needs; or he ended up being led by the group of gravediggers out of the camp. The quota was thirty to fifty dead per day.

There was no more room for me on the shelves, so the nurse advised me to lie down on the floor. And did I have a choice? I knelt down on the black floorboards, not far from the iron stove that stood in the middle of the hut. My bones trembled from cold and heat at the same time. I took off my clothes and put them on my fevered and frozen limbs. I was not left alone on the floor; soon several more patients were added and laid down next to me.

Fire burned in my body and suffocating dryness filled my throat and sparks of fire splashed against my eyes. I tried to get up and fell from exhaustion but, with sickly stubbornness I made an effort and crawled forward to the door of the shack. There, in the corner, stood a barrel full of water. As I did not have a cup, I dipped my face in the cold water and drank. I immediately got a double "fever" and my teeth were throbbing. I returned crawling to my "bed" and fell into a deep sleep.

After days, weeks, or months, I lost any sense of time, I opened my eyes and looked around me in wonder. Where am I? In the deep sleep that fell on me, that lasted for who knows how long, I was in another world, at my home, with my family, next to my friends and acquaintances, and I felt happy. I was very sorry, that my sweet dream stopped in the middle.

It was dark in the hut and the smell of mold and rot rose in my nostrils. The floor was full of patients who were writhing in pain and asking for help but, no one heard them.

My general feeling was very bad. The high fever did not go down and my aching bones, which had been lying on the floor for a long time, hurt me a lot. In addition to that, I was harassed by the passers-by in the hut, who stepped on my body during their passing from place to place. More than once, someone stepped on my feet with all their weight. It did not allow me to rest and strained my nerves to the point of exhaustion. I began thinking how to get out of the distress and be privileged, at least, to lie down in a more comfortable bed, on the planks of the shelves?

Every day, places on the shelves were vacated due to those who died or recovered but, the places that were vacated were immediately taken by patients who had the strength to get up and climb onto the shelves or they were confiscated by the doctor for privileged patients.

I came to the conclusion that I must reach a resting place at any cost, if I do not want to lose all hope of getting out of this barn alive.

It did not take long before I saw that not far from me, the "gravediggers" were "taking care" of one of the patients; I realized that this patient was no longer alive. I crawled closer there and I succeeded. I was the first to climb the shelf to the resting place.

[Page 419]

After I arrived at this desired place, my condition was even worse. I weakened to the point of exhaustion. I felt that I was about to die. In my previous place I could not concentrate and think about my condition because my nerves were troubled by too much worry, that my head and feet would not be prey to the soles of those walking on me; now my nerves reached the point of disintegration and revealed to me my true condition.

One day my illness got better. I was oppressed by the feeling of loneliness and I took out of my coat pocket a pamphlet, which contained several pages from *Masekhet Ketubot*. I once found it rolling around in the rag hut and now I looked it over. At that time, the head of the "gravedigger" group happened to pass by my bed and looked at me in confusion.

"What are the pages you're holding?" he asked me curiously. I showed him the pamphlet. He looked at them with great vigilance, sat down next to me and started investigating me. Who am I? In which *yeshiva* did I study? How did the pages come to me? Our conversation turned to *yeshiva* life in Poland and their ways of learning, to famous personalities in Polish and Lithuanian *yeshivas*, and so on. I was surprised to see in front of me a well read scholar, who recognized the subtle differences between the *yeshivas* of Poland and Lithuania and was well versed in them as if he felt at home. His face and rough clothes did not indicate at all that he belonged to the class of scholars.

Before parting with me he asked about the state of my illness and solemnly assured me that he would take interest in my fate and later that day he returned and approached me accompanied by the doctor. He gave the doctor a package full of medicines and injections and said, "These are intended for this friend of mine and I ask you to keep an eye on him". From then on, my condition changed for the better and there was a great improvement in my condition. The doctor and the nurse visited me often. I received various injections and medicines.

The doctor once explained this thing to me. He told me that this guy, by virtue of his role in burying the dead, visits at any time, freely, the nearest town, and there he buys the medicinal drugs.

As a result of this special treatment, my condition improved day by day, until I got up on my feet. On the day I left the hospital hut, the head of the "gravediggers" came to bless me and introduced himself to me – the former head of the *Beit Yosef Yeshiva* in the city of Ostrowiec, in the state of Poland.

One of the concentration camps

[Page 420]

In the Crematoria Oven
Fragment from a Poem

by Yosef Perlshteyn, Israel

Translated by Tina Lunson

Yosef Perlshteyn

He who has seen a crematorium with his own eyes,
Has long, long understood the sounds.
And I, although not in the oven myself,
Have taken in the horrifying story of the fire.

The crematory fire burns and hisses,
And snivels with flares and sizzles and gasps;
Like thousands of animals agitated
As this were a kettle of meat up for grabs.
Like hundreds of hades in thousands of degrees
Sends smoke out with terrible fumes;
As if the dead without end were gathered
And quietly stammered something…
---Ha -ha! Ha-ha!
---*Sha-sha! Sha-sha!*
A man-angel-corpse – the "pusher of death"
Shoves the skeleton into the oven, like bread:

Another one and another one and another one in!
Another one and another one and another one in!

A carcass– o heavens – only skin and bones,
With balled-up fists and gritted teeth:
A Jew – one can tell by the grizzled grey beard.
On the blue frozen lips a word

[Page 421]

Of a curse not delivered, or even a prayer,
From fear his hair has gone straight.
He probably suffered all his lived years,
And strove towards a proper grave among Jews,
But dying by fire surely not thought of,
And that on *Yon-kiper* – never meant to be!

After him a skeletal woman, her eyes running
From raising them to heaven in fear and despair;
Out of the lips, lament and screams, twisted,
The hair shorn off, to stuff mattresses;
The breasts bruised – not from a suckling child,
but in dying convulsions, legs bowed out;
Fingers clenched into hands – withered,
Stiffened in a prayerful gruesome crush.
It seems she would like more from life –
But she is quickly shoved in the oven.

A Jewish woman skeleton – a grandmother it seems.
One can see, from a fine Jewish house;
We see her heritage in the Jewish nuance
And it shines through her holy frame.
In old age she pursued Yiddish prayers,
And here – sent quickly into the oven.

Now here "comes" a young man – a blooming rose,
Killed by strangulation, how great a misfortune!
He seems to be a strong man –
better to die as a Partisan hero!

After him "goes" a girl, or engaged bride even,
Or a not-long married couple.
One can see her as the "young miss" of her *shtetl*,
But who could know how misfortune happens!

An infant child – just suffocated in the gas,
Not even rocked by a poor, sleepless mother,
A little crooked smile – in innocence dispossessed –
also shoved into the oven.

After them comes a body with a torn cross,
According to his moustache, a Gypsy or a Christian;
But that doesn't matter to the fire,
It's only a skeleton, maybe not even a Jew!

[Page 422]

*

Thus they slowly burn, carcass after carcass,
And blazing and scorching in flaming pleas,
and it flares and it broils, and it sobs and sizzles,
and hisses and stews, stews and gasps:
Hiss-ha! Gasp-ha!
Ha-ha! Ha-ha!

The air all round has a human stink
And the sky fevers red, like it's sick.
And it sizzles on wildly in the outdoors wind,
As if it wants to howl: *Oy vey iz mir* and alas
It's disgusting for me to carry the ash,
That becomes garbage nearby.
And despair steals into the day
And flabbergasts: *Oy* a catastrophe, oy a plague, oy a wail!
What do I see? I have never seen the like!
What is happening here? *Oy*, what is happening?!
Gevald, I feel like I'm burning!
Like I'm burning! Like I'm burning!
I am burning – not because they're broiling, roasting, searing me –
No, oh, almighty God! No, my God!
I am burning with shame, with disgrace, with rage and with hate,
Why have you served me such a hideous joke!

The "Pusher of Death" at work

[Page 423]

Hear O Israel...

by Rachel Auerbach, Israel

Translated by Mira Eckhaus

Edited by Tina Lunson

In those days, observant Jews were seeking a relief and refuge in prayer. And even among those who were not devout in religion, they often, in their last hours of life, clung to this age -old custom and together with all the others said *kadish* for the elevation of their own souls. Because by then, it was already known to everyone that there would be no more male sons left who would go every day to say *kadish* for the souls of their fathers and mothers. It was known that there would be left no elder nor young, neither children nor babies.

Some of the survivors tell how Jews were gathered inside the death wagons, before mass executions, and said *kadish* in public.

And sometimes Jews would recite psalms or, when they were already sitting in a mourning, sitting on the floors of the freight cars, they would begin by saying "Book of Lamentations" and lament. In the verses of Jeremiah the prophet and the verses of Judah Halevi, just before their own destruction, they would lament about the destruction of Jerusalem. With these lamentations they prepared themselves; they were saying goodbye to everything dear to them, as they set off on their last journey - to death. Even among those to whom the world of Judaism was already almost a stranger, there were a few who knew by heart some kind of a prayer. The others would stand and listen and like proselytes, they would repeat the verses word for word, in which they asked for an essential point of reference, some kind of a grip on something before their death.

While the former neighbors of my uncle, who lived in the village took him out of his hiding place and led him away to the Jewish cemetery to be shot dead, he pulled out a small prayer book from his coat pocket and said a prayer all along the way. He no longer wanted to gain even one glance at the view of the village; of the faces of those who led him; of those curious who looked at him as he walked towards death. The pages of the prayerbook were his last refuge in the world, the only refuge.

A young man who escaped from Treblinka told me about something he saw in a hut where those who were preparing to go to the "bath", the gas chambers, were taking off their clothes. There was a large group of women and children. Among them all, one tall woman stood out, whose head was wrapped in a handkerchief. She was standing in the corner, her face was turned towards the wall, to some hidden "east" she created in her imagination. Behind her stood the crowd of women and like her, they also turned their faces to that impure wall of the death hut.

As a cantor on *Yom Kipur*, as a public emissary of a group of women who were condemned to die, the woman stood on that day of judgment in Treblinka, on the day of the horrors of annihilation. In the melody of a prayer of the Days of Awe and in Yiddish words that came from her heart, she laid out her claims to God:

"Hear, O Israel, the Lord is our God, the Lord is one!", she cried comfortingly from her heart, "Lord of the world, you are our one and only father and we have no father but you. Open your eyes and see our poverty, look at our baseness and accept the cry of our children and babies. Remove from us all sin… so that we may be honored… like our ancestors

[Page 424]

Avraham, Yitskhak and Yakov, and as our mothers Sora, Rivke, Rokhl and Leye… may we be blessed… there… with all our loved ones… Merciful Father in heaven!"

A cry burst from her heart and she fell silent. And the whole hut was shaken for a moment by crying, similar to the crying in the holy Day of Awe in the women's section.

"And for the sake of God" the woman opened again with renewed strength "for the sake of your holy name in the world – take our revenge, demand our blood from the hands of our tormentors. Let not our sacrifice be in vain! The cry of the torture of our children, everything they did to us – may it be on their heads and on the heads of their descendants! On the sons and the children of the sons! Pursue them with your anger and destroy them! Uproot them, as they do to us! Merciful Father in heaven!"

With these words or something similar to them, the woman cried out her plea. She spread her hands towards heaven and the crowd of women stood behind her and with pale lips whispered every word with her. As in the blessing of the candles, their faces were covered with the palms of their hands, they moved their bodies silently and the tears were dropping down through their fingers as in the blessing of the candles.

And by chance, at that time, those who were taking care of the work of extermination did not look at that corner and did not desecrate it. Little by little, the voice of the women went silent until it was blended into the sound of the rest of the crowd.

And another incident was told to me that happened in Warsaw at the end of the first action days in September 1942.

One day an old Jew came out. Early in the morning, he emerged from his hiding place and decided that he was done with hiding in hiding places. Wrapped entirely in a white robe and a *talis*, as on the Day of Awe, while his lips were whispering a prayer, he went out into the street, to receive the fate destined for him. With his white beard, wrapped in a white robe, his entire appearance expressed a total whiteness and purity. He walked around in the panic that was on the street for a few moments. One executioner soldier or another passed by and did not harm the Jew, who seemed to no longer belong to this world. Finally, one aimed his weapon at him from a distance and shot him, as if he was afraid to look at the shining and bright face of the Jew wearing white.

Hear, O Israel, the Lord is our God, the Lord is one!

And one is your destiny, the people of Israel, among all the nations of the world.

Shema Yisroel - Hear O Israel

[Page 425]

Self-Sacrifice During Exile

by K. Neyekh, Israel

Translated by Tina Lunson

After a difficult weeks-long slog on beautiful Russian railroad cars, in dirt, hunger and thirst, we finally arrived in a "place of comfort".

I say "place of comfort". It was not any villa in Crimea on the Black Sea or a palace on Nevski Prospect in Leningrad. They threw us into a deep forest in Vologda province, USSR.

It was wintertime. The snow covered the world. Our eyes were pained from the blinding blue-white. The cold burned; cut into our limbs like needles.

In several wooden barracks that that we could barely see out of for the snow, we were quartered in small cabins about four by four. Close to seventy Jewish families with their wives, children and household goods were packed into the disgusting chambers with their bags and packs. There was no place to sit or even to stand.

The Jewish deportees were from Pultusk, Dlugashodle, Suvalk and other places. From Goworowo, there were five or six families. Besides them there were also some twenty Christian families, deported Polish officers and administrators.

Kamaritse was the name of the exile area in the Tatshimske region. In this primeval forest, we were to cut down trees. They were sawed and lugged on wagons to the nearest train station.

The grueling work in Egypt was a game compared to the penal colony labor in this place. From before dawn until late in the evening, the hungering, suffering people lifted and carried the loads like asses, without rest, without food to satisfy, under the rigorous watch of the N.K.V.D. And in the cold of 55 degrees. Our skin split under the pressure and our feet were swollen like puff pastries. And all this did not awaken a drop of mercy from the Russian supervisors, the N.K.V.D.

But I am not just describing the bundle of troubles of the deportation camp. I believe that there is enough material for a large book. Here I will only tell the chapter of strength of a Goworowo Jew, Reb Itsele, who had

[Page 426]

the moral devotion to lay *tfiln* and pray every day, although he knew that it could cost him his life.

The head of that camp was a certain Ivan, an N.K.V.D. officer, an extremely wicked man who had an allergic hatred for the Jewish faith. Nothing bothered him as much as a Jew donning *talis* and *tfiln* and praying.

I do not know why it fell to me, that Ivan made me responsible for the whole camp. Perhaps because I was the baker there and I served everyone their fresh roll. Ivan promised me that I should report to him when Jews prayed, in order for him to come and punish them. And he warned me that if ever I kept anything from him, he would take me out of the bakery and send me into the forest.

Yon-kiper came and *kol-nidrey*. I wrapped myself in my *talis* and buried myself in a corner. I would certainly not want Ivan to find out that I myself prayed. On the morning of *Yon-kiper,* the few Jews hid in a side room to pray. Ivan sought them but did not find them. He sent me to search. I went off and quickly told everyone to run away. I reported to Ivan that I did not find anyone. Then Ivan encountered a watchmaker from Suvalk, whom he saw was carrying a prayer book around. He gritted his teeth but he could do nothing to him. He had not caught him in the act.

Then once Ivan chanced to notice Itsele standing in *talis* and *tfiln*, praying. Raging blood pounded in his head. He ripped the *talis* and *tfiln* off him and attacked him like a thief, screaming and ranting. "One more time", he warned him, "I will see you begging in the street, you will never get out of prison."

We begged Reb Itsele to have mercy on himself and not to pray in *talis* and *tfiln*, because the murderer already had his eye on him. It was a death threat. Reb Itsele smiled and did not answer. In the morning, he again did what was his right, prayed in *talis* and *tfiln* as if nothing had happened.

Ivan made good on his threat. He found Reb Itsele praying again, He immediately arrested him and sent him to the Tatshimske prison.

Reb Itsele could not tolerate the conditions in the prison. He got sick there and died.

For all of us, it was clear that Reb Itsele had made an accounting of his deeds and he clearly knew that by praying in *talis* and *tfiln* he put his life in danger. He was, however, prepared to go as a martyr in God's name.

Certainly, such a case of heroic strength should be noted in Jewish history.

[Page 427]

Goworowo Without Jews

by Mordkhe Govartshik, Israel

Translated by Tina Lunson

It turned out that I was in Goworowo three times after the war and each time I went around as if in a cemetery. I could not make peace with the idea that there were no more Jews in the town.

The first time I was in Goworowo in 1947, along with Khayim Shmelts and Tuvye Bielik. It was a visit for personal purposes. The town was not recognizable. On every street stood several new houses on provisional foundations, built by Christians. That time I found the town in the following condition:

On Gedalye Grinberg's place and several places near it were built, provisionally of wood, the *Powshechna* school. The janitor was still the same one from before the war, Rorat. On Rozene's place was the township office. A little further on, on Shafran's place, there was a little shop. Across from that, on Verman Shikora's place, Stefan Vaytotski had made a business of hog products. After that, Tseglenski had built back his bakery. On Shaul Potash's place, another shop. On Ratenski's place one of his former employees had made a meat business. Khana Fridman's masonry house had only been half burned and the younger Rorat had repaired it and opened a hair styling institute there (see the photo on page 52). A little further on, Sobotka the "mayor" had established a shop and a restaurant. The priest's palace, the church and the whole *Probostva* remained untouched. The fire did not come here. Khayim Potash's shop was being run by a certain Yozefa from Bank Lane. The small mill of the Krulevitshes and Dronzd was specially lit afire and burned by the Germans. The larger mill of the brothers Rits was moved over to Bobovska's place on the Broad Street, apparently after the Germans. Dr. Glinka lived in his house above and under that was the *pasterunek*, the police station. Voytotski had built a business on Gerlits's place. Ratenski had built back his manufacturing business but on a smaller scale. The place of the study house was still fenced in with barbed wire then. The bricks from the building had been taken earlier by the

[Page 428]

Christians, who used them for their own houses. Where Yoelke's bakery had been there was another bakery belonging to a Christian. On Menashe Holtsman's place a Christian had made a shop. And on Gurki's place there already stood a little house. A gentile from Yavores had already begun building on the *Rov*'s place and that of Kosovski-Rozen. When I told him that the proprietors were still alive, he ran away. On the corner place of Gemora and Vishnia a *goy* from Yavores had built a restaurant. A Christian from Sukhtshits had bought the place near it and set up a shop there. On the Bank Lane, on Mordkhe Alek's place, one of Voytshik's sisters had put up a little house. Here and there, were a few other houses.

The cemetery was totally destroyed. (See photo on page 23.) The sole sign was the watchman's hut, which stood there as a remembrance.

The princely estates around Goworowo had been confiscated by the Polish government. Glinka's son Stanislav had become a registered manager for an estate in the Wroclaw area. All the villages around Goworowo remained untouched and did not suffer from the war. Thursday remained, as usual, the market day. The grain from the peasants was bought by cooperatives. The *goyim* took the produce to Warsaw. As a rule, all the commerce lay in Christian hands. But it was not the market day from before the war, with the Jewish merchants and craftsmen, with the shopkeepers and traders who brought life to the trading, initiative, and who were also good customers. Then, the peasant was also happy because he received earnings for his work, and with that money he could buy whatever he wanted.

I was also in Pasheki. The station master was still the same Yagella. But everything was dead. Now there were no Jewish expeditors or the wagons full of grain and wood that used to pass through every week on their way to Warsaw. And where were the wagons of coal, cement and other materials that used to arrive here for Goworowo, Ruzshan and other places around here?

A depression lay over the Christian population. It was hard for them to adapt to the new regime. They were afraid for the future. Also, the peasants lived in fear that their land would be nationalized and a *kolkhoz,* collective, would be instituted. The entire management was in the hands of the young Communists and workers.

I was in Goworowo again in 1948 and 1949. During that time another few Jews had sold their places there, but no great changes came about in the persona of the town. Here and there new houses were built, there were some *goyishe* craftsmen, but the ruin was still vividly evident.

I wander over the streets and sad thoughts come into

[Page 429]

my mind. I recall the bristling life of our purely Jewish *shtetl*, with the organizations and political parties, with the institutions and little prayer houses, with the merchants and tradesmen, fine Jews and laborers, and the fermenting youth, who were so bestially murdered by the Hitleristic hoards. I can still not abandon the thought that the *shtetl* where I was born and educated now remains without Jews forever.

Received by B. K.

Kadish

From a Eulogy at a Goworowo Memorial Evening

by *Rov* Meyshe Bernshteyn, Israel

Translated by Tina Lunson

Hebrew translated and annotated by Jerrold Landau

Rov Meyshe Bernshteyn speaks

The great Jewish prophet, the *novi* Yermiahu, who lived through the destruction of the First Temple, received from heaven the divine mission to lament that Jewish calamity. He composed the mournful scroll, "How lonely sits the city, that once was full of people has become like a widow". [Lamentations 1:1]. He spattered it with fiery lava. He found words to depict the catastrophe, the scope of the destruction; he found the appropriate curses for the gentile criminals; and in the end, he still sought in his arsenal of language for a few words of comfort for the tormented Jewish people.

We stand here today and think, what would Yermiahu the prophet say if he had experienced our calamity? Would he find the thunderous, flaming words to characterize even one tenth of the catastrophe? "Would it be that my head were water and my eyes a source of tears, that I might weep day and night for the slain of the daughter of my people!" [Jeremiah 8:23[1]] is absolutely not enough to lament six million martyrs who were killed by such barbaric tortures that Ashmoday[2] himself did not even think of.

[Page 430]

Could one mine out, from all the 70 languages of the world, such curses that would even a little ease the feelings of revenge against the Nazi persecutors? And are there any such words of consolation that could comfort such a grieving people?

The great poet *Rebi* Yehuda Haleyvi also lived in a tragic epoch. The huge troubles that were let loose on the heads of the Jews in Spain touched his sensitive heart and opened the muse of heavenly poetry. He mourned for the Second Destruction and created the elegy *Sha'ali Tsion*, which one recites along with the dirges for *Tishe B'ov*, with the finale "Lament oh Zion and her cities, like a woman in her birth pangs and like a maiden enwrapped in sackcloth for the husband of her youth."[3]

For our contemporary catastrophe the words are too pale. Can "like a woman in her birth pangs" be compared to the crematoria? Is "like a maiden enwrapped in sackcloth for the husband of her youth" a parable for Auschwitz, Dachau and Treblinka? Both the husband and the maiden in her youth were incinerated in the crematoria, along with their fathers, mothers, brothers and sisters together. There is much doubt, whether even that great, godly poet would have been able to gather the fitting words to depict the tragedy of our generation.

The national poet Khayim Nakhman Bialek experienced the horrifying pogroms in Ukraine and Russia. He wrote the *Megilas puranios* [Scroll of Tribulations] and mourned the Jewish tragedy. He shed a tear for Jewish troubles.

If he lived today, his tears would be turned into blood. He would break his pen and refuse to be a poet for Jews. For, how could one, with a human pen, express such inhuman murders and bestiality?

For our tragedy there is only one expression in the Torah. At the end of the "reproofs" in *parsha ki-savo* it is written, "the Lord will bring upon you all the other diseases and plagues that are not mentioned in this book of teaching". One cannot describe this. The *Midrash* on this says, "When they heard the one hundred minus two [i.e. 98) curses, their faces immediately became pale". The commentators ask, why does the Commentary ask, "Why does it say 'one hundred curses minus two, and not ninety-eight curses' as people usually count?". The commentators answer, that the "minus two" refers to the two terrible curses of "all the other diseases and plagues that are not mentioned in this book of teaching". If such curses exist, that the holy Torah itself has not found any suitable expression for them, it is a terrible thing for us. "Their faces became pale." "The faces of those who heard the unspoken curses turned green and yellow on account of that for which the Torah found no expression" – that is the greatest expression of our huge tragedy.

However great our tragedy, so great must our comfort be. Our most urgent request to the Master of the Universe is that He may transform the "hundred curses" into "hundred blessings". He should send down an abundance of so much good, even more

[Page 431]

than He promised us in His holy Torah. It should reinforce the strength of the Jewish land and a spirit of uplift should be sent down from heaven for the Jewish people.

But with only our comfort the tragedy is still not exhausted. We are still somehow guilty to the victims too. They were murdered as martyrs in sanctification of the Divine Name, not just for us but for the entire Jewish people. The Jewish homeland was established on their tormented souls. What must we do to eternalize and sanctify the memory of them?

When a father or a mother, heaven forbid, dies, the children, the orphans, rise up and say, "*Yisgadol v'yiskadeysh shemey rabo*". In essence the Master of the Universe has taken away the dearest that they had. A misfortune has befallen them. Instead of complaints for the Creator of the World, they go to praise and extol His name.

The truth is that the children feel the suspicion. But they consider the *kadish* as a sacred obligation over the fresh graves of their dear father and mother, who served the Master of the Universe with every fiber of their souls; and they promise that they will follow in the paths of their parents. With the death of a father or a mother there is a void in the Jewish world. A soldier in the divine army has fallen. It diminishes the power of the Creator, so to speak. A trusted servant is missing, who would extol and praise Him. In that, really, the innocent faith of our parents was very large. A father's prayer, an afternoon and evening prayer service. The Mama's reading out the *Tsene-u'rene*. The night after *Shabes*, when she closes her kosher eyes and whispers her quiet prayer, "*Got fun Avrom*, the holy *Shabes* is going away and the good week is coming to us, for us and for the entire Jewish folk". Such pure faith is not to be found in any other nation or language. Now come the children, the orphans, who promise that they will fill in the hollow place that has become empty with the death of their parents,"*Yisgadel v'yiskadeysh shemey rabo...*" May God's name be extoled and sanctified by His surviving children.

Let us now present what kind of gaps there are in the Jewish people after the horrifying death of six million fathers, mothers, children, brothers and sisters, scholars, cabalists, scientists, merchants and laborers. How small God's world has become.

Therefore our oath must be holy, "*Yisgadel v'yiskadeysh shemey rabo*". We, the survivors, the saved remnant, will fill the large rupture in the body of the Jewish people. We will build back the ruins in a physical sense and we will lift up the eternal Jewish spirit before the whole world. We will cry out, affirming in public, "*Yisgadel v'yiskadeysh shemey rabo!*"

Translator's notes:

1. From the *Haftara* reading for the *Tisha B'av* morning service
2. Also called *Asmodeus*, a king of demons in the legends of Solomon
3. *Shaali Tzion* was written by Judah Halevi. *Eili Tzion*, from which the last quote comes, is from a different elegy of unknown authorship and is the final elegy of the *Tisha B'av* morning service, recited with a unique melody.

[Page 432]

Elegy for David
(Psalms Chapter 16)

Composer: A. Y. Brukhanski

Translated by Mira Eckhaus

In memory of my father of blessed memory, my mother may God avenge her blood, and all my family members who perished in the Nazi Holocaust

[Page 433]

These Are Memorials

The memorial plaque in honor of the Goworowo martyrs
in the Holocaust Cellar on Mount Zion in Jerusalem

[Page 434]

Prayer for the Dead
God, Full of Mercy

Translated by Mira Eckhaus

Edited by Tina Lunson

Creator of the earth and the heavens, who hears the cry of the afflicted, the judgment of widows and orphans, please do not remain silent over the blood of your people Israel, which has been shed like water. Provide a proper rest upon the wings of the Holy Spirit, within the virtues of the holy and the pure, who shine like the starry heavens for the souls of six million of our sisters and brothers, and among them the members of our holy congregation of Goworowo and the surrounding area, hundreds of men and women, boys and girls, children and toddlers, who were killed and slaughtered and suffocated and drowned and burned and buried alive by the impure German Amalekites and oppressors – in the crematoria and the gas chambers in Auschwitz, Majdanek, Treblinka and the rest of the occupied lands under the hands of the Nazi enemy. All of them are holy and pure and among them are the mighty of the spirit, geniuses and righteous, innocent and sincere, rabbis and *hasidim*, mighty in the Torah and their scholars. May the Lord remember them favorably and may they rest in heaven, the Lord of Mercy will safeguard them secretly in his wings forever, and bind their souls in the bundle of life. May the Lord be their inheritance, and He will avenge their vengeance, and He will remind us of their sacrifice. And may their right will stand for our benefit and for the benefit of the entire people of Israel. O Lord, do not cover their blood, do not be a resting place for their screams. Thanks to them, the remnants of the people of Israel will return to their land, and the righteousness of these saints will always be remembered before God, may they rest in peace wherever they may be lying, and they will wake up and stand forever for the revival of their souls, and let us say, Amen.

[Pages 435-445]

List of the Slain

Transliterated by Haim Sidor

Note: Page numbers refer to pages in the original book

Family name(s)	First name(s)	Gender	Additional family	Remarks	Page
AGRADNIK	Yosef	M			435
AGRADNIK	Miriam	F			435
AGRADNIK	Yaakov	M			435
AGRADNIK	Rachel	F			435
AGRADNIK	Toiva	F			435
AGRADNIK	Berel	M			435
AUSLANDER	Haim	M			435
AUSLANDER	Devora Yitka	F			435
AUSLANDER	Avraham Yossel	M			435
AUSLANDER	Gittel	F			435
AUSLANDER	Shaina	F			435
OZDAVA	Kalman	M			435
OZDAVA	Vita	F			435
OZDAVA	Moshe David	M			435
OZDAVA	Yitzhak	M			435
OZDAVA	Yachat	F			435
OZDAVA	Devora	F			435
OZDAVA	Ezriel	M			435
OZDAVA	Necha	F			435
OZDAVA	Rashka	F			435

OZDAVA	Shimon	M			435
OZDAVA	Hannah Chaya	F			435
OZDAVA	Tzalka	F			435
OZDAVA		M		Tailor	435
EIZENBERG	Braina	F			435
ECKOLTSHIK	Mottel				435
OLIARZSH	Hershel	M			435
OLIARZSH	Toiva	F			435
OLIARZSH	Yisrael	M			435
OLIARZSH	Haim Leib	M			435
OLIARZSH	Pesha	F			435
OLIARZSH	Chaya Sarah	F			435
OLIARZSH	Esther	F			435
OLIARZSH	Yisrael Nachum	M			435
OLIARZSH	Tzalva	F			435
OLIARZSH	Yenta	F			435
OLIARZSH	Chava	F			435
ALECK	Mala	F			435
ALECK	Moshe	M			435
ALECK	Hannah	F			435
ALECK	Sarah	F			435
ALECK	Pesha	F			435
ALECK	Yehoshua	M	child		435
	Chava	F		husband's name Moshe. Maiden name ALEK	435
	Moshe	M		wife's name Chava	435
ALECK	Yakel	M			435
ALECK	Golda	F			435
ALECK	Hannah	F			435

ALECK	Devora	F			435
ALECK	Leah	F			435
OSTASHEVER	Yosef David	M			436
OSTASHEVER	Yitka	F			436
OSTASHEVER	Chaya Leah	F			436
OSTASHEVER	Esther Faiga	F			436
OSTASHEVER	Fishel Zvi	M			436
APPLEBAUM	Mordecai	M			436
BORSTEIN	Alter Moshe Mordecai	M		Rabbi	436
BATSHAN	Mendel	M			436
BATSHAN	Yosef	M			436
BATSHAN	Shlomo Eliezar	M	children	wife's name Liba	436
BATSHAN	Liba	F	children	husband's name Shlomo Eliezar	436
BARG	Velvel	M			436
BARG	Sima	F			436
BARG	Zvi	M			436
BARG	Feintsha	F			436
BARNIKAVITCH	Laizer	M			436
BARNIKAVITCH	Hannah	F			436
BARNIKAVITCH	Shmuelka	M			436
BORNSTEIN	Berish	M			436
BORNSTEIN	Chaya	F			436
BORNSTEIN	Simcha	M			436
BORNSTEIN	Yaakov	M			436
BORNSTEIN	Pesach	M	children		436
BORNSTEIN		F	children	husband's name Pesach	436
BONDA	Yaakov Yehoshua	M			436
BONDA	David	M			436

BORSTEIN	Yisrael	M	children		436
BORSTEIN		F	children	husband's name Yisrael	436
BIALIK	Zlata	F			436
BIALIK	Laizer	M			436
BIALIK	Rivka	F			436
BIALIK	Mirel	F			436
BIALIK	Moshe Mendel	M			436
BIALIK	Raichel	F			436
BIALIK	Shaina	F			436
BLUMSTEIN	Velvel	M			436
BLUMSTEIN	Faiga Nechama	F			436
BLUMSTEIN	Shmuel	M			436
BLUMSTEIN	Gershon	M			436
BLUMSTEIN	Devora	F			436
BLUMSTEIN	Arieh	M			436
BLUMSTEIN	Noah	M			436
BELFER	Fraida Shifra	F			436
	Chaya Raizel	F	children	husband's name Moshe. Maiden name BENGELSADAROF	436
	Moshe	M	children	wife's name Chaya Raizel	436
BERLINSKI-KLASS	Braina	F			436
BERLINER	Sarah	F			436
BERLINER	Haim	M			436
BERLINER	Chaya Sarah	F			436
BERLINER	Tcharna Leah	F			436
BERLINER	Leibel	M			436
BERLINER	Faiga	F			436
BERLINER	Meir	M			436

BERLINER	Yechiel Moshe	M			436
BERLINER	Gittel	F			436
BERLINER	Shaina	F			436
BERLINER	Simcha Hershel	M			436
BERLINER	Braindel	F			436
BERLINER	Yaakov Hersh	M			436
BERLINER	Zeiftel				436
BERLINER	Miriam	F			436
BERLINER	Rachel	F			436
BRAMBERGER	Yisrael Yitzhak	M	children	wife's name Leah	436
BRAMBERGER	Leah	F	children	husband's name Yisrael Yitzhak	436
BARZILAI	Avraham	M			436
BRICK	Feivel	M			436
BRICK	Esther Rivka	F			436
BRICK	Hershel	M			436
BRICK	Sarah Rivka	F			436
BRICK	Gittel	F			436
BRICK	Leibel	M			436
BRICK	Beinish	M			436
BRICK	Yitzhak	M			436
BRICK	Chaitsha	F			436
BRICK	Haim	M			436
BRICK	Moshe	M			436
BRICK	Necha	F			436
BRESSLER	Moshe Zindel	M			436
BRESSLER	Rachel	F			436

BESSERMAN	Shlomo Akiva	M			436
GOVARCHIK	Leah	F			437
GOVARCHIK	Aviezer	M			437
GOVARCHIK	Yisrael	M			437
GALANT	Avraham Yitzhak	M			437
GALANT	Hendel	F			437
GALANT	Moshe	M			437
GALANT	Rivka	F			437
GALANT	Haim	M			437
GALANT	Shlomo	M			437
GALANT	Yisrael	M			437
GOLAVINSKI	Chava	F			437
GOLAVINSKI	Simcha	M	children	wife's name Tshipa	437
GOLAVINSKI	Tshipa	F	children	husband's name Simcha	437
GORDON	Pesha	F			437
GORA	Sarah Roiza	F			437
GORA	Chaya Elka	F			437
GORMAN	Yaakov	M			437
GORMAN	Michael	M			437
GURFINKEL	Yiddel	M			437
GURFINKEL	Rivka	F			437
GURFINKEL	Sarah	F			437
GURFINKEL		M		mother's name Sarah. A child	437
GORKA	Mordecai Leib	M			437
GORKA	Devora	F			437
GORKA	Sender	M			437
GLOGOVER	Alta Chaya	F			437
GLOGOVER	David	M			437

GLOGOVER	Malka	F			437
GLOGOVER	Hershel	M			437
GLOGOVER	Baila	F			437
GELBARD	Shlomo	M			437
GERLITZ	Yechiel	M			437
GERLITZ	Rachel Leah	F			437
GERLITZ	Yitzhak Velvel	M			437
GERLITZ	Rachel	F			437
GERLITZ	David Hershel	M			437
GERLITZ	Mordecai	M	child		437
GRODKA	Avraham	M			437
GRODKA	Bina	F			437
GRODKA	Toiva	F			437
GRODKA	Liba	M			437
GRODKA	Hannah	F			437
GRODKA	Braina	F			437
GRODKA	Rachel	F			437
GRODKA	David Aharon	M			437
GRODKA	Tzirel	F			437
GRODKA	Zissa	F			437
GRODKA	Eliezar	M			437
GRODKA	Yechezkel	M			437
GRODKA	Haim Ber	M			437
GRODKA	Braina	F			437
GRODKA	Bracha	F			437
GRODKA	Rachel	F			437
GRAINER	Shalom	M			437
GRAINER	Leah	F			437

GRAINER	Braina	F			437
GRAINER	Berel	M	2 children		437
GRAINER		F	2 children	husband's name Berel	437
GRAINER	Esther	F			437
GREENBERG	Gedalyahu	M			437
GREENBERG-NIKS	Braina Perel	F			437
GREENBERG	Fishel	M			437
GREENBERG		M		Father's name Fishel	437
DEUTSCH	Velvel	M			437
DEUTSCH	Rivka	F			437
JIZA	Shlomo	M			437
JIZA	Baila	F	2 children		437
JIZA	Dan	M			437
JIZA	Chaya	F			437
DENDA	Pinchas	M		Pinchas	437
DENDA	Moshe	M			437
DENDA	Faiga	F			437
DROZED	Yehoshua Mordecai	M			437
DROZED	Baila	F			437
DROZED	Yerachmiel	M			437
DROZED-WALBERG	Sarah Leah	F			437
DROZED	Yosef	M			437
DROZED	David	M			437
DROZED	Esther	F			437
DROZED	Yaakov	M		married	437
DROZED		F		husband's name Yaakov	437
DREVIANKA	Litman	M			437
DREVIANKA	Rachel	F	2 children		437

HOLTZMAN	Menashe	M			438
HOLTZMAN	Esther	F			438
HOLTZMAN	Leib Hersh	M			438
HOCHSTEIN	Alter	M			438
HOCHSTEIN	Rivka Rachel	F			438
HOROWITZ	Haim	M			438
HOROWITZ	Hannah Shifra	F			438
HOROWITZ	Sarah	F			438
HOROWITZ	Hadassa	F			438
HOROWITZ	Moshe	M			438
HOROWITZ	Esther	F			438
HOROWITZ	Fradel	F			438
HOROWITZ	David	M			438
HERTZBERGER	Yishaya	M			438
HERTZBERGER	Tshipa	F			438
HERTZBERGER	Miriam Rachel	F			438
HERTZBERGER	Yachat	F			438
HERTZBERGER	Mordecai	M			438
HERTZBERGER	Nesha	F			438
HERTZBERGER	Natan	M			438
HERTZBERGER	Zelig	M			438
HERTZBERGER	Faiga	F			438
HERTZBERGER	Hershel	M			438
WANZSH	Avraham	M			438
WANZSH	Faiga	F			438
WASSER	Shimon	M			438
WASSER	Chaya Malka	F			438
WASSER	Hannah	F			438

WASSER	Dina	F			438
WASSER		M		mother's name Dina	438
WASSER		M		mother's name Dina	438
WOFNIAZSH	Yuspa				438
WOFNIAZSH	Gittel	F			438
WOFNIAZSH	Hannah	F			438
WOFNIAZSH	Shlomo	M			438
WEISBARD	Tema	F			438
WEISBARD	Chaya	F			438
WEISBARD	Yehudit	F			438
WEISBARD	Rachel Leah	F			438
WEISBARD	Avraham	M			438
WEISBARD	Daba	F			438
WISOTZKI	Hannah	F			438
WISOTZKI	Anshel	M			438
WISOTZKI	Elka	F			438
WISOTZKI	Zisel	F			438
WIROSLOV	Bertsha	F			438
WIROSLOV	Toiva	F			438
WIROSLOV	Yitzhak	M			438
WIROSLOV	Chaya Leah	F			438
WIROSLOV	Shaina Rachel	F			438
WIROSLOV	Bendit	M			438
WIROSLOV	Braina	F			438
WIROSLOV	Basha	F			438
WIROSLOV	Yehoshua David	M			438
WIROSLOV	Hamma	F			438
VISHNIA	Baila Rachel	F			438
VISHNIA	David	M			438

VISHNIA	Masha	F	child		438
WENGROV	Yaakov Hersh	M			438
WENGROV	Rivka	F			438
WENGROV	Hannah	F			438
WERMAN	Zalman	M			438
WERMAN	Sarah Dvasha	F			438
WERMAN	Yerachmiel	M			438
WERMAN	Meir	M			438
WERMAN	Izak	M			438
WERMAN	Laizer	M			438
WERMAN	Rachel	F			438
WERMAN	Shabtai	M			438
WERMAN	Hannah	F			438
WERMAN	Avraham	M			438
WERMAN	Tzirel Leah	F			438
WERMAN		F		mother's name Tzirel Leah	438
ZAMELSON	Yechezkel	M			438
ZAMELSON	Sima	F	2 children		438
ZILBER	Necha	F			438
ZILBERSON	Yonatan	M			438
ZILBERSON	Haim Eliezar	M			438
ZILBERSON	Meir	M			438
ZILBERSON	Rachel	F			439
ZILBERSON	Asher	M			439
ZILBERSON	Hersheleh	M			439
ZILBERSON	Moshe	M			439
ZILBERSON	Nechama	F			439
ZILBERSON	Yaakov	M			439
ZILBERSTEIN	Sarah	F			439

ZILBERSTEIN	Simcha	M			439
ZILBERSTEIN	Rivka	F			439
ZILBERSTEIN	Feivel	M			439
ZILBERSTEIN	Yocheved	F			439
ZILBERSTEIN	Yossel	M			439
ZILBERSTEIN	Golda	F			439
ZILBERSTEIN	Raizel	F			439
ZILBERSTEIN	Berel	M			439
ZIMAN	Anshel	M			439
ZIMAN	Braina	F			439
ZIMAN	Haim	M			439
ZIMAN-KLASS	Sarahtsha	F			439
CHEN	Yechezkel	M	children	married	439
CHEN		F	children	husband's name Yechezkel	439
CHETZRON	Faiga Shifra	F			439
TOIZ	Yakel	M			439
TOIZ	Faiga Pesha	F			439
TOIZ	Tzivia	F			439
TOIZ	Anshel	M			439
TOIZ	Rachel Leah	F			439
TOIZ	Elka	F			439
TOIZ	Sarahtsha	F			439
TOIZ	Velvel	M			439
TOIZ	Leibel	M			439
TOIZ	Rachel	F			439
TOIZ	Moshe	M			439
TOIZ	Rachel	F	2 children		439
TEITELBAUM	Roiza	F			439
TEITELBAUM	Hershel	M			439
TEITELBAUM	Esther	F			439

TEITELBAUM	Yechezkel	M			439
TEITELBAUM	Hannah	F			439
TEITELBAUM	Haim	M			439
TEITELBAUM	Shaina	F			439
TEITELBAUM	Hershel	M			439
TEITELBAUM	Zalman	M			439
TEITELBAUM	Avraham	M			439
TEITELBAUM	Hannah Gittel	F			439
TEITELBAUM	Peshka	F			439
TEITELBAUM	David	M			439
TEITELBAUM	Fradel	F			439
TEITELBAUM	Moshe	M			439
TEITELBAUM	Hannah	F			439
TEITELBAUM	Baruch Leibel	M			439
TEITELBAUM	Shlomo	M			439
TEITELBAUM	Yisrael Yitzhak	M			439
TROSHKEVITCH	Mordecai	M			439
TROSHKEVITCH	Gittel	F			439
TROSHKEVITCH	Avraham Yisrael	M			439
TROSHKEVITCH	Golda	F			439
TROSHKEVITCH	Roizka	F			439
TROSHKEVITCH	Hannah	F			439
TROSHKEVITCH	Liba	M			439
TROSHKEVITCH	Yoel	M			439
TROSHKEVITCH	Moshe	M			439
TROSHKEVITCH	Berel	M			439
TROSHKEVITCH	Meir	M			439

CHERVIN	Leibel	M			439
CHERVIN	Hinda	F			439
CHERVIN	Naftali	M			439
CHERVIN	Faiga	F			439
CHERVIN	Chaya	F			439
CHERVIN	Gittel	F			439
CHERVIN	Leah	F			439
YAGODNIK	Velvel	M			439
YAGODNIK	Shaina Tzirel	F			439
YAGODNIK	Chaya Hinda	F			439
YAGODNIK	Yenta	F			439
YARSCHAMAVEK	Nachman	M			439
YARSCHAMAVEK	Sarah	F			440
YARSCHAMAVEK	Shmuel	M			440
YARSCHAMAVEK	Malka	F			440
YARSCHAMAVEK	Rivka	F			440
YARSCHAMAVEK		M		mother's name Rivka. A child	440
YELLIN	Yoelka	M			440
YELLIN	Rivka	F			440
KASHER	Yaakov	M			440
KASHER	Rachel	F	2 children		440
KASHER	Moshe	M			440
KASHER	Baila	F	children		440
COHEN	Miriam	F			440
LUZIM	Avraham Yossel	M			440
LUZIM	Rachel	F			440
LUBELSKI	Feivel	M			440
LUBELSKI	Faiga Baila	F			440
LUBELSKI	Avraham Yosef	M			440

LEVER	Michael	M			440
LEVER	Hinda	F			440
LITMANOVITCH	Esther	F			440
LITMANOVITCH	Mordecai	M			440
LITMANOVITCH	Hannah	F			440
LITMANOVITCH	Braina	F			440
LITMANOVITCH	Chava	F			440
LITMANOVITCH	Meir Yakel	M			440
LEIBMAN	Haim Leib	M			440
LEIBMAN	Hannah Yeta	F			440
LEIBMAN	Yehoshua	M			440
LEIBMAN	Shimon	M			440
LEIBMAN	Faiga	F			440
LICHTMAN	Abba	M			440
LICHTMAN	Zissa	F			440
LICHTMAN	Leibel	M			440
LICHTMAN	Masha	F			440
LICHTMAN	Yitka	F			440
LICHTMAN	Mordecai	M			440
LICHTMAN	Chaya	F			440
LICHTMAN	Roiza	F			440
LICHTMAN	Masha	F			440
LICHTMAN	Yitka	F			440
LICHTMAN	Leibel	M			440
LICHTMAN	Yehoshua	M			440
LISS	Ziska	F			440
LISS	Esther	F	child		440
LEVKOWITCH	Devora	F			440
LEVKOWITCH	Efraim	M			440
LEVKOWITCH	Naomi	F			440

LEVKOWITCH	Rashka	F		440
LEVKOWITCH	Henech Yakel	M		440
LEVKOWITCH	Yiddel Leib	M		440
LEVKOWITCH	Aharon	M		440
LEVKOWITCH	Vita	F		440
MODRIKAMIAN	Yaska	M		440
MODRIKAMIAN	Miriam	F		440
MOLAVANI	Aharon	M		440
MOLAVANI	Sarah Sheindel	F		440
MOLAVANI	Rivka	F		440
MOLAVANI	Elisha	M		440
MOLAVANI	Miriam	F		440
MOLAVANI	Gedalyahu	M		440
MOLAVANI	Avraham	M		440
MOLAVANI	Mordecai	M		440
MOLAVANI	Shmuel	M		440
MOLAVANI	Yehoshua	M		440
MOLAVANI	Yocheved	F		440
MOLAVANI	Pesha Rivka	F		440
MOLAVANI	Braina	F		440
MOLAVANI	Shlomo	M		440
MONKETA	Natan	M		440
MONKETA	Aidel	F		440
MONKETA	Shlomo	M		440
MONKETA	Yehudit	F		440
MONKETA	Leib Hersh	M		440
MONKETA	Sarah	F		440
MAKAVIAK	Haim Matityahu	M		440

MAKAVIAK	Hinda	F			440
MAKAVIAK	Faiga	F			440
MAKAVIAK	David	M			440
MAKAVIAK	Moshe	M			441
MARIANSKI	Haim Leib	M			441
MARIANSKI	Bluma	F			441
MARIANSKI	Shlomo	M			441
MARIANSKI	Moshe	M	2 children	married	441
MARIANSKI		F	2 children	husband's name Moshe	441
MINTZ	Rachel	F			441
MINTZ	Itsha	F			441
MINTZ	Etka	F			441
MASHESON	Devora	F			441
MASHESON	Yisraelik	M			441
MASHESON	Rivkala	F			441
MISHNIOT	Yisrael Meir	M			441
MISHNIOT	Tzippora	F			441
MISHNIOT	Moshe	M			441
MISHNIOT	Leibel	M			441
MISHNIOT	Esther Leah	F			441
MISHNIOT	Hannah	F			441
NAIMAN	Sarah Leah	F			441
NAIMAN	Yechiel	M			441
NAIMAN	Pesha	F			441
NAIMAN	Necha	F			441
NIEDSHAVIETZKI	Haim	M			441
NIEDSHAVIETZKI	Basha	F			441
NIEDSHAVIETZKI	Hershel	M			441
NIEDSHAVIETZKI	Esther	F			441
NIEDSHAVIETZKI	Yitzhak	M			441

NIX	Clara	F		441
NIX	Rachel	F		441
SANDALA	Benzion	M		441
SANDALA	Roiza	F		441
SANDALA	Leibel	M		441
SANDALA	Perel	F	2 children	441
SANDALA	Hershel	M		441
SANDALA	Faiga	F	2 children	441
SARNA	Chaya Sarah	F		441
SARNA	Yitzhak	M		441
SEGAL	David	M		441
SEGAL	Yehudit	F		441
SEGAL	Hella	F		441
SEGAL	Moshe	M		441
SKASHINIA	Avraham	M		441
SKASHINIA	Braina	F	2 children	441
ENGEL	Anshel	M		441
ENGEL	Rachel	F		441
ENGEL	Pesha	F		441
POTASH	Haim	M		441
POTASH	Leah	F		441
POTASH	Naska			441
POTASH	Pesha	F		441
POTASH	Simcha	M		441
POTASH	Moshe	M		441
POTASH	Leah	F		441
POTASH	Faiga	F		441
POTASH	Fishel	M		441
POTASH	Chaya	F		441
POTASH	Haim	M		441

POTASH	Leah	F			441
POTASH	Braina	F		Maiden name LEVITAN	441
POTASH		M		wife's name Braina. Maiden name LEVITAN	441
FARBA	Hannah	F			441
FISH	Menashe	M			441
FISH	Sarah Rachel	F			441
FISH	Chaya	F			441
FISH	Faiga	F			441
FISH	Yeta	F			441
FISH	Elka	F			441
FISH	Yaakov	M			441
FISH	Gittel	F			441
FISH	Chaitsha	F			441
FISH	Gisha	F	2 children		441
FINEZEIG	Hersh Berel	M			441
FINEZEIG	Braina	F			441
FINEZEIG	Raichel	F			441
PLOTKA	Shalom	M			442
PLOTKA	Rachel	F			442
PLOTKA	Golda	F			442
PLOTKA	Faiga	F			442
PLOTKA	Moshe	M			442
FRASKA	Esther	F			442
FRASKA	Roiza	F			442
FRASKA	Chava	F			442
FRASKA	Yaakov	M			442
FRASKA	Elka	F			442
FRASKA	Hannah	F			442
FRASKA	Necha	F			442

FRASKA	Yermiyahu	M			442
FRASKA	Rashka	F			442
FRASKA	Moshe	M			442
FRASKA	Haim	M			442
FRASKA	Baila	F			442
FRASKA	Sarah	F			442
FRASKA	Yitka	F	husband	married	442
FRASKA	Shalom	M			442
FRASKA	Gisha	F			442
FRASKA	Chaya	F			442
FRASKA	Ezriel	M			442
FRASKA	Rashka	F			442
FRIED	Baruch	M	family		442
FRIED	Matityahu	M			442
FRIED	Braina	F	2 children		442
FRIED	Natan	M			442
FRIED	Yitka	F	2 children		442
FRIEDMAN	Raitza	F			442
FRIEDMAN	Shlomo Zalman	M			442
FRIEDMAN	Henech	M			442
FRIEDMAN	Miriam Yehudit	F			442
FRIEDMAN	Avraham Mordecai	M	child		442
FRIEDMAN	Hannah	F			442
FRIEDMAN	Faiga	F			442
FRIEDMAN	Shabtai	M			442
FRIEDMAN	Yehoshua	M			442
FRIEDMAN	Rivka	F			442
FRIEDMAN	Sarah	F			442

FRIEDMAN	Moshe	M			442
FRIEDMAN	Hannah	F			442
FRIEDMAN	David	M			442
FRIEDMAN	Chaya Etka	F			442
FRIEDMAN	Laizer	M			442
ZALKA	Avraham	M			442
ZALKA	Leah	F			442
ZALKA	Itsha	M			442
ZALKA	Shifra	F	2 children		442
ZODIKER	Shmuel	M			442
ZODIKER	Hannah	F			442
ZODIKER	Gedalia	M			442
ZODIKER	Mordecai	M			442
ZODIKER	Berel	M			442
ZWEIBAK	Alta	F			442
ZWEIBAK	Hershel	M			442
ZWEIBAK	Itsha	M			442
ZIMBAL	Shlomo Haim	M			442
ZIMBAL	Hinda	F			442
ZIMBAL	Yitzhakel	M			442
ZIMBERG	Leah	F			442
ZIMBERG		M		wife's name Leah	442
ZIRMAN	Yitzhak	M			442
ZIRMAN	Malka	F			442
KAVNER	Yehoshua	M			442
KACHAN	Yiddel	M			442
KACHAN	Sarah Rivka	F			442
KACHAN	Yakel	M			442
KACHAN	Sarah	F			442

KACHAN	Gittel	F			442
KACHAN	Eli	M			442
KASS	Yehudit	F			442
KASS	Leah	F			442
KASS	Devora	F			442
KASS	Yehuda Leib	M			442
KASS	Leah	F			442
KASS	Shlomo	M			442
KASS	Alta Sarah	F			443
KASS	Fruma	F			443
KASS	Nechemia	M			443
KASS	Etka	F			443
KASS	Shmuel	M			443
KASS	Eliezar	M			443
KASS	Rachel Leah	F			443
KASS	Bina	F			443
KASS	Necha	F			443
KASOVSKI	Fruma	F			443
KASOVSKI	Velvel	M			443
KASOVSKI	Yitzhak	M			443
KASOVSKI	Dina	F			443
KASOVSKI	Haim	M			443
KASOVSKI	Chaya	F			443
KORVAT	Betzalel Yosef	M			443
KORVAT	Sarah Leah	F			443
KORVAT	Moshe	M			443
KORVAT	Naftali	M			443
KORVAT	Pesha Tziel	F	husband & child	married	443
KORVAT	Miriam	F			443

KARLINSKI	Leibel	M			443
KARLINSKI	Chava	F			443
KARLINSKI	Naska	F			443
KARLINSKI	Artcha	M	child	married	443
KARLINSKI		F	child	husband's name Artsha	443
KUTNER	Asher	M			443
KUTNER	Rivka Perel	F			443
KUTNER	Pesha Gittel	F			443
KUTNER	Shmuel Feivel	M			443
KUTNER	Mordecai Leib	M			443
KUTNER-BORSTEIN	Gittel	F			443
KUTNER	Yocheved	F			443
KOKAVKA	Avraham	M			443
KOKAVKA	Perel	F			443
KOKAVKA	Ezriel	M			443
KOKAVKA	Hannah	F			443
KIRIS	Hannah	F			443
KIRIS	Raizel	F			443
KIRIS	Yehoshua	M			443
KIRIS	Hershel	M			443
KIRIS	Gittel	F			443
KLASS	Avraham	M			443
KLASS	Frieva	F			443
KLASS	Shlomo	M			443
KLASS	Reuven	M			443
KLASS	Esther	F			443
KLASS	Klaya	F			443
KLASS	Fraida	F			443

KLASS	Kalman	M			443
KLASS	Devora	F			443
KLEIN	Zalman	M			443
KLEIN	Tzirel	F	child		443
KLEMPNER	Chaya Zelda	F			443
KLAPPISH	Yakel	M			443
KLAPPISH	Necha	F			443
KLAPPISH	Hannah Leah	F			443
KLAPPISH	Rachel	F			443
KERSH	Yakel	M			443
KERSH	Tryna	F			443
KERSH	Faiga	F			443
KERSH	Yenta	F			443
KERSH	Chava	F			443
KERSH	Hannah	F			443
KERSH	Getzel	M			443
KERSH	Gittel	F			443
KERSH	Shifra	F			443
KERSH	Gittel	F			443
KERSH	Faiga	F			443
KERSH	Bluma	F			443
KERSH	Yitzhak	M			443
KERSH	Leah	F			443
KERSH	Hannah	F			443
KERSH	Sarah	F			443
KERSH	Hershel	M			443
KERSH	Avraham	M			443
KERSH	Baruch	M			443
KERSH	Haim	M			443
KERSH	Yitka	F			443

KERSH	Leibel	M			443
KERSH	Sarah	F	child		443
KRULEVITCH	Haim	M			444
KRULEVITCH	Tila	F			444
KRULEVITCH	Malka	F			444
KRULEVITCH	Aharon Meir	M			444
KROK	Avraham	M			444
KROK	Tzalva	F			444
KROK	Miriam	F			444
KROK	Menachem	M			444
KROK	Bracha	F			444
KROK	Rachel	F			444
KROK	Chaya	F			444
KROK	Miriam	F			444
KROK	Yisrael Leib	M			444
KROK	Yaakov	M			444
KROK	Avigdor	M			444
KASHANSHKA	Eliezar	M			444
ROZEN	Shaina	F			444
ROZEN	Yaakov	M			444
ROZENBERG	Avraham	M			444
ROZENBERG	Elka	F			444
ROZENBERG	Yisrael	M			444
ROZENBERG	Aitzel	M			444
ROZENBERG	Yenta	F			444
ROZENBERG	Yaakov	M			444
ROZENBERG	Yishaya	M			444
ROZENBERG	Leah	F			444
ROZENBERG	Yaakov	M			444
ROZENBERG	Dan	M			444

ROZENBERG	Tona	F			444
ROZENBERG	Hannah Aidel	F			444
ROZENBERG		M		mother's name Hannah Aidel	444
ROZENZWEIG	Zelig	M		married	444
ROZENZWEIG	Miriam	F	children	married	444
RAMANER	Meir	M			444
RAMANER	Raizel	F			444
RUBIN	Mendel Haim	M			444
RUBIN	Michla	F			444
RUBIN	Hershel	M	children	married	444
RUBIN		F	children	husband's name Hershel	444
ROZSHA	Avraham	M			444
ROZSHA	Gela	F			444
ROZSHA	Chaya Leah	F			444
ROZSHA		M		mother's name Chaya Leah	444
ROZSHA		M		mother's name Chaya Leah	444
ROITMAN	Izak	M			444
ROITMAN	Fraida	F			444
ROITMAN	Baruch	M			444
ROITMAN	Gittel	F			444
REITSHIK	Yitzhak	M			444
REICHMAN	Hannah	F	children		444
RITZ	Isser	M			444
RITZ	Yenta	F			444
RITZ	Yiddel	M			444
RITZ	Motka	M			444
RITZ	Moshe	M			444
RITZ	Baila	F			444
RITZ	Golda	F			444

RITZ	Fradel	F			444
RITZ	Neta	F			444
RITZ	Etel	F			444
RITZ	Hershel	M			444
RITZ	Yitzhak	M			444
RITZ	Hannah	F	children		444
RECHTSHEID	Yosef	M		married	444
RECHTSHEID		F		husband's name Yosef	444
SCHECHTER	Pesach	M			444
SCHECHTER	Nechama	F			444
SCHECHTER	Faiga	F	3 children		444
SCHECHTER	Haim Baruch	M			444
SHAPIRA	Elka	F			444
SHAPIRA	Bracha	F			444
SHAPIRA	Hannah Mirel	F			444
SHAFRAN	Avraham	M			444
SHAFRAN	Esther	F			444
SHAFRAN	Moshe	M			444
SHAFRAN	David	M			444
SHAFRAN	Binim	M			444
SHAFRAN	Devora	F			444
SHAFRAN		M		mother's name Devora. A child	444
SCHWARTZ	Meir	M			444
SCHWARTZ	Sarah	F			444
SCHWARTZ	Yisrael	M			444
SCHWARTZ	Raizel	F			445
SCHWARTZ	Leibel	M			445
SCHWARTZ	Liba	F			445
SCHWARTZ	Pesha	F			445

SCHWARTZ	Arieh	M			445
SCHWARTZ	Yechezkel	M			445
SCHWARTZ	David	M			445
SCHWARTZ	Perel	F	2 children		445
SCHWARTZ	Aharon	M			445
SCHWARTZ	Shaina Sarah	F	child		445
SCHWARTZ	Yechezkel	M	child	married	445
SCHWARTZ		F	child	husband's name Yechezkel	445
SHULMAN	David	M			445
SHULMAN	Bluma Hena	F			445
SHULMAN	Yisrael Moshe	M			445
SHULMAN	Haim Matityahu	M			445
SHULMAN	Sarah Hinda	F			445
SHULTZ	Yisrael Aharon	M	children	married	445
SHULTZ		F	children	husband's name Yisrael Aharon	445
STOCK	Meir	M			445
STOCK	Pesha	F			445
STOCK		M		mother's name Pesha. A child	445
STOCK		M		mother's name Pesha. A child	445
STERN	Shlomo	M			445
STERN	Rachel	F			445
STERN	Berel	M			445
STERN	Wolf	M			445
STERN	Mendel	M		Rabbi	445
STESHETSHINA	Yaakov	M			445
STESHETSHINA	Chava Tzirel	F			445
SHAINIAK	Gisha	F			445
SHAINIAK	Haim	M	family		445

SHIFFER	Avraham Yakel	M			445
SHIFFER	Toiva	F			445
SHIKARA	Pinchas	M			445
SHIKARA	Rachel Leah	F			445
SHIKARA	Yehudit	F			445
SHIKARA	Aviezer	M		married	445
SHIKARA		F		husband's name Aviezer	445
SHMELTZ	Leibka	M			445
SHMELTZ	Gittel	F			445
SHMELTZ	Leah	F			445
SHMELTZ	Moshe	M			445
SHMELTZ	Yechezkel	M			445
SHMELTZ	Fruma	F			445
SHMELTZ	Avraham Meir	M			445
SHMELTZ	Zelda	F			445
SHMELTZ		M		mother's name Zelda	445
SHMELTZ		F		mother's name Zelda	445
SHMELTZ-KLASS	Tcharna	F			445
SHMELTZ	Hannah Sarah	F			445
SHNIADOVER	Yitzhak	M			445
SHNIADOVER	Leah	F	2 children		445
SHNIADOVER	Faiga	F	son-in-law		445
SHNIADOVER		F		mother's name Faiga	445
SHETZECH	Sarah Leah	F			445
SHETZECH	Michael	M			445
SHERATA	Mordecai	M			445
SHERATA	SarahNecha	F			445
SHERMAN	Chaya	F			445

SHERMAN	Eliezar	M			445
SHERMAN	Pesha	F			445
SPITALEVITCH	Rivka	F			445
SPITALEVITCH	Kalman	M			445
SPITALEVITCH	Hersh Yitzhak	M			445
SPITALEVITCH	Braina	F	children		445
SHARON	Haim David	M			445
SHARON	Baila	F			445
SHARON	Yisrael Yitzhak	M			445
SHARON	Chaya Baila	F			445
SHARON	David	M			445
SHARON	Dan	M			445
SHARON	Raizel	F			445
SHARON	Shalom Hershel	M			445
	Shprintza	F			445
	Yakel	M	wife & children		445
TEHELIM	Meir Wolf	M			445
TEHELIM	Tzippora	F			445
TEHELIM	Yosef	M			445
TEHELIM	Necha	M			445
TEHELIM	Perel	F			445
TEHELIM	Haim Yehoshua	M			445

[Page 446]

Translations by Tina Lunson

Additional Hebrew text translated by Sara Mages

REMEMBER
6.000.000

Additional List

Here one may write in the names that were, for various reasons not included in the Goworowo list.

……………………………………………..….. ……………………………………………

……………………………………………..….. ……………………………………………

……………………………………………..….. ……………………………………………

……………………………………………..….. ……………………………………………

……………………………………………..….. ……………………………………………

……………………………………………..….. ……………………………………………

……………………………………………..….. ……………………………………………

……………………………………………..….. ……………………………………………

……………………………………………..….. ……………………………………………

……………………………………………..….. ……………………………………………

……………………………………………..….. ……………………………………………

[Page 447]

REMEMBER
6.000.000

Allon-Bachuth **[Weeping oak]**

In eternal memory of the souls of our parents, sisters, brothers-in-law,
and their holy and pure children
Who were murdered by the cursed oppressors in the Holocaust years:

Our father HaRav HaGaon
Rabbi **Alter Moshe Mordechai Burshtin**, may HaShem avenge his blood
President of the court of the Holy Community of Goworowo
Perished in Treblinka on 17 Av 5703

Our mother the rebbetzin
Mrs. **Ginendel** daughter of the Hasidic Rebbe, **R' Eviezer z"l** of Ruzhin
Passed away on 2 Iyar 5696 in Goworowo

Our sister **Bluma** and her husband Rabbi **Baruch Edelshtein** of Mława
And their children **Aviezer and Ester**
Perished in Belzec in 5703

Our sister **Yeta** and her husband Rabbi **Moshe Goldfeder** of Warsaw
And their children **Simcha, Chana and Feiga**

Our sister **Rachel** and her husband Rabbi **Zelig Frenkel** of Mława
And their children **Sara and Leah**

Our sister **Zelda** and her husband Rabbi **Yeshayahu Gotdold** of Warsaw
And their daughter **Ginendel**

Their sacred memory will never fade from our hearts
and God will avenge their shed blood

Aviezer Burshtin and his family
Haifa, Kfar-Sitrin

Chava and HaRav Moshe Burshtin
Tel-Aviv

[Page 448]

Dine of blessed memory

In Eternal Remembrance

R' Yitskhak of blessed memory

Our father and grandfather **R' Yitskhak Kosovski** of blessed memory
Died in Uzbekistan on 22 Elul 5702

Our mother and grandmother **Dine Kosovski** of blessed memory
Died in Uzbekistan on 8 Adar 5704

Khaye may God avenge her blood

Our brother and uncle **Khayim Kosovski**
And his wife **Khaye** may God avenge their blood

Perished in the Nazi Holocaust

Khayim may God avenge his blood

Elkhonen of blessed memory

Our brother and uncle **Nakhman** of blessed memory
Died in Warsaw on 7 First Adar 5695

Our brother, my husband, our father and uncle **Elkhonen** of blessed memory
Died in Israel on 16 Second Adar 5722

In mourning:
The Kosovski Family
Ramat-Gan, Israel

Nakhman of blessed memory

[Page 449]

It is a pity for those who are gone and no longer to be found

Our brother **Leyb Hersh**
of blessed memory
Died in Russian exile in the war years

Our beloved mother **Sore**
of blessed memory
Died on 22 Adar 5688 in Goworowo

Our father **R' Menashe** son of **R' Mayer Holtsman** of blessed memory
Died in Russian exile
On the eve of Rosh Chodesh Sivan 5702

In sorrow: **Yeta Galati-Holtsman**
Avrom Holtsman
And their families
in Israel

In memory
of my sister

Ester

of blessed memory

In perpetuity:
Yeshayahu Tsudiker
Israel

[Page 450]

Feyge Nekhame

In Eternal Remembrance

Velvl

Our parents: **Velvl and Feyge Nekhame Blumshteyn**

Sister: **Rokhl** and her husband **Yitskhak Velvel Gerlits**
And their children.

Brother: **Shmuel Blumshteyn**

Dovid Hershl and Mordkhe Gerlits

Shmuel

All murdered in the sanctification of God's name

In deep sorrow:
Avrom Kalman Blumshteyn
Yitskhak Blumshteyn
Dovid Blumshteyn
And their families in America

[Page 451]

In Eternal Remembrance

Our father **Meyshe Skurnik** of blessed memory
Died in Israel, 1952

Our mother **Blume Skurnik** of blessed memory
Died in Goworowo, 1935

Our sister **Gitel** with her husband **Ezra Bergman** and their daughter Sore
Who perished in the Nazi Holocaust, may HaShem avenge their blood

In mourning:
Rivke Bar-Kokhba–Skurnik, Israel
Sore Blumshteyn-Skurnik, USA
Khayim Skurnik, Israel
Yosef Skurnik, Israel
Adina Karzubar-Skurnik, France
And their families

[Page 452]

In Eternal Remembrance

Motl

Our father and grandfather **Mayer Romaner** of blessed memory,
Died at the beginning of the war.

Mother and grandmother **Reyzl**, murdered.

Mother and sister **Freydke** of blessed memory.

Reyzl

Freydke

Father and brother-in-law **Yisroel Leyb Tandaytshazsh** of blessed memory,
Died in Argentina in 1954.

Brother and uncle **Motl Romaner** of blessed memory.

Sister and aunt **Hinde Leye** and her husband **Shleyme Khayim Tsimbal**
And their little son **Yitsikh'l**
All murdered,
And their little daughter **Sore'le**, died.

Yisroel Leyb

Hinde Leye

Yitsikh'l

Sore

Shleyme Khayim

In sorrow:

Devore Shron-Romaner **Avrom Romaner, Canada**
Sore Tsimerman-Romaner **Yitskhak Romaner-Tandaytshazsh**

And their families

[Page 453]

Avrom Yitskhak

The children

Yehudis

In Eternal Remembrance

Mother: **Yehudis Galant**, murdered

Brother: **Avrom Yitskhak Galant**, murdered

His wife: **Feyge**, died before the war

Their children: murdered

Sister: **Bashe Miler-Galant**, died in America

Mourners:

Khane Leye Levin and family
Khaye Gitl and **Khayim Presberg**
Shmuel Hertsl Galant and family, Israel

Bashe

In Eternal Remembrance

Our father: **Yeshayahu Yom-tov** of blessed memory,
died before the war

Mother :**Khaye Sore** of blessed memory,
died in Russia

Brother **Yitskhak**, murdered

In grief:
Feyge-Urun-Sarne
Meyshe Sarne
Zalman Sarne
And their families in Israel

[Page 454]

In Eternal Remembrance

Father: **Yisroel Yitskhak Shron**
Murdered

Mother: **Khaye Beyle**
Died at the start of the war

Brother: **Dan** and his wife **Reyzl**
And their little son **Sholem Hershl**

Brother: **Dovid**
All murdered

In deep mourning:
Rokhl Leye Koskovitsh-Shron, America
Aron Shron, Israel
And their families

In Eternal Remembrance

Our father: **R' Aron Malovani**

Our mother: **Sore Sheyndl**

Our sister: **Devore Yetke** and with her husband

Khayim Oyslender, and their children **Avrom Yosef**, **Gitl** and **Sheyne**

Our sister: **Rivke**, our brother: **Elisha**

All perished in the Nazi Holocaust

In great grief:
Meyshe Dovid Malovani
Khave Vayner-Malovani
And their families in Israel

Devore, Gitl, Avrom Yosef

[Page 455]

In Eternal Remembrance

Our parents
Khayim Dovid and **Beyle Shron**

Our sister and brother-in-law
Rokhl Leye Shikora and her husband Pinkhas
And their children **Avieyzer** and **Yehudis**

Our sister **Malke Rozenberg** and her husband **Nakhman** and their children.

Our sister **Bashe Yismeyakh** and her husband **Yekhiel** and their children.

All killed by the Nazi murderers, may God avenge their blood.

In great grief:
Nathan and **Devore Shron**
and their family in Israel

In Eternal Remembrance

Our parents: **R' Yehoshe** and **Alte Rozen** of blessed memory

Sisters : **Khave** and **Sore Blume** of blessed memory

Brother: **Yankev** of blessed memory

In mourning
Leye-Tashe, Israel
Yetke, America
And their families

[Page 456]

Perl

In Eternal Remembrance

Our father and mother, grandfather and grandmother:
Eliyahu and **Perl Zshefa**

Eliyahu

Brother and uncle:
Avrom Zshefa and his wife **Dvore Rokhl** and their children **Yoske** and **Tsvia**

Sister and aunt:
Gitl Gerver, her husband **Mordkhe** and the children **Pinkhas** and **Blume**
All murdered, may God avenge their blood.

My husband and father:
Yitskhak Reytshik of blessed memory, died during deportation to Russia.
Daughter and sister **Rivke Nekhe** and her husband **Ayzik Frand** and
their child **Lili**, murdered in Camp Auschwitz

Lili Rivke Nekhe Ayzik

Mourners:
Khaye Sore Reytshik, Israel
Zelig Reytshik, Belgium
Perl Reytshik, Germany
Shleyme Reytshik, Israel
Golde Reytshik, America
And their families

[Page 457]

Peshe Tsirl

In Eternal Remembrance

Parents: **R' Beytsalel Yosef** and **Sore Leye Karvat**

Brother: **Yankev** and his wife and children

Sister: **Peshe Tsirl** and her husband and child

Brothers: **Meyshe Aron** and **Naftali**

All murdered

Beytsalel Yosef

Naftali

Mourners:
Khane Elke Shtetin, Canada
Noyakh, Dovid and **Khayim Karvat**, Israel
and their families

Meyshe Aron

In Eternal Remembrance

My husband and our father:
R' Yankev Ha'koen Shtetin of blessed memory

My daughter and our sister:
Chava Tsirl, may God avenge her blood
Perished in 5701

In deep grief:
His wife and her mother: **Chana Elka Shtetin**, Canada

The children: **Khaye Rivke Rozental, Shmuel Yitskhak Shtetin, Dine Sore Fayntsayg, Yesheyahu Nosn Shtetin** and families

[Page 458]

In Eternal Remembrance

Yisroel

Avieyzer

Leah

Mother and sister: **Leye Govartshik**

Sister: **Blume** and her husband **Dovid Shulman** and their little children –

Shmuel Meyshe, Khayim Matisyahu and Sore Hinde

Brothers: **Avieyzer** and **Yisroel**

All were killed by the Nazi murderers. May God avenge their blood.

Brother: **Yerakhmiel**, died in 1941 in Israel

Yerakhmiel

Blume

Shmuel Meyshe

With sadness:
Ester and **Note Tenenboym**, America
Gitl Pashkovski-Tenenboym, America
Yehoshe Mordkhe Govartshik, Israel
Avrom Govartshik, America
And their families.

[Page 459]

In Eternal Remembrance

Sore

Blume

Mordkhe

Our sister, brother-in-law, aunt and uncle

Sore and **Mordkhe Blum**

And their daughter **Blume**

All murdered

In grief:
Ester and **Note Tenenboym**
Gitl Pashkovski-Tenenboym
Yehoshe Mordkhe Govartshik
Avrom Govartshik
And their families

In Eternal Remembrance

My daughter and sister

Feyge the rabbi's daughter, may God avenge her blood

Who perished in the Holocaust

In mourning:
Her mother: **Devashe Hasenholtz**
Her brother: **Shmuel** the rabbi's son
And their families in Israel

[Page 460]

In Eternal Remembrance

With deep grief and great sorrow, we mourn the passing of the most beloved woman,

Mrs. Toybe Mozes, may she rest in peace

Who passed away in the United States and brought for burial in Jerusalem

Her husband: the slaughterer **Nisan Mozes**
Her sons: **Moshe, Yakov, Avraham, Menachem, Shmue**l and their families
Her daughter: **Feiga Rosen** and her family, USA

Remember

Khane Shapira

Beyle Rits

Rokhl Klepfish

[Page 461]

In Eternal Remembrance

Yehudis **Blume** **Alte Khaye**

Grandmother: **Alte Khaye Glogover**, murdered
Mother: **Blume**, died in 1946
Sister: **Yehudis**, died in 1956

Bashe with the children

Aunt: **Bashe** and her husband **Khayim Niedzshvietski**

And their children **Hershl, Ester Leye** and **Yitskhak**

Uncle: **Dovid Glogover** and his wife **Malke**

And their children **Hershl** and **Beile**

All perished

Dovid

In grief:
The **Gemora** family in Israel and Canada

[Page 462]

In Eternal Remembrance

Our parents: **R' Avrom** and **Bina Grudka**

Our brother: **Dovid Aron** and his wife **Tsirl** and their children **Zisa Elieyzer** and **Yekhezkel**

Our brother: **Khonen**, our sisters: **Tove, Libe, Brayne** and **Rokhl**

Who perished in the Nazi Holocaust

In great grief:
Yehude Grudka
Tsipore Kliborski-Grudka
And their families in Israel

In Eternal Remembrance

My dear parents

R' Khayim and **Khane Shapira**

My dear sisters

Sore and **Hadasa**

Who were tragically killed by the German murderers, may God avenge their blood.

In deep mourning:
Velvl Horovits, Israel

[Page 463]

Our father:
Khayim Leyb Prasko, may God avenge his blood

Mother: **Ester**

Sister: **Royze**

Yermiahu, Latka, Khayim, Solek, Pesa

Sister: **Khave** and her children **Khane, Yankev, Elke, Nekhe, Yermiahu, Rashke, Meyshe, Beyle**

Brother-in-law: **Yitskhak Odzoba [Ozdoba?]**, his wife **Yakhat**,
Their children: **Devore, Ezriel, Nekhe, Rashke**

Brother-in-law: **Avrom Kukovka**, his wife **Perl**,
Their children: **Ezriel** and **Khane**.

Royze and two Fleysher daughters

Ester

Brother: **Yermiahu**, his wife **Pesa**, their children
Latka, Solek, Khayim

Brother-in-law: **Leyb Hersh Fleysher**,
His wife **Rokhl** and their children.

All murdered may God avenge their blood.

Remembered by:
Yehudis Grudka-Proska
Rivke Vinderboym-Proska
Nemi Shtrasberg-Proska
and their families in Israel.

Grandchildren

[Page 464]

In Eternal Remembrance

My husband and our father
R' Dov Appelbaum
of blessed memory
Passed away in Israel 14 Sivan 5720

My son and our brother
Mordkhe Appelbaum may God avenge his blood
Perished in the Nazi Holocaust

Mourners:
Rokhl Appelbaum
Shleyme Appelbaum
Golda Dikshteyn- Appelbaum
And their families in Israel

My husband and father **Gedalye Grinberg** of blessed memory; son and brother **Avrom Leybl** of blessed memory

Daughter and sister **Rivke Rokhl**, her husband **Shmuel Gutenberg**, their child **Meyshe**

Daughter and sister **Malke Perl** – all murdered

Immortalizing:
Khane Grinberg, Israel
Sore Yisroel-Grinberg, Canada
Yitskhak Ayzik Grinberg, Brazil
Mordkhe Grinberg, America
And their families

[Page 465]

In Eternal Remembrance

Yehudis **Rokhl**

Velvl **Teme**

Father: **Velvel Vaysbord** of blessed memory
died before the war

Mother: **Teme**

Brother: **Avrom** and his wife **Doba**

Sisters: **Libe, Khaye, Rokhl, Yehudis,**

All murdered, may God avenge their blood

In grief:
Khane Vaysbord, Colombia
Yitskhak Vaysbord, Brazil
And their families

Avrom and Doba

In memory of our father **R' Chaim Dov** son of **Dovid Aharon Grudka**

Our mother: **Brayne** daughter of **R' Shmuel**

Our sister: **Leah**, her husband: **Yeshayahu Rozenberg** and their son: **Yakov**

Our sisters: **Brokhe** and **Rokhl**

Who perished in the Nazi Holocaust

In mourning:
Elka Brukhanski-Grudka
Menukha Zeltser- Grudka

[Page 466]

In Eternal Remembrance

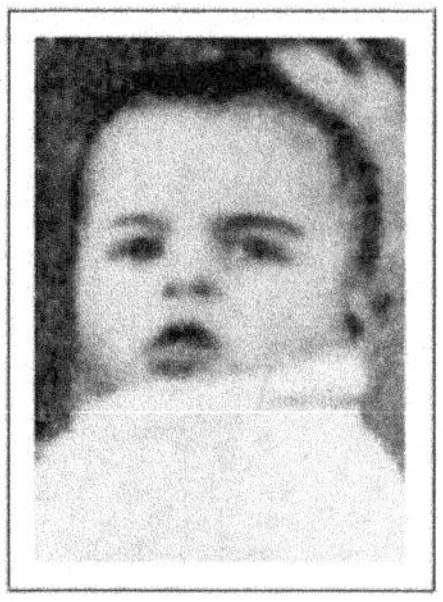

Tsvi

Our beloved father
R' Yehuda Ari Brak, may he rest in peace
Passed away in Goworowo
Was an honest and righteous man

Our beloved and faithful mother,
Hene, may she rest in peace
Passed away in Israel

Hene

Our beloved brother **Zev Brak**, his beloved wife **Sima**

Their son and daughter, young children, pleasant and lovely, **Tsvi** and **Pienza**

Who were destroyed and cut off in the Nazi Holocaust - their souls in paradise
May HaShem avenge their blood

Pienza

Sima Zev

Mourning in deep sorrow:
Pesia, Avrom and **Yafa**, Israel
Elka and **Yosef**, USA

Also, my grandfather: **R' Yehoshe Alek** of blessed memory, died before the war

Grandmother: **Mole Alek**

Uncles: **Meyshe Alek** and **Khone Alek**, and his wife **Sore**
And their three children, and **Khave Alek** – all murdered

In sadness,
Yente Reyt, Israel

[Page 467]

In Eternal Remembrance

Royze
may God avenge her blood

Leybl
of blessed memory

Khaye Elka

Our father **Leybl Gura** may his memory be for a blessing
Died in Israel

Our mother **Sore Royze Gura**

Our sister **Khaye Elka Gura**

Murdered by the Nazis. May God avenge their blood.

Immortalized by:
Meyshe Gura
Avrom Gura
And their families in Israel

[Page 468]

In Eternal Remembrance

Our parents:
Mordkhe and Ester Shmelts of blessed memory
Died in 1956 in Israel

In sadness:

Khayim Shmelts, Israel | **Shmuel Shmelts**, Israel
Mayer Shmelts, Canada | **Rokhl Grinboym-Shmelts**, Canada
Sholem Shmelts, Canada | **Meyshe Shmelts**, America

And their families

We will remember you forever!

Our tragically murdered little son and brother
Velvele may he rest in peace
Born 3 May 1935 – killed 8 June 1950

In great pain:
The parents: **Khayim** and **Khaye Shmelts**
Sister: **Rokhl**; brothers: **Yankev** and **Menakhem**

[Page 469]

Our parents
Hersh Yitskhak and **Hinke Malovani** of blessed memory
Died in America

Sister: **Peshe** and her family, murdered

Brayne, died in Russia

Brother: **Shleyme**, fought with the "Red Army", fell near Berlin

Hinke

Hersh Yitskhak

Shleyme

Peshe and Nakhman

Brayne

Immortalized by
Bashe Shafran-Malovani, Canada
Mayer Malovani, America
And their families

Remembrance

Hershl Aleyarzsh may God avenge his blood

His daughter **Khane Sore**
And **Mordkhe Litmanovits**
May God avenge their blood

[Page 470]

In Eternal Remembrance

Yekl

Mordkhe

Our parents: **Mordkhe** and **Bashe Alek** of blessed memory, died in Israel

Brother: **Yankl** and his wife **Golke**, their children **Khane** and **Devore**

Sister: **Gishe**, her husband **Sholem Proska**, their children **Khaye, Azriel, Rashke** – all murdered

Sholem

Gishe

Yekl's daughter

Sister: **Leye**, died in Russia

Brother: **Hershl**, died in America, buried in Israel

Hershl

Leye

In sadness:
Khane Berkovits-Alek
Yosl Alek, Meyshe Alek
And their families in Israel

[Page 471]

In Eternal Remembrance

Of our parents **Khayim Itshe** and **Feyge Shapira Khatsron** of blessed memory

Mourners:
Reyzl Alek-Khatsron
Tsipora Zilbershteyn-Khatsron
Dovid Khatsron
And their families in America

Peshe Gitl

In Eternal Remembrance

My father: **Asher Kutner**, his wife **Rivke**, murdered

Mother: **Yokheved**, died in 1917.

My wife: **Peshe Gitl** and the children **Shmuel Fayvl, Mordkhe Leyb**;

Sister: **Gitl Burshtin-Kutner**, her daughter **Yokheved**, all murdered

In sadness:
Avrom Yisroel Kutner
And families in Israel

[Page 481]

Landsmanshaftn: Associations of Fellow Countrymen

The *Yotse Goworowo* Organization in Israel

By Aron Shron, Israel

Translated by Tina Lunson

Aron Shron

The *Yotse Goworowo* Organization in Israel began its activities as soon as the first emigre groups from the surviving remnant after the great world destruction, began arriving. Before the First World War, there were only a small number of Goworowo Jews in the land, who were spread over various settlements, from Rehovot to Kfar Ata and in *kibutsim*. They kept in contact with one another but rarely met all together.

When the terrible reports about the destruction of Jews in Poland began to arrive, we wanted to do something, at least to know about the fate of friends and acquaintances. Our efforts did not bring any results. After some time we learned a few addresses of Goworowo deportees in Siberia. We began organizing the shipping of packages to the relatives.

At the end of 1948 the first of those rescued from the Holocaust arrived in the land. We tried to help each one with whatever we could. There were members living in one room residences who took in whole families and lived together until they had adapted a little to the land.

Khane Rokhl Kuperman developed an aid organization in America. She sent a large number of food packages for the new immigrants and we distributed them here according to the list included in the shipment. For the holidays, help also arrived from the Goworowo *landsmanshaft* in America – "Children of Aron Shleyme Tehililm" – of which her husband Borekh Kuperman, of blessed memory, was the head.

In 1949 there were already a large number of Goworowo Jews in Israel.

[Page 482]

What was needed now was an effective organization with an elected board of directors that could carry on the work. During the interim days of Passover of 1949, in the residence of Yekl Gurka and Avrom Romaner in Yafo, the first founding meeting took place. The following board was elected: Aron Shron, Avrom Holtsman, Tsipore Kliborski, Avrom Zakharihu and Yehude Gurka. At the assembly, a financial campaign was made and a certain sum of money was gathered to help the needy refugees.

In time the refugee families gradually settled in. People started to think about how to eternalize the memory of the victims and of the ruined *shtetl* . The 7th of Elul was designated as the memorial day, as that was the day when the first victim fell.

The first Goworowo "colony"

The first memorial day took place on the 7th of Elul that same year, in the venue of the *Beyt ha'khalutsot* in Tel Aviv. All of the Goworowo Survivors in the land took part. After the memorial prayers, plans were discussed about how to help the needy and create ties with the foreign *landsmanshaftn* and with individuals. Since then, a memorial service is held each year on that date, with the participation of a cantor and speakers. *Rov* Meyshe Bernshteyn often refers to the subjects of that day.

Over a few years, as more Goworowo families came into the land, the connections grew stronger and the council stayed in touch with everyone. New people were elected to the board and today it is composed of the following members: Aron Shron, Chairman, Avrom Levin, Avieyzer

[Page 483]

Burshtin, Berl Kosovski, Yosef Grudka, Yosef Zilbertson, Meyshe Sarne, Khave Bernshteyn, Naftali Shmelts, Yehude Gurka, Meyshe Dronitsa, Meyshe Granat and Avrom Holtsman.

In 1955 the organization founded an interest-free loan society, thanks to our *landsman* Meyshe Levin and his wife Sore from Cuba. They visited Israel then and offered a large sum of money as ground capital and thus the fund is named for their son Tsvi, of blessed memory, who died young. The council also raised money for that goal from members and friends in Israel, from our tourists, and from other sources.

In the last ten years a large number of Goworowo *landsmen* have visited Israel and for many of them the council made celebratory receptions. Coming from America: Avrom Kalman Blumshteyn, Sore and Yitskhak Blumshteyn, Sore Fridman, Libe Nadboy-Proske, Niske Koen, Ester and Note Tenenboym, Mariyam Blumshteyn-Papiertshik, the family Mozes, Simkhe Farba, Avrom Kshonzshka, Mayer Koen, Feyge Sheyniak, and others. From Canada: Rifke and Shmuel Rozenberg, Shmuel Shetsik and wife, Shtshetshina, Sore Israel-Grinberg, Libe Doytsh-Gemora, and others. From Belgium: Zelig Reytshik and family, From Colombia: Frume Tsuker-Vaysbord, Khane Vaysbord with her daughter and her husband. From Uruguay: Roman Beyle. From Argentina: Avrom Shvartsberd. From Australia: Yekhezkel Tehilim. From Germany: Berl and Yosef Kshanzshka. Most of all these guests gave money for the interest-free loan society and for the organization itself.

The founding assembly – Interim days of Passover 1949

[Page 484]

The council

First row, from right to left: Meyshe Sarne, Yosef Grudka, Meyshe Dranitsa, *Rov* Meyshe Bernshteyn, Khave Bernshteyn and Naftali Shmelts
Second row: Avrom Holtsman, Yehude Grudka, *Rov* Avieyzer Burshtin, Berl Kosovski and Aron Shron

In 1960 the organization installed a marble tablet in the "Holocaust Celler" on Mount Zion in Jerusalem, in memory of our destroyed *shtetl* Goworowo. For the World Congress of Polish Jews, which took place in Israel in 1961, the United Polish Refugees published a book titled *Landsmanshaftnin Israel*. Our organization supported the book and wrote a long article for it, with pictures of its activities and a general overview of Goworowo.

During all the days of remembrance and at other gatherings, people always spoke of the importance of publishing a *yisker-bukh* , according to the example of other *shtet* and *shtetlekh* in Poland. But the colossal difficulty and the huge financial costs that were associated with that stopped our carrying out the plan for a long time. Only in 1959, when our friends Rivke and Yisroel Rozenberg from Canada visited Israel for the first time, was the matter given a push forward. During a reception that was arranged in their honor at the home of the writer of these lines, people spoke about the great importance of a book of remembrance for our *shtetl* and the hard problems that stood in the way of realizing that. The guests promised us the necessary help and right after their return to Canada they indeed began their work. Rivke Rozenberg traveled down to New York specially for this and aroused the Goworowo Jews to the task. Active in this were the members: Sore and Yitskhak Blumshteyn, Yitskhak Shafran, Yitskhak Dovid Tehilim, Naftali Kuperman and others. All of these collected and sent money for the book. Avrom Kalman Blumshteyn was also among the first participants in the action. Here in Israel people also made the effort and we soon entered into the actual work.

[Page 485]

The first meeting of the editorial board took place in Kfar Sitron, at *Rov* Avieyzer Burshtin's and intensive and real work quickly began. Hundreds of circulars and letters were sent out to *landsmen* in Israel and in other countries and to several institutions. Dozens of meetings took place in the homes of Berl Kosovski, Yosl Gurka, Khave Bernshteyn and Avrom Holtsman. More Goworowo Jews were invited to become members: Yankev Gurka, Naftali Shmelts and among the local Polish *landsmanshaftn*. Contact was maintained with each Goworower individually, until the book was finally readied.

At a memorial service. The cantor recites *El mole rakhamim*.

The organization considered it an obligation to note with honor and thanks the members *Rov* Avieyzer Burshtin and Berl Kosovski, who dedicated enormous energies to write, edit and publish the book, without seeking any reward. There is absolutely no doubt that without them the book would not have been published. Just to edit such a book in Israel today would cost ten to fifteen thousand Israeli pounds and we had only about half of that and that had to pay for paper, printing, engraving, binding and other expenses that were involved. Many members helped at the beginning of the work, like Yosef Gurka and Avrom Holtsman. The writer of these lines was active the whole time and helped at every opportunity.

There is no doubt that the *yisker-bukh* was the crowning achievement of the organization but, the organization has other important goals for the future. We strive to be able to have our own apartment in Tel Aviv, from which all the activities of the organization could be conducted: the secretariat, the interest-free loan fund, a hall for meetings and a prayer room. When that plan is realized, we can trust that we have done all we can to reunite our beloved, ruined, *shtetl* Goworowo.

[Page 486]

The Interest-Free Loan Fund of the *Yotse Goworowo* Organization in Israel

by Avrom Levin, Israel

Translated by Tina Lunson

The interest-free loan society of the *Yotse Goworowo* Organization in Israel was founded in 1955. It happened during a visit in Israel by my children Meyshe and Sore Levin from Cuba. At the time, I held a meeting in my home with good friends from Goworowo, in which we spoke from our hearts. My son Meyshe told them of the great misfortune that he met with the death of his twelve-year-old son, my grandson Tsvi, of blessed memory, and he stated that he was prepared to financially support some kind of *mitsve* in the memory of his lost child. *Rov* Meyshe Bernshteyn proposed an interest-free loan fund in his name. The plan was promptly accepted. My son Meyshe contributed 500 Israeli pounds and a few months later he sent another 100 pounds. This was the foundation of the Goworowo interest-free loan fund.

Later, we also made a money collection among the Goworowo Jews in Israel. Each one contributed, some more, some less, and we received another 400 pounds. During my visit to Cuba in 1965, for the wedding of my grandson, I collected another 450 pounds from friends and acquaintances; and on my son Meyshe's second visit to Israel in 1958, he gifted it with another 350 pounds.

At the founding of the fund

[Page 487]

At the annual gathering

There were more gifts and contributions from friends and acquaintances until today, the fund holds 4,000 Israeli pounds.

The fund serves the Goworowo Jews. Whoever needs a loan of a few hundred pounds can receive the proceeds and pay it back in monthly payments.

Last year, 1965, the fund loaned out 5,500 Israeli pounds to 21 persons for necessary and productive uses.

The work of the interest-free loan fund gives us great satisfaction because we can help a person in a needy situation. The *mitsve* of *gemiles-khesed* stands above charity, because charity is only for poor people and *gemiles-khesed* â€“ is both for the wealthy and for the poor. We say it every day while praying, "and *gemiles-khesed*"; and the *Mishna* adds "The following are the things for which a man enjoys the fruits in this world while the principal remains for him in the world to come." [*Mishnah Peah* 1:1]. It is therefore a greater pleasure when a Jews asks for a loan and one can give it to him.

[Page 488]

Goworowo Societies in America

by Yitskhak Safran, Israel

Translated by Tina Lunson

Jewish America is famous for its *landsmanshaftn*. Almost every city and townlet in Europe has its society or community in America. Every Jew who came to America ten years ago quickly felt that "He might make thee know that man doth not live by bread only." [Deuteronomy 8:3] and that he would not exist just for making money. He also had a spiritual life and a spiritual life cannot be only individuals, but when one is organized in a community.

In order to grasp the concept of what was called "making money" then and how those "societies" were developed, we must turn back 60 or 70 years. And what was handed to our older *landslayt*.

Normal work hours then were between 60 and 70 hours a week, A [sewing] machine operator had to carry his own machine on his shoulders. After a hard day's work and after eating a cheap supper in a cellar restaurant, he began a new order of night work and extra hours.

One who worked until midnight received a nickel, five cents. That nickel back then had great value. One could get bread with herring and a glass of beer for it. But what did a Goworowo Jew, who left a wife and children in the old country, do? Better to save that nickel. He thought to himself,

Letterhead for the old organization, the Support Society
"Children of Aron Shleyme Tehilim for People from Goworowo"

[Page 489]

"I already ate supper, it is not long now until breakfast, it is better to save it for the family." As for sleeping, they slept in a cellar on an upright bed for fifty cents a month and that was not alone but along with another dozen *landslayt.*

One became so accustomed to saving, they could not stop saving… time for community activity. People organized and the older *landslayt* helped the Newcomers and work was more than enough. Almost every "greenhorn" needed some help, if not material help, then a kind word, some advice, encouragement, and the like. And they did not forget to share the last meal of the sabbath, to usher out the *Shabes* Queen, to study something, and so on. Consequently, the "societies" grew like mushrooms after a rain and their activity was of the first degree of importance.

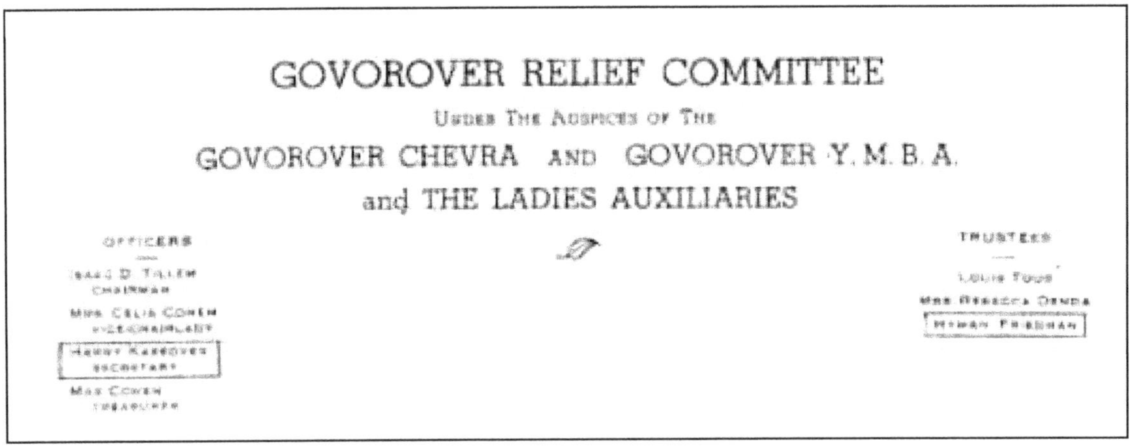
GOVOROVER RELIEF COMMITTEE
UNDER THE AUSPICES OF THE
GOVOROVER CHEVRA AND GOVOROVER Y. M. B. A.
and THE LADIES AUXILIARIES

OFFICERS
CHAIRMAN
MRS. CELIA COHEN
SECRETARY
MAX COHEN
TREASURER

TRUSTEES

Form for the partnering relief committee, of both societies

Our *shtetl* Goworowo has to this day two societies, an old one and a new one. The old has already existed here for 70 years. It is called in short "the old association" but the correct name is "Children of Aron Shleyme Tehilim for People from Goworowo". From its first pioneering founding we only know the name of Mendl Shults, Yisroel Yitskhak Vishnie, Khayim Dovid Fridman and Khone the kasha-maker. In the 1930s, when Borekh Kuperman of blessed memory came to America, he quickly became active in the leadership of the association. He was for many years the *gabay* of the Burial society and maintained that activity until his own passing. His wife Khane Rokhl, may her days be long, is today also leader of the Ladies Auxiliary.

The Association has its own *shul* for praying and studying and its own cemetery. The Association was once very active. Once a year they celebrated a big Burial Society feast, as in the old home. Several times a year there were smaller feasts. At all of these occasions, money was always collected for charity, the goal being to help the neediest *landslayt* in Goworowo.

[Page 490]

Mr. Y. D. Tehilim and his wife

But there was also a younger audience, among them many unmarried men, who did not want to be harnessed to the older association which only gave them the *shul* to pray in and sometimes, at the end of *Shabes*, the last meal. The young folk wanted a more modern communal work. Instead of a *Shabes* feast, they wanted a modern banquet with music and other things. That brought about the younger people making *Shabes* on their own and in 1909 they founded their own association under the name "Goworowo Young Men's Society".

In praise of both societies it must be said that thanks to the American democratic spirit, through all those 60 years of existence, there were no conflicts between the two *landsmanshaftn*. Many Goworower belonged to both societies. The chief task of both associations was to make it possible for all Goworower to maintain together, not be lonely, and to help one another when in need.

Among the founders and active members of the "Young Men's" it is worthwhile to mention Binyumin Aleirazsh, Louis Ashur, Yosef Burshtin and Meyshe Miller all of blessed memory; and may they live a good life Kalman Toyz, Yankev Bresler, Harry Nadel, Berish Granat, Sam Levin, Yankev Ribitsh, Max Kahn, and the brother Tehilim.

The "Young Men's" were active all their years in general communal areas. They consistently supported the Joint Distribution Committee, HIAS and others. Still today they give large sums annually to the United Jewish Appeal. The society, as well as the old association and many other *landsmanshaftn* in America, have their own cemetery. The "Young Men's" also involves a lot to help the lives of their members. So, for example, they have an aid fund for the ill. When a member becomes, heaven forbid, sick and cannot work, he receives a weekly stipend of 15 dollars.

[Page 491]

When Goworowo was still Goworowo, the two societies had a partnering relief committee and together sent the aid to Goworowo. We all remember well what was done in the *shtetl*, especially before Passover, regarding making the list of the poor people. Each person was judged according to his situation and importance. Of course, there were complaints about who got more and who got less. Many letters arrived in America with complaints, pleas and explanations from the town. The American committee had to make everything equal. It was a difficult piece of work with many arguments. The Goworower woman Khaye Sore Zeydler must be specially noted, as she gave large sums of money for the construction of the new study house.

After the great destruction of World War II, the relief committee was very active in sending packages and money to the Goworowo survivors, wherever they were. To this day we are still conducting productive work, but now not in the same volume as before. Until World War II there were always new *landslayt* coming to America, who were taken into the societies with great honor and helped in every way possible. With the last world war, when the Germans, may their names be blotted out, made a ruin of our town, the stream of new immigrants has almost completely stopped. There is no special Goworowo problem, but a general one of all Jewish societies in America that are gradually shrinking and without alternatives limit their activities. The "Young Men's" today has no more than 150 families and the old association, even fewer. But they work beyond their capabilities, in order maintain their existence.

The activists in today's "Young Men's" are Yankev Zemlovitsh, Chairman; Sam Epshteyn, Financial Secretary; Harry Miller, Recording Secretary; Yosef Bresler, Treasurer; Harry Berliner, Meyshe Izdoba and Yitskhak Dovid Tehilim, Trustees. Yitskhak Dovid Tehilim is also Chairman of the executive Board.

The activists in the old Association are Naftali Kuperman, President; Meyshe Dan, Vice President; Borekh Markovitsh, Trustee and Yankev Mozes, Recording Secretary.

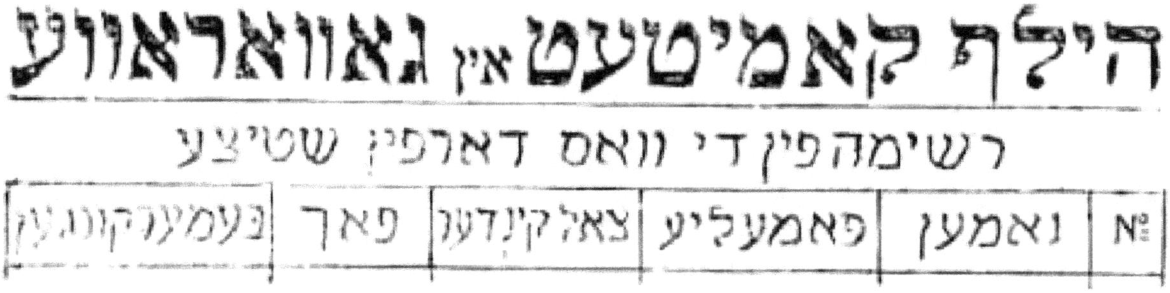
הילף קאמיטעט אין גאוואראווע

רשימה פין די וואס דארפין שטיצע

№	נאמען	פאמעליע	צאל קינדער	פאך	בעמערקונגען

Listing form for the Goworowo Aid Committee
Help Committee in Goworowo
List of those needing help
Remarks Occupation Children Family Name Name Number

[Page 492]

Goworowo *Landsmanshaftn* in Canada

by A. Ben-Mi'ir, Canada

Translated by Tina Lunson

The Goworowo *landsmanshaft* in Canada cannot be noted for its long years of history. In sum, most Goworowo families settled in Canada only after World War II. It took several years until they arranged a base from the financial standpoint and found a language with the strange new world. Of course, in the "green" years of adjustment into the new framework, they could not think about any kind of social work.

Sometimes one would meet a few *landslayt* at celebrations, at festive opportunities, or a temporary visit, but were still far from any organizing.

The first official meeting took place the 27th of November 1960, in the home of Leyb Gurman, after Rivke and Shumel Rozenberg returned from a visit in Israel. Some 40 people attended that meeting. Shmuel and Rivke Rozenberg presented a report about the Goworowo Jews in Israel and stressed the importance of publishing the planned *yisker-buch* that would be an eternal monument for our *Shtetl* Goworowo. Other speakers brought out memories of the former life and underlined the need for keeping in close contact with the Goworowo Jews across the whold world. The *landsmanshaft* in Canada was founded at that very meeting and the following committee was elected: Rikvke Rozenberg, President; Avrom Romaner, Secretary; Berl Leyb Girman, Treasurer; Leyb Gemora, Godl Teler, Hersh Zamek, Mater Shmelts, Yisroel Shafran, Yisroel Shtetin, and Shmuel Rozenberg.

One of the first assignments of the committee was to seek resources for publishing the *yisker-bukh.* To that end they took on the task of activating the New York *landslayt*. Rivke Rozenberg traveled to New York especially for that. She placed announcements in the two Yiddish newspapers, *Forverts* and *Tog Morgn-Zshurnal* calling for a meeting of the Goworowo Jews in New York. That effort brought results. A large sum of money was raised. Kalman Blumshteyn donated a golden women's watch and just like in the olden days we sold raffle tickets and designated that income for the book.

The Canada *landslayt* come together often until this day, in the home of the Rozenberg family. They deal with

[Page 493]

questions that are just local matters and everything that has to do with our ties to the other *landslayt* in all the other countries. Participating in one of the recent meetings were two Goworowo brothers, Yankev and Yitskhak Brik, from Montevideo, Uruguay.

They also plan to organize for and establish a *landsmanshaft* there.

As one can see from this story, the *yisker-bukh* was the thrust and the foundation on which the founding of the *landsmanshaft* in Canada was based.

The Committee

(From right to left) First row: Berl Leyb Gurman, Avrom Romaner, Leybtshe Gemora, Godl Teler, Rivke Rozenberg and Shmuel Rozenberg
Standing: Rokhl Gurman, Yisroel Shafran, Hershl Zamek, Etl Teler, Mayer Shmelts and Shmuel Shtetin

Goworowo in Other Countries

Translated by Tina Lunson

Besides the three countries of Israel, America, and Canada where there are large concentrations of Goworowo Jews, our *landslayt* are distributed throughout a number of countries across the whole world, in which there are found solitary and several families.

There are still several families in Russia from World War I. Goworowo families are also located in Uruguay, Brazil, Colombia, Australia, Argentina and Cuba. After the Second World War single families emigrated to Belgium, France, Italy, Poland and West Germany. It is also possible that individual families and persons who stem from Goworowo are to be found in other countries.

In the countries mentioned above, our *landslayt* do not direct any community activities. They meet seldom, mostly at happy occasions. The Goworowo thread binds them all together though. People stay in letter contact for many years and by visits to the countries where are others, each holding to his duty to visit a *landsman*, to talk a little about the past and exchange memories.

[Page 494]

Goworowo *landslayt* in Canada at a celebration

[Page 495]

Gratitude

Translated by Mira Eckhaus

Edited by Tina Lunson

It is a pleasant duty for us to express our gratitude and appreciation to the editors of the book, sons of our town:

Rov Avieyzer Burshtin, son of Rov Alter Meyshe Mordkhe, may God avenge his blood, studied at the yeshiva *Khokhmey Lublin* [Sages of Lublin), was crowned by the Sages and received the title of *Tsurba M'rabanan* in 1938. At the outbreak of World War II, he fled from Warsaw to Vilna, was in the Vilna, Grodno, and Bialystok ghettos, and in the extermination camps of Auschwitz and Dachau. After the liberation, he worked a lot to help the rest of the survivors and managed "The Salvation Committee" in Germany; he edited the newspaper *Dos Yidishe Vort* and the monthly newspaper *Netsakh Yisroel*.

He immigrated to Israel in 1949; founded and managed the *Talpiot* institution for immigrating youth in Jerusalem. Now he is the director of a *Torah U'molacha* [Torah and Craft] *yeshiva*, a vocational high school, in Kfar Tsvi Citrin, near Haifa.

In Israel, his following books were published: *Morey Deya, Gdoley Deya, Adirey Dea – Encyclopedia for the Greats of Israel* (Zioni Publishing House), and *Righteousness of the Wise* (Ohel Publishing House).

Dov Kosovski, son of the Reb Yitskhak of blessed memory, one of the founders of the Revisionist Zionist Alliance in the town and the commander of Betar, until the outbreak of the war. In the 1930s he participated in various sections of the newspapers *Hayntike Nayes, Far Ale* (Warsaw), *Yidishe Bilder* (Riga) and others.

After the liberation, he served as a member of the Central Committee for Liberated Jews in the British occupied area of Germany, a member of the Revisionist Zionist Alliance Center and the headquarters of the Betar district, Bergen Belsen. There he also edited the monthly newspapers, *Der Emes*, *Unzer Fraynt* and participated in *Vokhenblat* (Bergen Belsen), *Unzer Velt* (Munich) and other newspapers of the survivors of the Holocaust. He is the author of the *Bibliography of the Jewish publications in the British occupied area of Germany, 1945-1950.*

Our above- mentioned friends initiated the publication of this book, toiled, labored, and encouraged others to write, collected material and photos from various sources, and from scraps of rumors and testimonies erected an eternal tombstone to our hometown Goworowo. For this they will be blessed.

We also express our hearty gratitude to our friends Yosef Gurka, Meyshe Granat, Avraham Holtsman and others, who participated in articles and essays that added greatly to the content of the book.

The Goworowo Veterans Organization Committee

[Page 496]

An Expression of Thanks Goworowo

Translated by Tina Lunson

A huge thanks is due our *landslayt* and friends:

Mrs. Rivka and Shmuel Rozenberg of Monreal, Canada,
the first who properly valued the importance of the *yisker-bukh*.

Avrom Kalman Blumshteyn
Sore and Yitskhak Blumshteyn
Yitskhak Dovid Tehilim of the "Young Men's"
Naftali Kuperman of the "Society of the Children of Shleyme Tehilim"
Yitskhak Shafran, of America

And all our friends from Israel and other lands who supported
and made possible the publication of this ***Seyfer Yisker***.

Everyone – a hearty congratulation – may your strength only grow!

Council of the *Yotsey Goworowo* Organization in Israel

English Summary of the Book

Typed up by Genia Hollander

[Page I]

Forward

In profound awareness of the responsible nature of our task, we have undertaken to publish this Memorial Book, which is intended as a lament for our so tragically destroyed community and a headstone on the unknown graves of our martyred dear ones, whose ashes are strewn all over the fields and forests of Europe.

It is our sacred duty to remember, to carry our deep sorrow in our hearts and on our lips, together with an everlasting curse for the Nazi and their collaborators who so cruelly destroyed one third of our people.

*

Writing and editing this book has not been an easy assignment. All the historical sources and archives were destroyed together with the town. Some of the survivors have not been able to recall the events or to put them down on paper. Only the strong consciousness of our responsibility for keeping the memory of our destroyed town and its martyrs alive has given us the courage and strength to bring the work to a conclusion. With enormous trouble, bit by bit, we have succeeded in reconstructing the material: it is a memorial which had, so-to-say, to be put together brick-by-brick. We have made every effort to create an objective image of the town; of its institutions, parties and organizations; of its rabbis, community leaders, personalities and figures; of its general life and the circumstances of its death and destruction – always with the intention of bringing out what was specific for Govorovo.

It should be kept in mind that the financial means at our disposal would either have been sufficient to pay for the services of a professional editor, or for the cost of paper, blocks, printing and binding; in other words, we had to do everything ourselves as well as we could, or remain without a book. The choice was obvious. Our purpose was to construct a monument that would keep the memory of our town alive – and that, we believe, we have done.

*

While we have spared no time or effort to assure perfection, we are well aware that we are far from having achieved it. A large deal of documentary material and illustrations of social importance are lacking. In different descriptions, notes and lists, part of the names may well have been omitted or misspelled, and some of the dates mentioned may not correspond to the facts. To our regret, such blemishes are inevitable for a number of reasons, mainly because of the poor response and indifference of our compatriots who have not shown themselves sufficiently aware of the importance of this work. It should also not be forgotten that the whole enormous effort involved in publishing a book of this kind has fallen upon the shoulders of only two volunteers who undertook to edit the material, write a large part of it themselves and take care of all

[Page II]

the technicalities from the beginning to the end. With the best of intentions, they may well have allowed errors to creep in which could have been avoided if there had been more collective cooperation. We apologize for any offence caused for this or other reasons.

*

A summary of the book in English is provided for those who find it hard to read Yiddish and Hebrew. We want them, and particularly the younger generation, also to become acquainted, at least to some extent, with the town of their parents, its rabbis, prominent citizens and personalities, its parties, institutions and organizations, and above all, its tragic end which must never be forgotten.

The Editors

The Town

In the chapter: "A Few Notes on History", the authors describe Govorovo as a purely Jewish town in Congress Poland with a population of about 500 families. It lay on the railway line from Warsaw to Lomza, not far from the towns of Ostrolenka and Ostrow-Maz. It was part of the district of Ostrolenka and for many years of the Voivodate of Bialistok; a few years before the war, it was transferred to the Voivodate of Warsaw.

The only historical source available to the authors is *Slownik Geograficzny Krolewstwa Polskiego I Innych Krajow Slowianskich*, by Filip Sulimierski, Bronislaw Chlebowski and Wladislaw Waqleski, published in Warsaw in 1881. According to this work, Govorovo dates back at least to the 16th century. In 1821, it had 40 houses with 1485 inhabitants and the 'commune', i.e. the town together with its 14 surrounding villages, had 4747 inhabitants.

According to the tradition, there have been Jews among the population of Govorovo since its foundation. Old people still told stories about visits to Govorovo by Rabbi Abraham Danzig, the author of *Hayei Adam* (1748-1820) and the famous Rabbi Akiba Eger of Poznan (1761-1837). Presumably, part of the Jewish population lived in the village of Wolky, on the other side of the Hirsh River. There is an old manuscript which bears out this assumption.

During the Polish revolts against the Czarist domination (1794 and 1863), the Jews contributed to the successful outcome of the insurrections at the risk of their lives.

In course of time, the Jewish community became deeply rooted in the town and their numbers grew continuously. There are encyclopaedias which give the size of the Jewish population at the end of the 19th century as 1844 out of a total of 2139. In 1921, there were only 1228 Jews out of a total population

[Page III]

of 5299, probably because not all of them had returned after World War I.

During and immediately after World War I, the Jews suffered heavily: first from the retreating Russian army and the German army of occupation and later from the Polish revolutionary army and the German army of occupation, and later from the Polish revolutionary army, the so-called "Hallerczyki". When the latter was in control, the Jews were subjected to a flood of oppressive decrees and persecutions, accompanies by forced levies, cutting off of beards and attacks.

In time, the situation improved somewhat. The Jewish population, which had fled when the town was burnt down in World War I, gradually returned and conditions became more stable.

Under the Polish Republic of the 20's and 30's, until World War II, Govorovo's Jewish population mostly belonged to the middle class: artisans and shopkeepers, with a few great merchants and landowners. All Jewish political parties were represented in the town which also had the usual institutions and organizations, banks, schools, Hassidic *shtiblech* and so forth. All these will be described in detail.

Abraham Schwarzberg from Argentina writes about "Govorovo Half a Century Ago". He describes the old religious way of life and the penetration of the Haskala movement among the younger generation, in which Benjamin Ginzburg played a considerable part.

In "Once Upon a Time..." Moshe Granat brings back memories from a later period. He writes about life in town in general, the *cheders* and their *melamdim*, about life in the political parties and about the revolt of the younger generation who wanted a new dispensation.

"A Walk Through the Town" lists all those who lived there between the two wars. Starting with Welwel Blumstein, the "Walk" takes us past all the houses and through all the streets and lanes, down to the villages of Wolky and Paczeky, with a few words about everyone's occupation and habits.

Rabbis

This section (P.55), only describes the town's last three rabbis who are still remembered by the present generation.

Moshe Zinovicz writes about Rabbi Shlomo Zalman Klepfish, a great religious scholar and the author of a work named *Beth Aharon* and whose brother, Rabbi Samuel Zeinwel Klepfish, was one of the Chief Rabbis of Warsaw. He officiated in Govorovo until his death in 1885.

From the same pen we have a note about the 'Old Rabbi', R. Jacob-Judah Cahana-Batshan, who became Rabbi of Govorovo after the death of Rabbi Klepfish. Rabbi Batshan came from a famous rabbinical family and wrote a book named, *Veshav Hacohen*. He held office until his death in 1911. A few

[Page IV]

characteristic episodes in Rabbi Batshan's life was described by Rabbi N. Talmud who was an associate of his for many years.

An essay, "The Last Rabbi" by A. Avinoam, describes the personality of Rabbi Alter Moshe Mordechai Burstin, Rabbi Batshan's successor. Govorovo's last rabbi was a Jewish scholar of note famous for his wisdom and acuity and a leader of the community in the best sense of the word. He was killed in Treblinka in 1943.

An appreciation of the Last Rabbi is contributed by Rabbi Pardes, editor of *Pardes* journal of Chicago, U.S.A.

Religious Life

This section (p.66) starts with an article on "Jewish Life in a Little Town" by Joseph Gurka, which recalls the religious education of the younger generation, the good deeds of their pious elders and the general religious atmosphere of the town.

Abraham Levia presents us with a vivid description of R. Fishel Shapiro who later became Rabbi of Czervin and of other Hassidic figures who spent their life studying Tora. We are told of such customs of the *meclave malka* meal at the end of the Sabbath, of the Hassidic habit of using every opportunity for 'making a *lechayim*', of playing on Hanukah and of presenting *kvitlech*. The author makes us acquainted with a wide range of Hassidic personalities and has some amusing stories to tell about Hassidic life.

The next essay is Josef Givati's description of "The *Beth Midrash*", weekday and Sabbath prayers, the *gabbaim*, *hazanim* and other religious functionaries, travelling preachers and the *chevrot* or religious societies that used to meet for study between the afternoon and evening prayers.

Joseph Silberzahn writes about the Alexander *shtibel*, its founders and living members and about the people who used to travel regularly to the Alexander Rebbe.

A description of the Gerer *shtibel*, whose founders included Hassidim who had still visited the Old Rebbe of Ger, the author of' *Sfat Emet*, is provided by Josef Gur who mentions several Hassidim of standing who were also active in the Jewish community in general.

Yet another Hassidic group, the Vorker *shtibel*, which was also attended by the followers of the Rebbe of Skernievicz and of the Rebbe of Amshinov, is described by Abraham Holzmen, who also portrays Hassidic types from the times when this *shtibel* was founded until the outbreak of war.

In Govorovo there was also a Progressive *Minyan* which was mostly attended by younger people of a Zionist trend of thinking. This is described by G. Joseph.

[Page V]

Again from the pen of Joseph Gurka, we have a detailed description of "*Cheders* and *Melamdim*" which mentions the *melamdim* who lived and worked in Gorovovo between the two wars and who were responsible for the religious education of the community's children until they grew up and, in some cases, went on to a *yeshiva*.

A curious aspect of Jewish life before World War I is mentioned by Jacob Gurka who tells us of *kosher cheders*, which taught Russian for a couple of hours a day and *treife cheders* which objected to *goyish* subjects.

Joseph Gurka presents a number of students from Govorovo who attended different *yeshivot* in Poland; some of these became rabbis or principals of *yeshivot*. Bat-Yaacov Dov adds pen portraits of two more *yeshiva* students in "Two Brothers".

Rabbi Yitzhak Shafran, one of the Jewish community leaders in Govorovo, writes about the Beth Yaacov girls' school, its founders, supporters and teachers. The author was one of the active leaders of the school in 1932.

"Bar-Bi-Rav" tells us about the work of the *Chevra Kadisha*, the burial society, part of whose revenue was devoted to charity. He records the names of the society's presidents and describes its traditional annual dinner which was held on the eve of *Rosh Chodesh Shvat*. The author also recalls the famous Community Register which was kept by this Society.

Community Offices and Institutions

The functions and duties of the Town Council are the subject of an article by A. Bar-Even who relates how the Jews were tricked out of the office of Mayor even though the town was to all intents purely Jewish and how at certain times there were only a very few Jewish councillors. On the other hand, there was a stable Jewish Community Council. Bar-Even also tells how the police used to make trouble for the Jews.

The same writer describes the activities of the Jewish Community Board and the part it played in Jewish life and welfare activities. He lists part of the Board members from before World War I and nearly all from the years between the wars.

D. Baki presents an all-round paper on the Jewish schools and education system with its 7-year general elementary school and the private school of Alter Hochstem which taught in Yiddish and Hebrew in a Jewish national spirit. He recalls the teachers who came from other places to work in Govorovo and who taught Hebrew and Esperanto and conducted youth and adult courses. Finally, he tells of the unsuccessful efforts of some parties to establish kindergartens.

D. Ben-Yitzhak writes about the activities of the Merchants Association and

[Page VI]

Moshe Granat about the Artisans Association, their banks and their fight against the anti-Semitic boycott and the heavy tax assessments imposed on Jews. B. Alef describes the *Gmilut Chessed* small loans fund and the manner in which it provided help for the poor elements of the population.

The *Hachnassat Orchim* Society is described by B. Aviezer who tells how the Jewish community discharged its responsibility for poor transients, provided them with food, lodging and small amounts of money and assisted them in every way.

The voluntary principle was also the basis for provision for the sick. This was the task of the *Bikkur Cholim* and *Linat Hatzedek* Societies. A. Avi-Uriel describes how they used to mobilize the necessary medical instruments and equipment and even took care of night nursing.

Political Parties and Organizations

The general Zionist Organization, the oldest political organization in the town, is described by K. Ber (p.144) who tells how it was founded through the efforts of Benjamin Ginzburg. The young Zionists did not have an easy time; their orthodox parents made a good deal of trouble for them so that they could only work on a limited scale. Among the founders of the organization were: Bachman Tchechonover, Pessach Truchnovsky, Judith Rosen, Zlate Friedman, Haim Evron and Dinah Boines. Later, the *Tze'irei Zion* group headed by Hershel and Simon Farba became active within the Zionist Organization. In the 20's, the leadership was taken over by Moshe Dranitza, Aaron Grodka and others. In 1927, the right-wing *Poalei Zion* split off. In the early 30's, the Organization joined the Revisionist movement.

Rachel Brestel-Gurka writes about *Zukunft* and *Bund* activities and recalls such Bund leaders as Leibel Kersch, Moshe Olek, Simcha Silberstein, Leizer Friedman and others, thanks to whose dedicated efforts the organization came to rank among the most important in the town. Mrs. Brestel mentions well-known national Bund leaders who came to Govorovo as visiting lecturers: Herlich, Alter, Patt, Shefner, Kruk, Malkin and others and concludes with a short list of dedicated members who fell during the war.

Moshe Granat writes about the "Origins and Development of Poalei Zion Zionist-Socialists", their work and activities and their secession from the Zionist Organization in 1927. He mentions their cooperation with Bund in the matter of school and cultural affairs; their *Freiheit*, *Hechalutz* and Scouts youth movements; their theatrical and other performances. The movement had a large membership. Its leaders were: Shafran, Wiroslav, Granat, Shron, Blumstein, Sanne, Holzman and others.

The Revisionist Movement is dealt with by B. Kossovsky. He describes

[Page VII]

how a Revisionist group called *Haschachar* came into being within the Zionist Organization in the late 20's. It's founders were: Mates Mihsnayoth, Zadok Farba, Aviezer Shikora, Chava Burstin and the author. Later, the group took over the Zionist Organization. Its youth movement, *Betar*, was founded in 1931 with Judah Ritz at its head and whose place was later taken over by B. Kossovsky who continued to lead it until the outbreak of the war. The author describes the difficulties made by the Leftist element in the town when Betar founded its *hachshara* and writes about the first immigrants to Eretz Israel in the early 30's, work for the JNF and the *Tel-Hai* Fund. Other outstanding leaders, in addition to those already mentioned included: Shabtai Friedman, Josef Drozd, Mordechai Ritz, Shlomo Apelboim, Josef Krolevicz, David Blumstein and others.

J. Avi-Sarah writes about *Mizrachi*, *Hechalutz Hamizrachi* and *Hashomer Hadati*. We learn that the *Mizrachi* organization in Govorovo was founded in 1922 by Abraham Levin, Eli Grinberg, Yitzhak Tandeitchaz, Chanan Friedman, Israel Leib Kruk and Shmuel Zudiker. They set up their own *minyan* and Tora study group and were active in the cultural field. We are also told of famous Mizrachi leaders who visited Govorovo, such as Rabbi Hager, Rabbi Bronrot and others. In 1935, a *Tzeirei Mizrachi* group was founded, headed by Yerachmiel Drozd, Josef Gurka, Josef Silberzahn and Meyer Werman. The founders of *Hashomer Hadati* were: Jacob Kruk, Gedalia Zudiker, Mordechai Apelboim, Jacob Rosen, Shmuel Shmeltz znd others.

Next follows a description of the *Tzeirei Agudat Israel* movement which was founded in the early 30's as a reaction against the secular youth movements. Its first committee consisted of Levy Warszawiak, Moshe Moses, Itshe Shafran and Haim Kossowsky. *Tzeirei Agudat Israel* later became an element of considerable strength in the town with two representatives of its own on the Jewish Community Board. It also established its own *minyan* where Rabbi Naftali Gemara taught *midrash* every Sabbath. The article concludes by commemorating Hershel Rubin and Haim Kossowsky who were killed by the Nazi and Leib Hersh Holzman who died in Russia.

Mrs. Rivka Rosenthal-Stettin tells of the founding of the *Batya* and *Bnot Agudat Israel* organizations in Govorovo. They recruited their members mainly from along the girls of the *Beth Yaacov* school. The first committee consisted of Rivka Stettin, Eidel Kshonshka and Miriam Herzberg. Much help was given by the teachers of the *Beth Yaacov* School, all of whom had come from elsewhere. The two organizations succeeded in striking root among the Jewish girls of the town.

The *Hashomer Hatzair* organization which numbered 100 members immediately after being founded in 1927 is described by Eliezer Levin. Leaders of the organization included Hershke Granat, Moshe Levin, Feige Sheiniak,

[Page VIII]

Neche Shechter, Rachel Weisbard and later also the author. The group developed an intensive activity, achieved a leading position in collecting for the JNF, produced plays, took part in summer camps and so forth. It remained in existence until about 1933.

Noah Karvat writes about *Poalei Zion Left* at the head of which he stood since it was founded. Its committee included Abraham Weisbard, Tuvia Koss, Haya Weisbard, Alter Hochstein the teacher and others. It was a small party and conducted its activities in the homes of its members. National leaders of the party who visited Govorovo included Dr. Emanuel Ringelblum, Jacob Zerubavel, Peterseil and others.

Abraham Hozman tells the story of the Brenner Library which was maintained by the *Right Poalei Zion* and how he, together with Hershel Krolevicz, Israel Kutner and Jacob Drozd one night took all the books of the Zionist Organization and put them in the Brenner Library – a 'literary robbery' which ended up in court.

In his report on the *Falha hachshara kibbutz* in Czyrnia, Aaron Shron tells in great detail how the *kibbutz* was founded in 1925 by the central *Hechalutz* bureau in Warsaw and how eight boys from Govorovo, together with another 20 from Poznan, worked for half a year on the fields of the squire of Czyrnia in preparation for their immigration to *Eretz Israel*. The eight from Govorovo were Bunem Shafran, Zelig Herzberg, Yitzhak Spitalewicz, Selig Raiczik, Moshe Sarne, Israel Kutner, Berl Zudiker and the author.

The *hachshara* of the *Aguda* in Paszeki is described by Levi Warszaviak, its founder and chairman. The twelve-man group performed concrete work for Meyer Wolf Tehilim. Its four members from Govorovo were Levi Warszaviak, Moshe Moses, Josef Tehilim and Moshe Galant.

Abraham Hozman tells the story of the "'Dramatic Circles" of Govorovo. The most important of these were two which were active on a regular basis - one affiliated to the right-wing *Poalei Zion* and one with the *Bund*. Over the years, they presented scores of plays such as *Blameless-Guilty*, *The Father*, *God of Vengeance, On the Old Market*, etc. Their performances were always highly successful. Dramatic circles associated with other parties also presented plays from time to time.

"Work for the National Funds" is the title of an article by A.S. Menahem on JNI and *Keren Hayessod* work in Govorovo.

Scholars, Community Workers and Well-Known Figures and Types

This chapter (p.206) starts with a fragment from J.J. Tronk's book, *Poland* entitled "Nosske of Govorovo" which describes one Nosske – Katz,

[Page IX]

was his family name – as an odd type who was always to be found among Hassidic circles in Lodz, worked at a number of different jobs and finally wound up as the sexton of a *shtibel.*

This is followed by descriptions of leading Govorovo citizens, people who were active in community or party life and interesting figures. Thus, Moshe Granat writes about Moshe Yehoshua Ginzburg; A. Basham about Abraham Mordechai Friedman; Eliyahu Bruchansky about his father the cantor-slaughterer and Josef Silberzahn about his father Jonathan.

B. Itshes writes of Matityahu Rosen; B. Kossovsky of his parents Yitzhak and Dinah and of scenes from their lives. A Bashan describes Moshe Tennenbaum, the President of the Jewish Community; Abraham Hozman about his father Menahem and S. Yitzhaki writes of Abraham Shafran.

In an essay called "Five Generations" Chava Bat-Yaacov Dov preserves the memory of a Govorovo family of long standing – the Blumsteins. Yitzhak Shafran writes about Meir Wolf Tehillim and Menucha Selzer about her father Haim Ber Grodka. Baruch Mintz, Jacob Hersh Wengrov and Feivel Brik are commemorated by A. Bashan, Meir Romaner by A. Inbar and A. Bar-Even describes the interesting figure of Yoelke the baker who sacrificed his life to feed masses of Jewish children when the Germans burnt down the town.

Haim Skornik perpetuates the memory of his father, Moshe Skornik. D. Yerushalmi writes about Rabbi Haim Mordechai Bronrot, the Rabbi of Czechonow who was the son-in-law of a citizen of Govorovo and Moshe Haim Galant – about his father, Rabbi Abraham Mendel Galant who was born in Govorovo.

Josef Silberzahn describes well-known Hassidic figures: Isaia Eisenberg, Yechiel Gerlitz, Neta Ritz, Abraham Yitzhak Galant, Bertshe Viroslav and Abba Lichtman. A. Bashan writes about Avremke Tzalke, the popular chief sexton. The old Govorovo family Rosenblum is depicted in an article in Hebrew by Yitzhak Vardi-Rosenblum. Jacob Gurka evokes his father Efraim Leib Boines. A Bashan writes of Velvel Blumstein and J. Ben-Hassid of Mordechai Leib Gurka.

There are descriptions by M. Rimmon of Hershel Glogeuer and Elhanan Friedman and by A. Inbar of Israel Yitzhak Shron and Haim David Shron. J. Avi-Sarah describes the cantor-slaughterer Haim Leib Mariansky and A. Bar-Even, the Samoszcer Rabbi in Lublin, Rabbi Zvi Oleiarsz who was born in Govorovo and related to several of the town's families.

A.Bashan writes of Jacob Stettin and Josef Gurka of Isaia Herzberg; B. Avi of Yidel Sheiniak; Chava Bernstein-Burstin of her mother Genendel, the Rabbi's wife; B.P. Miriam of Chana Papiersztik; Chava Bat-Yaacov Dov writes in Hebrew about two interesting women: Rachel Shmilkes and Channa Rivka.

[Page X]

Baruch Kuperman is described by A. Beit; Asher Kutner by Abraham Alter Kutner, now rabbi in Lod, Israel. Ziporah Salzberg-Shachter writes of her grandfather Shlomo Leib Shacter and her father Chaim Shachter; G. Even writes about Gedalia Grinberg; Rivka Rosenberg-Shafran about her grandfather Jacob Shepsel Truchnovsky and A. Bashan about Yehoshua Rosen. J. Ben-Mordechai writes about Jacob Rosenberg; Rivka Vinderbaum-Praska about her home; H.S. Kashdan about Peshke Goldman and Chaya Shmeltz about her father-in-law Mordechai Shmeltz. Benjamin Ginsburg is described by Rivka Rosenberg-Shafran; Leibel Kersh by J.S. Herz and Feige Sheiniak and Hershke Granat by his brothers Moshe and Yitzhak. The list closes with Elhanan Kossovsky whose memory is perpetuated by D. Avi-Dani.

Scenes and Memories

This section starts on page 309 with an article entitled "I Remember You.." by the veteran leader of the left-wing *Poalei Zion* – Ahdut Avodah J. Zerubavel who assures us that he has not forgotten the large and small Jewish towns and recalls his visit to Govorovo on the occasion of a rally of party member's from Govorovo and Roznan.

A.Reis describes Govorovo as "A Jewish Folk Town" and evokes memories of *Poalei Zion* Zionist Socialist party work in the town and of the high opinion in which the party was held on account of its activities.

In an essay entitled "Govorovo", Israel Ristov describes a pre-war visit to the town on behalf of *Poalei Eion Z-S* for a lecture on *Eretz Israel.*

"My Comrades of *Betar* Govorovo" is the title of an article by Josef Chrost who describes the town, his meetings with fellow party members and particularly three of them with whom he was in close contact: Chava Burstin, Dov Kossovsky and Zadok Farba-Givner.

Nissan Moses, slaughterer of Govorovo writes of the visit to the town by the first rabbi of Amshinov, Rabbi Jacob David Kalish who came to settle a dispute between the slaughterers and tells how at the banquet in honour of the Rabbi, the Hassidim nearly ate *treife*.

The story of a "Cherem" from the beginning of the century is told by Yitzhak David Tehillim. Two householders took a dispute to the court of Rabbi Botshan who held office at the time and the one who lost the case, lost his temper and spoke rudely to the rabbi. For this sin, he was excommunicated with all due forms and ceremonies; only after the sudden death of his wife did the rabbi forgive him.

From the "Wilna Book" (1918), we reprint a story by S.L. Zitron from the times of the Russian occupation of Govorovo in World War I, relating how the Russian authorities arrested Rabbi Alter Moshe Mordechai Burstin

[Page XI]

with several householders for making an *eruv* in the town which they believed to be a secret telephone line for communicating with the enemy. Upon the intervention of Rabbi Rubinstein of Wilna, they were set free and the charges were withdrawn.

In "Once upon a Saturday Night", A. Bar-Even describes the traditional Saturday night teas at Isaia Eisenberg's home. He gives us a vivid portrait of the steady "tea drinkers" with their talk about politics and their anecdotes.

From the pen of Joseph Silberzahn, we have a description of "An Early Sabbath Morning in Winter": the whole town is still fast asleep, only those who are in the habit of attending early prayers are already on their way to the *Beth Midrash* to study a page of *Gemara* or a chapter of *Mishna*. A humorous note is provided by a picture of people exchanging the latest news from the fair in between prayers.

Feige Sheiniak contributes a poetic evocation of Sabbath in the old home: "everything clean and orderly, the tables covered with all that is good and father saying Kiddush".

"Youth Memories" way back from World War I are evoked by Sarah Zimmerman-Romaner who tells of home, of girl friends and acquaintances, of her teacher Alter Hochstein and of party life.

Rabbi Menachem Belfer, son-in-law of Nathan Farba, describes his four years in the town until its destruction and that terrible Sabbath of September 9, 1939 when the Germans arrested him with hundreds of other Jews and took them away to a camp in Germany.

Jacob Katz from Dlugoszodlo, recalls the young men from Govorovo who were his fellow-students at several *yeshivot*: Feivel Lubelsky, Fishel Krolevicz, David Shron, Yitzhak Shafran, Rabbi Eviezer Burstein and Nathan and Deborah Shron.

Rabbi Zvi A. Slushcz, the great-grandson-in-law of Rabbi Botshan of Govorovo writes of what he knows about the town by hearsay and about the duty to keep the memory of the Jewish towns alive.

"My Way to *Eretz Israel*" is described by Sarah Blumstein-Skornik. She describes her childhood among non-Jewish school children, anti-Semitism, joining *Hechalutz*, work for the JNF and immigration to *Eretz Israel* in 1932.

In "With the Rabbi's Permission", Yitzhak Blumstein tells how, before he left for *Eretz Israel*, his father made a journey to the Rabbi of Ger to ask whether he should allow his son to settle in the Holy Land and took the Rabbi's answer, "And if you say no, will it be any use?" to mean consent.

"A Jew Goes to Eretz Israel" is the title of Aaron Shron's memories from his visit to Palestine in 1932 on the occasion of the Maccabiah Games. He tells about looking for a day's work, of living in wooden huts, and how he found

[Page XII]

employment in the building trade and gradually made his way. The writer makes mention of immigrants from Govorovo who arrived before the outbreak of the war and tells how he managed to obtain a "certificate" (immigration permit) for his sister-in-law by passing her off as his fiancée.

Cantor Nathan Stolnitz from Canada tells how he used to visit Govorovo in his boyhood where he had relations. The title of his contribution is "Govorovo as I Saw It".

"A Story of *Chometz* on *Pessach*" by A.B. Shoshani tells of an incident which occurred in the days of Passover 1931 and led to an acrimonious battle between two newspapers, *Hajnt* and the Aguda organ *Tagblat*. In a feuilleton, *Hajnt* contributor Jeushson-Itchele had called for the abolition of the "second holiday" and specifically, the last day of Passover in the Diaspora. Some of Govorovo's pranksters sent a letter to the *Tagblat* claiming that on the strength of this proposal, the Zionist Organization had immediately arranged a dinner on the eighth day of Passover with *chametz* food and beer which gave the *Tagblat* the opportunity for a six-column spread, "Last Passover Day Abolished in Govorovo". The result was a newspaper duel between *Hajnt* and *Tagblat* with denials and explanations galore to the great excitement and entertainment of the good people of Govorovo.

H. Justus son of the journalist referred to in the previous paragraph and himself an editor of the Israeli evening paper *Maariv*, writes under the heading, "Remarks on an Article" that his father was a strictly religious man who had no impious intentions whatsoever when he wrote his piece on "The Second Holiday". In his articles in *Hajnt*, he always used to preach the Zionist cause which displeased his opponents on the *Tagblat*.

In "Nadliczbowy", B. Dines tells of his experiences when he tried to bribe his way out of the Polish military service with the help of a broker. The broker used to take money in the hope that, by some miracle, his client would be exempted because the contingent was full. Needless to add that the writer had to serve his full year and a half.

A.Govorover writers of the tricks the jokers of Govorovo used to play on the good townspeople. One of his stories relates to how Israel-Shepsel, the "Kadishsayer", filled the pipe of Yankel the butcher with gunpowder and how the resulting explosion caused a false air raid alarm.

Another story by the same author tells of a trick played on one of the householders of the town whom the young people disliked because he interfered with their Zionist activities. By way of revenge, they printed fictitious invitations to the wedding of the man's daughter, hired the town bands of Ostrolenka and Viskow and professional entertainers and invited a host of guests. When everyone arrived in Govorovo, they realized that they had been tricked but had no choice

[Page XIII]

but to stay over the Sabbath as guests of the pretended "father of the bride".

Jacob Gurka tells "Two True Stories". One is of the library which he and a few other young people founded in 1920 and which became a meeting place for boys and girls. The Orthodox element was far from pleased and matters came to the stage where the opponents of the library took away the doors and windows in midwinter. At last, the matter was taken to the Rabbi and a compromise was reached: the girls were permitted to exchange books but not to stay, and on Friday, the lights had to be lit before the beginning of the Sabbath. In the second story, the writer recalls how he taught a drunken hooligan a lesson when he started a quarrel with some Jews.

"Satan's Work" by Moshe Sarne is the true story of a town quarrel which occurred before World War I. It tells how one Jacob-Shlomo fell out with his neighbour Masha Leah over the buying of a load of hay. The families on both sides became involved in the fight and there were wounded on both sides. The end was that Masha Leah was found dead and Jacob-Shlomo's sons disappeared to America.

Two "Odd Stories" are told by Hannah Weisbard: How the "dead" caught the wife of Shmielke Cheisaks by her clothes when she stayed too late in the graveyard collecting herbs and how Israel Hersh recited the psalms one *Simhat Torah* with a "miraculous" tune. Finally, S.Z. recalls yet another odd story; how he once found Benjamin Ginzburg in the middle of the night washing his clothes in the pond.

Who in Gorovovo did not know Shlomo Akiva, the town fool and water carrier? A.B. Shoshani evokes memories of this colourful type and tells of some of his tricks and quips.

M. Rimmon contributes some notes on local folklore in an essay on nicknames and family names among the people of Govorovo – by trade, family, place of origin and physical particularities.

The section ends with reprints of two contributions to *Hatzefira* which appeared first in 1887.

Death and Destruction

This chapter begins (p.381) with a poem by Binem Heller: “In Polish Fields”.

Next comes a Hebrew article by Dr. Arye Leon Kubovy, President of Yad Vashem, entitled “Though Condemned to Death, We Did Not Lose God's Image”. Dr. Kubovy writes about the activities of Dr. E. Ringelblum and his friends in the Warsaw ghetto.

“I Seek My Brother” is the title of an article by Rabbi Yedidia Frenkel, who writes of his visit to Poland on the occasion of the 20th anniversary of

[Page XIV]

the revolt of the Warsaw ghetto and concludes with the words, “May the cry of those who cannot cry be heard in the Book of Govorovo”.

In “That Is How It Began”, Yitzhak Romaner recalls the events of the first days of the war and the entrance of the German troops in Govorovo.

Jacob Gurka's “Diary of an Enlisted Man” tells how he was called up for war service in the Polish army, how his unit was consistently pursued by the Germans and wandered all over Poland until he deserted in the midst of total confusion and managed to return to his family in Govorovo which was already under German occupation.

A detailed report on the destruction of Govorovo is presented by Moshe Malovany who described the first days of the German occupation, the killings, and the deportation of the Jews of the town to a camp in Germany, their liberation and how they eventually ended up on the Russian side.

“A Month With the German Beasts” is the title of a supplementary report by Shmuel Dranica who tells of the strafing of the town by German planes, of the entry of the German troops, of the first Jewish victims and of the time when the Germans drove all the Jews into the synagogue and were about to set fire to the building; miraculously, they were set free again and those who were of military age were taken prisoner.

In “Looking Backward”, Pessach Czerewin describes the last market day in Govorovo with its war mood; a walk through the town – later, after it had already been burnt down – and the melancholic thoughts it aroused; and finally, how he and his family left Govorovo forever.

“The Last *Kol Nidrei* Night” is a dramatic description by Chava Bernstin-Burstin of the occasion when the Germans took the few Jews who had met in Neta Ritz' house for the *Kol-Nidrei* prayer, together with her father the Rabbi, lined them up against a wall and pointed a machine gun at them. As the Jews were saying their last prayers, the Germans took a film of them and then shot their machine gun off in the air and disappeared.

In “That You May Remember”, Rabbi Yitzhak Shafran describes his experiences during the first days of the war which found him with his family in Ostrov-Maz. After reaching the ghetto of Shanghai in China, he eventually made his way to America. Rabbi Shafran concludes by expressing his gratitude for the fact that so many of the old comrades and the girls of *Bnot* had been spared.

An "Elegy" by A. Ben-Ir is followed by "In the Oven of the Crematorium" by Joseph Perlstein – a powerful description of "the shovel of death pushing the skeletons along like loaves of bread".

In "Shma Yisrael" (in Hebrew), Rachel Auerbach recalls the terrible experiences of the Jews under the rule of the Nazi and the cruel treatment

[Page XV]

which every single Jew had to expect from the German murderers who were helped by the local non-Jewish population. The writer also refers to the gas chambers.

K. Noach writes of "Self-Sacrifice During the Deportation" to the Russian camps where he and other Jews from Govorovo landed in the course of their wanderings. He tells of Itshe Reitzik who was persecuted by the camp commander for observing Jewish customs and eventually sent him to prison where he died.

"Govorovo Without Jews" is a description from the pen of Mordechai Govorczyk of Govorovo after its destruction. The author, who has visited Govorovo several times, mentions the names of non-Jews who have built houses and opened stores and workshops on plots which belonged to Jews. He describes the surrounding hamlets, which were not burnt down, the present occupations of the farmers, market day and the like.

Under the title "*Yitgadal Veyitkadash*", Rabbi Moshe Bernstein, son-in-law of the Rabbi of Govorovo, contributes passages from an address given by him at a memorial meeting for Govorovo in Israel.

The section closes with the psalm, *Michtam Ledavid*, especially set to music for the occasion by A.J. Bruchansky.

We Remember

After the traditional prayer for the dead, *El Malei Rachamim* (p.434) follows a list of more than 800 Jews from Govorovo who died in the ghettos and camps, on transport or as refugees during the war. The chapter concludes with a series of obituaries.

Landsmanschaften

The last pages of the book contain reports of the activities of former residents of Govorovo in other parts of the world.

Aaron Shron reports on the "*Irgun Yotzei* Govorovo in *Yisrael*". Starting from the arrival of the first Govorovers as illegal immigrants in the early 30's, he tells how the *Irgun* was founded in 1949; mentions its annual meetings to commemorate the martyrs of Govorovo and reviews its general activities up to the present. Mention is made of the project for a "Govorovo House" in the neighbourhood of Tel-Aviv which is designed to accommodate the *Irgun's* secretariat, its small loans fund and a synagogue and to provide a place for its functions.

The *Irgun's* Small Loans Fund (*Gmilut Chessed*) is described by Abraham Levin who reports that the Fund was founded in 1955 on the occasion of

[Page XVI]

a visit to Israel by his son Moshe and his wife who donated a large sum for the Fund and which bears the name of their late son Zvi. The fund provides loans up to IL500, repayable in monthly instalments to former Govorovers.

"The Govorover Societies in America" is the title of a report by Yitzhak Shafran. The report starts with a description of conditions in America 60 and 70 years ago when the first of these Societies was founded under the name of *Chevras Bnai Aharon Shlomo Tehillim Anshei Govorovo*. A second Society, Govorover Young Men's Society was established in 1909. Later, this was followed by a Ladies Auxiliary. The three organizations joined forces to form a Relief Committee with the purpose of helping new arrivals to America and sending assistance back to Govorovo for the local poor.

After the war, the Relief Committee also sent parcels and money for the surviving Govorovers. The present committee members of the Relief Committee are: Jacob Zemlovits, Chairman; Sam Epstein, Finance secretary; Harry Miller, Recording secretary; Joseph Bressler, Treasurer; Harry Berliner; Moshe Izdova and Yitzhak David Tehillim, Trustees. Mr. Tehillim is also chairman of the Executive Board. Committee members of the older Society are: Naftali Cooperman, President; Moshe Dan, Vice President; Baruch Marcovitz, Trustee and Jacob Moses, Recording secretary. Chairman of the Ladies Auxiliary is Mrs. Hannah Rachel Cooperman.

A.Ben-Meir reports on the Govorover "*Landsmanshaftn* in Canada" which, before its present intensive work in connection with the Govorovo Memorial Book, had no organized activities. Its Committee consists of: Rivka Rosenberg, President; Abraham Romaner, Secretary; Leib Gemara; Godel Teller; Hershel Zamek; Meir Schmelz; Israel Shafran; Samuel Stettin and Samuel Rosenberg.

In conclusion, there is a note about "Govorovo in other Countries".

At the end of the book, the *Irgun Yotzei* Govorovo acknowledges the contribution made by the editors, Rabbi Aviezer Burstin and Dov Kossovsky who gave their best efforts and time in order to create this monumental memorial for the Jewish born in Govorovo.

The *Irgun* also acknowledges the contributions of Rivka and Shmuel Rosenberg from Canada; of Kalman Blumstein; Sarah and Yitzhak Blumstein; Yitzhak David Tehillim; Naftali Copperman and Yitzhak Shafran, all from the United States and of all those others without whose efforts the work could not have been published.

*

The book is illustrated with a wealth of photographs of Govorovo, events in its social and political life, portraits of leading members of the community and of writers, facsimiles, sketches and drawings and with more than a hundred photographs of Govorovo's martyrs and war victims in the memorial section.

NAME INDEX

A

B

C

D

H

R

S

www.ingramcontent.com/pod-product-compliance
Lightning Source LLC
Chambersburg PA
CBHW062018090426
42811CB00005B/895
* 9 7 8 1 9 6 2 0 5 4 2 3 2 *